COLERIDGE
AND THE PANTHEIST
TRADITION

COLERIDGE
AND THE PANTHEIST
TRADITION

BY

THOMAS McFARLAND

OXFORD
AT THE CLARENDON PRESS
1969

Oxford University Press, Ely House, London W. 1

GLASGOW NEW YORK TORONTO MELBOURNE WELLINGTON
CAPE TOWN SALISBURY IBADAN NAIROBI LUSAKA ADDIS ABABA
BOMBAY CALCUTTA MADRAS KARACHI LAHORE DACCA
KUALA LUMPUR SINGAPORE HONG KONG TOKYO

79-444953

PRINTED IN GREAT BRITAIN

PREFACE

THIS book appears before complete texts of all Coleridge's writings have been published, and before many of the texts now available have received the benefit of modern re-editing. Not only were older editors in general more ready to normalize, to select, and to truncate than are their modern counterparts, but they were also less careful in their transcriptions from Coleridge's handwriting. Kathleen Coburn's edition of the notebooks, for instance, contains countless corrections of the texts in E. H. Coleridge's selection entitled *Anima Poetae*; E. L. Griggs's impeccable new edition of the letters does the same in terms of all previous collections except his own *Unpublished Letters*.

It might seem the part of wisdom, therefore, for a scholar to defer an assessment of Coleridge's intellectual position until the many new editions-in-progress are completed. An example may serve to indicate the dangers of working without adequate texts. In his respected book on Coleridge as a philosopher, Muirhead, writing in 1930, invokes Hort's opinion that Coleridge's moral philosophy was much like that of Bishop Butler, and he then comments on 'the singular fact', which Hort also noticed, 'of Coleridge's apparent entire ignorance of Butler'. But Muirhead was wrong. We can now easily verify, thanks to Griggs's editorial labours (and even without Hazlitt's testimony), that the youthful Coleridge not only knew Butler's thought, but even planned to re-edit his work. Nor does this example stand alone: similar misapprehensions, by other scholars, could be pointed out with respect to Coleridge's supposed ignorance of Shaftesbury, or of certain elements in Kant's philosophy. Sometimes such errors may be attributed to lack of proper indexes, or (as in the example from Muirhead) to the overlooking of texts that, though in print, are minor, piecemeal, and difficut to find. In all instances, however, they may be said to arise from lack of proper editions.

I have none the less chosen to proceed with my study. Doubtless many amplifying facts will become available within the next decade; doubtless some of our most cherished quotations from Coleridge will have to be corrected or understood in an altered context. But what Coleridge stood for in the life of the mind is, I am convinced, not likely to seem much different when we have a fuller documentation. The essentials of his thought are already presented to us in pages now in print and in handwritten sources easily accessible. Indeed, because Coleridge's mind was systematic and consistent, the principal task is not one of determining how many times, or in what precise language, he expressed himself on certain issues, but of interpreting what those issues meant for him in his own day, and what they still mean in ours.

The attempt at such an interpretation has involved this book in an unusually dense apparatus of notes, and for these I wish to make apology. As a reader, I have little fondness for texts barnacled with footnotes. But, as any student of Coleridge can testify, to enter upon the study of his mind is to wade into a morass. Coleridge is a writer almost unique in his special combination of allusiveness, fragmentariness of statement, complication of interests, and neurotic inability to attend to the demands of formal presentation. Such an unusual kind of intellectual surface requires an unusual approach on the part of a commentator. One need perhaps only cite the extensive documentation in the work of Lowes, or in Kathleen Coburn's editions, to convince the sceptic that Coleridgean scholarship tends naturally towards footnotes. In any event, my own system of annotation was adopted only after much experiment, and I hope that the notes in this volume may seem—at least in their more successful appearances—to be pilings driven down to the firm rock below the marshy texture of Coleridge's surface statements. If it be argued that the notes mar the writing and inhibit the reading of the volume, I should have to concede a measure of truth to the objection; indeed, in a certain lamentable sense it may be true that a book such as this one is not so much written as built, and is intended not so much to be read as to be analyzed and taken apart again.

I have been helped by many people, sometimes with points of specific information, sometimes with general criticisms of my position, sometimes simply with encouragement and good will. I wish, however, to offer special thanks to Frederick A. Pottle. It was in one of his memorable seminars that I first became intrigued by Coleridgean matters, and he himself has always been a model for me, both as a scholar and as a man. I take pleasure also in thanking W. K. Wimsatt, whose keenness, learning, and pedagogic skill have often been made generously available to me. Although I did not formally study under René Wellek, and although he figures somewhat in the role of devil's advocate in this book, I have none the less gained much from him, and I greatly respect his unparalleled learning in many literatures.

But my indebtedness is to friends as well as to teachers. I have a lasting sense of personal obligation for the unwavering support of Margaret Jane Fischer and of Ellene Winn. Many kindnesses, for which I am warmly grateful, have been shown me by Sears Jayne, by my former tutor, Albert B. Friedman, by my former colleague, W. Powell Jones, and by Albert Cook, with whom I have engaged in a running dialogue since our freshman year together in college. J. G. Bell read the typescript in an early version, and I have adopted many of his suggestions for its improvement. Robert Crawford not only discussed most of the book with me as it was being composed, but also contributed numerous translations from German and Latin. The entire typescript, finally, was worked through by Peter Sutcliffe, and his detailed criticisms, both of its style and of its content, were of inestimable value to me.

Although my mother died before this volume was accepted for publication, the dedication is retained as though she were alive, for such was the form in which she saw it.

THOMAS McFARLAND

CONTENTS

SELECT LIST OF WORKS CITED IN
THE TEXT AND NOTES

To avoid coded references, works are either cited in full where they appear in the text or notes, or are cited in self-identifying short titles. The short titles refer to the editions listed below.

ABRAMS, M. H.: *The Mirror and the Lamp: Romantic Theory and the Critical Tradition* (New York, 1953).

ALLSOP, T. (ed.): *Letters, Conversations, and Recollections of S. T. Coleridge* (New York, 1836).

ARNOLD, MATTHEW: *Essays in Criticism; First Series* (London, 1905).

BAADER, FRANZ VON: *Franz von Baader's sämmtliche Werke*, hrsg. Franz Hoffmann, Julius Hamberger, Emil August v. Schaden, Anton Lutterbeck, Christoph Schlüter, Friedrich von Osten (Leipzig, 1850–60).

BACON, FRANCIS: *The Works of Francis Bacon*, ed. James Spedding, R. L. Ellis, and D. D. Heath (London, 1857–74).

BARTH, KARL: *Credo*, trans. J. S. McNab (London, 1964).

BAUMGARDT, DAVID: *Franz von Baader und die philosophische Romantik* (Halle, 1927).

BAYLE, PIERRE: *Dictionaire historique et critique* (Rotterdam, 1697).

BERDYAEV, NICOLAS: 'Unground and Freedom', in *Six Theosophic Points and Other Writings by Jacob Boehme*, trans. J. R. Earle (Ann Arbor, Michigan, 1958).

—— *Dream and Reality; An Essay in Autobiography* (New York, 1951).

BERG, FRANZ: *Sextus, oder die absolute Erkenntniß von Schelling. Ein Gespräch* (Würzburg, 1804).

BESENBECK, ALFRED: *Kunstanschauung und Kunstlehre August Wilhelm Schlegels*, Germanische Studien, Heft 87 (Berlin, 1930).

BLOCH, ERNST: *Subjekt-Objekt; Erläuterungen zu Hegel*, erweiterte Ausgabe (Frankfurt am Main, 1962).

BOAS, GEORGE: *French Philosophies of the Romantic Period* (Baltimore, 1925).

BOLLNOW, OTTO FRIEDRICH: *Die Lebensphilosophie F. H. Jacobis* (Stuttgart, 1933).

BONJOUR, ADRIEN: *Coleridge's 'Hymn Before Sunrise'; A Study of Facts and Problems Connected with the Poem* (Lausanne, 1942).

BOOLE, GEORGE: *An Investigation of the Laws of Thought, On Which are Founded the Mathematical Theories of Logic and Probabilities* (New York, reprint of the 1854 edition).

BOSSUET, JACQUES: *Bossuet; textes choisis et commentés*, par Henri Brémond (Paris, 1913).

BOULGER, JAMES D.: *Coleridge as Religious Thinker* (New Haven, 1961).

BOYLE, ROBERT: *A Free Inquiry into the Vulgarly Received Notion of Nature*, in *The Works of the Honourable Robert Boyle. In Six Volumes. . . . A New Edition*, V (London, 1772).

BRANDL, ALOIS: *Samuel Taylor Coleridge and the English Romantic School*, English edition by Lady Eastlake (London, 1887).

BRYANT, JACOB: *The Sentiments of Philo Judaeus Concerning the ΛΟΓΟΣ, or Word of God* (Cambridge, 1797).

BUBER, MARTIN: *Between Man and Man*, trans. Ronald Gregor Smith (London, 1947).

BURNET, JOHN: *Platonism*, Sather Classical Lectures, vol. 5 (Berkeley, 1928).

BURTT, E. A.: *The Metaphysical Foundations of Modern Physical Science* (New York and London, 1927).

BUTLER, JOSEPH: *The Works of Joseph Butler, D.C.L.*, ed. Rt. Hon. W. E. Gladstone (Oxford, 1896).

CARLYLE, THOMAS: *The Life of John Sterling*, in *The Works of Thomas Carlyle in Thirty Volumes*, Centenary edition, XI (London, 1897).

CASSIRER, ERNST: *An Essay on Man; An Introduction to a Philosophy of Human Culture* (New York, 1953).

—— *Individuum und Kosmos in der Philosophie der Renaissance*, zweite Auflage (Darmstadt, 1963).

—— *Kants Leben und Lehre* (Berlin, 1918).

—— *The Philosophy of the Enlightenment*, trans. Fritz C. A. Koelln and J. P. Pettegrove (Princeton, 1951).

—— *The Platonic Renaissance in England*, trans. James P. Pettegrove (Austin, Texas, 1953).

CLARKE, SAMUEL: *A Demonstration of the Being and Attributes of God: More Particularly in Answer to Mr. Hobbs, Spinoza, and their Followers. . . . . The Third Edition, Corrected*, in *Clarke's Works*, IV (London, 1711).

COLERIDGE, SAMUEL TAYLOR: *Biographia Literaria, by S. T. Coleridge*, ed. with his Aesthetical Essays by J. Shawcross (London, 1907).

—— *Collected Letters of Samuel Taylor Coleridge*, ed. Earl Leslie Griggs (Oxford, 1956 ff.).

—— *The Complete Poetical Works of Samuel Taylor Coleridge*, ed. Ernest Hartley Coleridge (Oxford, 1912).

—— *The Complete Works of Samuel Taylor Coleridge*, with an Introductory Essay upon his Philosophical and Theological Opinions, ed. W. G. T. Shedd (New York, 1853).

—— *Critical Annotations of S. T. Coleridge*, ed. William F. Taylor (Harrow, 1889).

—— *Inquiring Spirit; A New Presentation of Coleridge from his Published and Unpublished Prose Writings*, ed. Kathleen Coburn (London, 1951).

—— *The Notebooks of Samuel Taylor Coleridge*, ed. Kathleen Coburn (New York, 1957 ff.).

—— *The Philosophical Lectures of Samuel Taylor Coleridge; Hitherto Unpublished*, ed. Kathleen Coburn (London, 1949).

—— *The Table Talk and Omniana of Samuel Taylor Coleridge*, arranged and ed. T. Ashe (London, 1888).

COTTLE, Joseph: *Early Recollections; Chiefly Relating to the Late Samuel Taylor Coleridge During his Long Residence in Bristol* (London, 1837).

CREUZER, FRIEDRICH: *Die Liebe der Günderode; Friedrich Creuzers Briefe an Caroline von Günderode*, hrsg. Karl Preisendanz (München, 1912).

CROCE, BENEDETTO: *Aesthetic; As Science of Expression and General Linguistic*, trans. Douglas Ainslie (New York, 1955).

DESCARTES, RENÉ: *Œuvres de Descartes*, ed. Charles Adam et Paul Tannery (Paris, 1897–1913).

DESCHAMPS, PAUL: *La Formation de la pensée de Coleridge (1772–1804)*, Librairie Marcel Didier, Études Anglaises 15 (Grenoble, 1964).

DE QUINCEY, THOMAS: *The Collected Writings of Thomas De Quincey*, ed. David Masson (Edinburgh, 1889–90).

DIELS, HERMANN: *Doxographi Graeci . . .* (Berolini, 1879).

—— *Die Fragmente der Vorsokratiker*, dritte Auflage (Berlin, 1912).

EDERHEIMER, EDGAR: *Jakob Boehme und die Romantiker* (Heidelberg, 1904).

EINSTEIN, ALBERT: *Essays in Science*, trans. Alan Harris (New York, n.d.).

—— *The World as I see it*, trans. Alan Harris (New York, 1949).

ELIOT, T. S.: *Selected Essays* (New York, 1932).

EMERSON, RALPH WALDO: *The Complete Works of Ralph Waldo Emerson*, Centenary edition, ed. E. W. Emerson (Boston and New York, 1903–4).

—— *Journals of Ralph Waldo Emerson*, ed. E. W. Emerson and W. E. Forbes, VIII (Boston and New York, 1912).

FÉNELON, FRANÇOIS DE LA MOTHE: *Œuvres de Fénelon . . . publiées d'après les manuscrits originaux . . .* (Versailles, 1820–30).

FEUERBACH, LUDWIG: *Das Wesen des Christenthums*, zweite vermehrte Auflage (Leipzig, 1843).

—— *Ludwig Feuerbach's sämmtliche Werke* (Leipzig, 1846–66).

FICHTE, J. G.: *J. G. Fichte Briefwechsel*, kritische Gesamtausgabe, hrsg. Hans Schulz (Leipzig, 1925–30).

—— *Johann Gottlieb Fichte's sämmtliche Werke*, hrsg. J. H. Fichte (Berlin, 1845–6).

—— *Grundlage der gesammten Wissenschaftslehre* (Leipzig, 1794).

FLAUBERT, GUSTAVE: *Œuvres complètes de Gustave Flaubert. Correspondance. Nouvelle édition augmentée* (Paris, 1926–33).

FOUCHER DE CAREIL, A.: *Réfutation inédite de Spinoza par Leibniz* (Paris, 1854).

FRAUNCE, ABRAHAM: *The Arcadian Rhetorike: Or the Praecepts of Rhetorike made plaine by examples Greeke, Latin, English, Italian, French, Spanish* (London, [1588]).

FREUD, SIGMUND: *Gesammelte Werke*, hrsg. Anna Freud et al. (London, 1940–52).

FREUDENTHAL, JACOB: *Das Leben Spinozas* (Heidelberg, 1927).

—— *Die Lehre Spinozas*, bearbeitet von Carl Gebhardt (Heidelberg, 1927).

FRIES, JAKOB FRIEDRICH: *Von deutscher Philosophie; Art und Kunst. Ein Votum für Friedrich Heinrich Jacobi gegen F. W. J. Schelling* (Heidelberg, 1812).

GILLMAN, JAMES: *The Life of Samuel Taylor Coleridge* (London, 1838).

GILSON, ÉTIENNE: *La Philosophie au moyen âge*, deuxième édition (Paris, 1944).

GODWIN, WILLIAM: *An Enquiry Concerning Political Justice, and its Influence on General Virtue and Happiness* (London, 1793).

GOETHE, J. W. VON: *Goethes Gespräche; Gesamtausgabe*. Neu herausgegeben von Flodoard Frhr von Biedermann (Leipzig, 1909–11).

—— *Gedenkausgabe der Werke, Briefe und Gespräche*, hrsg. Ernst Beutler (Zürich, 1948–60).

GOLDMANN, LUCIEN: *Le Dieu caché; Étude sur la vision tragique dans les Pensées de Pascal et dans le théâtre de Racine* (Paris, 1955).

GUHRAUER, G. E.: *Gottfried Wilhelm Freiherr v. Leibnitz. Eine Biographie* (Breslau, 1846).

GUEROULT, MARTIAL: *Descartes selon l'ordre des raisons* (Paris, 1953).

HAMANN, J. G.: *Johann Georg Hamann Briefwechsel*, hrsg. Arthur Henkel, IV (Wiesbaden, 1959).

—— *Johann Georg Hamann's, des Magus im Norden, Leben und Schriften*, hrsg. C. H. Gildemeister, V (Gotha, 1868).

HAMILTON, SIR WILLIAM: *The Works of Thomas Reid, D. D. Now Fully Collected, With Selections from his Unpublished Letters*. Preface, Notes, and Supplementary Dissertations, by Sir William Hamilton, Bart., sixth edition (Edinburgh, 1863).

HARNACK, ADOLF: *History of Dogma*, trans. James Millar et al., III, IV (London, Edinburgh, Oxford, 1897, 1898).

HAZARD, PAUL: *The European Mind (1680–1715)*, trans. J. Lewis May (London, 1953).

HAZLITT, WILLIAM: *The Complete Works of William Hazlitt*, ed. P. P. Howe, after the edition of A. R. Waller and Arnold Glover (London and Toronto, 1930–34).

HEGEL, G. W. F.: *Georg Wilhelm Friedrich Hegel's Werke*, vollständige Ausgabe durch einen Verein von Freunden des Verewigten: Ph[ilipp] Marheineke, J[ohannes] Schulze, Ed[uard] Gans, L[eo]p[old] v[on] Henning, H[einrich] Hotho, K[arl] Michelet, F[riedrich] Förster (Berlin, 1832–87).

HEIDEGGER, MARTIN: *An Introduction to Metaphysics*, trans. Ralph Manheim (New Haven, 1959).

—— *Sein und Zeit*, dritte Auflage (Halle, 1931).

HEIM, KARL: *Glaube und Denken; Philosophische Grundlegung einer christlichen Lebensanschauung*, dritte . . . Auflage (Berlin, 1934).

HEINE, HEINRICH: *Die romantische Schule* (Hamburg, 1836).

HEINEMANN, FRITZ: *Plotin; Forschungen über die plotinische Frage, Plotins Entwicklung, und sein System* (Leipzig, 1921).

HELMHOLTZ, ANNA AUGUSTA: *The Indebtedness of Samuel Taylor Coleridge to August Wilhelm von Schlegel* (Madison, Wisconsin, 1907).

HERDER, J. G. VON: *Aus Herders Nachlaß*, hrsg. Heinrich Düntzer und F. G. von Herder (Frankfurt am Main, 1856–7).

—— *Herders sämmtliche Werke*, hrsg. Bernhard Suphan (Berlin, 1877–1913).

HOBBES, THOMAS: *Hobbes's Leviathan; Reprinted from the Edition of 1651*, ed. W. G. Pogson Smith (Oxford, 1947).

HÖLDERLIN, FRIEDRICH: *Friedrich Hölderlin's sämmtliche Werke*, hrsg. Christoph Theodor Schwab (Stuttgart und Tübingen, 1846).

HOUSE, HUMPHRY: *Coleridge; The Clark Lectures 1951–2* (London, 1962).

HUSSERL, EDMUND: *Cartesianische Meditationen*, hrsg. S. Strasser, *Husserliana*, Band I (Haag, 1950).

—— *Ideas; General Introduction to Pure Phenomenology*, trans. W. R. Boyce Gibson (London and New York, 1958).

—— *Ideen zu einer reinen Phänomenologie und phänomenologischen Philosophie*, hrsg. Walter Biemel, *Husserliana*, Band III (Haag, 1950).

INGLEBY, C. M.: 'On Some Points Connected with the Philosophy of Coleridge', *Transactions of the Royal Society of Literature of the United Kingdom*, Second Series, IX (London, 1870).

JACOBI, F. H.: *Friedrich Heinrich Jacobi's auserlesener Briefwechsel*, hrsg. Friedrich Roth (Leipzig, 1825–7).

—— *Friedr. Heinr. Jacobi's Briefe an Friedr. Bouterwek aus den Jahren 1800 bis 1819*, hrsg. W. Mejer (Göttingen, 1868).

—— *Friedrich Heinrich Jacobi's Werke* (Leipzig, 1812–25). The fourth volume is in two parts, IV–1 and IV–2.

JAEGER, WERNER: *Aristotle; Fundamentals of the History of his Development*, trans. Richard Robinson (Oxford, 1948).

—— *The Theology of the Early Greek Philosophers*, trans. E. S. Robinson (Oxford, 1947).

JÄSCHE, GOTTLOB BENJAMIN: *Der Pantheismus nach seinen verschiedenen Hauptformen, seinem Ursprung und Fortgange, seinem speculativen und praktischen Werth und Gehalt. Ein Beitrag zur Geschichte und Kritik dieser Lehre in alter und neuer Philosophie* (Berlin, 1826–32).

JASPERS, KARL: *Schelling; Größe und Verhängnis* (München, 1955).

—— *Von der Wahrheit* (München, 1947).

JUNG, C. G.: *Modern Man in Search of a Soul*, trans. W. S. Dell and C. F. Baynes (New York, 1933).

KANT, IMMANUEL: *Immanuel Kants Werke*, in Gemeinschaft mit Hermann Cohen, Artur Buchenau, Otto Buek, Albert Görland, B. Kellermann, hrsg. von Ernst Cassirer (Berlin, 1912–22).

KIERKEGAARD, SØREN: *Concluding Unscientific Postscript*, trans. D. F. Swenson and Walter Lowrie (Princeton, 1944).

—— *The Journals of Søren Kierkegaard*, ed. and trans. Alexander Dru (London, New York, Toronto, 1951).

KLIBANSKY, RAYMOND: *The Continuity of the Platonic Tradition During the Middle Ages* (London, 1939).

KÖPKE, RUDOLF: *Ludwig Tieck. Erinnerungen aus dem Leben des Dichters nach dessen mündlichen und schriftlichen Mittheilungen* (Leipzig, 1885).

KOYRÉ, ALEXANDRE: *From the Closed World to the Infinite Universe* (New York, 1958).

—— *La Philosophie de Jacob Boehme* (Paris, 1929).

KRANTZ, ÉMILE: *Essai sur l'esthétique de Descartes, étudiée dans les rapports de la doctrine cartésienne avec la littérature classique française au XVIIe siècle* (Paris, 1882).

KRAUS, CHRISTIAN JACOB: *Vermischte Schriften*, hrsg. Hans von Auerswald (Königsberg, 1808–19).

KREMER, JOSEF: *Das Problem der Theodicee in der Philosophie und Literatur des 18. Jahrhunderts mit besonderer Rücksicht auf Kant und Schiller* (Berlin, 1909). Printed in Ergänzungsheft 13 of *Kantstudien*.

LAMB, CHARLES: *The Works of Charles and Mary Lamb*, ed. E. V. Lucas (London, 1903–5).

LAMPRECHT, J. F.: *Leben des Freyherrn Gottfried Wilhelm von Leibnitz* (Berlin, 1740).

LEIBNIZ, G. W. VON: *Die philosophischen Schriften von Gottfried Wilhelm Leibniz*, hrsg. C. J. Gerhardt (Berlin, 1875–90).

—— *Gottfried Wilhelm Leibniz sämtliche Schriften und Briefe*, hrsg. von der Preußischen Akademie der Wissenschaften (Darmstadt, 1923 ff.).

LOCKE, JOHN: *An Essay Concerning Human Understanding*, ed. A. C. Fraser (New York, 1959).

LOVEJOY, ARTHUR O.: 'Kant and the English Platonists', in *Essays Philosophical and Psychological in Honor of William James* (New York, London, Bombay, and Calcutta, 1908).

—— *The Dialectic of Bruno and Spinoza*, in *University of California Publications; Philosophy*, I (Berkeley, 1904).

MAIMON, SALOMON: *Versuch einer neuen Logik, oder, Theorie des Denkens*, Neudrucke seltener philosophischer Werke, hrsg. von der Kantgesellschaft, Band III (Berlin, 1912).

MALEBRANCHE, NICOLAS DE: *Œuvres de Malebranche*, nouvelle édition collationnée sur les meilleurs textes et précédée d'une introduction par M. Jules Simon (Paris, [1842]).

MASCALL, E. L.: *The Secularisation of Christianity; An Analysis and a Critique* (London, 1965).

MENDELSSOHN, MOSES: *Moses Mendelssohn an die Freunde Lessings* (Berlin, 1786).

—— *Moses Mendelssohn's gesammelte Schriften*, hrsg. G. B. Mendelssohn (Leipzig, 1843–5).

—— *Moses Mendelssohns Morgenstunden oder Vorlesungen über das Daseyn Gottes* (Berlin, 1785).

MILL, JOHN STUART: *An Examination of Sir William Hamilton's Philosophy and of the Principal Philosophical Questions Discussed in his Writings*, fifth edition (London, 1878).

—— *Dissertations and Discussions* (London, 1859).

MONTAIGNE, MICHEL DE: *Les Essais de Michel de Montaigne*, ed. Fortunat Strowski et François Gébelin (Bordeaux, 1906–20).

MORE, HENRY: *Henrici Mori Cantabrigiensis Opera omnia* (Londini, 1679).

MUIRHEAD, J. H.: *Coleridge as Philosopher* (London and New York, 1930).

NATORP, PAUL: *Platos Ideenlehre; Eine Einführung in den Idealismus*, zweite Ausgabe (Hamburg, 1961).

NETTLESHIP, R. L.: *Lectures on the Republic of Plato*, second edition (London, 1963).

NIETZSCHE, FRIEDRICH: *Nietzsche's Werke* (Leipzig, 1899–1926).

NORDEN, EDUARD: *Agnostos Theos; Untersuchungen zur Formengeschichte religiöser Rede* (Leipzig und Berlin, 1913).

NOVALIS: *Schriften*, hrsg. Paul Kluckhohn und Richard Samuel (Leipzig, [1929]).

ORSINI, G. N. G.: 'Coleridge and Schlegel Reconsidered', *Comparative Literature*, XVI (1964).

POHLENZ, MAX: *Die Stoa; Geschichte einer geistigen Bewegung*, zweite Auflage (Göttingen, 1959).

POLLOCK, SIR FREDERICK: *Spinoza; His Life and Philosophy*, second edition (London, 1912).

POPPER, K. R.: *The Open Society and its Enemies; Volume I; The Spell of Plato* (London, 1962).

PRIESTLEY, JOSEPH: *An Appeal to the Serious and Candid Professors of Christianity* ([London?]), 1771).

—— *Hartley's Theory of the Human Mind, on the Principle of the Association of Ideas; with Essays Relating to the Subject of It* (London, 1775).

PUFENDORF, SAMUEL: 'Briefe von Pufendorf', hrsg. und erläutert von Konrad Varren-trapp, *Historische Zeitschrift*, hrsg. Heinrich v. Sybel und Max Lehmann, LXX (München und Leipzig, 1893).

RAHNER, KARL: *Theological Investigations; Volume I; God, Christ, Mary and Grace*, trans. Cornelius Ernst (Baltimore and London, 1961).

RAYSOR, T. M. (ed.): *Samuel Taylor Coleridge; Shakespearean Criticism*, second edition (London and New York, 1960).

READ, HERBERT: *Coleridge as Critic* (London, 1949).

RENAN, ERNEST: *Nouvelles études d'histoire religieuse* (Paris, 1884).

ROBERTSON, JOHN MACKINNON: *New Essays Toward a Critical Method* (London and New York, 1897).

ROBINSON, HENRY CRABB: *Diary, Reminiscences, and Correspondence of Henry Crabb Robinson*, ed. Thomas Sadler (London, 1869).

ROYCE, JOSIAH: *The Spirit of Modern Philosophy* (Boston and New York, 1892).

RUSKIN, JOHN: *The Works of John Ruskin*, ed. E. T. Cook and Alexander Wedderburn (London, 1903–12).

SAINTSBURY, GEORGE: *Loci Critici; Passages Illustrative of Critical Theory and Practice from Aristotle Downwards* (Boston, 1903).

SANDERS, CHARLES RICHARD: *Coleridge and the Broad Church Movement; Studies in S. T. Coleridge, Dr. Arnold of Rugby, J. C. Hare, Thomas Carlyle, and F. D. Maurice* (Durham, N.C., 1942).

SAUSSURE, FERDINAND DE: *Course in General Linguistics*, ed. Charles Bally, Albert Sechehaye, and Albert Reidlinger, trans. Wade Baskin (New York, 1959).

SCHELER, MAX: *On the Eternal in Man*, trans. Bernard Noble (New York, 1960).

SCHELLING, F. W. J. VON: *Aus Schellings Leben. In Briefen*, hrsg. G. L. Plitt (Leipzig, 1869–70).

—— *Friedrich Wilhelm Joseph von Schellings sämmtliche Werke*, hrsg. K. F. A. Schelling (Stuttgart und Augsburg, 1856–61). The edition is in two *Abtheilungen*, the first consisting of volumes numbered 1–10, the second of volumes numbered 1–4. To avoid cumbersome identifications of *Abtheilungen*, I cite the first *Abtheilung* as volumes i–x, the second as volumes xi–xiv.

—— *F. W. J. Schelling's philosophische Schriften. Erster Band* (Landshut, 1809).

SCHILLER, J. C.: *Schillers Werke*, Nationalausgabe, hrsg. Julius Petersen et al. (Weimar, 1943 ff.).

SCHLEGEL, FRIEDRICH: *Friedrich Schlegel's philosophische Vorlesungen aus den Jahren 1804 bis 1806. . . . Aus dem Nachlaß . . . hrsg. C. J. H. Windischmann (Bonn, 1836–7).

—— *Friedrich Schlegel's sämmtliche Werke* (Wien, 1822–5).

—— *Kritische Schriften*, erweiterte Auflage, hrsg. Wolfdietrich Rasch (München, 1964).

—— *Literary Notebooks 1797–1801*, ed. Hans Eichner (Toronto, 1957).

SCHLEIERMACHER, FRIEDRICH: *Der christliche Glaube nach den Grundsätzen der evange-lischen Kirche im Zusammenhange dargestellt* (Berlin, 1821).

—— *Friedrich Schleiermacher's sämmtliche Werke* (Berlin, 1834–64).

SCHOLZ, HEINRICH: *Die Hauptschriften zum Pantheismusstreit zwischen Jacobi und Men-delssohn*, Neudrucke seltener philosophischer Werke, hrsg. von der Kantgesell-schaft, Band VI (Berlin, 1916).

SCHOPENHAUER, ARTHUR: *Arthur Schopenhauers sämtliche Werke*, hrsg. Paul Deussen (München, 1911–42).

SCHULZE, GOTTLOB ERNST: *Aenesidemus, oder über die Fundamente der . . . Elementar-Philosophie*, Neudrucke seltener philosophischer Werke, hrsg. von der Kantgesellschaft, Band I (Berlin, 1911).

SHAFTESBURY, THIRD EARL OF: *Characteristicks of Men, Manners, Opinions, Times* ([London], 1711).

SNYDER, ALICE D.: *The Critical Principle of the Reconciliation of Opposites as Employed by Coleridge* (Ann Arbor, 1918).

—— *Coleridge on Logic and Learning; With Selections from the Unpublished Manuscripts* (New Haven, 1929).

SOLGER, K. W. F.: *Solger's nachgelassene Schriften und Briefwechsel*, hrsg. Ludwig Tieck und Friedrich von Raumer (Leipzig, 1826).

SPIEGELBERG, HERBERT: *The Phenomenological Movement; A Historical Introduction*, second edition (The Hague, 1965).

SPINOZA, BENEDICT DE: *Opera*, im Auftrag der Heidelberger Akademie der Wissenschaften, hrsg. Carl Gebhardt (Heidelberg, [1925]).

SPRANGER, EDUARD: *Der unbekannte Gott* (Stuttgart, 1954).

—— *Wilhelm von Humboldt und die Humanitätsidee* (Berlin, 1928).

STALLO, J. B.: *General Principles of the Philosophy of Nature: With an Outline of Some of its Recent Developments among the Germans, Embracing the Philosophical Systems of Schelling and Hegel, and Oken's System of Nature* (Boston, 1848).

STEFFENS, HENRICH: *Was ich erlebte; aus der Erinnerung niedergeschrieben* (Breslau, 1840–4).

STENZEL, JULIUS: *Plato's Method of Dialectic*, trans. and ed. D. J. Allan (Oxford, 1940).

STEPHEN, LESLIE: 'Coleridge', *Hours in a Library*, III (New York and London, 1894).

STIRLING, JAMES HUTCHISON: 'De Quincey and Coleridge upon Kant', *Jerrold, Tennyson and Macaulay* (Edinburgh, 1868).

—— *The Secret of Hegel: Being the Hegelian System in Origin, Principle, Form, and Matter* (London, 1865).

STOKOE, F. W.: *German Influence in the English Romantic Period 1788–1818; With Special Reference to Scott, Coleridge, Shelley and Byron* (Cambridge, 1926).

TILLICH, PAUL: *Dynamics of Faith* (New York, 1957).

—— *Mystik und Schuldbewußtsein in Schellings philosophischer Entwicklung* (Gütersloh, 1912).

TULLOCH, JOHN: *Rational Theology and Christian Philosophy in England in the Seventeenth Century*, second edition (Edinburgh and London, 1874).

UNAMUNO, MIGUEL DE: *The Tragic Sense of Life in Men and in Peoples*, trans. J. E. Crawford Flitch (London, 1921).

UNDERHILL, EVELYN: *Mysticism; A Study in the Nature and Development of Man's Spiritual Consciousness* (New York, 1912).

URBAN, WILBUR MARSHALL: *Language and Reality; The Philosophy of Language and the Principles of Symbolism* (London and New York, 1951).

VOSS, GERARD: *Gerardi Ioannis Vossii de Theologia gentili, et physiologia Christiana; sive de origine ac progressu idololatriae; de que naturae mirandis, quibus homo adducitur ad deum, libri IX*, editio nova (Amsterdami, 1668).

WELLEK, RENÉ: *Immanuel Kant in England 1793–1838* (Princeton, 1931).

—— *A History of Modern Criticism: 1750–1950* (New Haven, 1955 ff.).

WHITEHEAD, ALFRED NORTH: *Process and Reality; An Essay in Cosmology* (Cambridge, 1929).

—— *Science and the Modern World* (Cambridge, 1926).

WILSON, THOMAS: *The Arte of Rhetorique, for the use of all suche as are studious of Eloquence, sette forth in English* ([London], 1553).

WITTGENSTEIN, LUDWIG: *Notebooks 1914–1916*, ed. G. H. von Wright and G. E. M. Anscombe (New York, 1961).

—— *Tractatus Logico-Philosophicus* (London, 1958).

WOLF, CHRISTIAN: *Theologia Naturalis, Methodo Scientifica Pertractata. Pars Posterior, Qua Existentia et Attributa Dei ex Notione Entis Perfectissimi et Natura Animae Demonstrantur, et Atheismi, Deismi, Fatalismi, Naturalismi, Spinosismi Aliorumque de Deo Errorum Fundamenta Subvertuntur* (Francofurti et Lipsiae, 1737).

WOLFSON, H. A.: *Philo; Foundations of Religious Philosophy in Judaism, Christianity, and Islam* (Cambridge, Mass., 1947).

—— *The Philosophy of Spinoza; Unfolding the Latent Processes of his Reasoning* (Cambridge, Mass., 1934).

—— *The Philosophy of the Church Fathers; Volume I; Faith, Trinity, Incarnation* (Cambridge, Mass., 1956).

ZELLER, EDUARD: *Die Philosophie der Griechen in ihrer geschichtlichen Entwicklung.* (Leipzig, 1920-23).

ZEYDEL, E. H.: *Ludwig Tieck, The German Romanticist* (Princeton, 1935).

ZIRNGIEBL, EBERHARD: *Friedrich Heinrich Jacobi's Leben, Dichten und Denken* (Wien, 1867).

INTRODUCTION

I

GEORGE LYMAN KITTREDGE'S classroom remark that 'Coleridge
was a great poet, and a considerable critic' rings strangely upon
our ears. Coleridge was not a great poet, although he wrote
one or two great poems and undeniably possessed the abilities to have
written more. Nor was he merely a considerable critic. The extraordinary
development of the techniques and methodology of criticism in recent
years has led to his recognition as the most profound of English critics,
not only in his practical judgements—an excellence generally conceded
by the end of the nineteenth century—but in his philosophic theories as
to the nature and function of the poetic faculty. In the words of R. P.
Blackmur: 'Coleridge began the whole business of the special techniques
of modern scholarship and criticism of poetry: all the expansions into the
psychology of language and imagination.'

Nevertheless, the traditional Anglo-Saxon dislike of abstract philosophy, combined with the far-reaching effects of Carlyle's malefic portrait, have even today a regrettable status in treatments of Coleridge.
Although modern commentators are certainly far from the extreme
opinion of the last century that Coleridge 'had the impudence to die in
his sixty-third year, with nothing to show for his life but a tiny handful
of poems, some of which he had not even the grace to finish', they are
perhaps not so close as they should be to Shawcross's quiet statement
that

the prejudice existing with regard to all Coleridge's speculative writings, that
they are dearly purchased at the expense of more poetry of the type of *Christabel*
or *The Ancient Mariner* . . . is an old one, and has received some countenance
from Coleridge himself; but it is not confirmed by the facts of his life, nor, if it
were, would it justify the neglect of his actual production.

We see a current example of the prejudice of which Shawcross speaks
in T. S. Eliot's insistence that 'it was better for Coleridge, as poet, to read
books of travel and exploration than to read books of metaphysics'.
Indeed, our attitude sometimes seems almost to be that Coleridge's philosophy was dearly purchased not only at the expense of his poetry, but at
the expense of his criticism as well. Eliot, for example, calls Coleridge, in
The Sacred Wood, 'perhaps the greatest of English critics', but apparently

finds no contradiction in speaking, in *The Use of Poetry*, of 'the stupefaction of his powers in transcendental metaphysics'. Dr. Leavis has, more trenchantly, expressed dissatisfaction with what he feels are the irrelevancies for literary criticism of Coleridge's philosophical interests. And even I. A. Richards, who has probably done more than any other critic to call attention to the usefulness of Coleridge's aesthetic theories, and who has insisted, perhaps more forcefully than any other commentator, on the necessity of understanding these theories in philosophical as well as in purely literary contexts, nevertheless asserts the view that most of Coleridge's thought was a 'huge ill-assorted fabric of philosophic and theological beliefs'.

II

The purpose of this essay is to indicate the fallacy of such an historically entrenched attitude. One might always feel justified, I suppose, in maintaining that Coleridge should have done more with his magnificent abilities than he did; but I do not think it can fairly be said that his philosophic viewpoints, as such, were 'ill-assorted' or inconsistent. I find in them a remarkable unity and cohesiveness, and I suspect the contrary opinion to be derived from the bibliographically diffuse nature of his production—lectures, marginalia, unfinished tomes, table talk, letters—rather than from a serious study of what he actually said.

Yet the multeity and disjointedness of Coleridge's utterance remain a serious hindrance to any attempt to assess his position; and the attempt is further complicated by another characteristic of his activity. I refer, of course, to his stupendous erudition and the problems it presents to commentators. When we are confronted by the bland insolence of the *Edinburgh Review*'s pronouncement that Coleridge was 'not deeply or critically learned', our indignation is far less strong than our devout wish that the statement were true. The *viri eruditissimi*, to use Burckhardt's phrase, put us uncomfortably on the defensive; for commentary implies, if not a superior knowledge on the commentator's part, at least a knowledge congruent to that possessed by the figure under consideration. When the figure, in those unusual cases of which Coleridge is an outstanding example, comes to us clothed in learning far brighter and more abundant than our own, our tendency is to salvage our egos at the expense of our scholarly effectiveness. We patronize our subject. We turn our backs on his learning and confidently assert that no learning can be seen. Thus, in the aggressive view of one modern commentator, Coleridge becomes 'a rather minor prophet furtively stuffing his shirt with other men's wisdom and giving himself the airs of an Aquinas or an Aristotle'—an opinion that might seem both foolish and spiteful did it not clearly define the limitations of the commentator rather than of Coleridge.

Alternatively, we concede the existence of the learning, but refuse to admit its pertinence. We recognize here the rationale for an edition of the *Biographia* which omits the chapters between four and fourteen with a fashionable sigh of regret that a man of Coleridge's powers should have devoted himself to non-essentials: philosophy, theology, and the theory of literature.

The particular quality of Coleridge's learning compounds the difficulty. Not all scholars shirk the problem, but despite the industry of Lowes, the sympathy of Muirhead, the vigour of Richards, the taste and discrimination of E. H. Coleridge and Shawcross—not to mention the more recent significant contribution of House, Deschamps, Beer, and above all, Coburn—we know today very little about Coleridge's thought, and much of what we claim to know is mistaken or out of focus. I am reluctant to admit that scholars of the calibre of those I have just named would be baffled by mere eclectic erudition. I feel rather that the peculiarly organic nature of Coleridge's knowledge, which places him among the select handful of history's truly learned men, is at the root of the commentator's difficulty. If, for instance, we possessed all the works of Varro—*doctissimus Romanorum*, to use Seneca's admiring epithet—his learning would excite wonder, but would scarcely, I think, pose a problem to scholars; for such learning is primarily an accumulation, which, theoretically at least, could be matched by an accomplished scholar willing and able to devote the time necessary to complete an equivalent amount of reading. And as with the learning of Varro, so with that of the polyhistors of our own era: Mommsen, Acton, Ranke, Toynbee. The learning of a man such as Coleridge, on the other hand, involves not only quantitative, but qualitative reading. A particular bit of knowledge rarely seems to lie loosely catalogued in Coleridge's mind; rather it seems to be bound firmly, in implicit comparison and contrast, to all other facts in his knowledge, the whole—both the direction of his reading in general and the stress of facts in particular—being subsumed under, and unified by, a group of organizing ideas. Varro's learning, being essentially an accumulation, could be segmented; if one scholar could not cope with it, a committee of scholarly specialists could treat it in parts, and the resulting whole would be theoretically congruent to the original. Coleridge's learning resists such an approach; a group of scholars could catalogue the facts available to Coleridge, but they could not—of this I am quite certain—reproduce the organized whole of his learning. The individual scholars who attempt to treat individual segments of Coleridge's thought seem, almost invariably, to become involved in distortion and inaccuracy. I. A. Richards—to cite a familiar, and perhaps too often derided example—sought to treat Coleridge's theory of imagination as distinct from his total position, and produced an interesting and in many respects valuable work that, unfortunately, is of only limited use as commentary on Coleridge or Coleridge's theory of imagination.

III

A recognition of the intensely organic nature of Coleridge's learning, and of the persistent interdependence of fact and idea in the body of knowledge with which he worked, will, I believe, prevent us from misinterpreting the significance of his fragmented modes of utterance. Most of us are aware that Arnold regarded Coleridge as merely the master of the fragment—an English Joubert; but it is significant that Mill, who possessed considerably more philosophical learning than Arnold, insisted that Coleridge was 'the most systematic thinker of our time'. The justness of Mill's opinion becomes apparent to us, when we consider more closely the nature of really good marginalia—the fragmentary form in which Coleridge excelled. We have all probably at one time or another attempted marginal annotation of our books. We have, in all likelihood, noticed that the quality was generally poor when we were reading on unfamiliar topics, but that it tended to improve in direct ratio to the comprehensiveness of our knowledge of the subject under comment. An extension of the principle would seem to suggest that a true master of the fragment, far from thinking in a fragmentary and eclectic way, would in fact have to be more than usually clear in his own mind as to the total implications of the point under consideration. The marginal note in its most finished form would, therefore, seem to indicate not a fragmentary and erratic power of insight, but exactly the opposite, an organic, coherent, and fully worked-out viewpoint that could be quickly focused on a given topic because all larger problems of structure had already been solved. This principle holds true to some extent, I think, even in deliberately aphoristic utterances—Goethe's maxims, the insights of Nietzsche, the *pensées* of Joubert. But I think the principle has its primary validity with respect to the kind of involuntary fragmentation typical of Coleridge, or of Leibniz, the thinker psychologically and bibliographically most like him (though no one, perhaps, has ever equalled Leibniz in range, and only few in subtlety). The personal notation, the letter, the unfinished essay, the commentary—these forms characterize both Coleridge and Leibniz, and it is significant that whereas there may remain today a substantial doubt as to the profundity and coherence of Coleridge's thought, and even in some quarters a certain scepticism as to the range and depth of his learning, the almost equally fragmentary Leibniz—thanks in part to the monumental labours of Erdmann—stands almost universally as the prime symbol of range and depth and organicism in learning.

Scholars of such fabulous industry as Erdmann are rare in any field; in

English literature they are virtually non-existent, and it is, therefore, not likely that Coleridge's learning will in the near future achieve recognition comparable to that accorded Leibniz's. It is, in fact, always difficult to distinguish grades of learning more advanced than our own. We may remember that T. S. Eliot, in at least one of his essays, expressed embarrassment at the tendency of eager critics to class him among the very learned, and hastened to reject the accolade. We may also recall, in this connexion, Johnson's disclaimer of knowledge in his celebrated interview with King George. Or we may recall the opinion of Johnson in another instance reported by Boswell:

> I always thought that [Johnson] did himself injustice in his account of what he had read, and that he must have been speaking with reference to the vast portion of study which is possible, and to which a few scholars ... have attained; for when I once asked him whether a person, whose name I have now forgotten, studied hard, he answered 'No, Sir; I do not believe he studied hard. I never knew a man who studied hard. I conclude, indeed, from the effects, that some men have studied hard, as Bentley and Clarke.'

We find such statements valuable precisely because, in comparison to most of us, Johnson was himself a learned man. We may find relatively little need for guidance in judging our own contemporaries; we can say quite independently that though Whitehead and Cassirer were both learned men, Cassirer was by far the more learned of the two. In more recondite instances, however, our own judgements cannot be trusted, and we find ourselves almost wholly dependent upon the judgements of the learned on themselves. In the discrimination of such matters most of us feel as helpless as, in the report of Mark Pattison, did poor King Henry of France:

> They told Henri that Lipsius was the most learned man of the age, and should be invited from Flanders. . . . The king took to the suggestion of Lipsius' name. 'I have been told', he said one day to Thiou des Portes, 'that Lipsius is the most learned man of the age.' Des Portes immediately named Scaliger, affirming that Scaliger possessed more knowledge of all sciences and all languages than Lipsius had of any one. Henri replied, 'They have never told me that.'

Thus though we often hear, and are certainly unable to judge for ourselves, that Selden was the true titan of English learning—'the chief of learned men reputed in this Land' says Milton—we should find it presumptuous to dispute Vico's unequivocal statement that Grotius— 'Hugoni Grotio viro eruditissimo' is Milton's admiring dative—was 'more learned and erudite' than Selden.

We do not possess such unassailably authoritative statements as to the extent and quality of Coleridge's learning. We do, however, have enough discriminating expressions of admiration to conclude that if Coleridge is not 'the chief of learned men', he is among those from whom the chief must be chosen. 'Coleridge', says Matthew Arnold, 'had immense reading.' 'Coleridge was a polymath', says Herbert Read—and then adds that 'it is never safe to assume that Coleridge had not read anything published before the year of his death'. '[I] have read almost every thing', writes Coleridge himself in 1796—and the claim receives the firm endorsement of Lowes as being 'a statement which few who know their Coleridge will seriously doubt!' And though the 'almost every thing' did not at the time —Coleridge was only twenty-four—necessarily encompass the best, we know from Lowes's massively documented study that quantitatively it was extensive indeed. And it must have grown ever more extensive, to judge by Coleridge's reading habits—some seven years later, for instance, he writes that he has 'not read on an average less than 8 hours a day for the last three years'.

Perhaps the most important, or at least the most unusual, testimony is, however, that of Coleridge's detractors. 'Hardly a speculation has been left on record from earliest time', writes Hazlitt, 'but it is loosely folded up in Mr. Coleridge's memory . . . scarce a thought can pass through the mind of man, but its sound has at some time or other passed over his head with rustling pinions.' 'Coleridge, we must conclude,' says René Wellek, speaking of the area where his own great learning is most profound, 'was an omnivorous reader well abreast of German aesthetics and philosophy.' And De Quincey, in the very essay in which he initiates the charges of plagiarism against Coleridge, provides us with a memorable portrait of Coleridge's learned theological disputes with the Bishop of Llandaff:

> Coleridge was armed, at all points, with the scholastic erudition which bore upon all questions that could arise in polemic divinity. The philosophy of ancient Greece, through all its schools, the philosophy of the schoolmen technically so called, Church history, &c., Coleridge had within his call. Having been personally acquainted, or connected as a pupil, with Eichhorn and Michaelis, he knew the whole cycle of schisms and audacious speculations through which Biblical criticism or Christian philosophy has revolved in Modern Germany. All this was ground upon which the Bishop of Llandaff trod with the infirm footing of a child. He listened to what Coleridge reported with the same sort of pleasurable surprise, alternating with starts of doubt or incredulity, as would naturally attend a detailed report from Laputa . . .

IV

If we agree to keep always in mind the simple fact of Coleridge's learning, we can, I believe, spare ourselves some rather common errors in our attempts to ascertain the essentials of his intellectual position. In the first place, if we prove wrong at a given point, we shall at least not compound our wrongness by an impudently superior attitude towards our subject. In a consideration of Coleridge's plagiarisms, for instance, we shall not only avoid the graceless *Schadenfreude* of a Ferrier, but, with a more cautious approach, perhaps be able to salvage something more from the discussion than the customary flotsam of triumphant accusation and indignant defence. In the second place, we shall find ourselves directed towards an organic, rather than a segmented assessment of Coleridge's thought. With an *a priori* awareness of his vast erudition, we shall be more appreciative of the pertinence of his own prime critical maxim— that until one understands a writer's ignorance, one should presume oneself ignorant of the writer's understanding—and in our attempts to reach the frontiers of his knowledge we shall, I think, tend to read ever further before allowing our opinions to assume their final form. In doing so we should become more aware of the organically interfused quality of his learning, and from that awareness we may possibly be able to penetrate to the great central ideas at the heart of the organism.

Once we realize the intrinsically organic quality of Coleridge's erudition, we shall have the basis for a genuine comprehension of his role and stature as a philosopher. René Wellek, the most learned among commentators on Coleridge, admits 'the fascination of the many historical problems' which are raised by Coleridge's 'eclectic use of sources', but also says that he has 'still to be convinced that Coleridge deserves a place among independent and original speculative philosophers'. Now it seems to me that the words 'original' and 'eclectic' are somewhat misleading— the former in relation to philosophy in general, the latter with respect to Coleridge in particular.

If we discard for a moment the honorific overtones of 'original', we shall agree, I think, that in the strict sense no philosopher is original. 'I am not at all of the humour of those who desire that their opinions may seem new', writes Descartes in May 1644. 'If', says H. A. Wolfson, 'we could cut up all the philosophic literature' available to Spinoza 'into slips of paper, toss them up into the air, and let them fall back to the ground, then out of these scattered slips of paper we could reconstruct his *Ethics*.' According to Diogenes Laertius, it was said by some in antiquity that Epicurus 'put forward as his own the doctrines of Democritus about atoms and of Aristippus about pleasure'. And according to Porphyry, Plotinus was accused 'of appropriating the ideas of Numenius'. Such judgements and accusations could be extended to cover every major philosophical figure, and, in fact, have been extended and definitively documented. Descartes, indeed, coolly asserts as one of the prime virtues of his *Principia philosophiae* the fact 'that this treatise contains no principles which are not universally received; and that this philosophy is not new. . . . I have . . . made use of no principle which was not received and approved by Aristotle, and by the other philosophers of all ages.' It is not merely that the structural activities of all human minds, fed by the *sensus communis*, and directed towards common problems, will produce basically similar results, but that philosophers have traditionally considered themselves to be striving less for originality than for truth. Thus, for example, Hegel's disciple, Karl Michelet, was annoyed by Eduard von Hartmann's charge, not that Hegel lacked originality, but, quite the opposite, that Hegel was too original to be significant. Hartmann attempted 'to tear Hegel out from the connexion of the history of philosophy— to isolate him'. Hartmann, says Michelet, not only 'grudges Hegel's agreement with Plato', but tries to separate Hegel from Kant, Fichte, and Schelling:

> The exposition, finally, of the philosophical systems of Kant, Fichte, and Schelling, as being perfectly separated from the Hegelian dialectic, bears testimony to the greatest ignorance—for everyone who has lived through this stage in the history of philosophy, or has restored it by study to new life within him, will have seen before his very eyes the gradual growth of the Hegelian dialectic from those standpoints.

The significance of Michelet's opinion does not depend upon its correctness as a statement of historical fact, but rather upon the point that a devoted disciple of a great philosopher should, in the heat of defensive polemic, abjure 'originality' for his master, and, indeed, appear to regard lack of 'originality' as the *sine qua non* of philosophical importance.

A similar example can be adduced from the controversies surrounding the philosophy of Schelling. In 1804 Franz Berg, announcing that 'I treasure Schelling, but I treasure the truth still more', launched an attack, in the form of a dialogue entitled *Sextus*, upon Schelling's *Bruno*. In the course of Berg's dialogue, the situation—quite strange to us with our notions of the value of originality—develops of Plotin (the character defending Schelling's thought) claiming Schelling as the philosophical heir of the ancient Greeks, and Sextus (Berg) high-handedly denying Plotin's contention. 'Do you really, in all seriousness,' says Sextus in utter disbelief, 'maintain that the ancient thinkers of Greece anticipated Schelling's Absolute Idealism?' Plotin proceeds to an elaborate justification of his contention, but Sextus cuts him off: 'Tell me just one thing: whether you really believe that the philosophers of Greece preceded Schelling in the invention of the Absolute.' Plotin, cornered, stoutly replies: 'I do believe it.'

A few pages later, the interlocutors begin to wrangle over whether Plato and Schelling represent the same philosophy. Again we find the strange situation of Schelling's opponent claiming 'originality' for Schelling—as the most damaging statement that can be made—and Schelling's defender vigorously asserting the identity of the philosophies of Schelling and Plato.

How damaging was Berg's ascription of 'originality' to Schelling may be seen from a ferocious dialogue entitled *Anti-Sextus*, written in 1807 by Johann Götz, a disciple of Schelling, in which much vehemence is expended in denying Schelling's 'originality'. 'Ach, armer Plato,' moans the distraught Götz, 'wie bist du unter die Mörder gefallen'—and he then proceeds to demonstrate the similarity of the doctrines of Schelling and Plato. He concludes with the unequivocal statement: 'This is Plato's true philosophy, set forth, to be sure, in non-technical language, but correctly described none the less. It is not in the slightest different from Schelling's thought. (*Nicht im geringsten ist sie verschieden von Schellings Lehre.*)'

In another sense, it is true, every great philosopher is an original. But his originality is never in the elements with which he works, nor in the conclusions he reaches, nor in the logic by which elements lead to conclusions, nor, indeed, except rarely, in the terminology he uses. Leibniz, for example, in his *Epistola ad Hanschium de philosophia platonica*, is at pains to state that 'the simple substances, which I call Monads' are identical with the 'objects of true knowledge' which Plato called 'τὰ ὄντως ὄντα'. And think of Eisler's monumental work on philosophical terminology in general, or of the many monographs, such as Richter's on the nature of Spinoza's terminology, that invalidate so thoroughly almost all claims, from whatever quarter, to terminological originality. 'Every philosophical thinker', says Kant in his *Logik*, 'builds, so to speak, his own work on the debris (*Trümmern*) of another.' A great philosopher's originality lies not in terminology, but rather in viewpoint and tone, and, above all, in the organic quality of his position. His historical importance doubtless depends upon factors of *race*, *moment*, and *milieu*, but his intrinsic quality, that which distinguishes him from other thinkers of similar persuasion, is almost wholly dependent upon the character of his work as an organism. As Hegel says,

> In the Platonic philosophy we see . . . many philosophemes which belong to an earlier time, but they are taken up into Plato's deeper principle, and therein united. This relation is possible from the fact that the Platonic philosophy exhibits a totality of the idea; hence, as a result, it includes in itself the principles of the previous philosophies. Plato in many of his works attempts nothing more than an exposition of the more ancient philosophies; and what there is peculiarly his own in these expositions consists only in the fact that he has expanded them.

Hegel's opinion on matters of philosophical history is, we may agree,

authoritative and weighty; and in this particular focus upon derivat-
iveness as a characteristic of great philosophy it can easily be reinforced
by ancient authority itself—note, for example, the evident pride with which
Porphyry reports that his master Plotinus, quite without originality,
'set the principles of Pythagoras and of Plato in a clearer light than anyone
before him,' and furthermore, continues Porphyry serenely, 'in Plotinus's
writings both the Stoic and Peripatetic doctrines are embedded; Aristotle's Metaphysic, especially, is condensed in them, all but entire.'

V

Such strictures on the nature and limitations of philosophical originality
should be valuable to us in determining our attitude towards Coleridge's
plagiarisms from the philosophies of his German contemporaries, especially his adoption of some of the idiosyncratic terminological units of
those philosophies. Despite the tendency of practising philosophers in
all times and all places to be, in Northrop Frye's phrase, 'terminological
buccaneers', some of the most persistent attacks on Coleridge have been
directed against his lack of an original terminology. Thus Wellek says
that 'one may take as ethically lenient as possible a view of Coleridge's
borrowings, but still one cannot deny the central fact that, on many
crucial issues and at many important points of his writings, Coleridge
adopts the words and terminology of other men'. Stirling employs a
more censorious tone to express the same attitude: Coleridge's philosophy is insignificant because it is not characterized by terminological
innovation. Stirling denies the legitimacy of Coleridge's use of such
polarities as 'subjective' and 'objective', 'transcendent' and 'transcendental', because they involve, he says, distinctions 'absolutely and exclusively Kant's'. 'Of *reason* and *understanding*', he continues, 'we may speak
in precisely the same tone. This distinction, also, is Kant's, and Kant's
alone.' But Stirling's claims are simply without historical validity. It is
a point of historical fact that 'reason' and 'understanding' were not 'Kant's,
and Kant's alone', but that, quite the contrary, the distinction formed the
very core of the philosophical thought of Kant's opponent, Jacobi. So
important, in fact, is the dichotomy for Jacobi's position, that the transcendentalist sophisticate Frederic Henry Hedge, who was the chief
purveyor of German culture to nineteenth-century America, even says
baldly that 'the distinction between reason and understanding, now so
widely accepted' was one that 'Jacobi was the first to point out, or, at
least, to make prominent'.

Wellek plays a different version of the same curious game of terminological precedences. For instance, Coleridge, in the *Biographia Literaria*,
after discussing 'the use of technical terms in philosophy', and deciding

that such terms are justified when they help preclude confusion or assist the memory, then says—somewhat disingenuously—that he will 'venture to use *potence*, in order to express a specific degree of a power. . .'. Wellek takes up the word. 'Even "potence" ', he notes, 'was suggested by Schelling's use.' No doubt it was. But if we play the precedence game, we should apply its rules fairly to all; if we question Coleridge's priority in 'potence', we must likewise question Schelling's priority in 'Potenz'. If we do so, meanwhile maintaining fond convictions as to Schelling's 'originality', we shall find ourselves much perplexed. For where Coleridge takes the word 'potence' from Schelling—and then, apparently finding no real use for it, lets it fade away—Schelling takes not only his word 'Potenz', but the specific pantheistic complex to which it refers, bodily from the 'potenza' described at length by Giordano Bruno in the third dialogue of his *De la causa*—takes the word, indeed, and uses it vigorously and centrally in various treatises. And lest anyone doubt whether Schelling was in fact familiar with Bruno's thought, it might be well to recall that in 1802 was published that dialogue of Schelling's that pleased Goethe so much: *Bruno; oder, über das göttliche und natürliche Princip der Dinge.*

But what is most humiliating for the faith in Schelling's originality demanded by the precedence game, is the fact, as certain as ever a fact can be, that not only did Schelling not 'originate' his word 'Potenz', but he did not, even, translate it from an Italian text of Bruno's dialogue; rather, he simply took it over, already translated as 'Potenz', from a work very much in his consciousness during his student days: namely, from the translated extract from *De la causa* that appeared as an appendix to the second edition of Jacobi's *Ueber die Lehre des Spinoza*. The date was 1789. The extract was appended, says Jacobi, both because of the 'Seltenheit'—the rareness—of copies of Bruno's dialogue, and because, together with the doctrine of Spinoza, it would provide 'gleichsam die Summa der Philosophie des ἕν καὶ πᾶν'—the 'Summa', as it were, of pantheist philosophy. In Jacobi's translation, therefore, we find not only the term 'Potenz', but its concept, conveniently Germanized for Schelling's use: e.g., 'Das Princip, welches Materie heisst, kann auf zweyerley Weise betrachtet werden. Einmal, als *Potenz*; hernach, als *Subject*', or, again, 'Das Universum, die unerzeugte Natur, ist . . . nur ein Schatten von dem Bilde des ersten Princips, in welchem thätige Kraft und Potenz, Möglichkeit und Wirklichkeit Eins und dasselbe sind.' So that the hurried reader would not fail to see the word, Jacobi obligingly incorporated it into a section heading: 'II. Von dem materiellen Princip überhaupt; hernach insbesondere von dem materiellen Princip als Potenz betrachtet.'

So much for 'Potenz'. It is not necessary, I hope, to insist that Bruno's own 'potenza', if pressed, would recede into the Latin 'potentia' of Nicholas of Cusa, and thence backward into the mists of scholastic controversy and ancient philosophy. To be sure, Coleridge—situated in England amid clamorous reviewers and, according to Matthew Arnold, provincially ignorant Romantic compeers—did, to satisfy the literary canons of English Romanticism, make some tentative and ambiguous claims about 'originality'; while Schelling, squarely in the middle of a hugely sophisticated philosophical tradition, could not, even had he so desired, so much as think of asserting terminological or other 'originality'. But surely the difference between the situations of Schelling and of Coleridge is irrelevant to our judgement of the intrinsic merit of either.

No, the tendency of German philosophy in its great age was to stabilize terminology, to attempt to make it public and precise. All the German philosophers were *au courant*: they all were in command of the history of philosophy, and they all read each brochure of their contemporary peers and rivals. In such a milieu it was simply pointless to play the provincial game of originality or priority, and it is a documentable fact of philosophical history that only very rarely did they play it. Though the polemics that stemmed from the combination of their intellectual intensity and their physical proximity often became bitter and even libellous, the one charge that almost never seemed to occur was the charge of plagiarism. 'Goethe', reminisces Henry Crabb Robinson, 'despised all imputations of plagiarism, and all disputes about originality', and Goethe's attitude was in this instance normative for his contemporaries. Kant, Herder, Schelling, Fichte, Hegel, Jacobi, Maimon used a common vocabulary of words and concepts without quarrelling about priorities. We find that such terms as 'reason', 'understanding', 'subject', 'object', 'idea', 'concept', 'imagination', are used by all these thinkers, not as their own terminological property, but as public words referring to the universal interests of philosophy. It is, for instance, difficult to imagine a term more idiosyncratic, more seemingly the sole property of its user, than was the term 'idea' for Plato. Yet we find Kant appropriating Plato's 'idea'—and not only the term, but the logical complex to which the term refers—as a public word referring to lasting and objective concerns of philosophy, as a word that later thinkers might therefore properly use, refocus, or even redefine.

For Kant regarded himself as a terminological focuser, not as a terminological innovator. Indeed, not only does he never reproach, say, Jacobi, for expropriating the distinction of 'reason' and 'understanding', but he leaves the position of Stirling and Wellek quite without support when he says, in the *Critique of Pure Reason*, that

to coin new words is to advance a claim to legislation in language that seldom succeeds; and before we have recourse to this desperate expedient it is advisable to look about in a dead and learned language, to see whether the concept and its appropriate expression are not already there provided. Even if the old-time usage of a term should have become somewhat uncertain through the carelessness of those who introduced it, it is always better to hold fast to the meaning which distinctively belongs to it . . . than to defeat our purpose by making ourselves unintelligible.

Thus, though Stirling and Wellek rebuke Coleridge for adopting 'the words and terminology of other men', for Coleridge not to have done so would, in the view of Kant, have been a 'desperate expedient'. Nor is Kant's opinion an eccentric one; it is rather the traditional view of practising philosophers. We find, for instance, our own contemporary, Gabriel Marcel, stating, in his preface to the English edition of his *Metaphysical Journal*, a similar opinion:

I must confess that I have never been fond of neologisms in metaphysics. They always seem to me barbarous . . . the mode of current expression, by the very fact that it has served for a multitude of different cases, has become charged with a genuine potential that neologisms lack. . . . The mind, that is to say, does not feel that it is 'at home'; it feels that it is 'nowhere', as in certain modern edifices that lack a past and a style.

VI

Such recurrent attitudes of the philosophical tradition apply, with what seems to me a controlling pertinency, to the explanation of Schelling's own mildness in the plagiarism charges against Coleridge. Jowett and Stanley report a conversation in which Schelling praises Coleridge and protests that it is 'an utter shame to talk of his having plagiarised from him, Schelling'. Though Robertson, unwilling to see Coleridge so easily absolved, suggests that 'it is not clear that Schelling knew all the facts', what is abundantly clear is Schelling's disinclination to admit the possibility of real plagiarism in a genuine thinker—and the less Schelling knew of the facts (to give tentative credit to Robertson's assumption that a man of Schelling's sophistication and acuteness would speak from ignorance on a matter touching his own philosophical reputation), the more integral to his philosophical stance does such a disinclination become. While it is true that Schelling accused Hegel of 'taking my ideas', we must view this unusual charge in the special context of the two men's former youthful friendship and subsequent intense rivalry. Heine, indeed, implies mockingly that Schelling makes himself foolish by the charge ('Nothing is more ridiculous than the claim of property rights to ideas. Hegel has certainly used a great many of Schelling's ideas in his philosophy; but Herr Schelling would never have known what to do with these ideas'). Far more representative of Schelling's attitude is his written exoneration of Coleridge, where, praising Coleridge as a 'many-talented Briton', he says that the 'unacknowledged borrowings from my writings' have been 'sharply, yes, too sharply, censured by his fellow countrymen. A really congenial thinker should not be charged in this way.' Yet Schelling was notoriously polemical—was a controversialist not renowned for generosity to his competitors. It should be evident that his unwillingness to charge Coleridge with plagiarism, regardless of the data on which it was based, can no more be discounted than can the conflicting fact that Coleridge did translate without proper acknowledgment portions of Schelling's philosophical works.

Coleridge did translate from Schelling, and Schelling did decline to make a charge of plagiarism. The seeming contradiction of the two acts suggests that the definition of plagiarism has not been satisfactorily drawn, and it suggests further that there is more to becoming the intellectual echo of another man than merely translating from his works. It seems to me, indeed, that Coleridge's total intellectual position is remarkably dissimilar to that of Schelling—that their thought is not only not identical, but also not even parallel. The relationship should rather be conceived as an athwartness; the lines of their philosophical consequence start from different backgrounds and personal presuppositions, approach one another in Coleridge's formulations around the year 1815, intersect in the Schelling translations of the *Biographia Literaria*, and then begin to diverge.

The true scheme of their relationship is therefore not identical lines as represented by the letter 'I', but intersecting lines as represented by the letter 'X'. Though Coleridge borrows from Schelling on other occasions, only the use of Schelling in the *Biographia Literaria*, I hope to show, can be regarded as relevant to the organization of his thought. And that use, almost beyond doubt, demonstrated to Coleridge, as it should to us, not the coincidence of the two men's philosophical concerns, but rather their hopeless irreconcilability.

I shall not, at the moment, insist upon this view. It seems more relevant for the present discussion merely to point out that Schelling is today almost wholly unread, while Coleridge remains a burning issue in modern literary studies. I intend no invidious comparisons—my respect for Schelling as an aesthetic philosopher approaches reverence—but surely we cannot reconcile the hypothesized point-for-point similarity between the thought of the two men with their strikingly dissimilar status in our own time. With the exception of Paul Tillich, I can bring to mind no modern thinker for whom Schelling has been of seminal importance. To some extent this state of affairs probably results from the fact that Schelling's major work has not been translated (although that fact in itself may be suggestive), but even in Germany Schelling is today only of academic interest. T. S. Eliot confesses that 'of Schelling I am entirely ignorant' and that, furthermore, Schelling 'is one of those numerous authors whom, the longer you leave them unread, the less desire you have' to read them. Though we may feel that the poet is the loser by his attitude, it is for all that typical. In a sense, too, the modern attitude can be seen not only as a vagary of historical taste, but as an implicit criticism of a certain deficiency in Schelling's work. 'Es ist ein sonderbares modernes Phänomen,' said Novalis as far back as 1798, 'das nicht zu Schellings Nachteil ist, das seine "Ideen" schon so welk, so unbrauchbar sind — Erst in neuesten Zeiten sind solche kurzlebige Bücher erschienen.'

Now it is interesting to speculate on whether this 'unusable', 'short-lived' quality that Novalis sensed in his contemporary's work has something to do with a lack of organicism in Schelling's thought. Schelling is ostensibly the most systematic and organic of thinkers, and seems particularly so in comparison with the apparently chaotic and fragmentary Coleridge. Yet, if we accept Coleridge's fragmentariness as in fact implying an extreme cohesion of thought, and if we accept organicism as the only true philosophic originality, the one guarantee against the ephemeral, we shall at least wonder whether Schelling's surface coherence of organization might not have been achieved by a studious rejection of elements and problems that did not readily fit his system. It is perhaps symptomatic that Karl Jaspers praises Schelling's insight most generously, but also asserts that he 'failed as creator of a system'. Novalis complains that 'in der Schellingschen Naturphilosophie wird ein beschränkter Begriff der Natur und der Philosophie vorausgesetzt'. And Hegel observes that Schelling's philosophy is 'nicht ein in seine Glieder organisirtes wissenschaftliches Ganzes'—not an organized, rigorous whole.

We do not necessarily need to subscribe to such objections to realize that Schelling is here being reproached with that same raw 'eclecticism' that Wellek finds in Coleridge. I question, therefore, whether 'eclecticism' is the proper term for Coleridge's use of his learning. The word implies the freedom to pick and choose, and thereby to reject, and it is a commonplace that for Coleridge the doctrine of the reconciliation of opposites was of primary importance, and that his persistent endeavour was to *make a place for* all facts and viewpoints, however varied. Was this not, in fact, to have been the characterizing principle of the *magnum opus*? He did, like Schelling, employ many sources; but—and the point, though almost a truism, has apparently not been stressed—the employment of a variety of sources is a mark of all powerful minds.

VII

Coleridge's thought demands for its assessment a recognition—and it is a recognition not usually accorded—that his intellectual endeavour constitutes an organic unity. There is in reality no tripartite division of rhapsodic poet, maundering metaphysician, and pious theologian; the same Coleridge philosophizes, poetizes, and theologizes, and, furthermore, the different fields of his interests are mutually interdependent—his poetry, both in theory and in practice, is essentially, not accidentally, involved with his philosophy, and his philosophy is reciprocally bound up with his theological interests.

Perhaps most of us would be willing to afford the foregoing claim an easy assent—is it not fashionable for every commentator to plead for his subject unity and profundity of thought and utterance? What I am urging, however, is rather different. I am saying that we have all forgotten how to think in systematic or organic terms in the sense that those terms had validity for philosophical minds from Descartes to Hegel. The two major modes of twentieth-century philosophizing, the existential and the positivist, derive more from a simple rejection of system than from any other single attitude; certainly both take their historical departure from the systems of German idealism, and in this sense both Kierkegaard and Mach, despite their wide differences in psychological orientation, have in common an almost compulsive need to strike from themselves what had apparently become the chains of the systematic. We find in Kierkegaard's triumphant philosophical dishevelment and ferocious denunciations of 'the System', a counterpart of Mach's anti-systematic credo in *The Analysis of Sensations*. 'The philosophical thinker', says Mach,

proceeds to make the single problem of the Ego . . . the starting-point for everything else. . . . When, therefore, speculative philosophers say 'Solipsism is the only logically consistent standpoint', their utterance is quite intelligible in view of their struggle to reach a closed, all-inclusive, complete system of the universe. . . . [But] the man of science is not looking for a completed vision of the universe . . . there is no such thing as 'the philosophy of Mach'.

And if for the father of modern positivistic thought 'there is no such thing as "the philosophy of Mach" ', it is likewise true that the existentialist tradition has also defined itself by its opposition to systematic thought. 'No existential system of philosophy is possible', says Kierkegaard in his *Concluding Unscientific Postscript*, and Kierkegaard's positivist/existentialist predecessor, Hamann, had even earlier, in 1786, written to Jacobi that 'we must be weaned from system'.

Certainly these two modes of thought, the positivist and the existential, have imparted important shadings to the intellectual spectrum of our century; in our historical consideration of thinkers of previous eras, however, they both serve as distorting and atomizing principles. One might call to mind briefly the almost total lack of historical sense in the writings of Bertrand Russell—a lack that in his history of western philosophy and his work on Leibniz results in judgements that might not unfairly be termed grotesque. Such reservations might be extended to include Wittgenstein or Carnap or Reichenbach. Wittgenstein, for instance, his brilliance notwithstanding, appears, in the portrait by Norman Malcolm, as a thinker almost unbelievably ill-read in the history of philosophy. Nor are the existentialists mighty historians.

No, we do not now fully understand the rules and aims of systematic thought, and we are consequently at a disadvantage when we try to understand what a mind like Coleridge's was attempting to do. To understand Coleridge's thought, both in its own structure and in its relationship to the thought of his contemporaries, it is necessary to refer all its manifestations constantly and explicitly to the systematic unity, the total organism which he, and almost all other thinkers of his era, accepted as the necessary condition of any intellectual activity at all. In a sense, when dealing with thinkers of Coleridge's time, we really do not care whether the system is articulated or merely implied. Mill reproaches Sir William Hamilton for being unable to draw the unexpressed corollaries of philosophical systems, and Kant was undeviating in his belief that the implications of a given philosophical position could be thought through by thinkers other than its author. 'Die menschliche Vernunft', said Kant in a statement utterly alien to twentieth-century predilections, 'ist ihrer Natur nach architektonisch, d.i. sie betrachtet alle Erkenntnisse als gehörig zu einem möglichen System'—human reason is by its nature architectonic, that is, looks upon all knowledge as belonging to a possible system. We today take something very much like pride in the limitations of our intellectual forays and in the lack of system in our thought. We are the heirs of a Mach who can suggest that 'the universe, as conceived by me, seems to be a chaos, a hopelessly tangled web of elements'. Psychologically, we are almost all random empirics, and we delight more in paradox than in harmony.

But for Coleridge, as for Kant, the architectonic concern was paramount, and perhaps the most important word in Kant's statement is 'possible'—for it reveals the omnipresence of system, whether, as in Hegel, fully enunciated, or, as in Coleridge, merely implied. Always it was to system, to the architectonic harmonizing of various elements, that thought bent its energies. And the urge to system is a reflection, in the special realm of philosophy, of a universal concern, the need to harmonize, to tie things together—what we may call the need for reticulation. 'Because man falls into self-contradiction', said Jacobi, 'therefore he philosophizes. In countless ways he loses the connexion of his truths . . . to philosophize is to recollect ourselves on all sides.' It is, indeed, possible that the whole thrust to unity so characteristic of Romanticism, as opposed to the classifying instinct of the eighteenth century, should be primarily seen—whether we think of the revival of the *coincidentia oppositorum* in minds as different as those of Hamann, Coleridge, Hegel, and Victor Hugo, or whether we think of the rise of pantheism in religion, of synaesthesia in art, of democracy in politics, of system in philosophy, of distinction-dissolving 'progressive Universalpoesie' in literature—as an intensification of the reticulative need.

In such a perspective this essay is, in its most general description, a study of the reticulation of Coleridge's thought. By using the term reticulation I intend to suggest a concern for as many interconnexions as possible: the interconnexions of his total activity with that of his contemporaries and with certain of the traditions of thought important in his time, as well as the interconnexions of the various modes—literary, theological, philosophical—of his intellectual vitality. Of the possible ways of entry into the study of these important but little understood relevancies, none is more dramatic than the questions raised by the problem of Coleridge's plagiarisms. So we will begin with that problem.

CHAPTER I

The Problem of Coleridge's Plagiarisms

WITH the appearance, in 1955, of the chapter on Coleridge in René Wellek's monumental history of modern criticism, the enthusiastic Coleridge revival of preceding decades seemed to have received a major check. Deriving its original impetus from the amazement aroused by Lowes's scholarly *tour de force*, and further focused by Richards's reappraisal of the aesthetic validity of Coleridge's theory of imagination, the honorific reconsideration encompassed successively Coleridge's poetry, his criticism, his philosophy, and his theology. His general reputation as an aesthetic theorist rose so high that the New Critics, casting about for anchorage in the critical tradition, adopted him almost unanimously as the founding father of the New Criticism, while scholars and historical critics discovered in his erudition and brilliant historical sense their own grounds for admiration. But then Wellek, in a work of immense scope and authority, disparages Coleridge as at best a second-hand thinker, a purveyor of borrowed ideas, and, at worst, and in many cases, as an out-and-out plagiarist.

So serious a charge cannot be ignored, and it serves to direct attention once more to a literary controversy that has raged with acrimony for over a century, that has involved important reputations, important thoughts, important historical precedents—and, judging by the viciousness of its central documents and by the virtual suppression of its existence in the consciousness of most modern students of English literature—important psychological biases. I refer, of course, to the controversy surrounding the nature and extent of Coleridge's plagiarisms from his German contemporaries.

The charge of plagiarism was initially made by De Quincey in an article —the first of a series occasioned by Coleridge's death—in *Tait's Edinburgh Magazine* for September 1834. According to De Quincey, Coleridge's old friend Thomas Poole 'furnished me with the first hint of a singular infirmity besetting Coleridge's mind'[1]—and De Quincey proceeds then to set forth a conversation between himself and Poole in which Poole mentions that 'our dear excellent friend Coleridge, than whom God never made a creature more divinely endowed . . . sometimes steals from other

---

[1] *De Quincey*, ii. 142.

people, just as you or I might do'[1]—and goes on to discuss the sense of *déjà vu* furnished by Coleridge's interpretation, in conversation, of the significance of Pythagoras's remark that a philosopher should beware of beans. 'Think, therefore,' De Quincey represents Poole as saying, 'if you have anywhere read a plausible solution.' 'I have,' replies De Quincey, 'and it was a German author. This German, understand, is a poor stick of a man, not to be named on the same day with Coleridge: so that, if Coleridge should appear to have robbed him, be assured that he has done the scamp too much honour'[2]—and De Quincey then explains the German author's interpretation, whereupon Poole is represented as saying, 'Well, then, Coleridge *has* done the scamp too much honour: for, by Jove, that is the very explanation he gave us.'[3] Continuing in a more serious vein, De Quincey says:

> Here was a trait of Coleridge's mind, to be first made known to me by his best friend, and first published to the world by me, the foremost of his admirers.... To forestall ... other discoverers, who would make a more unfriendly use of the discovery,—and also as matters of literary curiosity, I shall here point out a few others of Coleridge's unacknowledged obligations, noticed by myself in a very wide course of reading.[4]

De Quincey then lists four instances of Coleridge's plagiarism, beginning with the 'Hymn Before Sunrise in the Vale of Chamouni', which he identifies as in part an expansion, in part a translation, of Friederica Brun's ode to Klopstock. The fourth instance, however, is the one on which he appears willing to rest his case:

> All these cases amount to nothing at all as cases of plagiarism, and for this reason expose the more conspicuously that obliquity of feeling which could seek to decline the very slight acknowledgments required. But now I come to a case of real and palpable plagiarism; yet that, too, of a nature to be quite unaccountable in a man of Coleridge's attainments. It is not very likely that this particular case will soon be detected; but others will. Yet who knows? Eight hundred or a thousand years hence, some reviewer may arise who, having read the 'Biographia Literaria' of Coleridge, will afterwards read the 'Philosophical ——' [De Quincey's footnote for the blank space reads: 'I forget the exact title, not having seen the book since 1823, and then only for one day; but I believe it was Schelling's "Kleine Philosophische Werke" '] of Schelling, the great Bavarian professor—a man in some respects worthy to be Coleridge's assessor; and he will then make a singular discovery. In the 'Biographia Literaria' occurs a dissertation upon the reciprocal relations of the *Esse* and the *Cogitare*,—that is, of the *objective* and the *subjective*: and an attempt is made, by inverting the postulates from which the argument starts, to show how each might arise as a product ... from the other. It is a subject which, since the time of Fichte, has much occupied the German metaphysicians; and many thousands

---

[1] *De Quincey*, ii. 142.   [2] Ibid.   [3] Ibid., p. 143.   [4] Ibid.

of essays have been written on it, or indirectly so, of which many hundreds have been read by many tens of persons. Coleridge's essay, in particular, is prefaced by a few words in which, aware of his coincidence with Schelling, he declares his willingness to acknowledge himself indebted to so great a man in any case where the truth would allow him to do so; but, in this particular case, insisting on the impossibility that he could have borrowed arguments which he had first seen some years after he had thought out the whole hypothesis *proprio marte*. After this, what was my astonishment to find that the entire essay, from the first word to the last, is a *verbatim* translation from Schelling, with no attempt in a single instance to appropriate the paper by developing the arguments or by diversifying the illustrations? Some other obligations to Schelling, of a slighter kind, I have met with in the 'Biographia Literaria'; but this was a barefaced plagiarism, which could in prudence have been risked only by relying too much upon the slight knowledge of German literature in this country, and especially of that section of the German literature.[1]

De Quincey's accusation was ameliorated by an acute and sympathetic analysis of the possible pyschological explanation for Coleridge's actions, by a favourable attitude towards Coleridge's intrinsic originality, and finally, by a casualness that led him into citing Coleridge's source as Schelling's 'Kleine Philosophische Werke' (the work in question is actually the *System des transscendentalen Idealismus*).

A second attack was soon forthcoming, and it made no such mistakes. It was not casual, it was not favourable, and it was not sympathetic. In 1840, in an unsigned article in *Blackwood's Edinburgh Magazine* entitled 'The Plagiarisms of S. T. Coleridge', J. F. Ferrier launched a ferocious assault on Coleridge's honesty and philosophical reputation. Under the guise of prolegomena for a second edition of the *Biographia Literaria*, Ferrier demands 'some accurate notice and admission of the very large and unacknowledged appropriations it contains from the writings of the great German philosopher Schelling',[2] and then announces that he intends to 'do our best to supply the requisite information on this subject— tracing Coleridge's plagiarisms to their true sources, fixing their precise amount, or nearly so (as far, at least, as Schelling is concerned), and arguing the whole question on its broadest grounds, both literary and moral'.[3] He disclaims intent to damage Coleridge's reputation; yet he insists that

we are not going to sacrifice what we conceive to be truth and justice out of regard to the genius of any man, however high it may have been, or to the memory of any man, however illustrious and apparently unsullied it may be. Fair play is a jewel: and we think it our duty to see fair play upon all sides; and, if our admiration of Coleridge has whispered in our ear to keep this disclosure back, our admiration of Schelling (which we admit to be greater than that which

---

[1] Ibid., pp. 145–6.
[2] *Blackwood's Edinburgh Magazine*, xlvii (1840), 287. [3] Ibid.

we feel for Coleridge) was ever at hand, appealing to our conscience with a still louder voice to bring it forward, and to do justice to the claims of foreign philosophy and of individual genius, by showing that one of the most distinguished English authors of the nineteenth century, at the mature age of forty-five, succeeded in founding by far the greater part of his metaphysical reputation —which was very considerable—upon *verbatim* plagiarisms from works written and published by a German youth, when little more than twenty years of age![1]

Ferrier then explains that he is confining his accusation to the ' "first volume" of the "Biog. Lit." ',[2] and that he will refrain from entering into any discussion or 'explanation touching the transcendental philosophy in general',[3] but that 'we can at least state the exact pages of Coleridge in which the plagiarisms occur, and the corresponding pages of Schelling from which they are taken.'[4] Ferrier then embarks upon a tightly knit exposition that is rendered somewhat opaque by his method of describing rather than quoting the parallel passages involved. An arbitrary specimen will serve to convey the method:

The first instance in which we detect Coleridge translating closely from Schelling occurs in p. 130, beginning at the words 'how *being*'—the last clause is interpolated, we think not very wisely. This and the next sentence are to be found in Schelling's 'Transcendental Idealism', p. 113. The next two sentences ('Biog. Lit.,' p. 131) are to be found (slightly altered from the original) in 'Transc. Id.,' p. 112.—Then Coleridge interposes a short sentence of his own; after which we come to the words, 'Matter has no *inward*. We remove one surface but to meet with another.' This occurs in two places in Schelling's works; *vide* 'Phil. Schrift.,' p. 240, and 'Ideen', Introduction, p. 22. On turning over to p. 133, 'Biog. Lit.,' we find that nearly the whole of the first paragraph is taken from the 'Transc. Id.,' p. 113, though here the translation is not so close as usual.[5]

Ferrier makes little attempt to sustain his proclaimed impersonal attitude, and exhibits open glee at the especially blatant evidences of Coleridge's thefts:

We now pass on to the opening of Chap. X., B.L., p. 157. It commences in italics thus—the introductory words being put into the mouth of an imaginary reader: '*Esemplastic!—the word is not in Johnson, nor have I met with it elsewhere!*' 'Neither have I,' rejoins the author, Coleridge; 'I constructed it myself from the Greek words, εις ἐν πλαττειν, i.e. to shape into one.' To this we, taking up the cause and character of the imaginary reader, reply—'We beg your pardon, sir; but you did nothing of the sort—you met with it in Schelling's "Darlegung," p. 61. You there found the word "In-eins-bildung"—"a shaping into one"— which Schelling, or some other German, had literally formed from the Greek, εις ἐν πλαττειν, and you merely translated this word back into Greek, (a very easy and obvious thing to do,) and then you coined the Greek words into English, merely altering them from a noun into an adjective.' . . . Such, we will lay

[1] *Blackwood's*, p. 288.   [2] Ibid., p. 293.   [3] Ibid.   [4] Ibid.   [5] Ibid.

our life upon it, is the history of Coleridge's neology, in the instance of the word 'esemplastic'.[1]

And he manages often to be both gleeful and censorious:

We now pass on to what is, perhaps, the most singular case of plagiarism in the whole book. We find that the whole of p. 246, and the greater part of p. 247, B.L., are translated from the 'Phil. Schrift.,' pp. 327, 328, omitting three inter-polations, which rather detract from than add to the sense of the paragraph. The whole paragraph is occupied with a description of the kind of mind which is unfitted for philosophical speculations; and concludes (B.L., p. 247) in these terms: 'To remain unintelligible to such a mind (exclaims Schelling on a like occasion) is honour and a good name before God and man.' Exclaims Schelling on *a like* occasion!—why, this is the *very* occasion upon which Schelling utters that exclamation—the whole passage (with the slight exceptions mentioned) being a *verbatim* translation from him!! Can any thing beat that?—this is surely plagiarism out-plagiarised. . . . What can this mean?—is it humour, is it irony, is it dishonesty, or is it simple carelessness on the part of Coleridge?[2]

The final accounting of plagiarized passages in the *Biographia Literaria* is rendered by Ferrier as follows:

On looking back over the result of our researches, we perceive that we have traced the palpable presence of Schelling in thirty-three of Coleridge's pages. From these we will deduct two—rather more than the quantity he *admits* to have been translated *in part* from a 'contemporary writer of the Continent;'—thus leaving thirty-one pages faithfully transcribed, either wholly or partially, from Schelling. We perceive that the *continuous* whole pages so transcribed, amount to thirteen; that the *continuous* half pages so transcribed amount to six; and that the smaller passages under half a page interspersed throughout the work, amount to twelve. These latter may be calculated, on a very moderate computation, at three pages. So that we have the extraordinary number of nineteen full pages, copied almost *verbatim* from the works of the German philosopher, without one distinct word of acknowledgment on the part of the transcriber—an event in the history of literature altogether unprecedented, we believe; and in reference to the party chiefly concerned, we think we may add, quite unsuspected until now.[3]

Ferrier then concludes his attack (after a triumphant digression in which he identifies two of Coleridge's minor poems as translations from Schiller and Stolberg) with the warning that 'our purpose will have been answered, should any future author who may covet his neighbour's Pegasus or prose-nag, and conceive that the high authority of Coleridge may, to a certain extent, justify him in making free with them, be deterred from doing so by the example we have now put forth *in terrorem*. Let all men know and consider that plagiarism, like murder, sooner or later *will out*.'[4]

---

[1] Ibid., p. 294.   [2] Ibid., pp. 294–5.
[3] Ibid., p. 296.   [4] Ibid., p. 299.

Ferrier's article is central, both in tone and substance, to the entire tradition of anti-Coleridgean accusations of plagiarism, and it shares in the paradox that must inevitably inform all comment on the spectacle of an admittedly brilliant man involving himself in pointless and even stupid actions. Thus, while on the one hand it is impossible not to be impressed by the relentless documentation of Coleridge's pilfering, on the other it is surprising and rather anti-climactic to find that when the firing is over Ferrier has discovered no more than nineteen pages of plagiarism in the hundreds that make up the *Biographia Literaria*—and Ferrier's bombast seems to indicate that he himself felt the anti-climax: 'the extraordinary number of nineteen full pages, copied almost *verbatim* . . . an event in the history of literature altogether unprecedented'. In point of historical fact, of course, the event was not 'altogether unprecedented', and the 'extraordinary' number of nineteen pages somehow fails to justify Ferrier's massive shock and indignation.

The number of nineteen pages, however, was soon augmented. In 1846, in his Supplementary Dissertations to his edition of *The Works of Thomas Reid*, Sir William Hamilton took contemptuous note, in the course of a discussion of the history of association psychology, of the *Biographia Literaria*: 'In England, indeed, we have a chapter in Mr. Coleridge's "Biographia Literaria," entitled, "*On the law of Association—its history traced from Aristotle to Hartley*;" but this, in so far as it is of any value, is a plagiarism, and a blundering plagiarism, from Maass; the whole chapter exhibiting, in fact, more mistakes than paragraphs.'[1] To the word 'Maass' is appended a footnote, which begins:

'To be added to my friend Professor Ferrier's "Plagiarisms of S. T. Coleridge";' and which contains Hamilton's judgment that 'Coleridge's systematic plagiarism is, perhaps, the most remarkable on record,—taking all the circumstances into account, the foremost of which, certainly, is the natural ability of the culprit. But sooth to say, Coleridge had in him more of the ivy than of the oak—was better able to clothe than to create.'[2]

Hamilton, like Ferrier, was a Scot, and the traditional antipathy of the Scots towards the English, as well as a fierce local pride in Scottish philosophy, though not overt in Ferrier, clearly became in Hamilton a motive for the denigration of Coleridge: 'But, in truth,' says Hamilton at one point, apropos the use of the word *Idea* in Cartesian philosophy, 'it might be broadly asserted that every statement in regard to the history of this doctrine hazarded by British philosophers . . . is more or less erroneous.'[3] It is not wholly surprising, therefore, that the next major attack on Coleridge also bears marks of Scottish philosophical nationalism. In 1865

[1] Hamilton, ii. 890.
[2] Hamilton, p. 890, see note 1, p. 333.
[3] Hamilton, p. 890.

the Scottish popularizer of Kant and Hegel, J. H. Stirling, delivered himself, in his *Secret of Hegel*, of the following peremptory statement:

Coleridge, with all his logosophy, was no philosopher; and it is difficult to believe even that there is any single philosopher in the world whom he had either thoroughly studied or thoroughly understood. Schelling had both studied and originated Philosophy. Than Coleridge, he was infinitely profounder in acquisition, infinitely profounder in meditation of the same; he was infinitely clearer also, infinitely more vigorous, infinitely richer, and more elastic in the spontaneity of original suggestion and thought.[1]

Such an outburst of invidious hyperbole did not suffice Stirling for long; in 1867 he returned to the attack in an article in the *Fortnightly Review* entitled 'De Quincey and Coleridge upon Kant'. The article was ostensibly occasioned by De Quincey's Coleridge articles of 1834, where, in passing, De Quincey had repeated the early Mendelssohnian canard about Kant as the *alles zermalmender*, and had gone on, in truth quite ignorantly, to speak of Kant as the apostle of atheism and of annihilation after death. Such was the ostensible occasion; the actual purpose, it seems clear, was to discredit English writers as interpreters of German thought, and by implication to leave the Scots as the sole spokesmen for German culture to the English-speaking world. Carlyle had early pre-empted the role of interpreter of German literature, and Ferrier, Hamilton, and Stirling, apparently influenced both by Carlyle's success and by the historical connexion of the Scotsman Hume with Kant, staked a claim to German abstract thought.[2] In his article of 1867 Stirling belabours De Quincey for his errors, and, his arrogance whetted by the exercise, then turns upon the object of De Quincey's own assault, Coleridge, and adds some random but hearty blows:

The truth probably is, that Coleridge was not properly a student of philosophy, but rather a reader *carptim*. It pleased him, all the same, to sun himself, as quite a Brobdingnagian student, in the eyes of the innocent reader, by significant smiling nods to the fact of metaphysic and psychology being his 'hobby-horse'. In like manner it pleased him, too, to yield to such idle subjective fancies of the moment, as 'I believe in the depth of my being that the three great works since the introduction of Christianity are Bacon's *Novum Organum*, Spinoza's *Ethica*, and Kant's *Kritik*;' and to console his conscience, when it gnawed, by such images as, 'I have laid too many eggs in the hot sands of this wilderness, the world, with ostrich carelessness, and ostrich oblivion.' It is quite in keeping that Spinoza's should have been previously called an 'unwholesome book;' nor is it discrepant from such a nature that it should be very sharp on plagiarism in others, as in Hume and Aquinas, and about the line from Politian, and that it should whine pretentiously about taking 'a refuge from bodily pain

---

[1] Stirling, *The Secret of Hegel*, i. 28.   [2] See note 2, p. 333.

and mismanaged sensibility in abstruse researches'. . . . With faculty and law, mostly of mere receptivity and imaginative suggestion, what system of philosophy *could* Coleridge have thought out for himself? A procession of pictures he could give—to more he was incompetent. How, in this *Biographia Literaria*, he flows on in an endless prosing and prosiness, a dreamy, egotistic, querulous, plaintive prosiness—on and on, and round and round—his topics, fancy and imagination—Wordsworth, Southey, Lamb, the 'lyrical ballads,' the standards of criticism, Pope, Gray, Milton, Shakespeare, Plotinus, Proclus, Plato, Kant, Schelling—always in these last as if supporting a mighty weight, a something precious, mystic, unapproachable, of profound import, of prophetic power. . . . Finally he returns again to mumble and maunder about German philosophy, and that he had toiled it all out for himself; but that, in his laziness, he was magnanimous. Probably at bottom—we grieve to say so—it is a weak, self-indulgent, hollow nature this—a Harold Skimpole.[1]

Stirling's expression of grief was, in such a context, an insolently inadequate disclaimer; indeed, with his attack a certain shift in the focus of the accusations of plagiarism took place. Where Ferrier, despite his ferocity, had restricted himself rather scrupulously to the materials plagiarized, Stirling mentions the plagiarism in much less documented terms, and uses it really as only one gun in a general anti-Coleridgean fusillade.

The next accuser, the Scottish Shakespearian scholar C. M. Ingleby, tended to follow Stirling's method. In a lecture entitled 'On Some Points connected with the Philosophy of Coleridge', delivered before the Royal Society of Literature of the United Kingdom in 1870, Ingleby insists that it is to the earlier philosophy of Schelling 'that the little philosophical fragment, known to the world as "The Philosophy of Coleridge" actually belongs';[2] unwilling not to have his cake too, Ingleby also maintains 'that Coleridge never *thoroughly* understood Schelling'.[3]

Of Schelling's treatises, [he says], we are restricted to that called 'Ideen zu einer Philosophie der Natur' (1797), and that called 'System des Transscendentalen Idealismus' (1800), for, though Coleridge had evidently skimmed over some of the later writings of Schelling, it was from these two only that he derived his philosophical *pabulum*: I do not say philosophical method, for method, in the higher sense, he had none. . . . Much in Coleridge's works is *suggestive, stimulative, striking*; but the effect is as the manure, not as the seed: the seed must come from elsewhere.[4]

The last outburst of nineteenth-century Scottish spleen occurred in 1897, when, in his *New Essays Towards a Critical Method*, the Shakespearian

[1] J. H. Stirling, 'De Quincey and Coleridge upon Kant', pp. 219–20.
[2] C. M. Ingleby, *Transactions of the Royal Society of Literature of the United Kingdom*, Second Series, ix. 400.
[3] Ibid., p. 406.   [4] Ibid., pp. 400–1; p. 404.

scholar J. M. Robertson attributed Coleridge's faults to an inadequate childhood:

Certainly he was as ill-managed as such a child could be, with a commonplace and uneducated mother, a wool-gathering father, a jealous nurse, an average infant-schooling, and a free run in all sorts of imaginative juvenile literature; all this being followed later by months of strangely precocious tavern-haunting with an injudicious uncle, and then by the years of often unhappy schoolboyhood at Christ's Hospital, which were on the whole no better and no worse for him than the rest of his preparation. At no stage were his weaknesses corrected by kindly discipline. Always he was precociously intellectual, never sturdy or prudent; always excessive in sentiment, lacking anchorage, judgment, and organic tenacity.[1]

Convinced that 'the doctrinal influence of Coleridge was in certain ways harmful, and needed to be gainsaid',[2] Robertson used the plagiarism charge as a kind of crowbar in his attempt to dislodge Coleridge from his philosophical reputation: the fact is 'remarkable', he says, 'that Coleridge won and for a time kept his philosophic prestige despite of his being convicted of plagiarisms unparalleled in literary history'.[3] Summarizing the history of the charges, Robertson notes that it 'cannot judicially be questioned that Ferrier made out his case',[4] and he then takes up some further examples of plagiarism that had come to light since the time of Ferrier, some of them noted, in a tone sympathetic to Coleridge, for the first time by the German scholar Brandl.[5] Robertson, not at all sympathetic, focuses upon two damaging instances of Coleridge's plagiarism:

The worthlessness of his testimony on disputable points may be sufficiently seen from his explicit allegation:—'No one has charged me with tricking out in other words the thoughts of others,' when he has in the previous chapter [of the *Biographia*] admitted that he has been charged with plagiarism. Mr. Traill's statement that Coleridge knew nothing of Schlegel when he coincided with his views of Shakspere, is disproved by documentary evidence. Coleridge himself only claimed that he had anticipated Schlegel in early talk and in his first lectures at the Royal Institution, which (as usual) he misdated when making the claim. They were delivered in 1808, the year of Schlegel's lectures at Vienna. But Mr. Traill's denial refers to the preserved reports of the lectures of 1811–12 and the notes of 1818. Now Coleridge himself admits in his ninth lecture of the course of 1811–12 that he had seen Schlegel's book; and in a letter to Crabb

---

[1] Robertson, p. 133. The chapter on Coleridge was apparently written in 1893.
[2] Ibid., 'Preface', p. ix.   [3] Ibid., p. 154.   [4] Ibid., p. 157.
[5] See Brandl, *Coleridge and the English Romantic School*. Brandl's identifications of possible German sources for Coleridge's works have not fared well at the hands of other critics. In 1926 Stokoe, in an elegantly written work, examined and dismissed his allegations of German influence on *The Ancient Mariner* and other early poems (*German Influence in the English Romantic Period 1788–1818*, pp. 100–42). Raysor, again, says that 'None of the influences cited' in Brandl's book 'should be accepted without checking the facts' (*Coleridge, Shakespearean Criticism*, i. p. xxi, n. 3).

Robinson he accorded Schlegel unmeasured praise as a commentator. What seems true is that Coleridge as early as 1798 propounded to Hazlitt a view of Hamlet which anticipated Schlegel's. But the view in question was no very recondite reflection, being indeed only a pathetic interpretation of Hamlet in terms of Coleridge's own fatal tendency to talk rather than act; and the influence of Schlegel is clear on many other points.[1]

In addition to Coleridge's indebtedness to Schlegel on the interpretation of Shakespeare, Robertson notes 'one other decisive illustration',[2] which is 'a plain adaptation from Schelling' embodied at length in

Coleridge's so-called *Theory of Life*—that is, in the essay so entitled, published by Dr. Seth Watson in 1848, and described by him as a joint production of Coleridge and Dr. Gillman, but, in view of the style, probably . . . substantially Coleridge's. Gillman may have contributed some of the natural-history data; but it is incredible that anybody but Coleridge can have put together without acknowledgment such an undisguised compilation of the published views of another philosopher. Its main thesis is the ancient and familiar one, maintained by Goethe as well as Schelling, . . . that 'life' is not to be defined in terms of any merely biological data, but is to be regarded as embracing the whole field of things, and is to be defined as 'the principle of Individuation'. . . . It is hardly necessary to discuss the scientific value of this theorem, further than to say that it is a most instructive example of what can be done in the way of sham-definition and make-believe science by an elastic intelligence with great command of utterance and forms of dialectic, great confidence in its own guesses, and no concern whatever for scientific evidence. But whatever be its value, it is necessary to put distinctly on record, what Dr. Brandl only hints, that it is in every detail a simple restatement, albeit with oversights, of views advanced by Schelling in his *Ideen zur Philosophie der Natur* (1797), his *Von der Weltseele* (1798), his *Einleitung zu seinem Entwurf eines Systems der Natur-Philosophie* (1799) and his *Darstellung des Systems der Philosophie* (1801) and later works.[3]

With this scattered fire of German titles, the nineteenth-century Scottish attacks on Coleridge may be said to have come to an end.

In the twentieth century attitudes towards Coleridge's plagiarisms have been ambivalent. On the one hand, the accusers have continued to document his unacknowledged debts but have adopted a generally milder tone towards Coleridge himself; on the other, there has been a curious and very widespread tendency to gloss over, and even to suppress, the fact of the plagiarisms. Such an attitude, though, as I shall suggest, not without a kind of ultimate psychological justification, is no substitute for an orderly defence based on a consideration of the evidence. It has understandably aroused considerable annoyance in some critics not predisposed in Coleridge's favour, or conversant with the real extent of his plagiarisms (so far, that is, as that extent is known; numerous as his identified borrowings are, I believe they represent only a portion of the total number in his

---

[1] Robertson, pp. 154–5.   [2] Ibid., p. 158.   [3] Ibid., pp. 159–60.

writings). It was this 'reluctance of English writers to face the truth of
Coleridge's plagiarisms' that in 1942 spurred Joseph Warren Beach to an
article entitled 'Coleridge's Borrowings from the German', in which,
almost alone among twentieth-century commentators, he adopts the kind
of sharp and censorious tone so characteristic of nineteenth-century
accusers.[1] Beach, charging Coleridge with 'literary dishonesty' and 'vanity',
insists that 'in metaphysics and science he made pretensions to originality
which are not borne out by the facts'.[2]

Beach's discussion of Coleridge's obligations (he concentrates on the
debts to Schelling in the *Biographia*, the debts to Wilhelm Schlegel in the
Shakespeare lectures, and the debts to Schelling and Steffens in *Theory of
Life*) depends heavily on two earlier demonstrations of Coleridge's borrow-
ing practices, both of them more concerned to document than to accuse.
The first, a Bachelor of Arts thesis submitted in 1907 by Anna Augusta
Helmholtz, expands a hint by Ferrier and considers Coleridge's use of
A. W. Schlegel.[3] The second, an article of 1932 by the Swiss scholar
Henri Nidecker, documents the verbal indebtednesses of *Theory of Life* to
Steffens's *Beyträge zur innern Naturgeschichte der Erde*.[4] Both of these efforts
have the seemingly obvious—but, in the psychologically complex annals
of the plagiarism controversy, strangely rare—virtue of presenting their
evidence: the passages in question are printed in facing columns.

Another Swiss scholar, Adrien Bonjour, in a careful and sympathetic
thesis entitled *Coleridge's 'Hymn Before Sunrise'* (pp. 76–113), departs from
the fact originally noted by De Quincey, that the poem is an expanded
reworking of a German poem, and proceeds to account in psychological
terms for Coleridge's need to plagiarize. De Quincey had treated the
plagiarisms as a quirk, as a kind of intellectual kleptomania superfluous
to and outside of Coleridge's real achievement. Bonjour, on the contrary,

[1] Joseph Warren Beach, 'Coleridge's Borrowings from the German', *ELH*, ix (1942), 55.
[2] Ibid., pp. 50, 36.
[3] Helmholtz, *The Indebtedness of Coleridge to Schlegel*, pp. 273–370 of vol. 3, no. 4 of the Philology and Literature Series (No. 163), Bulletin of the University of Wisconsin. The hint from
Ferrier was as follows: 'Let us here make a passing remark upon what Coleridge says in reference to his "coincidences" with Schlegel. He tells us . . . that, as in reference to Schlegel, his
views upon dramatic art, so in reference to Schelling, his views on transcendental metaphysics
were matured before he knew any thing about either author. On the subject of his resemblances
to Schlegel, we are not prepared to speak. . . . But as he himself here perils the fact of his
priority to and independence of Schlegel upon the truth of what he says respecting his priority
to . . . Schelling, placing both instances upon exactly the same footing, we are entitled to say,
that *as*, in the case of Schelling, we know him to be a consummate plagiarist, and original in
nothing; *so*, in the case of Schlegel, we think it more than probable, that he has borrowed
ready-made from that author, every thing in which he "genially coincides" with him' (Ferrier,
p. 293).
[4] Henri Nidecker, 'Notes marginales de S. T. Coleridge, IV. En marge de Steffens', *Revue de
littérature comparée*, xii (Paris, 1932), 856–71. This article is one of a series by Nidecker, beginning
in 1927 and all printed in this same journal, that transcribe part of Coleridge's marginalia to
Schelling and to the *Naturphilosophen*: Schubert, Oken, and Steffens.

finds the plagiarism a compensation for that loss of the 'shaping spirit of imagination' that the poet bewailed in his *Dejection*, and thus a necessary factor in his continued intellectual activity.

Of all the twentieth-century writers on the plagiarisms, however, Wellek is the most significant—and indeed the most important accuser since Ferrier. His importance does not depend on the discovery of new evidence —for, like Beach, he is content to summarize what is already known—but rather because he speaks from a very wide background of reading in the literature and philosophy of German Romanticism, and because his denunciations have been persistent and powerfully stated. Thus the attack in the *History of Modern Criticism* does not represent a new departure in his views. On the contrary, his attitude towards Coleridge has been remarkably consistent throughout his career. As early as 1931, in *Kant in England*, he had formulated his opinions about Coleridge as a philosopher:

... we must insist on a fundamental lack of real philosophical individuality in Coleridge, whether his thought was fragmentary or not. This charge—if such a stress on a human limitation can be called a charge—is closely connected with the old charge of plagiarism and unoriginality. ... We know all that can be urged in Coleridge's defense: especially the weakening of his memory, possibly by opium and certainly by illness, his disorderly habits and his frequently very justifiable feeling of recognition. ... We have read the general acknowledgements Coleridge made so frequently; we know the fine phrase about truth, 'the divine ventriloquist'—all this is very well and even true in a sense, but there remains one simple fact which cannot be disputed away and which seems to us so much more important than the moralist's question about conscious or unconscious plagiarizing. ... It will sound paradoxical to those who see in him a master of subtle analysis and fine distinctions—but the truth is nevertheless this: Coleridge has little insight into the incompatibility of different trends of thought. He lacks a sense for the subtle shades of terminological differences in different thinkers, he seems sometimes almost blind to the wide implications in this or that idea. It is not the fact that several central passages in Coleridge are borrowed or paraphrased or influenced by other thinkers; it is rather the circumstance that these adaptations of other thought are heterogeneous, incoherent and even contradictory which makes the study of Coleridge's philosophy ultimately so futile. He was no doubt a great mediator of ideas, we feel also in most of what he wrote a certain unifying temperament which cannot be mistaken, but if we look more closely we find that Coleridge has built a building of no style, or rather of mixed style. We do not deny that he has built a complete building, we do not deny that *he* has built it, but we deny that it is a building in Coleridgean style. ... Coleridge's structure has here a storey from Kant, there a part of a room from Schelling, there a roof from Anglican theology and so on. The architect did not feel the clash of the styles, the subtle and irreconcilable differences between the Kantian first floor and the Anglican roof. He had vaguely in mind the type of building he wanted to build, but when he looked for material which he could not find in the quarries of his own mind, he took it from elsewhere thinking that it would perfectly fit the purpose for which he intends to use it. But these blocks of foreign marble or stone were not longer rough-hewn; they were thoroughly prepared to fit into another building and betrayed their origin also in Coleridge's house. . . . This fundamental inability to think systematically and therefore philosophically drove Coleridge to borrowings, conscious and unconscious and brought into his structure the feeling of instability and looseness.

All this might sound unnecessarily harsh, but one has to state this fact frankly in order to contradict the over-rating of Coleridge's philosophical thought which has begun recently as a reaction to a period of undue neglect.[1]

This statement marks an epoch in the controversy, for it is the first of the charges that attempts to confront plagiarism in any of its larger implications: what Wellek really accuses Coleridge of is not unethical appropriation, but a failure of the reticulative function. My whole essay, in a sense, is devoted to an attempt to discuss the matter on the grounds here chosen by Wellek, and the conclusion I shall attempt to justify is that it is not Coleridge who 'has little insight into the incompatibility of different trends of thought' or 'lacks a sense for the subtle shades of terminological differences' or who is 'heterogeneous, incoherent and even contradictory', but rather Wellek and the other accusers who fail to penetrate to the real subject of Coleridge's discourse, who fail to realize the small number of genuine positions possible in philosophy, and who fail to understand fully the rules, pertinencies, and historical traditions of syncretistic thought. I once suffered under a mathematics teacher who neglected to write on the blackboard every step in the progression of his algebraic manipulations, and I distinctly recollect my feeling of indignation and near suspicion of fraud at what seemed to me forced and inconsequent conclusions. What was really lacking (outside of pedagogic tact) was not the ability or correctness of the teacher, but the fullness of my own knowledge of algebra. Coleridge, I believe, exhibits the kind of instinctive jump from premiss to correct conclusion that we slower minds tend to regard with distrust. My hope in this book is to specify on the blackboard, as it were, some of the missing steps in his meditations.

In view of the clarity and control of Wellek's position in Kant in England, and also in his article of 1950 entitled 'Coleridge's Philosophy and Criticism', where he maintains 'the central fact that, on many crucial issues and at many important points of his writings, Coleridge adopts the words and terminology of other men',[2] and concludes 'on the whole' that 'Coleridge's thought cannot claim a high position in the history of philosophy',[3] it is unfortunate that the chapter in A History of Modern Criticism is his most

[1] Wellek, Kant in England 1793–1838, pp. 66–68.
[2] Wellek, 'Coleridge's Philosophy and Criticism', The English Romantic Poets; A Review of Research, ed. T. M. Raysor (New York, 1950), p. 96.
[3] Ibid., p. 107.

widely noticed statement; for in many ways it is the least impressive. It is marred by a strangely legalistic quibbling over sources and precedents —an attitude, incidentally, that Wellek does not extend to his consideration of German thinkers[1]—and by an uncharacteristically peremptory tone.

Despite these defects, the article in the *History of Modern Criticism* contains both a summary of the leading lines of defence so far pleaded for Coleridge, and the most comprehensive statement yet made of the range and significance of the plagiarism itself:

Constant references are being made to Coleridge's principle of the reconciliation of opposites, to his definition of the imagination, to the idea of the organic whole and to his distinction between symbol and allegory.

But if we look at Coleridge from an international perspective, fresh from our reading of Kant, Schiller, Schelling, the Schlegels, Jean Paul, Solger, and all the others, we must, I think, come to a considerably lower estimate of his significance, however great and useful his role was in mediating between Germany and England. It is not simply a question of plagiarism or even of direct dependence on German sources, though these cannot be so easily dismissed or shirked as it has become the custom of a good many writers on Coleridge to do. We need not reopen the question of plagiarism as an ethical issue and psychological problem. One should grant much to Coleridge's defenders. Coleridge's memory may have been weakened by ill health and opium; his habits of notetaking were such that he could have mistaken a translation of his own for original reflections; there are scattered acknowledgments in Coleridge's printed and unprinted writings; there was no need or even opportunity for citation of sources in public lectures, the notes for which were never meant for print and might never have been claimed by Coleridge as his own work. Besides, Coleridge held a theory of truth as the 'divine ventriloquist,' speaking from whatever mouth it chose. He was genuinely anxious to receive support from the agreement of other men, and often could justly feel that he had arrived at ideas and conclusions on his own, even though in his exposition he buttressed them with phrases from his German contemporaries.

Nevertheless, there remains a residue of indebtedness which cannot be eliminated. At crucial points in his writings Coleridge used Kant, Schelling, and A. W. Schlegel, reproducing the very pattern of sentences and the exact vocabulary. Whatever the ethics or psychology of the situation, it seems impossible to give Coleridge credit for ideas simply quoted literally. This is particularly true of the long passages from Schelling in chapters 12 and 13 of *Biographia*

---

[1] For example, he says 'there is scarcely any idea in Herder which could not be traced back to Blackwell or Harris, Shaftesbury or Brown, Blair or Percy, Warton or Young. Herder read them all, and of course he read his German predecessors and contemporaries, especially Lessing, Hamann, and Winckelmann. . . . But it would be a mistake to consider Herder merely the synthesizer of what could be vaguely called preromantic criticism in Europe. He is not only a synthesizer whom none of his predecessors could match in sweep and scope, he is also the first who sharply breaks with the neoclassical past...' (*A History of Modern Criticism: 1750–1950*, i. 181).

Literaria (1817) which lead up to the distinction between imagination and fancy and represent the most sustained attempt at an epistemological and metaphysical foundation for his theories. Much that has impressed I. A. Richards and Herbert Read—the discussion of the subject-object relation, their synthesis and identity, and the appeal to the unconscious—is simply the teaching of Schelling and cannot be made the basis of a claim for Coleridge's philosophical greatness. Coleridge's lecture 'On Poesy or Art' (1818), which has been used by several expositors of his aesthetics as the key to his thought, is with the exception of a few insertions of pious sentiments little more than a paraphrase of Schelling's Academy Oration of 1807. The series of papers 'On the Principles of Genial Criticism' (1814), which Coleridge considered 'the best things he had ever written', follow the distinctions drawn in Kant's *Critique of Judgment* at times so closely that Coleridge takes over even Kant's anecdotes and illustrations. In discussing the contrast between ancient and modern literature Coleridge reproduces a crucial passage from Schiller's *Naive and Sentimental Poetry*. The manuscript notes for the lecture on 'Wit and Humor' are a patchwork of quotations from Jean Paul's *Vorschule*. In many instances Coleridge borrowed from A. W. Schlegel. A lecture on Greek drama is simply a translation from Schlegel and 'ought not to be included in Coleridge's works at all.' Many crucial distinctions are derived from Schlegel. Thus, the formula for the distinction between 'mechanical regularity' and 'organic form' is a literal translation.

These are the main examples of direct quotations or paraphrase in Coleridge's aesthetic and critical writings. Many more could be drawn from his philosophical and scientific speculations. *Theory of Life* is merely a mosaic of passages from Schelling and Steffens; the lecture on Aeschylus' *Prometheus* paraphrases Schelling's *Gods of Samothrace*. The big two-volume 'Logic,' still unpublished for the most part, is largely an elaborate exposition of the *Critique of Pure Reason* with all its architectonics, tables of categories, and antinomies taken over literally. The history of association psychology in *Biographia Literaria* comes from Maass, an obscure German writer on imagination. The newly published *Philosophical Lectures* draw most of their information and learning from Tennemann's *History of Philosophy*. . . . In all the cases cited Coleridge must have had the actual texts in front of him or used detailed notes taken directly from them.[1]

Now, though one may deplore the accusations against Coleridge, it is a fact of literary history that no adequate defences have been constructed for him, even though scholars are generally disposed in his favour. We may identify two early and important reasons for this lack of a properly conducted defence.

First, the initial attacks—Ferrier's in particular—were directed against Coleridge as metaphysician, and in England the national pride of intellect has never been involved with philosophy as it has in Germany or Scotland. The English traditionally dislike and distrust metaphysics, particularly idealist speculations, and the plain fact seems to have been that very few of the English literati were averse to having Coleridge's metaphysics

[1] *History of Modern Criticism*, ii. 151–3.

declared, as it were, out of bounds—it then became no longer necessary to trouble one's head about such foggy and unrewarding matters. It is interesting to note that Coleridge's chief *literary* plagiarisms—those of Schlegel's Shakespearian criticism—though as well documented as his metaphysical plagiarisms from Schelling, touch upon the national pride of intellect and consequently have never commanded much credence at any time. I think that really no one, unless perhaps Wellek in the heat of controversy, actually subscribes to the belief—print as many parallel columns as one may—that Coleridge in any substantial way is dependent on Schlegel for his Shakespearian insights.[1] I do not sense any deep conviction even in Ferrier and Robertson.

In short, the English have been ready to stand up and fight for Coleridge the critic, for Coleridge the English man of letters, but have been content —even relieved—to lay the ghost of Coleridge the metaphysician by repeating Ferrier's incantation 'that Coleridge is indebted to Schelling for most of his philosophy'.[2] We see this ambivalent stand classically presented by the acute but so-British Sir Leslie Stephen:

> Coleridge has often been accused of plagiarism. I do not believe that he stole his Shakespeare criticism from Schlegel, and, partly at least, for the reason which would induce me to acquit a supposed thief of having stolen a pair of breeches from a wild Highlandman. But it is undeniable that Coleridge was guilty of a serious theft of metaphysical wares. The only excuse suggested is that the theft was too certain of exposure to be perpetrated. But as it certainly was perpetrated, this can only be an apology for the motive. The simple fact is that part of his scheme was to establish his claims to be a great metaphysician. But it takes much trouble and some thought to put together what looks like a chain of *a priori* demonstration of abstract principles. Coleridge, therefore, persuaded himself that he had really anticipated Schelling's thoughts and might justifiably appropriate Schelling's words. He threw out a few phrases about 'genial coincidence' —perhaps the happiest circumlocution ever devised for what Pistol called 'conveying'—and adopted Schelling in the lump.[3]

Notable in Stephen's attitude is not only the blank refusal to credit the literary Schlegel as a source for Coleridge, but, in the acceptance of the philosophical Schelling as a source, an underlying disbelief in the pertinence of such philosophy—the sardonic 'much trouble and some

---

[1] Thus even Beach, who is in no way predisposed in Coleridge's favour, feels that Coleridge did not really need Schlegel except as a crutch for the moment. While 'it is perfectly clear that, in preparing his later lectures', Coleridge did not feel himself 'quite capable of meeting the demands of the occasion without large drafts upon his German contemporary', he is none the less 'agreed to be a critic of greater subtlety and feeling than Schlegel' (Beach, 'Coleridge's Borrowings from the German', *ELH*, ix (1942), 52). Raysor, again, finds Coleridge's 'superiority over Schlegel' as an interpreter of Hamlet 'overwhelming' (*Shakespearean Criticism*, i. xlv). For the general question of Coleridge's indebtedness to Schlegel, see Excursus Note I, p. 258.

[2] Ferrier, p. 297.

[3] Leslie Stephen, 'Coleridge', *Hours in a Library*, iii. 356–7.

thought', and the fraud-hinting 'what looks like a chain of *a priori* demonstration', apply in context rather more to Schelling than to Coleridge.

Elsewhere in the same essay Stephen reveals even more explicitly the classic Anglo-Saxon scepticism about systematic philosophizing:

> . . . when we think what philosophical systems have so far been; what flimsy and air-built bubbles in the eyes of the next generation; how often we desire, even in the case of the greatest men, that the one vital idea (there is seldom so much as one!) could be preserved, and the pretentious structure in which it is involved permitted once for all to burst; we may think that another criterion is admissible; that a man's work may be judged by the stimulus given to reflection. . . . Upon that ground, Coleridge's rank will be a very high one. . . .[1]

The second reason for the ineptitude of the defences against the charges of plagiarism is that the early defenders devoted themselves—understandably enough in view of the fact that they were relatives and close friends of Coleridge—more to the salvation of Coleridge's ethical reputation than to the interpretation of his thought. And the ethical problem was made central not only by the filial interests of Coleridge's daughter, but by the prevailingly moralistic temper of Victorian England itself. One may feel, however, or at least hope, that our present intellectual world, freed from the rigid certainties of Victorian moralism by Freud, and from the inhumanities of Puritanism by modern theology, can summon little surprise and less indignation at the spectacle of a weak and fallen Coleridge, and only a bored scepticism about the existence—or pertinence—of the implied moral superiority of his accusers.[2] In any case, from the perspective of a later epoch, one wonders whether Coleridge the human being needs a moral defence: if translating some pages from his German contemporaries was his worst and blackest fault, then surely he was a prince among men.

To a certain extent the early defenders—notably Julius Hare and Coleridge's daughter Sara—do make out a case that mitigates the issue of moral culpability. But though they, and later Shawcross, present their cases with dignity and restraint, one senses that the charges have thrown them rather badly off balance. They seem to feel a necessity to concede Coleridge's intellectual bankruptcy in order to save his moral standing, and one wonders in that event if the game is worth the candle.

The first of the defences, Hare's, was published in 1835 and was, as its title 'Samuel Taylor Coleridge and the English Opium-Eater' indicates, occasioned by De Quincey's articles—not so much, however, by the accusation of plagiarism *per se* as by the generally patronizing tone assumed by De Quincey. 'Had Coleridge been alive', Hare remarks bitterly,

---

[1] Stephen, pp. 367–8.
[2] See note 3, p. 335.

and one suspects truly, De Quincey 'would not have dared thus to prate and chatter about him';[1] and De Quincey's aim, says Hare:

is not to delineate Coleridge's intellect, or his character, or to mark out the place he fills in the map of the human mind, or to determine the value of his labours in untwisting the gordian knot of thought . . . but he has turned away . . . to ransack the Monmouth-street of his memory for all the tattered tinsel he could pick up there. . . . Among the anecdotes related of Coleridge there are very few, of which the tendency is not to lower him in some way or other, to impair his claims to respect, to display his weaknesses, his failings, his distresses.[2]

Hare then takes up the plagiarism charge as a prime example of the Opium-Eater's malicious attempts to subvert Coleridge's reputation:

The dissertation in the *Biographia Literaria* . . . is asserted to be a translation from an essay in the volume of Schelling's *Philosophische Schriften*. True: the Opium-eater is indeed mistaken in the name of the book; but that is of little moment, except as an additional mark of audacious carelessness in impeaching a great man's honour. The dissertation, as it stands in the *Biographia Literaria* . . . is a literal translation from the introduction to Schelling's System of *Transcendental Idealism*. . . . [But] Coleridge . . . was so far from denying or shuffling about his debts to Schelling, that he makes over every passage to him on which the stamp of his mind could be discovered. Of a truth too, if he had been disposed to purloin, he never would have stolen half a dozen pages from the head and front of that very work of Schelling's which was the likeliest to fall into his reader's hands, and the first sentence of which one could not read without detecting the plagiarism. Would any man think of pilfering a column from the porch of St. Paul's? The high praise which Coleridge bestows on Schelling would naturally excite a wish in such of his readers as felt an interest in his philosophy to know more of the great German. The first books of his they would take up would be his *Naturphilosophie* and his *Transcendental Idealism*: these are the works which Coleridge himself mentions. . . . But even with the fullest conviction that Coleridge cannot have been guilty of intentional plagiarism, the reader will probably deem it strange that he should have transferred half a dozen pages of Schelling into his volume without any reference to their source. And strange it undoubtedly is. The only way I see of accounting for it is from his practice of keeping note-books, or journals of his thoughts, filled with observations and brief dissertations on such matters as happened to strike him, with a sprinkling now and then of extracts and abstracts from the books he was reading. If the name of the author from whom he took an extract was left out, he might easily, years after, forget whose property it was, especially when he had made it in some measure his own, by transfusing it into his own English. That this may happen I know from my own experience, having myself been lately puzzled by a passage which I had translated from Kant some years ago, and which cost me a good deal of search before I ascertained that it was not my

---

[1] J. C. H[are], 'Samuel Taylor Coleridge and the English Opium-Eater', *The British Magazine and Monthly Register of Religious and Ecclesiastical Information . . . etc.*, vii (1835), 16.
[2] Ibid., p. 18.

own. Yet my memory in such minutiae is tolerably accurate, while Coleridge's was notoriously irretentive.[1]

In terms of its occasion—the casual and inaccurate charges of De Quincey (Hare notes that De Quincey 'blurts out about German literature with the dashing ignorance he has often shown on that subject')[2]—this first defence is a very respectable effort, particularly in its assertion of the moral relevance of the fact that Coleridge showed little of the track-covering caution that might be expected of a deliberate thief.

Five years later, however, Ferrier launched his savage assault, and to that article Hare's brief statements were no adequate rejoinder.

'We are aware', [said Ferrier], 'that this subject is not now broached for the first time. It was mooted some years ago . . . Mr. De Quincey appearing . . . for the prosecution, and Mr. J. C. Hare . . . for the defence. But on both sides the case was very badly conducted; indeed we may say it was altogether bungled. Neither party appears to have possessed a competent knowledge of the facts. . . . [Hare] talks of Coleridge having transferred into his work "half-a-dozen pages", or little more, of Schelling. By our Lady! they are nearer twenty.'[3]

Ferrier's accusation, appearing as it did under the guise of information for a second edition of the *Biographia Literaria*, left the editors of that edition with no choice but to take notice of his charges. So, when in 1847 the second edition appeared, forty-four pages of Sara Coleridge's long and competent introduction were devoted to a rebuttal of Ferrier. The title of the section, 'Mr. Coleridge's obligations to Schelling, and the unfair view of the subject presented in Blackwood's Magazine', indicates the controlled resentment of its tone. The rebuttal is an intelligent and dignified statement that to a considerable extent succeeds in its principal aim, the vindication of Coleridge's moral reputation, but it is less successful in saving his philosophical reputation. The arguments are amplifications of those broached by Hare, and new light is largely confined to the quotation of two letters, one from Stanley concerning Schelling's own view of the plagiarism controversy, and one from Coleridge's philosophical disciple, J. H. Green, asserting the unfavourable opinion Coleridge came to hold of Schelling's position in philosophy. Stanley's remarks are interesting rather than conclusive:

Schelling's remarks about Coleridge were too generally expressed, I fear, to be of any use in a vindication of him, except so far as proving his own friendly feeling towards him. But as far as I can reconstruct his sentence it was much as follows, being in answer to a question whether he had known Coleridge personally. 'Whether I have seen Coleridge or not, I cannot tell; if he called upon me at Jena, it was before his name had become otherwise known to me, and amongst the numbers of young Englishmen, whom I then saw, I cannot recall

[1] Ibid., pp. 19–21.   [2] Ibid., p. 21.   [3] Ferrier, pp. 287–8.

the persons of individuals. But I have read what he has written with great pleasure, and I took occasion in my lectures to vindicate him from the charge, which has been brought against him, of plagiarising from me; and I said that it was I rather who owed much to him, and that, in the Essay on Prometheus, Coleridge in his remark, that 'Mythology was not allegorical but tautegorical,' had concentrated in one striking expression (*in einem schlagenden Ausdruck*) what I had been labouring to represent with much toil and trouble. This is all that I can be sure of.'[1]

The second testimonial, stemming as it does from Green's unique combination of philosophical training and intimate personal knowledge of Coleridge, is a judicious and important opinion that has never received as much attention as it deserves:

My acquaintance with S. T. C. commenced with the intention of studying the writings of Schelling; but after a few interviews the design was given up, in consequence of Coleridge declaring his dissent from Schelling's doctrines; and he began immediately the exposition of his own views.

This perhaps renders the *Biographia* more inexplicable. For herein S. T. C. assumes the originality of Schelling—which can only be received with great qualifications—and is content to have it admitted, that the agreements between himself and Schelling were the coincidences of two minds working on the same subject and in the same direction. Now this is the more remarkable, that it may be shewn, that many or most of the views entertained by Coleridge, at least at the period of our first acquaintance, might have been derived from other sources, and that his system differs essentially from that of Schelling. Some light might perhaps be thrown upon this interesting question by a knowledge, which unfortunately I do not possess, of the circumstances under which the fragment called the *Biographia* was drawn up. It is possible, no doubt, that Coleridge's opinions might have undergone a change between the period, at which the B. L. was published, and that at which I had the happiness of becoming acquainted with him. But at the latter period his doctrines were based upon the self same principles, which he retained to his dying hour, and differing as they do fundamentally from those of Schelling, I cannot but avow my conviction, that they were formed at a much earlier period, nay that they were growths of his own mind, growing with his growth, strengthening with his strength, the result of a Platonic spirit, the stirrings of which had already evinced themselves in his early boyhood, and which had been only modified, and indirectly shaped and developed by the German school.[2]

This seems to me an exceptionally penetrating statement. It not only adumbrates one of my central contentions in this book, but it avoids in an exemplary fashion the pitfalls of the plagiarism controversy. Green

---

[1] *Biographia Literaria* . . . Second Edition Prepared for Publication in Part by the late Henry Nelson Coleridge, Completed and Published by his Widow (London, 1847), i. xxxviii–xxxix. For the vindication to which Schelling refers, see Schelling, *Werke*, xi. 196 n.

[2] *Biographia*, Second Edition, i. xxxiv n.

does not, as is one temptation, deny the fact of Coleridge's borrowings; but he equally does not allow himself to be drawn into the ethical *cul-de-sac*—to him the translations exist, but he is content to regard their existence as, ambiguously, 'remarkable'. He points out that the coincidences with Schelling could be shown to be derived, or at least to be derivable, from other sources; he affirms his belief in the Platonic origin of Coleridge's fundamental attitudes. Finally, he asserts as his controlling justification the insight, achieved by no one else so far as I know, that the real measure of Coleridge's independence of Schelling is the blank fact that Coleridge's 'system differs essentially from that of Schelling'.

The year 1847, as the publication date of the second edition of the *Biographia*, marks an epoch in the controversy, for since that time, though special emphases have changed, no new defences have appeared for Coleridge. Two of the lines of argument current by 1847 are no longer frequently encountered: the ethical defence of poor memory, bad notes, and so forth, though not entirely invalidated, no longer commands the interest of commentators to any significant extent, while the defence implied by Green's opinion that Coleridge and Schelling were philosophers of essentially different positions has never been developed. The efforts of modern commentators are more generally clustered about a third and fourth line of defence, originally enunciated by Green and De Quincey respectively, the former of which is an affirmation of the view that Coleridge's philosophy has Platonic roots that render the German sources superfluous, and the latter a persuasively stated opinion, amounting to a credo, of Coleridge's philosophical independence. Neither of these views has been substantially developed beyond its original statement. Green maintains that Coleridge's doctrines 'were formed at a much earlier period', were 'the results of a Platonic spirit'.[1] De Quincey, on the other hand, in the article in which he promulgated the plagiarism charges, asserts that

after having read for thirty years in the same track as Coleridge—that track in which few of any age will ever follow us, such as German metaphysicians, Latin schoolmen, thaumaturgic Platonists, religious Mystics—and having thus discovered a large variety of trivial thefts, I do, nevertheless, mosth eartily believe [Coleridge] to have been as entirely original in all his capital pretensions as any one man that ever has existed.[2]

These two defences have dominated pro-Coleridgean statements during the twentieth century. But neither position, as it stands, is satisfactory; and the consideration of a pair of modern restatements of both positions may help to elucidate the prevalent weaknesses and faulty techniques in

---

[1] Ibid.   [2] *De Quincey*, ii. 147.

their handling. We may take a paragraph by Herbert Read as a rather distinguished avatar of the credo defence:

What Coleridge owed to the critical philosophy of Kant, or to the Transcendentalists as a school, cannot be established accurately. Let us realize, once and for all, that we are not dealing with the scholarly lucubrations of an academic coterie, in which priorities and credits are of some importance. Coleridge was involved in something much wider and more fundamental—in a revolution of thought such as only occurs once or twice in a millennium. Such revolutions do not come about as a result of individual efforts: the individuals are swept along in a current which they, least of all men, can control. Kant's philosophy is inconceivable without the stimulus of Hume; Fichte is inconceivable without Kant, and Schelling without Fichte. Let us rather visualize this whole movement of thought as a fleet of vessels moving towards new and uncharted seas. Kant and Fichte, Schleiermacher and Schelling; Herder and the two Schlegels; Goethe and Schiller; Tieck, Novalis and Wackenroder—so many vessels advancing in the stream of thought, flashing signals from one masthead to another, and all guided on their way by the lodestar of transcendental truth. As they proceed from some harbour in the Baltic, they are joined by solitary vessels from neighbouring countries, and Coleridge is one of these, already armed and provisioned, his course set to the same destination.[1]

Side by side with this modern restatement of the De Quinceyan credo, we may set M. H. Abrams's reformulation of Green's contention:

A. O. Lovejoy, in an early essay on 'Kant and the English Platonists', cited many parallels between Kant's 'transcendental idealism' and the writings— more abstract and less riotously metaphorical than Culverwel's or Sterry's—of such English Platonists as Cudworth, More, Burthogge, and Arthur Collier. . . . This essay . . . lends greater credibility than many students have granted to Coleridge's reiterated claim that through his early readings in Platonists and mystics, he had acquired the essentials of his idealism prior to his first knowledge of German philosophy.[2]

The exculpations of Read and Abrams share several weaknesses. Most

---

[1] Read, *Coleridge as Critic*, p. 15. For other examples of the credo defence see Enrico Pizzo, 'S. T. Coleridge als Kritiker', *Anglia; Zeitschrift für englische Philologie*, xl (June 1916); Helene Richter, 'Die philosophische Weltanschauung von S. T. Coleridge und ihr Verhältnis zur deutschen Philosophie', *Anglia; Zeitschrift für englische Philologie*, xliv (June 1920); J. H. Muirhead, *Coleridge as Philosopher* (New York, 1930); Kathleen Coburn, *The Philosophical Lectures of Samuel Taylor Coleridge* (London, 1949); and L. A. Willoughby, 'Coleridge and his German Contemporaries', *Publications of the English Goethe Society*, n.s. x (Cambridge, 1934), 43–62. Willoughby says, for instance, that though 'Kant, Jacobi and Schelling marked phases in [Coleridge's] philosophic development . . . he would seem justified in maintaining that the main and fundamental ideas of his philosophy were anterior to his acquaintance with German idealism' (pp. 59–60).

[2] M. H. Abrams, *The Mirror and the Lamp*, p. 346, n. 57. For other statements of the Platonic-origins defence, on the whole more weakly handled than the credo defences, see R. L. Brett, 'Coleridge's Theory of the Imagination', *English Studies 1949*, pp. 75–90; A. E. Powell, *The Romantic Theory of Poetry* (London, 1926); and Claud Howard, *Coleridge's Idealism: A Study of its Relationship to Kant and to the Cambridge Platonists* (Boston, 1924).

obvious is the fact that both, as they stand, are merely presentations of opinion (in the case of Abrams, someone else's opinion); they do not offer any valid reasons for honouring such beliefs. Their prototypes, the statements of De Quincey and Green, are likewise mere assertions, but the earlier statements command respect because they are based on an intimate knowledge of Coleridge's deepest intellectual attitudes. Neither Read nor Abrams has access to such knowledge, of course, and consequently some further confirmation is necessary. We need to know, in the one case, the precise goals and methods of the German metaphysicians —or, in terms of the metaphor, an exact description of the ships, their riggings, their crews and cargoes, and their ultimate destinations. And in the other case the Platonic anticipations need to be precisely identified, with reference both to their transmission in the Platonic tradition and to passages in Plato himself. No such chapter-and-verse elaboration is forthcoming in either statement, however, and both, as a result, take on an air of special pleading. Though Read's statement, for instance, is an effective piece of prose that makes good use of a striking metaphor, and is, we may grant, hypothetically a correct conclusion, it does not overtly consider the facts that might justify it. Indeed, the bundling together of 'Kant and Fichte, Schleiermacher and Schelling' as devotees of 'transcendental truth' suggests that it might be exceedingly difficult to develop a satisfactory context along these lines, for it is a byword of any serious study of German nineteenth-century philosophy—and will become, I believe, most apparent in the course of this book—that Kant was quite opposed in both aims and ultimate concepts to 'Fichte, Schleiermacher and Schelling' and the other—to use Coleridge's phrase—'post-Kantean anti-Kanteans'.

Nor does Abrams provide a convincing context for his avowal that the viewpoints of Kant and other German thinkers could have found their way into Coleridge's thought from Platonist sources. It might be possible to construct a vindication along these lines, but nothing remotely like it has yet appeared in English. There is, and the mere existence of the work is exciting in its implications, a lengthy, specific, and exhaustive comparison of the aesthetic of Schelling and that of Plotinus, with authoritative citation of both authors, by Fritz Heinemann, with the important conclusion that 'the substance, therefore, of the Schellingian position is thoroughly Plotinian';[1] but to adapt Heinemann's conclusion about Schelling and Plotinus to still another party, Coleridge, is a task that has not yet been undertaken. Abrams's invocation of Lovejoy's monograph does no service to the complexities of the problem.[2] In so far as the

---

[1] Heinemann, *Plotin*, p. 318.

[2] Merely to balance authority with authority, we may oppose Lovejoy by Tulloch, who says laconically that there is 'no warrant to look . . . for a Kant' among the Cambridge Platonists (John Tulloch, *Rational Theology and Christian Philosophy*, ii. 483).

English Platonists deal with the traditional matters and terminology of philosophy, one could perhaps find in their writings a doorway to any position whatever; but it would probably be more pertinent to say that the study of Kant can lead to an understanding of the relevance of English Platonism than vice versa.[1]

Perhaps these objections are acknowledged by the oblique, tentative tone of Abrams's statement—the shifting of the burden of proof to Lovejoy, the carefully worded 'greater credibility . . . than many . . . have granted'. A less qualified approach would have been more documented, and a more documented approach might have been able to take a more decisive stand by developing an explicit consideration of Coleridge's readings in the Cambridge Platonists, of the relationship of the Platonists to Shaftesbury, and then of the large role played by Shaftesbury's Neoplatonism in later eighteenth-century German thought. But the invocation of Lovejoy does not satisfy the requirements of such an arduous and delicate task.

It is difficult, in other words, to credit seriously any defence, however well intentioned, that in any way glosses over or attempts to extenuate the *fact* of Coleridge's borrowings. Ships flashing signals to one another, or discussions of Cudworth and More, are all very well, but it is salutary to keep before us specimens of Coleridge's actual practice. If we look at the twelfth chapter of the *Biographia Literaria*, we may, for instance, examine the passage that moved De Quincey to his initial charge, the 'dissertation upon the reciprocal relations of the *Esse* and the *Cogitare*'. In the middle of a paragraph in that chapter, Coleridge finishes a sentence with the phrase 'but both in one'. And then, without starting another paragraph, he produces the English sentence: 'All knowledge rests on the coincidence of an object with a subject.'[2] The first sentence in Schelling's *System des transscendentalen Idealismus* is the following: 'Alles Wissen beruht auf der Uebereinstimmung eines Objektiven mit einem Subjektiven.' Coleridge's

---

[1] The English Platonists are indeed significant—both for Coleridge's development and for the general history of ideas. Koyré has shown how important More was to Newton and the history of science; Feilchenfeld how important he was to Leibniz; in various places we shall suggest his importance as a transmitter of the doctrines of Boehme and the Cabala. Cudworth too is important. If he occupies a smaller role in the history of thought, he probably possesses more special relevance for Coleridge. His *Intellectual System* is virtually an encyclopaedia of ancient philosophical doctrine—one that, moreover, refers not generally but specifically to its sources. And like Kant, Cudworth is committed to the idea of the formative functions of mind. But it is Kant's systematic analysis of problems that cannot be found in English Platonism. Despite their learning, despite their value as custodians of the Neoplatonic tradition, the English Platonists are no substitute for Kant. And Coleridge, as we shall note, never thought they were. Ideas, information, points of view—all these he found in the Platonists. But coherence, rigour, control—in a word, reticulation—these he did not. For a concurring opinion see W. Schrickx, 'Coleridge and the Cambridge Platonists', *A Review of English Literature*, vii (1966), 91.

[2] The quotations from Coleridge are from *Biographia*, i. 174–6; the corresponding quotations from Schelling are from *System des transscendentalen Idealismus* (*Werke*, iii), pp. 339–41.

second sentence is not found in Schelling; with a curiously devious scrupulosity he places it in parentheses: '(My readers have been warned in a former chapter that, for their convenience as well as the writer's, the term, subject, is used by me in its scholastic sense as equivalent to mind or sentient being, and as the necessary correlative of object or *quicquid objicitur menti*.)' Having, as it were, glossed Schelling's 'Subjekt' and 'Objekt', Coleridge returns to his text: 'For we can *know* that only which is true: and the truth is universally placed in the coincidence of the thought with the thing, of the representation with the object represented.' The sentence is identical with Schelling's second sentence, except that Coleridge translates Schelling's plural 'der Vorstellungen mit ihren Gegenständen'—literally, 'of the representations with their objects'—by the free expansion 'of the thought with the thing, of the representation with the object represented'. Schelling's sentence is: 'Denn man weiss nur das Wahre; die Wahrheit aber wird allgemein in die Uebereinstimmung der Vorstellungen mit ihren Gegenständen gesetzt.' Coleridge's fourth sentence begins a paragraph: 'Now the sum of all that is merely OBJECTIVE we will henceforth call NATURE, confining the term to its passive and material sense, as comprising all the phænomena by which its existence is made known to us.' The first clause of Schelling's third sentence is: 'Wir können den Inbegriff alles bloss Objectiven im unserm Wissen Natur nennen'; Coleridge's English adds the 'now', the 'henceforth', and the qualification of the word 'Natur': 'confining the term to its passive and material sense, as comprising all the phænomena by which its existence is made known to us'. The second clause of Schelling's third sentence runs as follows: 'der Inbegriff alles Subjektiven dagegen heisse das Ich, oder die Intelligenz.' and is exactly translated by Coleridge's fifth sentence: 'On the other hand the sum of all that is SUBJECTIVE, we may comprehend in the name of the SELF or INTELLIGENCE.'

Schelling's fourth sentence, 'Beide Begriffe sind sich entgegengesetzt' is precisely rendered, except for the addition of the word 'necessary', by Coleridge's next sentence: 'Both conceptions are in necessary antithesis.' Schelling's fifth sentence is as follows: 'Die Intelligenz wird ursprünglich gedacht als das bloss Vorstellende, die Natur als das bloss Vorstellbare, jene als das Bewusste, diese als das Bewusstlose', and is, except for the 'ursprünglich', which Coleridge does not translate, and the 'Vorstellbare', which he loosely translates as 'represented' rather than 'representable', rendered verbatim by Coleridge's next sentence: 'Intelligence is conceived of as exclusively representative, nature as exclusively represented; the one as conscious, the other as without consciousness.' Coleridge's next two sentences are: 'Now in all acts of positive knowledge there is required a reciprocal concurrence of both, namely of the conscious being, and of that which is in itself unconscious. Our problem is to explain this

concurrence, its possibility and its necessity.' They are a faithful rendering, except for the addition of the phrase 'its possibility and its necessity',
of Schelling's sixth sentence: 'Nun ist aber in jedem Wissen ein wechsel-
seitiges Zusammentreffen beider (des Bewussten und des an sich Be-
wusstlosen) nothwendig; die Aufgabe ist: dieses Zusammentreffen zu
erklären.'

Coleridge's next sentence begins a new paragraph, as does Schelling's;
Coleridge says: 'During the act of knowledge itself, the objective and
subjective are so instantly united, that we cannot determine to which of
the two the priority belongs', which renders exactly Schelling's sentence:
'Im Wissen selbst—indem ich weiss—ist Objektives und Subjektives so
vereinigt, dass man nicht sagen kann, welchem von beiden die Priorität
zukomme.' Then Coleridge says: 'There is here no first, and no second;
both are coinstantaneous and one.' Schelling says: 'Es ist hier kein Erstes
und kein Zweites, beide sind gleichzeitig und Eins.' Coleridge says:
'While I am attempting to explain this intimate coalition, I must suppose
it dissolved.' Schelling says: 'Indem ich diese Identität erklären will; muss
ich sie schon aufgehoben haben.' Coleridge says: 'I must necessarily set
out from the one, to which therefore I give hypothetical antecedence, in
order to arrive at the other. But as there are but two factors or elements
in the problem, subject and object, and as it is left indeterminate from
which of them I should commence, there are two cases equally possible.'
And Schelling says: 'Um sie zu erklären, muss ich, da mir ausser jenen
beiden Faktoren des Wissens (als Erklärungsprincip) sonst nichts gegeben
ist, nothwendig den einen dem andern vorsetzen, von dem einen aus-
gehen, um von ihm auf den andern zu kommen; von welchem von
beiden ich ausgehe, ist durch die Aufgabe nicht bestimmt. Es sind also
nur zwei Fälle möglich.' Then Coleridge says: '1. EITHER THE OBJECTIVE
IS TAKEN AS THE FIRST, AND THEN WE HAVE TO ACCOUNT FOR THE SUPER-
VENTION OF THE SUBJECTIVE, WHICH COALESCES WITH IT.' And Schelling
says: 'A. *Entweder wird das Objektive zum Ersten gemacht, und gefragt: wie ein
Subjektives zu ihm hinzukomme, das mit ihm übereinstimmt.*' And Coleridge
says—to make this citation our last: '2. OR THE SUBJECTIVE IS TAKEN AS
THE FIRST, AND THE PROBLEM THEN IS, HOW THERE SUPERVENES TO IT A
COINCIDENT OBJECTIVE'—while Schelling says: 'B. *Oder das Subjektive wird
zum Ersten gemacht, und die Aufgabe ist die: wie ein Objektives hinzukomme, das
mit ihm übereinstimmt.*'

These selections from Coleridge's *Biographia* should not allow us to
forget, in their juxtaposition with the selections from Schelling's *Transcendental Idealism*, that the parallelisms of Coleridge and Schelling cannot,
where they occur, be dismissed as coincidence, but rather are almost
invariably literal, or near-literal, translations.

And yet I am convinced that Coleridge's thought, as Green originally maintained, is not only different from that of Schelling, but radically different; that Coleridge, squirrel-like, stockpiled terminology, phrasings, concepts, from other thinkers, but selected and arranged from these a reticulated pattern possessed of as much philosophical integrity as Schelling's own thought. We may regret the inconvenience of having to acknowledge that much of the twelfth chapter of the *Biographia* is translated from Schelling, that much of the fifth chapter is from Maass. Curiously enough, however, the addition of Maass as a source to Schelling does not add to the indictment of plagiarism, but tends rather to detract from it. A true plagiarist, a disciple, an echoing voice—these are the charges brought by the Ferriers and Robertsons and Inglebys—should translate only from Schelling. Discipleship implies for its definition the existence of a master. If Schelling is the master, what do we make of Maass? And as we inquire more deeply into Coleridge's unorthodox practice, we find that he also lays under intellectual taxation Jacobi, Wilhelm Schlegel, Herder, Kant, Steffens—these and many more. If Coleridge is the derivative, subordinate thinker, the disciple, who then is the master? The ideas and endeavours of these men are certainly not identical, and indeed not always reconcilable.

We are all familiar with the experience of the sudden coalescence of a series of intractable data around a particular datum, seemingly no more important than any other member of the series. For me, such an organizing and clarifying instance was Alice Snyder's comment, almost off-hand in its context, apropos of her examination of Coleridge's marginalia in Mendelssohn's *Morgenstunden*: 'It is, however, something of a surprise to discover in Coleridge's discussion of the syllogism in his manuscript "Logic" an "analysis of conceptions" taken over, much of it verbatim, from the *Morgenstunden*.'[1] This insight into Coleridge's borrowings-in-progress, as it were, with its concomitant image of the English thinker busily and methodically mining the German work, made sense for me—though certainly everyone must judge for himself—of the phenomenon of Coleridge's borrowings. For the very multiplicity of instances—far more than at first charged, and by no means as yet all identified—suggests the explanation, bizarre though it may seem, that we are faced not with plagiarism, but with nothing less than a mode of composition—composition by mosaic organization rather than by painting on an empty canvas.

We look too often for simple answers. Perhaps Bonjour's thesis that Coleridge plagiarized out of weakness and inadequacy is correct, but few of us will be satisfied that this is the whole answer. The psyche always has its rationalizations. A man may take raw material from other authors when

---

[1] Alice D. Snyder, 'Coleridge's Reading of Mendelssohn's "Morgenstunden" and "Jerusalem"', *JEGP*, xxviii (1929), 504.

he is confident of his ultimate ability to generate the flame necessary for a final transmutation of these materials into a *magnum opus*. Doubtless the *magnum opus*, projecting hypothetically into the future, was an important teleological rationalization, a psychic cover story, for Coleridge's borrowings.[1] Not that I mean to denigrate the good faith of the *magnum opus*; but once project such a work, as the fruition and reconciliation of all the elements of a variegated mind, and a new set of rules and tolerances might quite plausibly be set up.[2] Also tending to allow Coleridge to make his own rules was the philosophical vacuum of English thought in his time. Where there is a strong tradition, and where there are competent compeers, academic conventions quickly come into being: the rules are public and understood. But Coleridge, not only largely self-taught, but shut off from the kind of running colloquy that was so happily the cultural lot of his German contemporaries, would quite naturally tend to be less observant of the rules on that foreign ground than of those of his own situation.

So we may grant the facts. Firstly, Coleridge's borrowings are not only real, but so honeycomb his work as to form virtually a mode of composition. Secondly, he was, on the evidence, a deeply neurotic man. Thirdly, he expected much of himself and his friends expected much of him, but his blocks and frustrations compressed his powers in a humiliating and often impotent bondage—his dejection was indeed caused by his loss of the shaping spirit of imagination.[3] Fourthly, his cultural situation was isolated, and, compared with the philosophical activities of Germany, provincial.[4] 'Great indeed', said Coleridge, 'are the obstacles which an

---

[1] The conception of 'system' tends to depress the importance of originality and grant licence to borrowed, but in themselves not systematically arranged, materials. 'A System', says Coleridge, 'may have no new Truths for it's component Parts, yet having nothing but Truths may be for that very reason a new System' (*Letters*, ii. 700).

[2] Coleridge's faith in the value of reconciling and harmonizing activities of mind was so profound as to be literally religious, e.g.: 'To *reconcile* therefore is truly the work of the Inspired! This is the true *Atonement*—i.e. to reconcile the struggles of the infinitely various Finite with the *Permanent*' (*Notebooks*, ii. 2208). And as a kind of religious faith, his belief in the reconciling mission of his activities, culminating in his *magnum opus*, may well have seemed to provide a justification to dispense with older moralities and cleave to this new testament.

[3] As Carlyle says: 'To the man himself Nature had given, in high measure, the seeds of a noble endowment; and to unfold it had been forbidden him' (*The Life of John Sterling*, p. 60). Some of Coleridge's own statements of his sense of ineffectuality are of great poignance; e.g. 'A sense of weakness—a haunting sense, that I was an herbaceous Plant, as large as a large Tree, with a Trunk of the same Girth, & Branches as large & shadowing—but with *pith within* the Trunk, not heart of Wood/—that I had *power* not *strength*—an involuntary Imposter. . . . This on my honor is as fair a statement of my habitual Haunting, as I could give before the Tribunal of Heaven' (*Letters*, ii. 959. To Southey, 1 Aug. 1803). Again: 'I know, I feel, that I am weak—apt to faint away inwardly, self-deserted & bereft of the confidence in my own powers' (*Letters*, ii. 1054. To Sir George Beaumont, 1 Feb. 1804).

[4] Such at any rate was Coleridge's own conviction. He says, for instance, 'I am no Zealot or Bigot for German Philosophy, taken without comparison: tho' I shall always hold it my Duty to teach folks, as far as in me lies, to bow to their Betters—and in my conscience I think (*speaking of the last 50 years*) the very worst German Work of speculative philosophy or psychologic Observation better than the best that has been produced in London or Edingburgh

English metaphysician has to encounter.'[1] Then against these facts we have to take account of his huge erudition, his meditative habits, his flashing insight—even Carlyle concedes him 'a subtle, lynx-eyed intellect' and speaks of 'his pious, ever-labouring, subtle mind'.[2] Thus we can see, perhaps, the elements that might fuse into his unorthodox and disingenuous mode of composition: on the one hand, the sense of understanding and insight into problems that baffled lesser minds (and did not even exist for many), and on the other, the humiliation before his neurotic incapacity to perform the mere busy work necessary to body forth his insight. We may then be able to see in, say, the translations of the *Biographia*—a book, as Stephen notes, 'put together with a pitchfork'[3]— a kind of intellectual promissory note. We may be willing to concede that the psychological background of such borrowings was not a dearth of ideas, but a profusion of ideas along with a dearth of energy. Why, otherwise, 'plagiarize'? If one intends to steal the tiara, rather than merely borrow it, surely one does not keep it intact but rather dismantles it and resets its gems. Why lay oneself open to reproach? Why copy verbatim? If I, as the author of this essay, find myself inescapably dependent upon Schelling, I can, and will, so manage it, by the substitution of my own phrasings for his, that I will obviate reproach.

What, indeed, do we all learn in the course of a scholarly training, but the conventions and gentilities of using other people's thoughts? Some we encase in footnotes, some we read, digest, and restate, some we simply regurgitate, but few people in this world, very few indeed, really have more than a genuine idea or two in a lifetime. One musical idea can produce a Sibelius, one visual idea a Cézanne, one poetic idea a Vaughan. We all know many things, but only one or two of those things, or none at all, originates with any one of us. We all stand on the shoulders of others—of our predecessors and of our contemporaries—and we rightly condemn those who attempt to claim more. As Jung says,

widely accepted ideas are never the personal property of their so-called author; on the contrary, he is the bond-servant of his ideas. Impressive ideas which are hailed as truths have something peculiar to themselves. Although they come into being at a definite time, they are and have always been timeless; they arise from that realm of procreative, psychic life out of which the ephemeral mind of the single human being grows like a plant and blossoms, bears fruit and seed,

---

(i.e. Great Britain; and *Ireland*, inasmuch as o does not interfere with any numerical calculation)' (*Letters*, iv. 793). Arnold, in his *The Function of Criticism at the Present Time*, sees the whole English Romantic movement—with the exception of Coleridge—weakened because it 'did not know enough' (*Essays in Criticism; First Series*, p. 7), and in his *The Literary Influence of Academies*, as well as in *Joubert*, he again speaks of the provincialism of the British intellectual environment in the nineteenth century.

[1] *Biographia*, i. 191.
[2] Carlyle, *The Life of John Sterling*, p. 60.
[3] Stephen, *Hours in a Library*, iii. 355.

and then withers and dies. Ideas spring from a source that is not contained in one man's personal life.[1]

Nor are these the only considerations. The idea of originality grew slowly and confusedly in cultural history.[2] Who can read in the Church Fathers without faintness in the face of the laborious repetitions of opinion and phrase; who can read in critical history without quailing before the endless echoes of Horace or Aristotle by the literary theorists of the Renaissance and the Neoclassical era? What do we make of Johnson's *London* or of his *Vanity of Human Wishes*—are they 'original' poems, or 'translations', or 'plagiarisms' from Juvenal? (What, for that matter, do we make of Roscommon's urging, in his *Essay on Translated Verse*, that the translator should aspire to be 'No Longer his *Interpreter*, but *He*'?) What, further, do we make of the whole orientation of an age that defined its attitude towards originality by Pope's dictum, 'What oft was thought, but ne'er so well expressed'?

What—to become more specific—do we say, by the censorious standard of 'plagiarism', of Ben Jonson, whom Dryden praises as 'the most learned and judicious writer which any theatre ever had', as 'the greatest man of the last age', and also identifies, with unreproachful equanimity, as 'a learned plagiary', as 'a professed imitator of Horace'? Jonson, says Dryden, 'was deeply conversant in the Ancients, both Greek and Latin, and he borrowed boldly from them: there is scarce a poet or historian among the Roman authors of those times whom he has not translated in *Sejanus* and *Catiline*. . . . He invades authors like a monarch; and what would be theft in other poets, is only victory in him.'[3] And what is the ultimate significance of Jonson's 'robberies' in Dryden's view? Simply that these robberies are a testimonial to the superiority of the Ancients in the celebrated *querelle*.[4]

To be sure, Romanticism itself, perhaps beginning with Young's *Con-*

---

[1] C. G. Jung, *Modern Man in Search of a Soul*, p. 115.

[2] See, e.g., H. O. White, *Plagiarism and Imitation During the English Renaissance. A Study in Critical Distinctions* (Cambridge, Mass., 1933). Cf. Vida, writing in 1527: 'Come then, all ye youths! and, careless of censure, give yourselves up to STEAL and drive the spoil from every source! Unhappy is he . . . who, rashly trusting to his own strength and art, as though in need of no external help, in his audacity refuses to follow the trustworthy footsteps of the ancients, abstaining, alas! unwisely from plunder, and thinking to spare others. O vain superstition! . . . Not long do such men prosper—often they outlive their own works. . . . How [deeply] could they wish to have spared their idle labour and to have learnt other arts from their parents! Often I love to play on ancient phrase, and utter some far other thought in the same words. Nor will any wise man care to blame my self-confessing thefts—thefts open and to be praised and approved. . . . So far be it from me to wish to hide my stolen goods, and conceal my plunder from any fear of the penalty of infamy!' (Saintsbury, *Loci Critici*, pp. 85–86).

[3] Dryden, *Of Dramatic Poesy and Other Critical Essays*, ed. George Watson (London and New York, 1962), i. 69, 31, 69.

[4] Dryden himself, interestingly enough, was charged with plagiarism by one of his contemporaries. See note 4, p. 335.

jectures on Original Composition of 1759, increasingly treated literary originality as a virtue, and, indeed, sometimes as the only virtue. But we must not forget that Coleridge, as a founder of English Romanticism, was also a transitional figure from an earlier era. And though literature began to prize originality, philosophy, as I have suggested, did not.[1] So Coleridge, as not only a literary creator, but a philosophical systematist, was in the special position of being able to bestow his allegiance on whichever tradition suited the pressure of immediate circumstances, and had, additionally, the option of psychological escape into the literary attitudes of his Neoclassic predecessors. Finally, the deeply cherished Romantic, and Platonist, doctrine of organic form to some extent worked against, rather than complemented, the demand for originality.[2] 'It will not', says Coleridge, be 'by Dates, that Posterity will judge of the originality of a Poem; but by the original spirit itself.' He continues:

This is to be found neither in a Tale however interesting, which is but the Canvass, no nor yet in the Fancy or the Imagery—which are but Forms & Colors —it is a subtle Spirit, all in each part, reconciling & unifying all—. Passion and Imagination are it's *most* appropriate names; but even these say little—for it must be not merely Passion but poetic Passion, poetic Imagination.[3]

Thus the imagination-fancy distinction is presented as an adjunct to the organic form doctrine stemming originally from Plato, but as an opponent of originality.[4]

Coleridge speaks well in the foregoing passage, with the turn of phrase and gift for apt brevity that are so especially his characteristics as a commentator. He speaks well also in other passages where he expresses himself on the subject of originality and indebtedness. It is an interesting fact, and one that indicates strongly that his various borrowings were not to any substantial extent the mistaking of old translations for original notes, that Coleridge, before the charges of plagiarism—which, as we have seen, were not publicly instituted until after his death—virtually acknowledged that the charges inevitably would be made, and attempted to defend himself. One wonders why, in that event, he did not attempt to conventionalize his indebtedness in some way while he was still alive, if true

---

[1] Coleridge soon became sceptical about the possibility of philosophical 'originality'. In 1801, for instance, he writes that 'my Reading has furnished me with many reasons for being exceedingly suspicious of *supposed Discoveries* in Metaphysics' (*Letters*, ii. 675).

[2] Cf. Tillich on Schelling: It is possible, he says, to count off the 'supposed fathers' of Schelling's thought: 'Spinoza, Plato, Böhme, Baader, Hegel, Aristotle'. But if one merely thinks of these relationships in terms of 'influence', it will be impossible to talk of an 'inner dialectic' of Schelling's development. The error in such a procedure is the assumption that Schelling met each of these influences by chance. It was rather that the 'inner progress of Schelling's development' led him into proximity with these philosophers, from whom he then adopted 'homogeneous elements' (Tillich, *Mystik in Schellings Entwicklung*, pp. 10–11).

[3] *Letters*, iii. 361.

[4] Plato, *Phaedrus* 264 c: 'Every discourse should be a living creature'. The tradition of the cosmos itself as a living organism stems from the *Timaeus*.

plagiarism had been his necessity. A possible answer is that, while one can set right improper borrowing, either by proper acknowledgement or by revision so as to obliterate all marks of impropriety, one cannot change, *ex post facto*, an organic and persistent method of composition. And there can be little doubt that Coleridge's borrowings, though skirting and sometimes crossing the boundary of propriety, were not the thefts of a poverty-stricken mind, but the mosaic materials of a neurotic technique of composition. We see this mosaic organization, in fact, not only in a work like the *Biographia Literaria*, but as the central reality of the composition of such poems as *The Ancient Mariner*. Lowes's *Road to Xanadu* would not have been possible, there would have been no phrasings and snippets lifted from travel books, had not Coleridge's method of composition been to work with larger elements—phrases and connected image patterns—than is conventional.

If we examine some of the disclaimers broached by Coleridge himself, we find that he uses in one way or another all the defences later suggested for him. He insists on the integrity, and on the difference of his thought from that of the Germans, and he maintains the originality, or better, the organicism of his whole approach to life, of the central ideas of his thought —though conceding by implication that in at least the particularization and development of those ideas he is indebted to the German philosophers:

Of the three schemes of philosophy, Kant's, Fichte's, and Schelling's . . . I should find it difficult to select the one from which I *differed* the most, though perfectly easy to determine which of the three *men* I hold in highest honour. And Immanuel Kant I assuredly do value most highly; not, however, as a metaphysician, but as a logician. . . . I can not only honestly assert, but I can satisfactorily prove by reference to writings (Letters, Marginal Notes, and those in books that have never been in my possession since I first left England for Hamburgh, etc.) that all the elements, the *differentials*, as the algebraists say, of my present opinions existed for me before I had even seen a book of German Metaphysics, later than Wolf and Leibnitz, or could have read it, if I had. But what will this avail? A High German Transcendentalist I must be content to remain . . .[1]

In another place Coleridge avows that his 'opinions were formed before' he 'was acquainted with the Schools of Fichte and Schelling'.[2] The extent to which this statement is true, or can be true, is the extent to which it is true that, as Coleridge says, there is no 'system' of which 'the elements and the outlines' are 'not to be found in the Greek schools'.[3] Wellek tends to emphasize the differences of the German thinkers from their ancient prototypes, but the German thinkers themselves, as I suggested

---

[1] *Letters of Samuel Taylor Coleridge*, ed. E. H. Coleridge (London, 1895), ii. 735–6.
[2] *Letters*, iv. 792.
[3] *Notes on English Divines*, ed. Derwent Coleridge (London, 1853), ii. 144.

in the introduction, were eager to emphasize the similarities. 'Hegel', observes Emerson, 'pre-exists in Proclus, and, long before, in Heraclitus and Parmenides'[1]—and Hegel himself conceded that 'half' his system was in Parmenides.[2] 'Es ist weiter zu bemerken', says Hegel himself of Schelling, 'dass Schelling in neueren Zeiten der Urheber der Natur-Philosophie geworden ist; sie ist nicht neue Wissenschaft, wir hatten sie immer, bei Aristoteles u.s.w.'[3]—that Schelling has become the modern exponent of nature philosophy, which is not new knowledge, but has been always with us, from Aristotle on. And we are all familiar with Whitehead's oft-cited remark that the whole history of western philosophy is a 'series of footnotes to Plato'.[4]

To proceed to specific instances, consider the seeming fact that Coleridge's important imagination-fancy distinction, with its key proviso of the connexion of imagination to reason and of fancy to understanding, is derived directly from Schelling. I say Schelling, despite demonstrations that both 'imagination' and 'fancy' were terms in use in the native British critical tradition before Coleridge, for the specification of those terms, and the establishment of their relevance to the distinction between reason and understanding, could not have been supplied by the British tradition.[5] Schelling, on the other hand, is very exact: 'Einbildungskraft bezieht sich auf die Vernunft, wie Phantasie auf den Verstand. Jene produktiv, diese reproduktiv.'[6] But in this case it is very difficult to charge Coleridge with dependence, or impropriety, or lack of originality, if we are not willing to make the same charges against Schelling. For Schelling's *Einbildungskraft-Phantasie* distinction is explicitly dependent on Kant, as we see by his use of the Kantian words 'produktiv' and 'reproduktiv'. Schelling's 'Phantasie' is merely a reflex of Kant's 'reproductive imagination', which, in the *Kritik der reinen Vernunft*, is described as the faculty by which the manifold of intuition is schematized for the operation of the understanding (and hence, in its dimension in time, is a mode of memory),[7] and Schelling's 'Einbildungskraft' is a reflex of that creative imagination that Kant, in the *Kritik der Urteilskraft*, describes as 'free' from the law of association:

The imagination (as a productive faculty of cognition) is a powerful agent

---

[1] Emerson, 'Originality', *Complete Works*, viii. 180.

[2] Cited in F. M. Cornford, *Plato and Parmenides* (London, 1939), p. vi.

[3] Hegel, *Werke*, xv. 652.

[4] Whitehead, *Process and Reality*, p. 53.

[5] See John Bullitt and W. J. Bate, 'Distinctions Between Fancy and Imagination', *MLN*, lx (1945), pp. 8–15; Earl R. Wasserman, 'Another Eighteenth-Century Distinction Between Fancy and Imagination', *MLN*, lxiv (1949), pp. 23–25. See also Wilma L. Kennedy, *The English Heritage of Coleridge of Bristol, 1798. The Basis in Eighteenth-Century English Thought for his Distinction between Imagination and Fancy* (New Haven, 1947).

[6] Schelling, *Werke*, iv. 115 n. 1.

[7] Kant, *Kritik der reinen Vernunft*, *Werke*, iii. 622–5. These statements, Kant's most explicit, appear only in the first edition. But, in the second edition see iii. 97, 126–7.

for creating, as it were, a second nature out of the material supplied to it by actual nature. . . . We even use it to remodel experience, always following, no doubt, laws that are based on analogy, but still also following principles which have a higher seat in reason. . . . By this means we get a sense of our freedom from the law of association (which attaches to the empirical employment of the imagination), with the result that the material can be borrowed by us from nature in accordance with that law, but be worked up by us into something else—namely, what surpasses nature.[1]

Thus the priority in the imagination-fancy distinction, if not Coleridge's, is clearly not Schelling's either, just as 'potence', if taken by Coleridge from Schelling, is likewise taken by Schelling from Bruno. Schelling, indeed, was little concerned with priorities. In his first discussion of 'Einbildungskraft', for instance, he identifies his thought about it as arising from 'seeds' planted by Kant's 'immortal work', and expresses the hope that 'time' (not he himself or any other specified philosopher), which is the 'mother of every development' will 'nourish' our understanding of 'dieses wunderbare Vermögen'—this wonderful faculty:

Man darf hoffen, dass die Zeit, die Mutter jeder Entwickelung, auch jene Keime, welche Kant in seinem unsterblichen Werke, zu grossen Aufschlüssen über dieses wunderbare Vermögen, niederlegte, pflegen und selbst bis zur Vollendung der ganzen Wissenschaft entwickeln werde.[2]

Kant may have embodied this 'wonderful faculty' of *Einbildungskraft*, which can 'remodel experience', and can create 'a second nature' which 'surpasses nature', in a rigorous analysis of mental functions. And yet the general idea, the controlling notion of *Einbildungskraft*, that in which the power is likened to the creative power by which nature originally is founded, that in which its wielder, the poet, is represented as an analogue of the divine creativity, is not the property of Kant, but is an idea of great persistence and great antiquity, is, specifically, a Platonism, and, historically, infused German thought of the late eighteenth century expressly through the medium of Shaftesbury, who said:

I Must confess there is hardly any where to be found a more insipid Race of Mortals, than those whom we Moderns are contented to call *Poets*, for having attain'd the chiming Faculty of a Language, with an injudicious random use of Wit and Fancy. But for the Man, who truly and in a just sense deserves the Name of *Poet*, and who as a real Master, or Architect in the kind, can describe both *Men* and *Manners*, and give to an *Action* its just Body and Proportions; he will be found, if I mistake not, a very different Creature. Such a *Poet* is indeed a second *Maker*: a just PROMETHEUS, under JOVE. Like that Sovereign Artist or universal Plastick Nature, he forms a *Whole*, coherent and proportion'd in it-self, with due Subjection and Subordinacy of constituent Parts.[3]

[1] Kant, *Werke*, v, Section 49, 389.   [2] Schelling, *Werke*, i. 332 n. 1.
[3] *Characteristicks*, i. 207.

We see in Shaftesbury's 'insipid Race of Mortals . . . whom we Moderns
. . . call *Poets*' a refraction, through two millennia, of those truth-deprived
image-makers, the 'mimetic poets', who were so unremittingly the object
of Plato's disapproval,[1] while in Shaftesbury's 'second *Maker*', his 'just
PROMETHEUS, under JOVE', we see a refraction of Plato's true poet, who
not only 'puts together words' but 'creates' fables,[2] whose 'compositions are
based on knowledge of the truth'[3]—which is of 'the other world, the region
of purity, and eternity, and immortality, and unchangeableness'[4]—and
who is therefore 'to be called, not only poet . . . but [is] worthy of a higher
name . . . philosopher.'[5] In such terms it is possible to be emphatic about
Coleridge's independence of the German thinkers in the development of
his controlling ideas. Schelling, for instance, became seriously interested
in Plotinus mainly through Creuzer,[6] and in Boehme through Tieck,[7]
whereas Coleridge anticipated Schelling in his knowledge of both these
important figures. His native English tradition supplied him with a
Thomas Taylor to direct him to Plotinus, and with a William Law to
direct him to Boehme, and we know conclusively that his knowledge of
such central Platonic transmitters antedated that of Schelling.[8] The importance of Plotinus to German Romanticism in general has been carefully
studied.[9] We are advised by Max Wundt to regard 1799 as the time of the
first real discovery of Plotinus by the German intellectuals,[10] and to regard
Novalis as the true discoverer of Plotinus.[11] Yet we know, on Lamb's

---

[1] Plato, *Republic* 600 E, 602 A–B.   [2] Plato, *Phaedo* 61 B.
[3] Plato, *Phaedrus* 278 C.
[4] Plato, *Phaedo* 79 D.   [5] Plato, *Phaedrus* 278 C–D.
[6] See especially Creuzer, *Die Liebe der Günderode*, p. 35.

[7] Schelling apparently really became familiar with Boehme's work late in 1799, which suggests that Boehme confirmed rather than originated the pantheist mode of thought he had
already derived from Spinoza, Fichte, and his own apprehension of reality. Tieck seems to have
been mainly responsible for directing his attention to the mystic. Thus Plitt says that 'in
the summer of 1799 Tieck arrived in Jena for the first time to visit Schlegel. . . . In October
Tieck brought his family for a longer sojourn and stayed in Schlegel's house, which was
frequently visited by Novalis. He had won over Novalis, like Schelling, through his folk tales,
and now acquainted both new friends with Jacob Boehme. . . . Fichte wanted to know nothing
about this "confused dreamer", while Schelling revealed himself accessible to Boehmean
ideas . . . ' (Plitt, *Aus Schellings Leben*, i. 245–7). Tieck's own knowledge of Boehme, thinks
Ederheimer, is evident as early as 1792 (Ederheimer, *Boehme und die Romantiker*, pp. 3–4). Most
scholars, however, prefer a date no earlier than 1796. Boehme was mediated to the Germans by
F. C. Oetinger.

[8] In a letter to Tieck, Coleridge states that he 'conjured over' Boehme 'at School' in the
1780s (*Letters*, iv. 751). With respect to Coleridge's schoolboy knowledge of Plotinus, see
n. 3, p. 162. Inasmuch as it is established that Schelling had seriously studied neither Plotinus
nor Boehme much before 1800, Coleridge must be granted a precedence in his knowledge of
both thinkers.

[9] See P. F. Reiff, 'Plotin und die deutsche Romantik', *Euphorion*, xix (1912), 591–612; O.
Walzel, *Deutsche Romantik; I. Welt- und Kunstanschauung*, fünfe Auflage (Leipzig und Berlin,
1923), gp. 2–5, 46, 55; see also Excursus Note VI, p. 282.

[10] Max Wundt, 'Plotin und die Romantik', *Neue Jahrbücher für das klassische Altertum Geschichte und deutsche Literatur*, hrsg. Johannes Ilberg, xxxv (1915), 658–9.

famous testimony, that Coleridge was saturated with knowledge of Plotinus from his schooldays in the late 1780s.[1] Precisely because of such early and first-hand Neoplatonic knowledge, it seems, Coleridge paid little attention to Shaftesbury, and precisely because the Germans were late in pushing their own investigations back to the ancient sources, Shaftesbury loomed important for them.[2] And yet, in the following passage, Coleridge clearly participates in the Platonism of the 'second *Maker*', the 'just PROMETHEUS, under JOVE', though, we may believe, not as an echo of Shaftesbury:[3] 'Man . . . is urged to develop the powers of the creator, and by new combinations of those powers to imitate his creativeness.'[4] This Platonist echo clearly adumbrates Coleridge's later formulation in which the primary imagination is 'a repetition in the finite mind of the eternal act of creation', and the secondary imagination is an 'echo' of the primary, 'identical' in 'the *kind* of its agency. . . . It dissolves, diffuses, dissipates, in order to re-create. . . .'[5] It appeared in *The Watchman* in 1796, a date that places the conception unarguably prior to any possible German influence, because at the time Coleridge had not yet learned German. And Coleridge again, on 20 March 1796, clearly anticipates, in the word 'catenating', the organic nature of his subsequent theory of imagination, later conveyed by such words as 'esemplastic', 'synthetic', 'synergic', and 'coadunating'. The catenating faculty is, for the Coleridge of 1796, 'the silk thread that ought to run through the Pearl-chain of Ratiocination'.[6] Though these early emphases upon creative and organic formulations do not, of course, encompass fully the later imagination-fancy distinctions, they do the controlling attitudes and general ideas that characterize the later distinctions, and hence tend to justify Coleridge's contention that 'the elements, the *differentials*' of his 'opinions' existed 'before I had even seen a book of German Metaphysics, later than Wolf and Leibnitz, or could have read it, if I had'.

Even though the specifics of the theory of imagination were the work

[11] Ibid., p. 658. Novalis displays intense enthusiasm for Plotinus, and says that he was almost 'terrified' by the 'similarity' of Plotinus to 'Fichte and Kant'. See the letter of Novalis to Friedrich Schlegel in December of 1798: 'I don't know whether I wrote to you about my dear Plotinus. I became acquainted with this born-for-me philosopher out of Tiedemann's *History of Philosophy*—and I was almost terrified by his similarity to Fichte and Kant. . . . He is closer to my heart than either. . . . In Plotinus there is much still unused—and he would be, before all others, worth a new annunciation' (Novalis, *Schriften*, iv. 252).

[1] *The Works of Charles and Mary Lamb*, ii. 21.

[2] See note 5, p. 336.

[3] A good example, on the other hand, of a Platonism with the identifying insignia of transmission through Shaftesbury and the Germans is in Carlyle: 'A Hierarch, therefore, and Pontiff of the World will we call him, the Poet and inspired Maker; who, Prometheus-like, can shape new symbols . . .' (*Sartor Resartus* III. iii). Cassirer has demonstrated the development of the Prometheus-like Maker as a specific contribution of Renaissance thought (see Cassirer, *Individuum und Kosmos*, pp. 150–75).

[4] Coleridge, *The Watchman* [Bristol, 1796], p. 101.

[5] *Biographia*, i. 202.

[6] *Letters*, i. 193.

of Kant, and though Coleridge availed himself of the *Einbildungskraft-Phantasie* distinction of Schelling, the larger forms of such polar distinctions of mental powers had been always a characteristic of the Platonic tradition, and may have been subliminally the reason why he took up the *Einbildungskraft-Phantasie* polarity. Augustine, for instance, speaks of 'phantasmata', which are a function of the 'bodily senses', deal with 'bodily forms', and are a mode of 'memory'.[1] And Augustine likewise provides a prototype for 'reason' and 'understanding' in his distinction of 'sapientia' and 'scientia'.[2] Again, Aristotle's distinction between active and passive intellect, *nous poietikos* and *nous pathetikos*, was powerfully operant in the history of thought.[3] And perhaps the grand source of all such distinctions is Plato's conception of *phantastiké*, the faculty which images things phenomenologically, as they appear, as opposed to *eikastiké*, the faculty which images things as they are.[4]

It is difficult to say how well Coleridge knew such distinctions. But certainly 'imagination' itself has always been a recognized subject of philosophical inquiry (e.g. Aristotle, *De Anima* 428ᵃ–429ᵃ 10); likewise, the dichotomizing of problems for better analysis is a standard philosophical procedure. And Coleridge was usually ready to syncretize ancient and modern problems and terms. He says, for instance, that 'The grand problem, the solution of which forms, according to Plato, the final object and distinctive character of philosophy, is this: for all that exists conditionally . . . to find a ground that is unconditional and absolute.'[5] Since the terms 'conditional' (*bedingt*) and 'unconditional' (*unbedingt*) were brought into philosophical prominence by Kant, it might seem possible to interpret their ascription by Coleridge to Plato as simple ignorance on Coleridge's part. Wellek, indeed, implies as much.[6] But, as in the case of Stirling's terminological accusations noted in the introduction, historical considerations do not support such a view. For Coleridge was subscribing to the most sophisticated usage of his contemporaries. Kant himself has an idiosyncratic Kantian terminology for the description of Plato's objectives, thus providing a clear patent for the practice: 'Plato proceeds at least consequently with all these deductions. Without doubt the question confronted him, although in a dim way, "How are synthetic propositions *a priori* possible?"'[7] Inasmuch as any talk of 'synthetic propositions *a priori*' is a hallmark of Kantian analysis, Kant's suggestion of Plato's interest in the question is precisely the same kind of terminological syncretism that occurs in Coleridge's own use of 'unconditioned' with reference to Platonic goals. Jacobi, in fact, indicates the legitimacy of

---

[1] Augustine, *De vera religione* 18.   [2] Augustine, *De trinitate* xii. 25.
[3] Aristotle, *De anima* 430ᵃ 15. See note 6, p. 337.
[4] Plato, *Sophist* 235 D–236 D.   [5] *Works*, ii. 420.
[6] René Wellek, 'Emerson and German Philosophy', *The New England Quarterly*, xvi (1943), 42.
[7] Kant, *Werke*, vi. 479–80.

that very term for discussions of Plato: 'The empty chaos, the non-form, the completely undefined (Plato and the Pythagoreans called it the unbounded) is the unconditioned, the absolute of the understanding. . . .'[1] Coleridge thus found it proper to transpose problems to ancient proto-types, and vice versa; and such a procedure also accorded with his view of the nature of philosophical originality: 'As every man has a face of his own, without being more or less than a man, so is every true philosopher an original, without ceasing to be an inmate of Academus or of the Lyceum' (*Works*, iv. 400).

In addition to his implied plea of Platonic origins, Coleridge adduces several other kinds of apology. He claims, for instance, coincidence of background as the explanation of the coincidence of Wilhelm Schlegel's Shakespeare criticism and his own:

Schlegel & myself had both studied deeply & perseverantly the philosophy of Kant, the distinguishing feature of which [is] to treat every subject in refer-ence to the operation of the mental Faculties, to which it specially appertains— & to commence by the cautious discrimination of what is essential, i.e. explicable by mere consideration of the Faculties in themselves, from what is empirical— i.e. the modifying or disturbing Forces of Time, Place, and Circumstances. Suppose myself & Schlegel (my argument not my vanity leads to these seeming Self-flatteries) nearly equal in natural powers, of similar pursuits & acquire-ments, and it is only necessary for both to have mastered the spirit of Kant's Critique of the Judgment to render it morally certain, that writing on the same Subject we should draw the same conclusions by the same trains [of reasoning] from the same principles, write to one purpose & with one spirit.[2]

We may discern in this plea plausibility and disingenuousness in almost equal proportions. As founding figures and contemporaries in the Romantic movement, and as students of Kantian philosophy, Schlegel and Coleridge might indeed be expected to share important attitudes. But though similarity of background might lead to 'one purpose and one spirit', the suggestion that it is 'only' necessary to have read a treatise of Kant's to produce strikingly similar work seems rather strained, and Coleridge skirts the key point of the precise degree of similarity involved.[3]

---

[1] F. H. Jacobi, *Von den göttlichen Dingen und ihrer Offenbarung* (Leipzig, 1811), p. 181.

[2] *Letters*, iii. 360.

[3] There is some indication, however, that Coleridge is to some extent correct. More than seven years before he saw Schlegel's *Vorlesungen* he wrote to Sir George Beaumont: 'I shall both exhibit the characteristics of the Plays—& of the mind—of Shakespere—and of almost every character at greater or less Length [and provide] a philosophical Analysis & Justification, in the spirit of that analysis of the character of Hamlet, with which you were much pleased, and by being so, I solemnly assure you, gave me Heart & Hope/and did me much good' (*Letters*, ii. 1054). Thus Coleridge, at least as early as 1 Feb. 1804, was doing what he later claimed he learned from Kant, treating 'every subject in reference to the operation of the mental faculties' —that is, developing a technique of psychological character analysis, perhaps after the manner of Maurice Morgann, as the basis of his Shakespeare criticism; by that date too his analysis of the character of Hamlet was sufficiently developed to be impressive to a hearer.

The plea urged in the preceding passage is much the same as that put forward by Coleridge in the longest and best-known—one might also say the most notorious—of his defences, that in the ninth chapter of the *Biographia Literaria* regarding his relationship to Schelling:

In Schelling's 'NATUR-PHILOSOPHIE', and the 'SYSTEM DES TRANSCENDENTALEN IDEALISMUS,' I first found a genial coincidence with much that I had toiled out for myself, and a powerful assistance in what I had yet to do.... It would be but a mere act of justice to myself, were I to warn my future readers, that an identity of thought, or even similarity of phrase, will not be at all times a certain proof that the passage has been borrowed from Schelling, or that the conceptions were originally learnt from him. In this instance, as in the dramatic lectures of Schlegel ... from the same motive of self-defence against the charge of plagiarism, many of the most striking resemblances, indeed all the main and fundamental ideas, were born and matured in my mind before I had ever seen a single page of the German Philosopher; and I might indeed affirm with truth, before the more important works of Schelling had been written, or at least made public. Nor is this coincidence at all to be wondered at. We had studied in the same school; been disciplined by the same preparatory philosophy, namely, the writings of Kant; we had both equal obligations to the polar logic and dynamic philosophy of Giordano Bruno; and Schelling has lately, and, as of recent acquisition, avowed that same affectionate reverence for the labours of Behmen, and other mystics, which I had formed at a much earlier period. . . . Whether a work is the offspring of a man's own spirit, and the product of original thinking, will be discovered by those who are its sole legitimate judges, by better tests than the mere reference to dates. For readers in general, let whatever shall be found in this or any future work of mine, that resembles, or coincides with, the doctrines of my German predecessor, though contemporary, be wholly attributed to *him*: provided, that the absence of distinct references to his books, which I could not at all times make with truth as designating citations or thoughts actually *derived* from him; and which, I trust, would, after this general acknowledgment be superfluous; be not charged on me as an ungenerous concealment or intentional plagiarism.[1]

The curious mixture of frankness and of plain deceit in this passage leads us, if we examine it even briefly, into a veritable labyrinth of paradox. It may be useful to map a few of the psychological and logical mazes we find there. First: Coleridge argues his own originality, but at the same time criticizes the conception of originality and offers to attribute all similarities exclusively to Schelling. Secondly: Coleridge claims a common background for himself and Schelling, and we can verify that the two thinkers did indeed have parallel and independent derivations from Kant, Bruno, and Boehme. We might thus not only grant the possibility, but even expect the likelihood, of a certain amount of 'genial coincidence' of thought; yet surely we are not thereby prepared for Coleridge's translations of consecutive passages from Schelling's *System des transscendentalen*

[1] *Biographia*, i. 102–5.

Idealismus. Thirdly: if he was in fact completely dependent on Schelling's conceptions, why then did he not either (*a*) acknowledge his dependence by simply putting quotation marks around the passages he translated, or (*b*) conceal his dependence by the almost equally simple device—especially for a master of English prose style—of re-phrasing? In other words, why does Coleridge allow any 'striking resemblances' or any 'similarity of phrase'? If, indeed, Coleridge tells the truth, and 'all the main and fundamental ideas' were his without reference to Schelling, why this 'similarity'? Even if Coleridge lies, and 'all the main and fundamental ideas' are the property of Schelling, there is still no good reason for allowing the existence of 'similarity of phrase'. Fourthly: even granting that Coleridge lacked the power to achieve Schelling's mode of formal presentation, why does he think he needs such a mode? The *Biographia* does not claim to be a work of systematic philosophy, but merely 'biographical sketches' of Coleridge's 'literary life and opinions'; in the casual and non-rigorous context of 'sketches' and 'opinions' a systematic exposition is not only unnecessary but impossible. Fifthly: if plagiarism is actually being committed, why does Coleridge, the plagiarist, call attention to himself by using the words 'concealment' and 'plagiarism'? Sixthly: even if plagiarism has been both committed and charged, why does Coleridge then seem determined to help his accusers by supplying the names of both the author and the book to which he is indebted? And lastly—and most paradoxical: why does Coleridge translate from Schelling at all, inasmuch as it is demonstrable, and I hope so to demonstrate, that Schelling is alien to Coleridge's most deeply cherished philosophical and religious convictions?

I have no thread of Ariadne to lead us out of this labyrinth; we can do little but consider how very complex, how neurotic, and psychologically beclouded, Coleridge's unorthodox practices were. It is also clear how very inadequate is the simple term 'plagiarism' to describe them. In general, Coleridge presents us with the paradox of a burglar who seems more intent on setting off the alarm than on robbing the safe.

But a speculative answer to at least some of these questions might be outlined as follows. The particularly flagrant borrowings in the *Biographia Literaria* can be regarded as the failure, or perversion, of Coleridge's usual method of working with mosaic materials. At any rate, in later years he repudiated the 'metaphysical disquisition at the end of the first volume' of the *Biographia* as 'unformed and immature'.[1] But why should it have been unformed and immature as late as 1817? Examining the book and its date, we note two special points. First, the *Biographia* is a hastily assembled work; and secondly, Coleridge insisted, a dozen years earlier, that he habitually read 'for truth & self-satisfaction, not to make a book'.[2]

[1] *Table Talk*, 28 June 1834.   [2] *Notebooks*, ii. 2375.

Why, then, 'make' such a book? Perhaps Coleridge's financial embarrassments and his dependence on the generosity of others are one answer.[1] Such dependence would tend to goad a man's conscience and force him to make some attempt to justify his activity or lack of it.[2] And justification, for an intellectual whose whole security was based on his friends' belief that he was a genius, could only take the form of publication.[3] There was moreover, pressure from his detractors, who were ferociously articulate. The urge to 'show' them must have been very strong indeed.[4]

So, under great pressure to publish, Coleridge roused himself and heaped together the *Biographia Literaria*. And here we should note our second special point: the book is a product of Coleridge's hopeless middle years; its publication date of 1817 places it, not at the end of a period of cumulative development and coherence, but at the end of the most disconnected and opium-ridden time of Coleridge's life. In brief, Coleridge was badly off his philosophical form when he wrote the *Biographia*.[5]

But why plagiarize from Schelling rather than, say, Kant? Two answers present themselves. The first—which we shall discuss in detail later in this volume—is that Schelling, alone of contemporary thinkers, seemed to reconcile conflicting aspects of Coleridge's own thought. The second answer is more apparent and less important. Coleridge, in his lifelong struggle against English Philistinism, against the influence of Locke and Paley, of 'mechanism' and empiricism, needed allies.[6] Schelling and Fichte seemed to have all the necessary credentials. Schelling in particular was dramatic and satisfying in his scorn for 'Mechanismus', in his hailing of 'process', 'reciprocity', 'polarity', 'organism', the 'dynamic', 'freedom', 'ego', and other watchwords of the Romantic upheaval. Other men used such concepts—they were in the air all over Europe—but Schelling, as

[1] As early as 1801 he laments that 'I have not passed thro' Life without learning, that it is a heart-sickening Degradation to borrow of the Rich' (*Letters*, ii. 757).

[2] For instance, he writes to his benefactor, Josiah Wedgwood, in 1812 of his 'Hope' that 'I shall have a claim to an acknowlegement from you, that I have not misemployed my past years, or wasted that Leisure which I have owed to you, and for which I must cease to be before I can cease to feel most grateful' (*Letters*, iii. 421).

[3] Cf. the dreamy, associative musings of the tenth chapter of the *Biographia*: 'To have lived in vain must be a painful thought to any man . . .' (i. 148); 'But are books the only channel through which the stream of intellectual usefulness can flow?' (i. 149); 'Is the diffusion of truth to be estimated by publications . . . I speak . . . stung by accusation . . .' (i. 149); 'Would that the criterion of a scholar's utility were the number and moral value of the truths, which he has been the means of throwing into the general circulation . . .' (i. 149).

[4] Thus: '. . . the serious injury I have received from this rumour of having dreamed away my life to no purpose . . .' (*Biographia*, i. 150); 'Cruelly, I well know, have I been calumniated . . .' (*Letters*, iii. 421).

[5] 'Conceive a poor . . . wretch, who for many years has been attempting to beat off pain, by a constant recurrence to the vice that reproduces it. . . . In short, conceive whatever is most wretched, helpless, and hopeless, and you will form as tolerable a notion of my state, as it is possible for a good man to have' (*Letters*, iii. 511. To Josiah Wade, 26 June 1814).

[6] Thus: 'The pain I suffer & have suffered, in differing so much from such men, such true men of England . . . & their affectionate love of Locke . . .' (*Notebooks*, i. 1418).

Royce has said, was 'the prince of the romanticists'.[1] His treatises, particularly his *naturphilosophischen* writings, throb with repeated invocations of 'Polarität', 'Organismus', 'die Dynamik', 'organische Thätigkeit', 'Wechselbestimmung', 'eine dynamische Stufenfolge in der Natur', 'der dynamische Prozess', 'das dynamische Bestreben', 'ein freyes Spiel der dynamischen Kräfte', 'wechselseitige Entgegensetzung', 'Wirkung und Gegenwirkung anziehender und zurückstossender Kräfte', and 'Freiheit'. The theoretical groundwork of the organic-dynamic view of reality was laid by Kant's discussion of the organic in his *Kritik der Urteilskraft*, and by his discussion of the dynamic in his *Metaphysische Anfangsgründe der Naturwissenschaft*. But its hymns and paeans were Schelling's *naturphilosophische* writings. So Coleridge attempted to clothe his long-held anti-Lockian philosophical opinions in the language of this attractive and fashionable new dynamism, whilst seeking in Schelling's special reconciliation of 'ideal' and 'real' the solution to his own deepest philosophical perplexity. He began, as was his custom, to piece together materials for his book—neurotically attempting, at the same time, to protect himself from the anticipated attacks of his critics by insisting on his own 'originality'. But after translating some of Schelling, Coleridge began increasingly to realize that Schelling's thought was so alien to his own that no use could be made of it in his final reticulation. He therefore had no choice but to terminate his exposition of Schelling's transcendental idealism and proceed to other matters.

Such an explanation is supported by the very lameness and inconsequence of the use made of Schelling in the *Biographia*. Coleridge translates a few pages, supposedly towards a theory of imagination, then unaccountably breaks off, leaps helter-skelter to the theory—which does not proceed from anything that he has presented from or that we can find in Schelling—and then begins to talk about literature, Schelling's systematic exposition having been left dangling in its first premisses. If Coleridge were merely trying to puff up his reputation by pilfering from Schelling, he might well have continued with the translation: in for a penny, in for a pound.

So much for speculation. Coleridge's other arguments in his own defence are comparatively straightforward. We may note one that makes an implicit appeal to the justification of organic form, which is not wholly convincing, however, largely because of an exaggeratedly sardonic tone that seems to protest too much. But of particular significance is the suggestion that plagiarism, as commonly defined—or rather as commonly invoked without the trouble of exact definition—does not exist at all:

Excuse me, if I say that I have ever held parallelisms adduced in proof of

[1] Josiah Royce, *The Spirit of Modern Philosophy*, p. 181. See further Ludwig Noack, *Schelling und die Philosophie der Romantik. Ein Beitrag zur Culturgeschichte des deutschen Geistes* (Berlin, 1859).

plagiarism or even of intentional imitation, in the utmost contempt. There are two Kinds of Heads in the world of Literature. The one I would call, SPRINGS: the other TANKS. The latter class habituated to receiving only, full or low, according to the state of its Feeders, attach no distinct notion to living production as contra-distinguished from mechanical formation. If they find a fine passage in Thomson, they refer it to Milton; if in Milton to Euripides or Homer; and if in Homer, they take for granted it's pre-existence in the lost works of Linus or Musaeus. It would seem as if it was a part of their Creed, that all Thoughts are traditional, and that not only the Alphabet was revealed to Adam but all that was ever written in it that was worth writing.[1]

The heavy irony of the last two sentences may somewhat detract from the persuasiveness of the whole passage, but the daring suggestion that plagiarism, if it exists, must be something other than mere parallelism, is one to which we shall have occasion to return.

More impressive than the foregoing plea—which dates from about 1811—more impressive, in fact, than any other statement Coleridge or anybody else has made on his behalf, is one that was first printed in the *Anima Poetae*. It is an early entry in his notebooks, dating from December 1804. More emphatic than the defence in the *Biographia Literaria*, it is also less paradoxical and ambivalent. It is candid about its author's indebtedness and confident of his integrity. Taken with later statements, it reveals, for better or worse, a continuity in Coleridge's approach to composition, at the same time as it insists upon the fact of his organic independence. It is a powerful piece of prose, proud in tone, and fair, I think, with regard to fact:

In the Preface of my Metaphys. Works I should say—Once & all read Tetens, Kant, Fichte, &c—& there you will trace or if you are on the hunt, track me. Why then not acknowledge your obligations step by step? Because, I could not do in a multitude of glaring resemblances without a lie/for they had been mine, formed, & full formed in my own mind, before I had ever heard of these Writers, because to have fixed on the partic. instances in which I have really been indebted to these Writers would have very hard, if possible, to me who read for truth & self-satisfaction, not to make a book, & who always rejoiced & was jubilant when I found my own ideas well expressed already by others . . . & lastly, let me say, because (I am proud perhaps but) I seem to know, that much of the matter remains my own, and that the Soul is *mine*. I fear not him for a Critic who can confound a Fellow-thinker with a Compiler.[2]

There is much of interest in the passage: the distinction, orientated towards organic form, between 'fellow-thinker' and 'compiler'; the admission of 'obligations'; and, lastly, Coleridge's claim to have anticipated the German thinkers.

If our first reaction to this last claim is one of irritable disbelief, we should pause and reflect that Coleridge, if not entirely correct in his

[1] *Letters*, iii. 355.   [2] *Notebooks*, ii. 2375.

testimony, is at least consistent in his attitude, for he goes so far as to affirm that in thought he anticipated Plato himself:

Plato's works are preparatory exercises for the mind. He leads you to see, that propositions involving in themselves contradictory conceptions, are nevertheless true; and which, therefore, must belong to a higher logic—that of ideas. They are contradictory only in the Aristotelian logic, which is the instrument of the understanding. I have read most of the works of Plato several times with profound attention, but not all his writings. In fact, I soon found that I had read Plato by anticipation. He was a consummate genius.[1]

We should guard against misinterpreting this passage as arrogant pretence. Coleridge does not assert the ridiculous: that out of a clear blue sky, as it were, he found himself in *a priori* possession of the entire structure of Plato's thought, both controlling ideas and particular elaborations. He says rather that, given some initial stimulus to thought, and some inkling of Plato's attitudes, it is possible, and even inevitable, that one should think one's way through to further attitudes and to similar, if not identical, elaborations of them; and that this kind of anticipation is possible not from some sort of second sight, but because to some extent all minds think alike. 'All abstract philosophy', says Emerson, 'is easily anticipated,—it is so structural, or necessitated by the mould of the human mind.'[2]

If I seem to be involved in a paradox, that Coleridge is everywhere indebted, and most of all to Plato and Kant, while at the same time he owes nothing to anyone except himself, I would answer that the paradox is not of my making, but is inherent in the very existence of tradition in its relationship to individual talent. 'Ce n'est pas dans Montagne, mais dans moy', said Pascal, 'que je trouve tout ce que j'y vois.'[3] Flaubert writes in 1852 of his discovery that in one of Balzac's novels *'details are identical'* with his *Madame Bovary*.[4] 'Do they not', said Baudelaire, 'accuse me of imitating Edgar Allan Poe? And do you know why, with such infinite patience, I translated Poe? Because he was like me. The first time I ever opened a book by him, I discovered with delight and terror, not only subjects which I had dreamt, but whole phrases which I had thought, written by him twenty years before.'[5]

Perhaps the most profound aspect of the paradox is expressed in that 'favourite doctrine' of the Platonic Socrates, that all we can ever know is present in our minds from a prior existence, and that all learning is therefore in actuality a process of recollecting what we already know.[6] Surely we know, from our own experience, that we allow ourselves to see and hear and feel only those stimuli to which we are already prepared to react.

---

[1] *Table Talk*, 30 April 1830.   [2] Emerson's *Journals*, viii. 69.
[3] Pascal, *Pensées*, ed. H. F. Stewart (New York, 1950), p. 16.   [4] *Correspondence*, iii. 78.
[5] Quoted in Enid Starkie, *Baudelaire* (New York, 1933), p. 177.
[6] Plato, *Phaedo* 72 E–75 E. Also *Meno* 81 C–D.

This truth is nowhere more eloquently and insistently affirmed than in Emerson. 'No man', he says, 'can learn what he has not preparation for learning, however near to his eyes is the object.'[1] Or again, 'the Bacon, the Spinoza, the Hume, Schelling, Kant, or whosoever propounds to you a philosophy . . . is only a more or less awkward translator of things in your consciousness.'[2] It is a keystone of his thought: 'A man is . . . a selecting principle, gathering his like to him wherever he goes. He takes only his own out of the multiplicity that sweeps and circles around him.' 'We cannot see things that stare us in the face, until the hour arrives when the mind is ripened.'[3] Literary influence, in the light of these psychological truths, can never be more than the developing process that converts the image already on the negative into the finished print.

But the other aspect of the paradox, equally true and equally compelling, is that we all owe everything. 'People', said Goethe, 'are always talking about originality; but what do they mean? As soon as we are born, the world begins to work upon us, and this goes on to the end. And, after all, what can we call our own except energy, strength, and will? If I could give an account of all that I owe to great predecessors and contemporaries, there would not be much left over.'[4]

Convention supplies us with certain labels for intellectual interrelationships: originality, imitation, translation, influence, plagiarism. But these labels, though serviceable enough for some purposes, are ultimately misleading. 'Originality', for instance, is an error-freighted and ill-defined concept, and it takes only Goethe's question to reveal its insubstantiality. The label 'influence', as we have seen, bears most uneasily the scrutiny of an Emerson. Such labels are crude and makeshift; they arise from no genuine understanding of the symbolic functions of literary activity, and history itself is not long content with any of them. 'Imitation' or *mimesis* shifts precariously in its meaning from Plato to Aristotle, and from its general use in the eighteenth century has today declined into almost total obsolescence. 'Influence', once the dominating theme of scholarship, is rapidly drying up as a meaningful line of approach; titles beginning 'Der Einfluss . . .' today command only a small and restive audience.

Similarly, the concept of 'plagiarism' cannot stand the stress of historical examination. We encounter the term so rarely that we are perhaps not so critical of it as we should be. It applies mainly to the stricken efforts of undergraduates to meet demands far beyond either their abilities or their interests. But it has no proper applicability to the activities, however unconventional, of a powerful, learned, and deeply committed mind. Lest

---

[1] Emerson, 'Spiritual Laws', *Works*, ii. 146–7.
[2] Emerson, 'Intellect', *Works*, ii. 344–5.
[3] Emerson, 'Spiritual Laws', *Works*, ii. 144, 147.
[4] Goethe, *Gespräche*, iii. 204, no. 2331.

it seem I here open a special cultural category solely for the convenience of Coleridge, it may be of interest to direct our attention to one of the authentic demiurges of German culture itself, Lessing. A scholar named Albrecht, in three teutonic tomes entitled *Leszing's Plagiate*, provides a remorseless, parallel-columned citation of virtually the whole of Lessing's work as originating in various reaches of world learning, and concludes triumphantly 'dass—um es kurz zu sagen—der ganze LESZING von a–z zusammengestohlen ist'.[1] Despite such charges, however, Lessing's stature and role in cultural history can be described by Ernst Cassirer in these words:

All that Baumgarten considers as belonging to the character of the genuine aesthetician . . . is illustrated in Lessing's mind. In this one individual are embodied all the elements of richness, magnitude, truth, clarity, assurance, abundance, and nobility which Baumgarten demanded of the aesthetician. . . . It is this union of characteristics which constitutes the incomparable originality of Lessing's work, and which assured its place in the history of thought. If one considers merely the content of the various aesthetic concepts in Lessing's work, one does not find a sufficient explanation for the recognition accorded him. For he did not create this content but found it almost entirely ready at hand. There is scarcely a single aesthetic concept and scarcely a single principle in Lessing which did not have its exact parallel in contemporary literature, which could not have been documented in the writings of Baumgarten, the Swiss critics, Shaftesbury, Dubos, or Diderot. But it is a complete mistake to seek to raise objections to the originality of Lessing's basic thoughts on the grounds of any such documentation of his sources. Lessing's originality does not manifest itself in the invention of new ideas, but in the order and connection, in the logical arrangement and selection, which he accomplished with the materials already available. . . . The decisive aspect of Lessing's achievement does not lie in the matter of his concepts themselves, but in their form, not in what they are in the sense of a logical definition, but in their . . . transformation. . . . Every concept that enters the magic circle of his thinking begins at once to undergo a transformation. Instead of remaining mere end products, they again become original creative forces and directly moving impulses.[2]

Coleridge studies were unfortunately never graced by the attention of Cassirer, whose incredibly vast learning, particularly in German philosophy, and fine historical discrimination, would have lent his pronouncements a special authority. We can, however, see in his statement about Lessing his attitude towards the principle at issue in the Coleridge controversy—that it is possible for all a man's ideas to have an 'exact parallel in contemporary literature' and none the less to speak of his 'incomparable originality'. No, the label 'plagiarism' is inexact and misleading when applied to the activities of important minds. We may note, as an

[1] Paul Albrecht, *Leszing's Plagiate* (Hamburg und Leipzig, 1888–91), i. 73.
[2] Cassirer, *The Philosophy of the Enlightenment*, pp. 357–8.

illustration from another realm of thought, that 'simultaneous discovery' is a recurrent phenomenon in the history of science, and that, interestingly, in almost every documented case of such simultaneous discovery, the charge of 'plagiarism' was brought forward to explain the similarities involved, and was subsequently retracted upon closer knowledge of the facts.[1]

If we ask, then, whether 'plagiarism' has any historical validity, our answer must be that it has not when it is a question of the use of common materials by two or more individuals vitally involved in the culture of a period, but that it has a certain validity when defined as the mere repetition of borrowed materials without the achievement of reticulated pattern.

Such a definition is drawn—though without recourse to the word 'plagiarism', which might have been too crude a term for the techniques of irony involved—and placed in context by the crystalline intelligence of John Stuart Mill. But it is revelatory of the psychological tensions and profound paradoxes inherent in this whole question of indebtedness that Mill's focus for his definition of illicit borrowing is not Coleridge, whose work he knew so well, but a figure most unlikely, a figure we would, from the passages previously cited, least expect to be in any way open to such charges, who was himself an aggressive and important institutor of the charges against Coleridge—the righteous and acidulous Sir William Hamilton, who wrote, 'Coleridge's systematic plagiarism is, perhaps, the most remarkable on record'. It is this sanctimonious man whose pretensions and philosophical reputation Mill, in *An Examination of Sir William Hamilton's Philosophy*, coruscatingly and pitilessly destroys. Mill's most damning general point is that Hamilton borrowed without organizing, that he 'plagiarized' in the only true sense:

A second cause which may help to account for [Hamilton's] not having effected more in philosophy, is the enormous amount of time and mental vigour which he expended on mere philosophical erudition, leaving, it may be said, only the remains of his mind for the real business of thinking. While he seems to have known, almost by heart, the voluminous Greek commentators on Aristotle, and to have read all that the most obscure schoolman or fifth-rate German transcendentalist had written on the subjects with which he occupied himself; . . . while expending his time and energy on all this, he had not enough of them left to complete his Lectures. Those on Metaphysics . . . stopped short on the threshold of what was, especially in his own opinion, the most important

[1] The simultaneous discovery of the calculus by Newton and Leibniz, of biological evolution by Darwin and Wallace are rather familiar examples. Lancelot Law Whyte adduces also the very interesting case of the discovery of non-Euclidean geometry, where independent formulations were made by Gauss, a German, Bolyai, a Hungarian, and Lobachevsky, a Russian. Bolyai's bitter sense that his ideas had been stolen was, years later, proved wrong. (Lancelot Law Whyte, 'Simultaneous Discovery', *Harper's Magazine*, cc (Feb. 1950), 23–26. See also T. S. Kuhn, *The Structure of Scientific Revolutions* (Chicago, 1963), pp. 53–56.

part. . . . Those on Logic he left dependent, for most of the subordinate developments, on extracts strung together from German writers, chiefly Krug and
Esser; often not destitute of merit, but generally so vague, as to make all those
parts of his exposition in which they predominate, unsatisfactory; sometimes
written from points of view different from Sir W. Hamilton's own, but which
he never found time or took the trouble to re-express in adaptation to his own
mode of thought. In the whole circle of psychological and logical speculation,
it is astonishing how few are the topics into which he has thrown any of the
powers of his own intellect; and on how small a proportion even of these he
has pushed his investigations beyond what seemed necessary for the purposes
of some particular controversy. In consequence, philosophical doctrines are
taken up, and again laid down, with perfect unconsciousness, and his philosophy seems made up of scraps from several conflicting metaphysical systems.[1]

We note that Hamilton's 'plagiarism', in so far as Mill defines it as a
practice to be rebuked, does not consist in stringing together 'extracts'
from 'Krug and Esser', but in the use of such extracts without 'adaptation
to his own mode of thought'. That plagiarism is not the borrowing of
material, but the borrowing of material without attendant thought, is, therefore, the substance of Mill's definition. In a footnote accompanying the
foregoing passage, he makes the point with unequivocal succinctness. It
is, says Mill there, 'strikingly the case' that Hamilton 'lets Krug and Esser
think for him. Those authors stand to him instead, not merely of finding
a fit expression for his thoughts, but apparently of having any thoughts
at all.'[2] In terms of the particular requirements of philosophy, having no
thoughts at all means a failure of the reticulative function, a failure to
organize into a coherent whole those 'scraps from several conflicting
metaphysical systems'. It is this criticism that Mill dramatizes in the
dazzlingly destructive metaphor of missed connexions in the Mont Cenis
tunnel:

The reader must have heard of that gigantic enterprise of the Italian Government, the tunnel through Mont Cenis. This great work is carried on simultaneously from both ends, in well-grounded confidence (such is now the
minute accuracy of engineering operations) that the two parties of workmen
will correctly meet in the middle. Were they to disappoint this expectation, and
work past one another in the dark, they would afford a likeness of Sir W.
Hamilton's method of tunnelling the human mind.[3]

Thus our interest in Mill's attack is more than simply a kind of glee
at finding that if Coleridge is a black kettle then Sir W. Hamilton is a
black pot; that if Coleridge 'plagiarized' from a 'fifth-rate German transcendentalist' named Maass, then Hamilton plagiarized from two fifth-rate
German transcendentalists named Krug and Esser. What Mill's attack

[1] J. S. Mill, *An Examination of Sir William Hamilton's Philosophy*, pp. 637–8.
[2] Ibid., p. 638 n. *.   [3] Ibid., p. 639.

really does is to reiterate the central truth I have been at pains to stress: that no philosopher is original, that all philosophers use the materials afforded them by their traditions and their peers, that what has always been important in philosophy has been, not the originality of materials, but the coherence and consequence of the ordering of them—the reticulation of the materials. Mill says of Hamilton that he

would have been much at a loss if he had been required to draw up a philosophical estimate of the mind of any great thinker. He rarely seems to look at any opinion of a philosopher in connexion with the same philosopher's other opinions. Accordingly, he is weak as to the mutual relations of philosophical doctrines. He seldom knows any of the corollaries from a thinker's opinions, unless the thinker has himself drawn them; and even then he knows them, not as corollaries, but only as opinions.[1]

That reticulating characteristic of mind the lack of which Mill thus describes as Hamilton's fatal weakness is, I think, so abundantly present in Coleridge as to become almost the hallmark of his intellectual activity. Only the confident awareness of this reticulative power could allow him to say, or even think, that he had 'anticipated' Plato—whether he did or not is unimportant in this respect: or that he had 'anticipated' the German thinkers. In Mill's phraseology this is to say that he had drawn the 'corollaries' of Plato's opinions and attitudes, and of those of the Germans, and these were not mere opinions because he understood the 'mutual relations of philosophical doctrines'.

His view of the controlling, even the exclusive, importance of reticulation is clear and unmistakable. The structure of that complete philosophical system he was never to achieve was, indeed, to be a kind of monument to the importance of reticulation:

My system, if I may venture to give it so fine a name, is the only attempt I know, ever made to reduce all knowledges into harmony. It opposes no other system, but shows what was true in each; and how that which was true in the particular, in each of them became error, *because* it was only half the truth. I have endeavoured to unite the insulated fragments of truth, and therewith to frame a perfect mirror. I show to each system that I fully understand and rightfully appreciate what that system means; but then I lift up that system to a higher point of view, from which I enable it to see its former position, where it was, indeed, but under another light and with different relations; so that the fragment of truth is not only acknowledged, but explained.[2]

In this ideal, so similar to what Hegel actually achieved, Coleridge's 'plagiarisms' are those 'insulated fragments of truth' that are to be united in the perfect mirror of reality. And in such a union they would cease to be 'plagiarisms'.[3]

---

[1] Ibid., p. 643. [2] *Table Talk*, 12 Sept. 1831.
[3] Though Coleridge's neuroses complicate the whole question, the Romantic stress on

If we compare Coleridge's emphasis on system and coherence, on reticulation, with that of Schelling, we find that, whatever their ultimate differences, here the two thinkers were in profound agreement. Thus, in an important early testament, Schelling says:

In order to find what Leibniz found, that what is really philosophical in the most contradictory systems is also true, one must have before his eyes the idea of a universal system that gives all separate systems, however opposed they may be, connection and necessity in a system of human knowledge itself. Such an all embracing system can first of all fulfill the obligation of uniting the contesting interests of all other systems, of proving that none of those systems, no matter how much in opposition to common understanding it may seem, has achieved something really senseless, that therefore for every possible question of philosophy a universal answer is possible. For it is evident that reason can raise no question which might not be already answerable beforehand in itself. So, as out of a seed nothing develops that was not beforehand united in it, just so in philosophy can nothing (through analysis) arise, that was not previously at hand in the human spirit itself (the original synthesis). Therefore a common, ruling spirit permeates all separate systems, which merit the name; each individual system is only possible through discrepancy or deviation from the universal primary pattern (*Urbild*) to which all more or less approximate.[1]

We note without comment the omnipresent Romantic emphasis upon organic form, and also the emphasis upon the continuity of philosophical thought. The idea that philosophy was a communal endeavour in which thinkers both past and present constantly participated was characteristic of Coleridge too. This involvement in the historical dimension of philosophy brought upon him the charges of plagiarism; it is a tribute to the sophistication of the German philosophical tradition that Schelling's own reputation never had to withstand such charges, despite the uncontested fact that his many-sourced obligations mirror, at different stages in his thought, specific indebtednesses to Bruno, Boehme, Plotinus, and the Christian Mystics, as well as to Fichte and Kant.[2] No one was less 'original' than Schelling; so dependent, indeed, did he at times appear upon the

originality, in tension with this philosophical stress on the all-resolving system, made for ambivalence even in thinkers not labouring under his handicaps. Thus Victor Cousin—whose energy and industry have never been questioned—seems to share the predicament. 'Cousin never admitted in public', says Boas, 'the effect which Schelling had had upon his thought. . . . He must pretend that his interest in Schelling was similar to his interest in Plato and Aristotle. . . . Cousin was as impartial as anyone well can be in his historical sources . . . he tried to absorb all that was true in the past. He believed that each philosophy . . . had its contribution to make to human knowledge. . . . This, as Cousin said himself, was not "blind syncretism", but a fitting together of fragments into a whole' (Boas, *French Philosophies of the Romantic Period*, pp. 190, 209–10).

[1] Schelling, *Werke*, i. 457–8.

[2] Nicolai Hartmann, for instance, considers it an effect of the 'original vitality' of Schelling's thought that he worked into his philosophy ideas 'from Spinoza and Leibniz, from Plato and Plotinus, from ancient mythology as well as from orthodox Christianity and from the mystics' (Hartmann, *Die Philosophie des deutschen Idealismus* (Berlin und Leipzig, 1923–9), i. 125).

materials of other thinkers that his old Tübingen room-mate Hegel could say, in a famous gibe, that

Schelling hat seine philosophische Ausbildung vor dem Publikum gemacht. Die Reihe seiner philosophischen Schriften ist zugleich Geschichte seiner philosophischen Bildung, und stellt seine allmählige Erhebung über das fichte 'sche Princip und den kantischen Inhalt dar, mit welchen er anfing; sie enthält nicht eine Folge der ausgearbeiteten Theile der Philosophie nach einander, sondern nur eine Folge seiner Bildungsstufen.

that Schelling carried on his philosophical education before the public, that the sequence of his philosophical writings constituted a history of his philosophical self-education, representing a gradual departure from the Fichtian principle and Kantian content with which he began, and that these treatises were not worked-out parts of a completed philosophical system but a series of steps in his education.[1]

And yet even this cruel thrust is not a charge of plagiarism. Schelling emphasized the existence of a 'universal system' that is not invented, but discovered, by philosophical thought, which is not the creation of a given thinker, but a reality of the 'human spirit'. Such a view abrogates all philosophical property rights and leaves no room, we immediately realize, for any such category as 'plagiarism'—we cannot steal what we already own. The truth of things already exists, and the work of individual philosophers no more 'creates' the 'universal system' of philosophy than Columbus created America.

The nearest approximation Schelling ever achieved to the 'universal system' is his most ambitious and probably his greatest work, the posthumously published *System der gesammten Philosophie*, the very title of which proclaims its final importance among his treatises. Schelling utilized the thoughts and terminologies of many thinkers, but in this work the evidences of close indebtedness to a single mind, Spinoza, are particularly plain. Because the book was not polished for final publication by Schelling, its Spinozistic elements are especially striking, not only in the concepts but even in the phraseology—so striking, indeed, that if 'plagiarism' were a category relevant to philosophy it could be said that the heart and soul of *System der gesammten Philosophie* is 'plagiarized' from Spinoza. Thus, to cite very briefly, Schelling refers to 'Substanz oder Gott'[2]— substance or God—which is a direct echo of Spinoza's 'Deus, sive substantia'[3]—God, or substance. Schelling affirms that 'everything flows out of the idea of God',[4] which is a direct echo of Spinoza's statement affirming 'a summa Dei potentia . . . omnia necessario effluxisse'[5]—that from

---

[1] Hegel, *Werke*, xv. 647. [2] Schelling, *Werke*, vi. 198.
[3] Spinoza, *Ethica Ordine Geometrico demonstrata*, Pars I, Propositio 11.
[4] Schelling, *Werke*, vi. 182.
[5] Spinoza, *Ethica* I. 17 Scholium.

the supreme power of God all things have necessarily flowed. Schelling broaches a distinction between God creating (*Natura naturans*) and God reflected (*Natura naturata*) which is a clear Spinozism. Schelling says:

The totality of things—in so far as they are merely in God, have no being in themselves, and in their non-being are only the reflection of the All—is the reflected or imaged world (*Natura naturata*); the All, however, as the infinite affirmation of God, as that in which everything is that exists, is absolute All or the creating nature (*Natura naturans*).[1]

And Spinoza says:

Before proceeding further, I want to explain what we ought to understand by *Natura naturans* and *Natura naturata*. . . . By *Natura naturans* is to be understood that which is in itself . . . that is . . . God, so far as he is considered as free cause. By *Natura naturata*, however, I understand all that which follows from the necessity of God's nature, or of any of God's attributes. . . .[2]

Schelling says that 'jedes besondere Ding, das erscheint in der Endlichkeit, eine besondere Folge aus Gott ist'[3]—that every particular thing that appears in the temporal world is a particular effect of God—which echoes Spinoza's 'quo magis res singulares intelligimus, eo magis Deum intelligimus'[4]—the more we know particular things, the more we know God. Many more parallels could be added to these, if we wished to illustrate repetitively Schelling's dependence on the philosophy of Spinoza. But instead of adducing further parallels, it might be better to note Jacobi's summing up: that Spinoza was not merely a forerunner of Schelling's philosophy of identity, but was its founder and first exponent.[5]

If, then, Schelling's nearest approximation to his 'all embracing system' is both conceptually and verbally dependent upon the philosophy of Spinoza, and if, secondly, it is true that the relationship of Coleridge's thought to Schelling's is very difficult to define, or apparently has been difficult to define (whether that relationship be conceived, as it traditionally has been, as one of similarity, or, as I now maintain, as one of radical opposition), then it would seem to follow that an as yet unturned key to an understanding of Coleridge, and of the similarity or difference of his thought to that of Schelling, might be a comprehensive study of the philosophy of Spinoza and of the history of his influence.

[1] Schelling, *Werke*, vi. 199.
[2] Spinoza, *Ethica* I. 29 Scholium.
[3] Schelling, *Werke*, vi. 200.
[4] Spinoza, *Ethica* v. 24.
[5] Jacobi, *Von den göttlichen Dingen und ihrer Offenbarung* (Leipzig, 1811), p. 193. Cf. Franz Berg's statement to the interlocutor representing Schelling's philosophy: 'Ich sagte eben, du seyest Spinozen vertraut. Ich hätte wohl sagen sollen, du seyest Spinoza selbst'—I just said you are familiar with Spinoza. Perhaps I should have said, you are Spinoza himself (*Sextus*, p. 78). Again, Heine pointed out that Hegel certainly used a great many of Schelling's ideas, but that Schelling had borrowed more from Spinoza than Hegel had borrowed from Schelling (*Die romantische Schule*, pp. 175–6).

CHAPTER II

The Spinozistic Crescendo

'IT is impossible', said Coleridge once, 'to understand the genius of Dante, and difficult to understand his poem, without some knowledge of the characters, studies, and writings of the schoolmen of the twelfth, thirteenth, and fourteenth centuries. For Dante was the living link between religion and philosophy.'[1] I believe that Coleridge was the 'living link between religion and philosophy' for his own age.

The pertinent philosophy for his age, however, centred not upon the subtleties of the schoolmen but upon the great Romantic philosophical controversy over pantheism—the so-called *Pantheismusstreit*; and because the extent and significance, and in some cases, surprisingly enough, even the existence, of this controversy have been unknown to commentators on Coleridge (Shedd is a notable exception), the picture has been thrown seriously out of focus.

The *Pantheismusstreit* was, in its ontological ramifications, fundamentally a contest between the philosophy of Spinoza on the one hand and that of Kant on the other; in its ethical and eschatological implications, a struggle between Spinoza and Christianity; and in this dual contest the forced alliance of Kant and Christianity was continually on the defensive.

Spinoza was not, of course, the originator of the system of thought known as pantheism. But as the codifier and the purifier of all previous pantheistic views, Spinoza assumes a kind of absolute historical centrality, and it was his thought, and virtually his alone, that provided the impetus and occasion for the *Pantheismusstreit*. Thus when a theologian, in 1690, posed the rhetorical question 'Spinoza quis fuerit?' his answer involved as clear a delineation as we may ever expect to find of just those dichotomic elements that made up the *Pantheismusstreit*:

There are two, and only two, systems of philosophy that can be offered. The one posits God as the transcendent cause of things; the other makes God the immanent cause. The former carefully distinguishes and separates God from the world; the latter shamefully confounds God with the universe. The foundation of the former is the distinction between mind and body; that of the latter their confusion. The former derives all things from the free harmony of an infinite and omnipotent Mind; the latter from a certain brute and blind necessity of the divine nature or of the universe. The former looks at rest and motion as

---

[1] *Coleridge's Miscellaneous Criticism*, ed. T. M. Raysor (London, 1936), p. 147.

the effects of God; the latter as pertaining to the nature of God, or rather, as attributes of God. The former makes mind a thinking substance, and so it ascribes to the same mind, as thinking activities freely caused, such faculties as affirming and denying, willing and not willing; the latter, in considering mind a mode of God (of an immanent cause), transforms it into a spiritual automaton. The former establishes a foundation for every religious devotion and for all piety, and this the latter fundamentally overturns and takes away.[1]

That system here termed the 'latter', in which God is *causa immanens*, is the system represented by Spinoza, who wrote, 'Deus est omnium rerum causa immanens, non vero transiens'[2]—God is the immanent, not the transcendent, cause of all things. That is to say, he is not the creator of things but rather the things themselves.

It is not possible, in a brief summary, to convey the tone of Spinoza's thought: an almost unique combination of, on the one hand, coldly uncompromising clarity about the blindness of nature and the brevity and meaninglessness of human life, and, on the other, tremendous moral energy that rises to sublime heights of fervour and eloquence. We are confronted with icy scientism, with the denial of a benevolent deity, of a final cause for human endeavour, of beauty, nobleness, justice, harmony, and goodness; at the same time we are led from this remorseless naturalism towards the development of an ethical code of systematic self-interest that achieves, in its relentless exposition, a swelling conception of the human lot that is itself normative of the beautiful, the noble, and the harmonious.

Nor is it possible, in a brief summary, to examine the complete reticulation of Spinoza's system, a reticulation that aesthetically, if not logically, presents a pattern of great splendour.

It is necessary, however, to attempt at least some elucidation of Spinoza's central tenets, and of the ways in which these tenets cohere. Now if we agree with Aristotle that all philosophy begins in wonder, we must grant at the outset that we are beginning with two irreducible—or at any rate basic—elements: someone to wonder, and something to wonder at.[3] As Jacobi says, 'Ich erfahre, dass ich bin und das etwas ausser mir ist, in demselben unteilbaren Augenblick'—I realize that I am, and that something is outside me, all in the same indivisible moment.[4] All philosophical systems, in short, involve an account of the relation of the wonderer—the self, the ego, the individual consciousness—to the wondered at—the objective, the external, 'things'. From the interaction of wonderer and the wondered-at, a third basic category inevitably arises; from, on the one

---

[1] *Christoph. Wittichii Anti-Spinoza sive Examen Ethices Benedicti de Spinoza* (Amstelaedami, 1690), Praefatio. The author of the preface is not identified, but is clearly not Wittich himself.
[2] Spinoza, *Ethica*, I. 18.
[3] Aristotle, *Metaphysics* 982ᵇ 10–20. See also Plato, *Theaetetus* 155 D.
[4] Jacobi, *Werke*, ii. 175.

hand, the limitation of the wonderer's knowledge ('who am I?', 'why am I here?', 'where am I going?'), and on the other, the limitation inhering in the wondered-at ('what is it?', 'where did it come from?', 'why is it here?'). This third basic category of necessary philosophical involvement, arising as unbidden question from our immediate sense of limitation in our knowledge and our situation, constitutes that area of human concern termed the religious; and the most extended hypothetical answers to the totality of questions arising from these primal limitations are grouped under the symbolic term 'God'. 'To believe in a God', says Wittgenstein simply, 'means to see that the facts of the world are not the end of the matter.'[1]

Thus all systematic philosophy must account for the status and inter-relations of three entities, the ego or subject, the external or object, and the questions arising from the defining limitations of both subject and object, or the question of God.

We shall immediately see that only a limited number of basic positions can be established in terms of this requirement. We are granted as a beginning only two entities, the self and the not-self, and necessarily derive from our consideration of this first relation our idea of what the hypothetical answer to the questions arising from limitation is to be. Depending on whichever of our initial assumptions we treat as primary, the self or the object, the corollary which is God will assume the properties of a self or of an object. 'Es gibt', says Wittgenstein in one of his Delphic insights, 'zwei Gottheiten: die Welt und mein unabhängiges Ich'—there are two Godheads: the world and my independent I.[2] Furthermore, not only will God be the ultimate extension of all possible questions as defined by the emphasis upon whichever of the two primary starting-points is chosen, but the reality of the starting-point not chosen will be inevitably com-promised as a result of the emphasis upon the point that is chosen. To view the matter from the perspective of Descartes, who exemplifies the ontological presuppositions of all 'self' philosophy and is historically the prototype for much of that philosophy's development since the seven-teenth century, we begin, first and irreducibly, with the axiom of self-existence, as guaranteed by thought. This internal certainty alone is indubitable.[3] All external apprehensions fall before the scythe of scepti-cal doubt;[4] the reality of the whole external world is impeached and

---

[1] *Notebooks, 1914–1916*, p. 74e.   [2] Ibid.

[3] 'It is not possible for us to doubt that we exist while we are doubting, and this is the first thing that we know in the order of philosophizing. . . . And thus this knowledge, *ego cogito, ergo sum*, is of all things the first and most certain that occurs to one philosophizing formally' (*Œuvres de Descartes*, viii. 6–7).

[4] Descartes's own kind of scepticism, which is crucial for his entire position, is not mere Pyrrhonism; indeed, is not truly scepticism at all, for Descartes, underneath his surface, is a con-servative thinker. It is rather a coming to terms with scepticism at the outset, in order to protect his subsequent system against the ravages of sceptical criticism. He says that he does

compromised.[1] God, therefore, becomes an analogy of the logical *prius*, the self.[2] Hence the God of Descartes, invoked to reaffirm the reality of the external world—but only as subordinate to and dependent on the self— is characterized first and foremost by the attribute (clearly projected from the human psyche rather than derived from analogy with external pheno-mena) of honesty. This God, above all else, 'non sit fallax'—is not a deceiver.[3]

If, on the other hand, we take our departure not from the axiomatic reality of self but from the axiomatic reality of thing, the self will diminish to a mere category of thing, the ego will become an object—as in be-haviouristic psychology, or Communist philosophy, or the associationism of Locke and Hartley, or the necessitarianism of Godwin, or—to go far back—the philosophy of Aristotle, or—to come to the present—the philo-sophy of Bertrand Russell. 'Philosophy', writes John Locke, succinctly summing up the presuppositions of all subscribers to this second mode of thought, 'is nothing but the true knowledge of things.'[4] And the con-ception of God arrived at through the analysis of thing, of object, will itself be a conception of thing, lacking the characteristics of self—purpose, consciousness, will—or, in Christian terms, lacking 'person'.

There are thus, in their reductions to their ultimate ontological schemes, only two systematic philosophies possible: that arising from our intuitive knowledge 'I am' and that arising from our intuitive knowledge 'it is'. Many philosophies, of course, do not overtly concern themselves with ontology (most of our contemporary positivist or analytical works, for instance), restricting themselves to logic, or ethics, or, in many cases to epistemology; but nevertheless all these endeavours, whether overtly ontological or not, have ontological implications and can thus be described as either philosophies of 'I am' or philosophies of 'it is'. Thus Coleridge, in passages we shall later quote, divided all men into either Platonists (representing the 'I am' philosophy) or Aristotelians (representing the 'it

not imitate the Sceptics, who doubt only for the sake of doubting; on the contrary, all his design is to 'reietter la terre mouuante & le sable, pour trouuer le roc ou l'argile'—to reject the moving earth and sand in order to find the rock or clay (*Œuvres*, vi. 29). Accordingly it was 'cete verité: *ie pense, donc ie suis*' that was so firm and assured 'that all the most extravagant suppositions of the Sceptics were not capable of tearing it down' (*Œuvres*, vi. 32).

[1] Descartes doubts 'de rebus omnibus, praesertim materialibus'—all things, especially material things (*Œuvres*, vii. 12). All that he truly knows (omnia . . . quae vere scio) is that 'Ego sum res cogitans, id est dubitans, affirmans, negans, pauca intelligens, multa ignorans, volens, nolens, imaginans etiam & sentiens'—I am a thinking thing, that is, doubting, affirming, negating, knowing a little, ignorant of much, willing, not willing, imagining even and feeling (*Œuvres*, vii. 35, 34).

[2] Thus it is 'very likely' (valde credibile) that man is in some way an image and similitude of God, and that 'I perceive that similitude, in which the idea of God is contained, by the same faculty by which I perceive myself' (*Œuvres*, vii. 51).

[3] Descartes, *Œuvres*, vii. 79, ll. 22–23; also p. 80, l. 15; also p. 90, l. 11.

[4] *Essay concerning Human Understanding*, i. 14.

is' philosophy). Mill stressed the same distinction when he divided cultivated Englishmen of his day into Coleridgeans (representing 'I am' philosophy) and Benthamites (representing the dominance of the 'it is').[1]

The distinction assumes yet another of its protean shapes as the focal point of irreconcilability between the two major modes of philosophizing in our own century: the positivist-analytic and the existentialist. The apparent liberality of John Wisdom, for instance, in accepting various points of departure for philosophizing is actually an unequivocal insistence on the 'it is': 'Analytic philosophy has no special subject-matter. You can philosophise about Tuesday, the pound sterling, and lozenges and philosophy itself.'[2] The basic position of existentialism, on the other hand, is an Husserlian variant of the Cartesian *cogito* and hence an affirmation of the 'I am'.[3] As Sartre put it:

Our point of departure is, indeed, the subjectivity of the individual, and that for strictly philosophical reasons. It is not because we are bourgeois, but because we want a doctrine based upon the truth, and not an assemblage of fine theories, full of hope but without real foundation. There cannot be, at such a point of departure, any other truth than this one: *I think, therefore I am*, which is the absolute truth of consciousness attaining itself. All theory that deals with man outside this moment where he attains himself is therefore a theory that suppresses the truth, for, outside of the Cartesian *cogito*, all objects are merely probable. . . .[4]

As to which of these starting-points takes precedence over the other, the answer can be supplied neither by logic nor by an appeal to experience. Indeed, it must be stressed that though the 'it is' philosophers are declared empiricists—and could of course be nothing else—they do not thereby pre-empt the realm of experience. Historically, the 'I am' philosophers have also been dedicated empiricists, believing themselves capable of a more subtle apprehension of experience, and a more consistent responsibility to the structure of reality than the adherents of the 'it is' point of view. Descartes affirms that his rejection of the reality of the external world is precisely the result of experience: 'multa paulatim experimenta fidem omnem quam sensibus habueram labefactarunt'—many experiments

---

[1] *Dissertations and Discussions*, i. 397: 'Coleridge used to say that every one is born either a Platonist or an Aristotelian: it may be similarly affirmed, that every Englishman of the present day is by implication either a Benthamite or a Coleridgian' (first printed in the *London and Westminster Review*, March 1840). T. S. Eliot—whether with intended reference to the distinctions of Mill and Coleridge it is difficult to say—recasts the archetypal struggle into one between Bradley ('he replaced a philosophy which was crude and raw and provincial by one which was, in comparison, catholic, civilized, and universal') and the Utilitarian tradition, particularly those 'spiritual descendants of Bentham' who have in Eliot's time 'built anew, as they always will' (*Selected Essays*, p. 362). Eliot makes clear, both in his *Second Thoughts about Humanism* and in his *Thoughts after Lambeth*, that the chief of these 'spiritual descendants of Bentham' is, in his view, Bertrand Russell.

[2] *Problems of Mind and Matter* (Cambridge, 1934), p. 2.　　[3] See note 7, p. 337.

[4] *L'Existentialisme est un humanisme* (Paris, 1946), pp. 63–64.

gradually took away all the faith that I had in the senses.[1] And Kant, who together with Descartes compounds and sustains the humanistic implications of 'I am' thought, remarks sardonically that his concern is with experience and only with experience: 'High towers, and metaphysically great men resembling them, around both of which there is commonly much wind, are not for me. My place is the fruitful bottom land of experience. . . .'[2] Coleridge, again, maintains that Plato—the *Urvater*, as it were, of 'I am' extensions—is in his method consistently empirical: 'It is strange . . . that the writings of Plato should be accused of estranging the mind from sober experience and substantial matter of fact . . . Plato, whose method is inductive throughout, who argues on all subjects not only from, but in and by, inductions of facts. . . .'[3]

It is not, therefore, in a more or a less cavalier attitude towards experience, or towards logic, that we shall find the main differences between the 'I am' and the 'it is' thinkers. When Coleridge speaks of men as 'born' either Platonist or Aristotelian, he perhaps says as much about this important matter as anyone, at this stage of our history, is able to say.[4] Or perhaps we may prefer Freud's discussion, at the beginning of *Civilization and its Discontents*, of the possible reasons for the existence of a certain kind of ego rapture, an 'oceanic feeling' in which there seems no distinction between the ego and the external world. He postulates, in explanation of the persistence of this feeling in some adults, that in the infant

originally the ego includes everything, later it detaches from itself the external world. The ego-feeling we are aware of now is thus only a shrunken vestige of a far more extensive feeling—a feeling which embraced the universe and expressed an inseparable connection of the ego with the external world. If we may suppose that this primary ego-feeling has been preserved in the minds of many people—to a greater or lesser extent—it would co-exist like a sort of counterpart with the narrower and more sharply outlined ego-feeling of maturity, and the ideational content belonging to it would be precisely the notion of limitless extension and oneness with the universe.[5]

Perhaps future refinements of psycho-analytical observation will develop this hint into a precise description of the ways in which an infant's consciousness is conditioned so as, on the one hand, to make him as an adult so very certain of the over-riding importance of things, or, on the other, of the coruscatingly primary reality of his own existence. Whatever the aetiology of the 'I am' and 'it is' types, however, we have all noted their occurrence. We know people, for instance, to whom things, from automobiles or clothes to the whole complex of environmental claims (the demands of Freud's 'reality principle'), are of dominating importance.

[1] Descartes, *Œuvres*, vii. 76.
[2] Kant, *Werke*, iv. 129, n. 1.
[3] *The Friend*, Second Landing Place, Second Section, Essay VIII, *Works*, ii. 437.
[4] *Table Talk*, 2 July 1830.   [5] *Gesammelte Werke*, xiv. 425.

For them other people tend in subtle ways to be conceived as variants of things: 'a grocer', 'a dutiful daughter', 'an A student'. In such a psychological nexus the tendency in, say, matters of penology, would be for harshness towards 'criminals'. On the other hand, there are people to whom a 'self' is unique and prior to the claims of its conditioning environment. Such an attitude might reveal itself in ways ranging from carelessness in dress all the way up to the moral commitment of a Socrates or a Thomas More. The attitude of such people towards penology, to use the same example, would tend towards mildness in the treatment of offenders, because the 'criminal' is seen not as a thing, but as a variation of the potentialities of the self—for instance, in the Christian scheme, as a 'soul'.

To the apostle of 'it is' the 'Platonist' will seem hazy, soft-minded, given to foggy generalization, and often impractical or childish, while to the exponent of 'I am' the 'Aristotelian' will seem cloddish, incapable of abstraction, and materialistic. Neither will be able to see reasonableness in the irreducible axiom of the other. To the apostle of 'it is', the Cartesian proposition should be, as Hamann put it, 'nicht *Cogito, ergo sum*, sondern umgekehrt . . . *Est, ergo cogito*'—not 'I think, therefore I am', but the other way around, 'It is, therefore I think'.[1]

So much for some of the psychological attitudes underlying the choice of starting-point. In the history of thought the 'I am' position builds from Plato in ancient philosophy, and from Descartes in modern. It supports the great theological achievement of Augustine in antiquity,[2] and the great rationalistic achievement of Kant in the *Aufklärung*.[3] It is the necessary

[1] Hamann, *Leben und Schriften*, v. 81.

[2] See especially *De civitate Dei contra paganos*, xi. 26, where, after maintaining that we can recognize in ourselves an image of God, and identifying this image as a trinity (that 'we are, we know we are, and we care that we are and know'), Augustine not so much anticipates as surpasses Descartes—using the same hypothesis of being 'deceived': '. . . without any illusion or image, fancy, or phantasm, I am certain that I am, that I know, and that I love. In these truths I do not fear the arguments of the sceptical academics when they say: what if you are deceived? (Quid si falleris?). For if I am deceived, then I am. (Si enim fallor, sum.) For he who is not certainly cannot be deceived: so I am, if I am deceived. Because, therefore, I am if I am deceived, how can I be deceived that I am, when it is certain I am if I am deceived? Because, even if I were deceived, I would be he-who-was-deceived, doubtless I am not deceived in knowing that I am. (Quia igitur essem qui fallerer, etiam si fallerer; procul dubio in eo quod me novi esse, non fallor.) And it follows that when I know myself to know, I am likewise not deceived.' Augustine's anticipations of the *cogito* were pointed out to Descartes by Arnauld.

[3] Kant explicitly acknowledges his starting-point as the Cartesian *cogito*. He says (the passage appears only in the first edition of the *Kritik der reinen Vernunft*): '. . . we must necessarily distinguish two types of idealism, the transcendental and the empirical. By transcendental idealism I mean the doctrine that appearances are to be regarded as being, one and all, representations only, not things-in-themselves, and that time and space are therefore only sensible forms of our intuition, not determinations given as existing by themselves, nor conditions of objects viewed as things in themselves. To this idealism there is opposed a transcendental realism which regards time and space as something given in themselves, independent of our sensibility. The transcendental realist thus interprets outer appearances (their reality being taken as granted) as things-in-themselves, which exist independently of us and of our sensibility, and which are therefore outside us. . . . The transcendental idealist, on the other hand, may be an

background to the mathematical genius of Kepler and Leibniz.[1] Kepler, for instance, was a dedicated disciple of Plato.[2] Leibniz, though more complex in his attitude, was none the less, as we see in the following passage, no exponent of 'it is':

Thus the point noted by the ancient Platonists is very true and very worthy of consideration, that the existence of mental things and particularly of this 'I' that thinks and that is called spirit or soul, is incomparably more assured than the existence of external things; and that thus it would not at all be impossible, speaking with metaphysical rigour, that basically there are only mental substances, and that external things are only appearances.[3]

The philosophy of 'it is', conversely, can claim Aristotle, Locke, Mill, the major traditions of empiricism and experimental science, and the dominating strain of positivist-analytical philosophy in America and England today.

Now there is ostensibly still a third major category of speculative intelligences, usually referred to as 'pantheist', and numbering in its ranks such figures as Buddha, Plotinus, Lao-Tse, Proclus, Meister Eckhart, Scotus Erigena, Nicholas of Cusa, Giordano Bruno, Jacob Boehme, Zeno and Chrysippus and the other Stoic theorists, Schopenhauer, and Hegel. And Schelling. And, most of all, Spinoza. We are not truly justified, however, in placing these thinkers in a third category, for, as we shall see, their positions reveal themselves under scrutiny as ontological extensions of 'it is' philosophy. Empirical and positivist analysts of the 'it is' pride themselves on not pursuing final problems.[4] The watchword of this entire

empirical realist or, as he is called, a dualist; that is, he may admit the existence of matter without going outside his mere self-consciousness, or assuming anything more than the certainty of his representations, that is, the *cogito, ergo sum*. . . . From the start, we have declared ourselves in favour of this transcendental idealism' (Kant, *Werke*, iii. 647).

[1] Leibniz, throughout his life, exhibited a deep and instinctive sympathy for Plato's mode of thought. Plato was an 'auteur qui me revient beaucoup'—an author who means much to me (*Philosophische Schriften*, iii. 605). Leibniz had 'always been most satisfied, even from my youth, with the ethics of Plato, and in some ways with his metaphysics as well' (iii. 637). He was 'not at all for the *tabula rasa* of Aristotle, but there is something solid in that which Plato calls reminiscence' (v. 16). In his controversy with Locke, Leibniz identified himself as a follower of Plato, and then, by specifying Locke as an adherent of Aristotle, emphasized the archetypal 'I am'/'it is' nature of their opposition: 'our systems differ a great deal. Locke's relates more to Aristotle, and mine to Plato, although we both diverge in a good many ways from the doctrine of those two ancients' (v. 41).

[2] See, e.g., Burtt, *The Metaphysical Foundations of Modern Physical Science*, pp. 41–58.

[3] *Philosophische Schriften*, vi. 502–3.

[4] See, e.g., Bertrand Russell, *Sceptical Essays* (New York, 1928), p. 81: 'It has been generally regarded as the business of philosophy to prove the great truths of religion. The new realism does not profess to be able to prove them, or even to disprove them. It aims only at clarifying the fundamental ideas of the sciences, and synthesizing the different sciences in a single comprehensive view of that fragment of the world that science has succeeded in exploring. It does not know what lies beyond; it possesses no talisman for transforming ignorance into knowledge . . . it does not attempt to flatter human conceit as most philosophies do. If it is dry and technical, it lays the blame on the universe, which has chosen to work in a mathematical way rather than as poets or mystics might have desired.'

cast of mind is Wittgenstein's famous refusal to pursue non-semantic implications: 'Wovon man nicht sprechen kann, darüber muss man schweigen'—whereof one cannot speak, thereof must one remain silent.[1] Pantheism, on the other hand, pursues the syntactic implications of the 'it is' beyond the anchorage of the semantic, and thus may be defined as the ultimate expansion of the significance of 'it is' as the locus of reality. According to this definition pantheism is also identifiable as the ultimate systematic form of the scientific world view.[2]

In this context, the importance of Spinoza lies not in any 'originality' he may or may not have possessed, but in the consequence and coherence with which he followed implications open to everyone, and always present as a main channel of the possibilities of human thought. He is the greatest of the pantheist systematizers, the most compelling exponent of the philosophy of 'it is'. That is the reason why Coleridge says, in a statement of the most profound acumen, 'Did philosophy commence with an *it is*, instead of an *I am*, Spinoza would be altogether true.'[3]

Now we have noted that both the philosophy of 'I am' and the philosophy of 'it is' necessarily imply a religious perspective, even if the perspective is foreshortened into agnosticism. It is, however, a fact that only the conception of deity derived from analogy with the self, in short, the God-ideal of the alliance of Platonism and Christianity, has come to be associated in the western tradition with the word 'God' as it is commonly used.[4] The authority of Genesis assures us that God and man share the same image; God is dominantly the 'father' in Biblical theology, and in

---

[1] *Tractatus*, 7.

[2] Cf. Albert Einstein, *Essays in Science*, p. 11: '. . . a conviction, akin to religious feeling, of the rationality or intelligibility of the world lies behind all scientific work of a higher order . . . this may be described as "pantheistic" (Spinoza).' Elsewhere, we may note the precise congruence of Einstein's 'Weltbild' with the central tenets of Spinoza: 'In human freedom in the philosophical sense I am definitely a disbeliever. . . . I cannot conceive of a God who rewards and punishes his creatures, or has a will of the type of which we are conscious in ourselves. An individual who should survive his physical death is also beyond my comprehension, nor do I wish it otherwise. . . . Enough for me the mystery of the eternity of life, and the inkling of the marvellous structure of reality, together with the single-hearted endeavour to comprehend a portion . . . of the reason that manifests itself in nature' (*The World as I see It*, pp. 2, 5).

[3] Crabb Robinson, *Diary*, i. 400.

[4] For this alliance cf. Eusebius, who devotes the tenth to the thirteenth books of his *Evangelica praeparatio* to a particularization of the agreement of Plato with the Bible. Augustine makes a similarly extended comparison in the *De civitate Dei*, viii. 5–11. Psellos, in his letter to Xiphilinus, also asserts the congruence of the two bodies of thought (see Christian Zervos, *Michel Psellos* (Paris, 1920), pp. 217 ff.). Pico della Mirandola, in his *Oration on the Dignity of Man*, refers to 'Plato, whose principles are so closely related to the Christian faith that our Augustine gives immeasurable thanks to God that the books of the Platonists have come into his hands' (*The Renaissance Philosophy of Man*, ed. Ernst Cassirer, P. O. Kristeller, J. H. Randall (New York, 1948), p. 252). Cf. G. C. B. Ackermann, *Das Christliche im Plato und in der platonischen Philosophie* (Hamburg, 1835), p. 342: 'there has never been a more Christian philosophy, outside the Lord's church, than the Platonic'. For modern testimony, see Constantin Ritter, *Platon; sein Leben, seine Schriften, seine Lehre* (München, 1910–23), ii. 414, 502, 543 ff., 769 ff.

trinitarian Christianity is specifically 'personed'. The classic title of Anselm, *cur deus homo*, contains in its equation the central fact of God as analogized 'self'. Freud, in both *Totem und Tabu* and *Die Zukunft einer Illusion*, explicitly conceives the sense of God as an hypostasis of the father-image. And the most common and intuitive form of the conception of God for all of western culture is the anthropomorphic. As Kant says,

in analogy with realities in the world, that is, with substances, with causality and with necessity, I think a being which possesses all this in the highest perfection; and since this idea depends merely on my reason, I can think this being as *self-subsistent reason*. . . .[1] In thinking the cause of the world, we are justified in representing it in our idea not only in terms of a certain subtle anthropomorphism (without which we could not think anything whatever in regard to it), namely, as a being that has understanding, feelings of pleasure and displeasure, and desires and volitions corresponding to these, but also in ascribing to it a perfection which, as infinite, far transcends any perfection that our empirical knowledge . . . of the world can justify us in attributing to it.[2]

Thus the Platonic-Christian tradition expropriates all the common overtones of 'God' for the philosophy of 'I am'. And a corollary of this expropriation is the denial of 'God' in the religious implications of the philosophy of 'it is'.

Hence, though Spinoza says that 'the proper order of philosophic thinking' is for 'the nature of God' to be 'reflected on first',[3] he is forced to the important concession that 'my opinion concerning God differs widely from that which is ordinarily defended by modern Christians'.[4] For his opinion is that 'God' is the sum total of all things: 'All things . . . are in God, and all things which come to pass, come to pass solely through the laws of the infinite nature of God';[5] to God 'alone does existence appertain';[6] 'individual things are nothing but modifications of the attributes of God';[7] 'Whatsoever is, is in God, and without God nothing can be, or be conceived.'[8] Again, Spinoza says that 'substances' and 'modes' form 'the sum total of existence',[9] but since 'modes' are merely 'the modifications of substance',[10] and since 'besides God no substance can be granted or conceived',[11] then 'modes' become 'merely modifications of the attributes of God'[12] and we are left with only two basic entities,

---

[1] Kant, *Werke*, iii. 461–2.   [2] Ibid., pp. 474–5.
[3] Spinoza, *Ethica* ii. 10. Scholium. Contrast Kant's view: 'Es ist merkwürdig . . . dass die Menschen im Kindesalter der Philosophie davon anfingen, wo wir jetzt lieber endigen möchten, nämlich zuerst die Erkenntnis Gottes . . .' (*Werke*, iii. 569)—it is notable . . . that in the infancy of philosophy men began where we might rather end, namely, with the knowledge of God. . . .

[4] *Epistolae* LXXIII.   [5] *Ethica* i. 15. Scholium.
[6] *Ethica* i. 24. Corollarium.   [7] *Ethica* i. 25. Corollarium.
[8] *Ethica* i. 15.   [9] *Ethica* i. 15. Demonstratio.
[10] *Ethica* i. Definitio v.   [11] *Ethica* i. 14.
[12] *Ethica* i. 28. Demonstratio.

substance and God. The equation therefore reduces itself to 'the sum total of existence' equals 'God, or substance'.[1]

That this conception of 'God', placed first in response to 'the proper order of philosophic thinking', is actually a derivation from the original perception of an 'it is', Spinoza makes very clear. 'The first element', he says, 'which constitutes the actual being of the human mind, is the idea of some particular thing actually existing.'[2] From this initial emphasis we develop, by analysis of this 'particular thing', the conception of God. 'The more we know particular things', says Spinoza in the statement that was dearest of all to Goethe, 'the more we know God';[3] for 'individual things are nothing but modifications of the attributes of God'.[4] Hence Spinoza is inextricably bound to the category of 'thing' for his ultimate projection of God, and God becomes in this projection *res extensa*—an extended thing.[5]

We should at this juncture pause to examine more closely the precise meaning of *Deus*, and of *substantia*, which Spinoza so frequently uses in connexion with it. For it is probable that much of the difficulty of Spinoza's thought—and he is, as he himself proudly admits, a difficult thinker ('omnia praeclara tam difficilia quam rara sunt'[6]—all things excellent are as difficult as they are rare)—resides, first, in the seeming *petitio principii* of beginning, rather than concluding, his philosophy with the existence of God, and secondly, in confusing the meaning of 'substance' as Spinoza uses the term (and as the whole philosophical tradition from Aristotle through the schoolmen and Descartes uses it) with the meaning of 'substance' in common speech.[7] Schleiermacher has attempted to explain away the former difficulty by describing Spinoza's asseveration of God's existence as an axiom—daring and unconventional, to be sure, but none the less a primary and axiomatic assumption. I think, however, that this description fails to do justice to Spinoza's scientism, and that the matter is more comprehensible if we approach it from a different point of view. Spinoza defines God, at the outset, as 'a being absolutely infinite—that is, a substance consisting in infinite attributes, of which each expresses eternal and infinite essentiality'.[8] But this definition merely hypothesizes a God. Spinoza does not state that there is a God; rather he says that *if* there is

---

[1] *Ethica* I. 28. Demonstratio, and *Ethica* I. 11.
[2] *Ethica* II. 11.
[3] *Ethica* V. 24.
[4] *Ethica* I. 25. Corollarium.
[5] *Ethica* II. 2.
[6] *Ethica* V. 42. Scholium.
[7] Spinoza is indebted to a complex terminological tradition involving the Arabic, Jewish, and Scholastic thinkers of the Middle Ages, with antecedents reaching back to Aristotle. He probably, however, derived his specific conception most immediately from Descartes, who defines 'substance' as follows: 'Per *substantiam* nihil aliud intelligere possumus, quam rem quae ista existit, ut nulla alia re indigeat ad existendum' (*Œuvres*, viii. 24).—By *substance* we can mean nothing else than a thing which exists in such a way as to need no other thing for its existence.
[8] *Ethica* I. Definitio VI.

a God, *then* he must be conceived by this definition. In proposition 11 of the first part of the *Ethica*, however, Spinoza avers that 'God necessarily exists', and bulwarks the claim by adducing four 'proofs' or 'demonstrations' of a traditional kind—ontological, cosmological, and proof from sufficient cause all being included. We are here confronted with our first possibility of major misunderstanding, which we can attempt to avoid by thinking of the matter as follows. Spinoza does not start with an anthropomorphically coloured idea of God, and we must guard against projecting our own overtones and associations into his word. He is not 'proving' that God, an old man with a white beard, is somewhere 'up there'. Rather he starts with an unspecified concept, an empty pigeon-hole, labelled but otherwise unidentified, that indicates itself, by its name *Deus*, as the symbolic repository for the ultimate sum total of answers to all extensions of questions arising from the existence of things—but as in no other way defined or characterized. The whole task of Spinoza's thought, therefore, becomes the establishment of the contents of this pigeon-hole, of the characteristics of *Deus*. We might perhaps further simplify the matter for ourselves by substituting the word *beta*, devoid of overtones or emotional colouring, for Spinoza's *Deus*. The problem then is, defining β as the hypothetical form of answer to all unresolved questions arising from our perception of existing things, and defining 'I am' (understanding) and 'it is' (substance and modes) as the solely given, to determine what identities involving β may be derived. And one sees, by the elementary rules for the manipulation of equations, that statements for β are also values for 'I am' and for 'it is'. So when Spinoza 'proves' the existence of God in his eleventh proposition of the first part of the *Ethica*, he is not demonstrating the existence of that benevolent and anthropomorphic object of Christian faith, but merely saying that 'God', as symbolic terminus for all considerations arising from the interrelations of things and understanding, must be granted as much assumed reality as is granted to the assumption of the existence of the things and understanding with which we begin to philosophize.

If we now turn our attention to the meaning of 'substance', we will see that Spinoza defines this term as 'that which is in itself, and is conceived through itself; in other words, that of which a conception can be formed independently of any other conception'.[1] We should guard against confusion. 'Substance' thus defined is very different from the 'substance' of common speech—by which we usually mean a 'thing', and specifically a 'modified' thing, a grey metal, a viscous fluid, a white powder. But for Spinoza 'substance' is not a thing. It is the abstracted form of a thing, or, in line with his definition, the 'independent', unmodified, conception of a thing. He warns us, in fact, against confusing his abstraction 'sub-

[1] *Ethica* I. Definitio III.

stance' with the bethinged 'substance' of common speech, which he calls 'quantity':

If, then, we regard quantity as it is represented in our imagination, which we often and more easily do, we shall find that it is finite, divisible, and compounded of parts; but if we regard it as represented in our intellect, and conceive it as substance, which is very difficult to do, we shall then . . . find that it is infinite, one, and indivisible.[1]

In its form, Spinoza's substance, which must 'be conceived in and through itself', is therefore neither more nor less than the hypothetically most abstract answer to the question 'what is it?' If, for instance, I hand you a blue toothbrush with nylon bristles and ask you what it is, your answers would seek substantiality, but would in fact achieve no more than a modal transference. You might answer, 'Why that's an instrument for brushing your teeth', to which I might reply, 'I didn't ask you what it does, I asked you what it is'. So you might begin again: 'It is a piece of blue plastic, with nylon tufts.' To which I might reply, 'I'm not asking you what it's made of, or how it looks; I'm asking you what it really is——its blueness does not pertain to what it really is—it could be green, and still be what it is, or possibly you could be colour blind.' And, of course, this 'it' could be rubber rather than plastic, could have animal rather than nylon bristles, without affecting its substantiality. So, into the discard heap along with definition by function would go the modifiers: blue, plastic, nylon-tufted. And there too would go any attempts to identify the toothbrush by its position or size in space ('I didn't ask you where it was . . .') or its existence in time.

Now it is obvious that such a reduction, in which we reject all modal definitions—those which invoke the existence of something else beside the object under examination—tends systematically to strip the object of all the criteria of existence: the 'thing' is soon transformed into nothing. This transformation is precisely Spinoza's point. As Goethe said, 'vor seinem Blicke alle einzelne Dinge zu verschwinden scheinen'—before the gaze of Spinoza all individual things seem to disappear.[2] The existence of particular things is only modally possible; substantially, in terms of an answer to the question of what they really are, they have no existence as 'things'. And it further follows that the substance of any given thing, by this reduction, will be indistinguishable from the substance of any other thing, and that consequently, by the law of the identity of indiscernibles, there could not be a multiplicity of substances, or theoretical answers to the question 'what is it?', but one substance only. 'Setting the modifications aside', says Spinoza, 'and considering substance in itself, that is, truly, there cannot be conceived one substance different from another—

---

[1] *Ethica* I. 15. Scholium.   [2] Goethe, *Gedenkausgabe*, xviii. 851.

F

that is, there cannot be granted several substances, but one substance only.'[1]

The reductive process is crucial to Spinoza's thought. It is this reduction of the essence of all things to a unitary conception that Henry More, angrily but acutely, identified as 'fulcrum atheismi necessarium'—a necessary pivot of atheism.[2] For it is merely one short step for Spinoza then to say that 'substance is necessarily infinite'[3]—inasmuch as all other substances, which alone could limit a given substance, have been collapsed into one sole essence. And it is merely one short step beyond that, by adducing absolute illimitableness as an attribute of substance, for the concept of substance to be brought into congruence with the empty concept that Spinoza defined at the outset as 'God'. Thus the key fourteenth proposition: 'Besides God no substance can be granted or conceived.'[4]

The specific reductive instrument by means of which Spinoza constructs his 'fulcrum atheismi' is revealed in the first scholium to the eighth proposition of the first part of the *Ethica*: '. . . finite existence involves a partial negation, and infinite existence is the absolute affirmation of the given nature.'[5] The second clause here is both self-evident and traditional in philosophical and theological disquisition; it is to the first clause that we must direct our attention, and to the amplification of the statement of the first clause provided by a passage in Spinoza's fiftieth epistle, to Jarig Jelles, that achieves a summarizing formula: 'determinatio negatio est'— determination is negation.[6] The formula embodies concerns not unique to Spinoza: Wolfson cites its precedence in Aristotle,[7] and Kant describes its rationale very clearly:

. . . all negations (which are the only predicates by which all other things can be distinguished from the most real essence) are merely limitations of a greater, and ultimately of the highest, reality; therefore they presuppose this reality, and are, in regard to content, derived from it. All manifoldness of things is only a just so varied way of limiting the concept of the highest reality, which is their common substratum, just as all figures are possible only as different ways of limiting infinite space.[8]

---

[1] Spinoza, *Ethica* I. 5. Demonstratio.   [2] More, *Opera*, p. 619.
[3] Spinoza, *Ethica* I. 8.   [4] *Ethica* I. 14.
[5] *Ethica* I. 8. Scholium 1.
[6] 'As far as this is concerned, since shape (*figura*) is a negation, it is indeed not anything positive; it is evident that the whole of matter, considered indefinitely, cannot have any shape. Shape occurs only in limited, bounded bodies. For the person who says that he perceives shape means nothing else than that he perceives a limited thing and the means by which it is limited. Therefore this limitation does not apply to what a thing is but, on the contrary, to what it is not. Since therefore shape is nothing else than a limitation (*determinatio*) and a limitation is a negation, shape will not possibly be anything else than a negation, as I said' (Spinoza, *Epistolae* L, in *Opera*, iv. 240).
[7] *The Philosophy of Spinoza*, i. 134. Wolfson notes *Metaphysica* v. 22 and *De Interpretatione*, ch. 10.
[8] Kant, *Werke*, iii. 401–2.

We must understand the application of this point to Spinoza's thought, for the 'determinatio negatio est' is very important for Spinoza—'*Die Bestimmtheit ist Negation*,' said Hegel, in his *Wissenschaft der Logik*, 'ist das absolute Princip der spinozistischen Philosophie'—*determination is negation* is the absolute principle of Spinozist philosophy.[1]

What Spinoza means by 'determinatio negatio est' is that all determination—definition, description, identification, or the emergence into our consciousness of a thing as a thing—is not so much an affirmation of that thing as it is a negation of other things. For instance, to say that I have a blue nylon-tufted, plastic toothbrush is also to say that I do *not* have a yellow, animal-tufted rubber toothbrush, and, furthermore, is to say that I do *not* have a red, metal-jointed, oaken stool, and, ultimately, is *only* to say that I do *not* have all other things in the cosmos. In other words, every determination, or affirmation of the specific existence of any thing, is possible only through a countless multiplicity of negations of its identity with other things. If a table is a table, it is not a chair—nor is it a hymn, nor is it a wasp. Since, on the one hand, the essence of a thing, what 'it is', must, by the grammar of the question, imply an affirmation, and since all modification or relation is, by the *determinatio negatio est*, a form of negation, the form of ultimate abstraction from a thing must eschew modification or relation, and thereby all limit whatever, thus bringing us to the 'fulcrum atheismi', the identity of all substance. And since, on the other hand, Spinoza has accepted at the outset the traditional definition of God as the absolutely infinite—the being to whom neither negation nor limitation can be conceived as pertaining—then it follows that the sole substance, abstracted from the negational existence of thing, is identical with the absolute affirmation that we label 'God'.

Now in this development of a 'particular thing' into the 'sum total' of all things, into the 'extended thing' that Spinoza calls 'God, or Nature' ('Deus, sive Natura'), the unemphasized original element—the I, the self, the wonderer—is, as will always be the case finally in reasoning from the 'it is' axiom, ontologically demolished. Initially, and in accordance with philosophical convention, Spinoza assumes both the wonderer and the wondered-at, both the ego and the object: he says early in the *Ethica* that 'nothing is granted in addition to the understanding [the "I am"] except substance and its modifications' [the 'it is'].[2] But soon after he says that 'nothing is granted, save substances and their modifications.'[3] The 'understanding' is thus submerged into the formula 'substances and their modifications'. As Schelling acutely commented, the substance of Spinoza is a subject-object relationship, but one in which the subject gets totally lost.[4]

We can observe the submergence of the 'understanding', or subject, in

[1] Hegel, *Werke*, iv. 194.
[2] Spinoza, *Ethica* I. 4. Scholium.
[3] *Ethica* I. 6. Corollarium.
[4] Schelling, *Werke*, x. 38.

the following statements of Spinoza. 'There cannot exist in the universe two or more substances having the same nature or attribute',[1] or 'there cannot be conceived one substance different from another—that is, there cannot be granted several substances, but one substance only'.[2] This argument in turn leads to the statement that 'there is but one substance in the universe, and that . . . is absolutely infinite',[3] for 'every subtance . . . does not exist as finite, for . . . it would then be limited by something else of the same kind, which would also necessarily exist; there would be two substances with an identical attribute, which is absurd'.[4] It follows that substance is congruent to 'God', or, as Spinoza says simply, 'God is substance'.[5] But 'whatsoever is, is in God',[6] and also 'only one substance can be granted in the universe'; so, substituting in the equation 'God is substance', we and that 'whatsoever is, is "one" '. Thus we see emerging before our eyes the final equation of pantheism, the identity of the One and the Many. It is an equation that we also find in Schelling's ultimate thought: 'There is everywhere only One Being, only one true essence, the identity, or God. . . . God is plainly one, or: there is only one Absolute. For there is only one substance, which is God, the by-itself affirmed.[7] God is not the cause of all, but the All itself.'[8] And: '. . . Again, therefore, God also = the All, and there is no contradiction, but only absolute identity between both of them. Now for the first time is it clear how All is One and One is All.'[9]

These formulas are from the Würzburger Vorlesungen, posthumously published as *System der gesammten Philosophie*; they epitomize Schelling's thought. We can verify their typicality by turning to the *Darstellung meines Systems der Philosophie* where, in the specific terminology of the identity philosophy, the same exposition of Spinozistic pantheism is made. 'Alles, was ist,' says Schelling in this enchiridion, 'ist an sich Eines'—everything that is, is in itself One.[10] And also 'Alles, was ist, ist die absolute Identität selbst'—everything that is, is the absolute Identity itself.[11] 'Die Vernunft ist Eins mit der absoluten Identität'—reason is one with the absolute Identity.[12] Or, 'Die absolute Identität ist nicht Ursache des Universum, sondern das Universum selbst'—the absolute Identity is not the cause of the universe, but the universe itself.[13]

With Schelling, as with Spinoza, the negating process of the perception of any individual thing causes every individual thing to dissolve into the all of the universe, the identity of the One. 'The absolute Identity is absolute Totality. . . . I call the absolute Totality the Universe . . . what is

---

[1] Spinoza, *Ethica* I. 5.   [2] *Ethica* I. 5. Demonstratio.
[3] *Ethica* I. 10. Scholium.   [4] *Ethica* I. 8. Demonstratio.
[5] *Ethica* I. 19. Demonstratio.   [6] *Ethica* I. 15.
[7] Schelling, *Werke*, vi. 157.   [8] Ibid., p. 177.
[9] Ibid., p. 175.   [10] Schelling, *Werke*, iv, 119, Proposition 12.
[11] Ibid.   [12] Ibid., p. 118, Proposition 9.   [13] Ibid., p. 129, Proposition 32.

outside the Totality I call in this regard an *individual* being or thing.'[1] But 'there is no individual being or individual thing in itself',[2] for 'each individual being is as such a definite form of the being of the absolute Identity, not, however, in its being itself, which exists only in the Totality.'[3] All these subsidiary equations are restatements or corollaries of that one great equation, the alpha and omega of pantheism, the identity of the One and the Many.

In this final equation, the integrity of the 'I am' is swept away into the 'One', into 'das All'. As an 'I am' it has only a modal existence, as a wave momentarily cast up by the sea; its true existence, as substance, is the return and loss of its form in the sea again. Thus, of the individual personality, the self, Spinoza says: 'Being or substance does not appertain to the essence of man.'[4] Man, as man, is a fleeting and insubstantial vagary of nature: 'man is constituted by certain modifications of the attributes of God',[5] but we know that 'modifications' or modes are without existence in themselves, for Spinoza tells us that 'a mode exists in something else'.[6] 'The essence of man', therefore, 'does not involve necessary existence, that is, it may, in the order of nature, come to pass that this or that man does or does not exist.'[7] As flies to wanton boys, as Caliban to Setebos, are men to the Spinozistic God-Nature, and all their cherished hopes of personal immortality, of the uniqueness and indestructibility of the individual soul—all the guarantees of the Christian faith—are in this sombre apprehension of the interconnexion of man, world, and deity denied to them.

From this view of the brevity and the eschatological blankness of man's existence, Spinoza unflinchingly draws his conclusions. 'The human mind', he says in dismissal of the Cartesian *cogito*, is merely 'a part of nature',[8] and all that is supposed to distinguish and adorn it is imaginary. 'Only in relation to our imagination can things be called beautiful or deformed, ordered or confused',[9] and 'good and bad, right and wrong, praise and blame', all these treasured norms of humanity are mere 'prejudices'.[10] Man has no free will. 'Men think themselves free, inasmuch as they are conscious of their volitions and desires, and never even dream, in their ignorance, of the causes which have disposed them to wish and desire.'[11] We have no final control and no final choice: 'Men are mistaken in thinking themselves free; their opinion is made up of consciousness of their own actions, and ignorance of the causes by which they are conditioned. Their idea of freedom, therefore, is simply their ignorance of any cause for their actions.'[12] Nor is there eventual hope through the intervention of a benevolent deity,

[1] Ibid., p. 125, Propositions 26–27. [2] Ibid., Proposition 28.
[3] Ibid., p. 131, Proposition 38. [4] Spinoza, *Ethica* II. 10. Corollarium.
[5] Ibid. [6] Spinoza, *Ethica* I. 23. Demonstratio. [7] *Ethica* II. Axioma I.
[8] *Epistolae* XXXII. [9] Ibid. [10] *Ethica* I. Appendix.
[11] Ibid. [12] *Ethica* II. 35. Scholium.

for the God of Spinoza is mindless and soulless, vast and blank: 'neither intellect nor will', says Spinoza, 'appertain to God's nature',[1] and hence 'God does not act according to freedom of the will.'[2] 'I confess', says Spinoza, 'that the theory which subjects all things to the will of an indifferent deity . . . is less far from the truth than the theory of those, who maintain that God acts in all things with a view to promoting what is good.'[3] Thus in the system of Spinoza we are here not as inhabitants, bright even in our fall, of a world created for us by a loving and merciful God, whose image we see in our own likeness, but we are cast adrift, momentary and insignificant particles in the vast, blind efflux of deity. 'God', says Spinoza, 'is not affected by any emotion of pleasure or pain; consequently he does not love or hate anyone.'[4] We are not free to choose our destiny, but are bound fast by the iron chain of necessity: 'all things are conditioned to exist and operate in a particular manner by the necessity of the divine nature'.[5] And there is, finally, no hope in the future and no ultimate goal or meaning in life: 'nature has no particular goal in view, and . . . final causes are mere human figments'.[6]

This necessarily truncated discussion has not indicated the splendour of Spinoza's reticulation, nor the almost mystic calm of his ethical acceptance of man's hopeless situation. But perhaps something of the consequence, and the unblinking, unequivocal development of the implications of his initial standpoint, have been conveyed—enough at least to suggest why it can be argued that Spinoza is the very greatest of those thinkers who consider the 'it is' paramount in human experience. By this norm, even the father of modern empiricism, Bacon, is found by Spinoza in the final analysis to depend more on the 'I am' than on the 'it is':

. . . you ask me what errors I detect in the Cartesian and Baconian philosophies . . . they have wandered astray from the knowledge of the first cause, and of the human mind. . . . Of Bacon I shall say very little, for he speaks very confusedly . . . and works out scarcely any proofs: he simply narrates. . . . He assumes that the human intellect is liable to err, not only through the fallibility of the senses, but also solely through its own nature, and that it frames its conceptions in accordance with the analogy of its own nature, not with the analogy of the universe.[7]

Thus Spinoza would presumably have found himself in agreement with Coleridge that Bacon, as a representative of 'I am' philosophy, was, despite his empiricism of method, ultimately a follower of Plato.[8] And

---

[1] *Ethica* I. 17. Scholium.   [2] *Ethica* I. 32. Corollarium I.
[3] *Ethica* I. 33. Scholium 2.   [4] *Ethica* v. 17. Corollarium.
[5] *Ethica* I. 29.
[6] *Ethica* I. Appendix. Compare Goethe's statement, in a letter to Zelter of 29 Jan. 1830, that Spinoza had made him a believer in his hatred of the absurdity of final causes (Goethe, *Gedenkausgabe*, xxi. 889).   [7] Spinoza, *Epistolae* II.
[8] Coleridge habitually insisted that Bacon was a Platonist. See *Works*, ii. 437 ff. and *S. T. Coleridge's Treatise on Method*, ed. Alice D. Snyder (London, 1934), pp. 37-47, 51. For a more

since the greatest of those among Coleridge's immediate predecessors to assert the philosophy of 'I am' was Kant,[1] we may oppose these two chief exponents of 'I am' to Spinoza, the chief exemplar of 'it is', and understand the background of Coleridge's contention that 'the three greatest works since the introduction of Christianity' are 'Bacon, *Novum Organon*, . . . Spinoza, *Ethics*, . . . and Kant's *Critique of Pure Reason*.'[2] Perhaps too, if we understand the background, the ignorance underlying Stirling's airy dismissal of this contention as an 'idle subjective fancy of the moment'[3] may become apparent. This example of philosophical ineptitude on the part of one of Coleridge's shrillest critics is a sobering reminder that a few courses in the platitudes of philosophy, an academic success or two, a blustering ego, and the applause of one's fellows in ignorance, are scarcely sufficient equipment for judging the labours of a genius.

And nowhere is the philosophical genius of Coleridge more evident than in a brief statement from a manuscript notebook of about the year 1810. It is absolutely central to the whole of his thought and also, despite what at first sight may appear to be hyper-exclusiveness and over-generalization, is the kind of compressed and diamond-like insight that is achieved only as the end result of long hours of reading and longer hours of thought, combined with a very rare gift for pursuing the unstated implications of stated positions. The statement is one that draws an absolute opposition between the philosophy of Spinoza and the philosophy of Kant, and it is a remarkable testimony to the learning and insight of its author. The note says, 'only two *Systems* of Philosophy—(sibi consistentia) possible. 1. Spinoza. 2. Kant, i.e. the absolute & the relative, the κατ' ὄντως ὄντα and the κατ' ἄνθρωπον. Or 1. ontosophical. 2. the anthropological'.[4]

These two philosophies, however, though coequal antagonists, were not coeval; rather more than a century elapsed between the publication of Spinoza's *Ethica* and the publication of Kant's *Kritik der reinen Vernunft*. During that period historical considerations of great importance arose, and if we are to understand fully the complex attitudes of Coleridge towards both thinkers—and, incidentally, to see historically how fatuous is Stirling's chuckling superiority about Coleridge's reference to the *Ethica*

popular and conventional view, in which Bacon and Plato are regarded as 'diametrically opposite' thinkers, see Macaulay's essay, 'Lord Bacon', in *Critical and Miscellaneous Essays* (New York, 1857), ii. 378–87. See further F. H. Anderson, 'Bacon on Platonism', *University of Toronto Quarterly*, xi (1941–2), 154–66.

[1] See p. 62, notes 1 and 2.

[2] Flyleaf note on Schelling's *Philosophische Schriften* (Landshut, 1809) as printed in *Philosophical Lectures*, p. 454, n. 30.

[3] Stirling, 'De Quincey and Coleridge upon Kant', p. 220.

[4] *Philosophical Lectures*, p. 53. Cf. Fichte: 'Ich bemerke noch, dass man, wenn man das *Ich bin* überschreitet, nothwendig auf den Spinozismus kommen muss! . . . und dass es nur zwei völlig consequente Systeme giebt; das Kritische, welches diese Grenze anerkennt, und das Spinozische, welches sie überspringt' (*Grundlage der gesammten Wissenschaftslehre*, p. 17).

as an 'unwholesome book'[1]—we must examine with some care the meta-morphosis of Spinoza's reputation between his own era and the advent of Romanticism.

Spinoza, shortly before his death in 1677, fell into a deep and lasting philosophical and theological disrepute, punctuated at intervals by charges of atheism from the leading intellects of the time.[2] Spinoza, said the super-intellectual Leibniz, 'estoit veritablement Athée'.[3] He was, according to the great scholar and Newtonian apologist Clarke, 'the most celebrated Patron of Atheism in our Time'.[4] In an immensely influential attack, the sceptical encyclopaedist Bayle described him as an 'athée de systême'—a systematizer of atheism.[5] The Cambridge Platonist Henry More described him as 'in infimas Atheismi faeces immersus'—sunk in the deepest dregs of atheism.[6] Spinoza must be considered, said the Hebraic scholar and Christian theologian Buddaeus, 'pro atheorum nostra aetate principe'—the prince of atheists in our time.[7] His philosophy, said the philosophical academician Christian Wolf, 'tollit omnem actionum intrinsecam morali-tatem'—takes away all the intrinsic morality of our actions.[8] 'Huc nos ducit totum Systema Spinozae,' wrote Christopher Wittich sombrely, 'ut credamus, Mundum esse Deum, sicque verum Deum abnegemus'—to this point the whole system of Spinoza leads us, to believe the world to be God, and thus reject the true God.[9] According to Jean le Clerc, Bentley's victim, Spinoza was 'the most famous atheist of our time'.[10] If Spinoza's system were true, said the Archbishop of Cambrai, the famous Fénelon, 'tous les corps et toutes les pensées de l'univers ne faisant tous

---

[1] 'De Quincey and Coleridge upon Kant', p. 220.

[2] For the origins and development of anti-Spinozism see further Excursus Note II, p. 267.

[3] *Sämtliche Schriften und Briefe*, Zweite Reihe, i. 535. This opinion of 1683 is an amplification of Leibniz's judgement in a letter of 23 Sept. 1670, where he notes with approval Thomasius's attack on Spinoza, refers to the *Tractatus* as a 'book of intolerable licence', and sizes up Spinoza as a follower of Hobbes: 'I have recently seen a programme from Leipzig, undoubtedly your own, in which you gave that book of intolerable licence, de libertate philosophandi, just the treat-ment it deserved. The author seems not only in his politics but also in his religion a follower of Hobbes, who outlined his views rather fully in his *Leviathan*, a monstrous work, perhaps even evidenced by the title' (i. 66).

[4] Samuel Clarke, *A Demonstration of the Being and Attributes of God*, p. 28. See note 8, p. 338.

[5] *Dictionaire historique et critique*, ii. 1083. 'I believe', says Bayle, 'that he is the first who has reduced atheism to a system, and who has made of it a body of doctrine tied and woven together after the manner of the geometers; but otherwise his opinion is not at all new.' See note 9, p. 338.

[6] 'Demonstrationis duarum propositionum . . . quae praecipuae apud Spinozium Atheismi sunt Columnae, brevis solidaque Confutatio', in *Henrici Mori Cantabrigiensis Opera omnia* . . . p. 619.

[7] *Ioan. Francisci Bvddei . . . Theses theologicae de atheismo et svperstitione variis observationibvs illustratae*. . . . (Ienae, 1717), p. 163.

[8] *Philosophia practica universalis, methodo scientifica pertractata, Pars Prior* . . . Autore Christiano Wolfio . . . (Halae Magdebvrgicae, 1744), p. 211.

[9] *Christoph. Wittichii Anti-Spinoza sive Examen Ethices Benedicti de Spinoza et Commentarius de Deo et ejus attributis* (Amstelaedami, 1690), p. 9.

[10] Quoted by R. Meyer, *Leibniz und die europäische Ordnungskrise* (Hamburg, 1948), p. 76.

ensemble qu'un seul être simple, réelment un et indivisible'—all the objects and all the thoughts of the universe would make, all together, only one single, simple being, really one and indivisible.[1] And if Spinozism were true, continued Fénelon,

it would be necessary to overthrow all ideas, confound all natures and properties, renounce all distinctions, attribute to thought all the sensible qualities of bodies, and to bodies all the thoughts of thinking beings; it would be necessary to attribute to every body all the modifications of all bodies and of all spirits; it would be necessary to conclude that each part is the whole, and that each part is also every one of the other parts: and all this would constitute a monstrosity from which reason would recoil with shame and horror.[2]

The opinion that linked the pious Fénelon to the sceptic Bayle was shared also, so certain and unarguable did the maleficence of Spinozism seem, by Fénelon's opponent, the 'French Plato', Malebranche. 'We are a necessary emanation from the Godhead. . . . The infinitely perfect being is the universe, the assemblage of all that exists.'[3] So, tentatively, does Ariste, one of Malebranche's interlocutors, put forward the basic premiss of Spinozism. But he is crushed by the horrified reply of the representative of Malebranche's own opinion: 'comment aurait-il pu croire que tous les êtres créés ne sont que des parties ou des modifications de la Divinité? . . . Quel monstre . . . quelle épouvantable et ridicule chimère!' How can the Spinozist believe that all created beings are only parts or modifications of God? . . . what a monstrosity . . . what a wicked and ridiculous chimera![4] And, in more tactful tones, Henry Oldenburg, the Secretary of the Royal Society, informed Spinoza himself of learned discontent, and the grounds of that discontent, concerning Spinoza's treatment 'de Deo, & Natura; quae duo a te confundi, quamplurimi arbitrantur'—of God, and Nature; which two entities, in the judgement of a number of people, are confused by you.[5]

The authority of such figures paved the way for prolonged and often indiscriminate assaults by a horde of lesser men; indeed, Spinoza became the theological and philosophical scapegoat of his age.[6] Gottlob Spitzel of Augsburg stigmatized him with the epithet 'Satanam illum incarnatum'—

---

[1] Fénelon, 'Réfutation du Spinosisme', *Traité de l'existence et des attributs de Dieu*, in *Œuvres*, i. 194–5. This work, a posthumous publication, first appeared in 1718.

[2] Ibid. Fénelon, deeply involved with the Quietism of Madame Guyon—a religious attitude that in its implications was the same as Spinozism—was particularly sensitive, because of rebukes by the Church, to all that smacked of pantheism. None the less, it is questionable just how far he was ever able to withdraw from his Quietistic leanings; hence Jacobi, for one, insisted that the French bishop was almost as thorough a Spinozist as was Spinoza himself, and, as he told Fichte, had as a pet project the explicit demonstration of the similarity of the positions of the two thinkers (Jacobi, *Werke*, iii. 47).

[3] Malebranche, *Entretiens sur la métaphysique*, in *Œuvres*, i. 205–6.

[4] See note 10, p. 339. [5] Spinoza, *Epistolae* LXXI.

[6] See Excursus Note II, p. 261.

that incarnate Satan.[1] To Conrad Dippel he was a 'poisonous spider'.[2] Inevitably, the expulsion of Spinoza from his synagogue became a theme for pious Christian libel. Massillon thundered invective against 'ce monstre qui, après avoir embrassé différentes réligions, finit par n'en avoir aucune'.[3] But it remained for Christian Kortholt to achieve an arabesque of spite by sustituting 'Maledictus' for the 'Benedictus' that had Latinized the Hebrew 'Baruch' of Spinoza's given name.[4] Where there was not fear and hatred and loathing, there was ridicule. Pufendorf, the learned legal theorist and seventeenth-century existentialist who saw man as shipwrecked and abandoned, patronizingly averred that Spinoza had written 'nothing subtle'.[5] The erudite Göttingen historian of heresy Mosheim inquired rhetorically if anything could be more 'laughable' than Spinoza's belief that 'this world is God'.[6] And Voltaire ('einer der größesten Minuspoeten, die je lebten',[7] in Novalis's scathing opinion), clever as always, produced a famous poetic gibe:

[1] *Felix literatus ex infelicium periculis et casibus, sive de vitiis literatorum commentationes historico-theosophicae*, authore Theophilo Spizelio (Augustae Vindelicorum [Augsburg], 1676), p. 142. The context of the epithet is as follows: '. . . The books appearing in the shops that are part of the veritable farrago of conflicting treatises privately produced by the authors and that utter blasphemies, we have elsewhere reviewed at great length and utterly denounced. May the Lord rebuke that incarnate Satan who has held forth through a most calamitous and damnable booklet. . . . There appeared a few years ago a certain anonymous work under the title TRAC-TATUS THEOLOGICO-POLITICI, DE LIBERTATE PHILOSOPHANDI, the most unfortunate progeny of its author, who shuns the light (They say, however, he is Benedict Spinoza, a Jew by nationality, a man, as the matter itself attests, who has cast off all shame, a fanatic, hostile to every form of religion), and who has put his very finest effort into attacking the sacred text and rejecting all divine revelation, having advanced to such a state of impudence and impiety . . .' (pp. 142–3).

[2] See David Baumgardt, 'Spinoza und der deutsche Spinozismus', *Kantstudien*, xxxii (1927), 183; Freudenthal, *Die Lehre Spinozas*, pp. 224 ff. See especially M. Krakauer, *Zur Geschichte des Spinozismus in Deutschland* (Breslau, 1881), which provides a detailed examination of the careers of Dippel and his follower J. C. Edelmann.

[3] Massillon, *Œuvres* (Paris, 1842), i. 395.

[4] *De tribus impostoribus magnis liber*, cura editus Christiani Kortholti (Hamburgi, 1700), p. 75. 'Benedictus est de Spinosa (quem rectius Maledictum dixeris; quod *spinosa* ex divina *maledictione* terra (Gen. iii. 17. 18.) maledictum magis hominem, & cujus monumenta tot spinis obsita, vix umquam tulerit) vir initio Judaeus, sed postea, ob portentosas de ipso etiam Judaismo opiniones, ἀποσυνάγωγος, atque sic tandem nescio quibus artibus & fraudibus, inter Christianos nomen professus.' Kortholt's diction with reference to Spinoza's expulsion from the synagogue is virtually identical with that in which Graevius informed Leibniz, on 12 Apr. 1671, that 'the author of the *Tractatus* is said to be a Jew by the name of Spinoza, who was expelled from the synagogue (ἀποσυνάγωγος) recently because of the monstrous nature of his opinions . . .' (*Philosophiche Schriften*, i. 115)—and, in fact, the words of Graevius, with only slight variations, are repeated so often in the Spinoza polemics of the time as to assume almost a formulaic status.

[5] Letter to Thomasius, 19 June 1688, in 'Briefe von Pufendorf', p. 33: '*Spinosam* habe ich gekannt, der war ein leichtfertiger vogel, *deorum hominumque irrisor* und hatte das *novum Testamentum* und *Alcoran* in einen band zusammen gebunden. Ich finde auch nichts subtiles bei ihm, ist aber schon der muhe werth, dass man ihn *funditus* destruire.'

[6] J. L. von Mosheim, 'Die elende Thorheit der Religionspötter' [about 1725], in *Sämmtliche heilige Reden über wichtige Wahrheiten der Lehre Jesu Christi* (Hamburg, 1765), i. 311. See note 11, p. 340.

[7] Novalis, *Schriften*, ii. 328.

Alors un petit Juif, au long nez, au teint blême,
Pauvre, mais satisfait, pensif et retiré,
Esprit subtil et creux, moins lu que célébré,
Caché sous le manteau de Descartes, son maître,
Marchant à pas comptés, s'approcha du grand Être:
'Pardonnez-moi, dit-il en lui parlant tout bas,
Mais je pense, entre nous, que vous n'existez pas'.
Je crois l'avoir prouvé par mes mathématiques.[1]

Surely we sense here a whistling past the graveyard, this attempt to reduce the awful philosophy of Spinoza to a skit wherein the little, long-nosed, pale-faced Jew, 'less read than celebrated' and 'hidden under the mantle of Descartes', marches up to the Supreme Being and politely informs him that 'just between us, you do not exist'. Voltaire, at any rate, had his joke. But others found the implications of Spinozism a graver matter, as we may see in Christian Wolf's worried statement, free from denunciatory epithets, and occurring in the course of a long and careful refutation of Spinozism on both logical and moral grounds, that 'Spinosismus ab atheismo parum distat, & aeque noxius est, immo certo respectu magis nocet, quam atheismus'—that Spinozism, not far removed from atheism, is as harmful as atheism, and in a certain respect even more harmful than atheism.[2]

But that pre-Romantic era, though logically awake to the implications of Spinoza's thought, had as yet little inkling of his awesome psychological magnetism, and Wolf's fears perhaps seemed exaggerated. Even that near-professional heretic, the Irish Socinian John Toland—a man who, indeed, may have coined the very word 'pantheist'[3]—was not unduly impressed by the language and thought of the Jewish philosopher. While recognizing in Spinoza 'a great man', he said that Spinoza's '*system of matter without motion* is indigested and unphilosophical'.[4] And though he defended Spinoza's character and some parts of his philosophy,[5] he also observed superciliously that Spinoza's 'share of Learning (except in

---

[1] Voltaire, 'Les Systèmes', *Œuvres de Voltaire*, ed. Beuchot (Paris, 1829–40), xiv. 246–7.

[2] *Theologia Naturalis*, p. 729, Proposition 716. For Wolf's criticism of Spinoza, see further Excursus Note II, p. 263.

[3] 'TOLANDVS', roared Buddaeus, '... atheorum, quos nostra aetas tulit, facile impudentissimus'—Toland, of the atheists brought forth by our time, easily the most shameless (*Ioan. Francisci Bvddei ... Theses theologicae de atheismo ...* (Ienae, 1717), p. 8). For more about Toland and the origin of the word pantheism, see Excursus Note III, p. 266.

[4] John Toland, *Tetradymus* (London, 1720), p. 185.

[5] John Toland, *Letters to Serena* (London, 1704), p. 133: 'For my part, I shall always be far from saying that SPINOSA did nothing well, because in many things he succeeded so ill. On the contrary, he has had several lucky Thoughts, and appears to have bin a Man of admirable natural Endowments. ... I grant you likewise that he was truly sober, observant of the Laws of his Country, and not possest with the sordid Passion of heaping up Riches. ... I further agree ... that SPINOSA's adversarys have gain'd nothing on his Disciples by the contumelious and vilifying Epithets they bestow on his Person for the sake of his Opinions. ...'

some parts of the Mathematicks, and in the understanding of the Rabbins) seems to have bin very moderate';[1] and he could come to the final perverse opinion that 'the whole System of SPINOSA is not only false, but also precarious and without any sort of Foundation'.[2]

In this negative role Spinoza continued for approximately a hundred years after his death. While it is not correct to assert, with the Romantics, that he was neglected during this period[3]—he was the object of persistent clerical venom and also had from the first his surreptitious sympathizers[4]— it is probably true, as Voltaire said, that he was 'moins lu que célébré'. But he was read too, and Diderot's lengthy description in the *Encyclopédie* may be regarded as a summary of the pre-Romantic attitude. The article is partly a reprise of Bayle: like Bayle, Diderot says that Spinoza was 'un athée de système';[5] like Bayle, he emphasizes the similarity of Spinoza to certain ancient philosophers; like Bayle, he uses the argument about German and Turks killing one another; and he defends Bayle against the charge of having misunderstood Spinoza. It is also partly a whirlwind attack (John Morley speaks of its 'marked vigour of thrust' and 'marked energy of speech'), using arguments from a variety of sources, on Spinoza's logical distinctions.

Along about the time of this article, however, and roughly at the time of Voltaire, the emotional impact of Spinoza was beginning to be felt. Though the new attitude was culturally a manifestation of the 1750s, it appears, in a notably early adumbration of Romantic emotionalism, as an isolated phenomenon as far back as 1713. In that year the young Mairan writes to Malebranche:

Having passed, one or two years ago, from the study of mathematics and of physics to the study of religion, your works, Descartes, Pascal and Labidie were my principal conductors, and they managed soon to convince me of that which a good education and the reading of holy scripture had already made me love. I have rejoiced in this sweet conviction, without its having been troubled either by the arguments of unbelievers or by the mocking laughter of men of the world, until the works of Spinoza, and above all his *Ethic* or his philosophy chanced into my hands. The character of this author, so different from everything I had seen until then, the abstract form of his work, concise and geometric, the rigour of his reasoning, seemed to me worthy of attention. So I read him attentively, and he shocked me. I have since re-read him, and I have meditated in solitude and in what you call the silence of the passions; but the more I read him, the more I find him solid and full of good sense. In a word, I do not know where to break the chain of his proofs. The trouble, nevertheless, that this complete reversal of my primary and most cherished ideas produces in me, has made me

---

[1] Toland, *Letters to Serena*, p. 133. [2] Ibid., p. 135.
[3] See Excursus Note II, p. 264. [4] See Excursus Note II, p. 262.
[5] *Œuvres Complètes de Diderot*, ed. J. Assézat et M. Tourneux (Paris, 1875–9), xvii. 170. See note 12, p. 341.

at times resolve to abandon him. I made up my mind to forget him; but, when one is vitally touched by the desire of knowing the truth, can one forget that which has seemed evident? On the one hand, I cannot envisage without compassion for humanity and without sadness the consequences that follow from his principles; on the other, I cannot resist his demonstrations.[1]

No later testimonial to the emotional magnetism of Spinoza's thought, or to the conflict of head and heart induced in those who came under his spell, is more impressive, and Mairan's words might well, as we shall see, have been the words of a Jacobi or a Coleridge decades later. Mairan, however, was an exception to the historical progress of attitudes towards Spinoza, and we find no comparable statements among his contemporaries.

It is not until 1760 that we hear again that tone of awe in a brief digression in the work of the Abbé Lelarge de Lignac: 'Spinosa . . . n'étoit point un Athée, comme on le croit communément, mais un Spiritualiste outré. Il ne reconnoissoit que Dieu! le monde, les créatures spirituelles étoient pour lui les songes de la Divinité, semblables à ceux que nous avons pendant la nuit.'[2] In 1766 a more important statement, a worthy counterpart to that of Mairan in its emotional fervour, was made. In a tractate boldly entitled *Apologie de Spinosa et du Spinosisme*, the Abbé Sabatier de Castres sounded the keynote for a gathering orchestration of enthusiasm and wonder:

Although a Jew, Spinoza lived always as a Christian and was as versed in our divine Testament as in the books of the ancient law. If he had concluded, as one cannot doubt, by embracing Christianity, he would certainly have been placed in the ranks of the saints, rather than at the forefront of the enemies of God. O most falsely judged of sages, modest and virtuous Spinoza! forgive me for having partaken of the general error concerning thy works—before having read them—and receive today the tribute of thankfulness that I owe thee. If, in a century of corruption and frenzy, in the metropolis of talents and of voluptuousness, under the very pulpit of corrupters and sophists, I have remained firm in the faith of my fathers, I owe it to thee and thy oneness with this holy faith.[3]

We see in this fervent apostrophe the first clear sign of the almost frenzied enthusiasm that Spinoza, alone among philosophers, except perhaps for Plato, was able to inspire in his adherents. And when in 1778 Herder equated Spinoza with St. John himself as the apostle of love—indeed, termed Spinoza 'undoubtedly still more divine' than St. John—the shift of sensibility had become almost complete.[4]

The tinder awaited the spark. On the afternoon of 6 July and the morning of 7 July 1780 the philosophy of Spinoza—impelled by the

---

[1] Victor Cousin, *Fragments de philosophie cartésienne* (Paris, 1845), pp. 269–70.
[2] *Le Témoignage du sens intime et de l'expérience, opposé à la foi profane & ridicule des fatalistes modernes* (Auxerre, 1760), ii. 212.
[3] Sabatier de Castres, *Apologie de Spinosa et du Spinosisme* (Altona, 1805), pp. 13–14.
[4] Herder, *Vom Erkennen und Empfinden der menschlichen Seele, Werke*, viii. 202.

authority of the revered Lessing—burst forth upon the intellectual world with an impact that was to prove tremendous. The occasion was a conversation, paradoxically set in an almost ideal eighteenth-century situation of cosmopolitan order and elegance, between Lessing and his younger admirer, Friedrich Jacobi:

Lessing. . . . Die orthodoxen Begriffe von der Gottheit sind nicht mehr für mich; ich kann sie nicht geniessen. 'Εν και Παν! Ich weiss nichts anders. . . .

Jacobi. Da wären Sie ja mit Spinoza ziemlich einverstanden.

Lessing. Wenn ich mich nach jemand nennen soll, so weiss ich keinen andern.

Jacobi. Spinoza ist mir gut genug: aber doch ein schlechtes Heil, das wir in seinem Namen finden!

Lessing. Ja! Wenn Sie wollen! . . . Und doch . . . Wissen Sie etwas besseres?

Lessing. . . . The orthodox notions of the Deity no longer suit me; I cannot enjoy them. 'Εν και Παν! I know nothing besides this. . . .

Jacobi. In that idea you would be nearly in agreement with Spinoza.

Lessing. If I were to call myself after anyone, I know no other whom I should prefer to him.

Jacobi. Spinoza is good enough; yet it is a poor salvation that we find in his name!

Lessing. Yes, if you wish, but do you know any better?[1]

Here the conversation was interrupted, to be resumed in Jacobi's room after breakfast on the following morning:

Lessing. Ich bin gekommen über mein 'Εν και Παν mit Ihnen zu reden. Sie erschracken gestern.

Jacobi. Sie überraschten mich. . . . Freylich war es gegen meine Vermuthung, an Ihnen einen Spinozisten oder Pantheisten zu finden; und noch weit mehr dagegen, dass Sie mir es gleich und so blank und baar hinlegen würden. Ich war grossen Theils in der Absicht gekommen, von Ihnen Hülfe gegen den Spinoza zu erhalten.

Lessing. Also kennen Sie ihn doch?

Jacobi. Ich glaube ihn zu kennen, wie nur sehr wenige ihn gekannt haben mögen.

Lessing. Dann ist Ihnen nicht zu helfen. Werden Sie lieber ganz sein Freund. Es giebt keine andre Philosophie, als die Philosophie des Spinoza.[2]

Lessing. I have come to talk with you about my 'Εν και Παν. You were startled yesterday.

Jacobi. You surprised me. . . . I had certainly not expected to find in you a Spinozist or Pantheist, nor that you would admit it to me so frankly. My main reason for coming to you was to obtain help against Spinoza.

---

[1] Jacobi, *Werke*, iv-1. 54.   [2] Ibid., p. 55. See note 13, p. 341.

Lessing. Then you do know him?

Jacobi. I believe I know him as very few have known him.

Lessing. Then you are beyond help. Rather become wholly his friend. There is no other philosophy than the philosophy of Spinoza.

'There is no other philosophy than the philosophy of Spinoza.' The words are prophetic for the whole of nineteenth-century philosophy, except for such endeavours as those of Jacobi, of Coleridge, and of Kierkegaard.

Lessing died on 15 February 1781. In 1783 Jacobi heard from his friend Elise Reimarus that Moses Mendelssohn ('diesem ächten Verehrer und Freunde unseres Lessing') was planning a memorial essay on Lessing's character, and that she and Mendelssohn had been recently talking much about both Lessing and Jacobi.[1] Jacobi wrote to her, on 21 July of that year, that perhaps it would be well for Mendelssohn to know 'that Lessing in his last days was a decided Spinozist', and that consequently Mendelssohn should either avoid certain topics in his essay, or treat them with special care.[2]

Acting as intermediary, Elise Reimarus informed Mendelssohn and then, on 1 September 1783, wrote to Jacobi that Mendelssohn wished him 'to report explicitly what Lessing said, how he said it, and in what circumstances he expressed himself'.[3] Mendelssohn's scarcely veiled implication was that Jacobi's opinions, as those of a philosophical amateur, might not be reliable.[4] Mendelssohn himself, though a follower of Wolf rather than of Spinoza, was of course a philosopher of established reputation, and had furthermore been one of the very first thinkers of Germany to regard Spinoza as an important figure in philosophical history.[5]

On 4 November 1783 Jacobi obligingly furnished Mendelssohn with a long description of his conversations with Lessing. He said that Lessing had not only, as we have seen, avowed his Spinozism, but had insisted on the reciprocity of the thought of Leibniz and Spinoza, of the agreement of Luther and Spinoza in their denial of free will, and had once, 'with a half smile', suggested that 'he himself might be the highest being', a

---

[1] Jacobi, *Werke*, iv-1. 38–39.
[2] Ibid., pp. 39–40.
[3] Ibid., p. 45.
[4] See note 14, p. 342.
[5] As early as 1755 Mendelssohn had hailed Spinoza as one of the extenders of *Weltweisheit*— world wisdom—and as a sacrifice or martyr to the furthering of human understanding: 'Leibniz, Wolf, and various of their successors—to what perfection have they brought *Weltweisheit*! How proud can Germany be of them! Yet what does it avail to ascribe more to ourselves than is right? Let us always confess that someone other than a German—and I may add, someone other than a Christian—that Spinoza shared greatly in the advancement of *Weltweisheit*. Before the transition from Cartesian to Leibnizian *Weltweisheit* could take place, there had to be someone to plunge into the monstrous abyss lying between them. This unhappy lot fell to Spinoza. How very much is his fate to be regretted! He was a sacrifice for human understanding; but a sacrifice that deserves to be adorned with flowers. Without him *Weltweisheit* would never have been able to extend its bounds so far' (*Schriften*, 1. 204).

pantheistic variant that, said Jacobi, Lessing expanded in the manner of
Henry More and van Helmont. When Lessing did speak about a personal
divinity, Jacobi went on, he thought of it as a world-soul, according to
the analogy of an organic body. This idea, said Jacobi, Lessing returned
to frequently, 'now jokingly, now in earnest'.[1]

The playful spirits of the two did not, in Jacobi's report, desert them.
Sitting in the garden of the poet Gleim on a later occasion, Lessing said
to Jacobi, as it suddenly began to rain, 'You know, Jacobi, maybe it is
I that am doing that.' 'Or I', replied Jacobi, straight faced. Gleim, adds
Jacobi, looked on in wonderment, but without comment.[2]

In subsequent conversations, said Jacobi further, the two agreed that
a recent publication by the Dutch thinker Hemsterhuis was, notwithstanding the author's innocence of the fact (Diderot had assured Jacobi
that Hemsterhuis was not a Spinozist), pure Spinozism.[3]

Jacobi concluded his letter by saying that 'what I have recounted is not
a tenth of what I might have told you, had my memory been equal to the
task'—but that 'Lessing often and with emphasis cited the '$Eν$ $και$ $παν$ as
the essence of his philosophy and theology, several people can witness.
He said it and he wrote it, on various occasions, as his settled motto.'[4]
One fact was indisputably clear: '. . . Lessing believes in no cause of things
differentiated from the world; or, Lessing is a Spinozist.'[5]

Upon receipt of this letter—or essay, rather—Mendelssohn, in December 1783, wrote to Elise and apologized for having mistaken Jacobi for
a mere philosophical dabbler.[6] Then, eight months later, in August 1784,
he sent Jacobi himself a document specifying some objections to aspects
of Jacobi's view of the nature of Spinozism.[7] In the covering letter he
again apologized to Jacobi, praised his acuteness, averred that he did not
understand all of what Jacobi said, nor see the connexions in all of his
reasoning, and finally, in a respectful if fanciful vein, suggested that
Jacobi had delivered a kind of knightly challenge, that he, Mendelssohn,
was picking up the gauntlet, and that they should wage a 'metaphysischen
Ehrenkampf'—a chivalric struggle of metaphysics—under the eyes of the
lady treasured by them both (the lady apparently being 'truth'—die Wahrheit—rather than Elise Reimarus).[8]

In any event, Jacobi answered Mendelssohn, on 5 September 1784, that
perhaps his interpretation of Spinoza would be made more clear if he
enclosed a copy of a long letter he had recently written in French to
Hemsterhuis.[9] Jacobi further said that he did not realize he had issued a
knightly challenge, but if so he would not turn his back on the conflict;

---

[1] Jacobi, *Werke*, iv-1. 67–76, 79.   [2] Ibid., p. 79.
[3] Ibid., pp. 82–83.   [4] Ibid., p. 89.
[5] Ibid., p. 90.   [6] Ibid., p. 95.
[7] Ibid., pp. 103–19.   [8] Ibid., pp. 101–3.
[9] The letter occupies pp. 123–62 of the cited edition of *Ueber die Lehre des Spinoza*.

and he warned that his own thought was based not on the system of Spinoza, but on the attitudes of Pascal.[1]

The challenge having been thus duly acknowledged and accepted by both sides, another hiatus ensued. On 28 January 1785 Mendelssohn wrote to Elise apologizing for not having been more active in the controversy, saying that he worked with snail-like slowness ('schneckenartigen Langsamkeit') because of ill health and household business.[2] He inquired rather vaguely whether Jacobi's letters might some day be available for publication, and wondered who owed whom a formal letter in the controversy. Jacobi, meanwhile, using 'all my intellectual force . . . sparing neither pains nor patience', had been occupied in a new exposition of Spinoza's thought and its consequences, which he incorporated into forty-four propositions.[3] These he promptly sent to Mendelssohn.[4] But Mendelssohn, for his part, continued desultorily to fend off Jacobi by repeating that he did not understand much of what both Jacobi and Spinoza said. In the meantime, however, he finished and sent to the press, without consulting Jacobi or letting him see the manuscript, his *Morgenstunden oder Vorlesungen über das Daseyn Gottes*, in which work, among other matters, he broached the subject of Lessing's pantheism—without overt reference to his discussions with Jacobi—and attempted to extenuate the whole matter by postulating a morally and religiously acceptable 'purified pantheism' (geläuterter Pantheismus) as the sum and substance of Lessing's pantheistic allegiance. He concluded

that Lessing intended pantheism fully in the refined way that I have represented him—he thought of it in the best harmony with everything that can have influence on life and happiness; even that he was by way of binding together pantheistic concepts with positive religion: and indeed this was as possible for him as with the emanation system of the ancients, which has been accepted in religion through many centuries, and has been held as the sole orthodox doctrine.[5]

Jacobi, interpreting this unilateral publication as a violation of the rules of the controversy—'however unbounded my confidence in the rectitude and noble principles of my opponent was and will remain'—and feeling that his own views deserved clear public exposition, thereupon gathered together his letters, his two analyses of Spinoza's thought, and some final remarks on his own faith-philosophy.[6] Having shown this manuscript to Hamann and Herder, he sent it to press in Breslau, on 28 August 1785, under the title *Ueber die Lehre des Spinoza in Briefen an Herrn Moses Mendelssohn*.

---

[1] Jacobi, *Werke*, iv–1. 122.   [2] Ibid., pp. 163–5.
[3] Ibid., p. 172.
[4] The forty-four propositions occupy pp. 172–205 of the cited edition of *Ueber die Lehre des Spinoza*.
[5] *Morgenstunden*, p. 284.   [6] Jacobi, *Werke*, iv–1. 226–7.

The contents of this oddly constructed volume are designed, as Jacobi says, to prove six main points: (1) Spinozism is atheism; (2) the Jewish Cabala is, as philosophy, a confused Spinozism; (3) the philosophy of Leiniz and Wolf is no less fatalistic than Spinozism, and in its implications is tantamount to Spinozism; (4) any consequent demonstration in philosophy leads to fatalism or Spinozism; (5) all our knowledge is a knowledge of likenesses, based on agreements upon the truth of things, expressible only in tautologies; anything proved must be grounded in some prior proof, and the chain of proofs itself in something revealed; (6) all human knowledge is based on faith.[1]

However arguable the theoretical points in Jacobi's exposition, its historical contentions were so traditional, as we have seen, that we might have anticipated an unmurmuring acceptance by the philosophical public. Yet such was not the case. Jacobi's publication proved an epoch-marking event, for it brought into the open the underground current of Spinozist sympathy, where it rapidly revealed itself as having swollen to a Romantic tide. Mendelssohn died before his answer to Jacobi, *Moses Mendelssohn an die Freunde Lessings. Ein Anhang zu Herrn Jacobi's Briefwechsel über die Lehre des Spinoza*, was published in 1786; but his cause was taken up by younger partisans, who were made more fiery by the dramatic belief that his demise had been hastened by Jacobi's attack.[2] For his part, Jacobi, announcing that Lessing would have been a 'half-wit' to have subscribed to Mendelssohn's 'purified pantheism',[3] fought back in letters, conversations, and a second, amplified edition of *Die Lehre des Spinoza*.[4] He found himself, however, increasingly isolated. He looked to Kant for help, but Kant was, as Hamann suggested, too busy with his own system to take much interest in Spinoza's.[5] And Kant's own statements at the time seem to indicate

---

[1] Jacobi, *Werke*, iv-1. 216–23.

[2] The opinions of these partisans of Mendelssohn (Engel, Herz, and Friedländer) are summarized in an anonymous pamphlet called *Der entlarvte Moses Mendelssohn; oder völlige Aufklärung des räthselhaften Todverdrusses des M. Mendelsohn über die Bekanntmachung des Lessingschen Atheismus von Jacobi* (Amsterdam, 1786), pp. 11–17. The purpose of this sardonic little tract is to 'unmask' Mendelssohn so that 'these honourable gentlemen' will stop crying that 'Jacobi has vexed Mendelssohn to death' and that Mendelssohn 'out of pure . . . friendship' for his very dear and never to be forgotten friend Lessing 'departed this infamous world' (pp. 16–17).

[3] 'With the purified pantheism, which he is supposed to take for his recovery, Lessing would be, in my judgement, only a half-wit; and for that I do not want to have him educated after his death by Mendelssohn' (*Werke*, iv-2. 181).

[4] The major differences between the first and the second editions of *Die Lehre des Spinoza* consist of eight appendixes added to the second edition. The most interesting of these are the sixth (which contains a comparison of the systems of Leibniz and Spinoza, with the conclusion that though our knowledge of the development of Leibniz's monad doctrine is too circumstantial for flat statements, none the less Leibniz 'probably' could not have attained his pre-established harmony without Malebranche and Spinoza, and that 'eine grosse Analogie' exists between Leibniz and Spinoza in important particulars), the fourth and fifth, which contain a rebuttal of the Spinozism of Herder's *Gott*, and the first, which is an extract from Giordano Bruno.

[5] Thus on 3 Dec. 1785 Hamann writes to Jacobi: 'Kant has confessed to me that he has never studied Spinoza properly, and being occupied with his own system, has neither the time

that he thought Jacobi rather a nuisance.[1] Hamann himself, heretofore an intellectual soul-mate of Jacobi, was sympathetic, but did not really seem to understand the controversy.[2] The young Goethe, to whom Jacobi stood in the role of philosophical mentor, was indeed stimulated to begin reading the Jewish thinker, but then disappointed his teacher, and delighted himself, by finding that he was an instinctive and awed Spinozist.[3] 'I am reading', he wrote in November 1784, 'with Frau von Stein the *Ethic* of Spinoza. I feel myself very close to him, although his spirit is much deeper and purer than my own.'[4] And in January 1785 he wrote to Jacobi: 'I am busy with Spinoza—I am reading and rereading him, and I await with longing the breaking off of the quarrel over his dead body. I refrain from all judgement, but I must confess that I very much agree with Herder in this matter.'[5]

Such agreement was tantamount to a confession of Spinozism, for Herder, even before the actual publication of Jacobi's book, wrote expressing his opposition to its anti-Spinozistic stand:

'Εν και παν. . . . Seriously, dear Jacobi, ever since I've got things straightened up in philosophy, I've always been aware, and each time anew, of the truth of Lessing's proposition, that really only the Spinozistic philosophy is at one with itself. It's not as though I fully agree with it—for even Spinoza, it seems to me, has undeveloped concepts, where Descartes, upon whom he patterned himself, stood too near. I would therefore never call my own system Spinozism. . . . I have been intending for the last seven years or more to do a parallel of Spinoza, Shaftesbury, and Leibniz, and haven't been able to get to it. . . . Dear, best, extra-mundane Personalist . . . . if one doesn't have need of a 'deadly somersault' (*salto mortale*), why is it necessary to leap? And certainly we don't need such a leap, for we are in this world on level ground. The primary mistake, dear Jacobi, in your, and in every, anti-Spinozist system is that God, as the great being of beings, the eternally effecting cause of the essences in all appearances, is a zero, an abstract concept, as we form him to ourselves; He is, however, not that according to Spinoza, but rather the most real, most active One, who speaks to himself alone: 'I am that I am, and in all transformations of my appearance . . . will be what I will be.' . . . What, dear people, you want with existing outside the world, I have no notion. If God doesn't exist in the world, everywhere in the world, and indeed, limitless, whole, and indivisible, . . . then he exists nowhere.[6]

nor the wish to become involved with others' (Hamann's *Leben und Schriften*, v. 152). Again, on 9 April 1786, to Jacobi: 'Do not depend on our Critic [Kant], nor is it necessary. He is, like his system, no rock, but sand, in which one soon tires himself walking. . . . We must be weaned from system. . . . Kant's neutrality should therefore not upset you. . . . You must expect of every systematic thinker that he thinks about his system as a Roman Catholic does about the one true church . . .' (v. 284–5).

[1] e.g. 'This brainstorm of Jacobi's is not a serious, but only an affected outpouring of genius (*Genieschwärmerei*), in order to make himself a name, and it is therefore scarcely worth a serious refutation' (Kant, *Werke*, ix. 295).

[2] See note 15, p. 343.   [3] See note 16, p. 343.   [4] *Gedenkausgabe*, xviii. 811.

[5] Ibid., p. 834.

[6] *Aus Herders Nachlass*, ii. 251–5. The *salto mortale* to which Herder refers is Jacobi's most

Thus the contest went badly for Jacobi from the very outset. 'I know no extramundane God', said Herder in yet another long letter of 1784.[1] By 1786 Claudius was able to take special note of the 'very many voices' raised on Mendelssohn's behalf in the controversy.[2] By 1792 Maimon was saying it is 'inconceivable how anyone can make the Spinozistic system out to be atheistic'.[3] And in another place he observed, sardonically, that 'the profound Jacobi had a predilection for Spinozism, with which surely no independent thinker can find fault, and wanted to make out Mendelssohn, as well as his friend Lessing, to be Spinozists in spite of themselves'.[4]

Thus Jacobi's warning voice, which initially directed the attention of so many German intellectuals to Spinoza, was lost, as the 1780s gave way to the 1790s, and the 1790s to the 1800s, in a swelling chorus of acclamation of the great Jew and his philosophy of nature. 'Spinoza', said Lichtenberg in 1790, 'conceived the greatest thought that has ever come into a human mind';[5] and elsewhere Lichtenberg predicted that 'if the world is still standing in a countless number of years, then the universal religion will be a purified Spinozism. Reason left to itself leads to nothing else, and it is not possible that it could lead to anything else.'[6] 'Spinoza', said Novalis in a famous aphorism, was 'ein gotttrunkener Mensch'—a God-intoxicated man;[7] and Spinozism, far from being atheism, was 'eine Üebersättigung mit Gottheit'—a supersaturation with divinity.[8] In like manner Hegel, writing after the beginning of the nineteenth century, declared that those who charged Spinoza with atheism were wrong, that, quite the opposite,

dramatic single expression of the abandonment of connected reasoning towards philosophical system and the acceptance, in its stead, of faith. This 'deadly somersault' was invoked in response to Lessing's question as to how one escaped Spinozism. Jacobi said: 'My credo does not reside in Spinoza—I have faith in a conscious, personal cause of the world'. To which Lessing answered: 'O, so much the better! I'll get to hear something completely new.' Jacobi: 'Don't gloat. I escape my logical dilemma with a deadly somersault, and you are not accustomed to finding any special pleasure in a head-over-heels mode of reasoning.' Lessing: 'Don't say that; I enjoy it as long as I don't have to imitate it. And you will land on your feet once again' (*Werke*, iv–1, pp. 58–59). Later, after Jacobi explained his scepticism, his insistence on human freedom, and his need for faith, Lessing said: 'In general I don't mind your *salto mortale*; and I can understand how a man of reason could turn his reason upside down in order to get out of an intellectual quandary. Take me with you if it's all right.' Jacobi: 'If you want to tread on the elastic place of scepticism that gives me my impetus, you can make the leap automatically.' Lessing: 'But it would still be necessary to jump, and I can no longer expect such a jump from my old legs and my heavy head' (p. 74).

[1] *Aus Herders Nachlass*, ii. 263.

[2] Matthias Claudius, *Zwey Rescensionen in Sachen der Herren Leßing, M. Mendelssohn und Jacobi* (Hamburg, 1786), p. 9.

[3] Salomon Maimon, *Lebensgeschichte* (Berlin, 1792), i. 154.

[4] Ibid. ii. 184.

[5] *Georg Christoph Lichtenbergs Aphorismen*, hrsg. Albert Leitzmann (Berlin, 1902–8), iv. 56 (No. 277). For Lichtenberg's study of Jacobi's letters on Spinoza, see No. 130, p. 29.

[6] *Georg Christoph Lichtenberg's vermischte Schriften*, hrsg. L. C. Lichtenberg und Friedrich Kries (Wien, 1817), ii. 56.

[7] Novalis, *Schriften*, iii. 318   [8] Ibid., p. 317.

'bei ihm ist zu viel Gott'—with Spinoza there is too much God.[1] 'Have you read Spinoza, dear friend', asked Herder's Theophron, the interlocutor of a dialogue on God written after Jacobi's *Briefe* appeared. 'I have not read him', replied Philolaus:

who would, indeed, read each obscure book of a crazy man? I have heard, however, from the mouths of many, who have read him, that he is an atheist and pantheist, a teacher of blind necessity, an enemy of revelation, a mocker of religion, also a corrupter of the state and of all civil order, in short, an enemy of the human race, and that he died as such. He deserves therefore the hate and abomination of all men of good will of all true philosophers.[2]

But a different Philolaus returned from a reading of Spinoza's works· instead of 'Hass und Abscheu' for the 'Lehrer der blinden Nothwendigkeit', the 'Feind der Offenbarung', the 'Spötter der Religion', there was the amazement and swelling enthusiasm with which Romanticism rediscovered Spinoza:

Am I dreaming or did I read it? I believed I would find an impudent atheist, and I find almost a metaphysical-moral rhapsode. What an ideal of human nature, of knowledge, of the science of nature is in his soul! and he proceeds with such a thoughtful, careful-weighty step and style. . . .[3]

And later:

I come [says Philolaus] with my Spinoza; but almost more uncertain than I was before. That he is no atheist is evident on every page; the idea of God is for him the first and the last—I might even say the only—idea, because he connects to it knowledge of the world and knowledge of nature, consciousness itself, surrounding things, his ethics, and his politics. Without the concept of God his soul can do nothing, cannot even think itself, and it is to him almost inconceivable how men can make God merely the consequence, as it were, of other truths, and even of sensible perceptions, since all truth, as all existence, follows only out of the eternal truth, out of the infinite, eternal existence of God.[4]

These dialogues were first composed by Herder in 1787 and revised in 1800, and their dates signify, I think, the cresting of the Spinozistic tidal wave. In 1799 Schleiermacher invited the incoming century to offer with him

reverentially a lock to the manes of the holy, rejected Spinoza! He was filled

---

[1] Hegel, *Werke*, xv. 374.
[2] *Gott. Einige Gespräche über Spinoza's System*, in Herder's *Werke*, xvi. 412.
[3] Ibid., p. 430.
[4] Ibid., pp. 438–9. Jacobi's reaction to Herder's *Gott*, expressed trenchantly to Kant, was that it was beneath criticism: 'But the man [Herder] is wrong if he is not satisfied with me. I could have, like Aaron, burned his golden calf to powder and given it him to drink. Really, Herder's dialogue, regarded as philosophical criticism, is beneath all criticism, and contains scarcely a true word. For the rest, it is full of lovely things—the dialogue and the form of the whole excepted' (Kant, *Werke*, ix. 447).

with the lofty world-spirit, the infinite was his beginning and his end; the universe his only and eternal love. In holy innocence and deep humility he saw himself in the mirror of the eternal world, and saw how he too was its most lovely mirror; full of religion was he and full of holy spirit, and hence he stands there alone and unrivalled, master in his art, but exalted above the profane guild, without disciples and without civil right.[1]

Either Schleiermacher was carried away by his prose rhythms, or he was referring to Spinoza's expulsion from the synagogue, for Spinoza was, by the advent of the nineteenth century, neither rejected nor lacking in disciples. On the contrary, Spinozism seemed impeccably right in the Romantic rationale. 'I cannot say', wrote the young Goethe, 'that I ever read Spinoza straight through, that at any time the complete architecture of his intellectual system has stood clear in view before me. . . . But when I look into him I seem to understand him . . . I can always gather from him very salutary influences for my way of feeling and acting.'[2]

It is this emotional identification, this sense of congruency, that is most impressive about the Romantic attitude towards Spinoza; while philosophers were overpowered by his logic, artists and writers ordinarily beyond the pale of philosophic movements *felt* his truth. Thus the great poet Hölderlin, during his student days in Tübingen, about 1790, wrote to his mother that there had chanced into his hands

writings concerning and by Spinoza, a great and noble man of the last century, and, strictly speaking, a man who denies God. . . . I found that when one examines with precision, with the reason—a cold reason abandoned by the heart—one must arrive at the ideas held by Spinoza, especially if one wishes to explain and elucidate everything. But there remained to me still the faith of my heart, to which so indisputably is given the longing for the eternal, for God.[3]

---

[1] Schleiermacher, *Reden ueber die Religion*, in *Sämmtliche Werke*, Abtheilung I, i. 190.

[2] Brief an Jacobi, 9 Juni 1785, in Goethe, *Gedenkausgabe*, xviii. 851. We should note further that as late as 1816 Goethe wrote to Zelter that Spinoza and Shakespeare had made the two most profound impressions upon him (*Gedenkausgabe*, xxi. 191). And perhaps no testament to the emotional impact of Spinozism upon brilliant young minds in the latter part of the eighteenth century is more typical than Goethe's statement in *Dichtung und Wahrheit*: 'For a long time I had not thought about Spinoza, and now I was impelled to him by objections to his position. . . . My curiosity led me to the chapter on Spinoza in Bayle's Dictionary—a work as valuable and useful in its learning and acuteness as it is ridiculous and harmful in its chatter and twaddle. The article on Spinoza stirred in me unease and suspicion. The man is first presented as an atheist with highly objectionable opinions, but then it is admitted that he was a thoughtful, contemplative man, devoted to his studies, a good citizen, a communicating human being, a quiet individual. So the Biblical statement seemed to have been wholly forgotten: by their fruits ye shall know them!—for how can a life pleasing to men and to God arise from corrupted principles? I well remembered the peace and clearness that came over me when once upon a time I leafed through the posthumous works of this remarkable man. This effect was still clear to me, even though I could not have remembered specific details. I therefore hastened once more to the works to which I owed so much, and once more the same air of peace wafted over me. I gave myself to this reading and felt, while I looked into my inner self, that I had never seen the world so clearly' (*Gedenkausgabe*, x. 730–1).

[3] Hölderlin's *Werke*, ii. 7–8.

As for Hölderlin, so for the mainstream of the intellectual current in Germany. The serious, the almost worshipful, study of Spinoza became increasingly an indispensable groundwork for cultural sophistication in general. Thus, for instance, Solger, in a letter of 4 February 1807, remarks that

> I want no part of any disparagement of our common teacher, Spinoza. He dwells with me and occupies almost my whole forenoon each day, and my brother has already taught his three-year old son Albert that Spinoza is a smart fellow and that Uncle Charles says Spinoza knew everything better than anyone else. I am still busy with the *Ethic* and am writing now about what I consider of indispensable importance in its study. The deep-seeing clarity and peace of Spinoza's presentation charm me every day to a higher admiration. How very much his perfect calmness contrasts with the heaving and blustering of some of our most modern philosophers. . . .[1]

So flawlessly right did Spinoza seem to Solger that he adopted, to describe the aspirations of his own work, the sublimely humble-arrogant words of the Jew: 'Bald hoffe ich mit Spinoza sagen zu können: *Non dico me optimam invenisse philosophiam, sed verum me habere scio.*'—Soon I hope to be able to say, with Spinoza, that I do not claim to have found the best philosophy, but I know I have the truth.[2]

So too another intellectual with interests more literary than philosophical: Friedrich Schlegel. Observing invidiously that 'Die Philosophen sind mehr ephemerisch' than practitioners of the arts, he noted a single stark exception: 'nur Spinosa ausgenommen'.[3] In short, as an English traveller, himself the personification of non-philosophic John Bull, was told, and the information engraved itself deeply enough on his memory to be transferred to his memoirs, 'the greater part of the German literati were Spinozists'.[4]

But Spinozism, with all its logical and emotional rightness ('The inner consistency of the philosophy of this man', wrote Jacobi to Herder upon rereading Spinoza, 'has struck me anew and quite astoundingly')[5] involved, as we have seen, a dreadful set of corollaries, that not only subverted orthodox religion but struck at the very roots of man's emotional sense of self. For if God is immanent (*causa immanens*) in the world, rather than transcendent (*causa transiens*) or essentially separate from the world, man will have no personal identity, but will be only a finite mode of the world-substance that Spinoza calls God. As Kierkegaard says, 'So-called pantheistic systems have often been characterized and challenged in the

---

[1] *Solger's nachgelassene Schriften*, i. 145–6.   [2] Ibid., p. 152.
[3] *Literary Notebooks, 1797–1801*, No. 1929, p. 190.
[4] Clement Carlyon, *Early Years and Late Reflections* (London, 1856), i. 185. The same traveller has left a useful record of the Spinozist enthusiasm of Coleridge and Davy (pp. 193–4). For Coleridge's admiration of Davy's poem, 'Spinosism', see pp. 198, 235–8.
[5] Jacobi, *Briefwechsel*, i. 377.

assertion that they abrogate the distinction between good and evil, and destroy freedom. Perhaps one would express oneself quite as definitely, if one said that every such system fantastically dissipates the concept *existence*.'[1] Pantheism, as the hypothetically complete form of 'it is' thinking, wages mortal war with the sense of 'I am'.

Alternatively, as Kierkegaard concedes, the corollary of pantheism would be the destruction of man's freedom and of man's responsibility; for if everything is God all responsibility must be God's; there can be no right or wrong, for both right and wrong would be equally aspects of God. As Oldenburg asked of Spinoza himself, 'if we men are, in all our actions, moral as well as natural, under the power of God, like clay in the hands of the potter, with what face can any of us be accused of doing this or that, seeing that it was impossible for him to do otherwise? Should we not be able to cast all responsibility on God?'[2]

And finally, there would be no Christian eschatology of a personal life after death, for at death man would merely be reabsorbed by the world-substance. 'He is made one with Nature', says Shelley in Romantic elegy of the dead Keats,

> there is heard
> His voice in all her music, from the moan
> Of thunder, to the song of night's sweet bird;
> He is a presence to be felt and known
> In darkness and in light, from herb and stone. . . .

A poor exchange indeed for that Christian heaven where Lycidas is greeted by the community of saints,

> That sing, and singing in their glory move
> And wipe the tears for ever from his eyes.

There resulted from this 'rightness' of Spinozism on the one hand, and its dreadful consequences on the other, a philosophical and emotional schizophrenia that saturated both literature and philosophy. If, to 'a worshipper of Nature' like Wordsworth, nature appeared to be

> The anchor of my purest thoughts, the nurse,
> The guide, the guardian of my heart, and soul
> Of all my moral being,

there was also Tennyson's question:

> The wish, that of the living whole
> No life may fail beyond the grave,
> Derives it not from what we have
> The likest God within the soul?

Against this creed, said Tennyson, shrieked 'Nature, red in tooth and

---

[1] *Concluding Unscientific Postscript*, p. 111.   [2] In Spinoza, *Epistolae* LXXVII.

claw'. Thus those who had first welcomed the 'Εν και παν began to shift uneasily under its burden of implications, while those who opposed it on religious or ethical grounds were nevertheless continually haunted, as was Tennyson, by the feeling that Spinozism was the only and ultimate truth. 'It is delightful', said Schopenhauer sarcastically, 'to see how the professors of philosophy coquette with pantheism as with a forbidden thing which they have not the heart to seize.'[1] And, coquetting anxiously, Krause tried, by the coinage of a new term 'panentheism', to exorcize the dread corollaries of pantheism. But Krause's new word merely asserted a distinction without defining a difference (as had Mendelssohn's earlier euphemism, 'geläuterter Pantheismus'), for pantheism, name it as one would, was still pantheism: the philosophy of Spinoza.[2] 'And you are not a Spinozist, Jacobi?' queried Lessing sceptically; 'No, upon honour', came the answer, protesting too much.[3] Spinoza's emotional and logical inevitability compelled assent even while the human element and Christianity itself cried out against it.

It was in terms of this motif, and as a philosophical analogue of the Christian doctrines of free will and personal immortality that Kant seized the Romantic mind. The transcendent *Ding an sich*, extramundane, incommensurable, and unknowable, established by his epistemological criticisms offered the one logical escape from Spinoza. 'But in accordance with what conceptions then', Lessing had taunted, 'do you assume your personal, extramundane God? In accordance with the conceptions of Leibniz, perchance? I fear he was himself, at heart, a Spinozist.'[4] Jacobi agreed that Leibniz was at heart a Spinozist.[5] And so did Coleridge.[6] The judgement, indeed, was venerably old, and corruptingly widespread—most of the Romantics thought Leibniz a Spinozist.[7] And though the whole direction of Leibniz's thought tended demonstrably towards systematic anti-Spinozism, what he actually thought is not in this connexion so important as what he was thought to think.[8]

So when Lessing's words were spoken, in 1780, there seemed, among

---

[1] Schopenhauer, 'Einige Worte über den Pantheismus', *Parerga und Paralipomena: kleine philosophische Schriften*, in *Werke*, v. 106.

[2] For panentheism see Excursus Note IV, p. 268.

[3] Jacobi, *Werke*, iv-1. 69.   [4] Ibid., p. 63.

[5] The third of the six main propositions of *Die Lehre des Spinoza* maintained that 'Die Leibnitz-Wolfische Philosophie ist nicht minder fatalistisch, als die Spinozistische, und führt den unablässigen Forscher zu den Grundsätzen der letzteren zurück' (*Werke*, iv-1. 221-2).

[6] e.g. 'Leibnitz's doctrine of a pre-established harmony' was 'certainly borrowed from Spinoza' (*Biographia*, i. 89). Again: '. . . Leibnitz's pre-established harmony . . . originated in Spinosa' (*Works*, i. 361 n.).

[7] 'Ich bemerke noch,' said Fichte, '. . . dass das Leibnitzische System, in seiner Vollendung gedacht, nicht anderes sei, als Spinozismus' (Fichte, *Werke*, i. 101). Schelling, again, was of the opinion that we can regard 'den Leibnizianismus zunächst nur als einen verkümmerten Spinozismus' (Schelling, *Werke*, x. 54).

[8] See Excursus Note V, p. 271. 'Leibniz and Spinoza.'

the moderns, no philosophic refuge from Spinoza. But in 1781 Kant's *Kritik der reinen Vernunft* appeared, and though the work was not precisely understood until several years later, Hamann prophetically suggested its role in a letter to Herder of 10 May 1781: 'I am curious to hear your opinion of Kant's masterpiece. . . . Without his knowing it, his enthusiasm for the intellectual world beyond space and time is worse than Plato's.'[1] And when the *Kritik* was finally mastered by the intelligentsia, it became apparent that Kant's analyses, the most subtle ever propounded in philosophy, supplied the 'I am' conceptions that could be accommodated to the defence of a 'personal, extramundane' God. Kant himself, though not a man of faith, though an epistemologist rather than an ontologist, none the less made known where his own sympathies lay:

> One must be sufficiently convinced, by the whole course of our Critique, that, if metaphysics cannot be the foundation of religion, still it must always remain as the bulwark of religion, and that human reason, which is dialectical by nature, can never dispense with such a knowledge, which curbs it, and, by a scientific and fully elucidating self-knowledge prevents the devastations which a lawless speculative reason would otherwise quite certainly cause, in morals as well as in religion.[2]

When Kant, finally aroused by the issues of the *Pantheismusstreit*, turned his steely mind to the assessment of Spinoza's thought, it is quite clear that he found there that 'lawless speculative reason' that caused 'devastations' in 'morals as well as in religion'. Indeed, in 1786 Kant published a tractate, *Was heißt: sich im Denken orientieren*, for the specific purpose, as he wrote to Jacobi, 'of cleansing myself of the suspicion of Spinozism'.[3] So ministers, artists, and philosophers flocked to his logic for protection.

And Kant did seem to promise protection. He was in his own mind firmly convinced of the 'Ungereimtheit' of Spinoza's 'Grundidee'—the absurdity of Spinoza's fundamental idea—and he realized that in the system of Spinoza 'freedom could not be saved'. If one accepted Spinozism, 'man would be a marionette, or an automaton, carpentered together and put on strings by the highest master of all crafts, and though self-consciousness would make it a thinking automaton, the consciousness of its spontaneity, if this spontaneity were equated with freedom, would be a mere illusion.'[4] Kant said still more against Spinoza, and insisted on the radical opposition of their thought; but he never balanced the scales in any way by any friendly or praising word about his opponent nor in all his works ever incorporated a single quotation from Spinoza.[5] The magnetism of the great Jew had no purchase on the gemlike mind of the last and greatest product of the *Aufklärung*, and all the profound emotionalism of the

---

[1] Hamann, *Briefwechsel*, pp. 293–4.   [2] Kant, *Werke*, iii. 567–8.
[3] Ibid. ix. 433.   [4] Ibid. v. 110, 111.
[5] See Friedrich Heman, 'Kant und Spinoza', *Kantstudien*, v (1901), 273–339.

Romantic apprehension of Spinoza was to Kant an unreasoning rhapsody: 'der Spinozism', he said, leads 'gerade zur Schwärmerei'.[1]

So for a time the two antagonists seemed precisely matched, each in his way impregnable, each a final exponent of profoundly opposed ways of viewing all reality. As Maimon said, 'without Godhead no world can be thought'; but for a time, as Maimon also said, it was possible, on levels of equal modernity, to conceive of Godhead in two mutually opposed ways, either as raised above nature—completely separated from nature—or as diffused through nature.[2]

Such seemed at first the situation. But gradually the Kantian view began to lose its cogency for the Romantic mind, and there took place that curious phenomenon that had occurred once before, in the relationship of Neoplatonism to Plato, of the disciples arguing the master's position around to the exact and polar opposite of what it had originally been. As Plotinus, Porphyry, Jamblichus, and Proclus had, in the ostensible process of developing the position of Plato, actually achieved an elegantly co-ordinated anti-Platonist pantheism, so did Fichte, Schelling, Hegel, and Schopenhauer, though declared disciples of Kant, convert Kant's thought into an anti-Kantian variant of Spinozism.

The first thinker, however, to show the pantheists an Achilles heel in Kant's reasoning was not, curiously enough, one of the four great post-Kantians, but the anti-Spinozist apostle of 'I am', the brilliant and ubiquitous Jacobi, of whose criticisms of Kant one commentator says: 'If any one man succeeded in discovering the weaknesses that Kant's Critique of Pure Reason, and the whole critical philosophy founded on that book, hid in itself, that man was Friedrich Heinrich Jacobi.'[3] It was Jacobi's restless and probing philosophical insight that first understood that Kant's *Ding an sich* might be a conception open to dispute, in that it involved an assumption of external existence not logically connected with the postulates of the critical philosophy—that by Kant's own stipulation we are in total ignorance of anything behind the phenomena, and that this ignorance even extends to the assumption that anything behind them in fact exists at all. As Jacobi says, 'without the supposition that objects make impressions upon the senses' he could not enter the Kantian system, but *with* that supposition he could 'not remain in it'.[4]

We see how very damaging the intensification of such an attack could be, for the *Ding an sich* provided in its concept the solution to Mairan's perplexity as to 'where to break the chain' of Spinoza's demonstrations. Inasmuch as Spinoza's whole consequence consisted in a reduction of the implications of a concrete 'it is' to the abstraction of 'substance', the

[1] Kant, *Werke*, iv. 362 n.
[2] Salomon Maimon, *Versuch einer neuen Logik*, p. xx.
[3] Zirngiebl, *Jacobi's Leben*, p. iv.   [4] Jacobi, *Werke*, ii. 304. See note 17, p. 344.

postulate of the *Ding an sich*—the 'thing' in itself—by pre-empting the ultimate thingship of 'it is' as unknowable, blocked the Spinozistic *regressus* to 'substance', and at the same time cast the experiential form of 'it is' into a mind-controlled—therefore 'I am'-controlled—form as phenomenon. Once unblock the reduction from the 'it is' by invalidating the independent existence of the *Ding an sich*, and the Kantian philosophy, left not with unknowable externality but with incommensurable internality or consciousness as its ultimate postulate, could easily be transformed into Spinozism by merely relabelling the monistic substance as 'absolute Ego', as did Fichte and Schelling, or as 'absolute Idea', as did Hegel, or as 'Will', as did Schopenhauer, and describing all 'things' as merely ideational variations of the functions of hypostasized 'Ego' or 'Idea' or 'Will'. As Novalis said, 'it is all the same whether I posit the universe as in me or me as a part of the universe. Spinoza posits everything as outside—Fichte, everything as inside.'[1]

Thus, if the *Ding an sich* could be impeached, or relocated as internal consciousness rather than external thing—thereby making consciousness itself an 'it is'—the Kantian philosophy would not only offer no block to Spinozism, but its highly developed analytical instrumentation could be used in the service of an even more formidable variant—dynamic and evolutionary—of Spinozism. So Jacobi, looking backwards from the high efflorescence of idealistic pantheism, could say, 'thus there was founded, through our Kant, quite in opposition to his intention, a second Spinozism'.[2] The historical progress of this second Spinozism, said Jacobi, was that the Kantian criticism, followed through with strict consequence, had to have as its result the *Wissenschaftslehre* of Fichte, and this, in its turn, rigorously developed, resulted in the monism of Schelling, a turned-around or transfigured Spinozism, an idealistic materialism.[3]

Jacobi felt himself, therefore, forced to abandon Kant; but abandoning the rigour of Kant meant abandoning the whole subtly reticulated machinery of modern philosophy. This brave step Jacobi took: he retreated to the one remaining haven from Spinozism, the philosophy of Plato; he set up Plato as his guarantor of the personal, extramundane, theistic God:

And thus the philosophy of Plato is equally far removed from materialism and from idealism; it maintains the reality of the sensible world, its objectivity, asserts the reality of the highest cause, the truth of the ideas of the good and the beautiful, distinguishes the supernatural from the natural, the originating from the unoriginated, the universe from its creator; which means: the Platonic philosophy is decisively dualistic and theistic.[4]

---

[1] Novalis, *Schriften*, iii. 225.
[2] Jacobi, *Von den göttlichen Dingen und ihrer Offenbarung* (Leipzig, 1811), p. 196.
[3] Ibid., p. 124.
[4] Ibid., p. 222. Compare the unfriendly summary of Karl Popper: 'Looking back at this

Since, for Jacobi, 'toute ma philosophie repose sur le dualisme et l'antagonisme d'une nécessité aveugle et d'une liberté intelligent'—all my philosophy rests upon the dualism and antagonism of a blind necessity and an intelligent freedom;[1] and since 'ich läugne . . . dass es zwischen dem System der Endursachen, und dem System der bloß wirkenden Ursachen, ein . . . Mittelsystem geben könne'—I deny that, between the Christian system of final causes and the Spinozistic system of merely effecting causes, there can be any third or mediating system[2]—it followed that all theology reduced itself, not to an opposition of theism to atheism, but to an opposition of God-as-person to God-as-thing: 'Christianity is essentially anthropomorphic; it alone teaches a God who creates the world with knowledge and will. All non-Christian religion is cosmotheist'— preaches a world-god.[3]

This same opposition, transferred from theology to philosophy, revealed itself—Kant having been abandoned—as an antagonism of the thought of two great men, Plato and Spinoza. Thus, in a central realization of the irreducible opposition of 'I am' and 'it is' thinking, Jacobi insists that

There are only two philosophies essentially different from one another. I will call them Platonism and Spinozism. Between these two ways of thinking one can choose, that is, one can be gripped by one or the other in such a way that one cleaves to that one alone and must regard it alone as the spirit of truth. What decides the choice is a man's whole psyche. It is impossible to divide his heart between the two, and still more impossible really to unite them.[4]

If we compare this formula with Coleridge's statement reducing all philosophy to the opposition of Spinoza and Kant, we realize a major difference between Jacobi and Coleridge. Coleridge never gave up his allegiance to Kant, and thus never gave up his allegiance to system, while Jacobi, in abandoning Kant, abandoned all claims to philosophical reticulation, and was forced back to an increasing reliance on axioms that constituted, if not precisely mysticism (e.g. 'I undertand by the true

edifice, we may briefly consider its ground-plan. This ground-plan, conceived by a great architect, exhibits a fundamental metaphysical dualism in Plato's thought. In the field of logic, this dualism presents itself as the opposition between the universal and the particular. In the field of mathematical speculation, it presents itself as the opposition between the One and the Many. In the field of epistemology, it is the opposition between rational knowledge based on pure thought, and opinion based on particular experiences. In the field of ontology, it is the opposition between the one, original, invariable, and true, reality, and the many, varying, and delusive, appearances; between pure being and becoming, or more precisely, changing. In the field of cosmology, it is the opposition between that which generates and that which is generated, and which must decay. In ethics, it is the opposition between the good . . . and the evil. . . . In politics, it is the opposition between the . . . state . . . and the great mass of the people . . .' (*The Open Society*, i. 84–85).

[1] Jacobi, *Briefwechsel*, ii. 354. [2] Jacobi, *Werke*, iv-2. 92.
[3] Ibid., iv-1. xlviii–xlix.
[4] Ibid., vi. 239. As Spinoza wrote to Boxel in 1674, the authority of Plato carried little weight with him ('Non multum apud me Authoritas Platonis . . . valet'—*Epistolae* LVI).

something that is before and outside knowledge, that first gives worth to knowledge, and to the faculty of knowledge, the reason';[1] or 'But the GOOD—What is it?—I have no answer, if there is no God';[2] or 'The belief in God is no knowledge, but a virtue';[3] or 'I believe a conscious, personal cause of the world'),[4] at least an early and radical existentialism supported by a Socratic humility about our universal ignorance.[5] 'All my convictions', said Jacobi once, 'rest upon the single conviction that man is free; this concept is peculiarly my own and distinguishes my philosophy (if one wants to dignify a faith-teaching with that name) from all that have preceded it.'[6] Again, 'To me personality is the alpha and omega';[7] and again, 'my whole philosophy rests on the doctrine of freedom';[8] and yet again: 'There is no reason, except in the person; therefore, because reason is, there is a God and not merely something divine.'[9]

To save this existential personality and its freedom, Jacobi was forced to retreat completely from systematic concerns, for it was his conviction that the requirements of a systematic discourse, strictly observed, always reduced the 'I am' of a living personality (e.g. Unamuno's 'man of flesh and bone') to the 'it is' of a philosophically regarded thing (e.g. Fichte's 'ego')—a view in which Jacobi completely anticipated Kierkegaard—and thus that all demonstration in philosophy led, sooner or later, to Spinozism: 'Jeder Weg der Demonstration geht in den Fatalismus aus.'[10] Such a belief found an alternate expression in the statement that '. . . a philosophy all of a piece, a true system of reason, is only possible in the Fichtian way'.[11] And the way of Fichte, as we have seen, was Spinozism. As Novalis, with his customary acumen, remarked, 'Fichte's Ego is the Reason—his God and Spinoza's God have great similarity.'[12]

Now the mighty Kant should logically, if not psychologically, have been the natural philosophical ally of Jacobi, for Kant had placed his immense authority behind the proposition that 'the final aim to which the speculation of reason in its transcendental use is directed concerns three objects: the freedom of the will, the immortality of the soul, and the existence of

---

[1] Jacobi, *Werke*, iii. 32. Cf. Wittgenstein: 'If there is a value which is of value, it must lie outside all happening and being-so. For all happening and being-so is accidental. What makes it non-accidental cannot lie *in* the world . . .' (*Tractatus*, 6.41).

[2] Jacobi, *Werke*, iii. 36. [3] Ibid., p. 449.

[4] Ibid. iv–1. 59.

[5] The existentialism of Jacobi was, in regard to the fundamental doctrine of the priority of the existential subject, fully as well defined as that of Kierkegaard. As Zirngiebl says, 'It is a proposition of experience that underlies all Jacobi's philosophy: namely, as much and as far as we are capable of perceiving, we see all thought and action tied to the empirical individual . . .; it is the human being—the single individual, the single person, and not humanity as a generic character—who himself thinks and communicates what he thinks, as he understands what is communicated to him' (*Jacobi's Leben*, p. 169).

[6] Jacobi, *Werke*, vi. 231. [7] Jacobi, *Briefwechsel*, i. 436.

[8] In E. L. T. Henke, *Jacob Fries* (Leipzig, 1867), p. 317.

[9] Jacobi, *Werke*, iv–1. xxiv–xxv. [10] Ibid., iv–1. 223.

[11] Ibid., iii. 19. [12] Novalis, *Schriften*, iii. 266.

God.'[1] The failure of the two thinkers to realize their common cause, therefore, inevitably weakened the consequence and influence of Jacobi's position. As Bollnow puts it, 'the rift between Jacobi and his contemporaries, above all with Kant, threw him off his natural track'.[2]

So Jacobi early began to retreat from formal philosophy to a kind of emotional Platonism, fortified against the systems of other thinkers by perhaps the most devastatingly consistent Socratic-Pyrrhonist criticism of knowledge that any major thinker has ever held—a scepticism so intense that Hume himself seems credulous in comparison. 'We know that which is hardly worth knowing', says Jacobi in a climactic statement in his *Von den göttlichen Dingen*, and we

find ways of giving our ignorance infinite new forms. . . . Thus we do not perceive that, in the final analysis, we are only playing a game with empty ciphers. . . . This game with our ignorance is certainly the noblest of games, but it is none the less, clearly seen, only a game, a game with which we pass the time away, rather than truly fulfil it, or attain in it real, essential existence.[3]

Thus Jacobi in 1811. A dozen years earlier, in his *Brief an Fichte*, he had expressed the same opinion:

Our sciences, as such, are games which the human intelligence, to pass away the time, devises for itself. Devising these games, the intelligence only organizes its unknowingness, without coming a hair's breadth closer to knowledge of the truth. In a certain sense the mind even gets farther away from the truth, because when so occupied it no longer feels the pressure of unknowingness, even comes to love unknowingness, because that is—infinite; because the game becomes ever more complex, more delightful, huger, more enchanting.[4]

And ten years before that, in a letter of 16 November 1789, he had written to the great philosopher of Koenigsberg bidding farewell to the critical philosophy, saying that 'our knowledge might well be so wholly patchwork, that not even the knowledge of our not-knowledge could be excepted'—an attitude that out-Socratized Socrates.[5] To Fichte, again, Jacobi wrote: '. . . I have worn my not-knowledge on my sleeve in all my writings'.[6] And always Jacobi stressed our 'radicale Unwissenheit'—our radical unknowingness.[7] Hence his philosophy could make no claim to being a synthesis of knowledge, but had to remain, as he himself recognized, 'aphoristische'.[8]

With the retreat of Jacobi to Platonism, the critical philosophy lost a powerful ally, and the pressure of the young Spinozists upon Kant's philosophy became intensified to such a degree that for nearly a century

---

[1] Kant, *Werke*, iii. 536.
[2] Bollnow, *Die Lebensphilosophie Jacobis*, p. 7.
[3] Jacobi, *Werke*, iii. 305–6.
[4] Ibid., p. 29.
[5] Kant, *Werke*, ix. 447.
[6] Jacobi, *Werke*, iii. 44
[7] Ibid., p. 306.
[8] Ibid. ii. 107.

afterwards the dominant opinion in philosophical circles was that Spinozism, in the form of the Hegelian synthesis, had inundated Kant's thought.
An early example of this pressure occurred in 1786, when a reviewer of
Johann Schultze's *Erläuterungen über des Herrn Professor Kant Critik der
reinen Vernunft*, writing in Nicolai's *Allgemeine deutsche Bibliothek*, and sign-
ing himself merely 'Sg' (Vaihinger identifies him as Pistorius),[1] stated that
Kantianism in its consequences led to Spinozism:

There is rather, in so far as anything exists at all, only one single substance,
and this is the only *Ding an sich*, the only Noumenon, that is to say, the intelligible
or objective world. This limits itself, this is the sphere without beginning or end.
This is the sole ideal of pure reason. Therefore the ideas of pure reason would,
and would have to, in consequence of this theory of appearance and reality,
approximate the form given them by Spinoza. To him, as is well known, the
world is the sole substance, the self-completing series, or the unbounded sphere,
which occupies the place of Godhead. The author's theory would secure
Spinoza's pantheism against the important objection that an infinite thinking
substance may not be put together out of countless finite thinking substances,
for if, in accordance with the author's theory, our substantiality is merely logical
and apparent, if our ego is nothing but self-consciousness, and this only a subjective requisite of the connection of representations, a modification of other
modifications, what then keeps all these representations from being modifications of the sole substance? Likewise reason might find, if determinations in
time, and all the representations depending thereon, are merely seeming and
subjective, that all her demands are satisfied in Spinoza's system, and she would,
after such satisfaction, not be justified in still seeking a special kind of Godhead,
since the interests of truth demand no other Godhead than the world around us.
But, one will say, these are only inferences, and inferences, furthermore, that
place Herr Kant's theory in a hateful light; even though a pro-Spinozistic
deduction might be derived from Kant's theory—which Spinozism, so far as is
known, has not till now been able to claim—that certainly does not in itself
refute Kant's theory. True it is—they are only inferences, and I am very sorry
that they seem hateful, and likewise they ought, to that extent, to prove nothing
against the Kantian theory.[2]

Two years later 'Sg'—or Pistorius, if so he was—returned to the attack
in a long article in which he affirmed the 'Richtigkeit'[3] of his first article
and stated baldly this time 'that the critical philosophy of Kant specifically
encourages Spinozism'.[4] Yet again, in 1790, the itinerant Polish Jew,
Salomon Maimon, produced his *Versuch über die Transscendentalphilosophie*,
a work which he later described as 'die Vereinigung der *Kantischen Philosophie* mit dem *Spinozismo* versucht zu haben'—having attempted the union

---

[1] *Commentar zu Kants Kritik der reinen Vernunft*, hrsg. Dr. H. Vaihinger (Stuttgart, Berlin,
Leipzig, 1892), ii. 143.
[2] *Allgemeine deutsche Bibliothek*, lxvi (1786), 97–98.
[3] *Allgemeine deutsche Bibliothek*, lxxxii (1788), 427–70.   [4] Ibid., p. 429 n.

of Kantian philosophy with Spinozism—a Spinozistic loyalty, incidentally, that might have seemed ironically amusing to the lens-grinder, himself so indebted to the great Moses ben Maimon.[1]

In 1792 G. E. Schulze gave further comfort to the Spinozists by launching an attack, in a volume called *Aenesidemus*, on the 'Anmassungen'—the arrogances—of Kantianism. Schulze not only placed under heavy fire the conception of synthetic judgements *a priori*, but subjected the *Ding an sich* to the most searchingly unfriendly scrutiny it had yet received.[2] By 1795 the young Schelling, ostensibly a follower of Kant, and with Fichte a self-styled 'completer' of Kant's philosophy, prophesied that a new system of dogmatism was about to be constructed 'out of the trophies of the critical philosophy', and that this new system might well make every upright thinker wish to have the old building back.[3]

It must not be supposed that the aged Kant could not, or did not, defend himself against these assaults. In a tractate sarcastically entitled *Von einem neuerdings erhobenen vornehmen Ton in der Philosophie*—'concerning a recent "uplifted" "genteel" tone in philosophy'—he rejected Jacobi's faith-philosophy as 'mystic-platonic' and irritably declared 'Plato der Akademiker' to be—'ohne seine Schuld', through no fault of his own—'der Vater aller Schwärmerei mit der Philosophie'.[4] And to defend himself against whispered suggestions and overt charges of Spinozism, he produced his *Was heißt: sich im Denken orientieren?* In this essay he spoke strongly and unequivocally:

It is scarcely conceivable how thoughtful scholars could find support for Spinozism in the *Critique of Pure Reason*. The *Critique* wholly clips the wings of dogmatism in respect to the knowledge of supersensible objects, and Spinozism is in this respect so dogmatic that it even competes with the mathematician in regard to the strictness of its proof. The *Critique* proves that the table of pure concepts of the understanding must contain all materials of pure thought; Spinozism speaks of thoughts that think themselves, and thus of an accident that simultaneously exists for itself as subject: a concept not to be found in human understanding, and not to be introduced into it. The *Critique* shows that it does not suffice for claiming the possibility of a self-thought essence that nothing contradictory is in its concept (although it thereupon, if need be, remains permissible, of course, to assume this possibility); Spinozism, however, pretends to understand an impossibility: an essence whose idea consists of mere pure concepts of understanding, from which all conditions of sensibility have been taken away, and cannot support this presumption at all, which goes beyond all bounds. Precisely for this reason Spinozism leads straight to gush. There is

---

[1] *Magazin zur Erfahrungsseelenkunde*, ix (1792), ii. 143. Kant saw Maimon's book before its publication, and detailed his objections in a letter to Markus Herz, 26 May 1789. He suggested that 'Herrn Maimons Vorstellungsart' was 'of a piece' (einerlei) with 'Spinozism' (Kant, *Werke*, ix. 416).

[2] See note 18, p. 345.

[3] Schelling, *Werke*, i. 283.   [4] Kant, *Werke*, vi. 487.

H

no single certain means of pulling out all such *Schwärmerei* by the root except that limit-definition of the pure faculty of reason.[1]

In 1788, in the *Kritik der praktischen Vernunft*, Kant once more gave warning of the ethical ravages ensuing from Spinozism, and identified his *Ding an sich* as the final defence against the loss of freedom that follows from that philosophy:

If it be conceded that the intelligible subject can be free with reference to a given action, even though as a subject belonging to the world of sense it is mechanically determined in this action, it nevertheless appears that as soon as it is assumed that God as the Universal Primordial Being is the cause also of the existence of substance (and this assumption can never be given up without surrendering the concept of God as the Being of all Beings and thus His all-sufficiency, on which everything in theology depends), one must also grant that the actions of a man have their determining ground in something completely beyond his own power, i.e. in the causality of a Highest Being which is different from him and upon which his existence and the entire determination of his causality absolutely depend. Actually, if the actions of men, as they pertain to his determinations in time, were not merely properties of his being as appearance but also of his being as a thing-in-itself, freedom could not be saved. . . . Therefore, if the ideality of time and space is not assumed, only Spinozism remains, which holds space and time to be essential attributes of the Primal Being itself. . . .[2]

But Kant reserved perhaps his sharpest words for his 'disciples', the Fichte–Schelling axis ('the two daughters' of Kantian thought, said Jacobi, referring not to Goneril and Regan but to the daughters of Pelias)[3] that was by the late 1790s busily 'completing' the critical philosophy, reaching what Jacobi had predicted in 1787 would be its only logical development, 'the starkest idealism that has ever been propounded . . . a speculative Egotism'.[4] It was 'a second Spinozism'.[5] In a manifesto of 1799 entitled *Erklärung in Beziehung auf Fichtes Wissenschaftslehre*, Kant quoted the Italian proverb that says: we can probably take care of our enemies, but God save us from our friends.[6] The philosophical world must know, he insisted,

that I consider Fichte's Wissenschaftslehre a completely untenable system. For pure Wissenschaftslehre is nothing more or less than mere logic, which, by its principles, never goes as far as the materials of knowledge, but abstracts from content as pure logic, out of which the discernment of a real object is a vain and

---

[1] Kant, *Werke*, iv. 362 n.   [2] Ibid. v. 110–11.

[3] Jacobi, *Von den göttlichen Dingen und ihrer Offenbarung* (Leipzig, 1811), e.g. p. 116.

[4] Jacobi, *Werke*, ii. 310.

[5] Jacobi, *Von den göttlichen Dingen* (Leipzig, 1811), p. 196. The only distinction between the system of Spinoza and the 'second Spinozism' of Fichte and Schelling, said Jacobi further, was that the older system might be called 'Material-Idealism' and the newer, 'Ideal-Materialism' (p. 197).

[6] Kant, *Werke*, viii. 516.

therefore never attempted task, except where, in connection with transcendental philosophy, metaphysics must be infringed upon. . . . Therefore the question: whether I consider the spirit of Fichtian philosophy a genuine offspring of my critical philosophy, answers itself, without my having to pronounce on its worth or lack of worth. The argument of Fichtian philosophy does not concern, as in my philosophy, the means of judging an object, but rather concerns a judging subject, in which case it suffices for me to say that I want no part of that philosophy.

And I must further remark, that the nerve of imputing to me the intention of supplying, by my work, merely a propaedeutic to transcendental philosophy, rather than the system of transcendental philosophy itself, is simply inconceivable. No such intention could ever have come into my head, since I myself have extolled the completed whole of the pure philosophy in the Critique of Pure Reason as the best criterion of the truth of philosophy. . . . There are good-natured men, well-disposed towards us, who, at the same time, in their choice of a means of furthering our ends, behave perversely . . . and there are also, occasionally, deceitful, tricky, so-called friends, bent upon our ruin, who likewise employ the speech of well-wishers, of whom and of whose interpretative pitfalls one cannot be enough on his guard. Yet despite all this, the critical philosophy must feel itself convinced, through its irresistible tendency to the satisfaction of reason in its theoretical as well as in its moral, practical purpose, that no change of meanings, no subsequent improvements, no philosophical system formed in a different way, can supersede it; but rather that the system of critical philosophy, resting upon a fully secured base, fortified for ever, is indispensable to the highest purposes of mankind for all ages to come.[1]

Yet the age turned against Kant. The Spinozistic current, which had coursed through underground caverns until it issued forth into the sunlight of early Romanticism, now swelled to an all-inundating tide. All the philosophy of the nineteenth century, with rare exceptions such as Coleridge, Jacobi, and Kierkegaard, is, either in its open statement or in its implications, Spinozism. It is almost uncanny how Schelling, Hegel, Schopenhauer, starting from the logical elegance of a Kantian position, progressed to the dreaded but inevitable Spinozism; and how lesser thinkers, starting from this provincial insight or that emotional bias, found their way, uncertainly at first, and then with increasing assurance, from transcendental creek to Hegelian river and finally to the great monistic sea of Spinoza.[2]

[1] Ibid., pp. 515–16.

[2] As Feuerbach said in 1842, 'Spinoza is the real originator (*Urheber*) of modern speculative philosophy, Schelling its re-stater (*Wiederhersteller*), Hegel its completer (*Vollender*)' (*Werke*, ii. 244). Karl Joël, writing from the longer perspective of the year 1927, states the matter even more inclusively: 'We should not let ourselves be misled by the conventional differentiations of our philosophical handbooks: the thinkers of the nineteenth century, no matter how much they differ from one another as idealists and naturalists, all seek none the less the philosophical unity of their world and are from Schelling and Hegel through Comte and Lotze to Eduard von Hartmann, Spencer and Wundt saturated with the need to connect things into a unity; in short, they are more or less all monists and pay homage, from Schelling and Schleiermacher

An interesting example of such a minor and instinctive Spinozist of the early nineteenth century is John Stewart, known by the curious appellation 'Walking Stewart', whose works, as Bertrand Bronson says, 'give us an almost unique opportunity to sense the atmosphere of popular thought in the turbulent years 1790–1818'. Stewart's philosophy, which De Quincey called 'a sort of rude and unscientific Spinozism', is, says Bronson, 'an image, surprisingly free from literary influences, of the floating ideas of his time'.[1] Bronson's summary of 'the bare skeleton of Stewart's philosophy' provides us with ample evidence of the correctness of De Quincey's assessment:

The universe is altogether composed of eternal and indestructible matter. All matter is one infinite whole . . . which, if you will, may be called Nature. It is however, incessantly combining and recombining into forms, or 'modes'. When portions of it combine into the mode of man, it becomes active, or 'agent'; in all other forms it is passive. . . . It follows from this community of matter that the interests of the whole material universe are intimately the interests of every individual man. This is the basic truth of morality. . . . Walking Stewart . . . scoffed at the idea of the perpetuation of the individual consciousness after death. . . . Good itself does not remain constant, and no absolute standard of good can be established . . . the Child of Nature . . . will not look for reward to the consolations of a Christian or a pagan heaven, but he will find his adequate satisfaction in the joy that follows from the sublime contemplation of his unity with the whole sentient universe, as he feels his happiness in all things and all men through eternity.[2]

We may place beside this an example of instinctive Spinozism in an extremely sophisticated but naturally antiphilosophical mind, that of Matthew Arnold. Arnold's dislike of German thought is of course a commonplace, and his pragmatic, highly cultivated eclecticism was marked by disdain for philosophical formulations—as we see, for instance, in the insouciant imprecision of his 'sweetness and light', or of his 'touchstones'. Despite these antiphilosophical biases, however, Arnold could write of Spinoza, so mighty had that philosopher become by the middle of the nineteenth century, in these terms:

up to Fechner, Paulsen, Haeckel and even Nietzsche, to Spinoza—the archetype of pantheism.' The nineteenth century 'produced not a single great or original dualist'; the 'word Monism resounded triumphantly from the old-Hegelians to Ostwald, ultimately from India to America, from the materialists to the idealists . . . through all directions, all zones of the century' (Karl Joël, 'Die Ueberwindung des 19. Jahrhunderts im Denken der Gegenwart', *Kantstudien*, xxxii (1927), 477–8.) Again, compare Max Scheler: 'Pantheism was able . . . to express as it were the religious formulation of the German temperament so long as the nation's intellectual life was lost in dreams of an ideal world of the spirit, representing the true homeland of man . . . so long as the nation thought and felt itself to be first and foremost a *Kulturnation*. . .' (*On the Eternal in Man*, p. 114).

[1] Bertrand Bronson, 'Walking Stewart', *University of California Publications in English*, xiv (Berkeley and Los Angeles, 1943), 146–7.

[2] Bronson, pp. 143–6.

His short life—a life of unbroken diligence, kindliness, and purity—was passed in seclusion. But in spite of that seclusion, in spite of the shortness of his career, in spite of the hostility of the dispensers of renown in the 18th century . . . in spite, finally, of the immense weight of disfavour cast upon him by the long-repeated charge of atheism, Spinoza's name has silently risen in importance, the man and his work have attracted a steadily increasing notice, and bid fair to become soon what they deserve to become,—in the history of modern philosophy the central point of interest.[1]

In German philosophy, of course, as we have seen, Spinoza had long been 'the central point of interest', but that even a Matthew Arnold, little versed and less interested in formal philosophy, would note this point some two and a half generations later provides an impressive testimonial indeed to the continuing and, in fact, cumulative power of Spinoza. We also see in Arnold's attitude that almost worshipful emotional response, not necessarily accompanied by systematic interests, that Spinoza elicited in the nineteenth century:

A philosopher's real power over mankind resides not in his metaphysical formulas, but in the spirit and tendencies which have led him to adopt those formulas. . . . Propositions about substance pass by mankind at large like the idle wind . . . [but] Spinoza . . . has inspired in many powerful minds an interest and an admiration such as no other philosopher has inspired since Plato. The lonely precursor of German philosophy, he still shines when the light of his successors is fading away; they had celebrity, Spinoza had fame 'in my father's house are many mansions'; only, to reach any one of these mansions, there are needed the wings of a genuine sacred transport, of an 'immortal longing.' These wings Spinoza had; and, because he had them, his own language about himself, about his aspirations and his course, are true: his foot is in the *vera vita*, his eye on the beatific vision.[2]

So, in the main, the age turned against Kant. Arnold's statements are only one voice in a great chorus of praise for Spinoza. 'Il n'est plus aujourd'hui un esprit éclairé', wrote Renan in 1877, 'qui ne salue dans Spinoza l'homme qui eut à son heure la plus haute conscience du divin.'[3] Upon Taine, upon Bismarck and Nietzsche, George Eliot, Heine, Shelley, Lotze, Spencer, Wundt, as well as on countless literati and intellectuals unaware of the paradigm of their emotional or rational position, Spinozism exerted its massive nineteenth-century force.[4] Some, indeed, began—

---

[1] 'Spinoza and the Bible', *Essays in Criticism; First Series*, p. 308.

[2] Ibid., pp. 332, 340, 343.

[3] *Nouvelles études d'histoire religieuse*, p. 502.

[4] As Heine said in 1836, 'all our contemporary philosophers—perhaps often without knowing it—see through spectacles ground and polished by Baruch Spinoza' (*Die romantische Schule*, p. 176). Something of the extent of the dissemination of Spinozism, as well as its importance, is conveyed by Flaubert's report in 1848 about the death agony of his friend Alfred le Poittevin: 'As long as he was capable of doing anything, he read Spinoza in bed until one in the morning' (*Correspondance*, ii. 83). In sum, as Froude, who was a man of letters rather than a philosopher,

though with the exceptions of Jacobi and Coleridge, belatedly—to recognize and deplore the all-pervasiveness of Spinozism. Thus Friedrich
Schlegel, speaking with hindsight, and bearing still the scars of his own
early pantheism, noted that

> The high spirituality of that . . . error into which Spinoza leads one, might in
> return seem, for the deeper seeking person, to leave open several ways and
> means of raising himself once again to the truth. On the other hand, the more
> suited an error is for taking hold of the noblest and most spiritual minds, the
> more corrupting it is; the immediate consequences might possibly not be so
> damaging from a practical standpoint, but the corruption roots itself deeper
> inside, and works destructively, sooner or later, upon the whole of a nation or
> an epoch, like sickness in the human body that has infected the noblest organs
> of life. Such a penetrating spiritual sickness, deep in the centre of life, is the
> subtler pantheism, which, under many and various forms, has been reigning in
> Germany.[1]

Schopenhauer likewise, just that much younger than Schelling and
Hegel as to feel superior to them, allowed himself to realize the true
nature of the entirety of post-Kantian thought. Though blind to his own
Spinozistic beam,[2] he undeniably saw the Spinozistic motes of his great
seniors:

> In consequence of the Kantian criticism of all speculative theology, those
> philosophizing in Germany almost all threw themselves back upon Spinoza, so
> that the whole well-known series of bungled attempts that goes by the name of
> post-Kantian philosophy is a tastelessly dressed up and otherwise contorted
> Spinozism, enclosed in all kinds of impenetrable discourses.[3]

But these recognitions of the dangers of pantheism were tributes to its
pervasiveness, and, in so far as they might be viewed as attempts to dam
the current of Spinozism, they were swept away before a flood of Spinozistic affirmation. 'Spinoza ist Hauptpunkt der modernen Philosophie',

---

wrote in 1854, Spinozism had become by then 'a philosophy, the influence of which upon
Europe, direct and indirect, it is not easy to over-estimate' (J. A. Froude, 'Spinoza', *Short
Studies on Great Subjects* (London, 1909), i. 392).

[1] *Werke*, ii. 236–7. Cf. *Schelling. Briefe* . . . *I*. hrsg. H. Fuhrmans (Bonn, 1962, pp. 444–7.
[2] Schopenhauer's differentiation of his own thought from that of Spinoza is a marvel of
special pleading and purely verbal distinction: '. . . after I have shown the relationship of my
philosophy to pantheism in general, I want to point out how it relates to Spinozism in particular. It relates to Spinozism as does the New Testament to the Old. What the Old Testament
has in common with the New is the same God-Creator. Analogous to this, in my philosophy
and that of Spinoza, is the world, which exists through itself and an inner force. But Spinoza
has his *substantia aeterna*, the inner essence of the world, which he himself calls God, and in
terms of his moral character and worth is Jehova the God-Creator, who applauds his creation
and finds that all is excellently achieved. Spinoza has merely deprived Jehova of personality. . . .
In short, Spinoza's philosophy is optimism: therefore its ethical side is weak, as in the Old
Testament. Indeed, it is even false and to some extent disturbing' (*Die Welt als Wille und
Vorstellung, Werke*, ii. 738).   [3] Ibid., 737.

thundered Hegel, 'entweder Spinozismus oder keine Philosophie'—Spinoza is the central point of modern philosophy, either Spinozism or no philosophy.[1] 'Modern poetry begins with Dante', wrote Friedrich Schlegel, 'modern philosophy begins with Spinoza.'[2] 'I will have nothing to do with your immortality', wrote Byron, and 'as to revealed religion', he would sooner be a 'Spinozist'.[3] 'When philosophers become religious', wrote Schleiermacher, 'and seek God, like Spinoza, and artists become devout and love Christ, like Novalis, then will the great resurrection be celebrated for both worlds.'[4] 'The true philosophy', said Novalis, 'is realistic Idealism —or Spinozism.'[5] 'The theoretical part of my Wissenschaftslehre, as will be revealed at the proper time', wrote Fichte, 'is really systematic Spinozism.'[6] 'In general', wrote Hegel, 'it can be remarked that thinking must at one time stand upon the foundation of Spinozism; that is the essential beginning of all philosophizing. If one begins to philosophize, then one must first of all be a Spinozist.'[7] And Schelling wrote: '. . . probably no one can hope to progress to the true and complete in philosophy without having at least once in his life sunk himself in the abyss of Spinozism.'[8] Spinoza, said Goethe, 'beweist nicht das Daseyn Gottes, das Daseyn ist Gott. Und wenn ihn andre deshalb Atheum schelten, so mögte ich ihn theissimum ia christianissimum nennen und preisen'—does not prove the existence of God; existence is God. And when, therefore, others abuse him as atheist, I would like to call him, and value him, most theistic, yes, most Christian.[9]

The words of Goethe, like the words of Arnold, reveal a double aspect of Spinoza's hold upon the spirit of Romantics: for not only was Spinoza to them the ultimate philosopher, he was also the enunciator of a new religion. Thus in December 1798 Friedrich Schlegel broaches the plan for a new religion to be patterned on monistic nature philosophy:

I am planning to institute a new religion, or rather, to help in its annunciation. . . . If Lessing were still alive, I would not need to begin this work. . . . It seems to me that this new Evangelium already begins to stir itself. Besides those indications of philosophy and action in general, there is a stirring of religion in

---

[1] Hegel, *Werke*, xv. 374.

[2] *Literary Notebooks 1797–1801*, no. 1027, p. 111.

[3] *Letters and Journals*, ed. R. Prothero (London, 1922), ii. 18–22. We may perhaps be more impressed by the significance of this remark when we ponder the state of Byron's general philosophical sensibility as implied by Arnold's judgement that 'Byron, it may be said, was eminent only . . . by his inborn force and fire; he had not the intellectual equipment of a supreme modern poet; except for his genius he was an ordinary nineteenth-century English gentleman, with little culture and with no ideas' ('Heinrich Heine', *Essays in Criticism; First Series*, p. 193).

[4] *Reden ueber die Religion*, in *Sämmtliche Werke*, Abtheilung I, i. 190.

[5] Novalis, *Schriften*, iii. 347.   [6] Fichte, *Werke*, i. 122.

[7] Hegel, *Werke*, xv. 376. Compare Coleridge: 'Strong feeling and an active intellect conjoined, lead almost necessarily, in the first stage of philosophising, to Spinosism' (*Miscellaneous Criticism*, ed. T. M. Raysor (London, 1936), p. 253).

[8] Schelling, *Werke*, x. 36.   [9] Goethe, *Gedenkausgabe*, xviii. 851.

individuals who are particularly our contemporaries and belong to the few fellow citizens of the dawning period. A few examples. Schleiermacher (who if no apostle, is a born critic of anything having to do with the Bible, and, given the word of God, would preach mightily for it) is writing a work on religion . . . and does the synthesis of Goethe and Fichte amount to anything other than religion? . . . the seeds for the achievement of such a synthesis already lie in Lessing . . . not to mention Schelling and Hülsen, whom I think of as antennae on the snail of this new philosophy, stretching forth toward the light and warmth of the new day.[1]

Schlegel's confident projection was addressed to the young Novalis, a correspondent whose own nature—as his *Christenheit oder Europa* testifies —found religiosity congenial. Thus we can find Novalis speaking of the new nature-religion in the same tone as Schlegel, although with a different assemblage of prophets. The best in nature, says Novalis, is seen clearly by only a few. Those he cites as having the true vision of nature are by now familiar to us:

Fichte will in this regard shame his friends, and Hemsterhuis perceives this holy way to physical reality clearly enough. In Spinoza too lives this divine spark of the understanding of Nature. Plotinus, perhaps stimulated by Plato, was the first to enter with the true spirit this holy place, and even yet no one has pressed further into it than he.[2]

And Schelling, far too rapidly and decisively to justify a comparison to a snail, was indeed reaching toward the light and warmth of the 'new religion':

The seed of Christendom was the feeling of a separation of the world from God. . . . The new religion, which already announces itself in isolated revelations . . . will make itself known in the rebirth of Nature as the symbol of the eternal Oneness; the first reconciliation and resolving of the age-old discord must be celebrated in philosophy whose sense and meaning is grasped only by him who recognizes in such philosophy the life of the newly originated Godhead.[3]

We see that the 'new religion', as well as the philosophy that was to be its propaedeutic, was therefore neither more nor less than pantheism. And pantheism was ever and always, despite seeming changes and developments in his opinions, the sum and substance of Schelling's thought. There are different emphases and different equations, but all emphases and all equations resolve themselves into the Ἕν καὶ πᾶν. Thus in his early, Fichtian, *Vom Ich als Princip der Philosophie*, he says: 'Alles ist nur im Ich und für das Ich. Im Ich hat die Philosophie ihr Ἕν καὶ πᾶν gefunden'— everything is only in the Ego and for the Ego. In the Ego has philosophy found its Ἕν καὶ πᾶν.[4] The later *System des transscendentalen Idealismus* does

---

[1] In Novalis, *Schriften*, iv. 247–9.   [2] Ibid. iii. 266.
[3] Schelling, *Werke*, v. 117–20.   [4] Ibid. i. 193.

not, despite its confident expansions, abandon in any way this fundamental Spinozistic position; there, for example, Schelling says that 'transcendental philosophy is nothing other than a continuing elaboration
(Potenziren) of the Ego; its whole method consists in leading the Ego
from one step of self-realization to another.'[1] Nor in his summarizing
Darstellung meines Systems der Philosophie, 1801, had he in any way lessened
his reliance on Spinoza:

> Concerning my mode of setting forth my philosophy, I have in this work
> taken Spinoza as my pattern, not only because I believe I approximate him, in
> regard to content, most nearly in this system . . . but because this Spinozistic
> form at the same time permits the greatest brevity in my representation.[2]

We should not be surprised, therefore, that in the *System der gesammten
Philosophie* (1804) pantheism clangs forth as from an iron tocsin:

> Everything that is, is, in so far as it *is*, the absolute Identity. . . . There is
> everywhere only One Being, only one true essence, the Identity, or God as the
> affirmation of the same. . . . God is plainly one, or; there is only one Absolute.
> For there is only one substance, which is God, the by-itself affirmed. . . . God is
> not the cause of all, but the All itself. . . . The universe is likewise eternal with
> God. . . . It will be said that this system is pantheism. Supposing now that it
> actually were pantheism in your sense, what would it then be? Supposing, that
> precisely this system and no other followed from reason, must I not, despite your
> terror before it, maintain it as the only true philosophy? The most vulgar kind of
> polemic in philosophy is that which is carried on with certain terror-images
> (Schreckbildern) that have been ripped out of the history of philosophy and
> held up to each new system like so many Gorgon heads.[3]

We see Schelling here somewhat uneasily defending himself against charges
of pantheism. At the time he seemed to have little to fear, but in 1811
Lessing's old opponent, Friedrich Jacobi, still in the firing line after thirty
years, and the man whom Schelling himself, in friendlier days, had conceded to have 'seen most deeply into the innermost meaning of Spinozism',[4]
launched an assault, in a volume entitled *Von den göttlichen Dingen und ihrer
Offenbarung*, on the philosophy of Schelling, and specifically on that philosophy as the most modern avatar of pantheism, fatalism, and Spinozism.
'Spinoza', he said, 'was not merely the forerunner of Schelling's system
of absolute identity, but its inventor and first expositor.'[5]

Yet still the tide of battle ran against Jacobi. Schelling's ferocious
answer, *Denkmal der Schrift von den göttlichen Dingen*, seemed—and heads as
reverend as Goethe's nodded affirmation—to shatter once and for all the

---

[1] Schelling, *Werke*, iii. 450.   [2] Ibid. iv. 113.
[3] Ibid. vi. 156–77 *passim*.
[4] Schelling, *Fernere Darstellung aus dem System der Philosophie* (*Werke*, iv), p. 377.
[5] Jacobi, *Von den göttlichen Dingen und ihrer Offenbarung* (Leipzig, 1811), p. 193. See further
Resa von Schirnhofer, *Vergleich zwischen den Lehren Schelling's und Spinoza's* (Zürich, 1889).

claims of Jacobi as a philosopher.[1] In a different age, Schelling's *Denkmal* perhaps would have seemed scarcely to confront, much less to refute, Jacobi's charges.[2] But in 1812 Schelling's victory seemed complete, for, as Jacobi himself once wryly noted, 'that which is written in the taste of the times needs no justification; agreement takes the place of proofs, whereas the most profound opposition only excites anger'.[3] So almost everyone agreed that Schelling was in the right, and almost everyone became angry with Jacobi. A lonely and anachronistic figure on the German intellectual horizon, surrounded by a small band of unimportant disciples, Jacobi seemed, in the second decade of the nineteenth century, to have nothing more to offer the philosophical world. His 'not-knowledge' appeared a vain defence against the Spinozistic onrush of post-Kantian transcendental systematizing. Few if any found usable light in the existential radiance of those words he had written to Fichte in 1799—words that might serve as the epigraph to his whole philosophical endeavour: 'transcendental philosophy shall not tear my heart from its place'.[4] The publication of *Von den göttlichen Dingen* did nothing to affect the Spinozistic view of reality, which maintained its sway over the thought and the emotion of most of European culture.

[1] Virtually the only voice raised for Jacobi was that of Fries, and that more in the tone of 'a plague on both your houses' than of unequivocal support. (Fries decries 'die babylonische Verwirrung in unserm philosophischen Sprachgebrauch', which he blames on Fichte (*Von deutscher Philosophie*, p. 16).) By and large the cultivated public agreed with Steffens, who looked back on the *Denkmal* as 'one of the most intellectually powerful' writings 'that has ever been published'. 'Schelling', he says, 'has never written anything at once deeper and clearer. The essay must for ever be the object of earnest study; and whoever wants to understand Schelling must have thoroughly comprehended it. . . . Schelling is the classical prose stylist among the Germans. This essay is a masterpiece of German style' (Steffens, *Was ich erlebte*, viii. 378).

[2] See note 19, p. 346.   [3] Jacobi, *Werke*, vi. 159.

[4] Ibid. iii. 41. For a fuller discussion of Jacobi's role and influence, see Excursus Note IX p. 289.

CHAPTER III

Coleridge and the Dilemmas of Pantheism

THE role of Jacobi in German Romantic thought has been emphasized in order to place in perspective Coleridge's philosophical relationship with Spinoza and Schelling. A comparison of Coleridge and Jacobi illuminates the ambiguities of the English thinker's complicated response both to the 'I am' orientations of Kant and Plato and to the pantheistic 'it is' elaborations of Plotinus, Boehme, Bruno, and Fichte, as well as of Spinoza and Schelling. To take one instance, an understanding of the issues of the *Pantheismusstreit* reveals the meaning of the paradox in which —in the words of Crabb Robinson—Coleridge 'metaphysicized *à la* Schelling while he abused him'.[1]

So to metaphysicize and so to abuse, simultaneously, indicate not so much inconsistency or hypocrisy on Coleridge's part as an unresolvable tension of interests. This tension is not only relevant to but actually defines his philosophical position. Coleridge's ambivalences about Schelling, as we shall see, reflect his pervasive ambivalence about a greater thinker, Spinoza. 'Coleridge', reported Crabb Robinson on 3 October 1812, 'walked with me to A. Robinson's for my Spinoza, which I lent him. While standing in the room he kissed Spinoza's face in the title-page, and said, "This book is a gospel to me." But in less than a minute he added, "his philosophy is nevertheless false." '[2]

This inability either really to accept or wholeheartedly to reject pantheism is the central truth of Coleridge's philosophical activity. For Coleridge, as for Hamlet, another symbolic figure from our cultural past with whom, as we know, Coleridge identified himself, this seeming indecision before conflicting claims is a true emblem of his integrity. As with the dilemma of Hamlet, who, not indecisive *in himself*, is confronted with alternatives that *in themselves* admit of no right solution, so with the dilemma of Coleridge: he could not resolve the ambivalences of the *Pantheismusstreit* without diminishing one whole side of his awareness and vital commitment. And so he bore the pain of conflicting interests rather than choose the anodyne of a solution that did violence to the claims of either side in the conflict. Though, as we have seen, the ambivalences focused by the *Pantheismusstreit* were painful in some degree to almost every intellectual

---

[1] *Diary*, ii. 273.   [2] Ibid. i. 399–400.

of the late eighteenth and early nineteenth centuries, in every case but that of Coleridge the conflict was eventually resolved.

These resolutions were accomplished in one of two general ways: by illusion, or by withdrawal. As an example of the former method we may take the ingenious sophistries (some of which we have noted in the preceding chapter) by which Fichte, Schelling, Hegel, Schopenhauer—and lesser figures like Krause—managed to convince themselves that the interests of the 'I am' could co-exist, within a single system, with the interests of the 'it is'. More bleak, but also, perhaps, more tough-minded, was the other method adopted by the somewhat older generation of Kant, of Jacobi, and of Goethe, where the conflict was resolved by a heroic withdrawal from one or the other order of experience. Both Jacobi and Kant, despite their differences, withdrew from any vital relationship with the sum total of 'it is' concreteness called nature. Kant's refusal, in the course of an eighty-year lifetime, to leave the environs of Koenigsberg symbolizes the exclusiveness of his concern with the order of 'I am' abstractions. And Jacobi, confronted with the omnipresent Spinozism of an age that considered nature 'an infinitely divided God',[1] was forced to the essentially un-Christian counter position that 'nature conceals God'.[2] Consequently, in order to protect his moral concerns, he had to abandon nature.

Goethe, on the other hand, willingly sacrificed the whole realm of moral abstraction, which is projected only by the 'I am' in the consciousness of its primacy, in order to preserve the primacy and sanctity of nature. In this respect those favourite words from *Faust* represent his deepest beliefs: 'Grau, teurer Freund, ist alle Theorie, / Und grün des Lebens goldner Baum'—grey, dear Friend, is all theory, but green the golden tree of life. For Goethe the guarantee of Spinoza, that the more we know individual things the more we know God, was a password to the most intimate apprehensions of the warm contours of physical existence; whereas a novel like *Die Wahlverwandtschaften* was only a feeble and belated obeisance to the demands of moral abstraction.

Thus, leaving aside the sophistries of the post-Kantians, we may see Kant and Goethe as representing the two different ways of resolving the *Pantheismusstreit*.[3] The twin summits of 'Bewunderung und Ehrfurcht' are identified by Kant in a famous passage as 'der moralische Gesetz in mir'—the moral law within me—and 'der bestirnte Himmel über mir'—the starry heavens above me. If we regard these as symbols of the opposition of 'I am' and 'it is', we find that the whole testimony of Kant's major

---

[1] Schiller, *Werke*, xx. 124. Schiller, who thought of himself as an orthodox Kantian, shows a special propensity for the acceptance of Spinozism in sophistically ameliorated distinctions; he manages here, for instance, an affirmation of the dualist separation of God and the World at the same time that he blandly collapses its meaning into monism: 'Gott und Natur sind zwo Größen, die sich vollkommen gleich sind' (p. 123).

[2] Jacobi, *Werke*, iii. 425.   [3] See note 20, p. 347.

work is that a preoccupation with 'das moralische Gesetz in mir' leaves only nominal or schematic concern for 'der bestirnte Himmel über mir'.[1] The moral law within me makes exacting demands on living experience, while the full acceptance of the latter leads on the level of theory to the abandonment of free will, morality, and purpose in human life. When 'it is' thinkers involve themselves with ethics, their only historically viable alternatives seem to be the systematic self-interest and fortitude of Spinoza himself (or his Stoic predecessors), or a kind of 'inhibited-aim' Spinozism —the ethical relativism, for instance, of Charles Stevenson's *Ethics and Language*. Of similar purport are the frequent objections of Coleridge, John Sterling, and other religiously orientated English (and German) Romantics that Goethe was a pagan immoralist.[2] Wordsworth, with his confident advice to abandon grey theory ('quit your books') in favour of green and golden life

> Come, hear the woodland linnet,
> . . . Let Nature be your Teacher
> . . . One impulse from a vernal wood
> May teach you more of man,
> Of moral evil and of good,
> Than all the sages can

reveals his love of nature and his pervasive moral concern, but he was far too hopeful in his attempts to link the two. The nature-love of *Tintern Abbey* could allow to coexist with it only a singularly bleak, duty-bound, backward-looking moral Stoicism.[3] A Spinozistic ontology, however disguised and inexplicit, can lead only to a Spinozistic ethic. 'Nature', said Carlyle, seeing the skull beneath the smile after the first happy flush of Romantic nature-rapture had passed, 'as green as she looks, rests everywhere on dread foundations, were we farther down; and Pan, to whose music the nymphs dance, has a cry in him that can drive all men distracted.'[4]

In its ramifications, then, the problem cannot be resolved merely by an easy preference for green and golden life over grey and bookish theory; it is compounded into a gravely perplexing choice. The green and golden meadow beetles dreadfully over the abyss of moral nullity; opposed to it is a chill moral freedom which, though grey, may also be seen as the light of hopeful dawn. And to choose one is to reject the other.

Such a choice Coleridge refused to make. He would accept neither

[1] Kant, *Werke*, v. 174.　　　　[2] Cf., e.g., Goethe, *Gespräche*, ii. 62, 354, 396.
[3] The moral attitudes follow consistently from the attitudes towards nature, and parallel the larger conceptions of Stoic philosophy. The matter has been developed to some extent in Jane Worthington, *Wordsworth's Reading of Roman Prose* (New Haven, 1946). 'Tintern Abbey', 'Resolution and Independence', and the 'Ode to Duty' are especially characterized by ethical Stoicism. Compare the nature ethic of Vigny's *La Mort du Loup*.
[4] Quoted in Robert Gathorne-Hardy, *Recollections of Logan Pearsall Smith* (New York, 1950), p. 56. See note 21, p. 348.

alternative as finally satisfactory, or even as finally bearable, and yet, like Hamlet, he could not bridge the irreconcilability of his interests. Thus Coleridge could complete no *opus maximum*. He could produce no system. He has been scorned by the uncomprehending and the academically inert. But his mind played between its two poles with matchless vitality.

Coleridge lives and gains more life with each generation, not because he completed metaphysical systems, like Schelling, Fichte, and Hegel, whose Procrustean achievements only feebly command our attention today;[1] and not, as Dr. Leavis and T. S. Eliot and a hallowed tradition of Anglo-American commentary would have it, because he was a poet and critic in spite of his metaphysical preoccupations;[2] but because he honoured to the full the demands of a reticulated response to all the data of his consciousness—because, in short, his was a mind of rare integrity. He did not, like Goethe, stifle his metaphysical interests the better to breathe in the green world of things, and he did not, like the transcendental systematists, distort the texture of experience to achieve a completed network of abstraction.

Coleridge's endeavour was always towards system.[3] But this orientation was first of all the need to connect rather than the need to complete. Under the pressure of this need, his understanding expanded in all directions, both inward into the peculiarly human requirement of an architectonic of symbolic forms, and outward to a confrontation of the jaggedly incommensurable particularities of experienced reality.

Coleridge would sacrifice neither the one nor the other in the interest of completeness. We see this integrity, this stubbornness, most transparently in his notebooks, which are now, through the care and scholarly devotion of Kathleen Coburn, being made available in all their astonishing vitality. Though the notebooks are rather the front lines of the 'I am/'it is' confrontation than a systematic study—indeed are in a sense the very antithesis of system—their disorder bespeaks the need for system just as their fidelity of observation bespeaks the integrity of Coleridge's concern.[4]

And they are the best and most characteristic examples of his special virtues. They document the breadth, and likewise the intensity, of his mental engagement. 'Le trait le plus frappant de la personnalité de Coleridge', says Deschamps, 'est sans conteste la curiosité universelle qui le poussait à s'intéresser aux sujets les plus divers avec la même passion, le même désir de savoir, la même intense capacité d'attention et de réflexion.'[5] The notebooks confirm such a judgement. They also confirm House's insistence that Coleridge's thought and poetry are 'grounded in a minute analysis of

---

[1] For the decline of Schelling's reputation see Excursus Note XII, p. 303.
[2] For an early statement in this tradition see Hazlitt, *Complete Works*, xvi. 137.
[3] See note 22, p. 349.
[4] See note 23, p. 349.
[5] Deschamps, *La Formation de la pensée de Coleridge (1772–1804)*, p. 69.

the phenomena of sense. He is far more alert and sensitive to the modes in which sense-experience conditions the life of the mind than most technical philosophers. . . . His quivering alertness to every stimulus of sense was . . . the ground of his strengths and of his weaknesses.'[1]

It is the notebooks, moreover—where urine is reflected on with the same care as the Trinity, where the varieties of flowers are enumerated with the same urgency as the defects of his own personality, where trees and stones are observed with the same fidelity as the structure of dread—that furnish the deepest evidence of the fundamental incompatibility of Coleridge and Schelling. The notebooks record the collisions of a hugely developed sense of inner reality with a hugely developed sense of outer reality, with neither sense giving ground; Schelling's own personality, on the other hand, and his work and way of life were characterized, as Staiger has shown, by an imbalance in which the awareness of the outer world was almost overwhelmed by the energies of the inner personality. Schelling really lived his philosophical Egotism-Idealism.[2] And Jaspers, in this same context, provides bizarre examples of Schelling's 'Versäumen der Realitäten'—of his curious tendency to miss the structure of things and events as they really were.[3]

It was not so with Coleridge. The notebooks testify to a rare virtue, which allowed him to respond to the full range of our common need for connexions. Many have sensed this virtue in Coleridge, but none, I think, has been able to describe its significance, or to indicate its cause.

How many reserves must be made [says Matthew Arnold] in praising either his poetry, or his criticism, or his philosophy! . . . But that which will stand of Coleridge is this: the stimulus of his continual effort . . . crowned often with rich success, to get at and to lay bare the real truth of his matter in hand, whether that matter were literary, or philosophical, or political, or religious; and this in a country where at that moment such an effort was almost unknown . . . where ordinary minds were so habituated to do without thinking altogether . . . that any attempt to introduce within the domain of these the disturbing element of thought, they were prompt to resent as an outrage.[4]

And yet, though Arnold is able to bear witness, as it were, to Coleridge's vitality, his canons do not allow him, any more than they allow his pupil, Leavis, any explanation of what it means 'to get and lay bare the real truth of his matter in hand', nor of what 'the disturbing element of thought' actually was. He cannot explain why Coleridge's mental operations should be either more 'disturbing' or more worthy of the name 'thought' than

---

[1] House, *Coleridge*, p. 14.
[2] Emil Staiger, 'Schellings Schwermut', *Die Kunst der Interpretation* (Zürich, 1955), pp. 180–204.
[3] Jaspers, *Schelling*, pp. 247–59. As Jaspers drily concludes, 'Hegel ist gegen ihn ein Realist ersten Ranges' (p. 249).
[4] Arnold, 'Joubert', *Essays in Criticism; First Series*, pp. 274–5.

those of his intellectual English contemporaries. That special quality of 'thought' most unmistakably Coleridgean is its purposiveness towards system: the 'real truth' of Coleridgean 'matters at hand' was, I suggest, a continuing sense of *relevance* in a lifelong intellectual commitment.

That commitment was as concerned to preserve the 'it is' as it was the 'I am'. We realize, from the notebooks, that Coleridge, like Goethe, felt driven to seek 'das göttliche in *herbis et lapidibus*'[1]—the divine in plants and stones: that he could respond, like Goethe, to 'einem göttlichen Wesen'— a divine essence—'only in and through particular things . . . to the closer and deeper observation of which nobody can inspire me more than Spinoza himself'.[2] But Coleridge, more than Goethe, felt a kind of horror, recognizing that a concern with the 'it is' led towards a bleak pantheism that denied all the hopes and aspirations of the 'I am'.

But if Coleridge the Christian apologist and philosophical moralist recoiled in horror from the eschatological and ethical implications of pantheism, why then, we ask, did he not simply adopt the scepticism of a Jacobi and retreat into the moral fortress of the 'I am'? Why do we find pantheism so omnipresent in his thought? To answer these questions we need to consider another implication of the pantheist position: pantheism, of all ontological schemes, is the one most favourable, on the level of abstract justification, to the poet's art. And Coleridge was a poet, a poet by instinct and by choice, and a poet as much as he was a philosopher or theologian—'Samuel Taylor Coleridge—Logician, Metaphysician, Bard!', as Lamb put it, recalling his boyhood days at Christ's Hospital.[3]

We must emphasize the importance of this double commitment in Coleridge's conception of himself. Most poets are not philosophers, and most philosophers are not poets—notoriously so, in either instance. Most poets who philosophize do so badly, and most philosophers write indifferent poetry. Coleridge stands virtually unique in the depth of his dual involvement, as measured either by the world's opinion or by his own claims. Furthermore, his constant insistence that the two concerns are not alternatives, but interdependences, that a poem implies philosophy, and that philosophy implies poetry, is a warning that we must not attempt to consider either Coleridge's poetry or his philosophy in isolation—that is, if we wish to know what he was and what he really did.

He was, from first to last, always a poet and always a philosopher; the two functions were bound inseparably together. 'Philosophy', which he in his 'childhood woo'd' (his 'dawn of thought') then 'bore no other name than Poesy'.[4] He strongly endorsed Aristotle's definition of poetry as 'the

---

[1] Goethe, *Gedenkausgabe*, xviii. 852.
[2] Ibid., p. 851.
[3] *The Works of Charles and Mary Lamb*, ii. 21.
[4] 'The Garden of Boccaccio', ll. 48–51, *Poems*, i. 479.

most intense, weighty and philosophical product of human art'.[1] 'I feel strongly, and I think strongly'; he wrote early in his career, 'but I seldom feel without thinking, or think without feeling.'[2] Again,' I cannot write without a *body* of *thought*', and hence his '*Poetry* is crowded and sweats beneath a heavy burthen of Ideas and Imagery'.[3] A proposed '*series* of Love Poems—truly Sapphic' was to have 'a large Interfusion of moral Sentiment'.[4]

The interdependence of—the impossibility even of distinguishing between—poet and philosopher was one of his favourite tenets. Plato's philosophy was 'poetry of the highest kind'.[5] 'Plato', again, 'was a Poetic Philosopher, as Shakspeare was a Philosophic Poet';[6] and 'from Shakspeare to Plato, from the philosophic poet to the poetic philosopher, the transition is easy'.[7] Though verses were 'not logic', they should be 'the envoys and representatives of that vital passion, which is the practical cement of logic; and without which logic must remain inert'.[8] 'Why so violent against *metaphysics* in poetry?' he asks in May of 1796.[9] 'Metaphisics is a word, that you, my dear Sir! are no great Friend to', he says in 1802, 'but yet you will agree, that a great Poet must be, implicitè if not explicitè, a profound Metaphysician'.[10] He speaks approvingly of 'that delightful harmony which ever will be found where philosophy is united with... poetry'.[11] Elsewhere he expresses himself as 'convinced that a true System of Philosophy... is *best* taught in Poetry'.[12] And always the true poetic 'whole' is one 'in which the Thinker and the Man of Learning appears as the Base of the Poet'.[13]

Coleridge appears to have been particularly eager to impress upon his

---

[1] *Biographia*, ii. 101.

[2] *Letters*, i. 279. To Thelwall, 17 Dec. 1796.

[3] Ibid. i. 137. To Southey, 11 Dec. 1794.

[4] *Notebooks*, i. 1064.   [5] *Biographia*, ii. 11.

[6] *S. T. Coleridge's Treatise on Method as Published in the Encyclopaedia Metropolitana*, ed. Alice D. Snyder (London, 1934), p. 38.

[7] *The Friend*, Essay VII, *Works*, ii. 429.

[8] *Miscellaneous Criticism*, p. 277. This statement appears to be a reflex of the dictum Coleridge says he learned from Boyer: 'I learnt from him, that Poetry, even that of the loftiest and ... wildest odes, had a logic of its own' (*Biographia*, i. 4). It is interesting to note, however, that a cynical reviewer, obviously well informed, wrote, without further specification of the reasons for his opinion, that 'We may be sure ... Boyer never told his pupils that' (*The Athenaeum*, No. 4192, 29 Feb. 1908, p. 248). Strangely enough, there is evidence that the reviewer knew what he was talking about, for, some fifteen years before the appearance of the *Biographia*, Coleridge ascribes to Edward Young a statement very much like Boyer's alleged remark: 'Young somewhere in one of his prose works remarks that there is as profound a Logic in the most daring & dithyrambic parts of Pindar, as in the "Οργανον of Aristotle—the remark is a valuable one' (*Letters*, ii. 864).

[9] *Letters*, i. 215. To Thelwall, 13 May 1796.

[10] Ibid. ii. 810. To Sotheby, 13 July 1802.   [11] *Philosophical Lectures*, p. 395.

[12] *Letters*, iv. 687. To H. J. Rose, 25 Sept. 1816.

[13] *Unpublished Letters of Samuel Taylor Coleridge*, ed. E. L. Griggs (London, 1932), ii. 282. To Derwent Coleridge, 16 May 1821.

friends his status as poet-philosopher, for Gillman notes—in good
Coleridgean terminology—that Coleridge was 'born a poet, and a philosopher';[1] while Hazlitt speaks of him as 'a poet and a philosopher' and
remarks that in him 'Poetry and Philosophy had met together'.[2] Davy, 'in
the kindness of his heart', writes Coleridge, profoundly flattered, 'calls me
the Poet-philosopher'.[3] That the role of poet-philosopher was essential
to Coleridge's view of himself as a serious intellectual is further indicated
by his complaint, in 1821, that 'I must abrogate the name of philosopher
and poet, and scribble as fast as I can, and with as little thought as I can,
for Blackwood's Magazine'.[4] And the complaint echoes one from a
quarter of a century earlier, that he must go to London to write for the
Morning Chronicle: 'If I go, farewell Philosophy! Farewell, the Muse! Farewell, my literary Fame!'[5]

During the anxieties and insecurities that followed the breakdown of
his marriage and the confirmation of the opium habit, Coleridge for a time
lost—as he says in *Dejection*—his 'shaping spirit of Imagination.'[6] 'The
Poet is dead in me', he writes to Godwin in 1801, 'my imagination . . . lies,
like a Cold Snuff on the circular Rim of a Brass Candle-stick.'[7] To another
correspondent he says in 1802 that 'I have almost wholly weaned myself
from the habit of making Verses. . . . Poetic composition has become
laborious & painful to me'.[8] And in a self-blaming letter of 1806 ('. . . endless *heart-wasting* . . . irresolution, procrastination, languor, and former
detestable habit of poison-taking') he regrets that he had turned away
from 'poetry, and all the flowers & herbs that grow in the Light and
Sunshine—to be meanwhile a Delver in the unwholesome quick-silver
mines of abstruse Metaphysics'.[9]

Such was his opinion in his distress; but we note that even this lament
about 'unwholesome' metaphysics at the same time presupposes the poet-
philosopher conception and defines his malaise as its imbalance. In health
and happiness philosophy and poetry always shared his enthusiasm. When,
for instance, he writes to Southey in 1803 and speaks gaily of 'all the
alleviations' of his existence, these are identified as 'poetry, morals, metaphysics'.[10] Playfully he projects a fantasy in which 'I would write Odes

---

[1] Gillman, *Life of Coleridge*, p. 311.
[2] Quoted in Gillman, pp. 110, 112.
[3] *Letters*, ii. 668. To Poole, 1 Feb. 1801.
[4] *Letters, Conversations, and Recollections of S. T. Coleridge*, ed. T. Allsop, p. 98.
[5] *Letters*, i. 227. To Poole, 4 July 1796.
[6] 'Dejection: An Ode', l. 86, in *Poems*, i. 366. See further Bonjour's *Coleridge's 'Hymn Before Sunrise'*, pp. 13–75, and Marshall Suther, *The Dark Night of Samuel Taylor Coleridge* (New York, 1960) for special studies of this woe-filled time.
[7] *Letters*, ii. 714. See note 24, p. 349.
[8] *Letters*, ii. 903. To Mary Robinson, 27 Dec. 1802.
[9] Ibid. ii. 1178. To Stuart, 22 Aug. 1806.
[10] Ibid. ii. 911. To Southey, 8 Jan. 1803.

& Sonnets Morning & Evening—& metaphysicize at Noon',[1] and, again playfully, he identifies himself in 1800 as 'S. T. Coleridge, Esq. Gentleman-Poet & Philosopher in a mist'.[2] Even when dejected he was not able, such was his nature, to keep the two realms long apart. 'I wished to force myself out of metaphysical trains of Thought', he writes to Sotheby in 1802, but

when I wished to write a poem, beat up Game of far other kind—instead of a Covey of poetic Partridges with whirring wings of music . . . up came a meta-physical Bustard, urging it's slow, heavy, laborious, earth-skimming Flight, over dreary & level Wastes. To have done with poetical Prose (which is a very vile Olio) . . . first forced me into *downright metaphysics* for I believe that by nature I have more of the Poet in me.[3]

In the same letter Coleridge quotes some of his 'poem written during that dejection'—i.e. the dejection ode itself—and then concludes with the significant comment: 'Thank Heaven! my better mind has returned to me.'[4] In his 'better mind', we emphasize, he was 'a Poet & Reasoner'.[5] And if, when in his search for a covey of poetic patridges, up came a metaphysical bustard, conversely, when he examined his philosophical head, he always felt there the throbbings of a poetical heart. 'My philosophical opinions', he wrote, 'are blended with, or deduced from, my feelings'.[6] 'Believe me, Southey!', he says again, in an opinion more heavily stressed and more fully elaborated (in August of 1803), 'a metaphysical Solution, that does not instantly *tell* for something in the Heart, is grievously to be suspected',[7] and to this foreshadowing of Jaspers he adds an adumbration of Freud: 'Ideas *never* recall Ideas. . . . The Breeze . . . that runs thro' them . . . is . . . the state of Feeling'.[7]

Coleridge extended with special emphasis the conception of poet and philosopher to his assessment of Wordsworth, to whom, significantly, he had, during his mood of dejection, once left 'the higher & deeper Kinds' of poetry.[8] 'How shall he fully enjoy Wordsworth,' asks Coleridge, 'who has never meditated on the truths which Wordsworth has wedded to immortal verse?'[9] He praised Wordsworth as a 'great Poet by inspirations, & in the Moments of revelation' but also as a 'thinking feeling Philo-sopher habitually'. Wordsworth's 'Poetry' was 'Philosophy under the action of strong winds of Feeling',[10] and Coleridge's great admiration for his friend's achievement seems largely to have been based on this convic-

[1] Ibid. i. 223. To Estlin, 4 July 1796.
[2] Ibid. i. 614. To Purkis, 29 July 1800.
[3] Ibid. ii. 814. To Sotheby, 19 July 1802.   [4] Ibid., pp. 814–15.
[5] Ibid. ii. 863. To Sotheby, 10 Sept. 1802.
[6] Ibid. i. 279. To Thelwall, 17 Dec. 1796.   [7] Ibid. ii. 961.
[8] Ibid. i. 623. To Tobin, 17 Sept. 1800.   [9] *Omniana*, p. 407.
[10] *Letters*, ii. 957. To Wordsworth, 23 July 1803.

tion. Wordsworth, he says, 'is a Poet . . . he will hereafter be admitted as the first & greatest philosophical Poet—the only man who has effected a compleat and constant synthesis of Thought & Feeling and combined them with Poetic Forms . . .'.[1] And to Wordsworth's terror,[2] Coleridge

looked forward to the Recluse, as the *first* and *only* true Phil. Poem in existence. . . . I expected the Colors, Music, imaginative Life, and Passion of *Poetry*; but the matter and arrangement of *Philosophy*—not doubting . . . that the Totality of a System was not only capable of being harmonized with, but even calculated to aid, the unity . . . of a *Poem*.[3]

If we agree, therefore, that these multifarious statements, notwithstanding their differences in context and focus, serve to indicate a pervasive concern on Coleridge's part with both the claims of philosophy and the claims of poetry, together with a refusal to see these claims as excluding one another, we shall have provided ourselves with a basis for understanding the hypnotic attraction exerted upon him by pantheism. So far we have been at pains to investigate the central core of pantheistic assumptions as represented by the thought of Spinoza, and in doing so we have stressed the agreement of Spinoza's philosophy with the philosophy of Schelling. But now we must note an important discrepancy: although the two bodies of thought agree in their total implication, they differ in their explicit consequences. For where Spinoza presents the implications of a pantheistic ontology for ethics, Schelling directs his thought toward the realm of aesthetics. Instead of the dread conclusions with which Spinoza confronts the moralist, Schelling blandishes the poet with a siren song of the supremacy of art.

In the context, then, of Coleridge's instinctive, unequivocal, and lasting commitment to the conception of the poet-philosopher, we realize from, say, the conclusion of Schelling's *System des transscendentalen Idealismus*, how intensely seductive he must have found Schelling's special focus of pantheism; for Schelling states that

art is the only true and eternal organ and document of philosophy, which always and continually proclaims anew what philosophy cannot outwardly represent, namely, the unconscious in activity and producing and its original identity with the conscious. Just for this reason art is for the philosopher the highest thing, because it reveals to him, as it were, the Holy of Holies, where in eternal and original union burns in one flame what in nature and history is sundered, and what in life and action, just as in thought, must eternally flee itself. . . .

If, however, it is art alone that can succeed in making objective, with universal validity, that which the philosopher can represent only subjectively,

---

[1] *Letters*, ii. 1034. To Richard Sharp, 15 Jan. 1804.
[2] See *The Early Letters of William and Dorothy Wordsworth* (1787–1805), ed. E. de Selincourt (Oxford, 1935), p. 368, for Wordsworth's dependence on Coleridge's help.
[3] *Letters*, iv. 574. To Wordsworth, 30 May 1815.

then it is to be expected, as a corollary, that just as, in the childhood of knowledge, philosophy (and also all those sciences that are brought to fulfilment
through philosophy) was born from and nourished by poetry, so, after its
maturity, it will flow back as so many individual streams into the universal
ocean of poetry.[1]

Rather than pause at this juncture to examine the particular arguments
by which Schelling arrives at his special claim for the supremacy of art, we
may profit more by impressing upon ourselves two important considerations that make the connexion of poetry and pantheism, by whatever routes
of argument one may wish to proceed, so inevitable and vital. The first is
that the heart's blood of poetry is transfused from the realm of 'it is'. If
deprived of that sustenance for long, poetry ceases to be poetry. Even 'I
am' conceptions, moral or otherwise, require, for their transposition into
poetry, powerful fixations upon 'it is' phenomena—Eliot's conception of
the 'objective correlative' stands in the service of this truth, and Arnold's
notorious insistence that Dryden's verse is prose rather than poetry draws
much of its justification from the paucity of 'it is' concretenesses in that
verse. *The Hind and the Panther* and *Religio Laici* and *Absalom and Achitophel*
are masterpieces of the manipulation of language, for melody as well as
for meaning, but their texture consists predominantly of mental abstractions and generalities rather than naturalistically specified 'it is' images, and
this idiosyncrasy no doubt is what Arnold found unpoetic.[2] Likewise, the
human sense of time's corrosion is, by itself, merely a psychological
datum; it becomes a poetic apprehension only when it correlates itself
with a hurrying winged chariot, or swans on an Irish lake, or the counting
of a clock that tells the time, or a wrackful siege of battering days.

But we do not need a catalogue of examples; the indissoluble connexion
of poetry with the external world of 'it is' has been conceded by almost
everyone who has thought on the matter. Literary art, says Joseph Conrad
for instance, in a beautiful and impassioned essay, 'may be defined as a
single-minded attempt to render the highest kind of justice to the visible
universe'.[3] 'A Poet's *Heart & Intellect*', says Coleridge, 'should be *combined, intimately* combined & *unified*, with the great appearances in Nature'.[4]
Poetry, says Shelley in his *Defence*, is 'the perfect and consummate surface
and bloom of all things'. Art, affirms Ernst Cassirer from a different perspective, departs from our perception of existing outer things, and in its
function in a completed network of symbolic forms is not abstract but
concrete:

Language and art are constantly oscillating between two opposite poles, an
objective and a subjective pole. . . . Language originates in an imitation of sounds,

---

[1] Schelling, *Werke*, iii. 627.   [2] Cf. Wordsworth, *Early Letters*, p. 541.
[3] In the preface to *The Nigger of the Narcissus, Collected Works*, Memorial Edition (New York,
1925–6), iii. xv.
[4] *Letters*, ii. 864. To Sotheby, 10 Sept. 1802.

art is an imitation of outward things. . . . Language and science are abbreviations of reality; art is an intensification of reality. Language and science depend upon one and the same process of abstraction; art may be described as a continuous process of concretion.[1]

In brief, if poetic art has the special symbolic role of organizing imagistic concretenesses, and if these concretenesses are viewed in their abstract reference as derivations from 'outward things',[2] then we realize that the abstract accountings of pantheism and the concrete creations of poetry are structures that, though differing in design and use, are none the less reared upon a common foundation: the 'it is'.[3]

If their foundations are the same, so too are the licences by which they build: a free rearrangement of particularities under a universal guarantee of their reciprocal importance. In pantheism we are allowed to view all things as interchangeable and divinely important under the aegis of the ἕν καὶ πᾶν, of the *ex Toto quidem sunt omnia, et ex omnibus est Totum* of Stobaeus and Toland.[4] In the poetic, we find always a meaningful reciprocity of semantic references and syntactic organization within the framework of an understood language: a poem actuates the potentialities of a language and extends our sense of its oneness; in terms of its semantic content, it thus becomes co-ordinate with the ἕν καὶ πᾶν.

Perhaps we can elucidate this by invoking the general view of the Russian Formalists and their successors, the Prague Structuralists, as to the fundamental distinction between prose and poetry.[5] Prose is the use of words to indicate meaning, while poetry is a use of words both to indicate meaning and to act as a dam in the stream of language (linguistically, this view largely stems from the epoch-marking distinction of Saussure between *parole* and *langue*).[6] In Formalist theory, a poem is an artifact of words, an autonomous linguistic structure. It derives its autonomy from two kinds of thrusting against ordinary language: semantically, by juxtaposing against the expected and hence unspecial and unmemorable combinations of daily language a series of unexpected word combinations; syntactically, by imposing an expectation (rhythm) upon the chaotic and unmeasured flow of daily language. Prose dissipates itself in the indication

---

[1] *Essay on Man*, pp. 177, 184.

[2] Thus Croce frankly identifies 'intuitive' knowledge 'with the aesthetic or artistic fact', having first defined intuition as 'the undifferentiated unity of the perception of the real and of the simple image of the possible' (*Aesthetic*, pp. 12, 14).

[3] For additional discussion of the relationship between poetry and pantheism, see Excursus Note VI p. 274.

[4] Compare Proclus, *Elements of Theology*, Prop. 103: 'All things are in all things . . .'.

[5] My knowledge of this movement is mainly dependent on the account in Victor Erlich, *Russian Formalism; History, Doctrine* ('s Gravenhage, 1955), and on the collection of translated essays called *A Prague School Reader on Esthetics, Literary Structure, and Style*, ed. Paul Garvin (Washington, 1958).

[6] See de Saussure, *Course in General Linguistics*, pp. 9–15.

of meaning, while a poem both indicates meaning and resides memorably as a structural unity within the larger unity of language itself. The difference has nowhere been so explicitly stated as by Paul Valéry, who, though not a disciple of the Formalists, thinks much as they do:

Think of a very small child: . . . After a few months of life he has learned . . . to speak and to walk. . . . Having learned to use his legs, he will discover that he can not only walk . . . but dance. . . . He has at that moment both invented and discovered a kind of *secondary use* for his limbs, a generalization of his formula of movement . . . . whereas walking is . . . a rather dull . . . action, this new form of action, the Dance, admits of an infinite number of creations and variations or *figures*.

But will he not find an analogous development in speech? . . . parallel with *Walking* and *Dancing*, he will acquire and distinguish the divergent types, *Prose and Poetry*. . . . Walking, like prose, has a definite aim. It is an act directed at something we wish to reach. . . . There are no movements in walking that are not special adaptations, but, each time, they are abolished and, as it were, absorbed by the accomplishment of the act, by the attainment of the goal.

The dance is quite another matter. It is, of course, a system of actions; but of actions whose end is in themselves. It goes nowhere. . . . But please note this very simple observation, that however different the dance may be from walking and utilitarian movements, it uses the same organs, the same bones, the same muscles, only differently co-ordinated and aroused. . . .

Prose and poetry use the same words, the same syntax, the same forms, and the same sounds or tones, but differently co-ordinated and differently aroused. . . . But here is the great and decisive difference. When the man who is walking has reached his goal—as I said—when he has reached the place, book, fruit, the object of his desire (which desire drew him from his repose), this possession at once entirely annuls his whole act; the effect swallows up the cause, the end absorbs the means; and, whatever the act, only the result remains. It is the same with utilitarian language: the language I use to express my design, my desire, my command, my opinion; this language, when it has served its purpose, evaporates almost as it is heard. I have given it forth to perish, to be radically transformed into something else in your mind; and I shall know that I was *understood* by the remarkable fact that my speech no longer exists; it has been completely replaced by its *meaning*. . . .

The poem, on the other hand, does not die for having lived: it is expressly designed to be born again from its ashes and to become endlessly what it has just been. Poetry can be recognized by this property, that it tends to get itself reproduced in its own form: it stimulates us to reconstruct it identically.[1]

We can identify immediately some of the devices that 'stimulate us to reconstruct' a poem 'identically': rhyme, metre, alliteration, assonance, repetitions of various kinds—all those features of a poem that underscore its specialness and autonomy as a structure of language. More important

[1] Paul Valéry, 'Poetry and Abstract Thought', *The Art of Poetry*, trans. Denise Folliot (New York, 1958), pp. 69–72.

than any of these 'foregrounding' devices, however (all 'verse', we agree, is not 'poetry'), is semantic-syntactic reciprocity, that thrusts against the expectations of daily speech, that uniquely characterizes the language of poetry—that is, that maintains a poem as a poem even when rhyme, metre, and other foregrounding devices are absent—and that we all know in a special instance by Ruskin's phrase, 'pathetic fallacy'.[1]

In so describing the poetic ascription of emotions to things, Ruskin most certainly erred. The 'pathetic fallacy' is not a fallacy, but rather an exceptionally prominent instance of the semantic interchangeability, the unlimited possibility of new combinations, which are the hallmark of a poetic linguistic structure. Vaughan's line, 'Yet stones are deep in admiration', may be invidiously tagged as a 'pathetic fallacy', but the tag then means nothing at all; rather we all recognize the line as characteristically and powerfully poetic. More broadly, and departing from the specific limits described by Ruskin, an 'aged man' who is 'a tattered coat upon a stick' except that his 'soul' can 'clap its hands and sing'; a 'tiger' that is 'burning' in the 'forests of the night', a 'dwelling' that 'is the light of setting suns'; a 'fire' that is 'green as grass' are combinations of semantic references, made possible by the resources of the English language, that are all dislocated from the ordinary combinations of organized references, and are all at the same time admittedly from the high tradition of poetry.

Ruskin's 'pathetic fallacy', in short, is a critical *cul-de-sac*. He does see something important about poetic language, but he misinterprets what he sees as a deviation from, rather than as a special instance of, the truth. Far closer to an understanding of poetic language is Baudelaire's conception of *correspondances*, which, in his famous sonnet, becomes the text in all metapoetry for linguistic *laissez-faire*:

> La Nature est un temple où de vivants piliers
> Laissent parfois sortir de confuses paroles;
> L'homme y passe à travers des forêts de symboles
> Qui l'observent avec des regards familiers.
>
> .   .   .   .
>
> Il est des parfums frais comme des chairs d'enfants,
> Doux comme les hautbois, verts comme les prairies . . .

The synaesthesia of perfumes that are fresh as children's flesh, and soft as oboes, and green as meadows is not only possible but usual in poetic language, which consists not in special words but in special patterns of words, and especially in combinations that place unpredictable 'it is' specifications in a thoroughly predictable syntactic sequence. As Bacon says, the poetic 'Imagination' can 'make unlawful matches and divorces of things'.[2]

---

[1] The discussion occurs in *Modern Painters*, vol. iii, part iv, chap. xii. See Excursus Note VI, p. 276.   [2] *Works*, iii. 343.

Moreover we note, as we think of poetry and pantheism, that this semantic-syntactic tension, with its reciprocity of 'it is' content, is a consequence, in Baudelaire's own justification, of a unity of nature: 'Nature is a temple', and in the 'forests of symbols' that clothe her one tree is equal in dignity to the other, and all are parts of her garment. Thus, even if we were unaware of the historical fact that Baudelaire's poetic 'correspondences' are directly inspired by the pantheist 'correspondences' of Swedenborg, which themselves reflect the 'correspondences' of the pantheist Hermetic tradition, we would see that the metapoetic conception in its own implications is virtually synonymous with the *ex Toto quidem sunt omnia, et ex omnibus est Totum* that lies at the heart of philosophical pantheism.[1]

Again, Blake believed that he might 'see a World in a Grain of Sand'; this too is a Swedenborgian conception. It also expresses that pantheistic licence that allows him the semantic dislocation, in the symbolic realm of poetic language, of

> The Atoms of Democritus
> And Newton's particles of light
> Are sands upon the Red sea shore,
> Where Israel's tents do shine so bright.[2]

The poet, of course, does not explicitly show the connexion between a world in a grain of sand and Newton's particles of light as sands upon the Red sea shore. Discursive logic would find the actual similarity metaphorical, subliminal, and instinctive, though discursive logic is not inimical to the possibility that this similarity might also be demonstrated in formal terms. But it is not the rationalized, explicit, connexion of poetry and pantheism that concerns a poet—nor, except to the extent that we require demonstration for our own understanding, that concerns us in this volume. We are here interested in the *emotional* attraction of pantheism for Coleridge: on the *rational* level his attitude to pantheism is clear and unfailingly censorious. It is not so important to know just how a Schelling rationalized the common interest of poetry and pantheism as to realize that such a community of interest does exist, and has appeared over and over again, on whatever emotional or subliminal level, in the poetic tradition.

A poet, to be a poet, does not need a philosophical commitment, and many, perhaps most, poets are content to leave the book of abstraction firmly closed. In so far as a poet does feel the need for philosophical

---

[1] See Excursus Note VI, p. 280.

[2] Compare Coleridge: 'I have this morning been reading a strange publication—viz. Poems with very wild and interesting pictures . . . printed and painted by the Author, W. Blake. He is a man of Genius—and I apprehend, a Swedenborgian—certainly, a mystic *emphatically*' (*Letters*, iv. 833-4). Schorer too finds the debt of Blake to Swedenborg 'great' (Mark Schorer, 'Swedenborg and Blake', *Modern Philology*, xxxvi (1938), 177). For Swedenborg see Excursus Note VII, p. 283.

abstraction, however, his interest will tend, so the history of culture tells us, towards some variation of the pantheistic view. We have cited the importance of Swedenborg for Baudelaire, and for Blake. To these alliances of poetry and pantheism we may add almost at random: think of the importance of the Cabala for Milton, but also for Rimbaud; think of the importance of Plotinus for Yeats, but also for Goethe. Of first importance is the fact that in each instance the abstract pantheist interest enriches the concrete poetic production. Plotinus stands not behind, but within, Marvell's *Garden*—in its language as well as in its thought.[1] On the other hand, no philosophical interest except pantheism (and there are, of course, poets who philosophize without being pantheists) historically seems to co-ordinate itself with the poet as poet, however much it may ornament him as thinker.[2] A Newton may do much for the poet as physicist, but he does little or nothing for the poet as poet.[3] It is Wordsworth's symbolic utterance, not Newton's mind, that really voyages through strange seas of thought; and Newton's discursive abstractions are, for the poet, a single vision and a sleep. Among philosophers, only the apostle of the ἓν καὶ πᾶν sees what the poet sees. Keats says, as a poet, that 'Beauty is truth, truth beauty', but the equation is instinctive. When, however, a philosopher like Shaftesbury concludes that '. . . all *Beauty is* TRUTH',[4] the equation proceeds from argument, and the argument is based upon the ἓν καὶ πᾶν: 'ALL things in this World are *united*', says Shaftesbury, and '. . . in contemplating all on Earth, we must of necessity view *All in One*, as holding to one common Stock. . . . For scarce wou'd any-one, till he had well survey'd this universal Scene, believe *a Union* thus evidently demonstrable, by such numerous and powerful Instances of mutual Correspondency and Relation, from the minutest Ranks and Orders of Beings to the remotest Spheres.'[5] Or when Schelling says that 'Absolute Wahrheit und absolute Schönheit sind eins und dasselbe'[6]—absolute truth and absolute beauty are

---

[1] Though Milton Klonsky's 'Guide Through the Garden', *Sewanee Review*, lviii (1950), 16–35, has been criticized, the fault of the article is the mis-selection of pertinent passages in Plotinus rather than a general mistake in the identification of the poem's context of thought, which is supplied by the Garden of Zeus in *Enneads* iii. 5. 8–9. For our specific focus, moreover, we can readily equate Marvell's 'Mind, that Ocean where each kind / Does streight its own resemblance find' with the 'inépuisable fonds de *l'universelle analogie*' of Baudelaire, and with the 'mental images' which are 'forms existing in the general vehicle of *Anima Mundi*' of Yeats, and understand that all three poetic justifications find their paradigm in the pantheism of Plotinus.

[2] 'As a matter of fact I can scarcely conceive how a man can be a poet without honouring and loving Spinoza, and becoming wholly his' (F. Schlegel, 'Rede über die Mythologie', *Kritische Schriften*, p. 500).

[3] Compare Coleridge: 'I believe the Souls of 500 Sir Isaac Newtons would go to the making up of a Shakspere or a Milton' (*Letters*, ii. 709). Newton did, as a matter of fact, inspire a large amount of undistinguished poetry in the eighteenth century, but this effect, I believe, supports rather than refutes my contention. See, e.g., Marjorie Nicolson, *Newton Demands the Muse; Newton's Opticks and the Eighteenth Century Poets* (Princeton, 1946).

[4] *Characteristicks*, i. 142.   [5] Ibid. ii. 287–8.

[6] Schelling, *Werke*, vi. 574.

one and the same—or that 'Die höchste Schönheit und Wahrheit aller Dinge . . . wird angeschaut in einer und derselben Idee'[1]—the highest beauty and truth of all things is intuited in one and the same idea—his claim rests upon a discourse: 'jetzt hinaufsteigend und alles wieder auflösend in das Eine, die Natur in Gott, Gott aber in der Natur sehen'[2]—now climbing and reconciling everything in the One, seeing Nature in God, God in Nature. A poet sings, a philosopher defines; but singer and definer stand on the same ground in pantheism. Blake sings:

> To see a World in a Grain of Sand
> And a Heaven in a Wild Flower,
> Hold Infinity in the palm of your hand;

Schelling defines: '. . . das Unendliche endlich dargestellt ist Schönheit'[3] —the infinite finitely represented is beauty. The two statements, differing as poem and prose differ, none the less urge the same meaning, and bear witness to the tendency of pantheism to couple poetry and philosophy.

And so we return to the dilemma of Coleridge. As a poet, his linguistic many-and-one urge and his concern for the 'it is' wove themselves harmoniously about Schelling's philosophical ἕν καὶ πᾶν singing its siren song of art's supremacy and beauty's truth. But as Coleridge moved from the concreteness of his poetic to the rigorous abstraction of his philosophical involvement, the alluring flesh of Schelling melted to the white and dreadful skeleton beneath: Spinoza! And the siren song of art's supremacy changed to the harpy rasp of moral horror.

We may see in Coleridge's quandary an epitome of some of the largest perplexities of the European cultural situation for the two centuries preceding him. We have, in the foregoing chapter, taken the Cartesian *cogito* as the primary utterance, for modern times, of the idea of the priority of the 'I am'. But if to this philosophical context we add an historical context, we will, if we follow the high road of widely accepted historiographical generalizations, see in the *cogito* not simply an affirmation of the 'I am', but a retreat from the 'it is' as well.[4] If we accept the formula—first enunciated by Michelet, and later given currency by Burckhardt—*the discovery of the world and of man*, as a central description of that phenomenon we call the

---

[1] Schelling, *Bruno*, *Werke*, iv. 227.   [2] Ibid., p. 329.
[3] Schelling, *Werke*, iii. 620.
[4] E. A. Burtt, for instance, sees the whole tradition of 'modern metaphysics, at least beginning with the work of Berkeley and Leibniz'—and we could add Descartes—as 'in large part a series of unsuccessful protests against this new view of the relation of man to nature' (*The Metaphysical Foundations of Modern Physical Science*, p. 11), a view that he identifies as having behind it 'the great Newton's authority': it sees 'in man a puny, irrelevant spectator (so far as being wholly imprisoned in a dark room can be called such)', while the realm of 'it is' loomed dark and irrelevant to human longings: 'The world that people had thought themselves living in—a world rich with colour and sound, redolent with fragrance, filled with gladness, love and beauty' gave way to the belief that the 'really important world outside was a world hard, cold, colourless, silent, and dead' (pp. 236–7).

Renaissance, we can transpose it into our own terms and see the Renaissance as a dramatic acceleration of knowledge in the confidence of the twin integrities and mutual interplay of the 'it is' locus (the world) and the 'I am' locus (man).

But—and cultural historians can scarcely, I think, overstress the matter—the acceleration of insight into the realm of 'it is' resulted in the massive shock of the Copernican revolution, an event that tended to shatter the securities of the civilized mind of the sixteenth and seventeenth centuries.[1] Copernicus unaided could drive Montaigne to the sceptical nihilism of *Raimond de Sebond*; Copernicus verified by Galileo could drive a whole age into melancholy. The world had suddenly broken down ('And new Philosophy calls all in doubt; . . . 'Tis all in peeces, all cohaerence gone'); there were unbearable vistas of shards and emptiness ('Le silence éternel de ces espaces infinis m'effraye'). Against such a backdrop of a world and time out of joint, where the 'I am' could no longer maintain its former interplay with the 'it is' ('Man is out of order hurl'd', laments Herbert, 'Parcel'd out to all the world'; 'man', laments Donne, is 'contracted to an inch, who was a spanne'; 'L'homme', laments Pascal, 'ne sait à quel rang se mettre. Il est visiblement égaré, et tombé de son vray lieu sans le pouvoir retrouver. Il le cherche partout avec inquiétude et sans succès dans des ténèbres impénétrables')—against such a backdrop must we view the Cartesian *cogito*. It was a retreat for regrouping, a withdrawal from the shattered macrocosm into the microcosm, cold and bare, but intact. There new adjustments could take place, to issue forth in an ego-imposed formalism that in all its varieties we call Baroque, and, when its power begins to fade, Neoclassic. But this retreat into the *cogito* was a diminution of the possibilities of human experience, as well as a reassurance of security. 'Le cogito', says Faguet, 'assure l'homme de son existence comme être pensant, mais il l'enferme en lui-même'—the *cogito* assures man of his existence as a thinking being, but it shuts him up in himself.[2] Indeed Krantz, in a classic work, has attributed the impoverishment of the whole of seventeenth-century French literature in its response to nature largely to the 'subjectivisme excessif' of Descartes.[3] And, whether

---

[1] See Excursus Note VIII, 'The New Cosmology', p. 286.

[2] Émile Faguet, *Dix-septième siècle: études littéraires* (Paris, n.d.), p. 69.

[3] Émile Krantz, *Essai sur l'esthétique de Descartes, étudiée dans les rapports de la doctrine cartésienne avec la littérature classique française au* XVIIe *siècle*, p. 250. Krantz considers the 'true son of Descartes' to be Boileau (p. 61). And because 'the Cartesian spirit prefers the subject to the object, and indeed only wants to know the object by the traces it leaves in the subject' it follows that 'la nature extérieure n'est donc rien par elle-même' (p. 250). In short, 'in the Cartesian philosophy the world (that is to say, for artists, nature) is sacrificed to man and to God' (p. 251). Though often attacked, the book retains its usefulness. For a study of the diminished role of external nature in later seventeenth-century French literature see Phyllis Crump, *Nature in the Age of Louis XIV* (London, 1928); see also Grace Morley, *Le sentiment de la nature en France dans la première moitié du dix-septième siècle* (Paris, 1926).

we consider Descartes as cause or merely as emblem, we know that English literature also, for a century and a half following him, was unwilling, or unable, to keep its gaze steadily upon that great source of poetic imagery, external nature.[1] For to the Baroque sensibility external nature was the entrance to an abyss that underlay all the formal order of manifested culture. 'Si je jette la vue devant moi,' intoned Bossuet, amid the elegant formalisms of the refulgent court of the Sun King, 'quel espace infini où je ne suis pas! Si je la retourne en arrière, quelle suite effroyable où je ne suis plus! et que j'occupe peu de place dans cet abîme immense du temps! Je ne suis rien: un si petit intervalle n'est pas capable de me distinguer du néant.'[2]

Thus the dilemma. Either protect the ego, the 'roseau pensant', in its Cartesian fortress, or, venturing forth, surrender it to one of the subterranean pantheisms of the seventeenth century. The price of such surrender was all the dreaded moral corollaries of Spinozism, but the *gain* was the joyful enrichment of experience and of the poetical response to it. Thus Vaughan, escaping from the cagework of ego-spun decorums that both protected and imprisoned his contemporary Dryden, flung himself into the mystic depths of Hermetic pantheism and recovered there the rapturous sense of the ἕν καὶ πᾶν that erupted in a splendour of utterance that Dryden, with all his melody, his measure, his craft and wit, could never attain:

> So hills and valleys into singing break,
> And though poor stones have neither speech nor tong,
> While active winds and streams both run and speak,
> Yet stones are deep in admiration.

Vaughan could, however, poetize while leaving the thinking, as it were, to the future members of the Royal Society.[3] Standing apart from the chief engagements of his age, he seems neither culturally nor intellectually so important a figure as Dryden. But his poetry being so much to the good, we are able to find his pantheism little to the bad—if it fed his poetic faculty, blessings on it. It did not pose a formidable threat to the moral order.

For Coleridge, however, matters were not so simple. He shared the dominant poetic sensibility of his time, was indeed one of its law-givers. And in a general situation best summarized by Cassirer's dictum that 'To poeticize philosophy and to philosophize poetry—such was the highest

---

[1] See Basil Willey, *The Seventeenth Century Background* (New York, 1950), pp. 86–92. See also Marjorie Nicolson, 'The Early Stage of Cartesianism in England', *SP*, xxvi (1929), 356–74.

[2] Bossuet, *Sermon sur la mort* (1662), in *Bossuet; textes choisis et commentés*, ed. Henri Brémond, i.207. Cf. Pascal, *Pensées*, ed. H. F. Stewart (New York, 1950), p. 172, par. 312.

[3] See note 25, p. 350.

aim of all the romantic thinkers', he could not reduce his philosophical concerns to a merely heuristic function in the service of his poetry.[1] Indeed, the elucidation of the pressures that forced the interests of poetry and philosophy apart—notwithstanding his desire to reconcile them—constitutes the most important general task in a commentary on his intellectual position.

It is this irreconcilability of Coleridge's two great areas of commitment that accounts at least in part for his inability to complete his major work; it is also, more positively, responsible for the vital tension that has kept him alive and a centre of interest for us. Hence the importance of Spinoza, and of Jacobi. Commentary on Coleridge's philosophical interests has been traditionally concerned with Kant, on the one hand, and with Schelling, on the other. But without also taking into account the attitudes represented by Spinoza and by Jacobi, Coleridge's relationship to Schelling becomes merely a flaccid record of 'plagiarisms', and his relationship to Kant a dreary parroting of now-dead thoughts. Coleridge's connexion with Kant only becomes meaningful in terms of the counter-pull of Spinoza; his connexion with Schelling, only in terms of the counter-pull of Jacobi.

Jacobi, moreover, must be summoned up by our historical conscious-ness for still another reason. For not only do the *Von den göttlichen Dingen* and the *Jacobi an Fichte* focus for us the moralist's objections to the im-plications of post-Kantian pantheism, but Jacobi's *Ueber die Lehre des Spinoza* is historically necessary to the very definition of the opposition between Spinoza and Kant himself. Without that work, the problem of Spinozism would never have engaged Kant's mind. Jacobi, in short, more than any other philosopher, makes dramatic for us the supreme importance of pantheism for Coleridge. If it were not for Jacobi, we should be likely to toss away as a verbal pebble a word—pantheism—that actually con-stitutes a Himalayan reality in Coleridge's mental activity. Wellek, for instance, committed as he is to a conception of Coleridge as Schelling's disciple, seriously under-estimates, despite a formal awareness of pan-theism as a problem in Coleridge's thought, the scope and intensity of Coleridge's preoccupation with that problem. 'It would be a misunder-standing of the workings of Coleridge's mind', he says, 'to conclude that adherence to Schelling's views was only a passing phase: Coleridge simply wanted to separate himself from pantheism. . . . This did not prevent him

---

[1] *Essay on Man*, p. 199. Cassirer then quotes a well-known aphorism of Novalis that 'Poetry is what is absolutely and genuinely real. That is the kernel of my philosophy. The more poetic, the more true.' But this subordinates philosophy to poetry, while for Coleridge the two functions existed for the service of two needs. Again Novalis states elsewhere that 'poetry is the key, as it were, to philosophy—its goal and its meaning . . .' For an analogue to this attitude, compare A. W. Schlegel: 'Der Dichter kann wenig vom Philosophen, dieser aber viel von jenem lernen.'

from absorbing and using Schelling's ideas and vocabulary. . . '[1] In this view, Coleridge's rejection of Schelling as a pantheist is seen as merely another random Coleridgean quirk, not the massive, coherent, and reticulated opposition that, as we have seen from the preceding chapter, such a rejection would necessarily entail. 'To separate himself from pantheism' —because he 'simply wanted to'—becomes in a context without Jacobi an action of the same order as, when we are at dinner and the hostess asks if we will have some asparagus, to say, 'No thank you, I do not care for asparagus.'[2]

Our argument, on the contrary, is that Coleridge's rejection of pantheism was not the idiosyncratic rejection of a limited area of experience (like, for instance, his animus against Dr. Johnson), but rather a stand against a total ordering of symbolic forms that presented—at a price—a thinking man with a reticulation of reality: with a world of things and with a man's place in that world. This truth about the meaning of pantheism can scarcely be over-emphasized, especially in the light of the term's literary-historical status as one of those vast general words ('Platonism' and 'transcendentalism' are perhaps its two chief fellows) that we allow to be thrown about mightily by almost anyone able to string sentences together. It is almost as though literary commentators have entered a kind of silent conspiracy never to challenge one another as to the exact meaning of these ideas, or as to the appropriateness of their invocation. Indeed, it sometimes seems as though complete understandings of 'pantheism', of 'Platonism', and of 'transcendentalism' are, like freedom of speech and the franchise, the born rights of every citizen of a democracy.[3] In fact, however, all these cultural terms refer to the real and complex thoughts of real and complex people, and they should no more be sprinkled, undefined and unexamined, through literary history and commentary, than should formulas from quantum mechanics. And since our critical response to 'pantheism' is dulled by the conventions of literary historiography, it thus becomes useful to expand pantheism's implications by means of Jacobi.

Jacobi has, in fact, long been a figure standing mysteriously but importantly on the periphery of Coleridgean commentary. The first to take notice of his relevance was Shedd, who, noting a similarity of orientation between the *Aids to Reflection* and Jacobi's *Von den göttlichen Dingen*, went on to a broader comparison. . . . 'Speaking generally,' he said, 'Coleridge stands in nearly the same relation to English Philosophy, that Jacobi does

---

[1] Wellek, *A History of Modern Criticism 1750–1950*, ii. 154.

[2] Equally arbitrary is Max Schulz's statement that Coleridge's 'horror of pantheism is sufficiently pervasive in his writings . . . that it needs no documentation' (*The Poetic Voices of Coleridge* (Detroit, 1963), p. 41).

[3] Compare Montaigne's complaint, which applies today as well as it did in the sixteenth century: 'Voyes demener et agiter Platon. . . .'—Look at the way Plato gets thrown around; everybody wants him on his side, so he gets twisted around to fit (*Essais*, ii. 347).

to that of Germany. . . . The resemblance between Coleridge and Jacobi is very striking.'[1] In so far as Shedd identifies opposition to pantheism as the single, central, irreducible fact, and the motive force, of the philosophical thought both of Coleridge and of Jacobi, his judgement is correct and very useful. In so far, however, as we tend to read that judgement as indicating a similarity between Coleridge and Jacobi in the internal reticulation of their thought—in matters of style, tone, and emphasis—we shall be misled.

Our task, indeed, is not only to show Coleridge's similarity to central traditions of continental thought, but to indicate also the idiosyncratic differences that make it unrewarding to view him as merely an English voice for that thought. While Jacobi's mind was more orderly and precise, more focused and accurate than Coleridge's, Coleridge's mind possessed more colour, more nuance, and, above all, more range than Jacobi's. For Jacobi, the struggle to reject pantheism, difficult though it was, could be won at the cost of systematic involvements in philosophy. For Coleridge, the same struggle cost not only the fufilment of his commitment to system, but threatened the very life of his poetic faculty as well. Jacobi had no system because he abandoned system; Coleridge had no system because he was enmeshed in too full an allegiance to system.

Above all, Jacobi withdrew from a preoccupation with external nature, and therefore necessarily withdrew from a commitment to high art. 'Speculation', said Goethe once, if not fairly, at least not inaccurately, 'has been Jacobi's misfortune. . . . He has lacked knowledge of the natural sciences and has not been able to conceive a large view of the world by means of moral postulates alone.'[2] In terms of the common interest of the 'it is' and art that we have just stressed, such a lack would involve also a withdrawal from art. Novalis too said that Jacobi had no art sense.[3] Such, we suggest, is in substance the final and irreconcilable difference between Coleridge and Jacobi. Coleridge was—and so thought of himself—equally and inseparably poet and philosopher; while Jacobi was—and so thought of himself—almost exclusively a moralist.[4]

Because they had so much in common, and yet at the same time were so different, Coleridge's attitude towards Jacobi was naturally ambivalent. In a marginal note in Jacobi's *Werke*, for instance, Coleridge's tone is unfriendly: 'Jacobi too often betrays a captious envious bissigen Geist.'[5] Another is equally censorious: 'O shame to Jacobi! O shame and double shame to Schelling, his Antagonist!'[6] And remarks such as these led Lindsay to conclude, with Muirhead, 'that the whole trend of S. T. C.'s meta-

[1] Shedd, Introduction to *The Complete Works*, I. 26.
[2] Goethe, *Gespräche*, iii. 161, no. 2309.
[3] *Schriften*, iii. 312.   [4] See Excursus Note IX, p. 292.
[5] J. I. Lindsay, 'Coleridge Marginalia in Jacobi's *Werke*', *MLN*, l (1935), 219.
[6] Ibid., pp. 219-20.

physical thought is in conflict with the way of mysticism represented by Jacobi.'[1]

We may set Lindsay's opinion over against that of Shedd; we cannot, however, accept it as more than a portion of the truth. That aspect of Coleridge's intellectual involvement that made him a poet was indeed opposed to Jacobi's Pyrrhonism. Bollnow finds 'enmity to nature' a distinguishing fundamental of Jacobi's thought.[2] Coleridge, on the other hand, never rejected the external world, and, in fact, ultimately found neither Kant nor Plato sufficiently orientated towards nature to satisfy him—ultimately only Christianity satisfied him, and Christianity not only provides the strongest moral guarantees for the integrity of the human personality, but also, significantly, turns our eyes towards nature as the handiwork of God. 'A scheme of the Christian faith', said Coleridge, 'which does not arise out of, and shoot its beams downwards into, the scheme of nature, but stands aloof as an insulated afterthought, must be false or distorted in all its particulars.'[3]

In this stubborn insistence on rendering to both the ego and the external world the full due of each, we see not only Coleridge's harmonizing, outgoing concern, but, as its substructure, a primary attitude of intellectual conservatism. Coleridge was not by temperament a radical. Rather he tended, by instinct as well as by choice, towards a respectful defence of traditional premises: of the intuitive importance of nature, of established intellectual modes, of the authority supplied by minds of the past. Indeed, from some of his utterances we may even wonder if his bizarre methods of composition that we call 'plagiarism' are not largely explicable as a distorted reflection of his conservatism, of his instinctive respect for 'venerable Forefathers'. 'Those only', he says in November of 1803, 'who feel no originality, no consciousness of having received their Thoughts & opinions from immediate Inspiration, are anxious to be thought originals—the certainty & feeling is enough for the other, & he rejoices to find his opinions plumed & winged with the authority of venerable Forefathers.'[4] Coleridge, in any event, was a thoroughgoing intellectual conservative, with few rebellious impulses:

[1] Ibid., p. 224. The view that Lindsay supports is enunciated in Muirhead's article 'Metaphysician or Mystic?', in Coleridge; Studies by Several Hands on the Hundredth Anniversary of his Death, ed. Edmund Blunden and E. L. Griggs (London, 1934), pp. 179–97. Lindsay tends to deny any meaningful relation between Coleridge and Jacobi at all, apparently because he conceives 'relation' only as servicing the literary convention of 'influence', and if b-follows-a 'influence' is absent, then 'relation' is also absent: 'Instead of holding . . . that Coleridge's relation . . . to Jacobi was of longer duration and deeper than that to Schelling, I should prefer to believe that there was no important relation at all, and that even what knowledge he had of Jacobi was chiefly incidental to his one-time interest in Schelling and most casual' (Lindsay, pp. 225 n.–226 n.). It is not true, of course, that Coleridge's knowledge of Jacobi arose from his 'interest in Schelling.' See below, p. 131, note 4.

[2] Die Lebensphilosophie Jacobis, p. 244.   [3] Works, v. 113.

[4] Notebooks, i. 1695. It is unfortunate that Coleridge was under pressure from the Romantic

What is it [he asks], that I employ my Metaphysics on? To perplex our clearest notions, & living moral Instincts? To extinguish the Light of Love & of Conscience, to put out the Life of Arbitrement—to make myself & others ... *Worthless, Soul-less, God* less?—No! To expose the Folly & the Legerdemain of those, who have thus abused the blessed Organ of Language, to support all old & venerable Truths, to support, to kindle, to project, to make the Reason spread Light over our Feelings, to make our Feelings diffuse vital Warmth thro' our Reason—these are my Objects—& these my Subjects.[1]

Jacobi's temperament, on the other hand, was quite different. Not, as Lindsay thought, a 'mystic', he was rather, even in his *Gefühlsphilosophie*, a radical rationalist. Coleridge participated naturally in that upsurge of religiosity that marked early Romanticism in almost all its forms. Jacobi, on the contrary, was a product of the *Aufklärung*; he was by nature far closer to the religious scepticism of Diderot or Voltaire than to the piety of Novalis or Chateaubriand.[2] Though his faith goes beyond reason, it is built upon rational foundations; and his final assertions are not mysticism (which is, indeed, always a form of pantheism)[3] but a variant of the *credo ut intelligam*. Bollnow, in fact, goes so far in his recognition of the fundamental rationalism of Jacobi as to assert that he 'was basically—at least in a Christian sense—an unreligious man; that is decisive for our understanding of him'.[4] This sense of Jacobi, not as a Romantic but as an apostate from the *Aufklärung*, permeates, for instance, a conversation noted by Crabb Robinson:

An interesting chat with Fritz Schlosser about the men of the last age—our youth. He said that F. Jacobi anxiously wished to be a Christian, and would hail him as a benefactor who should relieve him from his doubts. . . . He hated Kantianism because he thought it wanted life and feeling. He loved Spinoza's

requirement for 'originality'. Otherwise he might have been able to justify his conservative tendency more wholeheartedly, and been spared the guilt and self-loathing ensuing from 'plagiarism'. 'I regard truth as a divine ventriloquist', he says in the *Biographia*, 'I care not from whose mouth the sounds are supposed to proceed, if only the words are audible and intelligible' (*Biographia*, i. 105). But we may perhaps infer the depths of the self-degradation that this urge, weighted down by the rhetoric and prejudices of Romanticism, plumbed in his tormented psyche; indeed, self-loathing seems poignantly present in another statement of the idea: '. . . from whatever dirty Corner, or Straw Moppet, the Ventriloquist Truth causes her words to proceed, I not only listen but must bear witness that it is *Truth* talking' (*Letters*, iv. 979). If only Coleridge had had another rhetoric of justification at his disposal—even Montaigne's puckish explanation would have been better than the spurious involvement in 'originality'. See n. 26, p. 351.

[1] *Notebooks*, i. 1623.   [2] See Excursus Note IX, p. 295.

[3] If we accept Underhill's distinction between 'mystic' and 'mystical philosopher' (*Mysticism*, p. 114), we might concede that the former, as he is defined only by the mystical experience, need not be a pantheist—but only because he is not a schematist at all, but a claimant to the ineffable. In that case he is of no cultural concern to us. Only the 'mystical philosopher' affects the stream of culture, and the 'mystical philosopher' is always a pantheist. There are, I think, no exceptions. 'The feeling of the world as a limited whole', says Wittgenstein simply, 'is the mystical feeling' (*Tractatus* 6. 45). See note 27, p. 351.

[4] Bollnow, p. 107. 'No other philosopher', said Schelling, 'conceded so much to pure rationalism as did Jacobi' (*Werke*, x. 168).

character, but thought himself wronged in being treated as his follower. He was fond of quoting Pascal and Hemsterhusius.[1]

Bollnow notes that whenever Jacobi utilizes 'specific Christian concepts' he 'secularizes' them, and that this secularization of religious concepts is the intrinsic character of the Jacobian faith philosophy.[2]

Thus we repeat that, however similar Jacobi and Coleridge are in some important respects, in other important respects they are not alike at all. While—as we shall presently see in more detail—Coleridge is at one with Jacobi on the magnitude of the pantheistic problem and the deadly effect of pantheism, his religiosity stands in contrast to Jacobi's secularity, his conservatism stands in contrast to Jacobi's radicalism, his commitment to system stands in contrast to Jacobi's rejection of system, his commitment to poetry and to external nature stands in contrast to Jacobi's aphoristic utterance and his retreat into the ego. If, as Faguet observes, the *cogito* both assures man of his existence and shuts him up in himself, we can well see this same ambivalence of strength and limitation in Jacobi's characteristic statement that 'Die Menschen suchen nicht Wahrheit, Gerechtigkeit, Freiheit; sie suchen nur sich selbst: und wüßten sie nur sich selbst recht zu suchen'—men do not seek truth, justice, freedom; they seek only themselves—and if they only knew how to seek themselves aright.[3] A beautiful statement, indeed, but at the same time far closer to the eighteenth century's belief that the proper study of mankind is man than to the attitudes of Romanticism.

But these differences between Coleridge and Jacobi, important though they are, still do not justify Lindsay's emphasis on the antipathy of Coleridge to Jacobi, nor do they justify his belief that Coleridge's knowledge of Jacobi's thought was superficial and not long standing.[4] In a note of 1810 Crabb Robinson says that 'Coleridge warmly praised Spinoza, Jacobi on Spinoza, and Schiller "Ueber die Sendung Moses," &c.'[5] Again, in 1812, Coleridge wrote to obtain Robinson's help in finding some books, and specified that Robinson should 'not forget Jacobi to Fichte'.[6] In his marginalia to a copy of the second edition of *Ueber die Lehre des Spinoza*, recently published by Schrickx, Coleridge's tone, furthermore, seems very respectful towards Jacobi—e.g. 'Here Jacobi's Eagle's wing seem to me to flag. . .'[7] And in a marginal note to a volume entitled *Lessing's Leben*, Coleridge emphasizes, in a tone sympathetic to Jacobi, details of Jacobi's

---

[1] Crabb Robinson, *Diary*, iii. 49.
[2] Bollnow, pp. 107–8.   [3] Jacobi, *Werke*, vi. 151.
[4] It is possible to identify—with considerable inferential certainty—the occasion of Coleridge's first acquaintance with Jacobi's work. See Excursus Note IX, p. 296.
[5] Crabb Robinson, *Diary*, i. 309.
[6] *Letters*, iii. 422.
[7] W. Schrickx, 'Coleridge and Friedrich Heinrich Jacobi', *Revue belge de philologie et d'histoire*, xxxvi, Pt. 3 (1958), 843.

thought that seem—to my ear at least—to indicate a very precise knowledge of the *Glaubensphilosophie*. Coleridge's statement, indeed, is so excellent an epitome that I suggest it implies an acquaintance not only with the
Ueber die Lehre des Spinoza but with Jacobi's important *David Hume* as well:

> This is not a fair Criticism on Jacobi. What was his Object? To prove, that
> FAITH, which the Philosophers of his Day, held in contempt, was sensuous
> Evidence, or Knowledge by immediate Beholding = Intuition? No! But to
> prove that the sensuous Evidence itself was a species of Faith and Revelation:
> therefore, that the *Genus* could not be despised, if any one Species were held
> in honor.[1]

Schrickx concludes that Coleridge knew more of Jacobi than has in the
past been thought, that his knowledge stemmed from a very substantially
earlier time in his career than has been thought, and that he was fundamentally more favourable to him than Lindsay was willing to concede.
Indeed, Schrickx feels it 'natural to suppose that Coleridge came into contact with Jacobi's thought at a much earlier date than 1810',[2] and even
that 'there is enough material to justify the view that Jacobi was the first
German thinker to really attract him after setting foot on German soil.'[3]
Though this latter contention is perhaps too broadly speculative—it is
based on what Schrickx feels are 'reminiscences' in Coleridge's early
writings of statements in Jacobi, and the similarities are really not conclusive enough to be introduced as evidence—Schrickx makes at least one
point which cannot be denied:

> But to say, as Lindsay also does, that Coleridge's interest in Jacobi was
> 'chiefly incidental to his one-time interest in Schelling and most casual', is to
> overlook, among other things, the fact that the Jacobi anecdote related in the
> *Biographia Literaria* (a work written in 1815) was borrowed from *Ueber die
> Lehre des Spinoza*, which did not become available in the collected *Werke* until
> 1819.[4]

Now the fact that most of Coleridge's adverse remarks on Jacobi
accreted around the time of the *Biographia* provides us, I think, with our
best inferential solution to the enigma of the 'plagiarisms' of Schelling.
We have noted in a preceding chapter some of the possible psychological reasons for Coleridge's utilization in the *Biographia* of what we

---

[1] Schrickx, pp. 815–16. Coleridge annotated the *David Hume*, according to Shedd. See
Lindsay, p. 217.

[2] Schrickx, p. 816.

[3] Ibid., p. 829. For my own conclusions as to the date of Coleridge's first encounter with
Jacobi's work, see p. 131, n. 4.

[4] Schrickx, p. 814. The deduction, incidentally, is confirmed by data printed for the first time
in Griggs's monumental edition of Coleridge's letters. On 4 September 1816 Coleridge writes
to Thomas Boosey to ask his son to obtain some German books for him, and says: 'I forgot
to desire young Mr Boosey to add . . . all the works of the *Philosopher*, Jacobi, *except* his Briefe
über die Lehre des Spinoza, which I have' (*Letters*, iv. 666).

consider the fundamentally alien thought of Schelling.[1] But what was Coleridge really trying to do? Leaving aside (although not dismissing) all explanations based on neurotic predilections, I suggest that the waxing of Coleridge's interest in Jacobi at the same time as the waxing of his interest in Schelling—that is, during the writing of the *Biographia*—is a phenomenon that urges us very strongly to look in the direction of the 'I am'/'it is' dichotomy for our explanation. That Coleridge's comment on Jacobi tended, at the time of the *Biographia*, to be unfavourable does not necessarily mean that he rejected Jacobi. Schrickx argues that it is 'natural for those who enrich books with their marginal comments rather to disagree with or counter the views of others to impose their own than to express enthusiasm for the author who is being annotated',[2] and if we allow the plausibility of this view, we might see Coleridge's adverse comments about Jacobi as constituting not the major part of his *interest* in Jacobi, but merely the major part of his *disagreement* with Jacobi. In a marginal comment in Schelling's *Denkmal*, Coleridge reprobates the 'indefiniteness, the golden mists of Jacobi's scheme',[3] but Lindsay has to concede that, on balance, even the marginalia in the *Denkmal* 'seem to show that Coleridge felt that Jacobi is to be preferred to Schelling'.[4]

Granted. But no amount of special pleading can explain away the apparent contradiction between Coleridge's preference for Jacobi over Schelling, and his utilization of Schelling more than Jacobi. Nor does Schrickx's plausible hypothesis about the special emphasis of marginalia extend to an explanation of the fact that not all of Coleridge's animadversions on Jacobi, at about the time of the *Biographia*, are in the form of marginalia. For instance, in 1817 Coleridge wrote slightingly to Green that Jacobi was 'a Rhapsodist, excellent in sentences all in SMALL CAPITALS . . .'.[5]

Can these discrepancies be resolved? They can, I believe, although not by a simple answer. We need here, as always, a solution that does justice to the paradoxes of Coleridge's struggle. We have noted that Coleridge was committed firmly and equally to poetry and to philosophy, and further to maintaining the connectedness of the two. We know that Coleridge preferred Jacobi to Schelling. We know that he 'plagiarized' from Schelling more than from Jacobi, most notably in the *Biographia Literaria*.

We have earlier stressed the common interest of poetry and pantheism, and we have noted that the 'I am', in its implications, retreats from art. We have also noted, in a preceding chapter, that the *Biographia Literaria*

---

[1] See above, Chap. I, pp. 40–42.
[2] Schrickx, p. 841.
[3] The marginal note is printed in the Appendix to volume iii of *Works*, p. 709.
[4] Lindsay, p. 222.
[5] *Letters*, iv. 792.

is, in its primary focus, not a work of abstract philosophy, but a series of sketches written about Coleridge's 'literary' life and opinions.

I suggest that all these facts fall into place if we consider the pantheist dilemma. Coleridge wrote the *Biographia* in his capacity as poet. Hence Jacobi, who had 'keinen Kunstsinn', was not prima facie relevant to the needs of the *Biographia*. On the other hand, the *Biographia*, which was rather a book *about* literature than a work of art, willy-nilly became involved, especially in the matrix of Coleridge's commitment to system, in the abstract relation of philosophy to art. The philosophy of Schelling, which apotheosized art, became, through the literary focus of the *Biographia*, as immediate and relevant as Jacobi was remote. Schelling's art-philosophy is inside, Jacobi's sceptical moralism outside, the chosen arena of the *Biographia Literaria*.

So we find Schelling inside the actual book, and outside, in its historical milieu, we find, in marginalia and letters, Jacobi—a Jacobi who, however irrelevant to a biography-*literary*, or to a Schelling-in-praise-of-art, was not irrelevant to system, or to a Schelling-as-pantheist. In this context Jacobi becomes a sort of censor in Coleridge's philosophical consciousness, a stern Cato demanding the destruction of pantheism, root and branch, and even in its fairest buddings as poetry.[1] His was a philosophical voice that could not be denied, because it was, on the implications of pantheism, Coleridge's own voice. Hence the carping, rather than reject-ing, tone of Coleridge's Jacobian animadversions; it is Jacobi's Rhada-manthine dignity as judge of pantheism that must be set askew, in order to let Schelling enter in with his philosophical emphasis on the importance of art.[2]

Such, I suggest, is a large part of the truth about the role of Jacobi, and some part of the truth about the role of Schelling, in the curious psycho-logical provenance of the *Biographia Literaria*. We can, however, under-stand still more from the middle chapters of this most vulnerable of masterpieces not merely about the work itself, but about Coleridge's mind and the tensions which drew it to its special harmonies. In particular, we may find it rewarding to concentrate upon three aspects of the Schelling-translations of the *Biographia*: first, upon any specific preliminary state-ment that might allow us to infer at least the rational urgencies of Coleridge's use of Schelling; secondly, upon the actual content of the Schelling-translations; and thirdly, upon the possible meaning of Coleridge's abandonment of the translation and his leap to his famous formulation of the primary and secondary imagination in the thirteenth chapter.

With regard to the first aspect, we find of immediate interest the fact that, just before this point in the twelfth chapter of the *Biographia* where

---

[1] See note 28, p. 352.   [2] See note 29, p. 353.

Coleridge launches upon the Schelling-translations that first elicited De Quincey's charge of plagiarism, he mentions that Schelling speaks of 'systems, which for successive generations have remained enigmatic. Such he deems the system of Leibnitz'.[1] Coleridge then observes that 'Leibnitz himself, in a most instructive passage, describes as the criterion of a true philosophy' that such a philosophy 'would at once explain and collect the fragments of truth scattered through systems apparently the most incongruous.'[1] Coleridge then delivers himself of one of his most characteristic utterances—indeed, in view of our study of the transformation of his thought that follows, an utterance not only characteristic but central to the documentable facts of his *biographia philosophica*. He says:

> The deeper, however, we penetrate into the ground of things, the more truth we discover in the doctrines of the greater number of the philosophical sects. The want of *substantial* reality in the objects of the senses, according to the sceptics; the harmonies or numbers, the prototypes and ideas, to which the Pythagoreans and Platonists reduced all things; the ONE and ALL of Parmenides and Plotinus, without Spinozism; the necessary connection of things according to the Stoics, reconcileable with the spontaneity of the other schools; the vital-philosophy of the Cabalists and Hermetists, who assumed the universality of sensation; the substantial forms and entelechies of Aristotle and the schoolmen, together with the mechanical solution of all particular phenomena according to Democritus and the recent philosophers—all these we shall find united in one perspective central point, which shows regularity and a coincidence of all the parts in the very object, which from every other point of view must appear confused and distorted. The spirit of sectarianism has been hitherto our fault, and the cause of our failures. We have imprisoned our own conceptions by the lines, which we have drawn, in order to exclude the conceptions of others. J'ai trouvé que la plupart des sectes ont raison dans une bonne partie de ce qu'elles avancent, mais non pas tant en ce qu'elles nient.[2]

The passage constitutes not only a credo for the accepting and reconciling spirit in philosophy, but also a fine avowal of the interests of system, as we have delineated those interests throughout our argument. But the passage is still more than a credo and an avowal. It is, in addition, a translation—or 'plagiarism'—verbatim from Leibniz. The French is from Leibniz untranslated; but all the English is a translation from Leibniz too. Shawcross, who with earlier commentators evidently did not realize this and did not appreciate that it is in fact the 'most instructive passage' of Leibniz mentioned by Coleridge, comments as follows:

Leibnitz himself, in a most instructive passage. Trois Lettres à Mr. Remond de Mont-Mort, 1741: *Œuvres*, ed. Erdmann, 1840, Pt. II, pp. 701–2 (ref. *Biog. Lit.* 1847).[3]

The note is incomplete; only the French words in Coleridge's passage are

---

[1] *Biographia*, i. 169.   [2] Ibid. i. 169–70.   [3] Ibid. i. 267 n.

from Leibniz's letters to Remond, while the entire preceding English portion of the passage is a translation from Leibniz's *Éclaircissement des difficultés que Monsieur Bayle a trouvées dans le systeme nouveau de l'union de l'ame et du corps*, written in 1698. In this tract we may read Leibniz's French as follows—and compare it with Coleridge's English as quoted above:

La consideration de ce systeme fait voir aussi que lorsqu'on entre dans le fonds des choses, on remarque plus de la raison qu'on ne croyoit dans la pluspart des sectes des philosophes. Le peu de realité substantielle des choses sensibles des Sceptiques; la reduction de tout aux harmonies ou nombres, idées et perceptions des Pythagoristes et Platoniciens; l'un et même un tout de Parménide et de Plotin, sans aucun Spinozisme; la connexion Stoïcienne, compatible avec la spontaneité des autres; la philosophie vitale des Cabalistes et Hermetiques, qui mettent du sentiment par tout; les formes et Entelechies d'Aristote et des Scholastiques; et cependant l'explication mecanique de tous les phenomenes particuliers selon Democrite et les modernes, etc. se trouvent reunies comme dans un centre de perspective, d'où l'object (embrouillé en le regardant de tout autre endroit) fait voir sa regularité et la convenance de ses parties : on a manqué le plus par un esprit de Secte, en se bornant par la rejection des autres.[1]

At this point Coleridge switches from Leibniz's *Éclaircissement* to his *Lettres à Remond*, and in doing so ceases to translate and merely quotes Leibniz's French. The recognition of this strange syncretism is important, for a Coleridgean locus that had earlier seemed merely incidentally related to Leibniz now becomes thunderously identical with Leibniz; Coleridge, in words that represent his philosophical position at its most characteristic, links himself here with one of his 'venerable forefathers', who has heretofore in scholarly commentary seemed at best peripheral to an understanding of the Englishman's mind.

Such, we suggested in our introduction, and now more emphatically assert, is not the case. We should, I think, interpret Coleridge's appropriations from Leibniz as an expression of fellow feeling of the same sort as Montaigne's towards Plutarch—for, as the Frenchman tells us, he could never go near Plutarch without thieving 'a leg or wing'.[2] We have been constantly occupied, in a *determinatio est negatio* sort of way, with limning Coleridge's philosophical features on the canvas of the philosophical tradition of Spinoza and Schelling. In comparing Coleridge with Jacobi, however, we noted that differences of temperament and psychological predisposition loomed as large on one side as did formal similarities of declared position on the other. 'Le cœur a ses raisons'—and Freud has taught us that we accept rationally only what we have first accepted emotionally. Historiography as a discipline is already by way of applying this lesson, and philosophy should, I suggest, learn to extend its investigations not only to an analysis of expressed thought, but to a consideration

---

[1] *Philosophische Schriften*, iv. 523–4.   [2] *Essais*, iii. 113–14.

of the role of the psyche in the aetiology of that thought. Those discursive webs of the *esprit géométrique* may be neither more nor less than transformations of the intuitions of the *esprit de finesse*.

Without some technique of deepening our portrait of Coleridge, in other words, the analysis of the formal doctrines of Jacobi and Kant on the one hand, of Schelling and Spinoza on the other, renders us merely a surface silhouette in two dimensions of *determinatio* and *negatio*. To add colour, shading, and perspective, we need to turn to Leibniz and a consideration of the temperamental relationship between the two men.

We have earlier urged the temperamental conservatism of Coleridge as opposed to the radicalism of Jacobi. It is a conservatism, I suggest, that finds its historical prototype more truly in Leibniz than in any other thinker, for it is not a reactionary conservatism, but rather a learned conservatism, a system-oriented and conciliating conservatism, a yea-saying conservatism rather than an out-of-bounds-declaring conservatism, that accepts modernism as a fulfilment rather than as a rejection of the past. 'I am as ready as any man', says Leibniz of the *querelle*, 'to do justice to the moderns. Yet I find that they have carried reform too far.'[1]

Such was his mature and considered attitude: 'I do not praise the new logicians who blame rather than improve the old.'[2] And he expressed the characteristic hope that his function would be to conciliate differences: 'I hope that what I have said, though longer than I expected, will be enough to make you understand my thoughts, so that they perhaps might serve for a conciliation or tempering, since both sides accept the theory of reason, even though you are looking for it in a kind of pure logic only...'.[3] To Wagner again, in a beautiful statement, he emphasized the respect due our 'venerable forefathers':

I confess that in my early youth I was inclined to reject much of what was introduced into the learned world. But, with maturity and deeper insight I have found the value of many things which previously I esteemed only slightly, and I learned not to despise anything easily, which rule I hold as better and surer than that of the Stoics, ... not to admire anything. I emphasized this to the so-called Cartesians in France and warned them that by attacking the schools they benefited neither themselves nor their studies, and would only make learned men bitter towards new and good ideas. ... And I have never been able to

---

[1] He maintained this opinion throughout his career. He states it, for instance, to Thomasius in a youthful letter of 1669 (*Sämtliche Schriften*, Zweite Reihe, i. 14), and again in the fully mature *Discours de metaphysique* of 1686: 'Il semble que les anciens aussi bien que tant d'habiles gens accoustumés aux meditations profondes, qui ont enseigné la theologie et la philosophie il y a quelques siecles, et dont quelques uns sont recommendables pour leur sainteté, ont eu quelque connoissance de ce que nous venons de dire, et c'est ce qui les a fait introduire et maintenir les formes substantielles qui sont aujourd'huy si decriées. Mais ils ne sont pas si eloignés de la verité, ny si ridicules que le vulgaire de nos nouveaux Philosophes se l'imagine' (*Philosophische Schriften*, iv. 434).

[2] *Philosophische Schriften*, vii. 526. [3] Ibid., pp. 526–7.

accord with Father Malebranche—otherwise my good friend—in his wanting
to cross off the criticism and investigation of Roman and Greek antiquity, and
the reading of rabbinical and Arabic books, and the industry of the astronomers,
and then something else, since surely all these things have their uses. . . .[1]

'Nicht leicht etwas zu verachten'—not to despise anything easily. The
words serve as a motto for Leibniz's deepest convictions about the proper
use of his mind, and we find them echoed again and again.[2] '. . . Je ne
meprise rien facilement', he writes to Remond '(excepté les arts divina-
toires, qui ne sont que des tromperies toutes pures)'—I do not despise
anything easily, except the divinatory arts, which are nothing but
plain cheating.[3] 'Itaque nihil puto contemnendum', he writes in another
context to Seckendorf, 'quod nobis usui esse possit'—thus I think nothing
ought to be despised that might be of use to us.[4] And in his *Specimen
Dynamicum*, the centrality of this belief for his whole intellectual effort
receives added testimony:

. . . for in the writings of eminent men both ancient and more recent (if you
take away those more severe things that they say against others) there is customarily much that is true and good and deserves to be dug up and replanted in
a public treasury. Would that men might choose to do this rather than waste
their time with criticisms that only cater to their vanity. Fortune, certainly, has
so favoured me with certain new things of my own that friends everywhere
bid me think on these alone; nevertheless I somehow take pleasure in most
opinions of others, and each, no matter how diverse, is judged by its own
value;—the reason probably being that I have learned in my several activities
not to despise anything.[5]

'Nicht leicht etwas zu verachten'—'nihil spernere'—'nihil . . . contemnendum'—'ne mepriser rien'. In whatever form this sentiment of Leibniz is
a fitting counterpart of Coleridge's *'golden rule'* of criticism—repeated on
so many occasions—that *'until you understand a writer's ignorance, presume
yourself ignorant of his understanding.'*[6]

If Coleridge and Leibniz shared the same tendency towards intellectual
conservatism, they also shared an undeviating insistence on the primacy

---

[1] *Philosophische Schriften*, vii. 515.

[2] 'One sees', wrote Fontenelle, 'that Leibniz, in his enormous reading, despised nothing;
and it is amazing how many mediocre and almost wholly unknown books he graced by
reading' (*Œuvres complètes*, i. 229). Moreover there was an equal absence, on the part of the
'most learned man in the world', of intellectual *hauteur* towards people: 'Il s'entretenait volon-
tiers avec toutes sortes de personnes, gens de cour, artisans, laboureurs, soldats. Il n'y a guère
d'ignorant qui ne puisse apprendre quelque chose au plus savant homme du monde' (Fontenelle, p. 250).

[3] *Philosophische Schriften*, iii. 620.

[4] *Sämtliche Schriften*, Zweite Reihe, i. 533.

[5] *Leibnizens mathematische Schriften*, hrsg. C. I. Gerhardt, vi (Halle, 1860), 235.

[6] *Biographia*, i. 160. 'Neglecting to make ourselves accurately acquainted with the opinions
of those who have gone before us,' says Coleridge elsewhere, in a statement that, in glossing
the formula, at the same time serves to emphasize its conservative background, is a 'pernicious
custom' (*Letters*, ii. 700–1).

of the 'I am.' They were, furthermore, in their general attitudes both Platonists, in the restricted sense of their Socratic insistence in the primacy of the self, the rejection of the 'it is', as a starting-point in philosophy.[1] Hence Leibniz, despite his consistently invidious comments on the great reputation of Descartes and his adverse criticism of some parts of Cartesian philosophy,[2] speaks warmly of his French predecessor when the 'I am' primacy is the issue: 'It cannot be denied that Descartes has brought forth some distinguished things, and most of all, that he has correctly restored the study of Plato by leading away the mind from the senses. . . .'[3] Again, commenting on the *cogito ergo sum*, he says approvingly that it is among the first of truths: 'Ego cogito, adeoque sum, inter primas veritates esse praeclare a Cartesio notatum est.'[4]

To these similarities between Leibniz and Coleridge, their conservative instincts and their shared 'I am' convictions, we may add another, which derives from these two—a peculiar outgoingness that manifests itself as a multifarious intellectual commitment based on erudition of most unusual depth and range. Such erudition is, I think, not so much an ornament as an essential of their systematic activity. Without it they might both be classed as exponents of that 'degenerate learning' with which Bacon taxed the schoolmen, 'who having sharp and strong wits . . . and small variety of reading' did 'out of no great quantity of matter, and infinite agitation of wit, spin out unto us those laborious webs of learning which are extant in their books. For the wit and mind of man, if it work upon matter, which is the contemplation of the creatures of God, worketh according to the stuff, and is limited thereby; but if it work upon itself, as the spider worketh his web, then it is endless, and brings forth indeed cobwebs of learning. . . .'[5] But Leibniz and Coleridge, unlike the schoolmen, worked with a large variety of reading and a large quantity of 'matter', and this characteristic had a great deal to do with the way they elaborated their thoughts. If one tends to travel light intellectually, to live, as it were, out of a suitcase—after the manner of Wittgenstein, or Schlick, or even of Socrates[6]—

---

[1] Compare Cassirer: 'In its earliest stages Greek philosophy seems exclusively concerned with the physical universe. Cosmology clearly predominates . . . [but] it is in the problem of man that we find the landmark separating Socratic from pre-Socratic thought . . . in [Socrates] all the former problems are seen in a new light because they are referred to a new intellectual centre. . . . Only one question remains: What is man?' (*Essay on Man*, pp. 18–19).

[2] Though agreeing with Descartes about the primacy of the 'I am', Leibniz was in many ways out of sympathy with him. For a discussion of the relationship between the two thinkers, see Excursus Note, X, p. 297.

[3] *Philosophische Schriften*, iv. 468.   [4] Ibid. iv. 357.

[5] *Advancement of Learning, Works*, iii. 285–6.

[6] It seems quite fitting, therefore, that Schlick not only regards Wittgenstein as a brother-in-arms—'I can hardly exaggerate my indebtedness to this philosopher' (Moritz Schlick, 'Meaning and Verification', *Gesammelte Aufsätze 1926-36* (Wien, 1938), p. 340)—but regards Socrates as the 'true father' of their kind of thinking: 'Parvenus à ce point de vue nous reconnaissons soudain le vrai père de notre philosophie, ce n'est ni un savant ni un logicien, ni Comte, ni

then no great housekeeping abilities are called for; but if one tends to admit intellectual responsibility for an enormous amount of data, with a continuing urge to accumulate still more, then the internal economy of this intellectual establishment becomes increasingly important. It is this principle of internal economy that we call system.[1]

Only for those who accumulate knowledge and experience, however, will system seem to be necessary. The excluding, analytic, nay-saying cast of mind that we in this century associate most dramatically with the Wiener Kreis, sets out to destroy all reticulative patterns; for philosophy as system is substituted philosophy as activity, that is, philosophy as propositional analysis.

I am convinced [says Schlick in *The Future of Philosophy*] that our view of the nature of philosophy will be generally adopted in the future; and the consequence will be that it will no longer be attempted to teach philosophy as a system. We shall teach the special sciences and their history in the true philosophical spirit of searching for clarity. . . . This is all we can do, but it will be a great step in the mental progress of our race.[2]

With their insistence upon philosophy as activity the positivists free themselves from the responsibilities of systematic endeavour.

The view which I am advocating [says Schlick] has . . . been most clearly expressed by Ludwig Wittgenstein; he states his point in these sentences: 'The object of philosophy is the logical clarification of thoughts. Philosophy is not a theory but an activity. The result of philosophy is not a number of "philosophical propositions", but to make propositions clear.' This is exactly the view which I have been trying to explain here.[3]

All metaphysical questions are declared out of bounds:

Metaphysics disappears [says Schlick in *A New Philosophy of Experience*], not

Frege, ni Poincaré, ni Russell, qui sont tous les anneaux tardifs d'une longue chaîne: c'est Socrate' (Schlick, 'L'École de Vienne et la philosophie traditionnelle', *Gesammelte Aufsätze*, pp. 395–6). Again: 'Socrates' philosophy consists of what we may call "The Pursuit of Meaning." He tried to clarify thought by analyzing the meaning of our expressions and the real sense of our propositions. . . . Socrates has set the example of the true philosophic method for all times' (Schlick, 'The Future of Philosophy', *Gesammelte Aufsätze*, p. 126).

[1] Thus Kant insists, not on the mausoleum of a completed system, but on systematic activity —that is, connexions and relevances—as central to philosophy. 'To philosophy according to the scholastic conception', he says, 'there belong two parts: first a sufficient stock of ideas (*Vernunfterkenntnissen*); secondly, a systematic connection of these ideas, or their union in the idea of a whole. Philosophy not only permits such a strict systematic connection, but it is indeed the only science that possesses a systematic connection in the proper sense and gives systematic unity to all other sciences. . . . For philosophy in its ultimate meaning is the science of the relation of all knowledge and mental usage (*Erkenntnisses und Vernunftgebrauches*) to the final goal of human reason. . . . The field of philosophy in this universal meaning is circumscribed by the following questions: (1) What can I know? (2) What ought I to do? (3) What may I hope? (4) What is man?' (*Werke*, viii. 343). Kant's final definition, accordingly, is that 'Philosophie ist also das System der philosophischen Erkenntnisse oder der Vernunfterkenntnisse aus Begriffen' (*Werke*, viii. 342).

[2] Schlick, 'The Future of Philosophy', *Gesammelte Aufsätze 1926-36* (Wien, 1938), p. 133.
[3] Ibid., p. 132.

because metaphysical problems [are] insoluble, as most of the old empiristic schools believed, but because there are no such problems. Where there are no questions, there can be no answers; it would be absurd to look for a solution where there is no problem. . . . In the older views the impossibility of metaphysics was due to some regrettable imperfection or incapacity of the human mind; in our view the impossibility is of a logical order, it is due to some intrinsic non-sense in the phrases which were supposed to express 'metaphysical problems.' To regret the impossibility of metaphysics becomes impossible; it would be the same as regretting the impossibility of a round square. All real questions . . . can in principle be answered . . . and they can be answered by experience only, by the methods of science. A heavy burden is taken from Philosophy, and it cannot quarrel any more with science. Its function is analytic and critical, it helps us to get rid of mere verbal disputes, and with unspeakable relief do we see great 'problems' vanish without leaving empty places.[1]

In line, finally, with this lightening of philosophy's burden and the dissipation of its problems is a moratorium on the primary concerns of ontology and epistemology: those questions that resist being declared nonsense are all referred to an axiomatic conception of reality that amounts more or less to the commonsense assumptions of Reid. It is 'one of the main theses of true positivism', says Schlick in *Meaning and Verification*, 'that the naïve representation of the world, as the man in the street sees it, is perfectly correct; and that the solution of the great philosophical issues consists in returning to this original world-view, after having shown that the troublesome problems arose only from an inadequate description of the world by means of a faulty language'.[2]

It is quite otherwise with the systematic conservatives—for such we may term Leibniz and Coleridge. Whatever they may have in common with the 'consistent empiricists' (to use Schlick's favourite description of

---

[1] Schlick, 'A New Philosophy of Experience', *Gesammelte Aufsätze*, pp. 148–9. More succinctly: 'Die Systeme der Metaphysiker enthalten manchmal Wissenschaft, manchmal Poesie, aber sie enthalten niemals Metaphysik' ('Erleben, Erkennen, Metaphysik', *Gesammelte Aufsätze*, p. 17).

[2] Schlick, 'Meaning and Verification', *Gesammelte Aufsätze*, p. 367. Because of his drastic rejection of systematic and metaphysical concerns, it is, in one sense, impossible to call Schlick a pantheist; in another sense, however, we are justified in drawing the implications of his standpoint whether he sanctions the procedure or not. Schlick hails the natural order and explicitly denies a two-world ontology—and no more is necessary to pantheism. Thus he speaks of 'the vain and absurd efforts of philosophers' who claim to be 'citizens of two worlds'. 'The setting-up of a second world' to resolve the problems of the first is the 'cheapest, most worn out philosophical trick' that small minds avail themselves of with 'such regularity and unscrupulousness' (Moritz Schlick, *Natur und Kultur* (Wien, 1952), pp. 20–21). For nature itself, however, he has a nineteenth-century combination of awe and love: 'Every independent mind must at one time tread, with wonder or terror, on the rim of the abyss which culture has opened up between him and nature: must shudder at the depths and look longingly across—longingly, even though it is not paradise that lies on the other side. For nature is as awful as she is mild and kindly; she endures struggle, pain, and death everywhere. She delivers the harmless antelope to the tearing teeth of the tiger. . . she allows pestilence and leprosy to rage, without giving terrified man the slightest sign of help or hindrance' (p. 11).

his school), they are, in their all-embracing, yea-saying concern, totally unlike the radical excluders. Where the positivists keep their intellectual house in order by briskly sweeping out and throwing away any unfashionable articles of intellectual furniture, the systematic conservatives labour for an harmonious assembly of all the furniture of their mind, whether already on the premises or brought in from outside, and would rather consider enlarging the house than abandoning a fine old piece that did not seem to fit. Thus for Coleridge philosophy was not an activity directed towards the clarification of propositions, but towards system. He sought 'an abiding place for my reason,' and in this quest 'began to ask myself; is a system of philosophy, as different from mere history and historic classification, possible? . . . I was for a while disposed to answer the . . . question in the negative, and to admit that the sole practicable employment for the human mind was to observe, to collect, and to classify. But I soon felt, that human nature itself fought up against this wilful resignation of intellect'.[1]

The primacy of his own individuality, the demand for connexions that refer always to that primacy, are emphasized by Coleridge in a way that shows him utterly and unbridgeably at variance with Schlick's cast of mind:

I am by the law of my nature a reasoner. A person who should suppose I meant by that word, an arguer, would not only not understand me, but would understand the contrary of my meaning. I can take no interest whatever in hearing or saying anything merely as a fact—merely as having happened. It must refer to something within me before I can regard it with any curiosity or care. My mind is always energic—I don't mean energetic; I require in everything what, for lack of another word, I may call *propriety*,—that is, a reason, why the thing *is* at all, and why it is *there* or *then* rather than elsewhere or at another time.[2]

We recognize such attitudes, and indeed the very language in which they are expressed, as close to Husserl, Jaspers and Heidegger; whilst such a passage resists, in all its axiological implications, any possible identification with the beliefs of Schlick and his colleagues.[3]

But even more than to modern phenomenology, it is to Leibniz that we look for historical correlatives of important features of Coleridge's orientation. The whole system, and the logical dependence of even the simplest assumptions upon at least the hypothetical existence of such a system, is summarized by Leibniz in a crucial statement:

We know only a slight part of an eternity stretching out into immensity, for how small is the memory of the few thousand years that history gives us. And yet from such small experience we judge at random of the unmeasurable and

---

[1] *Biographia*, i. 93.   [2] *Table Talk*, 1 March 1834.
[3] See note 30, p. 353

the eternal, as if men born and brought up in prison or in the subterranean salt mines of Sarmatia should think there was no other light in the world than that paltry lamp that is barely sufficient to direct their steps. If we look at a very beautiful painting, but cover the whole thing except for one small spot, what else will appear in it, even if we inspect it very carefully—and the more so the closer we look—than a kind of confused mixture of colours, without discrimination or art, while when the covering is removed, and the whole painting viewed properly, we see that what had appeared to be smeared at random on the canvas was made with the highest artifice by the author of the work.[1]

Leibniz's psychological Platonism is here particularly stark, and we might, indeed, gloss the passage as the allegory of the cave focused towards system. Certainly in this matrix 'great "problems" ' do not tend to 'vanish without leaving empty places'. And modern analytical thought, as described by Schlick, seems in Leibniz's context to have been largely concerned with closing off most of the painting (the systematic organization of hypothetical answers to the traditional questions of philosophy) the better to analyse its particularity, which attempt becomes, in the absence of the reticulative concern, merely the inspection of 'confusa quaedam congeries colorum sine delectu'—that is, the analysis of propositions chosen at random.[2]

We see in this important testimony to the outgoingness of Leibniz's thought the origins of one of the most inescapable dilemmas faced by a systematic conservative: that while his conservatism tends to expand his interests (his respect for 'venerable forefathers', for instance, obliges him to embody a mass of historical erudition in his philosophical deliberations), by the same token it renders more difficult his reticulative task. His need for system grows in direct proportion to the difficulty of achieving it, for his is a concern 'porrigendae in immensum'. Hence Leibniz confesses to Des Billettes that 'Mon systeme dont vous estes curieux, Monsieur, . . . n'est pas un corps complet de Philosophie'—my system about which you are curious, Sir, . . . is not a complete body of philosophy.[3] Leibniz was here writing in 1696; but even after his *Théodicée* he could not claim to have achieved his aim: as he then says to Remond, 'Il est vray que ma Theodicée ne suffit pas pour donner un corps entier de mon Systeme'—it is true that my *Théodicée* does not suffice to give the whole form of my system.[4] The more he read, and thought, and cared about, the more necessary, and paradoxically the more difficult, did the final reticulation become. If

---

[1] *Philosophische Schriften*, vii. 306.

[2] Such a limitation, of course, enormously diminishes the cultural role of the philosopher. Hence Ayer's statement of the function of philosophy resounds with unintentionally forlorn overtones: 'The most that philosophy can do, apart from seeing whether [a man's] beliefs are self-consistent, is to show what are the criteria which are used to determine the truth or falsehood of any given proposition . . .' (A. J. Ayer, *Language, Truth and Logic* (London, 1958), p. 48).

[3] Leibniz, *Philosophische Schriften*, vii. 451.   [4] Ibid. iii. 618.

system can be acclaimed as the habit of forming relevances, Leibniz's system, like that of Coleridge, is the marvellous achievement of a lifelong reticulative urge; but as with Coleridge, if system be thought of as completion, Leibniz finally had no system. We stress this specifically in regard to Leibniz, because Coleridge's neurotic inability to get down to business is assigned too facilely as the cause of his failure to complete his *magnum opus*. Sloth is only superficially the reason: he partly overcame the problem of sloth by his mosaic method of composition, and he probably over-dramatized his laziness in any event.[1] But even if sloth were the reason for his failure to complete, to what do we attribute the failure of his intellectual soul-mate Leibniz, a titan of intellectual industry?

We are, in this chapter, enmeshed in interwoven ironies, but to these we may add still another convolution by considering the implications of systematic conservatism when tied to the 'I am' starting-point. If we accept Jacobi's contention that all completed systems end in pantheism ('Jeder Weg der Demonstration geht in den Fatalismus aus'), then we will readily see that the 'I am' adherent would find it difficult, if not impossible, to complete a system that would not do violence to his primary concern. 'Si quelcun', said Leibniz, 'reduisoit Platon en systeme, il rendroit un grand service au genre humain, et l'on verroit que j'y approche un peu'—if someone would reduce Plato to a system, he would render a great service to humankind, and it would become apparent that my thought is a bit like his.[2] But Plato, we note, lived a long and full life; why did he not reduce his own thought to a system? His successor Plotinus provides us, in his name, with one of the most beautifully reticulated systems; it has all the emotional richness of Plato himself, but the system is pantheism.[3] And why did not Leibniz himself, who lived a long and busy life, not complete his own system? Certainly it was not for any lack of emphasis on the need for system; indeed, Fontenelle, in his *Éloge*, takes special heed of 'the spirit of system that Leibniz possessed to a sovereign degree'.[4] But to an even greater degree, I suggest, he possessed the spirit of 'I am', which he would not forfeit even for the completion of system—any more than Plato, or Coleridge, or Pascal.[5]

The systematic 'I am' thinker, in brief, is by the terms of his commitment perpetually committed also to paradox: the interests of system urge him to harmonize the realm of 'I am' and the realm of 'it is', while the moral

---

[1] See note 31, p. 354. [2] Leibniz, *Philosophische Schriften*, iii. 637.
[3] See note 32, p. 354. [4] *Œuvres complètes*, i. 229.
[5] Thus Goldmann argues that the fragmentary structure of the *Pensées* is less the effect of Pascal's untimely death than of the tragic and paradoxical fact that man and the world, in the Pascalian conception, are sundered from the 'hidden God'. The *Deus absconditus* makes 'le paradoxe et le fragment' the 'deux formes d'expression littéraire exigées par sa propre philosophie', and accordingly the *Pensées* 'sont en vérité, un chef-d'œuvre paradoxal, achevé de par son inachèvement' (*Le Dieu caché*, p. 220).

interests of the 'I am' draw back from the 'it is' and therefore conspire against completion. We can see both horns of the dilemma with great clearness in one of Leibniz's central statements:

I believe that everything really occurs mechanically in nature and is explicable by efficient causes, but that also, at the same time everything occurs morally, so to speak, and is explicable by final causes. And that these two realms, the moral one of spirits and souls, and the mechanical one of body, interpenetrate and accord with one another perfectly by means of the author of things, who is at once the first efficient cause and the last final cause.[1]

In Leibniz's invocation of the 'auteur des choses' we see the systematist's drive to harmonize the two realms, but in the very recognition of two realms we sense the existence of an intellectual rift. We see the same conflict of interests in Coleridge—in the famous comment to Mrs. Barbauld about the *Ancient Mariner*, for instance:

Mrs. Barbauld once told me that she admired the 'Ancient Mariner' very much, but that there were two faults in it,—it was improbable, and had no moral. As for the probability, I owned that that might admit some question; but as to the want of a moral, I told her that in my own judgment the poem had too much; and that the only, or chief fault, if I might say so, was the obtrusion of the moral sentiment so openly on the reader as a principle or cause of action in a work of such pure imagination.[2]

We note that on the one hand Coleridge implies that the 'moral sentiment' is an 'obtrusion' in a poem, and so confirms that the 'I am' and 'it is' theoretically do not coincide, while on the other hand he admits that 'the poem had', in fact, 'a moral', and so confirms that the reticulative impulse demands a harmony of all interests.[3] Presumably Coleridge knew before he wrote his poem—his greatest work—that the 'moral sentiment' should not openly obtrude, but none the less it does obtrude—was, furthermore, despite subsequent revisions, never made not to obtrude. Only the ambivalent explanation of the 'I am'/'it is' paradox can elucidate, I think, the ambivalence of Coleridge's attitude towards his creation.

The omnipresence of this ambivalence for a thinker committed on the one hand to the moral postulates of the 'I am', and on the other to system, can be seen—without the harmonizing interposition of deity—in still another statement by Leibniz:

The true middle ground that should satisfy both truth and religion is that all

[1] *Philosophische Schriften*, vii. 451.   [2] *Table Talk*, 31 May 1830.

[3] One must agree with Warren, who, arguing against Griggs's statement that there was 'no intention to give the poem a moral meaning', points out that Coleridge 'did not say that the poem as it exists has no moral, but says that it suffers from the "obtrusion of the moral sentiment so openly". Nor did he say or even imply that the poem would be better if there were *no* moral. He merely said that the "obtrusion of the moral sentiment" is too "open" ' (Robert Penn Warren, 'A Poem of Pure Imagination: An Experiment in Reading', *The Rime of the Ancient Mariner* (New York, 1946), p. 62).

the natural phenomena could be explained mechanically, if we understood them enough; but that the principles of mechanics themselves are not explicable geometrically, since they depend on principles more sublime, that signalize the wisdom of the author in the order and perfection of his work.[1]

Stated in this way, not only does the moral concern belong to a second realm as compared with the mechanical, but the corollary also becomes clear—that the Spinozistic reduction to substance can be blocked only by a means that likewise prevents system from being completed. In the tension between the 'I am' and the systematic, therefore, God will always be conceived as following the 'I am' in order of reasoning and experience, will be separate from the world, and will be free from all pantheistic conceptions. This ultimate disposition of 'I am' and systematic concerns Leibniz achieves in a statement that is the climax of his entire philosophy:

Besides the world, or aggregate of finite things, I assume a dominating One, not only as my mind dominates in me, or rather as my ego dominates my body, but in a much higher sense. For the dominating One of the universe not only rules the world but constructs or makes it, and is above the world—extramundane, so to speak—and is the final reason of things.[2]

This cosmological dualism is the only logical terminus possible for a series of reticulations beginning with the 'I am'. If it is not reached, then the true 'I am' philosophy, no matter what the initial statements of a thinker may be, has not been realized. Certain varieties of 'it is' thought begin with a nominal solipsism—the thought of Berkeley, for instance, or of Fichte, or of Schopenhauer—but they end in one-world cosmologies and thereby reveal their real structure.[3] But for Kant, and for Coleridge, as for Leibniz, the two-world conception exists as a final guarantee of the Platonic reticulation of thought.[4]

Now if the two-world cosmology logically terminates the series of 'I am' reasonings, it places the systematic adherent of 'I am' thought in a special quandary by virtue of, as it were, its built-in incompleteness. We might historically expect, therefore, that the systematic 'I am' thinker, in his constant urge to bridge the abyss between his sundered interests, would at crucial points in his reticulations veer towards pantheism, but that at the same time this flirtation with completeness would never seem to coincide wholly with his own authentic voice, because of the violence it does to his moral preoccupations. In this paradox lies our most general form of

---

[1] *Philosophische Schriften*, vii. 272. To realize the essential Platonism of this position, compare *Laws* 967 D: '. . . the soul is the eldest of all things which are born, and is immortal and rules over all bodies'.

[2] Leibniz, *Philosophische Schriften*, vii. 302.

[3] See Excursus note XI, p. 300.

[4] See the important article by A. O. Lovejoy, 'Coleridge and Kant's Two Worlds', *Essays in the History of Ideas* (Baltimore, 1948), pp. 254–76. Cf. Windelband: 'Thus there appears in Kant, in a new . . . form, *the Platonic doctrine of the two worlds* . . .' (*A History of Philosophy*, trans. J. H. Tufts (New York, 1958), ii. 555). See note 56, p. 368.

answer, I believe, to the curious combination of typicality and atypicality that characterizes Leibniz in his monad doctrine and Coleridge in his *Biographia Literaria*. In the former instance, we have Leibniz's most rigorous attempt at an ontologically grounded system—and the attempt led to charges of Spinozism.[1] In the latter instance, we see Coleridge involved in the attempt to reticulate his abstract philosophical and concrete artistic concerns, and this attempt led him to plagiarize a Spinozistic pantheist, Schelling. I suggest that we are justified in regarding, on at least one level of explanation, the two situations as reflecting the inauthenticity that each thinker felt, notwithstanding his urge towards system, as he approached most nearly the realm of completed system, that is, pantheism.

We will note—to extend our recognition of the similarity of Leibniz and Coleridge—that whereas they were very gingerly as they drew near to pantheism in its stark form as Spinozism, they were both able, to some extent, to ease the strain on their moral faculties by transferring their sympathies to the softer, more rapturous pantheism of Neoplatonism, uttered—to quote Berkeley—in 'the Lofty & Platonic' strain. In this regard, we may emphasize that Leibniz's enthusiasm for Shaftesbury was largely based on the fact that Shaftesbury provided 'L'Univers tout d'une piece,' a 'harmonie universelle,' while at the same time Leibniz characterizes Shaftesbury's rhapsodic utterance as 'le Platonisme noveau'.[2]

For his part, Coleridge regarded the work of Schelling as a Platonically ameliorated pantheism; he called it a 'Plotinised Spinozism'.[3] I suggest that he, like Leibniz in his quest for system, and idiosyncratically in his need for the reconciliation of his poetic with his abstract interests, drew so hopefully close to Schelling because of the same lure of harmony combined with the softenings of Neoplatonism. In this respect it is symptomatic that he did not restate, or break up in any way, the opening propositions of the *System des transscendentalen Idealismus* that he translates into the twelfth chapter of the *Biographia*. His translation, on the one hand, indicates that he did wish to make this viewpoint his own. His refusal in any way to restate or reorganize Schelling's argument indicates, on the other, that on at least some level of his intention he did not wish to make that viewpoint his own.

---

[1] Apparently the first printed charge that Leibniz's monad doctrine was tantamount to Spinozism was by Ruardus Andala in 1712, who asks: 'How compliant will the Spinozists be in accepting this new Leibnizian notion of *substance*?' Again: 'Who does not see the considerable agreement between this Spinozist *potentia* of anything or the *inclination* (*conatus*) by which it either does something by impulse or strives (*conatur*) to do it, and the Leibnizian active force which is furnished by impulse (*conatus*). . . .?' And finally quoting Leibniz ('. . . by the modification of the permanent divine substance; and because it returns to the same thing, nature itself or, if you will, the substance of all things is God'), he says flatly, 'This is *Spinozism* itself' (*Ruardi Andali . . . dissertationum philosophicarum pentas* . . .), Franequerae, 1712), pp. 20, 21, 22).

[2] *Philosophische Schriften*, iii. 429.

[3] *Letters*, iv. 883. To Tulk, 24 Nov. 1818.

The ambivalence may be more deeply outlined for us if we take up the second of our stipulated investigations with regard to this locus in the *Biographia*, that is, the question of the actual content of the translated passages. Because we quoted them at considerable length in the first chapter, and because of the elucidations since that point, it is now possible to speak somewhat summarily. De Quincey identifies the Schelling translations as 'a dissertation upon the reciprocal relations of the *Esse* and the *Cogitare*'.[1] The last word points us to the *cogito*, and the '*Esse*' to the 'it is'— in other words, we may say, following De Quincey, that the passage is a dissertation on the reciprocal relations of the 'I am' and the 'it is'. Schelling, in an extended either-or, purports to show that *it makes no difference* whether one starts from the 'I am' or from the 'it is': 'A. Entweder wird das Objektive zum Ersten gemacht, und gefragt: wie ein Subjektives zu ihm hinzukomme, das mit ihm übereinstimmt', 'B. Oder das Subjektive wird zum Ersten gemacht . . .'[2]

Now this *Entweder-Oder* represents the very kernel of Schelling's philosophical position. Almost from the outset of his career he had realized the incompatibility of 'I am' and 'it is' points of view. In his programmatic *Philosophische Briefe über Dogmatismus und Kriticismus* of 1795, he had mused on the opposition of Kantian criticism to Spinozistic dogmatism.[3] '. . . Criticism and dogmatism', he concluded, 'are nothing other than idealism and realism systematically thought through.'[4] But criticism and dogmatism had the 'same problem'. 'One of two things must happen. Either no subject and an absolute object, or no object and an absolute subject. How can this conflict be put right?'[5] The answer he provides is that 'the distinction between Idealism and Realism must dissolve as soon as the opposition between subject and object dissolves . . . in short, as soon as object and subject are identical.'[6]

In a philosophy of subject ('I am'), object ('it is'), and their absolute identity, therefore, Schelling early found the philosophical emphasis of his life: the *Identitätsphilosophie*, or the reconciliation of Spinoza and Kant in a single system by means of Fichte's fundamental principle—the law of identity. All his subsequent career he devoted to elucidating this threefold aspect of his thought: first the train of 'it is' consequences, under the banner of *Naturphilosophie*, then the train of 'I am' consequences, under the banner of *Transscendentaler Idealismus*, and finally, in a theosophic phase lasting from 1809 to his death in 1854, the absolute itself.

Schelling never allowed himself to doubt that he successfully discharged the task he set himself. In any case, he saw clearly that his cherished goal

---

[1] *Collected Writings*, ii. 145.   [2] *Werke*, iii. 340–1.
[3] He took his cue from Fichte, who in 1794 had insisted that 'there are only two systems, *das kritische* and *das dogmatische*' (*Werke*, i. 120 n.). 'In so far as dogmatism can be consequent', said Fichte, '*der Spinozism* is the most consequent product of dogmatism' (i. 120).
[4] *Werke*, i. 303.   [5] Ibid., p. 298.   [6] Ibid., p. 330.

of a completed system could not be achieved unless the reconciliation of Spinoza and Kant were somehow brought about, for the two systems were 'equally possible'. Though Kant believed himself to have overthrown dogmatism, Schelling was 'convinced that the completed system of criticism cannot theoretically refute dogmatism'.[1] Both series of consequence must therefore be retained. Yet Fichte's development of idealism had not managed to accomplish this feat. On the one hand it abandoned a living and dynamic view of nature, on the other it perverted idealism to Spinozism. 'Fichte's idealism', wrote Schelling, 'constitutes a turned-about Spinozism.'[2] 'It would be a mistake', he says in 1809, 'to believe that pantheism has been set aside and destroyed by idealism. . . . For it is immaterial to pantheism, as such, whether many individual things are conceived in an absolute Substance or many individual wills are conceived in one Primal Will. In the first case it would be realistic, in the second idealistic, but its fundamental concept remains the same'.[3]

His own solution was to set the external nature denied by Kant and Fichte in equipoise with the ego denied by Spinoza. The most cherished of his attitudes was one that maintained that Spinozism could be cleansed of fatalism by incorporating it as one part of a double system, the parallel part of which was a philosophy of 'I am'. 'Spinozism does not err at all in asserting . . . inviolable necessity in God,' he said, 'but only in taking this in a lifeless and impersonal way. Spinoza's system comprehends only one aspect of the Absolute—namely, the realistic side. . . '.[4]

Behind the 'ideal' side of his philosophy, moreover, Schelling nursed a magic secret: freedom. 'The beginning and end of all philosophy', he said in 1795, 'is—freedom!'[5] Of all the terms in his philosophical vocabulary, this one is the most emotionally charged. 'The essence of the ego is freedom. . . .'[6] Freedom would preserve his thought from Spinozistic fatalism.[7] There can be no doubt of his own conviction that he here possessed the secret of all reality, and the word itself was filled with the clean, bright hopes of the American and French revolutions. Thus, feeling himself buoyed by 'idealism' and 'freedom', Schelling early launched himself boldly into the laving depths of Romantic Spinozism: 'The more we know individual things, the more we know God, says Spinoza, and with constantly elevated conviction must we also now proclaim to those who seek the science of the eternal: come ye here to natural philosophy and

---

[1] Ibid., p. 296.   [2] Ibid. x. 92 n.
[3] Ibid. vii. 352.   [4] Ibid., p. 397.
[5] Ibid. i. 177. See further iii. 379.
[6] Ibid. i. 179. For a brief survey of the role of freedom in Schelling's whole range of thought see Hermann Zeltner, *Schelling* (Stuttgart, 1954), pp. 253–76.
[7] Schelling sometimes conceded that Spinoza implied a fatalistic view, but he argued (*a*) that pantheism and fatalism were not, as Jacobi had insisted, necessarily identical, and (*b*) that Spinoza's fatalism was merely an effect of his mechanistic physics and not an essential of his position. 'Spinoza's system', he says, 'is not fatalistic in that it lets things be conceived in God;

know the eternal.'[1] Such was the attitude underlying the *Naturphilosophie* as expressed in 1798. In 1800, in the *System des transscendentalen Idealismus*, Schelling sketched the subjective pole of his thought: the 'I am'. But still he had not developed this side of his thought as fully as he had his *Naturphilosophie*. Meanwhile, the charges of Spinozism increased in intensity. In 1809, accordingly, he produced one of his most dazzling performances, the *Philosophische Untersuchungen über das Wesen der menschlichen Freiheit*. The tract is at one and the same time an answer to Jacobi's *Ueber die Lehre des Spinoza*, a defence of Spinoza, a virtuoso development of the idea of freedom by means of the doctrine of organic form (freedom consists in acting according to the laws of one's nature and has meaning only in conjunction with the idea of dependence: an eye is an organ free and separate in the organism of the body, but at the same time functions meaningfully only in dependence on the body), a substitution of Boehme's dynamic pantheism for Spinoza's mechanistic pantheism, and the beginning of the final, theosophical phase of Schelling's thought. Moreover, as Schelling says, 'the present treatise is the first wherein the author offers with complete definiteness his conception of the part of philosophy which treats of the Ideal. . . . Though the author has up to now nowhere expressed himself on the chief points discussed herein—on freedom of the will, good and evil, personality . . . this has not prevented others . . . from ascribing definite views to him. . . .'[2] All his previous work, Schelling now says, affirms

a mutual interpenetration of realism and idealism. Spinoza's fundamental concept, spiritualized by the principle of idealism . . . was given a vital basis through the more elevated way of regarding nature, and through the recognized unity of what is dynamic with what is spiritual and emotional. From this there developed a philosophy of nature, which, as a mere physics, could indeed stand by itself, but which was always regarded, with respect to the whole of philosophy, as merely one of its parts . . . which could be raised into a genuine system of reason only by first being completed by an ideal part wherein freedom is sovereign.[3]

Now Coleridge, if we accept his statement of the matter, had at the time he wrote the *Biographia* seen seven of Schelling's treatises: the *Darlegung des wahren Verhältnisses der Naturphilosophie zu der verbesserten Fichte'schen Lehre*, the *Vom Ich als Princip der Philosophie*, the *Philosophische Briefe über Dogmatismus und Kriticismus*, the *Abhandlung zur Erläuterung des Idealismus*

---

for as we have shown, pantheism does not make formal freedom, at least, impossible. Spinoza must then be a fatalist for another reason. . . . The error of his system is by no means due to the fact that he posits all things in God, but to the fact that they are *things*. . . . Thus his arguments against freedom are altogether deterministic, and in no wise pantheistic.' (Schelling, *Werke*, vii. 349.)

[1] Schelling, *Werke*, ii. 378. [2] Ibid., vii. 334.
[3] Ibid., p. 350.

der Wissenschaftslehre, the *Ueber das Verhältniss der bildenden Künste zu der Natur*, the *Philosophische Untersuchungen über das Wesen der menschlichen Freiheit*, and the *System des transscendentalen Idealismus*.[1] We have noted that the concerns converging in the *Biographia* make the problem of Spinoza especially important to him at this time. The conflict between the moral interests of the 'I am' on the one hand, and nature and poetry on the other, though a lifelong constant in Coleridge's thought, here reached a special pitch of intensity.

And then, reading Schelling—and to read the Schelling of *System des transscendentalen Idealismus* and *Über das Wesen der menschlichen Freiheit* is to feel a most impressive and powerful mind at work[2]—Coleridge found the almost unbelievable good news: Spinoza and Kant could be reconciled, the moral 'I am' could be retained along with nature and poetry. 'Schelling's *Identitäts-System*', muses Royce in 1892, 'is really very deep and suggestive. . . . The thought that there must after all be some sort of synthesis possible of Kant and Spinoza, was indeed an important thought.'[3]

For Coleridge it was more than important; it was the promise of the resolution of his most agonizing conflict. Reassured, by *Das Wesen der menschlichen Freiheit*, that Spinozism could be retained without denying human freedom ('Immanence in God is so little contradictory of freedom, that freedom alone, and in so far as it is free, exists in God'),[4] Coleridge happily turned to the *System des transscendentalen Idealismus*, which, unlike the loosely-structured, almost vatic essay on freedom, is a *systematic* exposition of the 'I am' position as counterpart of the 'it is'. All knowledge, says Schelling in the *System*, rests on the coincidence of the subjective

---

[1] *Biographia*, i. 105.

[2] Curiously enough, the fact that Schelling often can be taxed with false logic does not invalidate the depth and power of his thought. As Whitehead notes: 'In the earlier times the deep thinkers were the clear thinkers—Descartes, Spinoza, Locke, Leibniz. They knew exactly what they meant and said it. In the nineteenth century, some of the deeper thinkers among theologians and philosophers were muddled thinkers. Their assent was claimed by incompatible doctrines; and their efforts at reconciliation produced inevitable confusion.' (*Science and the Modern World*, p. 115.)

[3] *The Spirit of Modern Philosophy*, p. 193.

[4] Schelling, *Werke*, vii. 347. As Schelling argues, 'Since freedom is unthinkable in contradistinction to omnipotence, is there any other escape from this argument than by placing man and his freedom in the divine being, by saying that man exists not outside God but in God, and that man's activity itself belongs to God's life?' (p. 339). And with the skill of the prestidigitator he insists that 'The procession of things from God is God's self-revelation. But God can only reveal himself in creatures who resemble him, in free, self-activating beings for whose existence there is no reason save God, but who are as God is' (p. 347). The fact that Schelling claimed to preserve human freedom in his system ('the true conception of freedom was lacking in all modern systems, that of Leibniz as well as that of Spinoza, until the discovery of Idealism' [p. 345]) would exert an enormous attraction upon Coleridge; for as Lovejoy sums up the matter, 'it is impossible to read Coleridge's more connected expositions of his moral and religious philosophy without recognizing his engrossing concern to establish the freedom of the will' (Arthur O. Lovejoy, 'Coleridge and Kant's Two Worlds', *Essays in the History of Ideas* (Baltimore, 1948), p. 255.)

with the objective; it is possible to depart from either pole: either the *objective* can be taken first, and then the problem is how to deduce the subjective, or the *subjective* can be taken first, and the problem is reversed. The *System des transscendentalen Idealismus*, accordingly, will do for the 'I am' what *Naturphilosophie* has done for the 'it is'.[1]

So Coleridge, reaffirming his own inviolable belief in the primacy of the 'I am' ('The postulate of philosophy and at the same time the test of philosophic capacity, is no other than the heaven-descended KNOW THYSELF!'),[2] starts to enlay Schelling's demonstration into the *Biographia*, and thereby to show how both the 'I am' and Spinozistic pantheism can coexist. But as he translates, his sense of philosophical form begins to return. Quite possibly he does not at that time clearly formulate his objections but merely senses that the exposition is not fufilling its promise. At any rate he abandons the translation and retreats in disorder.

It was probably not before 1818 that Coleridge became clear in his own mind as to why he could not use Schelling's demonstration. He had a twofold task: first, to think through his objections to Schelling's theory of freedom; secondly, to think through the logical objections to the systematic presentation in the *Transcendental Idealism*.

Now the 'freedom' which Schelling so passionately and eloquently advocated was only a formal freedom. I think it probable that during his youthful theological studies in the Tübingen *Stift* Schelling became impregnated with Luther's insistence that human freedom exists only in limited situations—that in final situations it disappears before God's omnipotence.[3] Schelling's scheme at any rate substituted, in the moral sphere, necessity for *Naturphilosophie*, freedom for *Transscendentaler Idealismus*, and transcended their opposition in the absolute. The 'opposition of nature and spirit', he proclaims in the essay on freedom, has 'been dislodged'; the 'time has come for the higher distinction, or rather, for the real contrast, to be made manifest, the contrast between necessity and

---

[1] 'To make the objective first, and deduce the subjective from it, is, as has just been shown, the task of *Natur-Philosophie*. Therefore, if there is a *Transscendental-Philosophie*, there remains open to it only the opposite direction: to depart from the subjective, as from the first and absolute, and to have the objective arise from it. *Natur-* and *Transscendental-Philosophie*, therefore, have divided among themselves the two possible directions of philosophy, and if all philosophy either must make an intelligence out of nature or a nature out of intelligence, then *Transscendental-Philosophie*, which has the latter task, is the other necessary and fundamental science of philosophy' (Schelling, *Werke*, iii. 342).

[2] *Biographia*, i. 173.

[3] Coleridge, significantly, despite his almost unbounded admiration for Luther, could not accept Luther's position on free will. 'Luther', he says, 'confounds free-will with efficient power, which neither does nor can exist save where the finite will is one with the absolute Will. That . . . he was driving at the truth, I see abundant reason to believe. But it is no less evident that he saw it in a mist, or rather as a mist with dissolving outline; and as he saw the thing as a mist, so he ever and anon mistakes a mist for the thing. . . . In fact, till the appearance of Kant's *Kritiques* of the pure and of the practical Reason the problem had never been accurately or adequately stated, much less solved' (*Works*, v. pp. 280–1). Cf. Kant. *Werke*, iii. 374–89.

freedom, in which alone the innermost centre of philosophy comes into view'.[1] But from early in his career he had cherished the secret of their reconciliation. 'Absolute freedom and absolute necessity', he said in 1795, 'are identical.'[2] In that same essay, however, he made a fateful concession: 'For many a one who finds Spinoza's doctrine objectionable on the ground that Spinoza conceives God as a being without freedom, it is not superfluous to remark that he too thought absolute necessity and absolute freedom identical.'[3] In short, despite his intense belief in freedom, despite his elegant discussions of the coincidence of freedom and necessity, Schelling never in any significant way distinguishes his position from that of Spinoza himself. In a note on the *Wesen der menschlichen Freiheit*, Coleridge wonders 'does not Schelling use Freedom often when he means no more than others mean by *Life*—that is, the power of originating motion.'[4] And a note on the *Philosophische Briefe über Dogmatismus und Kriticismus* shows that Coleridge eventually realized that Schelling's 'freedom' was not the kind of moral freedom the 'I am' must have: 'It is clear to me that both Schelling and Fichte impose upon themselves the scheme of an expanding surface, and call it Freedom. . . . P.S.—The above I wrote a year ago: but the more I reflect, the more convinced am I of the gross materialism, which lies under the whole system.'[5]

Coleridge gradually eroded his own early hopes for the validity of Schelling's demonstrations in the *System des transscendentalen Idealismus*. Schelling, all his own conviction and virtuosity of exposition notwithstanding, does not actually reconcile Kant and Spinoza, the 'I am' and the 'it is'; rather he gives two different deductions of Spinozism, two different versions of the 'it is'. His 'subjective' is a merely logical subject, not an existential subject, as it must be for the true validation of an 'I am' position. It is thus only verbally distinct from his 'objective'. And always Schelling is a monist. Thus in 1807, in some *naturphilosophischen* aphorisms not read by Coleridge until after he had written the *Biographia*, Schelling says:

> It is not our office now to penetrate deeper into the relations of the ideal world, but only to indicate here clearly . . . that there is only One Universe, thoroughly self-identical, only-begotten, at once Unity and Infinity, . . . from which everything born comes out and to which it returns.

And he then appends a footnote that reveals his whole scheme:

> We want to present, as a summary, our whole philosophy in the following general scheme, although we warn against its misuse. . . .

---

[1] Schelling, *Werke*, vii. 333. Cf. Herder, *Werke*, viii. 201–2.

[2] Schelling, *Werke*, i. 331. For example (as Schelling elsewhere points out) we paradoxically realize, in the case of a crime, that on the one hand the criminal had a choice of committing or not committing the crime, and that on the other he was necessitated by the whole course of his heredity, environment, and past existence to precisely this action. Cf. Kant, *Werke*, iii. 387.

[3] Ibid., p. 331 n. Compare Spinoza, *Epistolae* LVIII.

[4] Marginal note as printed in the Appendix to volume iii of *Works*, p. 692.

[5] Marginal note as printed in the Appendix to volume iii of *Works*, p. 701.

God

The All

relative-real All	relative-ideal All
gravity (A^1), matter	truth, science
light (A^2), motion	goodness, religion
life (A^3), organism	beauty, art

world-system	reason	history
man	philosophy	the state[1]

Thus we see that Schelling's division of philosophy into ideal and real, in all its manifestations, is merely a polar development of an 'it is' unity, the absolute. At the end of the *Transcendental Idealism* he reveals this fact: 'Philosophy', he says, 'goes out from an infinite division of opposed activities'.[2] But, as a later commentator says,

when we say that nature and intelligence are like two parallel lines, we virtually reduce intelligence to nature. Both must be explained as the manifestation of an activity which appears now as nature and again as intelligence . . . as a matter of fact the 'self' disappears and all that remains is the 'activity'. . . . The only wonder, in fact, is how Schelling did not see, at the time he wrote the *Transcendental Idealism*, that the parallelism of nature and intelligence necessarily carried with it the implication of a unity transcending both, a unity which for him could only be that in which they agreed, or their 'absolute indifference'. . . . This in fact is the source and rationale of his, as of all other pantheism. For, when intelligence and nature are so absolutely opposed, even the assertion that nature exists only for knowledge cannot prevent intelligence from being conceived as a finite subject, standing opposite to which is a world of finite objects; and hence the unity of both must be found in the conception of a power which manifests itself, now as thinking subjec t and again as thought object, neither the subject nor the object having any reality except as a phase of the Power which is over or behind both.[3]

Coleridge reached the same conclusion. In a note on the flyleaf of his copy of the *System des transscendentalen Idealismus* he says: 'In the very act of opposing A to B' Schelling 'supposes an X common to both viz. Being οὐσία; but this given, there is no necessary reason why Objectivity and

---

[1] Schelling, *Werke*, vii. 184. It is to such passages that Coleridge probably refers when, in 1818, he ruefully tells Green that Schelling would 'have put me on my guard' but for the fact that at first 'I knew little or nothing of any of his works, excepting his Transcendental Idealism. For as soon as he commenced the Objective or Natur-wissenschaft, he gave the Slip to the former [i.e. the 'I am' exposition of the *Transcendental Idealism*]—and in his Jahrbücher der Medicin [where this passage appears] fairly involved it [the 'I am'] in the latter [the Objective, or 'it is'] . . .' (*Letters*, iv. 874).

[2] Schelling, *Werke*, iii. 626. Such was always his conception. In 1795, for instance, he says the same thing in Fichtian language: 'The complete system of knowledge emanates from the absolute, all-contraries-excluding ego' (*Werke*, i. 176).

[3] John Watson, *Schelling's Transcendental Idealism. A Critical Exposition* (Chicago, 1892), pp. 200–1. See Excursus Note XII, p. 303.

Subjectivity should not both be predicable of both.'[1] Also, if the absolute is polar, then it is not absolute, and Coleridge, in a letter of 1818, therefore speaks of Schelling's 'inconsistency' in asserting 'Polarity' of the 'Absolute' to have 'Transcendental Idealism as one Pole and Nature as the other' was like 'putting the Candle horizontally and burning it at both ends.'[2] Conversely, if the absolute is absolute, then the polarities do not really exist, and the system is simple pantheism. Indeed, Schelling himself, near the end of the *Wesen der menschlichen Freiheit*, calmly admits that 'since all antitheses disappear with respect to the Absolute when regarded as such, whoever wishes to call this system pantheism should have this privilege. . . . The name does not matter. . . '.[3]

I suggest then that Coleridge, to whom the reconciliation of the 'I am' and the 'it is' was of such overpowering moment, approached Schelling's *Entweder-Oder* with the same mixture of expectant joy and a readiness for disillusionment with which a seventeenth-century mathematician must have approached a 'proof' for the squaring of a circle.[4] A consummation devoutly to be wished, but so far as Coleridge's own reasoning could lead him unlikely to be attained. If the circle of 'I am' could indeed be harmonized with the square of 'it is', its art of proof must be Schelling's art alone. Coleridge's viewpoints were not the same as Schelling's; but on this very important philosophical point Coleridge was willing to accept Schelling—even bow down to Schelling—if Schelling could do as Schelling claimed to do.

'My acquaintance with S. T. C. commenced', wrote Green, in a statement whose re-perusal in the light of these suggestions resolves its paradoxes,

with the intention of studying the writings of Schelling; but after a few interviews the design was given up, in consequence of Coleridge's declaring his dissent from Schelling's doctrines. . . . This perhaps renders the *Biographia* more inexplicable. For herein S. T. C. assumes the originality of Schelling—which can be received only with great qualifications—and is content to have it admitted, that the agreements between himself and Schelling were the coincidences of two minds working on the same subject and in the same direction. Now this is the more remarkable, that it may be shown, that many or most of the views entertained by Coleridge, at least at the period of our first acquaintance, might

---

[1] Marginal note on the flyleaf of Schelling, *System des transscendentalen Idealismus* (Tübingen 1800), in the British Museum. See note 33, p. 354.

[2] *Letters*, iv. 874. To J. H. Green, 30 Sept. 1818.

[3] Schelling, *Werke*, vii. 409–10.

[4] In a notation on the flyleaf of the *System des transscendentalen Idealismus* (Tübingen, 1800), Coleridge displays an almost this-did-I-fear resignation as he remarks that at page 54 'the *Spinosism* of Schelling's system first betrays itself . . .' (printed in Henri Nidecker, 'Notes marginales de S. T. Coleridge en marge de Schelling', *Revue de littérature comparée*, vii (1927), 743). The observation seems to have been written later than other notations on the same page.

have been derived from other sources, and that his system differs essentially from that of Schelling.[1]

But one of Schelling's views could be derived from no other source whatever: the reconciliation of the 'I am' and the 'it is'. In such a reconciliation Schelling would, if successful, have been matchlessly 'original'. Green was well aware that in no other reference could 'the originality of Schelling' be received except 'with great qualifications',[2] and so too was Coleridge, who recognized not without a certain contempt Schelling's indebtedness of style and matter. To cite a single instance, some seven years before the appearance of the *Biographia*, Coleridge told Crabb Robinson that 'Schelling's system resolves itself into fanaticism, not better than that of Jacob Boehme'.[3] Still more knowing is his sophisticated comment in the *Philosophical Lectures*: 'My time will not permit me to enter into any account of [Schelling] as I intended, but in truth I should be puzzled to give you a true account. For I might at one time refer you to Kant . . . another time to Spinoza . . . and then again I should find him in the writings of Plotinus, and still more of Proclus.'[4]

Thus, in any context other than that of the harmonization of the 'I am' and the 'it is', Schelling apparently seemed to Coleridge as at best an echo of various writers whom he had long known at first hand, and at worst as a patchwork pantheist. Coleridge's interest in Schelling would therefore be ultimately restricted to whether Schelling did or did not succeed in his attempt at reconciliation. So we come to the third of our investigations concerning Coleridge's Schelling translations in the *Biographia*—the question of the significance of Coleridge's abandonment of the translation and his helter-skelter leap (for it is nothing less than a philosophical rout, a mad dash from an untenable position) into the formulations about the imagination in the thirteenth chapter.

We are concerned in this volume with a large, but at the same time self-limiting task: the study of Coleridge's underlying ideas set against the central traditions of continental thought in his time. We have identified the dynamic polarity of his thought as consisting in an attraction–repulsion

[1] *Biographia*, 2nd edition (London, 1847), i. xxxiv n.

[2] Certainly in no other sense of the word did any sophisticated person ever think him original. See Excursus Note XII, p. 305.

[3] Crabb Robinson, *Diary*, i. 305. Compare Julius Hamberger: 'Schelling does not mention Boehme in the writings that appeared during his lifetime. This is quite especially conspicuous in his essay on *Das Wesen der menschlichen Freiheit*, where the influence of Boehme on Schelling's revised doctrine is so very evident . . .' (Baader, *Werke*, xiii. 162 n.). Compare Coleridge's comment on the *Wesen der menschlichen Freiheit*: 'How can I explain Schelling's strange silence respecting Jacob Boehme? The identity of his system was exulted in by the Tiecks at Rome in 1805, to *me*; and these were Schelling's intimate friends. The coincidence in the expressions, illustrations, and even the mystical obscurities, is too glaring to be solved by mere independent coincidence in thought and intention. Probably prudential motives restrain Schelling for a while . . .' (marginal note as printed in *Works*, iii. 695).

[4] *Philosophical Lectures*, p. 390.

tension of 'I am' and 'it is' consequences—a systole and diastole of his intellect, as it were—and we have seen this large problem as relevant to, though not identical with, the problems also faced by the intellectuals on the continent. Now a necessary corollary to such an investigation, which, dealing as it does with the foundations of Coleridge's thinking, emphasizes the intellectual points of rest provided by his peers and predecessors, is a demonstration of the internal reticulation of his interests. Such an investigation must be focused on Coleridge's conception of the imagination, to which he attached so much importance, and also on the imagination's function as mediator between his abstract moral interests and his poetic, objective interests. But precisely because of the importance of the imagination to Coleridge, it is not feasible in this volume to enter, in a significant way, a problem of such complex ramifications. We intend in our sequel to present a full investigation of the imagination, and of the theory of symbol, as well as a more careful investigation of the meaning of the Platonic backgrounds of Coleridge's thought, and we plan, finally, to demonstrate the ways in which his actual poetic production participated in the unity of his total effort.

For our present purposes it is enough to say that the imagination, either as posited in the thirteenth chapter of the *Biographia* or as elsewhere formulated, is conceived by Coleridge as functioning in a way that does not grow out of his Schellingian paraphrases, in a way that in fact frees him from dependence on such borrowings. For Coleridge the function of the imagination was to emancipate the poetic concern from any Spinozistic implications, or, to put it another way, to establish the harmony of the moral concern with poetry. Coleridge's formulations were not borrowed or fabricated in response to any temporary fashion or problem; they were gradually evolved as reflections of the deepest and most permanent needs of his intellectual awareness.[1] As early as 1796, before he had acquired a genuine knowledge of German or German thought, and long before his statements in the thirteenth chapter of the *Biographia*, Coleridge had put forward a theory of the imagination. Referring to the 'Godwinian System of Pride', which he clearly saw as 'Atheism' and as a system in which man was 'an outcast of blind Nature ruled by a fatal Necessity'[2]— a summing-up that could eloquently serve for Spinozism itself—he wrote in the Gutch Notebook: 'Doctrine of necessity rendered not dangerous by the Imagination. . .'[3] Such was the function of Coleridge's theory of

---

[1] Broadly speaking the function of the imagination for Coleridge was to connect the 'I am' with the 'it is', while maintaining the primacy and independence of the 'I am'. The 'imagination' —the faculty of images—is, as Bacon noted, 'not tied to the laws of matter' (*Works*, iii. 343), while as Kant points out, 'imagination' has the effect of 'creating a second nature out of the material supplied to it by actual nature' (*Werke*, v. 389). See Excursus Note XIII, 'Coleridge's Theory of the Imagination', p. 306.

[2] *Notebooks*, i. 174.   [3] *Notebooks*, i. 156. See note 34, p. 355.

imagination, and however it was elaborated it remained basically the same.[1]

Though deeply cherished by Coleridge as allowing a kind of working relationship between the abstract and the poetic, the theory was none the less clearly not adequate, nor in truth designed for, the reticulation of all his interests. Only a systematic justification could ultimately suffice, and it was in the hope of finding it that Coleridge welcomed Schelling. But it was only as the *soi-disant* reconciler of 'it is' and 'I am' thought (and to a less urgent degree as offering the aesthetic justification of artistic activity) that Schelling seriously engaged Coleridge's attention. In an 'examination of all the Systems', as he writes in 1818, Coleridge clearly reveals his hopes, for he identifies three systems as stemming 'from the pure Reason': the first is *'Objective'*, that is, as we see from our previous discussions, the philosophy of 'it is', which Coleridge therefore quite properly equates with 'Spinoza'; the second is 'Subjective' and is equated with 'Berkeley, Fichte'; the third is '. . . the Identity of both', which equals 'Schelling'.[2]

But as clearly as we here see Coleridge's hopes for Schelling as systematic reconciler, just as clearly do we see his built-in realization that such a reconciliation must of needs be specious; for 'Berkeley, Fichte', rather than Plato or Kant, are here identified as the exponents of the 'I am'. But Berkeley and Fichte are both only nominally 'I am' thinkers: that is, they both start from the 'I am' standpoint, but they do not verify the 'I am' systematic chain of consequences by coming to rest in a two-world cosmology, and hence, since both are really pantheists in their implication, both can be reconciled under the specious inversions of Schelling's *Entweder-Oder*.[3] We may say parenthetically that Schlick rightly reproves Carnap and Vaihinger for doing what Berkeley and Fichte do, that is, for attempting to connect a solipsistic ego philosophy with a positivist view of nature.[4]

It is further noteworthy that though Coleridge in his Godwinian days thought of Berkeley as the logical opponent of the system of nature, and even named a son for the Irish philosopher, Berkeley is rarely mentioned in his later writings and is specifically identified in the *Biographia* as one of the thinkers who had not provided him with 'an abiding place' for his 'reason'.[5] Moreover, Kant explicitly dissociated his own thought from that

---

[1] Coleridge's later distinction between imagination and fancy documents rather than contradicts this point. See Excursus Note XIII, p. 310.

[2] *Letters*, iv. 863.

[3] See Excursus Note XI, p. 300. See slso note 35, p. 355.

[4] Schlick, 'Meaning and Verification', *Gesammelte Aufsätze 1926–1936* (Wien, 1938), pp. 356–7.

[5] *Biographia*, i. 93. In a note of 1804 Coleridge uses such phrases as 'unphilosophical' and 'unworthy & sophistical mode' in describing some of the argument of Berkeley's *Principles* (*Notebooks*, i. 1842).

of Berkeley,[1] and Leibniz considered him lacking in high philosophical seriousness.[2] As for Fichte, whom Coleridge here seems to want to think of as an apostle of the 'I am', he was, as has been repeatedly emphasized in this volume, the chief link between Spinoza and the Schellingian form of pantheism.[3]

Coleridge's invocation of Schelling as the reconciler of 'objective' and 'subjective' philosophies is thus here, as it was in the *Biographia*, a wistful imposition of philosophical need upon logical fact, and such an imposition must necessarily be of brief duration. Coleridge had otherwise little use for the German, and was not in sympathy with him either in tone or in ultimate position. To Crabb Robinson in 1812 Coleridge spoke his true mind about the actual content of Schelling and Fichte, saying that 'from Fichte and Schelling' he had 'not gained any one great idea.'[4] Though he conceded, in another statement, that Schelling's thought was of 'a permanent value' as an 'attack on the mechanic and corpuscular Philosophy', in its inner reality—'as a *System*'—it was 'little more than Behmenism' and 'like Behmen's it is reduced at last to a mere Pantheism'.[5] Of Schelling's *Einleitung zu seinem Entwurf eines Systems der Naturphilosophie*, Coleridge wrote to Green in 1818 that he could 'see clearly the rotten parts and the vacua of his foundation.'[6] Coleridge's recognition of what Schelling stood for was sharply accurate when freed from the wishful distortion of his own craving to reconcile the moral and the poetic concerns. A 'Hylozoic Atheism', he says of Schelling's thought.[7] The 'entire principia philosophiae Schellingianae', he says, could be found 'in the fragments collected by Fr. Patricius from the Pagan and Christian Neo-platonists', especially 'Proclus'.[8] And

---

[1] Kant protests strongly against confusing his idealism with 'dem mystischen und schwärmerischen' idealism of 'BERKELEY'—against which, indeed, and against other similar mental cobwebs (Hirngespinste) his Kritik rather provides the remedy (Kant, *Werke*, iv. 43).

[2] Referring to Berkeley merely as 'Qui in Hybernia corporum realitatem impugnat,' Leibniz expresses himself as unsatisfied by the Irishman's reasons and explanations and says that he suspects Berkeley is the kind of man who wants to be known by his paradoxes (*Philosophische Schriften*, ii. 492).

[3] In this connexion it is interesting to note that Coleridge, in a marginal note on the flyleaf of Fichte's *System der Sittenlehre* . . . (Jena und Leipzig, 1798)—now in the British Museum—implies that Fichte's position leads to 'the old "Ἑν καὶ Πᾶν, into which all systems of Idealism must at length fall'. Again, in a note on the flyleaf of Fichte's *Grundlage der gesammten Wissenschaftslehre* (Leipzig, 1794)—also in the British Museum—Coleridge writes: 'Im absoluten Ich erkennt man Gott — nicht im Gotte erkennt man das absolute Ich, Ergo, Fichte und Schelling . . .=*Spinoza*??' For Coleridge's hope for Fichte as apostle of the 'I am' see *Biographia*, i. 101.

[4] Crabb Robinson, *Diary*, i. 380–1.   [5] *Letters*, iv. 883. To Tulk, 24 Nov. 1818.

[6] Ibid. iv. 873. To Green, 30 Sept. 1818.

[7] Ibid. 874. Hylozoism, the theory that matter is alive, is not a doctrine of Spinoza's. It is a tenacious legacy from antiquity. Coleridge would have known about its implications from early in his career, because both Berkeley's *Siris* and Cudworth's *Intellectual System* contain discussions of its role in ancient thought. Cudworth finds that 'the First and Chief Assertour of this Hylozoick Atheism was, as we conceive, *Strato Lampsacenus* . . .' (R. Cudworth, D.D., *The True Intellectual System of the Universe* . . . (London, 1678), p. 107). See note 36, p. 356.

[8] *Letters*, iv. 874. See note 37, p. 356.

if the philosophy of Schelling could be described from the ontological and theological standpoint as 'Hylozoic Atheism', from the historical stand-point it was, said Coleridge with precision, a 'sort of Plotinised Spinozism'.[1]

Thus, in the final analysis, we see that Schelling's thought possesses two kinds of relevance for the study of Coleridge: first, a general relevance for the 'I am'/'it is' tension that kept Coleridge's philosophical bow bent throughout his life, and secondly, a special relevance as a magnet for his literary interests at the time of the *Biographia Literaria*. But in the first instance Coleridge regarded Schelling's thought as one of several variants of Spinozism, much less important than Spinoza himself, than Plotinus, and probably than Boehme; somewhat more important, perhaps, than Bruno, Erigena, the Cabalists, the Hermetics, Swedenborg, and Proclus. And in terms of his special relevance, Schelling's importance has been over-emphasized, probably because of the drama of the plagiarism charges. His total importance is not to be dismissed entirely, but it needs to be more modestly assessed, and to be seen in these two aspects. The 'System' of Schelling was 'extremely plausible and alluring at a first acquaintance', said Coleridge.[2] But later acquaintance made him certain that with regard to Schelling and his followers his 'discrepances from the Doctors of the Absolute' were 'far more in number than our agreements';[3] and he had finally to confess that from his own 'confidence in others I was myself *taken in* by' Schelling, and that in adopting his thought 'in the metaphysical chapters of my Literary Life' he had been 'retrograding from my own prior and better Lights'.[4] And at a passage in the *Jahrbücher der Medicin als Wissenschaft*, where Schelling says that knowing and known are the same in reason, whose whole content is a self-confirmation of the absolute, Coleridge comments, in final and devastating dismissal: 'This is the Basis of the Schellingian Atheism, Σπινοσισμὸς πολύσαρκος, or the cloathed Skeleton of Spinoza!'[5]

So we may now return to Spinoza himself, for Spinoza is a far more con-stant factor in the development of Coleridge's thought.[6] Even the *Bio-graphia Literaria*, in the end, substitutes Spinoza for Schelling as the referent of Coleridge's 'it is' interest; with that substitution, furthermore, the 'I am'/'it is' literary reconciliation begins to come apart at its specious seams. For, following a summary of his Christian beliefs, Coleridge speaks of a reviewer's 'slander' (it was Hazlitt's) about 'my "potential infidelity" ',[7]

---

[1] *Letters*, iv. 883. Compare Friedrich Schlegel: 'Schelling's more recent works, which annul the earlier, seem to contain nothing other than a restoration of Spinozism and of Plotinian philosophy' (*Philosophische Vorlesungen*, i. 471).

[2] *Letters*, iv. 883. [3] Ibid. 876.

[4] Ibid. 874. See note 38, p. 357.

[5] Marginal note in *Jahrbücher der Medicin als Wissenschaft*, Zweyten Bandes zweytes Heft (Tübingen, 1807), p. 286. The volume is now in the British Museum.

[6] See note 39, p. 358.

[7] See Hazlitt, *Complete Works*, xvi. 106.

which, says Coleridge, can be attributed 'in part to the openness with which I have avowed my doubts, whether the heavy interdict, under which the name of BENEDICT SPINOZA lies, is merited on the whole or to the whole extent...'[1] But after this envoy, as it were, to his Spinozistic needs in a literary context, he concludes the whole work with an affirmation of Christianity—not, significantly, as a creed, nor again, as a way of life, but as a 'Scheme' in which 'link follows link by necessary consequence' —that is, as the system of philosophy that finally fulfils his requirements:

> This has been my Object, and this alone can be my Defence—and O! that with this my personal as well as my LITERARY LIFE might conclude! the unquenched desire I mean, not without the consciousness of having earnestly endeavoured, to kindle young minds, and to guard them against the temptations of Scorners, by showing that the Scheme of Christianity, as taught in the Liturgy and Homilies of our Church, though not discoverable by human Reason, is yet in accordance with it; that link follows link by necessary consequence; that Religion passes out of the ken of Reason only where the eye of Reason has reached its own Horizon; and that Faith is then but its continuation. . .[2]

With this triumphant reassertion of Christianity against Spinozism ('Unitarian*ism* ... PSILANTHROPISM and THEANTHROPISM as schemes of Belief'),[3] Coleridge brings to bear what sounds very much like an accommodated form of Jacobi's *Glaubensphilosophie*, and also brings to an end the *Biographia Literaria*.

Exactly when Coleridge began to read Spinoza is not known, and in view of his youthful saturation in the Neoplatonists is not very important. I should, indeed, argue that dates are only schematically, not substantively, important in examining Coleridge's development. We too often think of 'development' as a kind of progress up a series of steps, the improvement of one's position by the abandonment of a previous position. Actually the word implies an unwrapping of something already there. Its sister words in German and French suggest the same psychological truth: *Entwicklung* implies an unwrapping, *épanouissement*, a flowering from a bud. Such, I think, is the reality of all philosophical elaboration. Bacon never tires of stressing the psychological truth behind the Platonic doctrine of anamnesis, while Whitehead emphasizes that the minds of children are, in memory and logic, called upon to perform greater feats than the minds of adults.[4] The careful empirical investigations of Freud have demonstrated

---

[1] *Biographia*, ii. 217.   [2] Ibid. 218.   [3] Ibid. 217.
[4] Thus Whitehead: 'I commence by challenging the adequacy of some principles by which the subjects for study are often classified in order. . . . The first intellectual task which confronts an infant is the acquirement of spoken language. What an appalling task, the correlation of meanings with sounds! It requires an analysis of ideas and an analysis of sounds. We all know that the infant does it. . . . All I ask is that with this example staring us in the face we should cease talking nonsense about postponing the harder subjects' (Whitehead, *The Aims of Education and Other Essays* (New York, 1929), p. 25).

M

how relentlessly the bent twig inclines the grown tree; and for purposes of polemic I might even go so far as to say that our philosophical formulations are nothing more than an attempt to introduce connexions and order among the discrete phenomena that flow past us, but that what constitutes this connexion and order is really our sense of the coherence of later, more complex experience with our earliest psychological apprehensions. The child is father of the man. Indeed, in some minds the philosophical concern manifests itself almost simultaneously with youthful experience. Jacobi calmly tells Mendelssohn that an important part of his philosophical attitude was formed 'im achten oder neunten Jahre'.[1] 'I discovered Aristotle as a boy,' says Leibniz,'. . . and the Scholastics. . . . Plato too, and Plotinus. . . . I remember walking in a grove on the outskirts of Leipzig . . . at the age of fifteen, and deliberating, whether to preserve substantial forms or not.'[2] And Lamb testifies that at about the same age Coleridge entranced the casual passer through the cloisters with 'the mysteries of Jamblichus or Plotinus (for even in those years thou waxedst not pale at such philosophic draughts)' while the 'walls of the old Grey Friars re-echoed to the accents of the *inspired charity boy*!'[3]

The point should be stressed, because Wellek, in summarizing the difficulties of arriving at a full understanding of Coleridge's relation to German thought, notes that it would be necessary for an ideal commentator 'to pay considerable attention to the vexed question of chronology in Coleridge's thought',[4] and he rebukes Helene Richter for having 'no regard for chronology'.[5] Chronology, it is true, can often have a specific value; but its reverence by the scholarly tradition is largely a convention of that tradition, complementing the scholarly prejudices that require 'development' in the sense of progressive steps. The textbooks exult in the proliferation of developmental stages; but such stages do not allow us to see clearly the unfolding of a single, constant orientation to life. Though the data of the world change for us, and their connexions with our understanding, the eyes looking out from our time-eroded bodies are the lights of a soul that does not change. Who is to say the bloom is more truly the flower than is the bud?[6] Gillman testifies that

---

[1] Jacobi, *Werke*, IV–I, p. 48. Berkeley, again, says that he was 'distrustful at 8 years old; and conqseuently by nature diposed for these new doctrines', i.e. the opinions of 'Malbranch, Locke . . . that extension is not in matter . . . that colours are not in bodies' (*Berkeley's Commonplace Book*, ed. G. A. Johnston (London, 1930), p. 30, M. 275).

[2] *Philosophische Schriften*, iii. 606.

[3] *The Works of Charles and Mary Lamb*, ii. 21.

[4] René Wellek, 'Coleridge's Philosophy and Criticism', *The English Romantic Poets*, ed. T. M. Raysor, p. 101.

[5] Ibid., p. 100.

[6] To use a distinction of Nicholas of Cusa, the chronological development of a man's views is the *explicatio* of a *complicatio* that exists much earlier. The clear explications of maturity may be more important to others, but the intense complications of early experience are most meaningful to ourselves. The world applauds the 'hollow ghost / That blamed the

during the long period of their acquaintanceship Coleridge 'never deviated' from 'his philosophical views'.[1] Gillman speaks for the latter part of Coleridge's career, and we can recognize too the constancy of his orientation during the early and middle parts. To take two or three instances, each trivial, but perhaps for that reason the more impressive when constancy is the issue: first, at the end of the *Biographia*, Coleridge's last sentence rises to rhetorical fervour as follows:

It is Night, sacred Night! the upraised Eye views only the starry Heaven which manifests itself alone: and the outward Beholding is fixed on the sparks twinkling in the aweful depth, though Suns of other Worlds, only to preserve the Soul steady and collected in its pure *Act* of inward adoration to the great I AM, and to the filial WORD that re-affirmeth it from Eternity to Eternity, whose choral Echo is the universe.[2]

In this moment of final disposition of 'I am' and 'it is' concerns Coleridge, we note, refers to the starry Heaven and speaks of the stars as 'Suns of other Worlds'. This in the concluding sentence of a major work published in 1817. But it also occurs in a private notation in 1796, in the Gutch Notebook, as 'Stars twinkle upon us—Suns on other worlds.'[3] And still earlier, much earlier: 'I remember', Coleridge reminisces, 'that at eight years old I walked with [my father] one winter evening . . .—& he told me the names of the stars—and how Jupiter was a thousand times larger than our world—and that the other twinkling stars were Suns that had worlds rolling round them'.[4]

A second example can be taken from the discussion of the meaning of Don Juan in the twenty-third chapter of the *Biographia*, where Coleridge speaks against 'the (so called) *system of nature* (i.e. materialism, with the utter rejection of moral responsibility . . .)'.[5] In the Gutch Notebook of 1796 a short notation, reading 'Answer to the System of Nature—', shows clearly that he was thinking about the same issues, in the same words even, in 1796 as he was two decades later.[6] Thirdly, we may return to the

---

living man', laments Arnold. A man may write more clearly as he grows older, but if his experience has been authentic, he cannot change. An elm tree cannot grow from an oak's acorn. 'Only the lower natures', says Kierkegaard in *Fear and Trembling*, 'forget themselves and become something new. . . . The deeper natures never forget themselves and never become anything else than what they were.' Thus, though Coleridge can write in 1834 that 'it is wonderful to myself to think how infinitely more profound my views now are, and yet how much clearer they are withal' (*Table Talk*, 28 June 1834), a fortnight later, as he felt himself dying, he realizes that 'Youth and Hope' are the 'twin realities of this phantom world!' (*Table Talk*, 10 July 1834).

[1] Gillman, *Life of Coleridge*, p. 192.
[2] *Biographia*, ii. 218.   [3] *Notebooks*, i. 82.
[4] *Letters*, i. 354. See note 40, p. 358.
[5] *Biographia*, ii. 186.   [6] *Notebooks*, i. 161.

concluding chapter of the *Biographia*. There, immediately following his envoy to Spinoza, Coleridge says:

> With regard to the Unitarians, it has been shamelessly asserted, that I have denied them to be Christians. God forbid! . . . But this I have said, and shall continue to say: that if the doctrines, the sum of which I *believe* to constitute the Truth in Christ, *be* Christianity, then Unitarian*ism* is not . . .[1]

If we turn back twenty years to the Gutch Notebook, we find 'Unitarian/ travelling from Orthodoxy to Atheism—why, —&c.'[2]

Such evidence suggests that a man's deepest and most basic attitudes in relation to his total life activity should not be thought of as something superimposed by an adult sensibility. If it is not possible to trace mature attitudes back to premature attitudes, then we are likely to find that the mature attitudes are either not genuine or lack importance. Since our discussion has from the outset been centred upon the irreducible orientations of an instinctive sense of 'I am' as opposed to an instinctive sense of 'it is', it is admittedly possible to extend it into specifically psycho-analytical distinctions, although it would be difficult to apply a satisfactory analytical rhetoric to figures in the past. But the central point, that what is ultimately of importance in mature attitudes are intimations of reality recollected from earliest childhood, is one that Coleridge himself recognized. Crabb Robinson, for instance, notes in 1811 that he had a conversation with Coleridge

> on German metaphysics. He related some curious anecdotes of his son Hartley, whom he represented as a most remarkable child. A deep thinker in his infancy —one who tormented himself in his attempts to solve the problems which would equally torment the full-grown man. . . . When about five years old, Hartley was asked a question concerning himself by some one who called him 'Hartley.'—'Which Hartley?' asked the boy.—'Why, is there more than one Hartley?'—'Yes, there's a deal of Hartleys.'—'How so?'—'There's Picture Hartley (Hazlitt had painted a portrait of him), and Shadow Hartley, and there's Echo Hartley, and there's Catch-me-fast Hartley,'—at the same time seizing his own arm with the other hand very eagerly, an action which shows that his mind must have been led to reflect on what Kant calls the great and inexplicable mystery that man should be both his own subject and object, and that these should yet be one. 'At the same early age,' said Coleridge, 'he used to be in an agony of thought about the reality of existence. . . . Hartley, when a boy, had no pleasure in *things*; they made no impression on him till they had undergone a sort of process in his mind, and become thoughts or feelings.'[3]

It is against the background of such considerations as these that we asserted the precise date of Coleridge's first reading of Spinoza to be unimportant, especially in view of his youthful saturation in the Neo-

---

[1] *Biographia*, ii. 217.   [2] *Notebooks*, i. 80.
[3] *Diary*, i. 341–2. Compare also the letter to Dorothy Wordsworth of 9 Feb. 1801 (*Letters*, ii. 673).

platonists. What is important is that he did read, did think, and did realize the possibilities of reciprocal attitudes in which Neoplatonism, Spinozism, and the philosophy of Schelling all serve the same function. We can illustrate his tendency to view philosophies reciprocally by considering (but not otherwise judging) his claim, in 1817, that he had educated himself to certain ideas 'during the study of Plato, and the Scholars of Ammonius, and in later times of Scotus (Joan. Erigena), Giordano Bruno, Behmen, and the much calumniated Spinoza . . . long before Schelling had published his first and imperfect view'.[1]

Though we do not know exactly when Coleridge began to read 'the much calumniated Spinoza', it was certainly long before he began to read Schelling. Coleridge read and re-read and talked about the great Jew constantly. The famous '*Spy Nozy*' anecdote is significant: A government spy, come down to check on the loyalty of those two suspected Jacobins, Coleridge and Wordsworth, in the summer of 1797, was continually frustrated and professionally embarrassed over a space of three weeks because, said Coleridge, he 'often heard me talk of one *Spy Nozy*' and could not understand how he had given himself away.[2] 'As soon as I settle,' Coleridge announces in a letter to Davy in 1800, 'I shall read Spinoza';[3] and about a dozen years later he was still reading Spinoza, for Crabb Robinson, as we have seen, lent him his copy of Spinoza in 1812.[4] A letter to Southey shows him jocularly aware of the pitfalls of Spinozism: 'I however, sunk in Spinoza, remain as undisturbed as a Toad in a Rock',[5] and again to Southey: 'My Spinosism (if Spinosism it be and i' faith 'tis very like it) . . .'.[6] Countless brief invocations, often for comparison or contrast, show that Spinoza was never far from his mind: 'SHAKSPERE is the Spinozistic deity—an omnipresent creativeness';[7] '. . . I abide by a maxim which I learned at an early period of my theological studies, from Benedict Spinoza';[8] 'Sir T. Brown was a Spinosist without knowing it';[9]

---

[1] *Letters*, iv. 775. To Tulk, Sept. 1817.

[2] *Biographia*, i. 126–7. The spy actually existed, along with some darkly suspicious (and hilarious) official correspondence (see A. J. Eagleston, 'Wordsworth, Coleridge, and the Spy', *Coleridge; Studies by Several Hands*, ed. Blunden and Griggs, pp. 73–87). We may well doubt, however, as does Eagleston, the 'delightful story about Spinoza' (p. 86). Not only does the pun 'spy nosy' crop up in a jotting of 1799 (*Notebooks*, i. 432. 4), but there is a suspiciously similar story in which a librarian at Durham misunderstands Coleridge's request for 'Leibnitz' as '*live Nits*' and avers that 'We have no Museum in this Library for natural curiosities' (*Letters*, ii. 747).

[3] *Letters*, i. 590. [4] *Diary*, i. 399–401.

[5] *Letters*, i. 534. 30 Sept. 1799. The Paulus edition of Spinoza, which Coleridge borrowed from Robinson—'I return you (very reluctantly, I own) the two Volumes of Spinoza—reluctantly, because in England I cannot purchase them—' (to Robinson, 26 Nov. 1813, *Letters*, iii. 461)—was published in Jena in 1802–3, and it is therefore clear that Coleridge's interest in Spinoza preceded the availability of the standard Romantic edition.

[6] *Letters*, i. 551. 24 Dec. 1799. [7] *Table Talk*, 12 May 1830.

[8] *Works*, i. 320.

[9] *Coleridge's Miscellaneous Criticism*, ed. T. M. Raysor (London, 1936), p. 253.

'for the most part there is an absolute contrast, between Hobbes and Spinoza';[1] 'After the *Scienza Nuova* read Spinoza';[2] 'To rationalize this figment of his church, Bossuet has recourse to Spinosism'.[3]

Such a list of passing references can be augmented almost indefinitely; but of far more significance is a famous statement in the Tenth Chapter of the *Biographia*: 'For a very long time, indeed, I could not reconcile personality with infinity; and my head was with Spinoza, though my whole heart remained with Paul and John.'[4] Here are the grand ambivalences of the *Pantheismusstreit*. Pantheism against Theism. Atheism against Christianity. Personality against the outer world. The head against the heart. It is possible to go back through Coleridge's work for the period he describes and see the struggle as it took place. It is very clear in 1795 in 'The Eolian Harp':

> And what if all of animated nature
> Be but organic Harps diversely fram'd,
> That tremble into thought, as o'er them sweeps
> Plastic and vast, one intellectual breeze,
> At once the Soul of each, and God of all?

an example of pure Neoplatonic Spinozism that is immediately counterbalanced by the voice of the heart and of Christianity:

> But thy more serious eye a mild reproof
> Darts. . . . And biddest me walk humbly with my God.
> Meek Daughter in the family of Christ![5]

And in a letter to Thelwall in the autumn of 1797, the Spinozistic motif is very strong: 'My mind feels as if it ached to behold & know something *great*—something *one* & *indivisible*—and it is only in the faith of this that rocks or waterfalls, mountains or caverns give me the sense of sublimity or majesty'.[6]

Yet Christianity exerted a magnetism equally strong. 'Have you read over Dr Lardner on the Logos?' he asked Poole in March of 1796. 'It is, I think, scarcely possible to read it, and not be convinced. . . . I shall begin about my Christian Lectures';[7] and in September of that year he wrote Lamb a thoroughly Christian letter of consolation: 'You are a temporary sharer in human miseries that you may be an eternal partaker of the Divine nature'; 'We cannot arrive at any portion of heavenly bliss without in some measure imitating Christ'.[8] In a letter of January 1796, to Josiah

---

[1] *Omniana* p. 411.
[2] *Table Talk*, 23 April 1832.
[3] *Works*, v. 85. [4] i. 134.
[5] 'The Eolian Harp', ll. 44–53, *Poems*, i. 102.
[6] *Letters*, i. 349. [7] Ibid., p. 195.
[8] Ibid. p. 239.

Wade, Coleridge phrases the issues of the *Pantheismusstreit* very strongly—classically, even—and in doing so betrays his own perplexity:

> but *all at once he makes up his mind* on such important subjects, as whether we be the outcasts of a blind idiot called Nature [Spinozism], or the children of an all-wise and infinitely good God [Christianity]; whether we spend a few miserable years on this earth, and then sink into a clod of the valley, or only endure the anxieties of mortal life in order to fit us for the enjoyment of immortal happiness.[1]

And, more fancifully, the dilemma thrusts itself into a playful suggestion in the Gutch Notebook:

> Hymns to the Sun, the Moon, and the Elements—six hymns.—In one of them to introduce a dissection of Atheism—particularly the Godwinian System of Pride Proud of what? An outcast of blind Nature ruled by a fatal Necessity—Slave of an ideot Nature!
>
> . . . .
>
> In the last Hymn a sublime enumeration of all the charms or Tremendities of Nature—then a bold avowal of Berkley's System!!!!!![2]

At that time, as we know, 'Berkley's System' represented in its solipsism an impeccable 'I am' voice for Coleridge.[3]

These early formulations cast the issues of the *Pantheismusstreit* into Necessitarian and Neoplatonic pantheism, on the one hand, and into Berkleyan solipsism and Christianity on the other. None the less they reveal the full range of tensions of a more technically philosophical opposition between Spinoza and Kant, and do justice to all the corollary problems of pantheism. It would be easy to extrapolate for any one of them the most sophisticated kind of gloss from the high traditions of philosophy. Take, for instance, Coleridge's ambivalence about 'animated nature' as 'organic Harps . . . that tremble into thought, as o'er them sweeps / Plastic and vast, one intellectual breeze / At once the Soul of each, and God of all'—lines written in his twenty-third year (in a poem that he himself considered important: 'by the bye—that is my favorite of *my* poems . . .').[4] Coleridge's soulmate, Leibniz, writing in his full maturity in 1702, supplies the commentary:

> Several ingenious men have believed and still believe today that there is only one single spirit, which is universal, and which animates all the universe in all its parts, each according to its structure, following the organs that it finds, as the same wind makes the various pipes of an organ produce different sounds.[5]

---

[1] Ibid., p. 177.   [2] *Notebooks*, i. 174.
[3] e.g. 'I am a Berkleian' (*Letters*, i. 278. To Thelwall, 17 Dec. 1796); 'Bishop Taylor, Old Baxter, David Hartley & the Bishop of Cloyne are *my men*' (*Letters*, i. 245. To Poole, 1 Nov. 1796); '. . . those, who, like the Author [Coleridge], believe and feel the sublime system of Berkley. . .' (*Poems*, i. 124 n.).
[4] *Letters*, i. 295. To Thelwall, 31 Dec. 1796.
[5] *Philosophische Schriften*, vi. 529.

Such a view, Leibniz asserts, leads to a denial of personal immortality:

Thus they believe that when an animal has the right organs, the spirit makes the effect of a particular soul, but when the organs are destroyed, this particular soul returns to nothing or returns, so to speak, to the ocean of universal spirit.[1]

Leibniz, like Coleridge, was attracted by that corollary of the doctrine of a universal spirit by which nature becomes enriched with divinity, and by which all things are unified:

The doctrine of a universal spirit is good in itself, for all those who profess it admit in effect the existence of deity, be it that they hold that this universal spirit is supreme, in which case they hold that it is God himself, or that they believe with the Cabalists that God created it, which is also the opinion of the Englishman Henry More. . .[2]

But after this flirtation with Neoplatonist pantheism, Leibniz settles down to an unequivocal opposition to the further implications of the universal spirit, for they constitute Spinozism:

But when one goes on to say that this universal spirit is unique, and that there are no other souls or particular spirits at all, or at least that these particular souls cease to subsist, then I believe that one passes the bounds of reason. . . . Let us examine the apparent reasons upon which this doctrine rests—this doctrine that destroys the immortality of souls and degrades humankind, or rather all living creatures, from their proper place. . . . For it seems to me that an opinion of this weight must be proved, and that it is not enough to base it upon a lame analogy with a wind that animates musical organ pipes. . . . Spinoza has pretended to give a proof that there is only a single substance in the world, but his demonstrations are pitiable or unintelligible.[3]

Inasmuch as Coleridge's 'intellectual breeze' is specifically 'one', 'at once the Soul of each, and God of all', it would fall under Leibniz's interdiction, and would, in those terms, be tantamount to Spinozism. Elsewhere, Leibniz restates the identity of the implications of 'one intellectual breeze' with Spinozism:

Certain ancient and more recent thinkers have asserted . . . that God is a spirit diffused throughout the whole universe, which animates organic bodies wherever it meets them, just as the wind produces music in organ pipes. The Stoics were probably not averse to this opinion, and the active intellect of the Averroists, and perhaps of Aristotle, reduces to it, being the same in all men. . . . In another way Spinoza tends towards the same view. For him there is one substance, God. Creatures are his modifications, like figures in wax. . . .[4]

The 'I am'/'it is' tension is thus apparent in an early and Neoplatonic poem, 'The Eolian Harp'; it is present too in an even more youthful poem,

[1] *Philosophische Schriften*, vi. 529   [2] Ibid., pp. 530–1.   [3] Ibid., p. 531.
[4] *Gothofredi Guillelmi Leibnitii . . . Opera omnia . . . studio Ludovici Dutens* (Genevae, 1768), ii. 225.

the 'Religious Musings' written on Christmas Eve 1794, though derived from a different background of reading. Instead of 'all the strange phantasms that ever possessed your philosophy-dreamers from Tauth, the Egyptian to Taylor, the English Pagan'—that is, the fragmentary and corrupt Neoplatonisms that were Coleridge's youthful 'darling Studies'[1]— the reading that underlay the 'Religious Musings' was the tradition of eighteenth-century British materialism. Stemming from Newton and Locke, this line of thought became in its eighteenth-century expression undoubtedly one of the most provincial of all the traditions that the history of philosophy records, one that might be termed, not unfairly, a kind of bargain-basement Spinozism.[2] Its avatars, diminishing in importance as they manifested themselves in time, were Hartley, Priestley, and Godwin. Hartley's *Observations on Man, His Frame, His Duty, and His Expectations*, published early in 1749, was a compendium of Locke and Newton that attempted, with heroic inconsequence, to cover the philosophy of 'it is' with a fretwork of pious Christian avowals.[3] Priestley, the discoverer of oxygen, devoted a number of his multitudinous writings to an espousal of Socinian Christianity ('I think', says Coleridge in the *Table Talk*, 'Priestley must be considered the author of the modern Unitarianism').[4] And Godwin, in a work entitled *Enquiry Concerning Political Justice, and its Influence on Morals and Happiness*, was the rage of the 1790s in England, and became by his prominence and his manifest intellectual inferiority to the young Coleridge a kind of quintain that prepared Coleridge for his later jousts with Spinozism itself.[5]

[1] *Letters*, i. 260. To Thelwall, 19 Nov. 1796.
[2] See note 41, p. 359.
[3] See Excursus Note XIV, 'The Religious Heterodoxy of Hartley, Priestley, and Godwin', p. 311.
[4] *Table Talk*, 23 June 1834. The term 'Unitarian' (with Latin inflections) had been in use on the continent since around 1600; it first appeared in England, however, in 1673, where Henry Hedworth, in his *Controversie Ended* (part of a polemical dispute with William Penn occasioned by Hedworth's attack on George Fox) provides 'a short account of those men's opinion concerning Christ, who for distinction sake call themselves *Unitarians . . .* because they own but one Person, and one substance or Essence of the most High and Independent God and to distinguish them from other Christians, that hold three Persons and one Essence of God, and are therefore denominated Trinitarians' (Hedworth, p. 53; quoted in H. J. McLachlan, *Socinianism in Seventeenth-Century England* (London, 1951), p. 312). Though Unitarianism had existed in England for more than a century before Priestley, it was Priestley's indefatigable propagandizing that made it a formidable reality, and Coleridge's view is in this respect just.
[5] The youthful Franz von Baader, for instance, notes proudly in his diary: 'On April 10 (in the year 1793) began to read Godwin'—and then there follow no less than seventy pages (as printed) of extracts and comments on the *Political Justice* (Baader, *Werke*, xi. 210–80). Indeed, Godwin, despite his innocence of philosophical learning, presents himself as excitingly *au courant* with respect to the politico-intellectual modernities of his time: hence he says that his work was occasioned 'by the recent discussions of America and France', and that he 'derived great . . . instruction from reading the most considerable French writers upon the nature of man . . . *Système de la Nature*, Rousseau, and Helvetius', that he was influenced by 'ideas suggested by the French revolution'—which was at that time (1793) the very face and front of modernity (*Political Justice* I. vi. viii). See Hazlitt, *Complete Works*, xi. 16–17.

The tone and emphasis of the three thinkers differed somewhat: in Hartley, associationist psychology was presented in a Christian framework; in Priestley, a polemic for 'rational' Christianity was accompanied by Baconian progressivism; in Godwin, political anarchism and social utopianism were set forth without reference to Christianity. In all three, however, was a common denominator that they and others called 'necessitarianism', that is, a controlling conviction that reality was located in external circumstance that thereby necessitated or determined human action—in short, a Spinozism *manqué*.[1] And such was Coleridge's unvarying judgement in later years. In a note in the margin of Andrew Fuller's *Calvinsitic and Socinian Systems Examined and Compared*, he comments sardonically: 'in both systems'—that is, of Fuller and of Priestley:

man is annihilated . . . it is all God . . .—in brief, both systems are not Spinosism, for no other reason than that the logic and logical consequency of 10 Fullers+ 10×10 Dr. Priestleys, piled on each other, would not reach the calf of Spinoza's leg. Both systems of necessity lead to Spinosism. . . .[2]

As late as the *Aids to Reflection* Coleridge is still sardonically castigating Priestleyan necessitarianism as inconsequent Spinozism:

God (says Dr. Priestley) not only does, but is every thing. . . . And thus a system, which commenced by excluding all life and immanent activity from the visible universe, and evacuating the natural world of all nature, ended by substituting the Deity, and reducing the Creator to a mere *anima mundi*: a scheme that has no advantage over Spinosism but its inconsistency. . . .[3]

Such, however, was not his opinion in 1794. With Coleridge the emotional need for Christianity always came before the intellectual need for philosophy, but where the one went, the second was sure to follow.[4] If, as we have maintained at length, his orientation was towards a unity of his interests that would allow the poetry-feeding 'it is' to coexist with the moral 'I am', it would follow that the systems of Hartley and Priestley were peculiarly adapted, by their own inner inconsistencies that allowed Christian avowals side by side with an apotheosis of the 'it is', to disarm such an ardent but relatively unsophisticated intellectual. In his early days, therefore, Coleridge could triumphantly assert, under the aegis of Hartley, that he was a follower of the 'it is': 'I am a compleat Necessitarian—and understand the subject as well almost as Hartley himself—but I go farther

---

[1] See Excursus Note XIV, p. 313.

[2] *Works*, v. 449.

[3] *Works*, i. 361.

[4] 'It is the heart that lifts itself up to God' (*Works*, v. 341). 'The strongest argument for Xstianity' was that 'it fits the human heart' (*Notebooks*, i. 1123). 'Man may rather be defined a religious than a rational Creature: in regard that in other Creatures there may be something of Reason, but there is nothing of Religion' (*Notebooks*, ii. 2223). But '. . . without metaphysics there can be no light of faith' (*Works*, v. 259). Hence 'What is Christianity but a divine and pre-eminent Philosophy?' (*Inquiring Spirit*, p. 386).

than Hartley and believe the corporeality of *thought*.[1] At the same time, also under the aegis of Hartley, he could—or thought he could—maintain the Christianity so essential to his emotional being: 'My Wife was safely delivered of a boy. . . . I have named him David Hartley Coleridge, in honor of the great Master of Christian Philosophy.'[2] Coleridge's statements may sound befuddled, but the befuddlement inheres in the thought of Hartley rather more than in his own. It was Hartley who ostensibly united the necessitarian and the Christian, and when Coleridge rethought the chain of consequences he demonstrated his superior sense of reticulation by identifying 'Spinoza' and 'Hartley' as twin sharers of the 'system of necessity', and by abandoning Hartley.[3] As Willey remarks, speaking of Godwin—but granting licence to extend the point to Priestley and Hartley—'like the other eighteenth century necessitarians, Godwin tries to eat his cake and have it'; for, on the one hand, necessitarianism taught that 'the same laws of causation, which admittedly govern the universe, govern mind as well', but on the other it enabled Godwin 'to preach truth and justice . . . to believe in perfectibility, because "reason", "truth", "justice" are equivalent, for him, to "that which *must* prevail" .' Willey then wryly comments that it may seem strange that Godwin should have based his gospel of moral improvement 'upon the very philosophy which enables the assassin to excuse himself, and might give every man a pretext for staying as he is.'[4] The inconsistencies, however, troubled few in the England of the 1790s, and what seems remarkable, against that background, is not that Coleridge accepted this dominant native strain of philosophy for as long as he did, but rather that he did not accept it longer.

In 1794, however, he did accept necessitarianism, which forms the background of the 'Religious Musings'. We shall investigate other appearances of the 'I am'/'it is' tension, but these two poetic examples, 'The Eolian Harp' and the 'Religious Musings', are particularly edifying, for these early works are dramatic evidence of Coleridge's reticulative need, and of his refusal to compartmentalize his interests. Thus, from early to late, we find that his 'I am'/'it is' concern is not only enmeshed in his theory of poetic function, but appears in or alongside his poetic production itself. Accordingly, he considered 'THE FRIEND as the Main Pipe, from which I shall play off the whole accumulation and reservoir of my Head and Heart': this in 1808.[5] In 1817 he wrote to Poole that 'The Object of the

---

[1] *Letters*, i. 137. To Southey, 11 Dec. 1794.
[2] Ibid. i. 247. To Poole on 24 Sept. 1796 he announces the birth in a variant formula: 'It's name is DAVID HARTLEY COLERIDGE.—I hope, that ere he be a man, if God destine him for continuance in this life, his head will be convinced of, & his heart saturated with, the truths so ably supported by that great master of *Christian* Philosophy.' (*Letters*, i. 236.)
[3] Gillman, *Life of Coleridge*, pp. 319–20.
[4] Basil Willey, *The Eighteenth Century Background* (New York, 1953), pp. 228, 229.
[5] *Letters*, iii. 145.

third Volume of my Friend . . . is . . . that Morality without Religion is as senseless a scheme as Religion without Morality';[1] but, as he had written to Poole in 1809, he intended to publish 'all my poems in THE FRIEND, as occasion rises.'[2] Not only *The Friend*, but the *Biographia Literaria*—especially as prolegomena to his *magnum opus*—was explicitly conceived as uniting the philosophic and the poetic. Thus Coleridge speaks of the 'necessity of extending, what I first intended as a preface, to an Autobiographia literaria, or Sketches of my literary Life & opinions, as far as Poetry and *poetical* Criticism is concerned,'[3] and this work he considered as 'laying the foundation Stones of the Constructive or Dynamic Philosophy in opposition to the merely mechanic'.[4] Again, and even more explicitly, he says that 'instead of Poems *and* a Preface I resolved to publish "Biographical Sketches of my LITERARY LIFE, Principles, and Opinions, chiefly on the Subjects of Poetry and Philosophy. . . . To which are *added*, SIBYLLINE LEAVES, or a Collection of Poems". . . . The *Autobiography* I regard as the *main* work.'[5] And in 1816, in a projection of 'aspirations . . . toward the concentring my powers in 3 Works', he says that he is 'convinced that a true System of Philosophy . . . is *best* taught in Poetry as well as most safely'.[6]

Between these later statements and the early realities of 'The Eolian Harp' and 'Religious Musings' we may note various indicative remarks in his memorandum books: 'If I begin a poem of Spinoza. . . '[7] Again: 'A blank-verse, moral poem'.[8] Still again: 'Poem on Spirit—or on Spinoza'.[9]

The poem on Spinoza was never fully realized, doubtless because 'Spinosism with all it's Skeleton unfleshed, bare Bones and Eye-holes, as presented by Spinoza himself' would have revealed to Coleridge too dreadfully the ultimate incompatibility of his 'it is' and 'I am' drives.[10] The lesser Spinozisms—backing and filling, pious rather than logical—of Hartley and Priestley, on the other hand, did become the objects of his poetic effort. Thus in the 'Religious Musings' Coleridge speaks of him 'of mortal kind / Wisest, he first who marked the ideal tribes / Up the fine fibres through the sentient brain'[11]—and in a footnote identifies this 'of mortal kind wisest' as 'David Hartley.' And 'Priestley' is saluted in the same poem as 'patriot, and saint, and sage'.[12] While these enthusiasms are given the benefit of Christian pieties ('For in his own and in his Father's might / The Saviour comes!';[13] 'Lovely was the death / Of Him whose life was Love!'),[14] the poem reveals the pantheism of its ideas in a statement

---

[1] *Letters*, iv. 756.   [2] Ibid. iii. 235.   [3] Ibid. iv. 578–9.
[4] Ibid. 579.   [5] Ibid. 584–5.   [6] Ibid. 687.
[7] *Notebooks*, i. 556.   [8] Ibid. 330.   [9] Ibid. 1561.
[10] *Letters*, iv. 548.   [11] 'Religious Musings', l. 368–70, *Poems*, i. 123.
[12] Ibid., l. 371.   [13] Ibid., ll. 358–9, p. 122.
[14] Ibid., ll. 28–29, p. 110.

such as 'There is one Mind, one omnipresent Mind, / Omnific',[1] and, equally explicit if less embarrassing, ' 'Tis the sublime of man, / Our noon-tide Majesty, to know ourselves / Parts and proportions of one wondrous whole!'[2] Still more nakedly: 'But 'tis God / Diffused through all, that doth make all one whole'.[3]

Coleridge's own views on the poem are revealing both as to his constant involvement in its subject-matter and as to his growing conviction of its basic pantheism, which he saw would logically eventuate in Spinozism, however pious its language. 'I rest for all my poetical credit on the *Religious Musings*', he exults to Flower in 1796;[4] while to Poole in the same year he says the same thing: 'I pin all my poetical credit on the Religious Musings.'[5] To Thelwall he says that 'I build all my poetic pretentions on the Religious Musings—which you will read with a POET's Eye, with the same unprejudicedness, I wish, I could add, the same pleasure, with which the atheistic Poem of Lucretius. A Necessitarian, I cannot possibly dis-esteem a man for his religious or anti-religious Opinions.'[6] To Poole again, answering hypothetically a criticism that 'my religious Musings' were 'too *metaphysical for common readers*', he says proudly that 'the Poem was not written for common Readers'.[7] And to Cottle in February of 1797 he reveals the same preoccupation: 'The Religious Musings, I have altered monstrously, since I read them to you, and received your criticisms.'[8]

But the presence of alterations suggests a lack of complete satisfaction, and apparently this dissatisfaction deepened rapidly and importantly, for Cottle notes the curious fact that '. . . Mr. C. in his ever readiness to gratify me, by the recital of his various poems, never spoke of, nor repeated to me, one line of the "Religious Musings", till 1806'.[9] We have ample evidence why Coleridge began to look with disfavour on the 'Religious Musings'; it was the poem's pantheism rather than its lack of poetic stature that bothered him. De Quincey informs us that 'in an early poem entitled "Religious Musings," [Coleridge] has characterized Hartley as "Him of mortal kind / Wisest . . .". But at present [August 1807] all this was a for-gotten thing. Coleridge was so profoundly ashamed of the shallow Uni-tarianism of Hartley, and so disgusted to think that he could at any time have countenanced that creed, that he would scarcely allow to Hartley the

---

[1] Ibid., ll. 105–6, p. 113.   [2] Ibid., ll. 126–8, pp. 113–14.

[3] Ibid., ll. 130–1, p. 114. For other pantheisms in the poem, consider: 'Him Nature's essence, mind, and energy!' (l. 49, p. 111); '. . . plastic power, that interfused / Roll through the grosser and material mass / In organizing surge!' (ll. 405–7, p. 124). This latter passage of course faintly suggests Wordsworth's wonderful 'sense sublime of something far more deeply inter-fused' that 'rolls through all things' (*Tintern Abbey*), and it is interesting to note that Coleridge many years later implied Wordsworth's passage to be in 'language' (though not in intent) pantheistic, or, as he put it, a 'substitute for the Jehovah' of the 'Bible' (*Works*, i. 362).

[4] *Letters*, i. 197.   [5] Ibid. 203.

[6] Ibid. 205. Apr. 1796.   [7] Ibid. 207. 5 May 1796.

[8] Ibid. 309.   [9] Cottle, *Early Recollections*, ii. 52.

reverence which is undoubtedly his due.'[1] And Coleridge himself, writing to Cottle in 1814, subsumed the whole fault of the 'Religious Musings' under the grand paradigm of all 'it is' variants: Spinozism:

> The declaration that the Deity is 'the sole Operant' is indeed far too bold; may easily be misconstrued into Spinosism; and therefore, though it is susceptible of a pious and justifiable interpretation, I should by no means now use such a phrase. I was very young when I wrote that poem, and my religious feelings were more settled than my theological notions.[2]

Coleridge's last sentence goes to the heart of the matter; indeed, his whole intellectual activity might be described as a progressive attempt to find the philosophical system that would co-ordinate itself with his 'religious feelings'. He was, in truth, in the line of those Philonic thinkers that Wolfson posits as the absolute antithesis of the Spinozist.[3] If the existentialists preach existence before being, then Coleridge stands for feelings before notions—not, we emphasize, feelings without notions, in the manner of Jacobi, but an intellectual accounting in which feelings and notions cohere, with necessary alterations for this purpose occurring in the latter rather than in the former.

Of the three Necessitarians with whom Coleridge was principally involved, Godwin fell soonest into his disfavour, Priestley next, and Hartley last of all. Godwin, indeed, with no Christian avowal to mask the true consequences of his position, slipped almost immediately from grace and became something of a whipping boy for Coleridge, who could apparently discharge his anxieties upon Godwin and thus for a time preserve his illusions about Priestley and Hartley. As early as September 1794 Coleridge was hostile to Godwin's atheism ('Godwin *thinks* himself *inclined* to *Atheism*. . . . I set him at Defiance—tho' if he convinces me, I will acknowledge it in a letter in the Newspapers—I am to be introduced to him sometime or other'),[4] while he could none the less, in December 1794, purr that he was 'a compleat Necessitarian' of the order of 'Hartley himself';[5] could propagandize Southey ('I would ardently, that you were a Necessitarian');[6] and could proudly affirm himself to be 'a Unitarian Christian and an Advocate for the Automatism of Man.'[7] His attacks on Godwin became increasingly contemptuous: '. . . it is not his Atheism that has prejudiced me against Godwin; but Godwin who has perhaps *prejudiced* me against Atheism';[8] 'Why must every Man be Godwin —'tis the pedantry of Atheism';[9] 'My answer to Godwin will be a six

---

[1] De Quincey, *Collected Writings*, ii. 154.
[2] *Letters*, iii. 467. The 'sole Operant' phrase appears at line 56 of the poem (*Poems*, i. 111).
[3] See note 42, p. 360.
[4] *Letters*, i. 102.
[5] Ibid. 137.
[6] Ibid. 145. To Southey, 29 Dec. 1794.
[7] Ibid. 147.
[8] Ibid. 221. To Thelwall, 22 June 1796.
[9] *Notebooks*, i. 254.

shilling Octavo; and is designed to shew . . . the absurdities and wickedness of *his* System'.[1] These statements, from the years 1796–7, are rather
strong; but they are topped by even stronger language in 1804, when
Coleridge, after a fierce argument with Godwin one evening ('I begged
him for his own sake not to goad me . . . he . . . persisted—& then . . .
I did "thunder & lighten at him" with a vengeance, for more than an
hour & a half—every effort of self-defence only made him more ridiculous'),[2] describes the luckless Necessitarian as a 'dim-headed Prig of a
Philosophicide'.[3]

So for a while Coleridge was able to protect his esteem for Hartley and
Priestley by flaying Godwin. 'I do consider Mr. Godwin's Principles as
vicious', he writes in 1796, 'and his book as a Pander to Sensuality'—and
then he concedes thoughtfully: 'Once I thought otherwise'.[4] But in the
same letter he speaks of 'the great and excellent Dr. Hartley',[5] and a month
later, in May 1796, he still says flatly, 'I am a Necessitarian'.[6] Already,
however, in March of that year, Coleridge had caught a glimpse of
Priestley's Spinozism beneath the vesture of the Christian: 'How is it that
Dr Priestley is not an atheist?'—he asks in puzzlement. 'He asserts in
three different Places, that God not only *does*, but *is*, every thing.—But if
God *be* every Thing, every Thing is God—: which is all, the Atheists
assert—. An eating, drinking, lustful *God*—with no *unity* of *Consciousness*—
these appear to me the unavoidable Inferences from his philosophy.'[7]
The statement is extremely interesting, for here in March 1796 we see
that Coleridge's opposition to pantheism, and his analysis of pantheism,
were quite as well defined as in his most sophisticated statements of three
decades later. As we have repeatedly urged, Coleridge knew from the first
where he stood—or at any rate where he did not stand. His 'development'
entails the gradual adjustment of other sequences of thought to his own
axiomatic sense of reality; his philosophical biography records not an
access of wisdom, but a continuing process of elucidation of primary

---

[1] *Letters*, i. 267. To Flower, 11 Dec. 1796.

[2] Ibid. ii. 1072. To Southey, 20 Feb. 1804.

[3] Ibid. In 1811, after the need for a whipping-boy had gone, Coleridge apologized hand-
somely to Godwin: 'you', he said, are 'the Philosopher who gave us the first system in England
that ever dared reveal at full that most important of all important Truths, that Morality might be
built up on it's own foundation, like a Castle built *from* the rock & *on* the rock, with religion for
the ornaments & completion of it's roof & upper Stories . . .' (*Letters*, iii. 313–14). In a succeed-
ing letter, moreover, he said that 'Ere I had yet read or seen your works, I at Southey's recommendation wrote a Sonnet in praise of the author. When I had read them, religious bigotry,
the but half-understanding your principles, and the *not* half-understanding my own, combined
to render me a warm & boisterous Anti-Godwinist.' (*Letters*, iii. 315. To Godwin, 29 Mar.
1811.) See George Woodcock, *William Godwin; a Biographical Study* (London, 1946), pp. 167–73.

[4] Ibid, i. 199. To Caius Gracchus, 2 Apr. 1796.

[5] Ibid. 200.

[6] Ibid. 213. To Thelwall, 13 May 1796.

[7] Ibid. 192–3. Kant calls Priestley 'a genuine, consistent fatalist' (*Werke*, v. 108).

orientations. He is—we all are—the Lehrling of Sais. As a youth he was relatively unsophisticated about Priestley, indeed the concern with Priestley was in itself a mark of lack of sophistication. But he understood well enough the logical implications of what Priestley said. The phrase 'unity of Consciousness', for instance, grants full existential responsibility to the sort of critique of abstract 'subject' and 'ego' that is praised in Jacobi's 'Personalität' ('Mir ist Personalität α und ω')[1] or Unamuno's 'hombre de carne y hueso'. ('And note', says the latter, 'that in speaking of the "I", I speak of the concrete and personal "I", not of the "I" of Fichte, but of Fichte himself, the man Fichte.')[2]

By 1802, Coleridge, though his own Trinitarian Christianity had not assumed its enduring shape ('. . . you will see my *Confessio Fidei*, which as far as regards the Doctrine of the Trinity is *negative* Unitarianism'),[3] had nevertheless progressed so far from Priestley's brand of religion as to say:

> On the subjects of the original corruption of our Nature, the doctrines of Redemption, Regeneration, Grace, & Justification by Faith my convictions are altogether different from those of . . . Priestley. . . Neither do I conceive Christianity to be tenable on the Priestleyan Hypothesis.[4]

The rejection of Hartley was as final and as complete as of Priestley, and we may date Coleridge's disillusionment as culminating early in 1801, for in March of that year he wrote to Poole that: 'If I do not greatly delude myself, I have . . . overthrown the doctrine of Association, as taught by Hartley, and with it all the irreligious metaphysics of modern Infidels—especially, the doctrine of Necessity.'[5] Despite the finality of this rejection on ideational grounds, however, Coleridge never subjected Hartley, as a man, to the kind of abuse he showered upon Godwin, or even upon Priestley. As late, for instance, as the *Biographia Literaria*, though noting that it 'is fashionable to smile at Hartley's vibrations and

---

[1] Jacobi, *Briefwechsel*, i. 436.

[2] Unamuno, *The Tragic Sense of Life*, p. 8. Again: 'this "I" of flesh and bone, that suffers from tooth-ache and finds life insupportable if death is the annihilation of the personal consciousness, must not be confounded with that other counterfeit "I" which Fichte smuggled into philosophy' (pp. 28–29). See note 43, p. 360.

[3] *Letters*, ii. 821. To Estlin, 26 July 1802.

[4] Ibid. To Priestley, 'original sin' was 'this strange doctrine of the utter inability of men to do what God requires of them . . . a doctrine . . . injurious both to our Maker and ourselves. . . . My brethren, you find nothing like any part of this in your bibles. . . . It is allowed that we *suffer* by the sin of Adam, as any child may suffer in consequence of the wickedness of his ancestor; but it is not possible that we should have *sinned* in him. Wherever there is *sin*, there is *guilt*, that is, something that may be the foundation of *remorse* of conscience; something that a man may be *sorry for*, and *repent of*; something that he may wish he had not done; all which clearly implies that sin is something that a man has given his *consent* to, and therefore must be convinced of the reasonableness of his being punished for. But how can any man repent of the sin of Adam, or feel any thing like remorse of conscience for it; when he cannot but know that he never gave his consent to it . . .' (Priestley, *An Appeal to the Serious and Candid Professors of Christianity*, pp. 9–10).

[5] *Letters*, ii. 706.

vibratiuncles', he says with a trace of his old reverence that Hartley as a man was 'great' and as a thinker was 'coherent'.[1] In general, instead of abusing Hartley, Coleridge in later years contented himself with grouping him with Locke as a 'mechanic' philosopher ('the Mechanic, Locke, Hartley and Condilliac System'),[2] and when in an abusive mood he simply dropped Hartley's name from the rolls and concentrated his fire upon Locke himself (e.g. 'Locke and the stupid adorers of that *Fetisch* Earth-clod';[3] 'Mr Locke supposed himself an *adder* to Descartes—& so he was in the sense of *viper*').[4]

Though Coleridge's philosophical involvement with Godwin, Priestley, and Hartley dissipated itself in more or less rapid realizations of their Spinozistic implications, his involvement with the religious schematism for which Priestley and Hartley stood—that is, Unitarianism—lasted longer and went deeper, doubtless for the reason that the religious over-tones of Unitarianism as a church, associated with the schematic frame-work of the denial of Christ's divinity, made the intrinsic pantheism of the Unitarian arguments more difficult for Coleridge to recognize than merely philosophical pantheism. Even though pantheism is inescapably inherent in the monism of the Unitarian denial of the Trinity, the Socinian tradition, whether in an early manifestation such as Faustus Socinus's *De Christo Servatore* or in later works, was Bible-centred, and its purpose was exegetical and hermeneutic rather than cosmologically or ontologically speculative. It was, however, in line with Socinian apologetics that Toland supposedly coined the very word 'Pantheist'.[5] Unitarianism, in short, was historically destined to be a natural matrix for the 'I am'/'it is' collision of Coleridge's religious heart and philosophical head.

It would tend, furthermore, to assume special psychological importance for Coleridge in the light of his statement that 'my father had . . . resolved, that I should be a Parson'.[6] A Unitarian parson, however, Coleridge seemed strangely reluctant to become, even though he felt inexorably drawn towards precisely that position; and here again we can perhaps identify the opposing interests of the 'I am' and the 'it is', no matter how subliminal their influence. Thus Coleridge early adopted the curious notion—curious at least in the context of his poverty—that one should not teach the gospel for a living ('I deem that the teaching of the gospel for hire is wrong; because it gives the teacher an improper bias in favour

---

[1] *Biographia*, i. 76. [2] *Letters*, iv. 670.

[3] *Philosophical Lectures*, p. 460 n. 5. Coleridge almost always seems to have reserves of invective to lavish on Locke: e.g. 'the whole of Mr Locke's first Book is a jumble of Truisms, Calumnies, and Misrepresentations' (*Letters*, ii. 686); '. . . that same absurd Doctrine which Des Cartes is accused of having held concerning the Brutes, & which Mr Locke in his merry mood calls "a step beyond the Rosecrucians." This silly chapter . . .' (*Letters*, ii. 694); '. . . the sandy Sophisms of Locke . . .' (*Letters*, iv. 574).

[4] *Notebooks*, i. 857.

[5] See Excursus Note III, p. 266. [6] *Letters*, i. 354. To Poole, 16 Oct. 1797.

of particular opinions . . . where it is of the last importance that the mind should be perfectly unbiassed'),[1] a view that, whatever the merits of its inner logic, would, if accepted, effectively prevent Coleridge from following his father's intention and becoming a 'Parson'. None the less, on 29 December 1794 he writes to Southey that he is 'a Unitarian Christian'[2] (and yet the conjunctive clause following, 'and an Advocate for the Automatism of Man', is a storm cloud of tempests to come: compare Kant's statement of the central implication of Spinozism: 'Der Mensch wäre Marionette',[3] man would be a marionette or an automaton). And to Edwards on 29 January 1796 he says again that he is a 'Unitarian'.[4] An admission of reluctance, however, invades his statement when the stand-up-and-be-counted possibility of actually becoming a Unitarian minister is his subject: 'I might have a situation as a Unitarian minister,' he writes to Lloyd on 14 November 1796, but 'the Voice within puts a firm and unwavering negative.'[5] And with gloomy resignation he writes to Thelwall in October 1797 that: 'I have neither money or influence—& I suppose, that at last I must become a Unitarian minister as a less evil than starvation'.[6] His financial situation continuing to deteriorate, he braced himself, as it were, for the inevitable. To Josiah Wedgwood in January 1798 he announced that

I have conversed long, & seriously, & dispassionately with Infidels of great Talents & information—& most assuredly, my faith in Christianity [Unitarian] has been confirmed rather than staggered. In teaching it therefore, at present, whether I act *beneficently* or no, I shall certainly act bene*volent*ly. . . . It will be necessary for me, in order to my continuance as an Unitarian Minister, to believe that Jesus Christ was the Messiah—in all other points I may play off my intellect *ad libitum*.[7]

But then came the almost miraculous salvation. The bequest from Wedgwood was accepted with alacrity, and, the *Ancient Mariner* finished, Coleridge took ship later in the year for Germany, the Unitarian ministry behind him for ever.[8] Writing to Isaac Wood, after the receipt of Wedg-

---

[1] *Poems*, i. 117 n. 1.
[2] *Letters*, i. 147.   [3] Kant, *Werke*, v. 110.
[4] *Letters*, i. 178.   [5] Ibid. 255.
[6] Ibid. 349.   [7] Ibid. 366.
[8] It seems very likely that *The Ancient Mariner* reflects, perhaps both consciously and unconsciously, Coleridge's philosophical and religious preoccupations at this time. Coleridge was deeply committed to the Platonic tradition by which poetry was composed so as to convey an 'interior meaning' (*Letters*, ii. 866). The objection urged by House against Warren—'It is . . . tempting to use Coleridge's later distinctions between allegory and symbol in interpreting "The Ancient Mariner"; but they had not been expressed in 1797–8' (House, *Coleridge*, p. 93)— is only a very limited hindrance to explaining the poem as deliberately symbolic. Certainly the images in *The Ancient Mariner* are used elsewhere with a philosophical and theological significance (e.g. 'Mind, shipwrecked by storms of doubt, now mastless, rudderless, shattered,— pulling in the dead swell of a dark & windless Sea' (*Notebooks*, i. 932)). At the time of the poem's composition, moreover, there are indications of Coleridge's mental upheaval with regard to

wood's bounty, Coleridge, still in January 1798, protested once again his dedication to Unitarianism:

I have an humble trust, that many years will not pass over my head before I shall have given proof in some way or other that active zeal for Unitarian Christianity, not indolence or indifference, has been the motive of my declining a local and stated settlement as preacher of it.[1]

No excuse could sound more lame, and we, against the background of Spinozism, see Coleridge as prompted by the murmur of his heart—which was, as he says autobiographically, 'with Paul and John', against his head, which was 'with Spinoza'.[2] So much he himself later realized. Looking back after many years, he speaks of himself as having

said then plainly and openly, that it was clear enough that John and Paul were not Unitarians. But at that time I had a strong sense of the repugnancy of the doctrine of vicarious atonement to the moral being, and I thought nothing could counterbalance that. 'What care I,' I said, 'for the Platonisms of John, or the Rabbinisms of Paul?—My conscience revolts!' That was the ground of my Unitarianism.[3]

Though saved at the last moment from having to declare himself openly and irrevocably a Unitarian by accepting a post as a preacher, Coleridge seems to have been driven to a kind of crisis by the imminence of the threat, and it is at this point that the objections of his heart seem to rise up from their subliminal haunts to contest the Spinozistic reign of his head. At any rate, both his own evidence and other testimony confirm that his Bristol period was crucial in the evolution of his understanding of his religious sensibility. 'When Mr. Coleridge first came to Bristol,' recalls Cottle, 'he had evidently adopted at least to some considerable extent, the sentiments of Socinus. By persons of that persuasion, therefore, he was hailed as a powerful accession to their cause.'[4] And De Quincey recalls that he 'could not reconcile with my general reverence for Mr. Coleridge the fact, so often reported to me, that he was a Unitarian. But, said some Bristol people to me, not only is he a Unitarian—he is also a Socinian.'[5] Upon his return from Malta, however, Coleridge had worked his way round to a complete rejection of Unitarianism and an espousal of Trinitarian Christianity. When De Quincey spoke to him of the reports of the Socinianism of his Bristol days he found that 'he disowned most solemnly (and I may say penitentially) whatever had been true in these reports. Coleridge told me that it had cost him a painful effort, but not a moment's hesitation,

theological problems (compare, for instance, Cottle: 'Mr. C. up to this day, Feb. 18th, 1798, held, though laxly, the doctrines of Socinus', and on the same day a letter from Coleridge: 'Feb. 18, 1798 / My dear Cottle, / I have finished my Ballad, it is 340 lines . . .' (Cottle, i. 304,07)).

[1] *Letters*, i. 377. To Wood, 19 Jan. 1798.
[2] *Biographia*, i. 134. [3] *Table Talk*, 23 June 1834.
[4] Cottle, i. 177. [5] *Collected Writings*, ii. 154.

to abjure his Unitarianism'[1]—for which we may somewhat cynically substitute, certainly a painful effort to abjure his Unitarianism, but not a
moment's hesitation in accepting the Wedgwood bequest.

Coleridge himself, writing to George Fricker in October 1806, says that

> I was for many years a Socinian; and at times almost a Naturalist, but sorrow,
> and ill health, and disappointment in the only deep wish I had ever cherished,
> forced me to look into myself; I read the New Testament again, and I became
> fully convinced, that Socinianism was not only not the doctrine of the New
> Testament, but that it scarcely deserved the name of a religion in any sense.[2]

We can see the lack of co-ordination between head and heart, however,
in the fact that Coleridge seems to have abandoned the Unitarian position
before he was rationally prepared to substitute for it the Trinitarian position. For a time—roughly the period celebrated by his Dejection ode—he
was not only bereft of his shaping spirit of imagination, of his interest in
poetry, but was also negative in his religious beliefs. For instance, in an
oft-cited jotting, he reveals the beginnings of an overt dissatisfaction with
the precepts of Unitarianism, and a longing for a sequence of conceptions
more responsible to the psychic realities of his experience: 'Socinianism
Moonlight—Methodism &c A Stove! O for some Sun that shall unite
Light & Warmth'.[3] The wistful lament is repeated in 1802: 'Socinianism
moonlight—Methodism a Stove! O for some Sun to unite heat & Light'.[4]
On 1 July 1802 he betrays extreme perplexity: 'I have read carefully the
original of the New Testament', he says, and 'have convinced myself, that
the Socinian & Arian Hypotheses are utterly untenable; but what to put
in their place?'[5] And later in the same month he tells Estlin of his 'Confessio Fidei', which at that moment 'as far as regards the Doctrine of the
Trinity is *negative* Unitarianism—a non liquet concerning the nature &
being of Christ—but a condemnation of the Trinitarians as being wise
beyond what is written.' But simultaneously he expressed himself that
'neither do I conceive Christianity to be tenable on the Priestleyan
Hypothesis.'[6]

We should not wonder that Coleridge had so much trouble accepting
Trinitarianism to fill the vacancy left by Unitarianism.[7] His peculiar virtue
as an intellectual is his integrity: he would not cheat the head for the heart,
and on the other hand he would not cheat the heart for the head; he would

---

[1] *Collected Writings*, ii. 156.   [2] *Letters*, ii. 1189.
[3] *Notebooks*, i. 467.   [4] Ibid. 1233.
[5] *Letters*, ii. 807. To George Coleridge.
[6] Ibid. 821. To Estlin, 26 July 1802.
[7] Coleridge had been involved with the merely logical problems of Trinitarian thinking from
his schooldays on; for a long time, however, he could not dissociate this Trinitarianism from
pantheism. Thus as late as 1810 Robinson reports that Coleridge asserted 'Jesus Christ' to be
'a Platonic philosopher. And when Christ spoke of his identity with the Father, he spoke in
a Spinozistic or Pantheistic sense, according to which he could truly say that his transcendental
sense was *one* with God, while his empirical sense retained its finite nature.' (*Diary*, i. 307–8.)

not forsake the 'I am' for the 'it is', but on the other hand he would not abandon the 'it is'—like Berkeley—to fashion a verbal victory for the 'I am'. He would not abandon poetry for philosophy, nor philosophy for poetry. He would not abandon faith for reason; but he likewise would not abandon reason for faith. He always strove towards a systematic reconciliation of all his interests. Thus, though the Trinity is a doctrine that transcends reason, it could not contradict reason and still be acceptable to Coleridge; and Coleridge's slowness in believing the mystery indicates the full responsibility he assumed for exploring its meaning and place in the whole body of his thought. We can see, therefore, his initial rejection of Unitarianism gradually becoming more certain as he begins to see his way towards an acceptance of the mystery of the Trinity as faith's crown upon reason's head.

By 1804, for instance, he seems to have eroded the ground of his Unitarian commitments sufficiently to reject their necessitarian underpinning with even more confidence than he had rejected Hartley in 1801; for he writes approvingly to Poole that 'you never suffered either my Sublety or my Eloquence to proselyte you to the pernicious Doctrine of Necessity / all praise to the Great Being who has graciously enabled me to find my way out of that labyrinth-Den of Sophistry'.[1] With increasing sharpness he attacked Unitarianism itself: speaking of Middleton's book on the Greek article in the New Testament, he says, in 1808: 'I have received great & various Instruction from it, and see my own Scheme in a fuller light. And as to Socinian Textualism, *there* it lies! in shakes and shatters'.[2] To Poole in 1810 he writes: 'I feel convinced, that after a fair perusal of my Supplement you will perceive that Socinianism has not a pin's point to ground itself upon: and that No Trinity, no God—is a matter of natural Religion as well as of Christianity, of profound Philosophy no less than of Faith.'[3] And in a climactic letter to Cottle in 1814, he writes:

> You ask me my views of the *Trinity*. I accept the doctrine, not as deduced from human reason, in its grovelling capacity for comprehending spiritual things, but as the clear revelation of Scripture. But perhaps it may be said, the *Socinians* do not admit this doctrine as being taught in the bible. I know enough of their shifts and quibbles, with their dexterity at explaining away all they dislike, (and that is not a little) but though beguiled once by them, I happily, for my own peace of mind, escaped from their sophistries, and now, hesitate not to affirm, that Socinians would lose all character for honesty, if they were to explain their neighbour's will with the same latitude of interpretation, which they do the Scriptures.[4]

---

[1] *Letters*, ii. 1037. To Poole, 15 Jan. 1804.
[2] Ibid. iii. 69–70. To Southey, 13 Feb. 1808. See note 44, p. 361.
[3] *Letters*, iii. 283–4. To Poole, 28 Jan. 1810.
[4] Ibid. 480. To Cottle, April 1814.

His final acceptance of the Trinitarian position, accordingly, involved a complete and total rejection of Socinian belief. 'Socinianism', he says unequivocally in 1814, 'is not only not Christianity, it is not even *Religion* —it doth not *religate*, doth not bind anew—', and the statement prefixes a long explanation to Cottle of the ground of his acceptance of the Trinity.[1]

Along the way to this final form of understanding, however, Coleridge thought through the full sequence of Socinian-Unitarian implications and his conclusions make clear the basis for the instinctive reservations of his earlier years. They reveal, too, his sense of the final irreconcilability of the 'it is' starting-point with his deepest needs. '. . . I hold it demonstrable', he says, with profound insight, 'that a consistent Socinianism, following its own consequences must come to Pantheism'.[2] In a letter to Clarkson in 1806 he demonstrates his thorough understanding of Unitarian implications in words that both acknowledge Spinoza as the grand paradigm of 'it is' systems and explain the plaint of 1799 that 'Socinianism' was 'moonlight':

Unitarianism in it's immediate intelligential . . . consequences, is Atheism or Spinosism—God becomes a mere power in darkness, even as Gravitation, and instead of a moral Religion of practical Influence we shall have only a physical Theory to gratify ideal curiosity—no Sun, no Light with vivifying Warmth, but a cold and dull moonshine, or rather star-light, which shews itself but shews nothing else—[3]

Such was his logical understanding of the Socinian position. Having conclusively identified Unitarianism as Spinozism, however, Coleridge seemed reluctant to dismiss the Unitarian scheme altogether. Rather, like the persistence of sin in the life of the redeemed, Unitarianism survived as a kind of adverse terminus for his religious argument for the rest of his career. We may speculate that its function was, as Godwin's had been *vis-à-vis* Hartley, to provide a butt for his anti-Spinozistic sentiments while preserving the *Existenz* of Spinoza himself as an object of reverence.[4] Certainly, as we shall see, he found Spinoza lastingly worthy of reverence, and in those projections of his *magnum opus* that we shall presently consider he almost invariably suffixed a plan for a harsh treatment of Unitarianism to one for a gentle treatment of Spinoza. We have, indeed, already noted precisely this tendency in the envoy to Spinoza, accompanied by the attack on Unitarianism, that concludes the *Biographia Literaria*.

Again, perhaps his repeated and unequivocal rejection of Unitarianism

---

[1] *Letters*, iii. 479.   [2] *Works*, v. 406.
[3] *Letters*, ii. 1196. To Clarkson, 13 Oct. 1806.
[4] e.g. 'It is most necessary to distinguish Spinosism from Spinosa . . .' (W. Hale White, 'Coleridge on Spinoza', *The Athenaeum*, No. 3630, 22 May 1897, p. 681). '. . . I can see no reason for railing at Spinoza . . .' (ibid.).

was bound up with the reasons for his original embracement of that doctrine: it seemed close to Christianity. For Spinoza, for Plotinus, he always retained immense respect, and for such lesser 'it is' thinkers as Boehme and Swedenborg he always held an affection that never slipped below the level of tolerance. But he never seemed to be able to forgive Unitarianism for having led him so close to the perversion of his religious sensibilities.[1]

In this respect we may recall one of his encounters with his inimitable foil, Mrs. Barbauld. 'Mr. Coleridge', writes Gillman,

once met Mrs. Barbauld at an evening party. He had not long been present, and the recognition of mere acquaintanceship over, than, walking across the room, she addressed him in these words:—'So, Mr. Coleridge, I understand you do not consider Unitarians Christians.' 'I hope, Madam,' said he, 'that all persons born in a Christian country are Christians, and trust they are under the condition of being saved; but I *do* contend that Unitarian*ism* is not *Christianity*;' to which she replied, 'I do not understand the distinction.'[2]

Mrs. Barbauld would scarcely have been in character had she expressed a keener comprehension; yet few of us, for that matter, trouble our heads about such distinctions. If, however, we are to understand Coleridge, we must at least realize that he troubled his own head very much, and took these distinctions very seriously. As late as 1832, for instance, he was still actively concerned to be counted against Unitarian*ism*:

I make the greatest difference between *ans* and *isms*. I should deal insincerely with you, if I said that I thought Unitarianism was Christianity. No; as I believe and have faith in the doctrine, it is not the truth in Jesus Christ; but God forbid that I should doubt that you, and many other Unitarians, as you call yourselves, are, in a practical sense, very good Christians. We do not win heaven by logic.[3]

And in some of those beautifully phrased statements of his religious beliefs in the *Omniana*, he strikes again and again at the Socinian-Unitarian conceptions as irreligion masking itself as religion:

[1] For instance, in 1819 he writes of a conversation in which an interlocutor said that 'the Unitarians were not worth the stone that might be thrown at them—"they can do no harm" —' to which Coleridge replies, 'Aye, Sir! but the Spirit of Unitarianism (and I looked stedfastly at him as I spoke the words) Aye, Sir! but the *Spirit* of Unitarianism both can and does.—The most fanatical of those, who have excited so much alarm in your mind, are at worst but straw and Stubble set in a blaze on the outside of the Temple Walls, and you mistake the *reflection* for a conflagration in the Temple itself and cry out—Fire! Fire!—but the spirit of Unitarianism is the Dry Rot in the timbers of the Edifice, yea, in the very Beams and Rafters on the Roof of your Church' (*Letters*, iv. 965–6). Again, the 'spirit of Socinianism' was 'the dry rot in the beams and timbers of the Temple!' (*Works*, v. 156).

[2] Gillman, *Life of Samuel Taylor Coleridge*, p. 164. Coleridge attached great importance to the distinction and frequently invoked it. For a single instance, compare *Aids to Reflection* (*Works*, i), p. 238 n.: 'Resist every false doctrine: and call no man heretic. The false doctrine does not necessarily make the man a heretic; but an evil heart can make any doctrine heretical.'

[3] *Table Talk*, 4 April 1832.

VI. That Socinianism is not a religion, but a theory, and that, too, a very pernicious, or a very unsatisfactory, theory.

. . . . . .

VII. That Socinianism never did and never can subsist as a general religion.

. . . . . .

VIII. That Socinianism involves the shocking thought that man will not, and ought not to be expected to, do his duty as man; unless he first makes a bargain with his Maker, and his Maker with him.

. . . . . .

IX. That Socinianism involves the dreadful reflection, that it can establish its probability (its certainty being wholly out of the question and impossible, Priestley himself declaring that his own continuance as a Christian depended on a contingency,) only on the destruction of all the arguments furnished for our permanent and essential distinction from brutes. . . .[1]

Such arguments, wherever they appear in Coleridge's repeated rejections of Socinianism, are always special emphases or variants of his general form of rejection: that Socinian Unitarianism is a masked—and unworthy —Spinozism:

Upon my word, if I may say so without offence, I really think many forms of Pantheistic Atheism more agreeable to an imaginative mind than Unitarianism as it is professed in terms: in particular, I prefer the Spinozistic scheme in-finitely. . . . Unitarianism is, in effect, the worst of one kind of Atheism, joined to the worst of one kind of Calvinism, like two asses tied tail to tail.[2]

Though it was the most enduring religious analogue of Spinozism in Coleridge's consciousness, Unitarianism did not by any means pre-empt the energies he devoted to the 'I am'/'it is' tension. His wide erudition in secular philosophers led to subsumptions either of Kant or of Spinoza, and the conflict permeated his utterances even when specifically philosophic or religiously schematic distinctions were not present. It extended to the very roots of his being, and is identifiable, sometimes in opposed terms, sometimes as a favouring of one pole without overt mention of its opposite, in emotional statements that bear witness to the alternating, and sometimes simultaneous, intensity of his concern for both 'I am' and 'it is'. The need for pantheism, for instance, expresses itself blindly in a letter to Thelwall in 1797: 'I should much wish, like the Indian Vishna, to float about along an infinite ocean cradled in the flower of the Lotos.'[3] And to Sara Hutchinson, some five years later, he reveals the almost hypnotic train of pantheist associations suggested to his Romantic gaze by the sight of a cataract: 'What a sight it is to look down on such a Cataract!—the wheels, that circumvolve in it—the leaping up & plunging forward of that infinity of Pearls & Glass Bulbs—the continual *change* of the *Matter*,

[1] *Omniana*, pp. 420–1.   [2] *Table Talk*, 4 April 1832.
[3] *Letters*, i. 350. To Thelwall, 14 Oct. 1797.

the perpetual *Sameness* of the *Form*—it is an awful Image & Shadow of God & the World.'[1] In another place he allows himself a kind of exultation in a pantheist oneness with nature:

In simple earnest, I never find myself alone within the embracement of rocks & hills, a traveller up an alpine road, but my spirit courses, drives, and eddies, like a Leaf in Autumn: a wild activity, of thoughts, imaginations, feelings, and impulses of motion, rises up from within me—a sort of *bottom-wind*, that blows to no point of the compass, & comes from I know not whence, but agitates the whole of me; my whole Being is filled with waves, as it were, that roll & stumble, one this way, & one that way, like things that have no common master. I think, that my soul must have pre-existed in the body of a Chamois-chaser. . . . The farther I ascend from animated Nature, from men, and cattle, & the common birds of the woods, & fields, the greater becomes in me the Intensity of the feeling of Life; Life seems to me then a universal spirit, that neither has, nor can have, an opposite.[2]

Such feelings were especially benign for his poetic sense. 'I devote myself', he says, '. . . in poetry, to elevate the imagination & set the affections in right tune by the beauty of the inanimate impregnated, as with a living soul, by the presence of Life. . . .—I love fields & woods & mounta[ins] with almost a visionary fondness—'.[3]

Deep and instinctive, however, though this emotional pull towards pantheism was, equally deep and equally instinctive was his emotional sense of the primal sanctity of the 'I am'. 'I never', he writes to Poole autobiographically in 1797, 'regarded *my senses* in any way as the criteria of my belief. I regulated all my creeds by my conceptions not by my *sight*—even at that age.'[4] Coleridge was here referring to himself at the age of eight. As a full-grown man in 1801 he still could not accept sight and the senses as the masters of mind. 'Newton', he says with distaste, 'was a mere materialist—*Mind* in his system is always passive—a lazy Looker-on on an external World. If the mind be not *passive*, if it be indeed made in God's Image, & that too in the sublimest sense—the Image of the *Creator*—there is ground for suspicion, that any system built on the passiveness of the mind must be false, as a system.'[5] And whatever the pull of cataracts or mountains might at certain moments become, as

[1] Ibid. ii. 853–4. To Sara Hutchinson, 25 Aug. 1802.
[2] Ibid. 916. To Thomas Wedgwood, 14 Jan. 1803.
[3] Ibid. i. 397. To George Coleridge, 10 Mar. 1798.
[4] Ibid. i. 354. To Poole, 16 Oct. 1797. If Coleridge's conception of Hamlet reflects his own procrastinating temperament, it even more truly reflects the primal opposition of 'I am' and 'it is' that lies at the base of all his thought. 'In Hamlet', Coleridge says, Shakespeare 'wished to exemplify the moral necessity of a due balance between our attention to outward objects and our meditation on inward thoughts—a due balance between the real and the imaginary world. In Hamlet this balance does not exist—his thoughts, images, and fancy [being] far more vivid than his perceptions . . .' (Coleridge, *Shakespeare Criticism*, ed. T. M. Raysor, i. 34).
[5] *Letters*, ii. 709. To Poole, 23 Mar. 1801.

strong or stronger was the abiding sense that he communicated to his wife: 'I seem to exist, as it were, almost wholly within myself, in *thoughts* rather than in *things*'.[1] 'In looking at objects of Nature while I am thinking,' he says in a more complex statement, 'as at yonder moon dim-glimmering thro' the dewy window-pane, I seem rather to be seeking, as it were *asking*, a symbolical language for something within me that already and forever exists, than observing any thing new. Even when that latter is the case, yet still I have always an obscure feeling as if that new phaenomenon were the dim Awaking of a forgotten or hidden Truth of my inner Nature.'[2] 'The pith of my system', he says near the end of his life, 'is to make the senses out of the mind—not the mind out of the senses, as Locke did.'[3] And in his best-known statement, he intoned, 'O Lady! we receive but what we give, / And in our life alone does Nature live'.[4]

Inevitably, the two urges collided. Though Spinoza had demonstrated that 'the more we know individual things the more we know God'—that is, that the sense of the pantheist All is entered only by the door of the 'it is', Coleridge liked to think that his 'I am' orientation could complement itself with a unity of concepts about the 'it is': '. . . frequently *all things* appear little', he says, '—the universe itself—what but an immense heap of *little* things? . . . —My mind feels as if it ached to behold & know something *great*—something *one & indivisible*'.[5] But none the less he temporarily convinced himself that the way to the 'one & indivisible' was the way of the 'I am'. 'Those who have been led', he says, '. . . step by step thro' the constant testimony of their senses, seem to me to want a sense which I possess—They contemplate nothing but *parts*—and all *parts* are necessarily little—and the Universe to them is but a mass of *little things*.'[6] In later apprehensions, he showed a formal sense of the incompatibility of the two modes: 'First, then', he writes in a letter to Clarkson, 'what is the difference or distinction between THING and THOUGHT?'[7] But perhaps the most intriguing of all his non-schematic collisions of 'I am' and 'it is' interest finds expression in the emotionality of his musings about whether his son Hartley should be baptized a Christian or allowed to remain in the pristine matrix of a pantheistically invoked nature:

At times I dwell on Man with such reverence [that] . . . in that mood I exclaim, My boys shall be christened!—But then another fit of moody philosophy attacks me—I look at my doted-on Hartley—he moves, he lives, he finds impulses from within & from without—he is the darling of the Sun and of the Breeze! Nature seems to bless him as a thing of her own! He looks at the clouds, the mountains,

---

[1] *Letters*, ii. 881. To Mrs. Coleridge, 13 Nov. 1802.
[2] *Notebooks*, ii. 2546.   [3] *Table Talk*, 25 July 1832.
[4] 'Dejection: An Ode', ll. 47–48, *Poems*, i. 365.
[5] *Letters*, i. 349. To Thelwall, 14 Oct. 1797.
[6] Ibid. i. 354. To Poole, 16 Oct. 1797.
[7] Ibid. ii. 1194. To Clarkson, 13 Oct. 1806.

the living Beings of the Earth, & vaults & jubilates! Solemn Looks & solemn Words have been hitherto connected in his mind with great & magnificent objects only—with lightning, with thunder, with the waterfall blazing in the Sunset——then I say. . . . Shall I suffer him to see grave countenances & hear grave accents, while his face is sprinkled, & while the fat paw of a Parson crosses his Forehead?[1]

Such indications of the emotional omnipresence of the 'I am'/'it is' tension in Coleridge's consciousness are deeply interesting, especially as licence for their interpretation is granted by Coleridge himself. Writing in his time of dejection, he jots down in 1803: 'Seem to have made up my mind to write my metaphysical works, as *my Life*, & *in* my Life—intermixed with all the other events / or history of the mind & fortunes of S. T. Coleridge.'[2] But just as much a part of his life as these occasional and non-philosophical observations was his constant formal preoccupation with the history of philosophy, and our true understanding of the unity of Coleridge's effort resides most satisfyingly in the perception that Platonico-Christo-Kantism on the one hand, and Spinozism, on the other, subsume the complete schematism of the 'I am'/'it is' conflict. In his 'passage from Unitarianism (which as I have often said is the Religion of a man, whose Reason would make him an Atheist but whose Heart and Common sense will not permit him to be so) thro' Spinosism into Plato and St John',[3] he increasingly transposed the provincial formulas of his early involvements with the 'it is' into a recognition of their final abstract form as Spinozism. When we approach Coleridge out of his historical context, we seem to find a random eclectic moving in a cloud of heterogeneous names: Scotus Erigena, Plotinus, Boehme, Bruno, Swedenborg, Hartley, Godwin, Priestley, Schelling. But in fact all these thinkers, and many others, are connected, and mark stages in the unfolding of his philosophical understanding of the full implications of the 'it is'. We come to realize that the entire array of those philosophies that threaten the 'I am' march under the leadership of their commander in coherence, Spinoza, and that in such an exalted role Spinoza elicited the fullest measure of Coleridge's wondering respect and of his ultimately unequivocal opposition.

We must guard against the mistake—encouraged by Coleridge's own words at times—of confusing expressions of reverence for Spinoza with an acceptance of his philosophy. But no less a word than reverence really fits Coleridge's attitude towards the man:

It is a duty which we owe to truth [he says], to distinguish Spinoza from . . . the whole nest of *popular* infidels, to make manifest how precious a thing is the sincere thirst of truth for the sake of truth. . . . Now I affirm that none but an

[1] Ibid. i. 624–5. To Godwin, 22 Sept. 1800.
[2] *Notebooks*, i. 1515.   [3] Ibid. ii. 2448.

eminently pure and benevolent mind could have constructed and perfected such a system as that of the ethics of Spinoza.[1]

Again and again Coleridge displays the sort of emotional exaltation about Spinoza's *Existenz* that is the hallmark of the true Romantic: 'If he did not think as a Christian,' says Coleridge of the great pantheist, 'he felt and acted like one'.[2] 'I know but *one* instance (that of Benedict Spinoza)', he says apropos of Wordsworth's persecution by the reviewers, 'of a man of great Genius and *original* Mind who on those very accounts had been abused, misunderstood, decried and . . . persecuted, who has not been worried at last into a semblance of Egotism.'[3]

So great was his reverence for Spinoza ('He alone had the philosophic courage to be *consequent*'),[4] that at times he allowed himself to be led into assessments of Spinoza's position that were consequences of his own emotion rather than of Spinoza's thought. We see—in the *Biographia Literaria*, where Coleridge's poetic interests drew him closer to a reconciliation with pantheism than at any other time in his mature career— a wistful equivocation in his statement that 'The ETHICS of SPINOZA, may, or may not, be an instance' of a system 'capable of being converted into an irreligious PANTHEISM,' but 'at no time could I believe, that *in itself* and *essentially* it is incompatible with religion, natural or revealed'.[5] 'If Spinoza had left the doctrine of Miracles untouched,' he says hopefully in another place, '. . . his Ethics would never, could never, have brought on him the charge of *Atheism*.'[6] The equivocation recurs in other contexts; Coleridge expressed, at various times, the intention of showing that Spinoza had been calumniated, even that, properly viewed, his thought was not opposed to Christianity. He was always quick to defend Spinoza's personality and good will, and, in fact, would allow no one—no one else, that is—to criticize him.[7] 'I do not believe', he said, with Romantic ambivalence, that 'Spinoza would have acknowledged the system attributed to him by Jacobi.'[8] Again, '. . . I cannot accord with Jacobi's assertion, that Spinosism, as taught by Spinosa, is atheism'.[9] And, in an extreme moment, Coleridge said of Spinoza that 'to charge him with Atheism is a gross calumny'.[9]

Yet all these statements, their emphasis notwithstanding, testify rather to the persistence and depth of Coleridge's 'it is' concern than to his final and lasting opinions as to the real meaning of the philosophy of Spinoza. We have seen, in our discussions in the second chapter of this volume,

---

[1] Gillman, *Life of Coleridge*, pp. 321–2.   [2] *Philosophical Lectures*, p. 385.
[3] *Letters*, iv. 938.   [4] Ibid. 849.
[5] *Biographia*, i. 98–99.   [6] *Notebooks*, i. 1379.   [7] See note 45, p. 362.
[8] Marginal note at page 26 of Coleridge's copy of *Ueber die Lehre des Spinoza* (Breslau, 1789), now in the British Museum.
[9] W. Hale White, 'Coleridge on Spinoza', *The Athenaeum*, No. 3630, May 22, 1897, p. 681.

with what inescapable ambivalence the figure of Spinoza functioned in the intellectual ambiance of the Romantic era, and we therefore know the emotional basis for such statements. Even Jacobi, whose whole philosophical career can be seen as a resistance to Spinoza, said, quite simply, 'I love Spinoza'.[1] But in statements in which the interests of the 'I am' are predominant, Coleridge never allows his reverence for Spinoza to obscure the true issue. Thus he can at one and the same time speak as though Spinoza is a saint, and also speak of him as 'subversive of all virtue':

> Paradoxical, as it assuredly is, I am convinced that Spinoza's innocence and virtue, guarded and matured into invincible habit of being, by a life of constant meditation and of intellectual pursuit, were the conditions or temptations . . . of his forming and maintaining a system subversive of all virtue. He saw so clearly the *folly* and *absurdity* of wickedness, and felt so weakly and languidly the passions tempting to it, that he concluded, that nothing was wanting to a course of well-doing, but clear conceptions and the *fortitudo intellectualis*; while his very modesty, a prominant feature in his character, rendered him, as it did Hartley, less averse to the system of necessity.[2]

Again, though the anti-Spinozism of Wolf did not meet with Coleridge's approval when it was expressed by Wolf himself ('. . . a bitter inquisitorque abuse & atheizing of Spinosa', says Coleridge reprovingly of a section in Wolf's *Theologia naturalis*),[3] Coleridge's phrase, 'subversive of all virtue' none the less contains precisely the force of Wolf's 'tollit omnem moralitatem intrinsecam'.[4] Coleridge bridled too when Jacobi charged Spinoza with atheism, though he himself saw the consequences of Spinozism clearly—even when wistfully: 'it was pantheism,' he says of Spinoza's thought, 'but in the most religious form in which it could appear. . . . On the other hand I am far from hiding the inevitable consequences of pantheism in all cases, whether the pantheism of India or the solitary cases [*like that*] of Spinoza.'[5]

Thus, despite his admiration and respect for the quality of Spinoza's logical procedure ('his premiss granted, the deduction is a chain of adamant'),[6] the true issues were never really compromised. 'We must go', said Coleridge, 'either to the Trinity or to Pantheism.'[7] And he sounds for all the world like Jacobi when he says that

> The inevitable result of all consequent reasoning, in which the intellect refuses to acknowledge a higher or deeper ground than it can itself supply . . .

---

[1] Jacobi, *Werke*. iv–1, 70.   [2] Gillman, *Life of Coleridge*, pp. 319–20.

[3] *Notebooks*, ii. 2219.   [4] See above, Chapter II, p. 72, n. 8.

[5] *Philosophical Lectures*, p. 385.

[6] *Table Talk*, 23 July 1827. Again, 'Spinoza' is 'the Hercules' Pillar of human Reason' (Marginal note at page 40 of the first volume of the Law edition of Boehme's works in the British Museum).

[7] *Notebooks*, i. 922. Again, 'Trinity rejected, atheism, i.e. God = a blind unconscious Activity . . .' (*Notebooks*, ii. 3152). See note 46, p. 362.

is—and from Zeno the Eleatic to Spinosa, and from Spinosa to the Schellings
. . . of the present day, ever has been—pantheism, under one or other of its
modes . . . and in all alike . . . practically atheistic.[1]

This, it may be emphasized, was Coleridge's considered and final philosophical position. The 'arguments of Spinosa' were, 'in more appropriate
language, the *Atheistical system*'.[2] The 'Pantheism of Spinoza' was 'in
contrast with the Hebrew or Christian scheme'.[3] And when his literary
interests were not immediately involved, Coleridge's strictures against
Spinozism could be strong indeed. 'Spinozism', he said, 'consists in the
exclusion of intelligence and consciousness from Deity—therefore it is
Atheism.'[4] And 'Pantheism', he said still more strongly, 'is equivalent to
Atheism . . . there is no other Atheism actually existing, or speculatively
conceivable, but Pantheism.'[5]

Thus pantheism, the system of the 'it is', exerted the strongest possible
repulsion and the most extreme attraction upon Coleridge, and, while
unfolding itself for him in its most coherent and consequent form as
Spinozism, it was a crucial preoccupation throughout his career. We may
judge something of the continuousness of his involvement from a statement in which, defending himself in 1816 against a charge of keeping
borrowed books too long, Coleridge concedes only one instance in which
the charge might be true: 'the German complete Edition of Spinoza's
Works with his Life by Colerus, a work absolutely necessary to me in an
undertaking, which has occupied my best Thoughts for the last 10 years
& more'.[6]

The undertaking alluded to was, of course, the fabled *magnum opus*.

---

[1] *Works*, ii. 470–1. Compare Baader: 'The same pantheistic error emerged after all very
early in the Indian teachings as Buddhism, just as it already took root in the Jewish Cabala.
From this (consequently already corrupted) Cabala Spinoza created his own pantheism, which
receives its second edition in German *Naturphilosophie* (Schelling's), its third—and God willing
its last—in the philosophy of Hegel' (Baader, *Werke*, xiv. 472). Compare Jacobi's friend C. J.
Kraus: '. . . pantheism confirms itself as an authentic natural product of the human mind by the
fact that it has arisen on the Ganges as on the Rhine, and in the age of Xenophanes as in that
of Spinoza, and among Brahmins, Cabalists and mystics, theologians and philosophers—in
short, everywhere and always, and in all kinds of intellects' ('Ueber den Pantheismus', *Vermischte Schriften*, v. 12). Schelling himself notes that 'the Eleatic system' is 'wholly the same as
Spinozism' (*Werke*, vi. 93). Compare Schopenhauer: 'The ἐν καὶ πᾶν—that is, that the inner
nature in all things is absolutely one and the same—my age had already grasped and understood, after the Eleatics, Scotus Erigena, Giordano Bruno, and Spinoza had explicitly taught,
and Schelling had revived, this doctrine. . . . I myself have that ἐν καὶ πᾶν in common
with the pantheists. . .' (*Werke*, ii. 736).

[2] *Letters*, iii. 483. To J. Cottle, late Apr. 1814.

[3] *Table Talk*, 10 Mar. 1827.   [4] *Critical Annotations*, p. 32.

[5] *Works*, v. 406. It is possible to 'set out, like Spinoza, with all but the truth, and end with
a conclusion which is altogether monstrous . . .' (*Table Talk*, 14 April 1833).

[6] *Letters*, iv. 635. To John Murray, 26 Apr. 1816. Also see above, p. 165, n. 5.

CHAPTER IV

The Trinitarian Resolution

THE *magnum opus*, in whatever form it was projected, was neither more nor less than Coleridge's most cherished hope of achieving a systematic reconciliation of the 'I am' and the 'it is'. Against the background of the *Pantheismusstreit*, Coleridge's various listings of the aims and contents of his masterwork lose their chaotic irrelevance as a hodge-podge catalogue of unrelated philosophical personalities and problems, and become aspirations towards the resolution of the great tension that dominated his intellectual life. To resolve the tension, the systematic consequence of Spinozism had somehow to be retained, while the moral implications of Spinozism had to be changed from a message of death to a message of life.

Of his long-term reading in 'the Scholars of Ammonius' (that is, the Neoplatonists—Coleridge says that he had 'spent more time than I should be willing to acknowledge in reading the works of these men'),[1] and 'in later times' of 'Scotus (Joan. Erigena), Giordano Bruno, Behmen'—a list of pantheists that concludes with Schelling, Coleridge speaks in a way that indicates how necessary pantheism's apex, the system of Spinoza, was to his own hopes for system: 'the much calumniated Spinoza (whose System is to mine just what a Skeleton is to a Body, fearful because it is only the *Skeleton*)'.[2] In the very word skeleton we have his unresolvable ambivalence; for a skeleton is both a systematic network and a symbol of death. In one of his strictures against Calvinism, indeed, Coleridge reveals the full meaning of the image of the skeleton—and reveals too the poignancy of the inevitable defeat of his hopes for his great philosophical reconciliation. The words express the whole range of his conflicting attitudes towards Spinoza:

. . . I have taken my last Farewell of *Modern* Calvinism. It is in it's inevitable consequences Spinosism, not that which Spinosism, i.e. the doctrine of the Immanence of the World in God, might be improved into, but Spinosism with all it's Skeleton unfleshed, bare Bones and Eye-holes, as presented by Spinoza himself. In one thing only does it differ. It has not the noble honesty, that majesty of openness, so delightful in Spinoza, which made him scorn all attempts to varnish over fair consequences, or to deny in words what was affirmed in the reasoning.—I said, in one thing only. O I did injustice to thee, Spinoza!—

---

[1] *Philosophical Lectures*, p. 238.   [2] *Letters*, iv. 775. To Tulk, Sept. 1817.

Righteous and gentle Spirit, where should I find that iron Chain of Logic, which neither man or angel could *break*, but which falls of itself by dissolving the rock of Ice, to which it is stapled—and which thou in common with all thy contemporaries & predecessors didst mistake for a rock of adamant? Where shall I find the hundred deep and solemn Truths, which as so many Germs of Resurrection to Life and a glorified Body will make, sooner of later, 'the dry Bones live?'[1]

No words could better express the emotional life of the *Pantheismusstreit*. In the apostrophe 'O I did injustice to thee, Spinoza!—Righteous and gentle Spirit', we hear the singing wonder of Sabatier de Castres: 'O le plus mal jugé des Sages, modeste et vertueux *Spinosa*! pardonne-moi d'avoir aussi partagé l'erreur générale sur tes écrits.' In 'that iron Chain of Logic, which neither man or angel could *break*', we hear the proleptic awe of Mairan: 'je ne sais par où rompre la chaîne de ses démonstrations.'

To unstaple, not break, that 'iron Chain of Logic' from its 'rock of Ice' and restaple it to Christianity was Coleridge's purpose. But the hopelessness of achieving that purpose by means of systematic reason is made plain in the words: 'Where shall I find the hundred deep and solemn Truths which as so many Germs of Resurrection . . . will make . . . "the dry Bones live?" '

Perhaps now we can realize that the *magnum opus*, like Hamlet's hesitation, does honour to a man and to an ideal, whilst ironically bringing a course of action not a whisper nearer to an ideal resolution. The *magnum opus* could not have been written, even had Coleridge laboured like Hercules and not languished like Philoctetes. We have in its projections all that Coleridge—or unaided reason—could do. We realize, as we contemplate the irony that restricts the *magnum opus* to perpetual futurity, that Coleridge's formulations look backwards, on a life of vast erudition and the deepest intellectual and emotional commitment, rather than forwards to the making of a book.[2]

The book was a poignant illusion. It was to have been 'my most important Work,'[3] to have been 'a work, which has employed all my best thoughts & efforts for the last twelve years and more, and on which I would ground my reputation,'[4] to have been 'the Work, on which I would

---

[1] *Letters*, iv. 548. To R. H. Brabant, 10 Mar. 1815. The Spinozism of 'modern' Calvinism, the two chief exponents of which were 'Jonathan Edwards and the late Dr. Williams,' is referred to elsewhere: modern Calvinism 'supported the Necessitarian scheme,' it 'represents a will absolutely passive, clay in the hands of a potter,' and therefore 'it follows that all is nature' (*Works*, i. 206). Compare Inge: 'high Calvinism is simply Christian Stoicism. It has been called pantheistic because it admits only one Will in the universe' (*Christian Mysticism* (London, 1899), p. 121, n. 2). For Calvin's own reaction to the Stoic revival in the Renaissance, see Léontine Zanta, *La Renaissance du stoicisme au XVIme siècle* (Paris, 1914), pp. 52–68.

[2] See Excursus Note XV, p. 314.

[3] *Letters*, iii. 533. To Daniel Stuart, 12 Sept. 1814.

[4] Ibid. iv. 589. To John May, 27 Sept. 1815.

wish to ground my reputation with Posterity'.[1] It was to have been 'my Opus Maximum on which I chiefly rely for the proof that I have not lived or laboured in vain'.[2] It was first of all to have done justice to the systematic conservative's sense of history: 'It's Title will be Logosophia, or on the Logos human & Divine, in six Treatises.—The first, a philosophic Compendium of the History of Philosophy. . . . (No such work exists, at least in our language—for Brucker's is a Wilderness in six huge Quartos, & he was no Philosopher)'.[3] So Coleridge wrote to Stuart in October 1815. To John May in September 1815 he stated his plan in a way that emphasized his concern for system as well as his concern for history:

This work will be entitled LOGOSOPHIA; or on the LOGOS, divine and human, in six Treatises. The first, or preliminary treatise contains a philosophical History of Philosophy and it's revolutions. . . . (A perspicuous Compendium of the Hist. of Phil. has been long wanted: for Enfield's is a mere Bookseller's *Job* Abridgement of BRUCKER, a man of great Learning & unwearied industry, but scantily gifted with the true philosophic insight.)

The second Treatise is (Λογὸς κοινός) on the science of connected reasoning....[4]

Though the number of 'treatises' in the *magnum opus* varied, its general character did not; all the treatises together formed a system: 'a compleat and perfectly original system'[5] to which he had 'devoted 20 years' incessant Thought, and at least 10 years' positive Labor', and which was to include, as its crown, 'a detailed Commentary on the Gospel of St John'.[6]

St. John, however, had not always worn the crown. We will recall Coleridge's description of his early philosophical years as being a time in which 'my head was with Spinoza' while 'my whole heart remained with Paul and John'. And though Spinoza's rule of the head was by this time a thing of the past, what was Coleridge to do about the skeleton? So, in other formulations of the *magnum opus*, we find Spinoza once again standing opposite St. John—but this time in the projected hope of reconciliation and Christian resurrection. And not only Spinoza, as master of the 'it is', but, deployed under him, a retinue of pantheists, while, bringing up the rear, there was the pantheist sumpter-mule: Unitarianism.[7] Such is the form of one projection that speaks of

. . . 5 Treatises on the Logos, or communicative and communicable Intellect, in God and man. 1. Λόγος προπαιδευτικός. . . . 2. Λόγος ἀρχιτεκτονικός, or the principles of the Dynamic or Constructive Philosophy as opposed to the Mechanic. 3. Commentary in detail on the Gospel of St John—or Λόγος θεάνθρωπος. 4. Λόγος ἀγωνιστής Biography and Critique of the Systems of

---

[1] Ibid. p. 591. To Stuart, 7 Oct. 1815.
[2] Snyder, *Coleridge on Logic and Learning*, p. 155.   [3] Ibid., p. 591–2.
[4] Ibid. p. 589. To John May, 27 Sept. 1815.
[5] Ibid. p. 736. To Francis Wrangham, 5 June 1817.   [6] Ibid. p. 736, also iv. 592.
[7] Or perhaps Coleridge's own epithet is better: 'modern Unitarianism is verily the *sans-culotterie* of religion' (*Works*, v. 410).

Giordano Bruno, Behmen, and Spinoza. 5. Λόγος ἄλογος or the Sources and Consequences of modern *Unicism* absurdly called Unitarianism.[1]

In the plan communicated to John May in September 1815 we read of six treatises, the historical and systematic sections being followed by one on St. John reinforced by St. Paul, and then by the army of pantheists, with, lastly, Unitarianism:

IV. . . . a detailed Commentary on the Gospel of St John—collating the *Word* of the Evangelist with the Christ crucified of St Paul.
The Vth. (Λόγος ἀγωνίστης) on the Pantheists and Mystics; with the Lives and Systems of Giordano Bruno, Jacob Behmen, George Fox, and Benedict Spinoza.—
The VIth. (Λόγος ἄλογος) on the Causes & Consequences of modern Unitarianism.—[2]

Though the *magnum opus* could never be written, it existed—as heaven does in the minds of mortals—as the hypothetical servicing of Coleridge's needs; and it is therefore not merely a concrete plan dating from a certain period around the year 1815, but an omnipresent reality, even when imperfectly expressed. We see, for instance, the formulations of 1815 clearly foreshadowed in all their essentials by a rambling scheme of 1803:

On Man, and the probable Destiny of the Human Race.—
[*My last & great* work—always had in mind.]

Following this statement, we see:

The History of Logic with a Compendium of Aristotelian Logic prefixed.
History of Metaphys. in Germany

—and under this crossed out—but later to reappear as the title of one of the treatises of the *magnum opus*—the words *Organum vere Organum*. Then, a few lines farther down, a reference to 'Socinus, G. Fox', following which we have—inevitably—'Giordano Bruno, Jacob Boehmen, Spinoza.'— which is listed as the '10th' and last in the series of projections.[3]

Again, the plan expressed to H. J. Rose in 1816 prefaces 'The second work, 5 Treatises on the Logos, or communicative and communicable Intellect' with 'The first (for I am convinced that a true System of Philo-

---

[1] *Letters*, iv. 687. To H. J. Rose, 25 Sept. 1816.
[2] Ibid., pp. 589–90. To John May, 27 Sept. 1815.
[3] *Notebooks*, i. 1646. This early scheme provides interesting confirmation of Coleridge's various claims about his long labours towards the *magnum opus*: 'my last twenty years', he says in 1818 (*Letters*, iv. 889); 'for the last 15 years' (*Letters*, iv. 591); '20 years' incessant Thought, and at least 10 years' positive Labor'—this in 1817 (*Letters*, iv. 736). Another early projection of the *magnum opus*, a letter to Godwin on 4 June 1803, reveals plans to 'set seriously to work—in arranging what I have already written, and in pushing forward my Studies, & my Investigations relative to the omne scibile of human Nature—*what* we *are*, & *how* we *become* what we are; so as to solve the two grand Problems, how, being acted upon, we shall act; how, acting, we shall be acted upon' (*Letters*, ii. 948–9).

sophy . . . is *best* taught in Poetry as well as most safely) Seven Hymns with a large preface or prose commentary to each—1. to the Sun. 2. Moon. 3. Earth. 4. Air. 5. Water. 6. Fire. 7. God.'[1] These 'Hymns', we realize if we turn to the Gutch Notebook of the mid-1790s, are not a new idea but an expansion of an old and continuing involvement; for, in 1795–6, we find the sixteenth projection on a list (of which 'Jacob Behmen' is the fourth), to be

Hymns to the Sun, the Moon, and the Elements—six hymns.—In one of them to introduce a dissection of Atheism—particularly the Godwinian System of Pride Proud of what? An outcast of blind Nature ruled by a fatal Necessity—Slave of an ideot Nature!

.   .   .   .

In the last Hymn a sublime enumeration of all the charms of Tremendities of Nature— then a bold avowal of Berkley's System ! ! ! ! ![2]

In short, whether in the provincial opposition of Godwin to Berkeley, or in the sophisticated antithesis of Spinoza and St. John, as well as in countless intermediary alignments, Coleridge's mind was ruled, from early to late, by the tragic tension of the 'I am' and the 'it is'.

The Friend, the *Biographia Literaria*, the *Lay Sermon*, and later, the *Aids to Reflection* are preliminaries to the *magnum opus*—they are all like stones quarried and roughed out for the foundations of the edifice.[3] The *Lay Sermon*, for instance, was to be 'half a dozen theologico-metaphysico-political Essays,' showing that 'The Bible' was 'the Statesman's best manual &c', and incorporating an endeavour to 'explain myself at large on that distinction between the Reason and the Understanding, which I deem of such vital Importance—& with this some leading points of my scheme of philosophy, as contrasted with the Mechanic, Locke, Hartley and Condilliac System.'[4] This 'Mechanic . . . System', as we have seen, recedes into Unitarianism and then into Spinozism. Again, the *Biographia Literaria* and the *Friend* were to be co-ordinated in the foundation of 'the Dynamic Philosophy'—that is, the 'I am' system (wistfully equated about this time with the metaphorical dynamicisms of Schelling)—as opposed to the 'it is' system of 'Mechanic' philosophy:

In my literary Life you will find a sketch of the *subjective* Pole of the Dynamic

---

[1] *Letters*, iv. 687. To Rose, 25 Sept. 1816.

[2] *Notebooks*, i. 174.

[3] Coleridge himself customarily uses the notion of 'foundation' when speaking of his projects: '. . . it is essential to my plan, that I should first lay the *foundations* well, but the merit of a foundation is it's depth and solidity—the ornaments and conveniences . . . will come with the superstructure . . .' (*Letters*, iii. 237); 'Hitherto, my dear Sir, I have been employed in laying the Foundations of my Work' (*Letters*, iii. 257); '. . . laying the foundation Stones . . .' (*Letters*, iv. 579). By the same token, his philosophy itself was an 'Architecture' (*Letters*, iii. 127), while '*Biblical Theology*' was an 'ample Palace' that contained 'mansions for every other Knowledge' (*Letters*, iv. 953).

[4] *Letters*, iv. 670. To Rose, 17 Sept. 1816.

Philosophy; the rudiments of *Self*-construction, barely enough to let a thinking mind see *what it is like*—in the third Volume of the Friend, now in the Press, you will find the great *results* of this Philosophy in it's relation to Ethics and Theology. . . .[1]

We have earlier emphasized the necessity of the 'I am' as the guarantor of morality; thus the 'great *results* of this Philosophy' of 'the Dynamic' would be an affirmation of the 'I am' orientation : 'The Object of the third Volume of my Friend, which will be wholly fresh matter is briefly this—that Morality without Religion is as senseless a scheme as Religion without Morality. . .'[2] The moral view was, for Coleridge, an imperative, a psychic *donnée*—e.g. 'To return to the Question of Evil—woe to the man, to whom it is an uninteresting Question';[3] 'the impossibility of any man's being the good Poet without being first a good man';[4] 'The sum total of moral philosophy is to be found in this one question, Is *Good* a superfluous word, —or mere lazy synonyme for the pleasurable. . ?' In order to affirm the reality of this moral view it was everlastingly necessary to reject pantheism; and such a rejection, therefore, was as much the object of the third volume of *The Friend* as was the establishment of 'Morality': 'By the bye,' said Coleridge in 1818, 'at my first leisure I will transcribe for you a paragraph to be inserted at p. 263—and unfortunately omitted—it's object being to preclude all suspicion of any leaning towards Pantheism, in any of it's forms.'[5] And in another statement he expresses himself more fully:

I have sent the three volumes of the *Friend*, with my MS. corrections, and additions. . . . The largest . . . had a twofold object—to guard my own character from the suspicion of pantheistic opinions, or Spinozism . . . and next, to impress . . . the conviction that true philosophy, so far from having any tendency to unsettle the *principles* of faith . . . does itself actually require them as its premises. . . .[6]

If *The Friend* thus stands as a document in the tension of the 'I am' and the 'it is', so also, as we have seen, does the *Biographia Literaria*. Coleridge himself says that the 'disquisition on the powers of association, with the History of Opinions on this subject from Aristotle to Hartley, and on the generic difference between the faculties of Fancy and Imagination' in that work was extended and elaborated 'as laying the foundation Stones of the Constructive or Dynamic Philosophy in opposition to the merely

[1] *Letters*, iv. 767. To Tulk, Sept. 1817.   [2] Ibid., p. 756. To Poole, 22 July 1817.
[3] *Notebooks*, i. 1622.
[4] Ibid. 1057. This oft-repeated and highly typical statement is from the dedication to Jonson's *Volpone* (as in this citation he acknowledges) and is a fine example of Coleridge's adeptness in finding appropriate mosaic fragments. Elsewhere he says that Jonson translated the passage from Strabo (*Miscellaneous Criticism*, p. 427).
[5] *Letters*, iv. 894. To W. H. Coleridge, 8 Dec. 1818.
[6] *Biographia Epistolaris*, ed. A. Turnbull (London, 1911), ii. 175. To Allsop, 20 Mar. 1820.

mechanic'.[1] The difficulties in 'laying the foundation stones' we have discussed at length, but the intent revealed contributes to our understanding of the unity of Coleridge's intellectual effort.

This unity, as distinguished by the concerns of the 'I am' and those of the 'it is' ('it being the business of philosophy ever to distinguish without unnaturally dividing'),[2] is apparent in his intellectual disposition of thinkers not explicitly summoned to reconciliation in the *magnum opus*. Some, as we shall see, like Plotinus, were read so early, and pondered so long, that they survived residually in all his thought. Others, especially Schelling and 'the Doctors of the Absolute'—Steffens, Oken, Baader, Schubert, Creuzer—were approached in the middle of his career, and then assumed a special, and indeed over-emphasized, importance in his systematic plans. Spinoza, of course, was omnipresent. But some thinkers —Scotus Erigena, for example—enter Coleridge's ken at a given time, are thought through, and are seen to interest him specifically for their relevance to the criteria of 'I am' and 'it is', of Christianity and pantheism.

Coleridge began the serious study of Erigena in 1803. 'If you find my paper smell, or my Style savour,' he wrote to Godwin on June 4, 'of scholastic quiddity, you must attribute it to the infectious quality of the Folio, on which I am writing—namely, Jo. Scotus Erigena de divisione Naturae, the fore runner, by some centuries, of the Schoolmen.'[3] With his customary enthusiasm when on a new intellectual tack, he gave Southey, on 29 June, a kind of report of progress: 'I have received great delight & instruction from Scotus Erigena.'[4] But his delight did not obscure from him the implications of Erigena's thought: 'He is clearly the modern founder of the School of Pantheism—indeed he expressly defines the divine Nature, as quae fit et facit, et creat et creatur—& repeatedly declares Creation to be *manifestation*. . . . The eloquence with which he writes, astonished me. . . .'[4] For his own use he jots down in his notebooks: 'Creation explained by Jo. Scot. Erig. as only a manifestation of the unity of God in forms—et fit et facit, et creat et creatur. Lib. I. p. 7.—p. 8. a curious & highly philosophical account of the Trinity, & compleatly Unitarian—'.[5] Fifteen years later Erigena is referred to, in the *Philosophical Lectures*, in admiring words: 'The most extraordinary man, perhaps, of his age, and the first philosopher that arose after the suspended animation of philosophy, was Johannes Scotus ERIGENA. . . . A wonderful man he must have been'.[6] In that vein of enthusiasm Coleridge contented himself with gently chiding Erigena for having been 'somewhat dazzled with the splendour of the Eclectic philosophy [i.e. Neoplatonism—Erigena was

---

[1] *Letters*, iv. 579. To Brabant, 29 July 1815.
[2] *Philosophical Lectures*, p. 268.
[3] *Letters*, ii. 949. To Godwin, 4 June 1803.
[4] Ibid., p. 954. To Southey, 29 June 1803.
[5] *Notebooks*, i. 1382. See note 46, p. 362.
[6] *Philosophical Lectures*, p. 270.

influenced by Proclus and the pseudo-Dionysus] and in some points to have come too near pantheism'.[1]

But Coleridge's annotation in his personal copy of *De divisione naturae* indicates, along with such approbation for Erigena's mind, a far, far deeper concern with the implications of Erigena's philosophy:

> How is it to be explained that S. Erigena with so many other Christian Divines and Philosophers should not have perceived that pious words and scriptural phrases may disguise but cannot transubstantiate Pantheism—a handsome Mask that does not alter a single feature of the ugly Face it hides? How is it to be explained that so comprehensive and subtle an Intellect as Scotus Erigena, should not have seen, that his 'Deus omnia et omnia Deus' was incompatible with moral responsibility, and subverted all essential Difference of Good and Evil, Right and Wrong?—I can suggest no other solution, but the Innocence of his Heart and the Purity of his Life—[2]

The annotation, springing from Coleridge's most radical objection to pantheism, its subversion of morality—we sense Coleridge's intensity by his excusing Erigena in much the same tone that he excuses Spinoza himself, —becomes at this point a kind of autobiographical confession:

> . . . so many young men in the unresisted Buoyance of their Freedom embrace without scruple the doctrines of Necessity and only at a later and less genial Period learn, and learn to value, their free-agency by its struggles to maintain itself against the increasing encroachments of Nature and Society. It is a great Mercy of God that a good Heart is often so effective an antidote to the heresies of the Head. I could name more than one learned, godly and religious Clergyman, who is a Pantheist thro' his zeal for the *Trinity*—without suspecting what neverthless is demonstrably true, that Pantheism is but a painted Atheism and that the Doctrine of the Trinity is the great and only sure Bulwark against it.[2]

Such a 'learned, godly and religious Clergyman' was apparently the Reverend John Oxlee, for in another work Coleridge notes the implications of Erigena's thought in the following terms:

> STRANGE—yet from the date of the book of the Celestial Hierarchies of the pretended Dionysius the Areopagite to that of its translation by Johannes Scotus Erigena . . . and from Scotus to the Rev. John Oxlee in 1815, not unfrequent—delusion of mistaking Pantheism, disguised in a fancy dress of pious phrases, for a more spiritual and philosophic form of Christian Faith! Nay, stranger still:—to imagine with Scotus and Mr. Oxlee that in a scheme which more directly than even the grosser species of Atheism, precludes all moral responsibility and subverts all essential difference of right and wrong, they have found the means of proving and explaining, 'the Christian doctrines of the Trinity and Incarnation,' that is, the great and only sufficient antidotes

---

[1] *Philosophical Lectures*, p. 271.   [2] Ibid., p. 433 n. 17.

of the right faith against this insidious poison. For Pantheism—trick it up as you will—is but a painted Atheism.[1]

Coleridge's assimilation and disposition of the thought of Scotus Erigena can thus be clearly traced. On the other hand his reaction to Plotinus is more difficult to discover, though we can see that he rejected Plotinus as surely as he did Erigena.

Plotinus, surprisingly, rarely figures overtly in Coleridge's discourse, and there seem to be four main reasons for this. First, Coleridge read Plotinus so early in his career that Plotinus became a part of the sub-stratum of his thought (as we recognize in 'The Eolian Harp'),[2] rather than, like Erigena and Schelling, who came relatively late to his attention, remaining on the surface while he analysed their implications. Secondly, he covered Plotinus with the emotional mantle of Plato and so was able to sidestep the necessity of a head-on confrontation with Plotinus's pantheism. Thirdly, Plotinus—and to some extent Plato—did not figure in the special modernity, the contemporaneity, of the *Pantheismusstreit* in the way Schelling and Kant, and also Spinoza did. Fourthly, Coleridge was able to make a mental arrangement by which he simply set aside—much as one cherishes a favourite memory—the pantheist consequences of Plotinus, thereby making him a kind of ineffectual angel, but also an enduringly beautiful one.

We see this last attitude clearly in a statement in which Coleridge assumes the 'untenable transcendency' of Plotinian thought, thus sustaining his reverential tone without, as in the case of Erigena, being forced into a more censorious analysis. He chides Tennemann for the

cold, praiseless, fault-finding spirit, with which he quotes passage after passage from Plotinus, which (*granting* their untenable transcendency) state in the most beautiful language the only possible Form of a Philosophic Realism, and demonstrate its conditional necessity by one of the most masterly pieces of exhaustive Logic, found in ancient or modern writings.[3]

By thus disclaiming responsibility for the consequences of Plotinus (we might describe Coleridge's attitude as one of 'just looking, not buying'), he could indulge to the full his admiration for Plotinian logic. And that admiration, without doubt, was one of the eight deepest enthusiasms of

---

[1] *Works*, v. 457.

[2] Plotinus, indeed, seems to have been both one of the earliest and most poetically influential of Coleridge's youthful readings. Speaking of Coleridge's 'rage for metaphysics' before his 'fifteenth year' (Gillman, pp. 23, 25), Werkmeister concludes that 'it is evident that his "rage for metaphysics" could have been only a "rage for Neoplatonism"', and that 'until 1789 Coleridge's thinking is thoroughly Plotinian; and, even when it deviates from Plotinus, as it does after that time, the deviation is in the nature of a personal critique' (Lucyle Werkmeister, 'The Early Coleridge: His "Rage for Metaphysics"', *The Harvard Theological Review*, liv (1961), 108–9). Werkmeister finds explicit Plotinian content in a number of Coleridge's earliest poems.

[3] Marginal note in Tennemann's *Geschichte der Philosophie*, printed in *Philosophical Lectures*, p. 428 n. 20.

his life—his love of Plato, Kant, Spinoza, Shakespeare, Milton, Paul, and John providing its only parallels. 'Plotinus', Coleridge says with un-qualified esteem, 'was a man of wonderful ability, and some of the sublimest passages I ever read are in his works.'[1] And again:

> Let the attempt of Plotinus have ended in a failure—yet who could see the courage and skill with which he seizes the reins, and vaults into the Chariot of the Sun, with what elegance he curbs and turns the ethereal steeds, without sharing in his enthusiasm—and taking honor to the human mind even to have fallen from such magnificent Daring![2]

In one important discussion, however, Coleridge distinguishes Plotinus from Plato, albeit as gently as possible. The distinction clearly reveals the ineradicable opposition, distributed in terms of the contrary consequences of 'I am' and 'it is', of the successors of Plato from Plato himself. Coleridge first describes Plato as proceeding from the affirmation of the 'I am', and by systematic progression arriving at a logical need for something outside the system on which to ground the system. He then compares the thought of Plotinus, and thus makes explicit the radical un-Christianity of Neo-platonism, notwithstanding its near-Christian intensity of moral fervour:

> The same doctine [i.e. as that of Plato] was taught by Plotinus . . . but with this remarkable inversion of order—[he] began first with the knowledge of the Supreme Being, not in our Christian sense of the word, not as a belief that such a being exists whom we are to obey, and under whom perform our duties, no—but . . . men were to arrive at a communion—that is to say at an intellectual, a positive, possession of this Supreme Being which would supersede all know-ledge by giving them a higher one. . . . Beautiful passages there are in Plotinus—exquisite morality—fine observations so that you would believe him to be a Christian. . . . But this is the difference between the works of Plotinus (and in speaking of Plotinus I speak of almost all that follow him) and those of the ancient philosophers: in the works of Plato and Aristotle you see a painful and laborious attempt to follow thought after thought and to assist the evolution of the human mind from its simple state of information to the highest extent its faculties will reach; but in the works of Plotinus it is all beginning, no middle, no progress. . . . In short the Eclectic philosophy might be contrasted in its distinctions alike from genuine philosophy and Christianity.[3]

Though Coleridge declines to explain the consequences of Plotinus's 'remarkable inversion of order' in beginning 'first with the Supreme Being', it is possible, by reference to the Kant–Spinoza paradigm of the 'I am'/'it is' opposition, to realize that such a description is tantamount to describing Plotinus as an 'it is' thinker tending ultimately to pantheism, his Platonic rapture of language notwithstanding. Thus Kant, as the paradigm of the 'I am' position, writes that 'it is noteworthy . . . that men

---

[1] *Table Talk*, Sept. 24, 1830.   [2] *Philosophical Lectures*, p. 428 n. 20.
[3] Ibid., pp. 241–2.

in the early stages of philosophy began where we would rather end, namely with the knowledge of God';[1] while, conversely, Spinoza, as the paradigm of 'it is' thought, states that the 'proper order of philosophic thinking' is for the 'nature of God' to be 'reflected on first'.[1] In other words, the 'I am'/'it is' opposition can be alternatively projected as philosophies-ending-with-God (we recall that Descartes's ontological proof is a corollary function of the *cogito*) versus philosophies-starting-with-God.

The importance of the distinction, which Coleridge recognizes as vitally important, is that if God is posited prior to self, he must be posited as an object—an extension of an 'it is'—while if He is posited as the anchor of a chain of consequences proceeding from the 'I am', he possesses the character of—in Coleridge's words—'the great I AM'. Thus as Coleridge says,

No man in his senses can deny *God* in some sense or other . . . but it is the *personal, living, self-conscious* God, which it is so difficult, except by faith of the Trinity, to combine with an infinite being infinitely and irresistibly causative. Τὸ ἕν καὶ πᾶν is the first dictate of mere human philosophy. Hence almost all the Greek philosophers were inconsistent Spinozists.[2]

'Spinoza', said Coleridge in another statement, 're-codified the pantheism of the old Greek philosophy.'[3]

If we accept this invitation to transpose the problem into Spinozistic terms, we can see the specific equating of a philosophy-beginning-with-God, such as he ascribes to Plotinus, with a pantheist expansion of an 'it is'. 'Spinoza's System', jots Coleridge, 'rests on his Deism/Subst. ad se subsistet.'[4] And elsewhere he identifies this substance-God starting-point, or 'Deism', as the 'prime error' of Spinoza:

The πρῶτον ψεῦδος of Spinoza is not his first definition; but one in which all his Antagonists were as deeply immerged as himself. He alone had the philosophic courage to be *consequent*. . . . The πρῶτον ψεῦδος consists in the assumed Idea of a pure independent *Object*—in assuming a Substance beyond the I; of which therefore the I *could* only be a modification.[5]

This succinct statement applies also to the consequences of Plotinus. But perhaps the most revealing elucidation of all is Coleridge's own gloss to 'the rock of Ice' ('O I did injustice to thee, Spinoza! . . . where should I find that iron Chain of Logic, which neither man or angel could *break*, but which falls of itself by dissolving the rock of Ice, to which it is stapled —and which thou . . . didst mistake for a rock of adamant?')—for in a footnote to 'rock of Ice' Coleridge says, 'viz. God as an *Object*'.[6] Thus Plotinus

---

[1] See above, Chapter II, p. 62 , n. 3.
[2] *Notes on English Divines*, ed. Derwent Coleridge (London, 1853), ii. 67.
[3] *Coleridge's Miscellaneous Criticism*, ed. T. M. Raysor (London, 1936), p. 185.
[4] *Notebooks*, i. 1500. [5] *Letters*, iv. 849. To Pryce, Apr.
[6] Ibid., p. 548 n. To Brabant, 10 Mar. 1815. This goes to the very heart of Spinozism. Compare some of Coleridge's other statements: 'The impossibility of an absolute thing

lay beneath the waterline of the Spinozistic 'rock of Ice', and hence was not summoned to the epiphanic reconciliation of the *magnum opus*.

But at the same time we notice the absence there also of the two greatest representatives of 'I am' philosophy, Plato and Kant. This omission does not indicate a dissatisfaction with or rejection of what they stood for in philosophy. They are not mentioned because neither, in consequence of the paradoxes attendant upon an 'I am' anchorage to an extramundane ground, completed a system; and the *magnum opus* was above all else to be a system. Some of the great pantheistic opponents of Plato and Kant— Spinoza, Bruno, and Boehme—are named in the plan for the *magnum opus*, because, since Coleridge accepted the Jacobian view of pantheism as the only possible system of philosophy, these thinkers presented systems that needed only to be re-stapled to Christianity. Kant and Plato, on the other hand, were both conceived by Coleridge as constituting logical prolegomena for the true system which, transcending its philosophical bases, completed itself in Christianity. It was St. John who elucidated for Coleridge—against the Socinianism of his youth—the 'selfness' of God by his insistence on the mystery of Christ as both man and God. St. John provided the link between the mundane and the extramundane that allowed Coleridge the vision of a possible completion of system that resisted Spinozism, and therefore his name represents the conciliating 'I am' philosophy in Coleridge's final projection. Kant and Plato represented all that philosophy unaided could do with the 'I am' position; but the true consummation of the 'I am', Coleridge came to believe, moved out of the sphere of philosophy into the sphere of religion.

Thus the very title of the *magnum opus*, in one description, was 'Christianity the one true Philosophy'.[1] 'I wished to prove', wrote Coleridge in 1808, '. . . that true philosophy rather leads to Christianity, than contained anything preclusive of it'.[2] To Cottle in 1815 he wrote of his intent 'to finish my greater Work on Christianity, considered as Philosophy and as the only Philosophy.'[3] 'There can be', he wrote to W. H. Coleridge, 'no Philosophy without Religion'.[4] He lectured in 1819 on 'Our Lord as a

---

(substantia unica) . . . as well as its utter unfitness for the fundamental position of a philosophic system, will be demonstrated in the critique on Spinozism in the fifth treatise of my Logosophia' (*Biographia*, i. 182 n.); '. . . Spinoza begins with the Phantom of a Thing in itself, i.e. an Object. But an Object implies a Subject . . .' 'The Truth is, Spinoza in common with all the metaphysicians before him (Böhmen perhaps excepted) began at the wrong end—commencing with God as an *Object*.' (W. Hale White, 'Coleridge on Spinoza', *The Athenaeum*, No. 3630, 22 May 1897, p. 681.)

[1] *Letters*, iii. 533. To Stuart, 12 Sept. 1814. Compare Coleridge's statement of 1810: 'I mean to publish, as a Supplement to THE FRIEND . . . all my philosophical principles of Morals & Taste . . . as "The Mysteries of Christianity grounded in, & correspondent to, the Mysteries of Human Nature." ' (*Letters*, iii. 272–3.)

[2] *Letters*, iii. 155. To Thomas Wilkinson, 31 Dec. 1808.

[3] Ibid. iv. 546. To J. Cottle, 7 Mar. 1815.

[4] Ibid., p. 848. To W. H. Coleridge, 1 Apr. 1818.

Philosopher, as the Union of the Truths and the Supplement of the inherent imperfections of Philosophy'.[1] And, climactically, he insisted that 'then only will true philosophy be existing when from philosophy it is passed into that wisdom which no man has but by the earnest aspirations to be united with the Only Wise, in that moment when the Father shall be all in all.'[2]

Because, then, of 'the inherent imperfections of Philosophy' on the one hand, and the pantheism of all possible resolutions on the other—with pantheism's attendant denial of morality and human personality—Coleridge needed Trinitarian Christianity as the 'Supplement' of 'I am' schematisms. Neither Plato nor Kant could appropriately be nominated to head the 'I am' interests of the *magnum opus*, because completed system was the characterizing principle of that work, and neither philosopher represented such a completion. Conversely, there was no need to nominate either thinker as a subject for reconciliation, as was the case with Spinoza, Boehme, and Bruno, because neither Plato nor Kant stood out against the schematism of Christianity, but rather were associated, in Coleridge's mind, with its philosophical underpinning. He accepted both thinkers, not as exponents in themselves of a final philosophy, but as propaedeutic elucidators of that philosophy.

Coleridge was undeviating in this idea. Though one must agree with Richards that 'of all the knowledge with which Coleridge worked none went deeper or did more than what he had learned from Plato',[3] it does not follow that Coleridge ever accepted Platonism as a philosophical goal. He rather treasured it as an indispensable philosophical instrument. Thus in a playful statement to Thelwall in 1796 he says 'I love Plato' but immediately appends the laughing dismissal: 'his dear *gorgeous* Nonsense'.[4] Again, speaking sardonically of the malignity of the *Edinburgh Review* with respect to *Christabel,* he says:

But, in my own instance, I had the additional misfortune of having been gossiped about, as devoted to metaphysics, and worse than all, to a system incomparably nearer to the visionary flights of Plato, and even to the jargon of the Mystics, than to the established tenets of Locke.[5]

Though he here ruefully concedes that his 'system' is 'incomparably nearer' to Plato than to Locke, there is nevertheless a reservation: 'nearer to' is not 'identical with'. And again in the *Biographia* he expresses both his admiration for Plato as a philosophical instrumentality leading towards Trinitarian modes of thought, and his reservations about Platonism—

[1] Ibid., p. 913. To Rose, Jan. 1819.
[2] *Philosophical Lectures*, p. 226.
[3] I. A. Richards, ed., *The Portable Coleridge* (New York, 1950), p. 45. Compare Coleridge: 'if there be any two subjects which have in the very depth of my Nature interested me, it has been the Hebrew & Christian Theology, & the Theology of Plato' (*Letters*, ii. 866).
[4] *Letters*, i. 295. To Thelwall, 31 Dec. 1796.   [5] *Biographia*, ii. 212.

though close to Christian thought, none the less it was not Christian thought: 'I was', he says of his early philosophical years, '. . . though a Trinitarian (i.e. ad normam Platonis) in philosophy, yet a zealous Unitarian in Religion'.[1]

His view of Plato as logically propaedeutic rather than systematically final is central to any understanding of the meaning of Platonism for Coleridge. 'Plato's works', he says, 'are preparatory exercises for the mind. He leads you to see, that propositions involving in themselves contradictory conceptions, are nevertheless true; and which, therefore, must belong to a higher logic.'[2] Again, he says that 'Plato's works are logical exercises for the mind. Little that is positive is advanced in them. Socrates may be fairly represented by Plato in the more moral parts; but in all the metaphysical disquisitions it is Pythagoras.'[3]

The implications of this view are made explicit in various other statements. Coleridge asserts that '. . . the true idea of Plato's genius and system is to be found in the union of Pythagoras with Socrates', and goes on to explain the nature of that union.[4] Socrates, says Coleridge, 'was a man . . . who generally appears to have possessed a fine and active but yet not very powerful imagination—an imagination instrumental and illustrative rather than predominant and creative'.[5] He was characterized, says Coleridge with continuing coolness, by 'the UNCOMMON excellence of common sense. . . . This without genius would have been the character of a wise, natural, unaffected man; but Socrates doubtless possessed genius in a high degree'.[5] His 'whole life', says Coleridge, 'was one contest against the sophists', but, he adds—ever-mindful of Christianity—that life 'marked the necessity of revelation by an intermixture of weakness, nay even of sophistry, in his own mode of contending against them.'[5] Socrates 'gave currency to a mode of argument which may be as easily, perhaps more easily, adapted to delusion than to sound conviction. It has the misfortune at least, by entangling a man in a number of questions the answers to which he does not anticipate, of leaving a final conviction, as if the man were cheated INTO A conclusion though he could see no HOLE afterwards to escape from it.'[6] And this defect of systematic method ultimately, in Coleridge's opinion, disqualified Socrates from the first rank as a philosopher, although not as a human being. 'He did the best it was possible for unassisted man to do', says Coleridge generously but not without reservation—'He lived holily and died magnanimously'.[7]

Not only did Coleridge feel in general that '. . . Socrates himself was not free from the errors which it was his object to oppose',[8] but Socratic

---

[1] *Biographia*, i. 114.   [2] *Table Talk*, 30 Apr. 1830.
[3] Ibid., 8 May 1824.   [4] *Philosophical Lectures*, p. 177.
[5] Ibid., pp. 136-7.   [6] Ibid., p. 137.
[7] Ibid., p. 136.   [8] Ibid., p. 148.

thought was to him weakened by three special limitations. First of all 'Socrates himself had no system',[1] a fact which would certainly not have recommended him to Coleridge. (Thus, for instance, Coleridge, despite his love of Jeremy Taylor, felt that Taylor's virtual Pelagianism—very like the moral position of Socrates—masked errors that would have become explicit had Taylor been more systematic: 'All hangs together. Deny Original Sin, and you will soon deny free will;—then virtue and vice;—and God becomes *Abracadabra*; a sound, nothing else.')[2]

Secondly, there was the fact that Socrates, in advocating the philosophy of 'I am', turned away from external nature. This reversal of the direction of pre-Socratic philosophizing is signalized by a famous passage in the *Phaedrus*, where Socrates declines to speculate about mythological explanations of natural phenomena: οὐ δύναμαί πω κατὰ τὸ Δελφικὸν γράμμα γνῶναι ἐμαυτόν· γελοῖον δή μοι φαίνεται, τοῦτο ἔτι ἀγνοοῦντα τὰ ἀλλότρια σκοπεῖν—for I am not yet capable, according to the Delphic writing, of knowing myself; so it seems silly to me, while ignorant of that, to investigate other things[3]—and that φιλομαθὴς γάρ εἰμι· τὰ μὲν οὖν χωρία καὶ τ δένδρα οὐδέν μ' ἐθέλει διδάσκειν, οἱ δ' ἐν τῷ ἄστει ἄνθρωποι—I am a lover of learning; but the country places and trees will not teach me, as do the men of the city.[4] For Coleridge, on the contrary, one of the prime functions of Christianity was to reconcile man with nature: '. . . if Christianity is to be the religion of the world . . . so true must it be that the book of nature and the book of revelation, with the whole history of man as the intermediate link, must be the integral and coherent parts of one great work'.[5] And he feels rapture at the thought of 'Nature, looking at me with a thousand looks of Beauty, and speaking to me in a thousand melodies of Love.'[6] Thus, apparently with reference to the 'τὰ μὲν οὖν χωρία καὶ τὰ δένδρα οὐδέν μ' ἐθέλει διδάσκειν', Coleridge jots in his notebook, 'Die Bäume und die Felsen sagen mir nichts, said Socrates', and then comments: '. . . the endless superiority of Christ over him in this respect'.[7] Coleridge could no more accept the Socratic exclusiveness in favour of the 'I am' at the cost of nature ('. . . in his philosophy he had the design, and he certainly produced the effect, of making the moral being of man the especial and single object of thought')[8] than he could accept the Spinozistic exclusiveness of the 'it is' at the cost of human personality.

Thirdly, and most strongly stated of all, was Coleridge's conviction that Socrates, despite the admirableness of his personal morality, had, by his neglect of systematic consequence, allowed himself to posit a moral view that, in denying the reality of evil, implied a denial of the reality of

---

[1] *Table Talk*, 24 Sept. 1830.   [2] *Works*, v. 217.
[3] Plato, *Phaedrus* 230 A.   [4] Ibid., 230 D. Cf. Aristotle, *Metaphysics* 987^b 1–5.
[5] *Works*, v. 113.   [6] *Letters*, i. 271. To Poole, 12 Dec. 1796.
[7] *Notebooks*, i. 1686.   [8] *Philosophical Lectures*, p. 139.

good as well, and thus became tantamount to Stoicism—or, as we transpose the statement, to Spinozism.[1] The 'grand error of Socrates himself' —and 'The Stoics adopted it'—was that 'the definition of virtue is to live according to Nature, without considering the double constitution of man, his spirit and his body—in one part indeed the creature of Nature but in another constituted above Nature. . . '. This 'grand error', in short, 'confounded God and Nature.' In another place, Coleridge notes that the 'great point which Socrates laid down was this, that ignorance was the ground of all vice and therein of all misery, and that knowledge on the contrary was the source of all virtue and therein of all happiness.' But, says Coleridge, such a doctrine either 'was an argument in a circle' or 'it led to the destruction of the very essence of virtue.' Socrates 'failed', therefore, in 'his own logic': 'some error like this Socrates seems to have fallen into in the groundwork of his argument, namely, that pleasure is the ultimate object of all our pursuits'. On crucial questions of moral implication, 'Socrates was constantly vacillating. At one time things were to be revered and honoured for their utility. . . . At other times . . . he speaks with true piety of blessedness but again relapses and considers this but another mode of pleasure.' Consequently, says Coleridge, 'from the laxity of the Socratic moral with regard to the subject of utility,' systems destructive of true morality are allowed to rise up.

If this was the Socrates who constituted 'the more moral parts' of Plato's expressed thought, it is easy to see why Coleridge did not find Platonism interchangeable with Christianity. In the 'metaphysical disquisitions' of Plato's thought, however, which Coleridge attributed to Pythagoras, the basic systematic requirement of 'I am' thought was observed. Coleridge's tone in invoking Pythagoras is reverent: 'Pythagoras' was 'something like one of the most extraordinary human beings that has ever astonished and perplexed the world.'[2] 'Pythagoras', again, was 'the proper founder of philosophy'.[3] What such a tribute means is that Pythagoras understood the systematic consequence through which the implication of the 'I am' would necessarily come to rest in a disjunctive ground. Pythagoras 'proposed the whole problem, the attempt to solve which constitutes the philosopher, namely the connexion of the visible thing, the phaenomenon, with the invisible thing, under a cause common to both and above both.'[4] And this insight—so elegantly stated by Coleridge—constituted the chief debt of Plato to Pythagoras: 'Plato, with

[1] See note 47, p. 362.

[2] *Philosophical Lectures*, pp. 219–20, 150–1, 141–3, 97.

[3] Ibid., p. 145. It is interesting to note that Coleridge conceived one of Pythagoras's chief virtues to be freedom from pantheism. Thus it was 'to the honour of Pythagoras' that his doctrine 'did not in the least partake of Pantheism, but still kept the Deity at a distance from his works' (*Philosophical Lectures*, p. 109).

[4] *Philosophical Lectures*, p. 145.

Pythagoras before him, had conceived that the phenomenon or outward appearance, all that we call thing or matter, is but as it were a language by which the invisible (that which is not the object of our senses) communicates its existence to our finite beings'[1]—a statement of philosophical transcendence that would serve as well for Jaspers' *das Umgreifende* as for the ideas of Plato or the noumena of Kant.

In Coleridge's opinion it was the Pythagorean understanding of the importance of consequence that allowed Plato to accept the 'I am' position of Socrates without becoming disastrously involved in the reticulative breakdown that led Socrates to an implied perversion of moral agency:

> Socrates rose as a reformer and in the heat of reform he confined all philosophy to the knowledge of our own nature. . . . Plato, his great disciple, perceived that this were true if it were possible, but that the knowledge of man by himself was not practicable without the knowledge of other things, or rather that man was that being in whom it pleased God that the consciousness of others' existence should abide, and that therefore without natural philosophy and without the sciences which led to the knowledge of the objects without us, man himself would not be man.[2]

Platonic philosophy, therefore, in Coleridge's view, logically prepared the way for the Trinitarian Christianity that grounded the interests of the 'I am', along with the interests of the 'it is', in a personalized extramundane deity. 'We feel', said Coleridge, that 'our being is nobler than its senses', and this 'craving for something higher than what could be imagined in form' could—'Plato himself . . . told us'—only be satisfied 'by the Realizer, by Him who was the fountain of all and who in the substance superseded the shadow—I mean the Founder of the Christian religion.'[3]

Plato was eminently a prolegomenon to Christianity, and whatever in his thought did not seem to serve this role Coleridge explained as a consequence of Plato's true system not actually being stated in his dialogues:

> . . . this appears to me to have been the object of Plato—to have published for the advantage of all his countrymen that which being studied by docile minds would lead them to seek further. All that could be safely entrusted to men at large he, under the name of Socrates . . . truly representing his opinions, has given us in the most enchanting form, but all as the introduction to something.[4]

This something, said Coleridge, Plato declined to publish: 'But what this philosophy is, you look for in vain in the writings of Plato. . . . And if a man should take up the writings of Plato expecting to find the proper system of Platonism, he will feel himself much in the same state that our amiable countryman—our sweet poet and scholar, Gray, seems to have found himself after a most laborious and elegant abstract of the writings of Plato.'[5] That state, so Coleridge tells us in the marginal note to Gray's

[1] Ibid., p. 187. [2] Ibid., p. 176. [3] Ibid., pp. 168-9.
[4] Ibid., p. 163. [5] Ibid., pp. 164-5.

Platonica, was that 'whatever might be expected from a scholar, a gentle-man, a man of exquisite taste', Gray had performed, and

The poet Plato, the orator Plato, Plato the exquisite dramatist of conversa-tion. . . . Plato the high-bred . . . republican, the man . . . stands full before us. . . . But Plato the philosopher, but the divine Plato, was not to be comprehended within the field of vision, or to be commanded by the fixed immoveable tele-scope of Mr. Locke's human understanding. . . . The little, according to *my* convictions . . . , the very little of proper Platonism contained in the *written* books of Plato, who himself, in an epistle, the authenticity of which there is no tenable ground for doubting, as I was rejoiced to find Mr. Gray acknowledge, has declared all he had written to be substantially Socratic, and not a fair exponent of his own tenets. . . .[1]

Coleridge, in short, maintained (as do some of the best modern scholars)[2] 'that the works of Plato contain the opinions of Socrates, but they by no means convey the opinions of Plato. I do not mean that they convey different opinions but they do not convey the peculiar opinions of Plato.'[3] The peculiar opinions might, said Coleridge, to some extent reside in Speusippos, likewise in Plotinus and his successors, but ultimately they resided in Christianity.

The positive use of Platonism, Plato's 'peculiar opinions' aside, was for Coleridge twofold. First of all '. . . Platonism at least predisposed the most effective means' that prepared the mind for 'Christianity'.[4] It did so by two emphases, that of the 'I am' ('. . . Plato began in meditation, thought deeply within himself of the goings-on of his own mind . . . and then looked abroad to ask if this were a dream, or whether it were indeed a revelation from within. . . . He employed his observation as the interpreter of his meditation . . .');[5] and that of the systematic necessity for grounding the consequences of the 'I am' in an extramundane, supra-discursive idea:

Plato had taught men that after going through all the highest exertions of the faculties which nature had given them, cultivating their senses, their under-standings, their reason and their moral powers, yet still there was a ground wanting, a something that could not be found within the sphere of their know-ledge. Yet knowledge led men to ask for that ground, and this he placed in the Supreme Being as the final result of all human effort and human reasoning.[6]

Such a ground having been indicated by Plato, Christianity, in Coleridge's view, then stepped forward to occupy the ground and fulfil the system: 'that which combines all the common sense of the experimental philo-sopher with all the greatest prospects of the Platonists—that we find in Christianity.'[7] With this view—of Christianity as 'the proper supplement of philo-

---

[1] *Coleridge's Miscellaneous Criticism*, ed. T. M. Raysor (London, 1936), p. 308.
[2] See note 48, p. 363.   [3] *Philosophical Lectures*, p. 156.   [4] Ibid., p. 157.
[5] Ibid., p. 186.   [6] Ibid., p. 241.   [7] Ibid., p. 223.

sophy', uniting all philosophy into 'one systematic and coherent power'[1] —Coleridge comes so close to a formulation of the aim of the *magnum opus* that we realize that Plato is absent from the various schemes for the work because he was already a part of its very conception. The *magnum opus* was, indeed, essentially an expansion and elaboration of Platonism.[2]

Secondly, Plato was useful for Coleridge as the guarantor of a unique and valuable tone for philosophical discourse. The special vocabulary of Platonism, with its array of emotionalized abstractions—justice, beauty, the good—and its constant sense of unexpressed significance, its dramatic intensity, its appeal to the sense of rapture, has, in all ages, been the mark of an orientation opposed to limited, drily technical or cognitive modes of philosophizing. It has been especially favourable to the emotionalizing of philosophy.[3] 'Plato', says Coleridge—and he expresses the truism as well as anyone ever has—'was a poet of such excellence as would have stood all other competition but that of his being a philosopher. His poetic genius implanted in him those deep impressions and the love of them which, mocking all comparison with after objects, leaves behind it thirst for something not attained, to which nothing in life is found commensurate and which still impels the soul to pursue.'[4] It was this special tone of Platonism—more than any arguments from logic—that kept 'alive the *heart* in the *head*' during Coleridge's early involvements with pantheistic variants; it was this tone that, occurring in the mystics, worked against the implications of their pantheism and 'acted in no slight degree to prevent my mind from being imprisoned within the outline of any single dogmatic system'.[5] 'The early study of Plato and Plotinus,' says Coleridge, '. . . contributed to prepare my mind for the reception and welcoming of the "Cogito quia sum, et sum quia Cogito".'[6] This Platonic tone, it should

---

[1] Ibid., pp. 233–4.

[2] Thus Coleridge says flatly that in 'my *Logosophia*' he 'shall give (deo volente) the demonstrations and constructions of the Dynamic Philosophy scientifically arranged. It is, according to my conviction, no other than the system of Pythagoras and of Plato revived and purified from impure mixtures' (*Biographia*, i. 179–80). Elsewhere, more obliquely, Coleridge, after speaking of 'the unwritten dogmata of Plato,' the 'interior doctrine,' muses that some 'future' philosophical palaeologist might 'make up the whole system and reproduce the Platonic philosophy for us as it then existed.' As groundwork for this possibility he mentions a fragment in Stobaeus in terms suggestive of the syncretisms that always occur in his projections of the *magnum opus*: 'I refer to the passage in which we are told that the intelligential powers, by the Pythagoreans and Anaxagoras called the *Nous*, (the *Logos* or the *Word* of Philo and St. John) is indeed indivisibly united with, but yet not the same as the absolute principle of causation, THE PATERNAL' (*Philosophical Lectures*, p. 175).

[3] See note 49, p. 363.

[4] *Philosophical Lectures*, p. 158. From such a statement we may conclude that the Platonic motifs of 'longing'—ὀρέγεσθαι (*Republic* 572 A; *Phaedo* 65 C) and the 'beyond'—ἐπέκεινα (*Republic* 509 B) were of vital importance for Coleridge. As Adam says, 'ὀρέγεσθαι expresses the instinctive and unconscious turning of the soul toward the fountain of her being . . .' (*Republic*, ed. James Adam (Cambridge, 1965), ii. 321 n. 2).

[5] *Biographia*, i. 98.

[6] Ibid., pp. 94–95. This formulation, which probably derives from Fichte's '*Ich bin schlechthin,*

be noted, was treasured by Coleridge as something quite apart from any technical commitment to philosophy, as the indispensable prelude to significance. Thus he praises Sir Joshua Reynolds, who, mired in the eighteenth-century rationalistic environment that Coleridge despised ('in evil days, and with every obstacle around him'[1]), had 'drunk deeply of Platonism, at least of what is best of all the vital feelings of Platonism, in his early youth' and had hence been able to provide 'the mark of a better taste' in eighteenth-century art.[1]

Accordingly, it was Platonism's affirmation of the whole man—not just man thinking, but man thinking and feeling and longing—that Coleridge emphasized. Plato is explicitly opposed not to Spinoza, as with Jacobi, but rather to Aristotle; and Coleridge's well-known formulas of the opposition of the two thinkers bring out the psychological predisposition of the 'I am'/'it is' tension more than its logical elaborations.

Every man [says Coleridge] is born an Aristotelian, or a Platonist. I do not think it possible that any one born an Aristotelian can become a Platonist; and I am sure no born Platonist can ever change into an Aristotelian. They are the two classes of men, beside which it is next to impossible to conceive a third. . . . I believe that Aristotle never could get to understand what Plato meant by an idea. . . . With Plato ideas are constitutive in themselves.[2]

Coleridge repeated the distinction (in which he had been anticipated by Goethe) on more than one occasion; in all its forms, however, the psychological opposition is stressed in contradistinction to the logical opposition of the Kant-Spinoza paradigm.

There are, [says Coleridge] and can be, only two schools of philosophy, differing in kind and in source. Differences in degree and in accident, there may be many; but these constitute schools kept by different teachers with different degrees of genius, talent, and learning;—auditories of philosophizers, not different philosophies. . . . Schools of real philosophy there are but two,—best named by the arch-philosopher of each, namely, Plato and Aristotle. Every man capable of philosophy at all . . is a born Platonist or a born Aristotelian.[3]

weil ich bin' (Werke, i. 98), substitutes 'quia' (because) for Descartes's 'ergo' (therefore). See Excursus Note XVII, 'Coleridge and Descartes', p. 320.

[1] Philosophical Lectures, p. 194.

[2] Table Talk, July 2, 1830. Coleridge's claim that Aristotle did not understand Plato's doctrine of ideas has been repeatedly put forward, and as often denied, in the history of thought. Apparently the Neoplatonist Syrianus was the first to make the charge; the counter-argument is that Aristotle, as a pupil of Plato, must have been privy to Plato's deepest attitudes. Cherniss points out, however, that 'certainly Speusippus and Xenocrates would have been unimpressed by the much repeated modern argument that Aristotle's long association with Plato guarantees his correct understanding of the latter's philosophy, (Harold Cherniss, Aristotle's Criticism of Plato and the Academy (Baltimore, 1944), p. xi). For a summary of the history of the debate, see Cherniss, pp. ix–xxi. Natorp, like Coleridge, finds that Aristotle did not understand Plato, and attributes the 'error' to 'the eternal incapacity of dogmatism to transpose itself into the viewpoint of the critical philosophy in general' (Platos Ideenlehre, p. 385). For Natorp's substantiation of the charges, see pp. 384–456.

[3] Works, v. 37. Cf. Unpublished Letters, ed. E. L. Griggs (London, 1932), ii. 265.

But Coleridge, while continuing to stress the psychological opposition of Plato and Aristotle, makes it clear that he conceives it as logically entailing the formal tension of 'I am' and 'it is':

The difference between Aristotle and Plato is that which will remain as long as we are men and there is any difference between man and man in point of opinion. . . . Aristotle . . . affirmed that all our knowledge had begun in experience, had begun through the senses, and that from the senses only we could take our notions of reality. . . . this would necessarily have led to atheism and an utter destitution of all religion and all morality. . . . [So] two opposite systems were placed before the mind of the world. One, whether or not, in order to arrive at the truth, we are in the *first* place (for there is no doubt among thinking men that both must be consulted—the question of priority is the point) whether or not in the *first* place, and in order to gain the principles of truth, we are to go into ourselves and in our own spirits to discover the law by which the whole universe is acting . . . or whether on the contrary we are to regard, with Aristotle, the mind as being a blank or empty receiver, distinguished from it indeed by a strange and mysterious propensity of being filled. . . .[1]

The opposition of Plato and Aristotle was conceived by Coleridge in terms not merely of psychological predispositions, or even of logical starting-points, but of ultimate systematic implications. The opposition finally reveals itself, characteristically, in terms of Coleridge's preoccupation with pantheism. 'God', says Coleridge, 'is confounded with (and everywhere, in Aristotle's genuine works), included in the universe: which most grievous error it is the great and characteristic merit of Plato to have avoided and denounced.'[2]

Aristotle and the *tabula rasa* lay behind the psychological presuppositions of the 'it is', and the *tabula rasa* lay behind the Locke-Hartley-Priestley-Godwin naturalism that Coleridge struggled with in his early philosophical quest. Yet however clearly Coleridge understood the implications of Aristotle as leading to pantheism, it was none the less not Aristotle, but Spinoza, who caught men's minds in the Romantic era, and it was not Aristotle, but Spinoza, who posed the most consequent and powerful threat to Coleridge's requirement of moral agency, and at the same time presented the most seductive lure of system fulfilled and nature dignified.

It was, in short, the impetus of the Spinozistic onrush in Romantic philosophizing that forced Coleridge to add Kant to Plato as propaedeutic for his Christian acceptances and ultimate systematic reconciliation. Though Plato, and the platonist tradition, provided him with his earliest

[1] *Philosophical Lectures*, pp. 186–9.

[2] *Works*, i. 264 n. Compare Boyle: 'I know *Aristotle*, and his commentators . . ., do not directly idolize nature . . . but yet I doubt they pose further than they can justify . . . when they most commonly call the works of God the works of nature, and mention him and her together, not as a creator and a creature, but as two co-ordinate governors, like the two Roman consuls.' (*A Free Inquiry*, p. 185.)

realizations of the unsatisfactoriness of any form of necessitarian hypothesis, the tremendous upsurge of Spinozism in the sophisticated ramifications of post-Kantian terminology made it almost mandatory for Coleridge to conduct his counter-war in the matrix of those same sophistications. We may therefore differentiate the role of Plato from that of Kant by saying that, though both served as prolegomena to the true system, Plato served the heart and Kant the head.[1] The discussions of Plato, embedded in irony, paradox, and dramatic situation, could only with difficulty be related to the defence against Spinozism, especially in its transcendental form; on the other hand, Kant provided for Coleridge the intellectual armoury by which he was able to maintain the systematic interests of the 'I am' against the formidable Spinozism of his German Romantic contemporaries.

The precise role played by Kantian distinctions—the double function of imagination, the synchronism of reason and understanding, the elucidation of phenomenon and thing-in-itself, the differentiation of idea and concept—will be taken up in our sequel, dealing with the internal reticulation of Coleridge's thought and also the specific implications of Platonism. For our purposes here we will stress only the general form of Kant's usefulness.[2]

Now Coleridge, despite his affection for the Cambridge Platonists, did not find their Platonic transmissions a suitable philosophical groundwork for his system. Though Henry More's theological writings contained 'original, enlarged, and elevating views of the Christian dispensation',[3] though he had fine imagination, and 'both the philosophic and the poetic genius, supported by immense erudition',[3] he was made largely useless for Coleridge (as he was for Leibniz) by his lack of a sense of systematic implication.[4] The poet and the philosopher in More 'did not amalgamate'.[5] They did not for three reasons: because More's Platonism was 'a corrupt, mystical, theurgical, pseudo-Platonism'[6] ('With his *semi*-Cartesian, *semi*-Platonic, *semi*-Christian notions, . . . More makes a sad jumble . . .');[7] because More was ignorant of 'natural science';[8] and, most important, because More was afflicted by a 'want' of 'searching logic',[9] of the propaedeutic function which Coleridge sees as hinted at by Bacon ('the English

---

[1] See note 50, p. 364.

[2] The fullest discussion of Coleridge's use of Kant is provided by Elisabeth Winkelmann, *Coleridge und die kantische Philosophie. Erste Einwirkungen des deutschen Idealismus in England,* Palaestra Heft 184 (Leipzig, 1933). See also Wellek, *Kant in England,* pp. 65–135.

[3] *Works,* v. 112.   [4] See note 51, p. 365.   [5] *Works,* v. 112

[6] Ibid., p. 114. See note 52, p. 365.

[7] *Works,* v. 117. Compare Cassirer: 'As to the writings of Henry More, they not only exhibit . . . the lack of any sense of structure and proportion in the presentation of an argument; but this weakness bears with it another, a lack of proper intellectual form. . . . In More's complete works his cabbalistic writings occupy no less space than his metaphysics, ethics, and nature philosophy, and the latter also show the constant intermixture of quite heterogeneous mystical elements.' (*The Platonic Renaissance,* p. 143.)

[8] *Works,* v. 113.   [9] Ibid. See note 53, p. 366.

Plato') but not systematically presented until Kant. Thus Coleridge reproves More for

the want of that logical προπαιδεία δοκιμαστική, that critique of the human intellect . . . that fulfilment of the heaven-descended *nosce teipsum*, in respect to the intellective part of man, which was commenced in a sort of tentative broadcast way by Lord Bacon in his *Novum Organum*, and brought to a systematic completion by Immanuel Kant in his *Kritik der reinen Vernunft, der Urtheilskraft, und der metaphysische Anfangsgründe der Naturwissenschaft.*[1]

And in his notes on John Smith, Coleridge extends this dual emphasis—the similarity of the Cambridge Platonists to Kant, side by side with their inferiority to Kant—to the whole 'Latitudinarian party at Cambridge':

The greater number were Platonists, so called at least, and such they believed themselves to be, but more truly Plotinists. Thus Cudworth, Dr. Jackson . . . Henry More, this John Smith, and some others. . . . What they all wanted was a pre-inquisition into the mind, as part organ, part constituent, of all knowledge, an examination of the scales, weights, and measures themselves abstracted from the objects to be weighed or measured by them; in short, a transcendental aesthetic, logic, and noetic. Lord Herbert was at the entrance of, nay, already some paces within, the shaft and adit of the mine, but he turned abruptly back, and the honor of establishing a complete προπαιδεία of philosophy was reserved for Immanuel Kant, a century or more afterwards.[2]

Kant thus stood for a modernization of concepts, a systematic articulation of distinctions.

The writings of the illustrious sage of Königsberg, the founder of the Critical Philosophy, [says Coleridge in the *Biographia*], more than any other work, at once invigorated and disciplined my understanding. The originality, the depth, and the compression of the thoughts; the novelty and subtlety, yet solidity and importance of the distinctions; the adamantine chain of the logic; and I will venture to add . . . the *clearness* and *evidence*, of the 'CRITIQUE OF THE PURE REASON;' of the 'JUDGEMENT;' of the 'METAPHYSICAL ELEMENTS OF NATURAL PHILOSOPHY;' and of his 'RELIGION WITHIN THE BOUNDS OF PURE REASON,' took possession of me as with a giant's hand.[3]

We should be perfectly clear, however, that Kant provided Coleridge with instruments, not with a philosophical orientation—he 'invigorated and disciplined my understanding'. Indeed, in the light of our contention that Coleridge's philosophy was a systematic elucidation of unchanging and deeply felt, even when not clearly articulated, commitments, we can see, in those cases where we can trace the origins of his interest in a thinker, that the interest almost always preceded his actual knowledge of the contour of the thinker's work. It was as though his own inner lucubrations opened a realm of discourse first, and then invited the contributions of other thinkers. Thus his enduring involvement with Lessing appeared

---

[1] *Works*, v. 112–13.   [2] Ibid., pp. 266–7.   [3] *Biographia*, i. 99.

full-blown, antecedent to any knowledge of the German intellectual, as a result of his hearing that Lessing was the 'most formidable infidel'.[1] Similarly he seemed to know from afar that he was headed towards Kant, long before he could possibly have been acquainted with the details of Kant's work. He was aware of his own philosophical problems and knew that he needed help. So by December 1796, though knowing no German, he was already writing to Thelwall of '. . . the most unintelligible Emanuel Kant'—and the word 'unintelligible' is surely a challenge and a foreshadowing.[2]

Indeed on 5 May 1796 Coleridge had complacently written to Poole that he was studying German '& in about six weeks shall be able to read that language with tolerable fluency', and that he was planning to go to Germany and 'bring over with me all the works of Semler & Michaelis, the German Theologians, & of Kant, the great german Metaphysician.'[3] After which, said Coleridge—faintly foreshadowing the *magnum opus*—he would start a school, to teach the following studies in order: '1. Man as Animal. . . . 2. Man as an *Intellectual* Being: including the ancient Metaphysics, the systems of Locke & Hartley,—of the Scotch Philosophers—& the new Kantian S[ystem—] 3. Man as a Religious Being. . . '.[4] Then, as soon as he got to Germany, Coleridge wrote back to Poole of a long interview with Klopstock, and already his possessiveness about Kant is apparent. 'Of Kant', Klopstock said, reports Coleridge, 'that he was a Mountebank & the Disgrace of Germany—an unintelligible Jargonist.—And that his New Lights were going out very fast in Germany. (N.B./ *I* meet every where tho', with some SNUFFS that have a live spark in them —& fume under your nose in every company.—All are Kantians whom I have met with.)'[5]

When Coleridge began to read Kant in earnest, the use to which the German analyst could be put was already apparent. A letter to Godwin in June 1803 indicates that Coleridge was working on Bacon and Plato: 'I am now . . . ready to go to the Press, with a work which I consider as introductory to a *System*, tho' to the public it will appear altogether a Thing by itself.' This work would contain a section described as 'Lord Bacon—or the Verulamian Logic', which would be followed by a section described as 'Examination of the same, & comparison of it with the Logic of Plato (in wĉh I attempt to make it probable, that tho' considered by Bacon himself as the antithesis & Antidote of Plato, it is bonâ fide the

---

[1] *Letters*, i. 197. To Flower, 1 Apr. 1796. See note 54, p. 366.
[2] Ibid., p. 284 n. To Thelwall, 17 Dec. 1796.
[3] Ibid., p. 209. Obviously, however, he failed to realize his plan for quick 'fluency', for two years later (3 Aug. 1798), he writes Poole that 'With regard to Germany, these are my intentions . . . . stay 3 or 4 months, in which time I shall at least have learnt the language . . .' (*Letters*, i. 414).
[4] Ibid., p. 209.   [5] Ibid., p. 444. To Poole, 20 Nov. 1798.

same, & that Plato has been grossly misunderstood.)'[1] This propaedeutic, as we know, was still occupying Coleridge by the time of *The Friend*—and later, too. But as early as 1807 Kant had allowed him to glimpse a much grander fulfilment of the defence of free moral agency against Spinozism. To John Ryland in 1807 he writes that he is 'convinced that Kant in his Critique of the pure Reason, and more popularly in his Critique of the Practical Reason has completely overthrown the edifice of Fatalism, or causative Precedence as applied to Action.'[2]

Although it is not our present purpose to examine the specific function of Coleridge's Kantian adaptations, it will be useful, both as testimony to the unity of his effort under the conception of the *magnum opus*, and as an indication of the great importance he attached to the Kantian arsenal of distinctions in his lifelong struggle to preserve the conception of a moral self within a philosophical system, to consider a few of his statements with regard to one prime Kantian distinction, that of 'reason' and 'understanding'.[3] We have earlier noted the coherence of all Coleridge's work, both prose and poetry, as foundation stones for the systematic *magnum opus*. So we will not be surprised that one of the objects of *The Statesman's Manual* was also one of the objects of the *Aids to Reflection*. To Rose in 1816 Coleridge says that in the former work he 'endeavoured to explain myself at large on that distinction between the Reason and the Understanding, which I deem of such vital Importance'.[4] Likewise, one of the aims of *Aids to Reflection*, in 1825, was '3. To substantiate and set forth at large the momentous distinction between reason and understanding'— which was followed by '4. To exhibit a full and consistent scheme of the Christian Dispensation'.[5] He refers elsewhere to the distinction in still more serious tones, speaking, for instance, of the 'unspeakable importance of the Distinction between the Reason and the Human Understanding, as the only Ground of the Cogency of the Proof *a posteriori* of the existence of a God'.[6] He even says that 'all the labors of my life' will have 'answered but one end, if I shall have only succeeded in establishing the diversity of Reason and Understanding'.[7] The importance of this polarity in Coleridge's thought, which he so much emphasized, is explained in a footnote to *The Friend*: the distinction enables him to steer the ship of religion past the rocks of pantheism:

By the 'understanding,' I mean the faculty of thinking and forming judgments

---

[1] Ibid. ii. 947. To Godwin, 4 June 1803.

[2] Ibid. iii. 35. Cf. Kant, *Werke*, iii. 374–89; v. 103–13.

[3] Perhaps the most satisfactory presentation of Coleridge's views on 'Reason' and 'Understanding' is to be found in Sanders, *Coleridge and the Broad Church Movement*, pp. 35–48. For Coleridge's invocation of the distinction, see, e.g., *Letters*, ii. 1198; *Works*, v. 181, 286, 514–15, 561; ii. 143–50; i. 241–53.

[4] *Letters*, iv. 670. To H. J. Rose, 17 Sept. 1816.   [5] *Works*, i. 115.

[6] *Inquiring Spirit*, p. 382.   [7] Snyder, *Coleridge on Logic and Learning*, p. 135.

on the notices furnished by the sense. . . . By the pure 'reason,' I mean the power by which we become possessed of principles,—the eternal verities of Plato and Descartes. . . . To many of my readers it will, I trust, be some recommendation of these distinctions, that they are more than once expressed, and everywhere supposed, in the writings of St. Paul. I have no hesitation in undertaking to prove, that every heresy which has disquieted the Christian Church, from Tritheism to Socinianism, has originated in and supported itself by arguments rendered plausible only by the confusion of these faculties.[1]

This Kantian distinction, in other words, allowed Coleridge to focus a whole unexpressed range of 'it is'/'I am' implications in a manner that favoured Christianity and blocked Spinozistic consequences.

Though Kant provided Coleridge with the most effective set of distinctions for coping with Spinozism, and to that extent differed from Plato, he was none the less, in his essentials, considered by Coleridge as having a great deal in common with Plato—a view, incidentally, that later received weighty confirmation from the Marburg School.[2] The logical importance of Plato was his indication of the necessity of a ground of being outside any chain of consequent reasoning; the final characteristic of Platonic thought was that the 'mind always feels itself greater than aught it has done'. Such a supersensible ground was indicated also by Kant in his conception of the *Ding an sich*, and Coleridge regarded that as he did the implications of Platonism, as an invitation to substitute Christian hypotheses.

I soon found, [said Coleridge, that there] were hints and insinuations referring to ideas, which KANT either did not think it prudent to avow, or which he considered as consistently *left behind* in a pure analysis. . . . In spite therefore of his own declarations, I could never believe, that it was possible for him to have meant no more by his *Noumenon*, or THING IN ITSELF, than his mere words express.[3]

---

[1] *Works*, ii. 164 n. Though almost certainly Kant's analytic use of 'Reason' and 'Understanding' first alerted Coleridge to the theological importance of the distinction, he later came to insist that the dichotomy existed in the very nature of the human mind and therefore had been known and expressed by various thinkers before Kant (see, e.g., *Works*, v. 81–82). In one place, in fact, Coleridge paraphrases Jacobi's view—'I should have no objection to define reason with Jacobi . . . as an organ bearing the same relation to spiritual objects, the universal, the eternal, and the necessary, as the eye bears to material and contingent *phenomena*. . . . Thus, God, the soul, eternal truth, &c., are the objects of reason; but they are themselves reason' (ii. 144–5)—and we recognize that the statement is simply an accommodation of Plato's equation in which *eikasia* (imaginative conjecture) relates to *pistis* (trustful certainty) proportionately to the relation of *dianoia* (intellect) to *noesis* or *episteme* (divine knowledge) (*Republic* 509 D). Nettleship, indeed, specifically suggests that we equate *dianoia* with Coleridge's 'understanding' and Kant's 'Verstand', *episteme* with Coleridge's 'reason' and Kant's 'Vernunft' (*Lectures on the Republic of Plato*, p. 249 n. 2).

[2] See note 55, p. 367.

[3] *Biographia*, i. 99–100. Again: 'I could never believe, that it was possible for him to have meant no more by his *Noumenon*, or Thing in itself, than his mere words express.' (J. I. Lindsay,

But the true congruence of Kant and Plato exhibits itself more fully in Kant's *Kritik der Urteilskraft* than in the *Kritik der reinen Vernunft*, and it was for this reason, I believe, that Coleridge found the former work the most amazing of Kant's treatises. 'Of Kant C[oleridge] spoke in terms of high admiration', records Robinson in 1810, '. . . and intimated that he should one day translate his work on the Sublime and Beautiful. His *Critik der Urtheilskraft* he considered as the most astonishing of his works.'[1]

The virtuosity of the systematic analysis in this remarkable work reaches its climax, and its unalterable and mystic limit, in Kant's discussion of the sublime. The critique of reason might in logic point the same way as Plato, but its dryness of tone is the antithesis of Platonic vitality;[2] in the *Kritik der Urteilskraft*, however, emotional incommensurabilities are central to Kant's discourse, and it is for that reason unique among Kant's works. The aim of the third critique, in short, is the commensurating of the incommensurable—such hitherto affective commonplaces as 'taste', as the 'beautiful', are brought by the titanic ordering power of Kant's mind into systematic focus. The crown of the whole achievement, and the analogue of the supradiscursive *Ding an sich* of the first critique, is posited by Kant as '*das Erhabene*'—'the sublime'. Raised above all its fashionable eighteenth-century antecedents—from the tepid Longinianism of Boileau to the clever antitheses of Burke[3]—the 'sublime' becomes the tribute of reason to that which encompasses reason, an acknowledgment of Plato's overriding principle that the 'mind always feels itself greater than aught it has done'. Such is the testimony of Kant's sublime: 'Erhaben ist, was auch nur denken zu können ein Vermögen des Gemüts beweiset, das jeden Maßstab der Sinne übertrifft'—the sublime is that, the mere capacity of thinking which evidences a faculty of mind transcending every standard of sense.[4] Again and again the luminous intellect of Kant flashes forth with its testimony of the mind's abundance: '. . . the true sublime cannot be contained in any sensuous form, but rather concerns ideas of reason, which, although no commensurate representation of them is possible, by their very incommensurability, which is itself representable, are aroused and called into mind.'[5] The 'sublime' is thus at one and the same time hyper-Platonic in its reference to the 'something more', and absolutely

'Coleridge Marginalia in Jacobi's *Werke*', *MLN*, l (1935), p. 221). And again: '. . . hints and insinuations referring to ideas, which Kant either did not think it prudent to avow, or which he considered as consistently *left behind* in a pure analysis, not of human nature *in toto*, but of the speculative intellect alone' (Lindsay, p. 218). Kant's friend and biographer, Jachmann, reports that 'in the true sense he was a worshipper of God'. See note 56, p. 368.

[1] *Coleridge's Miscellaneous Criticism*, ed. T. M. Raysor (London, 1936), p. 386.

[2] Compare Kant: 'If we set aside the exaggerations in Plato's methods of expression, his spiritual flight from the ectypal mode of reflecting upon the physical world-order to the architectonic ordering of it according to ends, that is, according to ideas, is an enterprise which calls for respect and imitation.' (Kant, *Werke*, iii. 259.)

[3] See note 57, p. 369.   [4] Kant, *Werke*, v. 322.   [5] Ibid., pp. 316–17.

anti-Spinozistic in its rejection of the finality of 'res singulares' (*Ethica* v. 24) and of nature itself. 'Dass das Erhabene also nicht in den Dingen der Natur,' says Kant, 'sondern allein in unsern Ideen zu suchen sei, folgt hieraus'—it follows that the sublime is not to be sought in the things of nature but in our own ideas (a central adumbration, we cannot doubt, for Husserl's *eidos*, as *das Erhabene* in general must surely be for Jaspers's *das Umgreifende*).[1] So the sublime is a function of the irreducible primacy of the 'I am':

... the broad ocean agitated by storms cannot be called sublime. Its aspect is horrible, and one must have previously in the mind a set of ideas if such an intuition is to raise it to the pitch of a feeling which is itself sublime, in that the mind has been stimulated to abandon sensibility and occupy itself with ideas that contain higher purposiveness.[2]

Not only does the sublime involve a repudiation of the finality of nature, it also fulfils two other requirements important for an 'I am' system; it has as its basis the capacity for moral feeling: 'the sublime ... has its foundation in human nature, and indeed in that part of human nature that, with the natural understanding, one can at the same time expect and demand of everyone: namely, in the tendency to a feeling for (practical) ideas, i.e. for the moral.'[3] And secondly, it takes its existence specifically from the reticulative requirements of mind:

... precisely because there is a striving in our imagination towards progress *ad infinitum*, while reason demands absolute totality, as a real idea, that same inability on the part of our faculty for the estimation of the magnitude of things of the world of sense to attain to this idea, is the awakening of a feeling of a supersensible faculty within us; and it is the use to which judgement naturally puts particular objects on behalf of this latter feeling, and not the object of sense, that is absolutely great, and every other contrasted employment small. Consequently it is the disposition of a soul evoked by a particular representation engaging the attention of the reflective judgement, and not the object, that is to be called sublime.[4]

We see, in this key statement, that not only does the sublime proceed from the 'I am', but it exists as a consequence of the imagination's 'Bestreben zum Fortschritte ins Unendliche' and reason's 'demand for absolute totality'—that is, it exists as a function of the mind's reticulative propensities.

When, therefore, Coleridge syncretizes the language of Kant with the name of Plato in indicating reason's demand for system, and the necessity of anchoring that system in a supralogical, extramundane ground, he does

---

[1] Kant, *Werke*, v. 321. Husserl says that he uses 'eidos' because Kant's 'idea' had become a spent term. I suspect that he was encouraged to use a Platonic term by Natorp's work, which he admired.

[2] Kant, *Werke*, v. 317.   [3] Ibid., p. 337.   [4] Ibid., pp. 321–2.

so with complete propriety.[1] The passage indicates his sense of the congruence of Kant and Plato in their propaedeutic function for Christianity, and the necessity of their thought as an antidote to Spinozism:

The grand problem, the solution of which forms, according to Plato, the final object and distinctive character of philosophy, is this: for all that exists conditionally (that is, the existence of which is inconceivable except under the condition of its dependency on some other as its antecedent) to find a ground that is unconditional and absolute, and thereby to reduce the aggregate of human knowledge to a system.[2]

Though Coleridge's esteem for Kant was very great indeed, we should not make the mistake of thinking that Kant for that reason did more for him than serve as herald of Christianity. 'I reverence Immanuel Kant with my whole heart and soul', he writes to Green, 'and believe him to be the only Philosopher, for *all men* who have the power of thinking. I can not conceive the liberal pursuit or profession, in which the service derived from a patient study of his works would not be incalculably great, both as cathartic, tonic, and directly nutricious.'[3] Strong though the statement is, its last three modifications suggest Kant's preparatory rather than substantive role. This emphasis is still more clear in another statement: 'Kant had 1. to overthrow, 2nd. to build the best possible temporary Shed and Tool-house. . . . Lastly, in this Shed to give the Hints and great Ideas for the erection of the new Edifice.'[4] And Coleridge makes the implied reservation more explicit in a letter of 1825, for there, while he restates his reverence for the German thinker, he equally emphasizes that he accepts Kant as a logical prolegomenon (like Bacon, who for Coleridge implied Plato too) but not as a final philosophy:

Of the three schemes of philosophy, Kant's, Fichte's, and Schelling's . . . I should find it difficult to select the one from which I *differed* the most, though perfectly easy to determine which of the three *men* I hold in highest honour. And Immanuel Kant I assuredly do value most highly; not, however, as a metaphysician, but as a logician who has completed and systematised what Lord Bacon had boldly designed and loosely sketched out in the Miscellany of Aphorisms, his Novum Organum.[5]

---

[1] See note 58, p. 369.   [2] See note 59, p. 370.
[3] *Letters*, iv. 792. To Green, 13 Dec. 1817.
[4] *Inquiring Spirit*, p. 122.
[5] *Letters of Samuel Taylor Coleridge*, ed. E. H. Coleridge (London, 1895), ii. 735. To J. T. Coleridge, 8 Apr. 1825. Coleridge was undeviating in this assessment. Thus Robinson records that in 1812 Coleridge informed him that 'to Kant his obligations are infinite, not so much from what Kant has taught him in the form of doctrine, as from the discipline gained in studying the great German philosopher' (Crabb Robinson's *Diary*, i. 381). Again, in his *Logic* Coleridge says that 'the Critique of the pure reason . . . would have been open to fewer objections, had it been proposed by the author under the more appropriate name of Transcendental Logic. For considered as *Logic* it is irrefragable: as philosophy it will be exempt from opposition and cease to be questionable only when the Soul of Aristotle shall have become one with the Soul of Plato . . .' (MS. Logic in the British Museum, vol. ii, Egerton 2826, p. 330).

True philosophy was furthered by both Plato and Kant, but not to be found in either. It could be found only in Christianity. 'And why is Philosophy for ever to be set up as the Rival rather than the Friend and natural Companion, of Christianity?', Coleridge asks, and then, in direct opposition to the later emphasis of Ritschl and in our day of Barth, he asks: 'What is Christianity but a divine and pre-eminent Philosophy?'[1]

We are not concerned here with the inner organization of all Coleridge's attitudes towards Christianity. It can be said in general, however, that he regarded himself as an orthodox, rather than a latitudinarian, Church of England man (and in any event the Thirty-Nine Articles present Anglican orthodoxy as something larger than a straitened creed); that the scholarly studies of his Christianity, which place him in the rather limp context of nineteenth-century Anglican theology, are not wholly satisfactory; that the potentially most interesting study of his role *qua* theologian would not be with respect to the Anglican tradition but with respect to the dynamic changes in the theological climate on the continent between Schleiermacher and Barth—with particular attention to Feuerbach; and that such a study would reveal Coleridge, in his general opposition to the stream of continental theology, to be a far more important figure than the eccentric latitudinarian and avuncular predecessor of Maurice that he now appears.[2]

As a philosophy, Coleridge's Christianity is important in four respects. First, he posited Christianity axiomatically, as a need of the human heart co-ordinate with the sense of the 'I am'. Secondly, Christianity's initial demand upon our consciousness expressed the basic truth of morality—the reciprocity of guilt and responsibility. Thirdly, Christianity was a 'scheme', or 'system'; it 'all hangs together'. Finally, it did not hang together for Coleridge until, by his rational acceptance of the Trinity, he found a way to staple the chain of 'I am' consequences in an extramundane ground, thus at one and the same time guaranteeing the free agency of his moral being and the reality of external nature.

As we have seen, Coleridge's development was a series of unfoldings of the meaning of his initial commitment. That commitment, in its most irreducible form, was the emotional sense of the self as a moral agent: the sense of the heart. Nothing that ever conflicted with that sense, even when imposed by reason itself, was allowed to stand. For Coleridge 'the heart, the moral nature' was 'the beginning and the end', and 'truth, knowledge, and insight were comprehended in its expansion'.[3] It is significant, for

---

[1] *Inquiring Spirit*, p. 386.

[2] See Excursus Note XVI, p. 316, for Coleridge and the later course of theological thought.

[3] *Works*, i. 226; *Inquiring Spirit*, p. 397. Again: 'So true is it, that the faith, which saves and sanctifies, is a collective energy, a total act of the whole moral being; that its living sensorium is in the *heart*; and that no errors of the understanding can be morally arraigned unless they have proceeded from the heart.' (*Biographia*, i. 84.)

instance, that his *Confessio Fidei* of 1816 begins as follows: I BELIEVE that I am a free agent, inasmuch as, and so far as, I have a will, which renders me justly responsible for my actions, omissive as well as commissive.'[1] He begins, in short, not with faith, not with God, not with the church, not with Schleiermacher's *Abhängigkeitsgefühl* (feeling of absolute dependence) and its pantheistic implications, but with the self and its moral agency. Following this statement, there is a recognition of the mind's urge to reticulation: 'Likewise that I possess reason . . . which, uniting with my sense of moral responsibility, constitutes the voice of conscience.'[1] (The meaning of this passage is expanded in the *Aids to Reflection*, where it testifies to the absolute centrality of the reticulative need: 'It is the office, and as it were, the instinct of reason, to bring a unity into all our conceptions and several knowledges. On this all system depends; and without this we could reflect connectedly neither on nature nor our own minds.')[2] Next in order is the realization that the systematic projection— reason's action—of the concerns of the 'free agent' must necessarily find its completion only in God: 'Hence it becomes my absolute duty to believe, and I do believe, that there is a God. . . .'[3] (A continuation of the passage just adduced from the *Aids to Reflection* provides a supporting gloss: 'Now this ["the instinct of reason, to bring a unity into all our conceptions"] is possible only on the assumption or hypothesis of a One as the ground and cause of the universe. . . . The One must be contemplated as eternal and immutable.')[4]

This order of belief is parallel to that of Descartes, in that it begins with the 'I am' and proceeds to God; it is parallel also to that of Kant; but it is not parallel to that of a mystic, or a pantheist, who begins first with the sense of God. Coleridge starts with the sense of self, and finds that that sense resides in his capacity for moral choice—one of the titles of the *magnum opus*, for instance, was 'The Mysteries of Religion grounded in or relative to the Mysteries of Human Nature: or the foundations of morality laid in the primary Faculties of Man.'[5]

But the next item in Coleridge's *Confessio Fidei* finds no parallel in Descartes, and Kant, and, indeed, constitutes much of the reason why neither of these philosophers, nor Plato himself, was ever wholly satisfactory to him. It explains too why he would never abandon Spinoza; secure as a corollary of Christian faith, and free from pantheism, it recognizes the importance of the external order of nature: 'The wonderful works of God in the sensible world are a perpetual discourse, reminding me of his existence, and shadowing out to me his perfections.'[6] Such an

---

[1] *Works*, v. 15.   [2] Ibid. i. 210.   [3] Ibid. v. 15.   [4] Ibid., i. 210–11.
[5] *Letters*, iii. 279. To Lady Beaumont, 21 Jan. 1810. The title may be an echo of a subtitle in Butler's *Fifteen Sermons*: 'Upon Human Nature, or Man Considered as a Moral Agent'.
[6] *Works*, v. 15.

opinion was not a corollary of Cartesian philosophy. On the contrary, 'Descartes was the first man who made nature utterly lifeless and godless, considered it as the subject of merely mechanical laws.'[1]

Such, in brief, is the essential scheme of Coleridge's Christianity. All was connected, the moral sense was primary, the dignity of nature was necessary, and God was the anchor of the whole system.

Of these irreducibles, it was the conception of God that gave Coleridge most trouble in his theological development. His heart never wavered in his emotional acceptance of the efficacy and primacy of Christian commitment; but his early conception of a unitary God led his mind to necessitarian and Spinozistic contradictions, whereby the emphasis on external nature turned against the moral agency of the self. Coleridge's theological development, therefore, can be seen as a continuing attempt, effectuated by the movement from a unitarian to a trinitarian conception of deity, to remove the internal contradictions of his heart's convictions. And what is really most important—and though almost blindingly clear, rarely seen by us today—is that the meaningfulness of the difference between the two conceptions of deity for Coleridge arose from and was a function of his rendering absolute allegiance to the sovereignty of systematic consequence. Most of us, I dare say, can very comfortably accommodate a vague kind of anthropomorphic authority-reverence (so many of us are so truncated in our care for existence that monotheism would be too strong a word) with whatever at all we deign to think about free will or its lack, the dignity of nature or the terror of nature, and any other item we pack into the portmanteau, or, more likely, do not recognize as belonging in the portmanteau. I remember vividly a funeral oration for an elderly and futile scholar, where on a bleak winter day a man, attired as a Protestant Christian minister, stood up in church and earnestly assured us—his bored and careless auditors—that in a sense the old gentleman was immortal, that all his molecules were indestructible and would come to rest or continue to function in rivers and rocks and trees and winds—a thought that comforted us no more than it did the prisoner Claudio; and then, proceeding from this raging Spinozism to an equally forthright and equally unconscious Socinianism, our Bossuet *manqué* began to exhort us about the dignity of human life, which he found summed up in the 'three greatest men in history: Socrates, Jesus, and Dwight D. Eisenhower'.

Well, as Coleridge said, we do not win heaven by logic. But in our mortal frame logic—if not always the discrete propositional analyses of contemporary philosophy (which too often seem a perpetual clearing of the throat while we raptly wait for speech)—is important; and for Coleridge, logic, or rather consequence, the reticulation of concerns, was inseparable from the possibility of mental activity at all. For Coleridge,

[1] *Philosophical Lectures*, pp. 376–7. See Excursus Note XVII p. 320.

then, the problem of God-conception was to define God in such a way as to guarantee both the living richness of the world and the moral freedom of the person.

It is not our task here to investigate the complicated, but historically accessible, background of Coleridge's Trinitarian meditations. We know in general that he was helped by the Anglican theologians Bull, Waterland, and Leighton.[1] We know that he came to accept the logic as well as the mystery of the Trinity. We know that he came to believe that '. . . there neither is, nor can be, any religion, any reason, but what is, or is an expansion of the truth of the Trinity; in short . . . all other pretended religions, pagan or *pseudo*-Christian (for example, Sabellian, Arian, Socinian), are in themselves Atheism'.[2] In a long letter to Cottle in April of 1814, Coleridge concludes that 'The Trinity . . . from its important aspects, and Biblical prominence, is the grand article of faith, and the foundation of the whole christian system.'[3] And, as an old man, he said that he was 'resting my whole and sole hope of salvation and immortality on the divinity of Christ, and the redemption by his cross and passion, and holding the doctrine of the Triune God as the very ground and foundation of the Gospel faith'.[4] Still again, he said that the 'doctrine of the Trinity' was 'the foundation of all rational theology, no less than the pre-condition and ground of the rational possibility of the Christian Faith, that is, the Incarnation and Redemption'.[5]

These statements could hardly be weightier or more emphatic. The 'foundation of the whole christian system', however, was not in place—was quite absent from his Christian beliefs—during his Socinian days in the 1790s, for he writes to Thelwall in December, 1796:

You say the Christian is a *mean* Religion: now the Religion, which Christ taught, is simply 1 that there is an Omnipresent Father of infinite power, wisdom, & Goodness, in whom we all of us move, & have our being & 2. That when we appear to men to die, we do not utterly perish; but after this Life shall continue to enjoy or suffer the consequences & [natur]al effects of the Habits, we have formed here, whether good or evil.—This is the Christian *Religion* & all of the Christian *Religion*.[6]

Elsewhere in the same letter we see Coleridge's emphasis on morality and Christian sentiment, side by side with a total lack of sympathy with—or even awareness of—the radical paradoxicality of Christianity in all its great moments, especially with regard to the mystery of faith. Socinian Christianity had found, in Toland's rubric, 'Christianity Not Mysterious',

[1] See note 60, p. 370.   [2] *Works*, v. 404–5.
[3] *Letters*, iii. 486.   [4] *Works*, v. 78–79.
[5] Ibid., p. 397. Again '. . . I hold the Nicene Faith, and revere the doctrine of the Trinity as the fundamental article of Christianity . . .' (v. 431).
[6] *Letters*, i. 280.

and though Coleridge's heart is strong, his head is here full of the 'reason' of Priestley:

Is it a despicable trait in our Religion, that it's professed object is 'to heal the broken-hearted, and give Wisdom to the Poor Man?'—It preaches *Repentance*—what repentance? Tears, & Sorrow, & a repetition of the same crimes?—No. A 'Repentance unto good works'—a repentance that completely does away all superstitious terrors by teaching, that the *Past* is nothing in itself. . . . Christianity regards morality as a process . . . . let me explain the word Faith—by Faith I understand, first, a deduction from experiments in favor of the existence of something not experienced, and secondly, the motives which attend such a deduction.[1]

Coleridge's transition from this kind of simplified moralizing under the name of Christianity to his acceptance of the mysteriousness of the Christian dispensation under the Trinity was not a result of any sudden conversion. It was, rather, a slow, complicated, process, with tentative advances and retreats, and with progress on one issue of the Christian schematism not always accompanied by progress on the others. Characteristically, his first objections to simple Socinianism were based on his sense of individual moral responsibility. '*Guilt* is out of the Question', he wrote imperiously to Thelwall in May 1796, 'I am a Necessarian, and of course deny the possibility of it.'[2] But his heart refused to be muffled by this central tenet of Priestleyan Unitarianism, and by March 1798, though not ready totally to reject its pious optimism, he renders it practically null by a by-passing affirmation of original Sin:

Of GUILT I say nothing; but I believe most stedfastly in original Sin; that from our mothers' wombs our understandings are darkened; and even where our understandings are in the Light, that our organization is depraved, & our volitions imperfect; and we sometimes see the good without *wishing* to attain it, and oftener *wish* it without the energy that wills & performs—And for this inherent depravity, I believe, that the *Spirit* of the Gospel is the sole cure—[3]

What is here enunciated is, without doubt, the basic and irreducible ground of Coleridge's religious sensibility.[4] It deepens with the years, and its latent existence in the early 1790s made the halter of Necessitarian optimism irksome to Coleridge, even before he specifically rejected it. It is also the reason why the great Leibniz, in so many other ways his soulmate, does not figure more overtly in Coleridge's religious expression; Coleridge loved the Leibniz of the *Nouveaux Essais*, but he could not accept the optimistic theodicy of that magnificent mind.[5]

[1] *Letters*, i. 282–3. See note 61, p. 371.
[2] *Letters*, i. 213. Compare Godwin: '. . . under the system of necessity the ideas of guilt, crime, desert and accountableness have no place' (*Political Justice*, i. 314).
[3] *Letters*, i. 396. To George Coleridge.
[4] See Excursus Note XV, p. 314.   [5] See note 62, p. 371.

Coleridge soon broke through the optimism of the Unitarian view, but he experienced far more difficulty in substituting the Trinitarian conception of God for the Unitarian hypotheses.[1] In particular, he found the personality of the Christ a stumbling block, and he could also only proceed slowly towards an acceptance of Christ's place in the Godhead. The Socinian insistence on Jesus as a mere man, as simply a good example, lingered on to prevent a whole-hearted acceptance of the Trinity even after he had become dissatisfied with Priestleyan Christianity in general. So, in a letter to his wife in April 1799, he shows—under the stress of the death of his infant son—the deepest discontent with Necessitarian implications, and at the same time an unwillingness to accept the personality of Christ:

That God works by *general* laws are to me words without meaning or worse than meaningless . . . —What and who are these horrible shadows necessity and general law, to which God himself must offer *sacrifices* . . . ?—I feel a deep conviction that these shadows exist not. . . . —I confess that the more I think, the more I am discontented with the doctrines of Priestley.[2]

But in the same letter he says:

. . . although the *Man* Jesus had never appeared in the world, yet I am Quaker enough to believe, that in the heart of every Man the Christ would have revealed himself, the Power of the Word. . . .[2]

For a while he tried to tell himself that the emphasis on the 'personality' of God smacked of idolatry:

. . . I am sometimes jealous, that some of the Unitarians make too much an *Idol* of their *one* God. Even the worship of one God becomes Idolatry, in my convictions, when instead of the Eternal & Omnipresent, in whom we live, & move, & *have* our Being, we set up a distinct Jehovah tricked out in the *anthropomorphic* Attributes of Time & *Successive* Thoughts—& think of him, as a PERSON, *from* whom we *had* our Being. The tendency to *Idolatry* seems to me to lie at the root of all our human Vices—[3]

He followed this line of thought to its absolute conclusion, for on 5 December 1803 he wrote to Matthew Coates thanking him for 'that article of my Faith . . . which is the nearest to my Heart . . . —I mean, the absolute Impersonality of the [D]eity.'[4]

From this theological dead end he recoiled, and by 1806 he had worked himself around much closer to the Trinitarian position. In a letter to George Fricker, in which he concedes some of the objections to miracles, he adds:

Still must thou repent and be regenerated, and be crucified to the flesh; and this not by thy own mere power; but by a mysterious action of the moral Governor on thee; of the Ordo-ordinians, the Logos, or Word. Still will the

---

[1] See note 63, p. 372.   [2] *Letters*, i. 482. To Mrs. Coleridge, 8 Apr. 1799.
[3] Ibid. ii. 893. To Estlin, 7 Dec. 1802.
[4] Ibid., pp. 1022–3. Cf. Emerson, *Works*, i. 130.

eternal filiation, or Sonship of the Word from the Father; still will the Trinity of the Deity, the redemption, and the thereto necessary assumption of humanity by the Word, 'who is with God, and is God,' remain truths: and still will the vital head-and-heart FAITH in these truths, be the living and only fountain of all true virtue.[1]

But in a letter to Fricker five days later he reveals that the head was not yet quite so certain as the heart:

I fear, you rather misunderstood one part of my Letter. I by no means gave that extract, as containing the whole of my Christian Faith; but as comprising such doctrines, as . . . would prepare the way for the *peculiar Doctrine* of Christianity, namely, Salvation by the Cross of Christ. I meant these doctrines as the Skeleton, to which the death & Mediation of Christ with the supervention of the Holy Ghost were to add the Flesh, and Blood, Muscles, nerves, & vitality.— God of his goodness grant, that I may arrive at a more living Faith in these last, than I now feel. What I now feel is only a very strong *presentiment* of their Truth and Importance aided by a thorough conviction of the hollowness of all other Systems.[2]

That conviction, as we have seen, was notably enhanced during these days by Kantian analyses; and we must not forget that Coleridge's passage from Unitarianism to Trinitarianism was also being worked out through Plato and Bacon. It was, of course, grounded in the Trinitarian defences of the Anglican bishops of the seventeenth and eighteenth centuries, as well as in ancient patrology and its matrices—'. . . I should use Philo (who has not been used half enough) to demonstrate that the Socinian interpretation of John's Gospel *must be false*'.[3] But also, as Coleridge said, the 'doctrine of the Trinity' demanded 'power and persistency of abstraction, and a previous discipline in the highest forms of human thought'.[4]

The Trinity, however, is a Christian mystery, and, to that extent, its apprehension must be an act of faith as well as of logic. Coleridge's acceptance of it cannot, therefore, be seen simply as the rational fulfilment of his philosophical need. 'The Trinity, as Bishop Leighton has well remarked,' emphasized Coleridge, 'is "a doctrine of faith, not of demonstration," except in a *moral* sense.'[5] In 1825 he again invoked the mysteriousness of the doctrine as a limit on its discussion: 'I have not entered on the doctrine of the Trinity, or the still profounder mystery of the origin of moral Evil. . . . These doctrines are not, in strictness, subjects of reflection.'[4]

The schematic function of the Trinity in Coleridge's thought can be understood, however, in relation to three central facts: first, that the original impetus was negative—Coleridge was pushed away from Uni-

---

[1] *Letters*, ii. 1189–90. [2] Ibid., p. 1192.
[3] Ibid. iv. 803. See note 64, p. 372. [4] *Works*, i. 204.
[5] *Letters*, iii. 481. To Cottle, Apr. 1814.

tarianism by its pantheistic implications before he was ready to accept the solution offered by the Trinity;[1] secondly, that the Trinity solved the methexic question for him; it provided a conception that guaranteed the existence of both the Many and the One, and so allowed him to anchor his complete system (if not to our edification at least to his own) in an extramundane ground without abandoning the reality of the natural world; thirdly, that his final acceptance of the uniqueness of the Trinitarian solution was made possible by a process of deepening elucidation of the meaning of the 'I am' starting-point, so that the Trinity became for him a peculiarly satisfying and appropriate doctrine in terms of his emotional as well as his logical orientation.

Coleridge was initially impelled towards the Trinity by his conviction that all other systematic possibilities led to Spinozism. One of his finest appreciations of this truth occurs in the *Aids to Reflection*, where he says, first, that the 'hypothesis of a One as the ground and cause of the universe' is necessary to bring 'unity into all our conceptions and several knowledges. . . . The One must be contemplated as eternal and immutable.' Then he goes on to say that

the idea, which is the basis of religion, commanded by the conscience and required by morality . . . can be expressed in no other terms. . . . It comprehends, moreover, the independent (extra-mundane) existence and personality of the Supreme One, as our Creator, Lord, and Judge.

The hypothesis of a one ground and principle of the universe . . . is thus raised into the idea of the Living God. . . . Religion and morality do indeed constrain us to declare him eternal and immutable. But if from the eternity of the Supreme Being a reasoner should deduce the impossibility of a creation; or conclude with Aristotle, that the creation was co-eternal; or, like the later Platonists, should turn creations into emanation, and make the universe proceed from the Deity, as the sunbeams from the solar orb;—or if from the divine immutability he should infer that all prayer and supplication must be vain and superstitious; then however evident and logically necessary such conclusions may appear. . . . [they] must be false. For were they true, the idea would lose the sole ground of its reality. . . . The very subject of the discussion would be changed. It would no longer be the God, in whom we believe; but a stoical Fate, or the super-essential One of Plotinus, to whom neither intelligence, nor self-consciousness, nor life, nor even being can be attributed; or lastly, the World itself, the indivisible one and only substance (*substantia una et unica*) of Spinoza, of which all *phaenomena*, all particular and individual things, lives, minds, thoughts, and actions are but modifications.[2]

In the discussion that follows this quotation, Coleridge affirms that the

[1] As he said in retrospect, 'A more thorough revolution in my philosophic principles, and a deeper insight into my own heart, were yet wanting. Nevertheless, I cannot doubt, that the difference of my metaphysical notions from those of Unitarians in general contributed to my final re-conversion to the whole truth in Christ . . .' (*Biographia*, i. 137).

[2] *Works*, i. 211. Cf. Plotinus, *Enneads*, v. 1. 6; v. 2. 1; v. 3. 13.

only way to maintain the necessary hypothesis of a One as the ground cause of the universe, and at the same time to keep it free from Spinozism, is by the Trinity. He is 'clearly convinced, that the Scriptural and only true idea of God will, in its development, be found to involve the idea of the Triunity.'[1] And again, the 'Idea of the Trinity' is 'that Idea, in which alone' the 'divinity of our Lord' can 'be received without breach of the faith in the unity of the Godhead'.[2]

Coleridge became convinced, in other words, that 'There is, there can be, no *medium* between the Catholic Faith of Trinal Unity, and Atheism disguised in the self-contradicting term, Pantheism; for every thing God, and no God, are identical positions.'[2] He became convinced, to cite a still more succinct statement, that '. . . the Trinity is the only form in which an idea of God is possible, unless indeed it be a Spinosistic or World-God.'[4] He was, accordingly, censorious of the attempt—begun during the the Renaissance[5]—to associate the Cabala ('this patchwork of corrupt Platonism or Plotinism, with Chaldean, Persian, and Judaic fables and fancies')[6] with Christianity. 'It is not,' he says, 'half a dozen passages' about the

first three *proprietates* in the Sephiroth, that will lead a wise man to expect the true doctrine of the Trinity in the Cabalistic scheme; for he knows that the scholastic value, the theological necessity, of this doctrine consists in its exhibit-ing an idea of God, which rescues our faith from both extremes, Cabalo-Pantheism, and Anthropomorphism. It is, I say, to prevent the necessity of the Cabalistic inferences that the full and distinct development of the doctrine of the Trinity becomes necessary in every scheme of dogmatic theology.[6]

The 'Cabalistic theosophy', on the other hand, was 'Pantheistic, and Pan-theism, in whatever drapery of pious phrases disguised, is (where it forms the whole of a system) Atheism, and precludes moral responsibility, and the essential difference of right and wrong.'[6] And then the final demytho-logizing: 'Spinoza himself describes his own philosophy as in substance the same with that of the ancient Hebrew Doctors, the Cabalists—only unswathed from the Biblical dress.'[7]

The primary *impetus* towards the Trinity, therefore, was supplied by the need to protect systematic reason from pantheism. The primary *attraction*, however—the lure of the Trinity even before Coleridge was able to accept the doctrine as an article of faith—was that it solved the methexic problem

---

[1] *Works*, i. 216.   [2] Ibid., p. 220.   [3] Ibid. v. 406.

[4] Ibid., p. 36. Again: 'Even while my faith was confined in the trammels of Unitarianism (so called) with respect to the doctrines of Sin and Grace, I saw clearly, as a truth in philosophy, that the Trinitarian was the only consequent Medium between the Atheist and the Anthropo-morph.' (Marginal note at page 40 of the first volume of the Law edition of Boehme's works in the British Museum.)

[5] See Joseph L. Blau, *The Christian Interpretation of the Cabala in the Renaissance* (New York, 1944).

[6] *Works*, v. 462–3.   [7] Ibid., p. 463. See note 65, p. 374.

that lies at the root of all reticulative philosophy.[1] Though pantheist philosophies were capable of system, they all obliterated the substantial existence of the Many in order to maintain the One. For Coleridge, however, no solution was acceptable that did not guarantee the substantial existence of both the Many and the One, together with their essential unity. We see him worrying about the problem in 1799:

I would make a pilgrimage to the burning sands of Arabia, or &c &c to find the Man who could explain to me there can be *oneness*, there being infinite Perceptions—yet there must be a *oneness*, not an intense Union but an Absolute Unity.[2]

And he is worrying no less intensely in 1803:

I would make a pilgrimage to the Deserts of Arabia to find the man who could make understand how the *one can be many*! Eternal universal mystery! It seems as if it were impossible; yet it *is*—& it is every where!—It is indeed a contradiction *in Terms*: and only in Terms![3]

Both of these statements occur, significantly, as afterthoughts to musings about the possibility of a poem on Spinoza. But Spinozism, though it raised very strongly the question of the One and the Many, did not, could not, answer it to Coleridge's satisfaction, for Spinozism dissolved the Many to maintain the One.

The Trinity, however, suspended in its mystery both One and Many, and once Coleridge became involved in its acceptance we find in his writings no more offers to make pilgrimages to Arabia for his methexic answer.[4] The God of the Trinity is at one and the same time a guarantee of that necessary conception of the One that the mind hypothesizes for its systematic concerns, and of the substantial existence of the Many: Father, Son, and Holy Ghost. It is, indeed, precisely the ὁμοούσιον τῷ Πατρί of the Nicene Creed that guarantees the *substantial* existence of the Many at the same time that it denies Arian Unicism. Coleridge, in accepting 'the Trinity, as the Supreme Being, his reflex act of self-consciousness and his love, all forming one supreme mind', found, in the very terms of that acceptance, the guarantee of the joint reality of the One as One and the Many as Many.

---

[1] As the Platonic Socrates says, '. . . if all things partake of both opposites, and are enabled by their participation to be both like and unlike themselves, what is there wonderful about that?' but 'if anyone showed that the absolute like becomes unlike, or the unlike, like, that would, in my opinion, be a wonder', and 'if he shows that absolute unity is also many and the absolute many again are one, then I shall be amazed' (*Parmenides* 129 B). Thus Coleridge speaks of 'the exceeding difficulties of admitting a one Ground of the Universe (which however *must* be admitted) and yet finding *room* for any thing else' (*Letters*, iv. 849). Cf. *Enneads*, v. 1. 6.

[2] *Notebooks*, i. 556.   [3] Ibid. 1561.

[4] Indeed, to judge by the metaphor, his interest in Schelling may be seen as an attempt to find help with the methexic problem: '. . . long before Schelling had published his first and imperfect view—. If I had met a friend & a Brother in the Desart of Arabia, I could scarcely have been more delighted than I was in finding a fellow-laborer . . .' (*Letters*, iv. 775).

This solution clearly related to Coleridge's unstapled chain of consequences—'the chain, of which Christ is the staple and staple ring'.[1]
Though both Platonism and Kantian analysis, as we have seen, indicated
the reasonableness of the need for stapling the chain in an extramundane
ground—a need which, as we have argued from Leibniz, distinguishes
the true 'I am' system from the merely nominal 'I am' contentions of
Berkeley, Fichte, or Carnap—neither Plato nor Kant was able finally to
secure the chain. Only the Trinity could do so.[2] By the idea of the Incarnation the reason of man was able, to change the metaphor, to plant one
foot firmly in this world, and by the idea of God the Father to plant the
other on extramundane ground; and the idea of the Holy Ghost—especially in view of the Anglican acceptance of the *filioque* clause—was a
guarantee of the dynamic unity-in-diversity of the two steps.

St. John was vital to Coleridge in this respect. 'St. John', he says, 'had
a two-fold object in his Gospel and his Epistles,—to prove the divinity,
and also the actual human nature and bodily suffering, of Jesus Christ,—
that he was God and Man.'[3]

This conception, orthodox as it is, sounds with comforting familiarity
in our ears, and we may wonder why Coleridge—like countless other
Christians—could not simply accept it as a dogma. The answer should by
now be clear. Coleridge's mature conception of faith was not as a low-
probability belief, but as something much closer to Tillich's 'ultimate
concern'.[4] Thus he warns us against confounding 'the act of faith with
the assent of the fancy and understanding to certain words and conceptions.'[5] And he warns against 'a confusion of faith with belief'.[6] 'Faith', on
the contrary, 'is the *apotheosis* of the reason in man, the complement of
reason, the will in the form of the reason.'[7] 'Faith', again, 'seems to me the
co-adunation of the individual will with the reason, enforcing adherence
alike of thought, act, and affection to the Universal Will, whether revealed

[1] *Works*, v. 88.

[2] Coleridge recognized that all dichotomous thinking is in a sense trichotomous thinking
(see, e.g., *Works*, v. 355), for to think of a polarity of A and B is not only to think of A, and
to think of B, but also to think of a third, their relationship. Thus the dualism necessary to
validate the systematic extension of the 'I am' position (see Excursus Note XI, p. 302) becomes
automatically a trinalism.

[3] *Table Talk*, 6 Jan. 1823. See note 64, p. 373.

[4] *Dynamics of Faith*, p. 1: 'Faith is the state of being ultimately concerned: the dynamics of
faith are the dynamics of man's ultimate concern.'   [5] *Works*, v. 92.

[6] Ibid. Elsewhere he speaks of 'the practical mischiefs resulting from the confusion of
Belief and Faith. . . . Yet how early the dangerous identification of the two words began, we
learn from the Epistle of James, who, arguing *ex absurdo* on the assumption, that Faith means
Belief, justly remarks—The Devils believe, and so thoroughly too, that they believe and
tremble. Belief, therefore, can not be the proper and essential ground of Salvation in the soul.
But Faith *is*, and by Christ himself is solemnly declared to be so. Therefore, Belief can not be
the same as Faith! though the Belief of the truths essential to the Faith in Christ is the necessary accompaniment and consequent of the Faith.' (*Works*, v. 530–1.)

[7] *Works*, v. 107.

in the conscience, or by the light of reason.'[1] Or, 'FAITH may be defined, as fidelity to our own being'.[2] In another sense, '. . . faith is fidelity, fealty, allegiance of the moral nature to God. . . . The will of God is the last ground and final aim of all our duties. . . . But the will of God, which is one with the supreme intelligence, is revealed to man through the conscience.'[3] '. . . Faith is properly a state and disposition of the will, or rather of the whole man, the I.'[4] And finally,

> Faith subsists in the *synthesis* of the reason and the individual will. By virtue of the latter therefore it must be an energy, and inasmuch as it relates to the whole moral man, it must be exerted in each and all of his constituents or incidents, faculties and tendencies;—it must be a total, not a partial; a continuous, not a desultory or occasional energy. And by virtue of the former, that is, reason, faith must be a light, a form of knowing, a beholding of truth.[5]

It is quite clear, therefore, that for Coleridge an act of faith could in no sense by-pass the claims of reason; it represented the utmost exertions of reason in the quest for deity. It was necessary for him to examine the systematic implications of the Trinity, their coherence and their usefulness to his heart's concerns, in order to be able to accept the dogma and its mystery by his will.

In other words, Coleridge did indeed accept the Trinity as a dogma of faith. But for him, as for the author of *Hebrews*, Christian faith was an epistemological function. Coleridge's system-craving reason had to see how—in what Husserl calls 'syntaktische Gegenständlichkeit'—the dogma arranged itself systematically.[6] *Credo quia absurdum* was no part of Coleridge's creed.[7]

Thus, if one were a man, in Coleridge's phrase, of 'discontinuous mind' —as most men are—the Trinity could be accepted, or more likely rejected, by a blank statement of assent or dissent; its syntactic problems, which involve the age-old considerations connected with οὐσία or *substantia*, could be airily dismissed by a waiver such as Arnold's 'Propositions about substance pass by mankind at large like the idle wind'.[8] But if one were a man of 'continuous' mind[9]—and as such a man Coleridge regarded himself

---

[1] Ibid., p. 106.   [2] Ibid., p. 557.   [3] Ibid., p. 564.
[4] Ibid., p. 91.   [5] Ibid., p. 565.
[6] 'I was never so befooled as to think that the author of the fourth Gospel, or that St. Paul, ever taught the Priestleyan Psilanthropism, or that Unitarianism (presumptuously, nay, absurdly so called), was the doctrine of the New Testament generally. But during . . . my aberration . . . I presumed that the tenets of the divinity of Christ, the Redemption, and the like, were irrational, and that what was contradictory to reason could not have been revealed by the Supreme Reason. As soon as I discovered that these doctrines were not only consistent with reason, but themselves very reason, I returned at once to the literal interpretation of the Scriptures, and to the Faith.' (*Works*, v. 405.)
[7] See note 66, p. 375.
[8] 'Spinoza and the Bible', *Essays in Criticism; First Series*, p. 340.
[9] *Notebooks*, ii. 2112.

—substance would be of much greater moment. Coleridge's compeer of 'continuous' mind, Leibniz, gently rebukes Shaftesbury's dismissal of the importance of 'substance', and his attitude can certainly be ascribed to Coleridge as well:

One should of course reject sterile philosophizing; but I am of the opinion that true ideas of space, of matter, and above all of substance (sometimes thought of as useless, but by no means so common or so well known as might be imagined), would be knowledge with much to recommend it. . . . The agreement and disagreement of ideas are not known by a simple confrontation of our imaginations; analysis is necessary—a fact not sufficiently known to Mr. Locke, able though he was. On the knowledge of substance, and consequently of the soul, depends the notion of virtue and of justice, and the corollary question of the reasonableness of risking one's life for the good of another.[1]

In such terms we can see that the Trinity, which was developed historically to protect monotheism on the one hand, and confer permanent dignity upon Jesus's role as redeemer on the other, is an exceedingly delicate doctrine that threads a course through a philosophical field heavily mined with antique heresy. The literature on the subject is inconceivably vast, and the distinctions and sub-distinctions are sometimes so encrusted with factionalism as to be almost impossible to understand. There were the Macedonians, or Pneumatomachi, who, though in the opinion of Gregory Nazianzen 'sound in regard to the Son', reputedly imagined the Holy Ghost as a creature. There were the ever-threatening Arians, who, with their conception of a subordinate Christ, were most emphatically *un*sound in regard to the Son. There were the Sabellians (the most important of whom, in Coleridge's day, was Schleiermacher), who over-rationalized the mystery by making the persons of the Trinity merely modal distinctions of the Godhead (Coleridge laments the use of Latin *persona* (mask) in Trinitarian discussion);[2] and the Tritheists, who leaned over backwards to protect themselves against Sabellianism, and in so doing fell into polytheism (Coleridge brusquely rejects 'the oscillatory creed of Sherlock, now swinging to Tritheism in the recoil from Sabellianism, and again to Sabellianism in the recoil from Tritheism').[3] And there were more.

These ancient factions bear testimony to the complexity of the Trinitarian balance of conceptions, and their arguments remain paradigms for the full understanding of the dogma.[4] Rather, however, than engage in

---

[1] Leibniz, *Philosophische Schriften*, iii. 427–8.

[2] *Works*, v. 174. Another possibility, however, is that Coleridge is here inveighing against the implied Sebanthropism of 'person', as against the 'hypostasis' of the Greek formulation.

[3] *Works*, v. 76.

[4] For a general historical orientation see Harnack, *History of Dogma*, iii. 121–315; iv. 1–267. For a discussion of the historical formation of the arguments and terminologies involved, see Wolfson, *Philosophy of the Church Fathers*, pp. 141–493. For works in antiquity itself see Augus-

a discussion of the historical antecedents of the Trinitarian formulation, we may, for our purposes here, be content with a briefer kind of analysis. Coleridge, we have seen, always thought of his commitments in terms of what Jaspers calls the polarity of *Vernunft* and *Existenz*—of head and heart. Both aspects of his commitment were necessary, but, as his long inner dialogue attests, they were difficult to maintain in harmony. Emanating from these two realms of commitment—which were fused by faith— was a claim of the head upon God as the 'One', and a claim of the heart upon the need for a Redeemer. The first of these claims was a matter of philosophy; the second was the specific content of the Christian Religion.

Now we have devoted much argument to Coleridge's conception of systematic reason as that which ultimately dictated the necessity of an extramundane One. We should also insist on the emotional autonomy of his need for Christianity, which was a function of his axiomatic sense of fallenness and sin. Leibniz was probably as deeply committed to Christianity as Coleridge himself, and as theologically sophisticated; but Leibniz's Christianity did not involve this primal, palpable anxiety, which looks forward to Heidegger's fearfulness of existence, and backwards to Boehme.[1] 'Observe,' says Coleridge, '. . . once for all, that I do not pretend to account for Original Sin. I declare it to be an unaccountable fact.'[2]

tine, *De Trinitate*, which served as the foundation for most medieval thought on the subject. See too the orations of Athanasius, *Contra Arianos*, which contain the germs of most of Coleridge's arguments. In the general context of Coleridge's involvement with trinal schematisms outside the specific formulations of the fourth-century councils, a useful aid to comprehension is the three-volume work of F. C. Baur, *Die Christliche Lehre von der Dreieinigkeit und Menschwerdung Gottes in ihrer geschichtlichen Entwicklung* (Tübingen, 1841–3), which deals not only with the trinitarian formulations of the church fathers, and with those of medieval and Reformation Christianity, but also with those of the mystics and pantheists, including Boehme, Schelling, and Hegel. Lastly, for a modern work that is at once concise and authoritative, see J. N. D. Kelly, *Early Christian Doctrines* (New York, 1958), pp. 83–137, 223–79.

[1] In a striking summary of Boehme's position, Franz von Baader, his most dedicated interpreter, speaks in the very language of Heidegger: 'At the basis of J. Böhme's philosophy there lies the observation, evident everywhere, that all life rises out of *Angst* (birth fear), founders (suffocates) in *Angst* (death fear), and consequently consists only in a constant suspension of *Angst*. In this suspension Jacob Böhme calls this *Angst* the closed Centrum Naturae' (Baader, *Werke*, ii. 300). Compare Boehme: 'The eternal Mind stands thus in the Darkness, and vexes itself, and longs after the Light . . . and the Anguish is the Source . . .' (*Of the Threefold Life of Man*, xi. 15). The congeniality of Boehme's emphasis on *Angst* to Coleridge is evident from a pregnant statement in the notebooks: 'It is a most instructive part of my Life the fact, that I have been always preyed on by some Dread, and perhaps all my faulty actions have been the consequence of some Dread or other on my mind / from fear of Pain, or Shame, not from prospect of Pleasure /—So in my childhood & Boyhood the horror of being detected with a sorehead; afterwards imaginary fears of having the Itch in my Blood—/then a short-lived Fit of Fears from sex—then horror of DUNS, & a state of struggling with madness from an incapability of hoping that I should be able to marry Mary Evans . . . had all the effects of direct Fear, & I have lain for hours together awake at night, groaning & praying . . . then came Rob. Southey's alienation / my marriage—constant dread in my mind respecting Mrs Coleridge's Temper, &c—and finally stimulants in the fear & prevention of violent Bowelattacks from mental agitation / then . . . night-horrors in my sleep . . .' (*Notebooks*, ii. 2398).

[2] *Works*, v. 203.

'. . . I profess a deep conviction', he says, 'that man was and is a fallen creature, not by accidents of bodily constitution or any other cause, which human wisdom in a course of ages might be supposed capable of removing; but as diseased in his will, in that will which is the true and only strict synonyme of the word, I, or the intelligent Self.'[1] Again: 'A Fall of some sort or other—the creation, as it were, of the non-absolute—is the fundamental postulate of the moral history of Man. Without this hypothesis, Man is unintelligible'.[2]

The sense of fallenness was thus an imperative, and its demand was for a mode of redemption to assuage the pain of existence. Where Leibniz's religious sensibility was apparently actuated by a sense of reverence similar to that which he had felt for his father, Coleridge's took its departure from anxiety. The reasoning head can be satisfied by a 'One'—by a philosophical God that serves as terminus to a chain of rational consequences—but the fallen heart cries out for redemption. 'The two great moments of the Christian Religion are,' said Coleridge, 'Original Sin and Redemption; that the ground, this the superstructure of our faith.'[3] It was the 'actual existence' of 'Original Sin' that was 'the antecedent ground and occasion of Christianity,' while 'Christianity itself, as the edifice raised on this ground' was 'the faith in Christ, as the remedy of the disease—the doctrine of Redemption.'[4] 'On the doctrine of Redemption', said Coleridge again, 'depends the faith, the duty, of believing in the divinity of our Lord. And this again is the strongest ground for the reality of that Idea, in which alone this divinity can be received without breach of the faith in the unity of the Godhead. But such is the Idea of the Trinity.'[5]

We can see, therefore, why a Unitarian deity could never really serve Coleridge's philosophico-religious needs, and why the very bifurcation of those needs made the doctrine of a multiform deity theoretically acceptable. During his early years, however, when his head had been with Spinoza, or at least with Socinus, Coleridge had concurred in the 'Socinian' belief that interpreted Jesus's function to mean 'only that a good and gifted teacher of pure morality died a martyr to his opinions'.[6] His problem, then, lay not in accepting a multiform deity, but in overcoming his Socinian prejudice about Jesus—in realizing, in short, that only a Redeemer could bring redemption. The real difficulty concerned the 'personality' of Godhead: why the conception of God needed to be amplified by the conception of the Father, and that of the Redeemer by that of Jesus (the Holy Ghost, as the binding principle, caused Coleridge

---

[1] *Works*, i. 195–6.   [2] *Table Talk*, 1 May 1830.
[3] *Works*, i. 300. Compare Pascal: 'Car la foi chrestienne ne va presque qu'à établir ces deux choses: la corruption de la nature, et la rédemption de J[ésus] C[hrist].' (*Pensées*, ed. H. F. Stewart (New York, 1950), p. 106.)
[4] *Works*, i. 290.   [5] Ibid., p. 220.
[6] *Works*, v. 167.

no worry—once personality was accepted, then the Holy Ghost rode in on the same arguments as did the Son).[1]

We may take a passage from the *Aids to Reflection* as a clue to the mental process by which Coleridge resolved his difficulties on this key issue. After affirming his faith in the 'idea of the Triunity', he says: 'But I am likewise convinced that previously to the promulgation of the Gospel the doctrine had no claim on the faith of mankind'.[2] Coleridge, in short, accepted (against the Socinian interpretation) the theological arguments by which the Trinity is adumbrated in the New Testament,[3] but he declined to accept arguments (also available) that located the doctrine in the Old Testament.[4] He found this difference of crucial importance. If the Trinity, as the only possible amplified conception of divinity, was not enunciated before the New Testament, how could the Old Testament serve its religious needs? By, says Coleridge, the Mosaic I AM that I AM:

> I form a certain notion in my mind, and say: This is what I understand by the term, God. . . . I then apply the rules laid down by the masters of logic, for the involution and evolution of terms, and prove (to as many as agree with me in my premisses) that the notion, God, involves the notion, Trinity. I now pass out of the Schools, and enter into discourse with some friend or neighbor . . . unused to the process of abstraction . . . but sensible and single-minded . . . trusting in *the Lord God of his fathers, even the God of Abraham, of Isaac, and of Jacob*. If I speak of God to him, what will he understand me to be speaking of? . . . An accident or product of the reasoning faculty. . .? No. By God he understands me to mean an existing and self-subsisting reality, a real and personal Being—even the Person, the I AM, who sent Moses to his forefathers in Egypt.[5]

'The Person, the I AM.' The circle is complete, Coleridge ends where he began. Challenged by a theologico-historical question, Coleridge in his search for an answer uncovers the existential premise of Christianity—reveals that God must be not merely an abstraction of *Vernunft* ('product of the reasoning faculty') but a given in *Existenz* (a discovery from 'discourse with some friend or neighbour').

Coleridge had once gone so far as to denounce personality in religion as a form of idolatrous anthropomorphism.[6] But having reached the end of that alley, and found it blind, he retraced his steps and proceeded in the opposite direction. For what is clear about his final acceptance of the Trinitarian position is that by re-thinking the bases of the 'I am' starting-point, he came to a conclusion of the non-thingness, the incommensurability, of the

---

[1] See note 67, p. 375.   [2] *Works*, i. 216.   [3] See note 68, p. 376.
[4] 'Solely in consequence of our Redemption does the Trinity become a doctrine, the belief of which as real is commanded by our conscience' (*Works*, v. 17). The Old Testament possessed a 'Messianic *Spirit*' and an 'onward-looking *character*' (*Letters*, iv. 802), and though the Trinity itself existed 'in all ages, under more or less disfigurement, by *Tradition*' (*Letters*, iv. 895), not until the incarnation did it become an article of necessary faith. See note 63, p. 372.
[5] *Works*, i. 217–18.   [6] See note 69, p. 376.

personality. It was this that made it for him a unique principle, one that could not be transformed or translated in any final equation, and that had necessarily to be incorporated, in the absence of any possible alternatives, in the terminus of 'I am' considerations, that is, into God-head itself. Hence, what had seemed in 1802 a debilitating emphasis upon 'PERSON' in the Christian scheme, came to seem the key to the under-standing of the Trinity. 'I CAN NOT meditate too often,' he writes, 'too deeply, or too devotionally on the personeity of God, and his personality in the Word . . . and thence on the individuity of the responsible creature.'[1] The conception of God as extramundane ground was, therefore, joined, both logically and emotionally, by the conception of God as 'I am': '. . . I have . . . earnestly endeavored to show, that *Deus est ens super ens*, the ground of all being, but therein likewise absolute Being, in that he is the eternal self-affirmant, the I Am in that I Am'.[2]

Our understanding of how Coleridge actually re-worked the 'I am' posi-tion must be necessarily inferential, for he customarily presents us with completed opinions based on unexpressed arguments rather than with the process of argument itself. But I suspect that the process, in formal terms, would bear a close resemblance to the kind of extended re-thinking of the implications of the *cogito* that Husserl labours towards in his *Ideen zu einer reinen Phänomenologie und phänomenologischen Philosophie*, and in his *Carte-sianische Meditationen*; and, in *Existenz* terms, to the discourse of Jaspers and his central definition of self as *das Umgreifende, das ich bin* (the encom-passing, that I am).[3] Certainly Coleridge speaks the language of twentieth-century phenomenology when he asks, 'Who can comprehend his own will; or his own personeity, that is, his I-ship (*Ichheit*); or his own mind, that is, his person; or his own life? But we can distinctly apprehend them.'[4]

The question is basic. In its assertion of the incommensurability of the 'I', it provides the ground, in what Husserl calls 'primordial experience', for the recognition of the untranslatability of consciousness. In our own day, this untranslatability has been affirmed in the vatic sentences of Martin Buber's *Ich und Du*, and theologically in the work of Karl Heim—though for a long time neither thinker realized that the 'Copernican revo-lution' of their I-Thou distinction was actually a legacy from Jacobi's wars against Spinozism, and not the invention of Feuerbach in 1843.[5] For

---

[1] *Works* v. 269.   [2] Ibid., p. 103.

[3] Jaspers, *Von der Wahrheit*, p. 49 *et passim*.

[4] *Works*, v. 410. Similarly, 'It is one thing to *apprehend*, and another to *comprehend*. Reason apprehends the existence of the Supreme Being, though that Being alone can comprehend it.' (*Works*, v. 537.) The term 'Ichheit', which frequently occurs in Fichte and Schelling, was first used philosophically, according to Baader, by Meister Eckhart (Baader, *Werke*, ix. 73.) For the distinction between 'comprehend' and 'apprehend' compare Kant: 'Auffassung (*apprehensio*), und Zusammenfassung (*comprehensio aesthetica*)' *Kritik der Urteilskraft*, *Werke*, v. 323).

[5] See note 70, p. 377.

Buber the principle of the incommensurability of the 'I' is expressed by its dimensionality as 'Duwelt', while the formal 'I' of science and philosophy implies a wholly different meaning in a different realm, the 'Eswelt'.[1] It is the 'Dusagenkönnen' (the capability of saying 'Thou') that marks the truly human; we experience things, but we encounter a 'Thou'—and 'alles wirkliche Leben ist Begenung' (all real life is encounter):[2]

> Standing face to face with a human being as my 'Thou', speaking the basic word I-Thou to him, then do I find that he is no thing among things, and that he does not consist of things.
>
> He is not a 'he' or a formal 'you', bounded by other 'he's' and 'you's', a point registered in a world network of space and time; and he is not a state, describable, experiencable—a loose bundle of designated qualities. But uniquely and untranslatably is he Thou, and he fills the circle of heaven. Not as though nothing else existed except him: but rather as though all else lives in his light.[3]

And to Buber this irreducible principle finds its culmination in the conception of God, not as a final 'it', but as an eternal 'Thou':

> The eternal Thou cannot become It, because it cannot be posited in measure and bound, not even in the measure of unmeasurableness and the bound of boundless being; because it is not a sum of qualities—cannot even be conceived as an infinite sum of qualities raised to transcendence; because it can be met with neither in nor outside the world; because it cannot be experienced, cannot be thought; because we err when we say, 'I believe, that He is'—even 'He' is a metaphor, but not 'Thou'.[4]

To Buber the testimony of the real locus of human life as I-Thou rather than I-it arises from the phenomenon of speech: 'Geist ist Wort'—spirit is word. 'Geist ist nicht im Ich, sondern zwischen Ich und Du'[5]—but just as words do not arise from the confrontation of I and it, but only from the encounter of I and Thou, so too does the human spirit find its only mirror, its only realization, in the Thou that alone expresses the meaning of I.

Some such understanding Coleridge came to for himself. Perhaps extended reflection on the *Logos* of St. John—particularly as reinforced by reading Philo and the Christian fathers of Alexandria—gave him his clue. Or perhaps he picked up his needed emphasis from Jacobi ('... ohne Du,

---

[1] 'Ich nehme etwas wahr. Ich empfinde etwas. Ich stelle etwas vor. Ich fühle etwas. Ich denke etwas. . . . All dies und seinesgleichen zusammen gründet das Reich des Es.

'Aber das Reich des Du hat anderen Grund. Wer Du spricht, hat kein Etwas zum Gegenstand. . . . Wer Du spricht, hat kein Etwas, hat nichts. Aber er steht in der Beziehung. . . . Im Anfang ist die Beziehung. . . . Die Eswelt hat Zusammenhang in Raum und in der Zeit.

'Die Duwelt hat in beiden keinen Zusammenhang. . . . Ohne Es kann der Mensch nicht leben. Aber wer mit ihm allein lebt, ist nicht der Mensch.' (Martin Buber, *Ich und Du* (Leipzig, 1923), pp. 10, 11, 25, 42, 43.)

[2] Ibid., pp. 24, 18.   [3] Ibid., p. 15.   [4] Ibid., p. 129.

[5] Ibid., p. 49.

ist das Ich unmöglich'—without Thou, the I is impossible).¹ Perhaps he
was able to develop a statement such as Friedrich Schlegel's 'Nur in der
Antwort seines Du kann jedes Ich seine unendliche Einheit ganz fühlen'—
only in the answer of its Thou can every I wholly feel its infinite unity.²
Perhaps his own reflection on the needs of his own nature supplied the
doctrine.³ In any event, he found the I-Thou principle the keystone and
completion of his Trinitarian speculations: the 'I AM' of the Old Testament
contained in itself the central reality of the word: that anything spoken
implies a 'Thou'. For Coleridge, the sense of moral responsibility, which
was a function of the mystery of Original Sin, initially awakened the
human 'I' to its sense of incommensurability as personality.⁴ 'It appears,
then,' he says, 'that even the very first step, that the initiation of the
process, the becoming conscious of a conscience, partakes of . . . an act.
It is an act, in and by which we take upon ourselves an allegiance. . . .
It is likewise the commencement of experience.'⁵ Brutes are merely
'scious'; only human beings with 'conscience' are conscious.⁵ Coleridge
continues:

Now the third person could never have been distinguished from the first but
by means of the second. There can be no He without a previous Thou. . . .
This is a deep meditation, though the position is capable of the strictest proof,—
namely, that there can be no I without a Thou, and that a Thou is only possible
by an equation in which I is taken as equal to Thou, and yet not the same. . . .
I do not will to consider myself as equal to myself, for in the very act of constituting myself *I*, I take it as the same, and therefore as incapable of comparison,

¹ Jacobi, *Werke*, iv-1. 211. Jacobi's earliest formulation, however, occurred in a letter of 16
October 1775, which he quotes to Lavater in 1781: 'I open eye or ear, or I stretch forth my
hand, and feel in the same moment, inseparably, Thou and I; I and Thou. . . . Thou,
Thou! givest life.' (*Briefwechsel*, i. 330.) Again, in 1811: 'We must first really experience our
existence through another. For this reason: since without the exterior there is for us no interior,
without Thou no I is either present or possible; thus we are as certain of the other as of our
own selves, and love it, as we love life, which in conjunction with the other becomes part of
us.' (*Werke*, iii. 292.)

² Friedrich Schlegel, *Lucinde; Ein Roman* (Berlin, 1799), p. 221. Schlegel apparently was
impelled to his own version of the I-Thou formulation by a proto-Lawrentian realization of the
wonder of sexual union: 'Liebe ist höher als Anmuth und wie bald würde die Blüthe der
Schönheit fruchtlos welken ohne die ergänzende Bildung der Gegenliebe! Dieser Augenblick,
der Kuss des Amor und der Psyche ist die Rose des Lebens.—Die begeisterte Diotima hat
ihrem Sokrates nur die Hälfte der Liebe offenbart. Die Liebe ist nicht bloss das stille Verlangen
nach dem Unendlichen; sie ist auch der heilige Genuss einer schönen Gegenwart.' (p. 219.)

³ See note 71, p. 378.

⁴ 'I rather think that conscience is the ground and antecedent of human (or self-) consciousness, and not any modification of the latter. . . . for if I asked, How do you define the human
mind? the answer must at least contain, if not consist of, the words, "a mind capable of conscience."' (*Works*, i. 185.) Compare Heidegger: 'Das Gewissen ruft das Selbst des Daseins auf
aus der Verlorenheit in das Man. . . . *Das Dasein ruft im Gewissen sich selbst.*' (*Sein und Zeit*,
pp. 274–5.) Compare Butler: 'We are plainly constituted such sort of creatures as to reflect
upon our own nature. . . . This principle in man, by which he approves or disapproves . . .
is conscience; for this is the strict sense of the word . . .' (*Fifteen Sermons, Works*, ii. 41–42).

⁵ *Works*, v. 559.

that is of any application of the will. . . . the equation of Thou with I, by means of a free act, negativing the sameness in order to establish the equality, is the definition of conscience. . . . the conscience is the root of all consciousness . . . the precondition of all experience,—and . . . can not have been in its first revelation deduced from experience.[1]

We note that the I-Thou of Coleridge differs, in its initial emphasis, from the I-Thou of Buber by being a deduction from the nature of consciousness rather than, as in Buber, an axiom of experience. The step with which Buber begins: one human confronting another as an I to a Thou, is for Coleridge a secondary realization of a polarity that has arisen in the individual consciousness itself.

The difference is significant for our understanding of Coleridge's mental process. The possible sources of the I-Thou doctrine as cited above, though adequate for Buber's formulation, can be in Coleridge's version no more than hints, requiring a much more rigorous body of argument for their full realization. Such an argument did exist, and was available to Coleridge. It was the theory of apperception (*Apperzeption*) that Kant developed in the first and second editions of the *Kritik der reinen Vernunft*.

Apperception, as Kant defines it, is 'the consciousness of self', the 'simple representation of the "I" '.[2] In an examination of the structure of apperception, Kant finds that it takes a double form: 'empirical apperception', which is 'consciousness of self according to the determinations of our state in inner perception',[3] and 'pure apperception', which is 'the abiding and unchanging "I" ',[4] or 'transcendental apperception', which is 'pure, original, unchangeable consciousness'.[5] Kant says,

It must be possible for the 'I think' to accompany all my representations; for otherwise something would be represented in me which could not be thought at all. . . . All the manifold of intuition has, therefore, a necessary relation to the 'I think' in the same subject in which the manifold is found. But this representation is an act of spontaneity, that is, it cannot be regarded as belonging to sensibility. I call it pure apperception, to distinguish it from empirical apperception . . . because it is that self-consciousness which, while generating the representation 'I think' (a representation which must be capable of accompanying all other representations, and which in all consciousness is one and the same), cannot itself be accompanied by any further representation. The unity of this apperception I likewise entitle the transcendental unity of self-consciousness, in order to indicate the possibility of *a priori* knowledge arising from it.[6]

The relationship between apperception considered as a transcendental unity (that is, the 'I' of the Cartesian *cogito*) and empirical apperception is that of object and subject:

---

[1] Ibid., pp. 559–60.   [2] *Werke*, iii. 76.
[3] Ibid., p. 616. 'No fixed and abiding self', says Kant, 'can present itself in this flux of inner experiences.' Kant took the term 'apperception' from Leibniz.
[4] Ibid., p. 625.   [5] Ibid., p. 616.   [6] Ibid., pp. 114–15.

The transcendental unity of apperception is that unity through which all the manifold given in an intuition is united in a concept of the object. It is therefore entitled objective, and must be distinguished from the subjective unity of consciousness, which is a determination of inner sense. . . . Only the [transcendental] unity is objectively valid; the empirical unity of apperception, upon which we are not here dwelling, and which besides is merely derived from the former under given conditions *in concreto*, has only subjective validity.[1]

We may assume that Coleridge was well aware of the importance of Kant's analysis. Kant emphasizes that 'the principle of apperception is the highest principle in the whole sphere of human knowledge',[2] and Coleridge specifically invokes 'what Kant calls the great and inexplicable mystery that man should be both his own subject and object, and that these should yet be one.'[3] Compare Kant:

How the 'I' that thinks can be distinct from the 'I' that intuits itself . . ., and yet, as being the same subject, can be identical with the latter; and how, therefore, I can say: 'I, as intelligence and thinking subject, know myself as an object that is thought . . . and yet know myself, like other phenomena, only as I appear to myself, not as I am to the understanding'—these are questions that raise no greater nor less difficulty than how I can be an object to myself at all, and, more particularly, an object of intuition and of inner perceptions. (*Werke*, iii. 129.)

We need not assume, however, that Coleridge was indebted to Kant alone. Indeed, not only is the double awareness of self a feature of much mystical thought of the past, but it is a feature of our common experience. When we admonish or berate ourselves, stand in front of a mirror and admire or deplore our appearance, consult with ourselves before making a decision —or, like Mr. Flood, give ourselves a lonely party—we treat ourselves as a double consciousness, as an 'I' confronting a 'Thou'.[4]

Thus the importance of Coleridge's independent meditations upon the nature of the 'I am' as the source of his I-Thou doctrine cannot be dismissed, although it seems likely that these meditations were focused by his study of Kant. Or even more likely, that his own thought, stimulated by Kant, absorbed still further syncretisms. Such a pattern would have been in keeping with his mental habits, and quite possible in terms of the knowledge available to him.

We can, for instance, discern the outline of such a possible syncretism in his knowledge of Philo. It was from 'the consideration' of 'the essential meaning of *personality*', he says, that 'Plato and Philo Judaeus deduced the necessity of a Deus alter et Idem'.[5] Inasmuch as both Plato and Philo wrote in Greek, it is difficult to understand the pertinence of Coleridge's Latin

---

[1] *Werke*, iii. 119.
[2] Ibid., p. 116. For Coleridge's early awareness of Kant's 'apperception' see *De Quincey*, ii. 202, also *Biographia*, i. 99.   [3] Robinson, *Diary*, i. 341.
[4] Fichte notes that 'the concept of the Thou arises through the union of the It and the I' (*Werke*, i. 502).   [5] *Letters*, iv. 632.

formula, and perhaps impossible to recover exactly the process of his reasoning. But if we realize that at the time this statement was made, 1816, he was in command of Kant's philosophy, we may find it interesting to consider some well-known passages in Philo. In broaching the idea that no created thing is complete in itself, Philo says that 'through reciprocity and combination' created things should 'come to concord and form a single harmony'.[1] He then adds to this statement of a universal necessity for subject-object relationship some thoughts on the nature of the 'I am'. By doing so he discovers a difference in past existence, which pertained to a previous 'I', and present existence:

> What has become of the changes produced by life's various stages in the seemingly permanent self? Where is the babe that once I was, the boy and the other gradations between boy and full-grown man? Whence comes the soul...? Can we tell its essential nature?... The soul knows us, though we know it not; it lays on us commands, which we must fain obey...[2]

As Goodenough says, in commenting on Philo's assumption of a 'double mind', the 'personality, which Philo comes nearer to recognizing as a problem than any of the ancients, is not in the higher mind, but in the mixture, that is in the composite of bodily parts, soul, and mind'.[3] Coleridge, in some of his statements, seems to assume a distinction between 'personeity' and 'personality',[4] and if we think of 'personeity' as analogous either to Philo's soul (which is that part of our 'I' that belongs to God) or to Kant's transcendental unity of apperception, the connexion between such formulations and the I-Thou structure of self is not difficult to make.

In any event, Coleridge, using the *alter et idem* formula, anticipates Feuerbach's whole philosophy of community that Buber hails so enthusiastically:

> Unlike a million of tigers, a million of men is very different from a million times one man. Each man in a numerous society is not only coexistent with, but virtually organized into, the multitude of which he is an integral part. His *idem* is modified by the *alter*. And there arise impulses and objects from this *synthesis* of the *alter et idem*, myself and my neighbour.[5]

But such a communal realization, we must not forget, was an extrapolation of polarities uncovered in the individual self, and the direction of Coleridge's interest was less sociological than theological.

Having related the sense of person as primordial mystery (Coleridge laments that Jeremy Taylor had not 'meditated in the silence of his spirit on the mystery of an I AM! He would have seen that a person, *quoad* person, can have nothing common or generic')[6] to an understanding that

---

[1] *De Cherubim*, xxxi. [2] Ibid. xxxii.
[3] E. R. Goodenough, *An Introduction to Philo Judaeus* (New Haven, 1940), p. 151.
[4] *Works*, v. 269. [5] Ibid., p. 563. [6] Ibid., p. 218.

all self-realization involves 'consciousness' first stepping into 'conscience' to look back upon itself as 'Thou', Coleridge was ready for his Trinitarian resolution. When God, from the unfathomable depths of his being, broke forth into utterance—'I AM'—he activated the mystery of person as I-Thou, and posited himself as both Father and Son.

This is the corner-stone of my system, ethical, metaphysical, and theological [Coleridge says]—the priority, namely, both in dignity and order of generation, of the Conscience to the Consciousness in Man—No I without a Thou, no Thou without a Law from Him, to whom I and Thou stand in the same relation. Distinct Self-knowledge begins with the Sense of Duty to our neighbor: and Duty felt to, and claimed from, my Equal supposes and implies the Right of a Third, superior to both because imposing it on both.[1]

God could not be God, by the logic of 'Personalität', if he were simple and Unitarian; God *had* to be Christ in order to be God.[2] We may see something of the aetiology of Coleridge's argument in a note of 1805:

Thinking during my perusal of Horsley's Letters in Rep. to Dr P[riestley] objections to the Trinity on the part of Jews, Mahometans, and Infidels, it burst upon me at once as an awful Truth what 7 or 8 years ago I thought of proving with a *hollow Faith* and for an *ambiguous purpose*, my mind then wavering in its necessary passage from Unitarianism (which as I have often said is the Religion of a man, whose Reason would make him an Atheist but whose Heart and Common sense will not permit him to be so) thro' Spinosism into Plato and St John / No Christ, No God![3]

To this inquiry into the psychology—or, to use Brentano's special term, the 'Psychognosie'—of the I-Thou *Grundwort* as elaborated by the etymological play of con-*science* (axiomatically given)[4] as being the first *concretum* and activating principle of that knowledge called *con*-sciousness (knowing-withness as the governing condition of human personality), Coleridge added also a grammatical schematism. A 'father' can, in strictness, not be a father unless he has progeny. Now, though a 'son' *in tempore* follows a father, in logic, which in Bolzano's insistence is characterized by being outside time, a 'person' could not be conceived with the predicate 'father' except under the prior condition of our thinking of

[1] Coleridge, Notebook 26, as printed in Appendix I to Boulger, *Coleridge as Religious Thinker*, p. 227. The 'Trinity' was 'the Supreme Being, his reflex act of self-consciousness and his love, all forming one supreme mind . . .' (*Works*, v. 398). Again: 'In the Trinity there is, 1. Ipseity. 2. Alterity. 3. Community.' (*Table Talk*, 8 July 1827.)

[2] 'No Trinity, no God—is a matter of natural Religion as well as of Christianity, of profound Philosophy no less than of Faith.' (*Letters*, iii. 283–4. To Poole, 28 Jan. 1810.)

[3] *Notebooks*, ii. 2448.

[4] 'This then is the distinction of moral philosophy . . . I assume a something, the proof of which no man can give to another, yet every man may find for himself. If any man assert that he can not find it, I am bound to disbelieve him. . . . If . . . he will not find it, he excommunicates himself. He forfeits his personal rights, and becomes a thing . . .' (*Works*, i. 193).

'son'.[1] Therefore, against Arian subordinationism, and very much in line with Augustinian filiationism, the 'son', existed for Coleridge with as much necessity as did the 'father', and both 'father' and 'son' being givens of the Trinitarian problem, the problem was thereby resolved. 'St. John', says Coleridge in 1826, 'would have taught' English theologizers, who unwittingly argued towards pantheism,

a deeper philosophy, and the only one compatible with a *moral* religion. . . . $\Theta\epsilon\delta\varsigma$ [God] becomes δ $\pi\alpha\tau\dot{\eta}\rho$ [the Father] by the act of realizing in the Son. It sounds paradox, but it is most certain truth, that in order of thought, under the intrusive form of *Time*, the Father is a reflex from the Son—and that if it does not appear so in human relations arises from our Fathers having had Fathers— The man is called Father by anticipation grounded on a Past. But in the Idea of a Christian Deity the order is as the Evangelist gives it—1. $\Theta\epsilon\delta\varsigma$. 2. δ $\check{\omega}\nu$, δ $\mu o\nu o$-$\gamma\epsilon\nu\dot{\eta}\varsigma$. 3. δ $\pi\alpha\tau\dot{\eta}\rho$. Plato was a prophetic Anomaly—all the prior Theologians of Greece . . . were $\phi\upsilon\sigma\iota o\lambda\delta\gamma o\iota$ [reasoners about nature]—Their first principle was —$''E\sigma\tau\iota$ [it is]—the first of the Christian Scheme $E\dot{\iota}\mu\dot{\iota}$ [I am]—The former deduced the Persons—the latter begins with and from the Personal, or rather the Personality itself.[2]

This extrapolation of the transcendence of the 'I am' starting-point constitutes, I think, the very peak or limit of Coleridge's systematic reasoning. 'We begin with the I KNOW MYSELF, in order to end with the absolute I AM. We proceed from the SELF, in order to lose and find all self in GOD.'[3] He did not linguistically elaborate the insight in the style of twentieth-century phenomenology, but it apparently lay just below the surface of his conscious intent as the final reconciling principle by which Spinoza's rock of ice would be dissolved and the chain of consequences restapled where it belonged, in Christ. We have at least two hints that it was the personality of Spinoza himself—Spinoza's *Existenz*—that Coleridge intended to develop in contradistinction to the closedness of the Spinozistic system. 'The $\pi\rho\hat{\omega}\tau o\nu$ $\psi\epsilon\hat{\upsilon}\delta o\varsigma$ of Spinoza', he says in 1818, '. . . consists in the assumed Idea of a pure independent *Object*—in assuming a Substance beyond the I; of which therefore the I *could* only be a modification.'[4] But

---

[1] Compare Clement of Alexandria, *Stromata* v. 1: 'Nor is the Father without the Son . . . And that we may believe in the Son, we must know the Father. . . . Again, in order that we may know the Father, we must believe in the Son. . .'. Compare Athanasius, *Contra Arianos* i. 8: 'how can he discourse about the Father who denies the Son, since it is from the Son we derive knowledge of the Father?' As Tixeront says, 'the characteristic teaching of the Alexandrian school in opposition to the Apologists' is the Son's 'eternal generation'. 'This generation not only preceded creation; it had no beginning, no starting point . . . for the Father is Father only on condition that He has a Son.' (J. Tixeront, *History of Dogmas*, trans. H. L. B. (Baden, 1910), p. 248.)

[2] *Unpublished Letters of Samuel Taylor Coleridge*, ed. E. L. Griggs (London, 1932), ii. 372. Compare Athanasius: 'The generation of the Son is not like that of a man, which requires an existence after that of the Father, but the Son of God must, as such, have been begotten of the Father from all eternity.' (*Contra Arianos* i. 14, compare also i. 21.)

[3] *Biographia*, i. 186.   [4] *Letters*, iv. 849. To Pryce, Apr. 1818.

'Spinoza, at the very end of his life, seems to have gained a glimpse of the truth. In the last letter published in his works, it appears that he began to suspect his premiss. His *unica substantia* is, in fact, a mere notion,—a *subject* of the mind, and no *object* at all.'[1] And the 'rock of Ice' itself was, says Coleridge, the conception of 'God as an *Object*, forgetting that an Object as much presupposes a Subject, as a Subject does an Object. Spinoza's is a World with one Pole only, & consequently no Equator. . .'[2] In all these criticisms, struggling for terminological emergence, are the criteria behind the development of the existentialist watchword, existence before being.

Spinoza, [says Unamuno], the most logical and consistent of atheists—I mean of those who deny the persistence of individual consciousness . . .—and at the same time the most pious, Spinoza devoted the fifth and last part of his *Ethic* to elucidating the path that leads to liberty and to determining the concept of happiness. The concept! Concept, not feeling! . . . And against Spinoza and his doctrine of happiness there is only one irresistible argument, the argument *ad hominem*. Was he happy, Benedict Spinoza, while, to allay his inner unhappiness, he was discoursing on happiness? Was he free? . . . Was he happy, the poor Jewish intellectualist definer of intellectual love and of happiness? For that and no other is the problem.[3]

By wrenching the argument to its full premisses of *Existenz*, Coleridge could begin to work loose the staple from the rock of Ice.[4]

It was, I think, this same elation about the extended implications of the 'I am' as the incommensurable that led Coleridge to include, as well as Spinoza, three of his favourite pantheists in the reconciling scheme of the *magnum opus*. We remember that as early as 1803, 'G. Fox', along with 'Giordano Bruno, Jacob Boehmen, Spinoza',[5] appeared in a projection of the task before him. Later formulations also included these names, always with an emphasis on their 'lives' as well as their 'systems'—for example, 'Biography and Critique on the Systems of Giordano Bruno, Behmen, and Spinoza',[6] or, again, 'the Lives and Systems of Giordano Bruno, Jacob Behmen, George Fox, and Benedict Spinoza.'[7]

---

[1] *Table Talk*, Apr. 30, 1830. Compare Husserl: 'The objective world, the world that exists for me, that always has and always will exist for me, the only world that ever can exist for me, —this world, with all its objects, I said, derives its whole sense and its existential status, which it has for me, from me myself, from me as the transcendental Ego . . .' (*Cartesianische Meditationen*, p. 65).

[2] *Letters*, iv. 548 n. To R. H. Brabant, 10 Mar. 1815.

[3] Unamuno, *Tragic Sense of Life*, pp. 97–99.

[4] '. . . thank heaven there is a glorious inconsistency in human nature; through the mercy of our Creator, a man's head will frame this and that cobweb, but his heart will whisper better things, his moral feelings will wish them and he will contradict himself, and with the common sophistry try to reconcile the one with the other; and thus it is with the natural influence of pantheism, or the belief of God as identical with the world' (*Philosophical Lectures*, p. 127). Coleridge in other words, relies on the distinction between logical subject and existential subject that became so important for Kierkegaard and for the whole movement of existentialist thought in the twentieth century. See note 72 , p. 379.

[5] *Notebooks*, i. 1646.   [6] *Letters*, iv. 687.   [7] Ibid., p. 590.

Now there were other pantheists—Erigena, Swedenborg, Zeno—whom Coleridge respected, but they are passed over; only Fox, Boehme, and Bruno seem to be singled out for special treatment. Doubtless to some extent it was because of the particular *Existenz* situations of all three; but also we may infer that Coleridge felt himself under a particular obligation to these men. There 'exist folios on the human understanding', he says in a key passage in the *Biographia Literaria,*

which would have a far juster claim to their high rank and celebrity, if in the whole huge volume there could be found as much fulness of heart and intellect, as burst forth in many a simple page of GEORGE FOX, JACOB BEHMEN, and even of Behmen's commentator, the pious and fervid WILLIAM LAW.

The feeling of gratitude, which I cherish towards these men, has caused me to digress further than I had foreseen or proposed; but to have passed them over in an historical sketch of my literary life and opinions, would have seemed to me like the denial of a debt, the concealment of a boon. For the writings of these mystics acted in no slight degree to prevent my mind from being imprisoned within the outline of any single dogmatic system. They contributed to keep alive the *heart* in the *head*; gave me an indistinct, yet stirring and working presentiment, that all the products of the mere *reflective* faculty [i.e. the understanding, as opposed to the reason] partook of DEATH, and were as the rattling twigs and sprays in winter. . . . If they were too often a moving cloud of smoke to me by day, yet they were always a pillar of fire throughout the night, during my wanderings through the wilderness of doubt, and enabled me to skirt, without crossing, the sandy deserts of utter unbelief. That the system is capable of being converted into an irreligious PANTHEISM, I well know.[1]

The singling out of Boehme and Bruno (the obligation to Fox's Quakerism seems to have been a short-term debt, and as Fox was not really a systematic thinker it will not concern us here)[2] for *Existenz* salvation in the *magnum opus* seems, therefore, to have been largely due to their having helped his 'heart' (they 'enabled me to skirt . . . the sandy deserts of utter unbelief') even while they assailed his 'head'. It seems likely that both Bruno and Boehme were able to play such a role, despite their pantheism, because they were both heirs of the Platonic tone that Coleridge considered so important—the 'thirst for something not attained' that kept system from being totally enclosed in pantheism, even when the 'head' saw pantheism and pantheism alone.[3] Historically, both thinkers were fertilized by

---

[1] *Biographia*, i. 98.

[2] It seems clear, however, that Coleridge came to regard Quakerism, in its implications, as a form of pantheism. 'I should call modern Quakerism,' he says, 'so far as I know it as a scheme of faith, a Socinian Calvinism. Penn himself was a Sabellian, and seems to have disbelieved even the historical fact of the life and death of Jesus—most certainly Jesus of Nazareth was not Penn's Christ, if he had any.' (*Table Talk*, 12 Jan. 1834.) Quakerism, in short, was a 'representative of self-oracled Enthusiasm that uses the Bible as a cushion to doze and dream upon', a 'tubercular State' of the 'breath of Spiritual Life' (*Letters*, iv. 845–6).

[3] See note 73, p. 380.

Nicholas of Cusa, who, as Klibansky says, provides us with 'the fullest documentation' of the 'unbroken Platonic tradition', and was 'in the judgement of his contemporaries the "grande Platonista" '.[1] Thus Coleridge notes 'that the first principles of Behmen are to be found in the writings of the Neo-Platonists after Plotinus'.[2] Likewise, when in 1801 he encountered Bruno's *de Monade*, he immediately commented that 'it read very much like Thomas Taylor & Proclus',[3] while in the *Biographia Literaria* Bruno—as 'the philosopher of Nola'—is listed with the Platonists ('Plato and Plotinus . . . the illustrious Florentine [Ficino] . . . Proclus, and Gemistius Pletho') as one of those who 'contributed to prepare my mind for the reception and welcoming of the "Cogito quia sum, et sum quia Cogito" '.[4]

There was, however, probably a second reason for the honour accorded Bruno and Boehme; namely that next to Spinoza himself they were the most important of the historical figures who were drawn into the pantheistic structure of German Romanticism. Bruno seemed especially glamorous. In the second edition of the *Ueber die Lehre des Spinoza*, Jacobi had appended a long extract from Bruno's *De la causa, principio, et uno* with the avowed intent of providing thereby, in conjunction with Spinozistic doctrine, 'gleichsam die *Summa der Philosophie des 'Εν και Παν'*—the summa, as it were, of pantheism.[5] Jacobi had praised Bruno as an archetypal exponent of pantheism ('Schwerlich kann man einen reineren und schöneren Umriss des *Pantheismus im weitesten Verstande* geben, als ihn Bruno zog'),[6] and had commented on the 'gegenwärtige Seltenheit'[7]—the rareness at the present time—of Bruno's works. Such credentials could not fail to make Bruno an intriguing figure for the German *literati* ('ja, in unsern Zeiten,'

---

[1] *The Continuity of the Platonic Tradition During the Middle Ages*, pp. 29–30. Bruno's debt to Cusanus is well known. That of Boehme is probably more indirect, and it is not clear that Boehme knew Cusanus's thought first hand—indeed the whole of Boehme's intellectual background is cloudy. Koyré, however, suggests that Boehme's doctrine of imagination may have been derived from Cusanus's *De Mente*. (*La Philosophie de Jacob Boehme*, p. 347, n. 3.)

[2] *Works*, v. 325. See note 74, p. 380.

[3] *Notebooks*, i. 928.

[4] *Biographia*, i. 94–95.

[5] Jacobi, *Werke*, iv–1. 10. The actual relationship of Spinoza and Bruno is a matter of speculation. Freudenthal notes that 'Spinoza hat den Namen Bruno nie genannt' (*Die Lehre Spinozas*, p. 249 n.). Pollock, however, says, 'We have no direct evidence that Spinoza was acquainted with Giordano Bruno's writings; but the want of such evidence counts for very little. . . . We are free, then, to take at its full worth the internal evidence for Spinoza's knowledge of Bruno; and it is of such strength as to carry all but irresistible conviction' (*Spinoza*, p. 97). Again, Lovejoy (apparently without knowledge of Jacobi's contention) argues that Spinoza and Bruno have 'a demonstrably similar dialectic'. 'My thesis', he continues, 'is that the more general and fundamental principles of Spinoza's metaphysics are in no respect original; that he is, like Bruno, a consistent Neo-Platonist of the Renaissance type; that his way of dealing with the problem of the relation of substance to its attributes is one already fore-shadowed in Plotinus, fully worked out by mediaeval theologians, and much used by Bruno . . .' (*The Dialectic of Bruno and Spinoza*, p. 145). So also Sigwart, Avenarius, but not Martineau.

[6] Jacobi, *Werke*, iv–1. 10.   [7] Ibid., p. 8.

Jacobi had said, 'beynah für nothwendig');[1] and so in 1802 Schelling, with an obeisance to Jacobi, produced his dialogue of 'Plotinised Spinozism' entitled *Bruno, oder, über das göttliche und natürliche Princip der Dinge*.[2] The impact of this work on the Romantic sensibility can perhaps be judged from Goethe's enthusiastic statement to Schiller that the *Bruno* 'accords with my deepest inner convictions'.[3]

In view, therefore, of the modishness of Bruno in the context of the *Pantheismusstreit*, we can see Coleridge's interest as to some extent reflecting an understandable desire to be fully *au courant*. Thus his comments on Bruno emphasize, with quiet pride, the rareness of that philosopher's works. In the *Omniana*, for instance, he quotes verses from Bruno at length, defends him against the 'charge of impenetrable obscurity'[4] ('Alle klagen', said Jacobi, 'über die undurchdringliche und mehr als Heraklitische Dunkelheit des Mannes. Brucker vergleicht sie mit Cimmerischer Finsterniß; und Bayle versichert, des Bruno vornehmste Lehrsätze wären tausendmal dunkler und unbegreiflicher, als das unbegreiflichste'),[5] and says that 'the work from which' the verses 'are extracted is exceedingly rare (as are, indeed, all the works of the Nolan philosopher)'.[6] In *The Friend*, after quoting a long Latin passage from Bruno ('let the sublime piety of the passage', he says, always awake to pantheism, 'excuse some intermixture of error'),[7] he adds, in a footnote:

> Giordano Bruno, the friend of Sir Philip Sidney and Fulk Greville, was burnt under pretence of atheism, at Rome, on the 17th of February, 1599–1600. . . . His works are perhaps the scarcest books ever printed. They are singularly interesting as portraits of a vigorous mind struggling after truth, amid many prejudices, which from the state of the Romish Church, in which he was born, have a claim to much indulgence. . . . The most industrious historians of speculative philosophy, have not been able to procure more than a few of his works. Accidentally I have been more fortunate in this respect, than those who have written hitherto on the unhappy philosopher of Nola; as out of eleven works, the titles of which are preserved to us, I have had an opportunity of perusing six.[8]

---

[1] Ibid., p. 10. Thus Dilthey identifies Bruno as the 'first link in the chain of pantheistic thinkers' which runs 'through Spinoza and Shaftesbury, through Robinet, Diderot, Deschamps and Buffon, through Hemsterhuys, Herder, Goethe and Schelling to the present' (Wilhelm Dilthey, 'Giordano Bruno und Spinoza', *Archiv für Geschichte der Philosophie*, vii (1894), 269).

[2] Thus Schelling speaks of the 'geistreichen Auszug, welcher von seinem Werk: Von der Ursache, dem Princip und dem Einen, als Anhang zu den Briefen über die Lehre des Spinoza von Jacobi, gegeben worden ist' and that this extract (from which he quotes) reveals 'wie Jordanus Brunus die Lehre vom Universum dargestellt hat', which 'Lehre' Schelling says he will 'am meisten annähere' in 'die folgende Darstellung'—will for the most part approximate in the following presentation (Schelling, *Werke*, iv. 330).

[3] So Goethe: 'Schelling hat ein Gespräch geschrieben: Bruno, oder über das göttliche und natürliche Prinzip der Dinge. Was ich davon verstehe, oder zu verstehen glaube, ist vortrefflich und trifft mit meinen innigsten Überzeugungen zusammen' (*Gedenkausgabe*, xx. 887).

[4] *Omniana*, p. 368.   [5] Jacobi, *Werke*, iv–1. 8.
[6] *Omniana*, p. 367.   [7] *Works*, ii. 109.
[8] Ibid., pp. 110 n.–111 n.

Just as Bruno was a very elegant item in the German pantheist inventory, so Boehme—'this greatest of all mystics', as Berdyaev calls him,[1]—infiltrated German Romanticism. 'Since Leibniz', noted Baader, 'all German philosophers with the exception of Kant . . . have taken one thing or another from Jacob Boehme, sometimes without naming him'.[2] By *literati* as well as philosophers, moreover, Boehme was cherished; and his status was as a kind of warbler of Spinozist woodnotes wild.[3] The similarity of Boehme and Spinoza had early been noted by Henry More ('En purum putum Behmenismus!'—behold! plain and simple Behmenism—More had said of one of Spinoza's central conceptions),[4] but it was Tieck the littérateur, rather than any practicing philosopher, who actually set the fashion of reading the Görlitz cobbler in Germany ('Tieck is studying Jacob Boehme with great love', noted Friedrich Schlegel approvingly in 1798. 'He is there certainly on the right path.')[5] And Coleridge concedes Tieck's special authority when he asks Robinson to be 'so good as to ask Mr Tieck. . . . whether there were any Followers of Jacob Behmen, of any note or worth, about the same time?'[6]

It seems probable, however, that because of the availability of Boehme through William Law's collection of translations, Coleridge read the German visionary before the German Romantics did.[7] He informs Tieck

---

[1] *Dream and Reality*, p. 179. Cf. Friedrich Schlegel, *Philosophische Vorlesungen*, i. 424: Boehme is 'ohne Zweifel der umfassende, reichhaltigste und mannigfaltigste von allen Mystikern'.

[2] Baader, *Werke*, xiii. 162–3.

[3] 'What was intuition . . . in Boehme', said Schelling to his students, 'appears in Spinoza . . . as developed rationalism' (*Werke*, xiii. 123). 'Among the madnesses of the Romantic School in Germany', recalls Heine, 'the incessant extolling and praising of Jacob Boehme deserves special mention. His name was, as it were, the Shibboleth of these men. Whenever they uttered the name, Jacob Boehme, they put on their most thoughtful expressions.' (*Die romantische Schule*, p. 170.)

[4] More, *Opera*, p. 619.   [5] Novalis, *Schriften*, iv. 249.

[6] *Letters*, iv. 742. To answer Coleridge's question, we may cite the names of Abraham von Franckenberg (Boehme's biographer), Johann Theodor von Tschech, Johannes Heermann, and Daniel von Czepko. (See, e.g., Richard Newald, 'Die Nachfolge Jakob Böhmes', *Die deutsche Literatur von Späthumanismus zur Empfindsamkeit 1570–1750* (München, 1960), pp. 235–43.) Though Coleridge deferred to Tieck's erudition on the subject of Boehme (he deferred to no one on the issues of Boehme's thought), Tieck met his match in Baader. Köpke reports that at the first meeting of Tieck and Baader in 1804 each found with delight that the other was a devotee of Boehme, but in the ensuing conversation about mystical matters, Tieck was—to use the American slang word that alone fits the situation—'snowed' by Baader in a three-hour monologue (Köpke, *Ludwig Tieck*, i. 312).

[7] *The Works of Jacob Behmen, the Teutonic Theosopher . . . with Figures, illustrating his principles*, left by the Reverend William Law, M.A. (London, 1764–81), 4 vols. Coleridge annotated a set of these important and rather rare volumes, now in the British Museum, and the marginalia, which occupy approximately 150 pages, were apparently composed over a number of years—1812 to 1827 might be a reasonable guess. He had, furthermore, done considerable reading in Boehme from early boyhood. The Germans themselves were rather slow in coming to Boehme. It can be argued that either Tieck or Baader was the first of the Romantic Behmenists in Germany: Zeydel thinks that Tieck did not begin his study of Boehme before about 1796 (*Tieck*, p. 359 n. 28); Baumgardt, on the other hand, while saying that Baader's serious study of Boehme could scarcely have begun before 1798, states that Baader 'probably' preceded Tieck

that he had studied Boehme during his school days at Christ's Hospital (' . . . Behmen's Aurora, which I had *conjured over* at School');[1] and one of the projects listed in the Gutch Notebook in 1795–6 is 'Jacob Behmen'.[2] In 1810 he wrote to Lady Beaumont that 'Of Jacob Behmen I have myself been a commentator. . . . But for myself I must confess, I never brought away from his Works any thing I did not bring to them. . . . Yet Jacob Behmen was an extraordinary man. . . . Either in this or in some after Number of the Friend I shall give the character of Jacob Behmen & compare him with George Fox—and both with Giordano Bruno.'[3]

Even so, Coleridge's debt to Boehme was much the deeper obligation.[4] Bruno was modish; Bruno lived—and especially died—in intensely dramatic fashion; Bruno was both poet and philosopher. Bruno used the 'polar logic' that fitted so well with Coleridge's inclusive and reconciling temperament. But these matters are really on the surface.[5] With Boehme, Coleridge's intellectual relationship lasted over three decades, and the voluminous notes in the Law collection of Boehme's tracts show how often he returned to study him. Apart from the fillip that Boehme gave to Coleridge's scientific pretensions—a matter now of no importance except as an expression of Coleridge's concern with the 'it is'[6]—his main interest in Boehme was as a trinitarian thinker. Corollary to this interest was an involvement with Boehme's stress on the will. Just possibly, too, Coleridge's doctrine of the primary imagination owed something to Boehme.[7]

Yet Coleridge became fully aware that Boehme and Bruno, however much he might like their Platonic tone, were both pantheists. It is true that he habitually treated them gently: 'Synesius was . . . never . . . arraigned or deemed heretical for his Pantheism, tho' neither Giordano Bruno, or Jacob Behmen ever avowed it more broadly. . . . Pantheism is therefore not necessarily irreligious or heretical; tho' it may be taught atheistically.'[8]

in such study (*Baader und die philosophische Romantik*, pp. 220, 224). In any case, it seems that neither can be said to have preceded Coleridge in any substantial way.

[1] *Letters*, iv. 751.   [2] *Notebooks*, i. 174.

[3] *Letters*, iii. 278–9.

[4] In a marginal note of 1818 Coleridge refers to them both, admitting that his knowledge of them was by no means equal: '. . . the Errors of this extraordinary Man [Boehme] fall under two heads . . . in both instances, the same as that of Schelling and his followers. What resemblance it may have to the system of Giordano Bruno, I have read too few of Bruno's writings to say, and read them at a time, when I was not competent to ask the question . . .' (on pages 126–7 of vol. i of the Law edition).

[5] See note 75, p. 381.

[6] Not all scholars would accept this summary dismissal. Thus Muirhead agrees with Miss Snyder 'that there can be no adequate account of [Coleridge's] metaphysical system that does not recognize his participation in contemporary scientific discussions, and his sense of their philosophic implications' (*Coleridge as Philosopher*, p. 119). For a further discussion of Coleridge's scientific interests see Excursus Note XVIII, p. 323.

[7] See 'Coleridge and Boehme', Excursus Note XIX, p. 325.

[8] *Biographica*, i. 169 n.–170 n.

And of Boehme he could speak with eloquence: '. . . I have felt my own mind much indebted to him', he says.[1] In a marginal note he remarks that

when I recollect the notions held and doctrines enforced by the contemporary Divines, Civilians and Philosophers; and then reflect on the rank and means of *this* man . . . it seems to me, that many assertions, that have been favorably received by the Learned of the present day, have met a more decisive oppugnancy on the part of my Reason and Feelings, than the Belief . . . that Jacob Behmen was favored with a portion of the same spiritual gift, the outbreathings of which in John and Paul we pronounce Θεοτοτα, and designate by the name of Inspiration. *S.T.C.*[2]

And in the *Philosophical Lectures* his attitude is still more affirmative:

He was indeed a stupendous human being. Had he received the discipline of education, above all had he possessed the knowledge which would have guarded him against his own delusions, I scarcely know whether we should have had reason to attribute greater genius even to Plato himself.[3]

But whatever his enthusiasm or indebtedness, Boehme's pantheism was ultimately clear in Coleridge's mind. At the end of *Aids to Reflection* he posits a possible objection that what he has said may be called 'mysticism, all taken out of William Law, after he had lost his senses in brooding over the visions of a delirious German cobbler, Jacob Böhme',[4] and then he continues:

Of poor Jacob Böhme I have delivered my sentiments at large in another work. Those who have condescended to look into his writings must know that his characteristic errors are: first, the mistaking the accidents and peculiarities of his own overwrought mind for realities and modes of thinking common to all minds: and secondly, the confusion of Nature, that is, the active powers communicated to matter, with God the Creator.[5]

Nor was his awareness of Boehme's pantheism merely a passing judgement on a quirk of mind. Boehme's pantheism was finally just as much a trap as Spinoza's. To Lady Beaumont, after praising Boehme as an 'extraordinary man', he adds musingly, 'I do not think, you will derive any advantage from his works'.[6] In a note on Boehme's *Aurora*, he speaks of his early intoxication with 'the vernal fragrances & effluvia from the flowers and first fruits of Pantheism, unaware of its bitter root',[7] and then—in a passage that might serve as a rebuke to 'panentheist' quibbles—he speaks of himself as 'pacifying my religious feelings meantime by the dim

---

[1] *Philosophical Lectures*, p. 327.
[2] Marginal note at page 211 of the third volume of the Law edition of Boehme's works.
[3] *Philosophical Lectures*, p. 329.
[4] Hazlitt had spoken of Coleridge 'going up in an air-balloon filled with fetid gas from the writings of Jacob Behmen and the mystics' (*Complete Works*, xvi. 118).
[5] *Works*, i. 350.   [6] *Letters*, iii. 279.
[7] Marginal note at page 127, first volume of the Law edition.

distinction, that tho' God was = the world, the World was not = God—
as if God were a Whole composed of Parts, of which the World was one!'[1]
The error of Boehme, said Coleridge again, was not only 'the same as that
of Schelling and his followers', but was 'radically the same as that of
Spinoza'.[2] And he confesses that 'I myself have partaken of the same error'
as Boehme,[3] and that Boehme approaches 'perilously near to Pantheism'.[3]
But he says, significantly, in 1818, that from Boehme's 'errors . . . I have
extricated myself'.[4] For 'SPINOZA and BEHMEN were, on different systems,
both Pantheists'.[5]

So much for the presence of Boehme and Bruno in the scheme of the
magnum opus. They contribute, as do all the transformations provided by
the action of Coleridge's intense concern upon his vast reading, to our
understanding of the systematic coherence and lasting dignity of his effort.
In the final accounting, Coleridge's thought, with Plato and Kant dissolved
into the arguments of the Trinity, with Boehme and Bruno giving way to
the hypostasis of pantheism, with Schelling rejected, always remained true
to the two great poles of its activity, the 'I am' and the 'it is', Christianity
and Spinozism:

Not one man in a thousand [Coleridge said] has either strength of mind or
goodness of heart to be an atheist. I repeat it. Not one man in ten thousand has
goodness of heart or strength of mind to be an atheist.

And, were I not a Christian . . . I should be an atheist with Spinoza. . . . This,
it is true, is negative atheism; and this is, next to Christianity, the purest spirit
of humanity![6]

And there it is. Christianity, as an expansion from the 'I am', was Coleridge's lifelong commitment, in philosophical as well as religious terms:[7]

---

[1] Ibid.

[2] Marginal note printed in A. D. Snyder, 'Coleridge on Böhme', *PMLA*, xlv (1930), p. 617.

[3] Ibid., p. 616.

[4] Ibid. Boehme 'preposterizes the Consequent of the Fall into the absolute First, and
ignorant of the only sense, in which it is other than an abstraction, he makes it a mere abstraction, and then by a second . . . abstraction, that of Subject and Object from the idea of the
Absolute, he identifies the former with God as Omneity, out of which the living Godhead
evolves . . .' (marginal note, pp. 126–7, vol. i). This long note, to which the Snyder citation
above refers, is concluded by a postscript that emphasizes Coleridge's eventual rejection of
Boehme's pantheism: 'P.S. I earnestly intreat of whoever may hereafter chance to peruse *this*
Copy of Behmen's works, that if he should find in the marginal MSS Notes, preceding or
following the present Note, any positions or opinions contradictory to it and partaking of the
error . . . here exposed, he will attribute them to the earlier date, at which they were written.
S. T. Coleridge, Highgate—27 August, 1818.'

[5] *Biographia*, ii. 112. See Excursus Note XIX, p. 332.   [6] Allsop, p. 61.

[7] Its twin bases were the need for redemption and the sense of moral responsibility ('. . . a
law in the nature of man resisting the law of God. . . . It follows necessarily from the postulate
of a responsible will. Refuse to grant this, and I have not a word to say') (*Works*, i. 285).
Another passage throws light on this: 'The removal of this *antithesis* of the creature to God is the
object of the Redemption, and forms the glorious liberty of the Gospel' (*Works*, v. 68). Compare

'. . . I do not hesitate to assert, that it was one of the great purposes of Christianity, and included in the process of our redemption, to rouse and emancipate the soul from . . . debasing slavery to the outward senses, to awaken the mind to the true *criteria* of reality . . . will manifested in act, and truth operating as life.'[1] This commitment was in continual tension with his poetic concern, emanating from the 'it is', and the tension is the secret of his wonderful vitality. The experience of nature filled him with rapture:

> . . . I am *blessed* in worshipping the Loveliness of Fields, Lakes, Streams, ancient Trees, mountains, & Skies . . .[2]

> O that Sky, that soft blue mighty Arch, resting on the mountains or solid Sea-like plain/ what an aweful adorable omneity in unity[3]

> Every season Nature converts me from some unloving Heresy—[4]

But the threat of pantheism, and the call of the 'I am', always summoned him back:

> Now the very purpose of my system is to overthrow Pantheism, to establish the diversity of the Creator from the sum whole of his Creatures, deduce the personeity, the I Am of God, and in one and the same demonstration to demonstrate the reality and originancy of Moral Evil, and to account for the fact of a finite Nature.[5]

His poet's eye delighted in nature: 'The prospect around us', he writes almost gloatingly in 1795, 'is perhaps more *various* than any in the kingdom—Mine Eye gluttonizes.—The Sea—the distant Islands!—the opposite Coasts!—I shall assuredly write Rhymes—let the nine muses prevent it, if they can—/.'[6] But another voice always said:

> That which we find in ourselves is . . . the substance and the life of all our knowledge. Without this latent presence of the 'I am,' all modes of existence in the external world would flit before us as colored shadows, with no greater depth, root, or fixture, than the image of a rock hath in a gliding stream. . .[7]

Boehme: 'Human life is placed in a counterstroke to the divine will, in and through which counterstroke God wills . . .' (*On the Divine Intuition*, ii. 14).

[1] *Works*, i. 363.
[2] *Notebooks*, ii. 2647.
[3] Ibid., ii. 2346.
[4] Ibid. i. 1302. Cf. the enormous vividness of his description of a walk: '. . . a wearisome road indeed but I took it leisurely, & came in to the Monastery cool / O what a lovely place / Birches or Aspens; for it seemed Birch trunks with Aspen leaves—. & Pine trees before the white seeming large Farmhouse behind & around vineyards & woody hills & vine clad hills. the vines growing in the powdered Lava, a marvel for it exactly resembles the Dross-dust before a Forge Door / no particle of vegetable mould to be seen / I ascended the Hill, the ground scorching my feet, & joyously entered the wood on the Top . . .' (*Notebooks*, ii. 2169).
[5] Coleridge, Notebook 35, f. 25ᵛ. Printed in Boulger, *Coleridge as Religious Thinker*, p. 129.
[6] *Letters*, i. 160.
[7] *Works*, i. 465.

Always the images of nature pressed in on him with a religious joy:

> So will I build my altar in the fields,
>   And the blue sky my fretted dome shall be,
> And the sweet fragrance that the wild flower yields
>   Shall be the incense I will yield to Thee,
> Thee only God![1]

But always the consequences drew him back; and his imagination was stirred by darker musings about the cost of a total commitment to nature:

> IF dead, we cease to be; if total gloom
>   Swallow up life's brief flash for aye, we fare
> As summer-gusts, of sudden birth and doom,
>
> .   .   .   .   .   .
>
> If even a soul like Milton's can know death;
>   O Man! thou vessel purposeless, unmeant,
>
> .   .   .   .   .   .
>
> Surplus of Nature's dread activity, –
> Which, as she gazed on some nigh-finished vase,
> Retreating slow, with meditative pause,
>   She formed with restless hands unconsciously.
> Blank accident! nothing's anomaly!
>   If rootless thus, thus substanceless thy state,
> Go, weigh thy dreams . . .
>   Why rejoices
> Thy heart with hollow joy for hollow good?
> Why cowl thy face beneath the mourner's hood?
>
> .   .   .   .   .   .
>
> Be sad! be glad! be neither! seek, or shun!
> Thou hast no reason why![2]

Against this creed of the final meaning of 'it is', ultimately the destruction of human meaning, Coleridge's religious heart asserted its counter-truths: 'No, not from any external impulses, not from any agencies that can be sought for' did life and meaning derive, for 'man comes from within, and all that is truly human must proceed from within'.[3]

We can see Coleridge's failure as an explicit systematist to be a paradox inherent in his needs, in his ambivalent position as both moralist and poet, rather than as a failure of his reticulative faculty. In the perspective of the opposed interests of the *Pantheismusstreit*, we can see in the paradox of

---

[1] 'To Nature', ll. 9-13, *Poems*, i. 429.

[2] 'Human Life; On the Denial of Immortality', ll. 1–28, *Poems*, i. 425–6. The conflict in the attitudes of the two poems can be paralleled from many places in Romantic literature. Compare, for instance, the double attitude of Vigny in *La Maison du berger*: 'La Nature t'attend dans un silence austère', but then: 'Ne me laisse jamais seul avec la Nature; / Car je la connais trop pour n'en pas avoir peur'. Vigny's nature-horror can be contrasted with Lamartine's nature-rapture.

[3] *Philosophical Lectures*, p. 226.

his acceptance and rejection of Spinoza, on the memorable occasion reported by Robinson, not the confusion of its surface reflection, but rather a testimonial to his insight, engagement, and philosophical integrity:

Coleridge walked with me to A. Robinson's for my Spinoza, which I lent him. While standing in the room he kissed Spinoza's face in the title-page, and said, 'This book is a gospel to me.' But in less than a minute he added, 'his philosophy is nevertheless false. Spinoza's system has been demonstrated to be false, but only by that philosophy which has demonstrated the falsehood of all other philosophies. Did philosophy commence with an *it is*, instead of an *I am*, Spinoza would be altogether true.' And without allowing a breathing time, Coleridge parenthetically asserted, 'I, however, believe in all the doctrines of Christianity, even the Trinity.'[1]

Thus we see in this pregnant moment in Coleridge's life a microcosm of his total philosophical commitment, with the irreducible tensions that constituted its distinctive character. These tensions did not suddenly appear at this particular moment on 3 October 1812; they were there from first to last. Hence through all the transformations of his 'it is'/pantheist interests on the one hand, and of his 'I am'/moral interests on the other, he remained true to the ineradicable fact of their tragic opposition—longing for their reconciliation, but foundering, as do we all, before the mysteries of existence.

In this equipoise Coleridge's philosophical achievement is both of its time and out of its time. His thought shares with that of his German contemporaries an emphasis upon the central importance of Spinozistic pantheism. But it differs in its idiosyncratic refusal to decide, either by pantheism or by solipsistic scepticism, that which cannot be decided.

For this man, so tormented in his personal life, so protean in his intellectual attainments, was a man who cared—who cared too much to resolve the unresolvable, either by Procrustean system or by an irresponsible refusal to recognize the meaning of the disharmony. And so it was throughout his life. 'But *all at once he makes up his mind*', he says, in 1796, in shocked comment on Dr. Darwin, 'on such important subjects, as whether we be the outcasts of a blind idiot called Nature, or the children of an all-wise and infinitely good God'.[2] The intensity of his concern constitutes his dignity as a man; and Leibniz's holy words can justly be claimed for him too: 'Most men have no earnestness. They have never tasted truth,

---

[1] Crabb Robinson, *Diary*, i. 399–401. Commenting on this passage, Deschamps suggest thats 'la philosophie "qui démontra la fausseté de toutes les autres philosophies" est évidemment la critique kantienne' (*La Formation de la pensée de Coleridge (1772–1804)*, p. 434, n. 112). But though the philosophy of Kant fits the purely schematic requirements of opposition to Spinoza, it seems to me that the dramatic qualities of the opposition here suggest, not Kantian criticism, but 'Christianity the One True Philosophy'.

[2] *Letters*, i. 177.

and are stuck in a secret unbelief. Let each examine himself whether he has faith and life; if he find any joy greater than in the love of God and the glorification of his will, he does not know Christ enough, and does not feel the stirring of the Holy Spirit.'[1] Coleridge's high seriousness, his capacity for suspending the immediate claims of his own philosophical egotism and accepting the intrinsic difficulties of the problem, is part of that ability to see feelingly that is his peculiar virtue as a mind.

It is a capacity that raises him to a special place in the history of thought. In 1797, in a verbal picture of Thelwall, he draws, as in a mirror, a memorable portrait of himself, in his care, his patience, and his intellectual constancy:

John Thelwall is a very warm hearted honest man—and disagreeing, as we do, on almost every point of religion, of morals, of politics, and of philosphy; we like each other uncommonly well. . . . He is prompt to *conceive*, and still prompter to *execute*—. But I think, that he is deficient in that *patience* of mind, which can look *intensely* and *frequently* at the *same subject*. He believes and disbelieves with impassioned confidence—I wish to see him *doubting* and *doubting*.[2]

In German philosophy in the 1790s and 1800s the brilliant young Schelling, conceiving promptly and executing still more promptly, turned out tractate after confident tractate; but these efforts soon, as Novalis said, began to seem faded, unusable, and short-lived. In England, however, Coleridge, endowed with matchless 'patience of mind, which can look intensely and frequently at the same subject', bore lifelong witness to the claims and dignity of both external nature and the human personality. By the constancy of his doubt he made his way into the minds and hearts of posterity, where the effect of his name, and the meaning of his concern, live and grow with the passing years.

---

[1] 'Den meisten Menschen ist es kein Ernst. Sie haben die Wahrheit nicht gekostet, und stecken in einem heimlichen Unglauben. Jeder prüfe sich selbst, ob er Glauben und Leben habe; findet er einige Freude und Lust grösser, als diese in der Liebe Gottes und Verherrlichung seines Willens, so kennt er Christus nicht genugsam, und fühlet noch nicht die Regung des heiligen Geistes.' (Leibniz, *Von der wahren* THEOLOGIA MYSTICA, in *Leibniz's deutsche Schriften*, hrsg. Dr. G. E. Guhrauer (Berlin, 1838–40), i. 413).

[2] *Letters*, i. 339.

EXCURSUS NOTE I

Coleridge's Indebtedness to A. W. Schlegel

THE real question of Coleridge's indebtedness to Schlegel more or less reduces itself to whether Coleridge did or did not derive his conception of 'organic form' from Schlegel's dramatic lectures. It is interesting to pursue this problem, because it sheds light both on the meaning of Coleridge's borrowing, and on the various biases of his commentators. Though Helmholtz in 1907, Beach in 1942, and Orsini in 1964 have all printed both the English and the German of the passage in question, it is probably correct to say that scholarship at large does not want to see the facts. Thus Raysor says that 'as Mrs. von Helmholtz-Phelan's monograph is easily accessible . . . there can be no longer any need of giving in full detail the evidence of Schlegel's influence. For this reason I have frequently contented myself with a reference in the notes to the parallel passage in Schlegel's works, without quoting' (Raysor, 'Preface (1930)', i. ix). But alas, without quoting, one is much too tempted to forget the facts. To Coleridge's definition of 'organic form' (where Coleridge, in an acknowledgment deleted by H. N. Coleridge and restored by Raysor, speaks of a 'continental critic'— i.e. Schlegel), Raysor comments: 'This passage again is a striking illustration of Coleridge's relations with Schlegel. The idea of the next two sentences is entirely Schlegel's; the eloquence, which begins here and continues to the end, is entirely Coleridge's' (Raysor, i. 198 n. 2). In fact, however, the 'eloquence' is Coleridge's only in so far as the translation is a good one. Coleridge says: 'The form is mechanic when on any given material we impress a pre-determined form, not necessarily arising out of the properties of the material. . . . The organic form, on the other hand, is innate; it shapes as it develops itself from within, and the fullness of its development is one and the same with the perfection of its outward form' (Raysor, i. 198). Schlegel says: 'Mechanisch ist die Form, wenn sie durch äußere Einwirkung irgend einem Stoffe bloß als zufällige Zuthat, ohne Beziehung auf dessen Beschaffenheit ertheilt wird. . . . Die organische Form hingegen ist eingeboren, sie bildet von innen heraus, und erreicht ihre Bestimmtheit zugleich mit der vollständigen Entwickelung des Keimes' (A. W. von Schlegel's sämmtliche Werke, hrsg. E. Böcking (Leipzig, 1846–7), vi. 157). Though Raysor provides the citation in Schlegel's works, by neglecting to quote the actual passage he leaves the ambiguous impression that what is in fact a simple translation is somehow something more.

This continuing 'considerable reluctance' of scholarship to 'accept the fact' of Coleridge's translation is rightly protested against by G. N. G. Orsini, who, noting the persistence of the attitude even among contemporary scholars (whom he names), finds it necessary once more to set up the passages in parallel columns (and at greater length than we adduce them). As he says, 'The reader can see for himself that Coleridge was following Schlegel step by step, sentence by sentence, and finally word for word. The all-important definition of organic form in the last paragraph is a faithful translation from Schlegel, with the alteration of only one word of the original; "soft mass" (*weichen Masse*) in Schlegel is replaced by "mass of wet clay" ' (G. N. G. Orsini, 'Coleridge and Schlegel Reconsidered', *Comparative Literature*, xvi (1964), 102).

Orsini treats the matter as one not of plagiarism, but of literary influence. As he emphasizes, 'the object of this analysis is not to put Coleridge in the dock and indict him for felonious misappropriation of other men's thoughts. There is no question here of plagiarism. Apart from the fact that these are private notes, not prepared for publication, there is the clear reference to the "Continental critic" as the author of the formula' (Orsini, p. 102). He asserts rather that the 'introduction of the concept of organic form led to the solution of a long-standing problem in Shakespearean criticism—the problem of Shakespeare's dramatic form' (Orsini, p. 115); and he insists that the 'demonstration of Shakespeare's dramatic unity was finally provided by the Schlegels through the concept of organic form' and that 'This Coleridge saw and introduced into English literature—which constitutes one of his great merits as a critic' (Orsini, p. 118).

But I cannot agree. I believe that such a position—which is virtually the same as that of Wellek—is almost as misleading as the refusal to recognize the facts of Coleridge's borrowing. Orsini clears Coleridge of 'plagiarism'—at least on this central issue of organic form—but substitutes a conception in which Coleridge is absolutely obligated for the idea—a conception that urges that in 1811 the magic spark of 'organic' form passed from Germany to England as August Wilhelm Schlegel transmitted it to S. T. Coleridge: 'My purpose is . . . to show how a great idea passed from one brilliant mind to another brilliant mind, and thereby effected a revolution in literary criticism' (Orsini, p. 102). This view can no more be maintained than the view that Coleridge did not translate from Schlegel. The translations from Schlegel testify to Coleridge's compulsive intellectual symbiosis; they show also that he habitually enlaid his mosaic patterns with whatever pertinent or attractive statements he found at hand. They do not show that Schlegel taught him how to read Shakespeare; and they do not show that Coleridge learned about organic form from Schlegel.

On the contrary, Coleridge almost certainly knew about organic form already, and the idea was not in any case the property of Schlegel. If, as Orsini urges, the problem is 'purely a question of sources, which is a matter both of historical fact and of historical justice' (p. 112), then we must insist that not only is Schlegel here utilizing what had become a Romantic commonplace, but in general, as a commentator stresses, 'complete originality of thought is a rarity with Wilhelm Schlegel. He constantly needed stimulation and achieved his best in the borrowing or refutation of something offered him from elsewhere' (Besenbeck, *Kunstanschauung und Kunstlehre August Wilhelm Schlegels*, p. 13). And Heine, as is well known, savagely attacks Schlegel's reputation as an original critic (though Heine is not fair). In any event, the idea of organic form was so much 'in the air' during the Romantic era that Whitehead has in effect defined Romanticism itself as a 'protest on behalf of the organic view of nature' against the mechanic view (Whitehead, *Science and the Modern World*, p. 132). Though Orsini wants to divorce the 'organic form' of literary criticism from the organic view of nature ('the organic simile', he says, 'is not the concept of organic *form*'), organic form is in fact an obvious corollary of the 'organic simile' and historically cannot be separated from it. As Spranger says, 'the organic analogy' is one of the three main analogies according to which Romantic man conceived himself and his situation: 'To be sure the structure of the organism was not yet scientifically grounded. But there was a consciousness of its special nature: reciprocal conditioning of its parts, ability to reproduce, inner purposiveness. People realized that it was only with such structures that the spiritual life could be compared. The individual, as well as the spirit of the people, is an organism, filled with a living urge to form, which conditions growth, development and form by teleological instincts and drives. Aristotelian thoughts are revived. All parts hang together in an inward, spiritual whole—organically. People discover a duality of forces (polarity). People believe in life force. . . . The organic principle is raised to be the universal principle of the world' (Spranger, *Humboldt und die Humanitätsidee*, p. 23).

When Carus, therefore, in his *Grundzüge allgemeiner Naturbetrachtung*, says that 'the flowing' (*das Flüssige*) is 'the elemental fact of all organic development', we may feel that his argument stems from the tradition of Schelling's *Naturphilosophie*. But when Wordsworth, in 1800, defines poetry as the 'spontaneous overflow' of powerful feelings, we recognize the metaphor as equal to Carus's specification for the organic, and at the same time as being quite independent of any German influences. Likewise, when Keats, in a letter of 27 February 1818, says that one of his axioms is that 'if Poetry comes not as naturally as the Leaves to a tree it had better not come at all', we realize that the doctrine of organic form has been invoked in terms of another metaphor, and that its invocation very probably owes nothing to 'influence'. Again, Coleridge, in a letter of 19 April 1819, says that 'The Tree is not indeed dead; but the Sap is all sunk down to the root—and I think it better to wait for it's reascension into the Head and Branches; than to anticipate its product by Buds and Blossoms, however faithful Copies or Fac Similes they might be of the natural Growth' (*Letters*, iv. 935). Here too we realize that the doctrine of organic form has been invoked, and here too we surmise that there is no question of influence. Yet, on the other hand, should one desire to go searching for priorities, they could be turned up in numerous instances in French and English writings antedating formulations by Schlegel or any other German Romantic. To cite a single example, Robinet, in 1765, says that 'La force évolutive des germes domine la matiere de leur développement', and in this context he speaks explicitly of 'L'énergie du germe, ou sa force organique'. He finds that 'La force évolutive agit par elle-même, selon une certaine mesure & dans des bornes réglées par sa propre nature' (*De la nature* (Amsterdam, 1761–66), iv, 138). 'La forme est dessinée dans le germe, comme le corps parfait y est ébauché ou esquissé' (p. 136). For early English statements see Abrams, e.g., pp. 165, 167, 199.

Organic form, in short, was every intellectual's possession, and Coleridge enunciated it as he needed it, in terms of whatever books and occasions involved him at a given time. In *On Poesy or Art* he writes that 'there is a difference between form as proceeding, and shape as superinduced;—the latter is either the death or the imprisonment of the thing;—the former is its self-witnessing and self-effected sphere of agency' (*Biographia*, ii. 262). At this time he was reading Schelling's essay on nature and art, and the formulation may thus be an accommodation of Schelling's statement that the essence of a work of art 'might well be damaged by form which is pressed on it, but never by that which flows out of it' (*Werke*, vii. 303). On the other hand, he may have simply been developing his own note of February 1805—written some two years before Schelling's essay, and considerably before Schelling's *Vorlesungen*—as to the 'difference' between 'Fabrication and Generation': the 'Form' of the latter is 'ab intra, *evolved*, the other ab extra, *impressed*' (*Notebooks*, ii. 2444). This distinction expresses in full the meaning of the doctrine of organic form.

To be sure, Schelling had been saying this kind of thing since the 1790s. For example, in his *Ideen zu einer Philosophie der Natur* of 1797 (which Coleridge annotated in the second edition of 1803), there occur numerous succinct formulas: e.g. 'in the organic product form and matter are inseparable' (*Werke*, ii. 41); 'form and matter relate to one another reciprocally' (*Werke*, ii. 42). Similar formulas occur in Schelling's *Von der Weltseele, eine Hypothese der höheren Physik zur Erklärung des allgemeinen Organismus*, which was published in 1798 and eventually read by Coleridge. A formula of 1795 asserts that 'True art, or rather the divine (θεῖον) in art, is an inner principle. It forms the material from within outward, and counteracts all-powerfully every crude mechanism, every irregular aggregation of materials from outside' (*Werke*, i. 285). An especially satisfying statement appears in the *Abhandlung zur Erläuterung des Idealismus der Wissenschaftslehre* (1796–7)—which was probably one of the first of Schelling's works that Coleridge read: 'If the human spirit is a self-organizing nature, then nothing comes to it from outside, mechanically; what is in it has formed itself from within outwards, according to an inner principle. Everything in the human spirit therefore strives toward system—that is, toward absolute purposiveness. Everything, however, that is absolutely purposive is in itself whole and complete. It bears in itself the origin and final goal of its existence. . . . In that which is purposive form and matter, concept and intuition, interpenetrate' (*Werke*, i. 386).

Though all these formulations antedate Schlegel's *Vorlesungen*, I doubt exceedingly that Coleridge had read them by 1805. Coleridge was, moreover, well aware that Schelling had not originated such ideas. Thus at a passage where Jacobi says that when Lessing wanted to represent a personal divinity 'he thought of it as the soul of the all; and conceived the whole thing according to the analogy of an organic body', Coleridge comments: 'This with indeed most of the other essential Thoughts of Lessing has been adopted by Schelling . . .' (marginal notation in the British Museum copy of Jacobi, *Ueber die Lehre des Spinoza*, neue Ausgabe (Breslau, 1789), p. 46). As Spranger says, the insistence that 'the whole of the world be understood as a work of art, as a closed organic unity' was the 'genial intuition' of earlier thinkers such as 'Herder, Moritz, Goethe'; Schelling's role was that he 'systematized these intuitions' (Spranger, p. 15). Thus Oskar Walzel delivers himself of the dictum that 'Der Organismusgedanke ist der Schlüssel der romantischen Weltanschauung' (*Deutsche Romantik*; *I. Welt- und Kunstanschauung*, fünfte Auflage

(Leipzig und Berlin, 1923), p. 15). He says that 'it is a very difficult task to determine how far the Romantics were indebted to Schelling for the conception and application of the organic hypothesis. Unquestionably no one developed it as logically in all its phases as did Schelling. But equally certain is it that Friedrich Schlegel's line of thought was from the very first directed to the same end. He applied very early the aesthetic conception of organism, which has a long previous history in the philosophy and art of the eighteenth century and which was handed over to Schelling, as well as to Friedrich Schlegel, in highly perfected form by Goethe, Herder, and Moritz' (p. 43). Walzel finds that the 'Gedanke des Organismus'—'applied to nature and to art'—goes back to 'Shaftesbury, and through him to Plato and Neoplatonism' (p. 16). Noting that Schelling 'was induced to conceive of nature and humanity as a single, mighty, unified organism' specifically through 'the lectures given in 1793 by Kielmeyer, *Über die Verhältnisse der organischen Kräfte* . . .', he points out that Schelling himself traced 'Kielmeyer's train of thought back to Herder' (p. 14). And as to Wilhelm Schlegel, Walzel speaks both of his 'allseitiger Aufnahmefähigkeit'— his capacity for taking things from all kinds of sources—and of the fact that, in his Berlin lectures, he rendered 'almost rapturous thanks' to Moritz. In the latter's *Über die bildenden Nachahmung des Schönen* (1788), 'the Romantic doctrine of organism, in its aesthetic application', found terse and easily understood expression (pp. 12, 16).

Moritz, indeed, had written to Mendelssohn as early as 1785 that the 'aesthetic object must be something complete in itself', and that 'the true artist will seek to achieve the highest inner purposiveness or perfection in his work' (Karl Philipp Moritz, *Schriften zur Ästhetik und Poetik*, kritische Ausgabe, hrsg. Hans Joachim Schrimpf (Tübingen, 1962), pp. 6, 8). And if we keep in mind Walzel's specification (Walzel, p. 43) that 'the chief characteristic of the organic point of view is the wish to conceive an appearance as a whole (*Ganzes*)', we find Moritz very explicit in his *Über die bildende Nachahmung des Schönen*: 'Each beautiful whole (*Ganze*) that comes from the hand of the plastic artist is therefore a copy in miniature of the highest beauty in the great whole of nature' (*Schriften*, p. 73). 'For the plastic artist, the horizon of his active force must extend as far as does nature itself—that is, the organization must be as finely woven and offer as infinitely many contact points as all-streaming nature . . .' (p. 76).

It is not clear how much of Schelling Coleridge had read before he saw Schlegel's *Vorlesungen*. According to statements in the *Biographia* (i. 105, 171), he had read the *Abhandlung* and the *Philosophische Briefe* before composing that work, but apparently not the *Ideen* or the *Weltseele*. But Schlegel himself had read Schelling long before his own *Vorlesungen* appeared. And Coleridge, Schlegel, and Schelling had all three read Kant. In the *Kritik der reinen Vernunft*, in one of the most famous of all definitions of organic form, Kant insists that a 'system' must be a 'whole', and that 'Das Ganze ist also gegliedert (*articulatio*) und nicht gehäuft (*coacervatio*); es kann zwar innerlich (*per intus susceptionem*) aber nicht äusserlich (*per appositionem*) wachsen, wie ein tierischer Körper . . .'—that this whole is organically structured (*articulatio*) and not assembled (*coacervatio*); it can, like an animal body, grow from within (*per intus susceptionem*) but not from without (*per appositionem*) (Kant, *Werke*, iii. 557). Moreover, the most important single impetus to the Romantic use of organic form was supplied by Kant's discussion of 'inner purposiveness' (innere Zweckmäßigkeit) in the *Kritik der Urteilskraft*. 'An organic being', he there says, 'is not merely a machine . . . it possesses a forming power in itself' (Kant, *Werke*, v. 452).

These citations alone invalidate any belief that A. W. Schlegel originated the idea or introduced Coleridge to it. Yet they by no means exhaust Coleridge's possible sources. Before Kant's work, and before Coleridge's knowledge of that work, for instance, there appeared a discussion of organic form that was full and unequivocal. In a 'Digression concerning the Plastick Life of Nature', Cudworth discusses 'a Plastick Nature, that acts ἕνεκά του, *for the sake of something*' (Ralph Cudworth, *The True Intellectual System of the Universe . . .* (London, 1678), p. 147). Cudworth concludes that 'the first General Conception of the *Plastick Nature*' is 'That *it is Art it self, acting immediately on the Matter as an Inward Principle*' (p. 155). '*Nature* Acts Immediately upon the Matter as an Inward and Living Soul, or Law in it' (p. 156). 'Indeed *Humane Artists* themselves do not Consult properly as they are *Artists*, but when ever they do it, it is for want of *Art*, and because they are to seek, their Art being Imperfect and Adventitious: but *Art it self* or *Perfect Art*, is never to seek, and therefore doth never *Consult* or *Deliberate*' (p. 156). This view, maintains Cudworth, is that of Aristotle, whose meaning 'is that Nature is to be conceived as *Art* Acting not from without and at a Distance, but *Immediately* upon the thing it self which is Formed by it' (p. 155). It is, again, the view of Plotinus (and inasmuch as Heinemann has demonstrated that Schelling's essay on art and nature is almost wholly dependent on Plotinus, it is interesting to compare Cudworth's translation of Plotinus with Schelling's art-and-nature formulation adduced above): '. . . it is manifest that the Operation of Nature is different from Mechanism, it doing not its Work by Trusion or Pulsion, by Knockings or Thrustings, as if it were withoutthat which it wrought upon' (Plotinus, *Enneads*, iii. 8. 1; Cudworth, p. 156).

Such statements must have been well known to Coleridge. Not to mention his youthful saturation in Plotinus himself, he had Cudworth's *Intellectual System* in his possession from 15 May to 1 June 1795, and again from 9 November to 13 December 1796 (George Whalley, 'The Bristol Library Borrowings of Southey and Coleridge, 1793–8', *Transactions of the Bibliographical Society. The Library*, September 1949, pp. 120, 124).

EXCURSUS NOTE II

The Reaction Against Spinoza

ANTI-SPINOZISM as an historical movement originated not with the appearance of Spinoza's chief work, the *Ethica ordine geometrico demonstrata* (published posthumously in 1677 through the agency of Spinoza's friends Jarig Jelles,

Georg Schuller, and Lodewijk Meijer—for the complicated provenance of its printing see Carl Gebhardt, 'Die Drucklegung der Opera Posthuma', Spinoza, *Opera*, ii. 311–19)—but with the anonymous publication, early in 1670, of the *Tractatus theologico-politicus*, a work that passed through four new printings before the end of 1671 and was immediately denounced as atheistic by savants such as Jacob Thomasius (Leibniz's teacher), Friedrich Rappolt, Fridericus Miegius (*ordinarius* at Heidelberg), the theologian Johannes Melchior, and the philologist Burman. For a detailed discussion see Freudenthal, 'Kämpfe um den theologisch-politischen Traktat', *Das Leben Spinozas*, pp. 217–52.

The immediate influence of Spinoza's views was great, and seemed even greater than it was. Thus Roell speaks of 'whole armies' of Spinozists: 'Utinam inauditum esset in Belgica nostra exsecrabile illud Spinosae nomen, quem tota armenta sequuntur ducem!' (*Herm. Alexandri Roëll Dissertatio de religione rationali*, editio quarta (Franequerae, 1700), p. 166). Despite a flood of anti-Spinozistic literature, there was apparently an animated pro-Spinozistic propaganda carried on by word of mouth; hence Velthuysen reports in 1680 that Spinoza's way of thinking is by no means hidden in the obscurity that some people suppose, but has trickled through to many persons, 'especially from the discussions of Spinoza's followers' (praesertim ex sermonibus sectatorum *Spinozae*), and has 'corrupted young men very greatly' (juventutem tantopere infecit) (*Tractatus de cultu naturali, et origine moralitatis. Oppositus Tractatui Theologico-Politico, & Operi Posthumo B. D. S.*, in *Lamberti Velthuysii, Ultrajectini, Opera Omnia* . . . (Roterodami, 1680), ii. 1370). To avoid reprisals the adherents of Spinoza sometimes published their work anonymously, e.g. *Specimen artis ratiocinandi naturalis et artificialis* (Hamburgi, 1684)—as Dunin-Borkowski says, 'from Heinrich Künrath in "Hamburg", the masked publisher of the theological-political tractate, there appeared in 1684 an anonymous book. . . . The philosophical apprentice who wrote it did not remain unknown. He was soon discovered to be Abraham Joh. Cuffeler' (Stanislaus Von Dunin-Borkowski, 'Nachlese zur ältesten Geschichte des Spinozismus', *Archiv für Geschichte der Philosophie*, xxiv (1911), 76–77; the section on Cuffeler, which is entitled 'Ein christlicher Spinozist', extends from page 76 to page 89)—and sometimes assumed the protective colouring of ostensible anti-Spinozism, most notably Boulainvilliers, *Réfutation des erreurs de Benoit de Spinoza* (Bruxelles, 1731). The success of this latter title in concealing its author's real views may be gauged from the statement of a recent writer who says that 'no less than four' of Boulainvilliers' works 'are devoted to Spinoza, and it seems quite in keeping that one should be a translation of the *Ethics* and another a refutation of the system expounded in that treatise' (Vincent Buranelli, 'The Historical and Political Thought of Boulainvilliers', *JHI*, xviii (1957), 476, n. 4). The savants, however, were less easily misled. Compare, for instance, the statement of Mosheim in his Latin translation of Cudworth (p. 339, note 9), or the authority of Brucker, who speaks of the 'Refutation of the Count Boulainvilliers, or more accurately, the exposition of the Spinozistic system' (*Iacobi Bruckeri* . . . *Historia critica philosophiae* (Lipsiae, 1766), iv. 683). Again, Freudenthal: 'Of greater importance is the fact that a famous scholar and free-thinker in the literary circles of Holland and France, the Count Boulainvilliers, provided—in the guise of an opponent—an illuminating exposition and explanation of Spinozist philosophy' (*Die Lehre Spinozas*, p. 219). See further Ira O. Wade, *The Clandestine Organization and Diffusion of Philosophic Ideas in France from 1700 to 1750* (Princeton, 1938), pp. 97–140.

Yet the supporters of Spinoza, both overt and secret, were vastly outnumbered by his detractors. In addition to the works to which I refer in the text, the following early anti-Spinozistic tracts should at least have their existence noted: Pierre-Daniel Huet, *Demonstratio evangelica* (Paris, 1679); Pierre Yvon, *L'Impiété convaincue . . . réfutation du livre impie de Spinoza* . . . (Amsterdam, 1681); Noël Aubert de Versé, *L'Impie convaincu ou Dissertation contre Spinoza dans laquelle on réfute les fondements de son athéisme* (Amsterdam, 1684); Franciscus Cuperus, *Arcana atheismi revelata, philosophice et paradoxè refutata, examine Tractatus Theologico-Politici* (Roterodami, 1676); *Petri Poireti Cogitationum rationalium de Deo . . . nec non B. de Spinoza Atheismus et . . . errores, funditus extirpantur* (Amstelodami, 1685); Michael Berns, *Altar der Atheïsten, der Heyden, und der Christen . . . Wider die 3 Erz-Betrieger, Hobbert [Herbert] Hobbes und Spinoza* . . . (*Hamburg*, 1692); Friedrich Ernst Kettner, *De duobus impostoribus B. Spinosa et B. Bekkero dissertatio historica* . . . (Lipsiae, 1694); François Lamy, *Le Nouvel athéisme renversé, ou Réfutation du sistème de Spinoza, tirée pour la plupart de la connaissance de la nature de l'homme* (Paris, 1696); John Howe, *The Living Temple*, Part II (London, 1702); Christianis Benedictus Lucius, *B. de Spinoza, Atheismi convictum* . . . (Vitembergae, [1705]); Charles Gildon, *The Deist's Manual: or, a Rational Enquiry into the Christian Religion. With some Considerations on Mr. Hobbs, Spinoza, etc.* (London, 1705); Jean Coler, *La Vérité de la Résurrection de Jesus Christ défendue contre Benedict de Spinoza et ses sectateurs. Avec la vie de ce fameux philosophe* (La Haye, 1706); William Carroll, *A Dissertation upon . . . Mr. Locke's Essay Concerning Humane Understanding; Wherein that Author's Endeavours to Establish Spinoza's Atheistical Hypothesis are Confuted* . . . (London, 1706); Johannes Musaeus, *Spinosismus: hoc est, Tractatus theologico-politicus, quo . . . B. Spinoza . . . demonstratum ivit, libertatem philosophandi . . . posse concedi . . . ad veritatis lancem examinatus . . .* (Jenae, 1674 and Witebergae, 1708); [William Carroll?], *Spinoza Reviv'd; A Treatise, Proving the Book, Entitled, The Rights of the Christian Church, &c.* [by Matthew Tindal] . . . *to be the Same with Spinoza's Rights of the Christian Clergy, &c. And that both of them are grounded upon downright atheism . . .* (London, 1709); Philippe Naudé, *Examen de deux Traittez. . . . Avec une addition, où l'on prouve contre Spinoza que nous sommes libres*, 2 vols. (Amsterdam, 1713); Alexander Innes, Ἀρετη Λογια or, *An Enquiry into the Original of Moral Virtue; Wherein the False Notions of Machiavel, Hobbes, Spinoza, and Mr. Bayle are Examined and Confuted* (Westminster, 1728). I have not seen all these works, but those I have seen impress me by two predominant qualities: analytical keenness and a tone of abuse. All of them are of historical interest, and some of intellectual interest. In this latter respect one should be especially noted: the tractate by Musaeus, who was professor of theology at Jena, is characterized by learning and logical sophistication, especially in its demonstration of the deficiencies of Spinoza's understanding of the New Testament.

None of these attacks, however, were as powerful as one mounted by Christian Wolf. The most important German philosopher between Leibniz and

Kant, Wolf provides perhaps the most formidable critique ever directed against Spinoza—a critique closely reasoned and massive in content, and noteworthy among anti-Spinozistic utterances by its tone of calm objectivity and its relative lack of abuse. Wolf's objections focus on the moral implications of Spinoza's cosmogonic philosophy, but his most telling points are attacks on logical fallacies in Spinoza's deductive process. He concludes that 'Spinosa *fatalista universalista* est' (*Theologia Naturalis*, p. 721, Proposition 709), and that Spinoza's logical ground is 'slippery': 'Videmus itaque quam lubricum sit totius Spinosismi fundamentum' (p. 693). The examination is conducted as a careful, point by point, unfriendly analysis of almost every Spinozistic supposition. Thus, at random, 'Spinoza has not shown that all substance is by necessity infinite' (p. 713, Proposition 702); 'Spinoza has not shown that substance exists by necessity' (p. 711, Proposition 700); 'Spinoza has not proved that in the universe it is not possible to have two or more substances of the same nature or attribute' (p. 706, Proposition 697); 'Spinozism rests on doubtful principles, confused and also ambiguous' (p. 692, Proposition 687); 'Spinoza has incorrectly and even ambiguously defined finite or limited' (p. 687, Proposition 685); 'Spinoza confounds substance with being itself' (p. 687, Proposition 684). The logical objections, many of them precise and searching, incorporated in these propositions are in each case amplified by a discussion following the statement of the proposition.

Wolf's critique was published sixty years after Spinoza's death, and along with the other anti-Spinozist literature, shows that there was really no cessation of interest in Spinoza at any time, even though the Romantics liked to think there was—Schelling, for instance, laments that 'Spinoza hat unerkannt gelegen über hundert Jahre' (*Werke*, ii. 71). But as Freudenthal says: 'Nothing is . . . less correct than the oft-heard assertion that during the first eighty years of the eighteenth century Spinoza was forgotten and unnoticed. Spinoza was never less forgotten than during the time when his name was covered with insult and disgrace' (*Die Lehre Spinozas*, pp. 217–18).

References to Spinoza during the eighteenth century are, indeed, too numerous to attempt to review here (for discussion of the neo-Spinozistic pantheism of such figures as Robinet and d'Holbach see the second volume of Paul Vernière, *Spinoza et la pensée française avant la révolution* (Paris, 1954)). One refutation of his thought, however, deserves to be noted, not only because of its similarity to Wolf's logical attacks, but also because of its complete freedom from abuse. In 1749 Condillac, in his *Traité des systèmes*, examines, among other things, Spinoza's philosophy, with the general design of showing that 'abstract principles' are 'useless and dangerous'. 'Plus on avance', he says, 'plus Spinosa est aisé à réfuter, parce que les vices de ses raisonnemens se multiplient, à proportion que ses dernières preuves supposent un plus grand nombre de propositions', and he concludes that 'Spinosa n'a nulle idée des choses qu'il avance; que ses définitions sont vagues, ses axiomes peu exacts, et que ses propositions ne sont que l'ouvrage de son imagination, et ne renferment rien qui puisse conduire à la connaissance des choses' (*Œuvres complètes de Condillac* (Paris, 1822), ii. 214, 250).

Condillac's rather detailed analysis scores a number of points against Spinoza's logic, as had Wolf's. Indeed, that logic, notwithstanding Romantic admiration for its consequence, is really somewhat vulnerable. In the nineteenth century Boole demonstrates its insufficiency (see below, p. 338, n. 8), as did also John Dewey, in a youthful article in the *Journal of Speculative Philosophy*. There is an impressive unity in Spinoza, but it derives as much from his emotional certainty and serenity as from his reasoning. His apologists in the nineteenth and twentieth centuries go too far when they dismiss the early attacks as simple misunderstandings of his doctrine. By and large, the authors of the early tracts understood him very well; they simply could not accept him. We know from Freud that emotional acceptance must precede rational acceptance, and very few people before the late eighteenth century were emotionally prepared for Spinoza's vision of reality. More equivocating pantheisms, yes; Spinozism, no. But the early attacks are, despite their ferocity, keen attacks, and it distorts history to deny them merit. Huet, a studious churchman of colossal although inert learning ('Cet homme', said Sainte-Beuve, 'décidément avait trop lu') brings vast erudition to bear in a counter-examination of matters of Biblical scholarship; Lamy, the spokesman for the Catholic establishment, argues as confidently from his postulates as Spinoza does from his own; Velthuysen argues against Spinoza on Cartesian grounds that foreshadow the distinctions of Husserl. There can be little doubt that Spinoza not only loved what he thought to be truth, but also that he had a strong emotional bias against organized Christianity; this all his early adversaries well understood. He became angry when Velthuysen wrote to a mutual friend that the doctrine of the *Tractatus theologico-politicus* 'omnem cultum & religionem tollit, atque funditus subvertit, clam Atheismum introducit'—overthrows and fundamentally subverts all worship and religion, and secretly introduces atheism—and 'tectis, & fucatis argumentis merum Atheismum docere'—teaches pure atheism by hidden and disguised arguments (Spinoza, *Epistolae*, xlii; Spinoza's reply is xliii). But Velthuysen, from his Christian and Cartesian standpoint, is as justified in his charge as Spinoza is in his resentment.

The early history of Spinozism has been treated in a number of books and monographs: most useful, in addition to Vernière, is Max Grunwald, *Spinoza in Deutschland* (Berlin, 1897); but see also L. Bäck, *Spinozas erste Einwirkungen auf Deutschland* (Berlin, 1895); G. Jenichen, *Historia Spinozismi Leenhofiani* (Lipsiae, 1707); A. van der Linde, *Spinoza. Seine Lehre und deren erste Nachwirkungen in Holland* (Göttingen, 1862); M. Francès, *Spinoza dans les pays néerlandais de la seconde moitié du XVIIᵉ siècle* (Paris, 1937); P. Janet, 'Le Spinozisme en France', *Revue philosophique*, xiii (1882), 109–32; F. Pillon, *L'Évolution de l'idéalisme au XVIIIᵉ siècle; la critique de Bayle; critique du panthéisme spinoziste* (Paris, 1899); L. Brunschvicg, *Spinoza et ses contemporains* (Paris, 1923); P. Siwek, *Spinoza et le panthéisme religieux* (Paris, 1937); G. Friedmann, 'Spinoza, scandale de son temps', *Revue de métaphysique et de morale*, li (1946), 37–48; P. Hazard, 'Voltaire et Spinoza', *Modern Philology*, xxxviii (1941), 351–64; L. Stein, *Leibniz und Spinoza* (Berlin, 1890); G. Friedmann, *Leibniz et Spinoza* (Paris, 1946); F. Erhardt, *Die Philosophie des Spinoza im Lichte der Kritik* (Leipzig, 1908), pp. 1–35; G. Pape, *Christophe Wittichs Anti-Spinoza* (Berlin, 1910); M. Krakauer, *Zur Geschichte des Spinozismus in Deutschland* (Breslau, 1881); E. Altkirch, *Spinoza im*

Porträt (Jena, 1913); *Maledictus und Benedictus* (Leipzig, 1924); D. Baumgardt, 'Spinoza und der deutsche Spinozismus', *Kantstudien*, xxxii (1927), 182–92; R. Colie, 'Spinoza and the Early English Deists', *Journal of the History of Ideas*, xx (1959), 23–46; J. S. Spink, *French Free-Thought from Gassendi to Voltaire* (London, 1960), pp. 238–99.

EXCURSUS NOTE III

Toland and the Origin of the word 'Pantheism'

JOHN TOLAND, a learned, independent, and contentious free-thinker, composed for himself a famous and often-reprinted epitaph, in which he spoke of knowing ten languages and affirmed that he did not believe in immortality; a counter-view by a 'late weekly Writer', in the manner of eighteenth-century 'character' attacks, deserves to be remembered along with the self-laudatory epitaph: Toland's 'Misfortunes are to be ascribed to his Vanity; he affected singularity in all things (an easy way of being distinguished), he would reject an Opinion, merely because an eminent Writer embraced it; he had a Smattering in many Languages, was a Critick in none; his Style was low, confused, and disagreeable; he prefix'd affected Titles to his Tracts, in imitation of some ancient Philosophers, in which he loved to talk of himself, and that in a most complaisant manner. Dabbling in Controversy was his Delight, in which he was rude, positive, and always in the wrong. His being known to the world, is owing chiefly to the Animadversions of learned Men upon his Writings, among whom 'twas a common trick in their Disputes with one another, to charge their Adversary with an agreement to, or resemblance of Mr. TOLAND's Notions, as the greatest Infamy, and the surest *Criterion* of Error. No man that wrote so voluminously against Religion, has ever done so little mischief.' (Quoted in *Some Memoirs of the Life and Writings of Mr. John Toland*, in *A Collection of Several Pieces of Mr. John Toland, Now First Publish'd from his Original Manuscripts . . .* (London, 1726), i. xc–xci.)

The word 'pantheist' occurs in the title, and once in the text, of a pamphlet of 1705: 'After this Reflection I did further assert, as you may remember, that those cou'd be found in the World (particularly the PANTHEISTS) who not only were, but also appear'd intirely unconcern'd in all Disputes, of which number I profess my self to be one. Their *System of Philosophy* I did in confidence communicate to you . . .' (*Socinianism truly Stated; BEING An Example of fair Dealing in all Theological Controversys. To which is prefixt, Indifference in Disputes: Recommended by a PANTHEIST to an Orthodox Friend . . .* (London, 1705), p. 7). I am not entirely convinced, however, that Toland did coin the term—I suspect rather that it might have first appeared in one of the seventeenth-century Latin tracts that no one now reads. At any rate, not only does Toland's statement seem to indicate an earlier currency for the word, but the historians of philosophy who attribute the coinage to him are quite vague on the matter. Thus Eisler says that 'pantheist' was first used by Toland in 1705, but then erroneously cites as source the *Pantheisticon*, which was not published until 1720 (Rudolf Eisler, *Wörterbuch der philosophischen Begriffe*, Vierte völlig neubearbeitete Auflage, weitergeführt und vollendet durch Dr. Karl Roretz (Berlin, 1929), II. 375). Of more interest really than the exact date of coinage is the fact that Toland uses the word 'pantheist' as an exact synonym for 'Spinozist': 'Moses was, to be sure, a Pantheist, or, if you please, in more current terms, a Spinosist . . .' (*J. Tolandi Dissertationes Duae, Adeisidaemon et Origines Judaicae* (Hagae-Comitis, 1709), p. 117). This use receives, in 1717, the sanction of his violent antagonist, Buddaeus, who says: 'Naturalism, and pantheism too if it be the same thing, agrees well with atheism, or at least is a species of atheism'—and then amplifies his opinion in a note: 'The most crass indeed of those who acknowledge no other god than nature, or this very universe, is he who is accustomed to come under the name of pantheist, and in honor of the principal renovator of the impious error, Spinozist. . . . Simple naturalism does not concern us here. That its most crass form, pantheism if you will, does not differ from atheism is self-evident' (*Theses theologicæ de atheismo* (Ienae, 1717), pp. 211–12).

Toland's fullest statement concerning pantheism is incorporated into his *Pantheisticon* of 1720, where he gives ample justification for Buddaeus's scornful surmise (Buddaeus, p. 196) that Toland himself was in the camp of the pantheists. In the *Pantheisticon* Toland defines the 'Pantheistae' as a new Socratic society who hold as their central belief the view, in the words of Stobaeus, that '*Ex Toto quidem sunt omnia, et ex omnibus est Totum*' (John Toland, *Pantheisticon, sive formula celebrandae sodalitatis Socraticae* (Cosmopoli [London?], 1720), p. 6)— a statement of the identity of the one and the many necessary, as we have noted earlier, to any formulation of pantheism. Toland elaborates: 'They claim that the universe . . . is infinite both in extension and virtue, but one, in the continuation of the whole and contiguity of the parts: immovable according to the whole, for beyond it there is no place or space; but mobile according to the parts, or by distances in infinite number: incorruptible and necessary both ways: eternal in existence and duration, intelligent also by an eminent reason, and not to receive its denomination from our intellectual faculty, unless by a slight similitude: lastly, that in the universe the integrant parts are always the same, the constituent parts always in motion' (pp. 6–7). The 'force and energy of the whole,' says Toland, 'the creator and ruler of all, and always tending to the best end, is God, whom you may call the mind, if you please, and soul of the universe; and hence it is, that the Socratic sodality . . . are called PANTHEISTS, this force, according to them, being not separated from the *Universe* itself, except by a distinction of reason alone' (p. 8). Toland is specific about the identification of God and nature, of the one and the many: 'all things in the world are one, and one is all in all things' intones the mystic moderator; and the response of the others in the society then equates divinity with this primary equation of the one and the many: 'what is all in all things is GOD, eternal and immense, neither born nor ever to die' (*Pantheisticon*, p. 54). And Toland seems to adumbrate the raptures of Romanticism when he states explicitly that the pantheists may rightly be called the mysts and hierophants of Nature: 'Naturae Mystae ac Hierophantae merito vocari possunt PANTHEISTAE' (*Pantheisticon*, p. 77).

EXCURSUS NOTE IV

Panentheism

K R A U S E's system of philosophy, which is a Schellingian variant that he calls *Wissenschaft*, is attained by means of a method of 'inspection of being' (*Wesenschauung*). Where 'pantheism teaches that all and everything is God', in *Wesenschauung* the reverse reveals itself, for there it is found that 'nothing is God, as God alone; everything finite however is indeed in God, but essentially different from God'. *Wesenschauung* does not maintain 'that One and All are the same, that One is the All and All the One, after the manner of the Eleatic assertion: ἕν καὶ πᾶν'. 'One' is essentially different from 'All' because the thought 'All' already has the thought of 'multitude' (*Vielheit*) in it. But Krause finds that 'being, as the One' is 'in itself, among itself and through itself all things' and is also 'the content of everything finite', so it can be said that 'the One in itself and through itself also is the All'; and since in *Wesenschauung* it is perceived that 'God also is All in, among, and through himself', *Wissenschaft* could be called '*Panentheismus*' (K. C. F. Krause, *Vorlesungen über das System der Philosophie* (Göttingen, 1828), pp. 255–6). The following year Krause argued that 'the accusation of atheism, pantheism, and fatalism in regard to my *Wissenschaft* is wholly without sense'. It is true that 'God is the whole ground and content of *Wissenschaft*' and that 'God in, within and through himself (*an, in und durch sich*) also is all things (*Alles was ist*)'. None the less, claims Krause, *Wissenschaft* should not be reproached with being 'Pantheismus' or 'Allgottlehre' in the sense of 'the confusion of the world, or nature, or finite things in general with God', for *Wissenschaft* rather perceives 'everything finite as in, or as within God, and as through God as ground and cause'. *Wissenschaft* should therefore be called 'Panentheismus' or 'Allingottlehre' (Krause, *Vorlesungen über die Grundwahrheiten der Wissenschaft* (Göttingen, 1829), p. 484).

Krause's position, in short, can be summarized as asserting that though All Things are God, God is not equal to All Things. As such it is an attractive formulation—as are most formulations that allow us to have it both ways. Indeed, both Leibniz and Coleridge at times enunciate similar conceptions. Some theologians, moreover—particularly those with nineteenth-century backgrounds—defend the orthodoxy of panentheism (for instance, Dean Inge says that 'the belief in the *immanence* of a God who is also transcendent' should be 'called *Panentheism*, a useful word coined by Krause, and not Pantheism. In its true form it is an integral part of Christian philosophy, and, indeed, of all rational theology' (W. R. Inge, *Christian Mysticism* (London, 1899), p. 121). And the term has been taken up by literary scholars as though it does in fact assert an essentially different view from pantheism; thus Bernbaum, in his bibliographical résumé of modern research on Wordsworth, sums up a whole line of literary opinion when he says that one of the studies he reviews errs 'by confusing pantheism, a heresy into which Wordsworth did not consciously deviate, with his panentheism, which is certainly orthodox' (*The English Romantic Poets: A Review of Research*, ed. T. M. Raysor (New York, 1950), p. 49).

Despite this tradition, however, I should maintain that 'panentheism' cannot be distinguished from 'pantheism' and also cannot be considered as in any way an orthodox Christian conception. Indeed, the enormous burden that Krause places on mere prepositions should make us suspicious of his method of thought; it implies exclusively material and physical conceptions (e.g. God as receptacle). But more formally, I would urge four considerations against the orthodoxy of panentheism and against its being different from pantheism itself. In the first place, Spinoza himself speaks of God as containing 'infinita attributa', of which the only two we know are extension and thought—and therefore Spinoza asserts precisely what Krause asserts: that God is all things, but all things do not exhaust God. Secondly, Biblical authority does not support either the orthodoxy of panentheism or the distinction of panentheism and pantheism. It is true that Paul's statement that 'in him we live, and move, and have our being' (Acts xvii. 28), as well as his 'One God and Father of all, who is above all, and through all, and in you all' (Ephesians iv. 6) might seem to provide Biblical sanction for panentheism. But if Paul be so interpreted, then he must also be interpreted as providing sanction for pantheism itself—indeed, Spinoza himself sardonically says, 'I claim that all things are in God and move in God, thus agreeing with Paul . . .' (*Epistolae*, lxxiii). But such passages provide no sanction *either* for pantheism *or* for panentheism: they mean rather that we live, move, and have our being in the spirit ('God is a Spirit and they that worship him must worship him in spirit' (John iv. 24)). Paul, in fact, expressly warns, immediately after the passage in Acts, that we must not confuse God with any material manifestation: 'we ought not think that the Godhead is like unto gold, or silver, or stone . . .' (Acts xvii. 29). And if Paul has been invoked, however unjustifiably, by both pantheists and panentheists, John is unequivocal in his separation of God and world: 'I am not of the world,' says Christ (John xvii. 16); 'My kingdom is not of this world' (John xviii. 36); 'I am the living bread which came down from heaven' (John vi. 51); 'Ye are from beneath; I am from above; ye are of this world; I am not of this world' (John viii. 23).

Thirdly, there are logical objections. To conceive all things as God, but God as more than all things, is to conceive a part-whole relationship. But God cannot be conceived as a 'whole', for 'whole' implies limitation, and God is by theological definition illimitable and infinite. Likewise, that which is infinite can have no 'parts'—an eighth of infinity is an impossible conception ($1/8 \times 1/0$ is a meaningless statement in mathematics). Furthermore, when we say that all things are equal to God, or are 'in' God, we say that each individual thing is God, or 'in' God. If a thing—a frying-pan, for instance—is God totally, then the grandfather clock, by the principle of contradiction, is barred from being God. If, however, the frying-pan is only 'part' of God, then we both diminish and lessen God and attempt to modify infinity. If, however, we emphasize the preposition 'in', then we must think of a thing as 'in' God as a cork is in the sea, or a grape is in a bowl—in any event, we must think of the thing as in a physical relationship to another *thing* (and even if we think of a thing as *in* God the way iron filings are *in* a magnetic field, we are still conceiving physical relationships). As Pascal saw, 'if there is a God, He is infinitely incomprehensible, because, having neither parts nor limits (*n'ayant ni parties ni bornes*), he has no relationship (*rapport*) with us' (Pascal, *Pensées*, ed. H. F. Stewart (New York, 1950), p. 116). And Coleridge, in 1818, speaks contemptuously of the 'dim distinction, that tho' God was = the world, the World was not = God—as if God were a Whole composed of Parts, of which the World was one!' (marginal note at page 127 of the first volume of the Law edition of Boehme's works in the British Museum). But how do we relate to God, if not by knowledge (*Wissenschaft, gnosis*)? The true answer of religion is, by faith.

Fourthly, against the kind of theological authority represented by the statement of Dean Inge, we may summon both ancient and modern countertestimony. 'What do I love when I love thee?' asks Augustine. 'I asked the earth, and it said, I am not it; and whatever is on earth made the same confession. I asked the sea and the abyss and the creeping things of animal life, and they answered, We are not your God; seek above us. I asked the winds that blow, and the whole air with its denizens said, Anaximenes was wrong; I am not God. I asked the heaven, the sun, the moon, the stars: Nor are we God whom you seek, said they. And I said to them all . . . Tell me about my God, since you are not he. . . . And they cried out with a loud voice, He himself made us' (*Confessions* x. 6). As Barth puts it, for the Christian 'creaturely reality means reality on the basis of a *creatio ex nihilo*, a creation out of nothing. Where nothing exists —and not a kind of primal matter—there through God there has come into existence that which is distinct from Him' (Karl Barth, *Dogmatics in Outline*, trans. G. T. Thomson (London, 1949), p. 55). But the panentheist argues the opposite: 'Creation, as ordinarily understood, is denied by Krause. . . . Creation as of a world, made out of nothing, the Work of pure will, subsisting out of God, is for Krause contrary to the infinity, plenitude and perfection of Deity' (James Lindsay, 'The Philosophy of Krause', *Archiv für Geschichte der Philosophie*, xxvii (1913), p. 82).

For the panentheist, as for the pantheist, God must be somehow in all things —be these things themselves. For the Christian, however, as Barth has insisted, God must be conceived as a being *totaliter aliter*—of a totally different manner. 'Creation is grace', says Barth. 'God does not grudge the existence of the reality distinct from Himself.' 'This world', he insists, 'is not God himself, as pantheistic confusion again and again wishes to assert.' 'It is not, as ancient and modern gnosis claims, that . . . the Son is fundamentally the created world, or that the world is by nature God's child. Nor is it that the world is to be understood as an outflow, an emanation from God as something divine which wells out of God like a stream out of a spring . . . creation means something different; it means a reality distinct from God.' 'God', summarizes Barth, 'is one; and heaven and earth, man and the universe are something else, and this something else is not God' (Karl Barth, *Dogmatics in Outline*, pp. 54–55).

Panentheism, therefore, is no more reconcilable with Christianity than pantheism itself. The reason why Wordsworth is not a pantheist is that he held no systematic position, not that he was instead a panentheist. Without challenging Ferry's division of his attitudes towards nature into 'mystic' and 'sacramental' (David Ferry, *The Limits of Mortality; An Essay on Wordsworth's Major Poems* (Middletown, Conn., 1959), pp. 29–50), I none the less maintain that in so far as he was a 'worshipper of nature' he was a pantheist and not a Christian; for a Christian worships God through Christ. Rather than using 'panentheism' to defend the naturalism of Wordsworth and other nineteenth-century literary figures, we should do well to adopt the wry insight of Coleridge: 'I will not conceal from *you'*, he says in 1820, 'that this inferred dependance of the human soul on accidents of birthplace and abode, together with the vague, misty, rather than mystic, confusion of God with the world, and the accompanying nature-worship . . . is the trait in Wordsworth's poetic works that I most dislike . . . while the odd introduction of the popular, almost the vulgar, religion in his later publications (the popping in, as Hartley says, of the old man with a beard) . . . conjures up to my fancy a sort of *Janus* head of Spinoza and Dr. Watts' (*Letters, Conversations, and Recollections of S. T. Coleridge*, ed. Thomas Allsop (New York, 1836), p. 71). For one of the few modern studies of Wordsworth that realizes the irrelevance of any attempt to distinguish pantheism from panentheism, see Melvin Rader, *Wordsworth; A Philosophical Approach* (Oxford, 1967), pp. 59–60, 199–200.

EXCURSUS NOTE V

Leibniz and Spinoza

THOUGH Lessing's taunt to Jacobi, affirming that Leibniz was 'at heart a Spinozist', was tantamount to saying that Leibniz did not in fact believe in a 'personal, extramundane God', the view would seem to be contradicted in precisely Lessing's terms by explicit statements by Leibniz himself. Thus in the *Théodicée* Leibniz uses the actual word 'extramundane'—with specific reference, incidentally, to the Platonic tradition—for his definition of God: 'Dieu, selon nous, est Intelligentia extramundana, comme Martianus Capella l'appelle, ou plustost supramundana' (*Philosophische Schriften*, vi. 248). Earlier, in 1697, he had said: 'The One, being master of the Universe, not only rules the World but also frames or makes it, and is both above the world and, so to speak, outside it (extramundanum) . . .' (vii. 302). To these thoroughly unequivocal statements might be added, furthermore, Leibniz's insistence, in his controversy with Clarke, that God is outside the world. Clarke intimates that the conception of God as extramundane leads to a sterile Deism: 'The notion of the world's being a great machine, going on without the interposition of God, as a clock continues to go without the assistance of a clockmaker . . . tends (under pretence of making God a *supra-mundane intelligence*,) to exclude providence and God's government in reality . . .' (*The Leibniz–Clarke Correspondence*, ed. H. G. Alexander (New York, 1956), p. 14). To which Leibniz replies: 'I don't think I can be rightly blamed, for saying that God is *intelligentia supramundana*', and, showing himself alert to the pantheistic pitfall, continues: 'Will they say, that he is *intelligentia mundana*; that is, the soul of the world? I hope not' (p. 19). Clarke then responds with the insistence that 'God is neither a *mundane intelligence*, nor a *supra-mundane intelligence*; but an omnipresent intelligence, both in and without the world. He is in all, and through all, as well as above all' (p. 23). Leibniz then observes that Clarke 'strives in vain to criticize my expression, that God is *intelligentia supramundana*. To say that God is above the world, is not denying that he is in the world' (p. 29), and when Clarke (p. 34) rather grudgingly accepts the term under this qualification, Leibniz returns to his original emphasis on God's supramundaneity, with special notice of the danger of pantheism inherent in any other conception: 'Those who undertake to defend the vulgar opinion concerning the soul's influence over the body, by instancing in God's operating on things external; make God still too much like a soul of the world. To which I add, that the author's affecting to find fault with the words, *intelligentia supramundana*, seems also to incline that way' (p. 41).

Despite these statements the notion that Leibniz was in fact a Spinozist had a persistent historical currency. Leibniz himself, furthermore, seems in places to lend countenance to the charge. He says at one point that Spinoza 'has many beautiful thoughts, which correspond to my own' (cited by Ludwig Stein, *Leibniz und Spinoza. Ein Beitrag zur Entwicklungsgeschichte der Leibnizischen Philosophie* (Berlin, 1890), p. 308); he admits, in the *Nouveaux Essais*, that he once inclined towards Spinozism: 'Vous savés que j'estois allé un peu trop loin ailleurs et que je començois à pencher du costé des Spinosistes . . .' (*Philosophische Schriften*, v. 65); he knew and was interested in Spinoza personally. Yet we must set against these not very compromising facts such a thoughtful and emphatic disclaimer as this one, in a letter to Bourguet in 1714: 'Je ne say, Monsieur, comment vous en pouvés tirer quelque Spinosisme; c'est aller un peu vite en consequences. Au contraire c'est justement par ces Monades que le Spinosisme est detruit, car il y a autant de substances veritables, et pour ainsi dire, de miroirs vivans de l'Univers tousjours subsistans, ou d'Univers concentrés, qu'il y a de Monades, au lieu que, selon Spinosa, il n'y a qu'une seule substance. Il auroit raison, s'il n'y avoit point de monades; alors tout, hors de Dieu, seroit passager et s'evanouiroit en simples accidens ou modifications, puisqu'il n'y auroit point la base des substances dans les choses, laquelle consiste dans l'existence des Monades' (*Philosophische Schriften*, iii. 575). For another explicit statement, occurring a dozen years before the disclaimer to Bourget, see *Philosophische Schriften*, vi. 529–31. In short, not only was Spinoza not the teacher of Leibniz, but, in Friedrich Schlegel's penetrating statement, was rather Leibniz's 'invisible, dreaded opponent'. (Schlegel, *Sämmtliche Werke* (Wien, 1822), ii. 238: 'the literary sceptic Bayle, and Locke, the founder of the doctrine of sense-experience, were the chief opponents of Leibniz. . . . The noblest of all, however, is Spinoza, with whom Leibniz so often—even where he does not name him—contends, as if with an invisible, dreaded opponent.')

But how did Leibniz ever come to be identified with his adversary? We can suggest at least four reasons: (1) Leibniz's vast knowledge, which supplied him with view points whose genesis could readily be mistaken; (2) Spinozism as an archetypal form of reproach during Leibniz's own time—hence the term would naturally tend to be cast about in polemics; (3) the eagerness of the Romantics to see Spinozism as the only possible system of thought; (4) Leibniz's concern not to exclude the divine presence from the world, as Descartes had done. In addition, Leibniz himself displayed at times a certain lack of candour about his thorough acquaintance with Spinoza's thought and about his personal acquaintance with Spinoza himself: the world of learning has never been entirely at ease with the duplicity with which Leibniz could address Spinoza himself in language of the most refined and courtly politeness and also write to Thomasius of Spinoza's 'monstrous' opinions. In this instance, however, his seeming duplicity can be seen, I think, less as hypocrisy than as genuine ambivalence of attitude, stemming, on the one hand, from his unfailing respect for intellectual excellence, and, on the other, from his deep-seated aversion to pantheism. One of his early tracts was a *Confessio naturae contra atheistas*, and we may also recall his quick anger, in his correspondence with Arnauld, at Arnauld's virtual accusation of atheism (*Philosophische Schriften*, ii. 16 ff.). In place of the Romantic opinion as to the identity of the thought of Leibniz and Spinoza, therefore, I should, with Georges Friedmann, substitute an assessment in which Leibniz appears, like Coleridge, as a thinker conservative and harmonizing in his tendency, never far from the Christian description of the human situation: 'One of the conclusions that imposes itself when one penetrates the thought of the young Leibniz . . . is the extraordinary precocity of that thought: we are obliged to go back very far in his life, always farther back, in order to find the first germs of the ideas he much later definitively matured and integrated into his system. And these ideas all converge toward a primal nucleus, an original centre . . . the centre of a thought essentially harmonious, religious, substantially united to a Christian vision of man, of his destiny terrestrial and extraterrestrial, of the civilization that men of goodwill ought to work to perfect and to extend throughout the planet. Leibniz was from the beginning essentially different from Spinoza' (Friedmann, *Leibniz et Spinoza* (Paris, 1946), p. 204). To this opinion we may add the even more authoritative view of Freudenthal: 'However many threads bind Leibniz to Spinoza's thought, none the less he never accepted Spinoza's fundamental position; he was never a Spinozist. . . . According to Spinoza, God is the substance of the world, to whom no kind of will and thought pertains. For Leibniz a God lacking understanding and will is unthinkable. In Spinoza all individuality disappears in the one infinite substance; in Leibniz the simple, single existence is the true reality' (*Das Leben Spinozas*, pp. 272–3).

If Leibniz's opposition to Spinoza is emphasized in his expressed opinions, so, too, does opposition inhere in the unexpressed implications of his central conception, that of the monad. Perhaps the term 'monad' came from Bruno, and this might seem to taint it with pantheism; certainly its central emphasis took up Aristotle's 'entelechy' (*Philosophische Schriften*, vi. 609), and this might seem to involve 'it is' presuppositions. Nevertheless, the monad can be conceived in only one way, as an analogy with the self. 'Among all the philosophers', says Durkheim, 'Leibniz is one of those who have felt most vividly what a personality is; for before all, the monad is a personal and autonomous being' (*The Elementary Forms of the Religious Life*, trans. J. W. Swain (London and New York, n.d.), p. 270). The monad is alive and one, and its aliveness is the condition of its oneness. 'Leibniz', says Gottfried Martin, 'regards living creatures as the only unities which are wholes, and he uses for them the term *monads*' (*Leibniz; Logic and Metaphysics*, trans. K. J. Northcott and P. G. Lucas (Manchester,

1964), p. 117). Each monad is a 'living mirror' of 'the universe' (*Philosophische Schriften*, vi. 616), and 'represents the universe according to its point of view' (vi. 599). There 'are as many concentrated universes as there are monads' (iii. 575). If these specifications are to mean anything, it is difficult to see how, except by analogy with human existence, wherein each mind perceives, from its own experience of life, the sum total of all things that are, the concept of the monad could be maintained. As Martin says elsewhere, 'the archetype of unity for . . . Leibniz is the living human being in the comprehensive unity of his existence' (*Kant's Metaphysics and Theory of Science*, trans. P. G. Lucas (Manchester, 1961), p. 1). Thus is it not merely that the monad doctrine opposes a principle of plurality to Spinoza's monism of substance; it also hypostasizes the 'I am', and therefore rejects the thought of Spinoza in its deepest meaning. As Herbart concluded, in the course of an analysis of Spinoza's logic and a comparison of Leibniz and Spinoza, 'the agreement between Leibniz and Spinoza in respect of the pre-established harmony is not decisive, but merely superficial; and one does Leibniz wrong—yes, one does not even understand him—if one seeks real Spinozism in Leibniz's philosophy' (Johann Friedrich Herbart, *Allgemeine Metaphysik* (Königsberg, 1828–9), i. 175). For more of Leibniz's adverse judgements on Spinozism, see *Philosophische Schriften*, iv. 568, 590; vi. 217, 336 ff. For his study of Spinoza's writings, see *Philosophische Schriften*, i. 119, 150–2; Stein, *Leibniz und Spinoza*, pp. 62, 99 ff., 103, 287, 289; Foucher de Careil, *Réfutation inédite de Spinoza par Leibniz* (Paris, 1854).

EXCURSUS NOTE VI

The Connexion between Poetry and Pantheism

POETRY and pantheism have much in common both structurally and historically. Though Urban states that 'Poetry is primarily revelatory of the life and spirit of man', he realizes that 'life and spirit are parts of nature in the sense of reality as a whole' and that 'poetry has much to say about nature': for the poet 'the river runs, the brook ripples and even sings, the mountains rear their head, the sea roars. Even where metaphors are not used, where merely the intuitive language of poetry is employed, this language conjures up a living universe' (*Language and Reality*, pp. 496–7).

The analogies of structure are of three general kinds. First of all, both poetry and pantheism tend to make particular awarenesses involve, or symbolically imply, more extended awarenesses, the extensions being none the less validated by some kind of relationship that they hold in common. As the pantheistic Hermetic tracts say, 'God is in all things, as their root and the source of their being. . . . The Lord manifests himself ungrudgingly through the universe. . . . God contains all things, and there is nothing which is not in God, and nothing in which God is not. Nay, I would rather say, not that God *contains* all things, but that, to speak the full truth, God *is* all things' (*Hermetica*, ed. W. Scott (Oxford, 1924–36), i. 155, 157, 185). In similar manner poetry, as Shelley says in his *Defence*, 'awakens and enlarges the mind itself by rendering it the receptacle of a thousand unapprehended combinations of thought'. Or as Allen Tate says, 'the meaning of poetry is its "tension", the full organized body of all the extension and intension that we can find in it. The remotest figurative significance that we can derive does not invalidate the extensions of the literal statement. Or we may begin with the literal statement and by stages develop the complications of metaphor' ('Tension in Poetry', *Critiques and Essays in Criticism*, ed. R. W. Stallman (New York, 1949), p. 60). Both poetry and pantheism, in short, tend to move the mind from a focal object to more inclusive realizations.

Take, for example, Blake's 'poetic' apprehension by which he sees 'a World in a Grain of Sand'. The meaning compressed into the statement is expanded by Fichte into a specifically 'pantheist' apprehension: 'In every moment of her duration Nature is one connected whole; in every moment each individual part must be what it is, because all the others are what they are; and you could not remove a single grain of sand from its place, without thereby, although perhaps imperceptibly to you, changing something throughout all parts of the immeasurable whole. But every moment of this duration is determined by all past moments . . .; and you cannot conceive even the position of a grain of sand other than it is in the present. . . . Make the experiment, for instance, with the grain of quick-sand. Suppose it to lie some few paces further inland than it does—then must the storm-wind that drove it . . . have been stronger than it actually was [and so on]. . . . How can you know . . . that in such a state of weather as may have been necessary to carry this grain of sand a few paces further inland, some one of your forefathers might not have perished from hunger, or cold, or heat . . . and that thus you might never have been at all, and all that you have ever done, or ever hope to do, must have been obstructed in order that a grain of sand might lie in a different place' (*Werke*, ii. 178–9).

A second similarity between poetry and pantheism is that both tend to allow a scrambling, as it were, of ordinary reference. If, for pantheism, all things are conceived as really one, there is no reason to prefer one to the other, or for aligning or arranging them in any special way, or for regarding any existing alignment as more than temporary and adventitious.

And thirdly, both poetry and pantheism tend to obliterate the boundaries between the realm of thing and the realm of mind: for poetry, objects are invested with meaning, spiritual states are correlated with states of nature, emotions evoke things or the memory of things, while for pantheism either matter is conceived as an appearance of spirit, or spirit as an extension of matter, or both are conceived as variations of a third reality.

With regard to the second similarity, we should remind ourselves that one of the hall-marks of poetry is its habit of presenting combinations of words with words, and of word references to things, that are not encountered in daily speech: 'The mules that angels ride come slowly down/The blazing passes, from beyond the sun'; 'Garlic and sapphires in the mud/Clot the bedded axle-tree'; 'Take this Sea, whose diapason knells/On scrolls of silver snowy sentences.' As Bacon says, 'Poesy is a part of learning in measure of words . . . and doth truly refer to the Imagination; which, being not tied to the laws of matter, may at pleasure join that which nature hath severed, and sever that which nature hath joined, and so make unlawful matches and divorces of things' (*Works*, iii. 343). And Coleridge says that 'In my opinion, Poetry justifies, as *Poetry* independent of any other Passion, some new combinations of Language' (*Letters*, ii. 812). Again, metaphor is 'the heart and core of imaginative process', says Cleanth Brooks ('Metaphor, Paradox, and Stereotype', *British Journal of Aesthetics*, v (1965), 323); and the language of poets, as Shelley says, is 'vitally metaphorical; that is, marks the before unapprehended relations of things and perpetuates their apprehension'. If the poet, therefore, seeks 'unapprehended relations of things' by means of metaphorical language, he finds a natural ally in the pantheist, for whom, in the words of the Hermetic tracts, 'God is the All; and there is nothing that is not included in the All . . . for God is all, and the All permeates all things, and has to do with all things' (*Hermetica*, i. 237, 239).

The 'new combinations of language' that express the 'unapprehended relations of things' have been recognized as necessary to poetry by almost all theoreticians of the subject. We may look almost at random in the history of poetic theory and find illustration of this truth. As the Renaissance rhetorician, Thomas Wilson, says, Cicero advised for poetic discourse 'that woordes translated from one significacion, to another (called of the Grecians, Tropes) bee used to beautifie the sentence, as precious stones are set in a ryng, to commende the golde' (*The Arte of Rhetorique*, Fol. 88). Proceeding then to 'The division of Tropes', Wilson analyzes some of the characteristic figures ('A figure is a certaine kinde, either of sentence, oration, or worde, used after some new or straunge wise, muche unlike to that, which men communely use to speake' (Fol. 89)), which we see to be such poetic staples as catachresis and metonymy, i.e., 'when for a certaine proper woorde we use that whiche is most nighe unto it: As in callyng some water, a fishe ponde, though there be no fishe in it at all' (Fol. 93); and 'when a woorde hath a proper signification of the owne, & beyng referred to an other thyng, hath an other meanyng' (Fol. 93). Such attempts at the analysis of what we would call poetic language are repeated frequently in the rhetorical investigations of the time (Fraunce, for instance, discusses 'two kindes of tropes'. The 'first cōteineth *Metonymia* . . . and *Ironia*. the second . . . *Metaphore* and *Synecdoche*' (*The Arcadian Rhetorike*, The First Booke, Cap. 2., A3)); and their repetition bears witness to the fact that poetic language is characterized by tropes and other juxtapositions, which, as guarantee that such manipulations of the linguistic code will not forfeit meaning, always imply as their condition a systematic unity of reference outside the code. In philosophical terms, what is most closely analogous is pantheism's readiness to construe heterogeneous matters as a unity, to dissolve the many into the one.

From this point of view we may approach Ruskin's 'pathetic fallacy'. Quoting a couplet, 'The spendthrift crocus, bursting through the mould/Naked and shivering, with his cup of gold', Ruskin comments: 'This is very beautiful, and yet very untrue. The crocus is not a spendthrift, but a hardy plant; its yellow is not gold, but saffron. How is it that we enjoy so much the having it put into our heads that it is anything else than a plain crocus?

'It is an important question. For, throughout our past reasonings about art, we have always found that nothing could be good or useful, or ultimately pleasurable, which was untrue. . . . If we think over our favourite poetry, we shall find it full of this kind of fallacy . . . this fallacy is of two principal kinds. Either, as in the case of the crocus, it is the fallacy of wilful fancy, which involves no real expectation that it will be believed; or else it is a fallacy caused by an excited state of the feelings, making us, for the time, more or less irrational. . . . I want to examine the nature of the [second] error . . . in *Alton Locke*—

> They rowed her in across the rolling foam—
> The cruel, crawling foam.

'The foam is not cruel, neither does it crawl. . . . All violent feelings have the same effect. They produce in us a falseness in all our impressions of external things, which I would generally characterize as the "pathetic fallacy".

'Now we are in the habit of considering this fallacy as eminently a character of poetical description, and the temper of mind in which we allow it, as one eminently poetical, because passionate. But, I believe, if we look well into the matter, that we shall find the greatest poets do not often admit this kind of falseness,—that it is only the second order of poets who much delight in it' (*Works*, v. 204–5). Now, while it is true that a 'crocus' is 'not a spendthrift', Ruskin confuses a weak metaphor with a principle of poetry in general. But not to labour the crocus, let us turn to Tennyson's 'flower in the crannied wall'. By Ruskin's implied standards, it would seem a falseness to say '*if* I could understand/What you are, root and all, and all in all, I should know what God and man is'. But I would hazard that on whatever day of our youth we first encountered this little poem, we gave immediate and instinctive assent to its affirmation of the necessary, systematic interrelation of every 'it is' in a total unity. It is a 'poetic' statement, and it is closely parallel to a 'pantheistic' one. 'Each several thing', says Plotinus (*Enneads*, iv. 4. 32), 'is affected by all else in virtue of the common participation in the All.' Leaving aside the vulnerability of Ruskin's moralizing assumptions about the nature of the 'good', the 'useful', and the true, we realize that to accept his literal-minded contentions about proper poetic reference, we must reject Wordsworth in his deepest moments. The 'cruel, crawling foam' can hardly be held up as exciting metaphor, but its predication of emotions for things constitutes no violation in principle—no 'pathetic fallacy'. We have here not an instance of a fallacy, but of a weak observance of a norm.

If Ruskin is disappointing in his treatment of poetic language and reference, his grasp of what art really is seems much surer when he speaks of his beloved architecture. Though 'Architecture', as Coleridge says (*Biographia*, ii. 261), 'exhibits the greatest extent of the difference from nature which may exist in works of art', though it 'involves all the powers of design' and 'shews the greatness of man', it none the less involves a coming together and interfusion of the world of thing and the world of mind: the building or statue possesses a content of stone or other natural material; its form, however, arises in man's mind. This reality Ruskin honours: 'There are but two strong conquerors of the forgetfulness of men, Poetry and Architecture; and the latter in some sort includes the former, and is mightier in its reality: it is well to have not only what men have thought and felt, but what their hands have handled, and their strength wrought, and their eyes beheld, all the days of their life' (*Works*, viii. 224). What he here enunciates is the third main structural similarity of art and pantheism—the tendency, that is, to obliterate distinctions between the internal and external, to join together nature and mind. 'Art', as Coleridge says, 'used collectively for painting, sculpture, architecture and music, is the mediatress between, and reconciler of, nature and man' (*Biographia*, ii. 253). 'In every work of art there is a reconcilement of the external with the internal' (*Biographia*, ii. 258).

But what Ruskin and Coleridge find true for the plastic arts is true also in the symbolic realm of poetry. 'To end this eternal conflict between our Self and the world', sighs Hölderlin from his poet's heart, 'to re-establish the peace above all peace, which passeth all understanding, to unite ourselves with Nature, into one infinite entity, that is the aim of all our aspirations' (quoted in *Hölderlin; His Poems Translated by Michael Hamburger; With a Critical Study* (New York, 1952), p. 85). All poets know the truth of the statement; the structure of poetic image, which is simultaneously a reproduction of things and a vehicle for meaning, legitimizes it; our own experience as lovers of poetry attests it. 'To make the external internal, the internal external,' says Coleridge, 'to make nature thought, and thought nature,—this is the mystery of genius in the Fine Arts' (*Biographia*, ii. 258).

This statement, as likewise those statements by Coleridge in the preceding paragraph, is from 'On Poesy or Art', where he is paraphrasing leading ideas from Schelling's *Ueber das Verhältnis der bildenden Künste zu der Natur*. And Schelling, in his own formulation of these ideas, often is providing, as Heinemann says, 'merely a translation' of Plotinus (*Plotin*, p. 211). The congruences, I suggest, simply testify to the common interest of poetry and pantheism.

Indeed, we should realize that Schelling completes his system with an apotheosis of art not because he derives the theory of art from other forms of philosophical reasoning, but rather because he takes as given and apparent the fact that nature and mind coincide in art, and therefore art exhibits a pre-formed similarity to the structure of his ontological thought. In one of the briefest, deepest, and surely most eloquent of all expositions of philosophies of the Romantic era, Ricarda Huch identifies Schelling's position as virtually synonymous with Romanticism itself: 'For the Romantics, however, this was the most important thing: that the feeling which was inborn for them—to see nature and spirit as one, was confirmed and raised to a formal viewpoint by Schelling' (*Blütezeit der Romantik*, dritte Ausgabe (Leipzig, 1905), p. 173). If the oneness of nature and spirit was a virtually unanimous Romantic intuition, and if 'poesy' (or art) is the confluence of nature and spirit, then it would seem in some sense to follow that Romanticism and poetry would themselves stand on common ground; and in this context the famous statement of Friedrich Schlegel's Fragment 116 takes on added meaning: 'The Romantic style of poetry is the only one which is more than a style, and which is, as it were, poetry itself; for in a certain sense all poetry is, or should be, Romantic.'

But even if we do not wish to adopt a Romantically coloured view of *Natur* and *Geist* as actually one and the same, even if we have no emotional or formal commitments outside the strict province of poetry and its criticism, we find that poetry takes place at the common threshold of the world outside and the world inside. 'Every art', says Dewey, 'does something with some physical material' (*Art as Experience*, New York, 1934, p. 47). 'Poetic structure', says Wimsatt, 'is always a fusion of ideas with material, a statement in which the solidity of symbol and the sensory verbal qualities are somehow not washed out by the abstraction' (*The Verbal Icon* (Lexington, Ky., 1954), p. 115). Or consider Ransom: 'To say "metaphor" tirelessly, with brutal repetition, is one militant way of defending nature as the element to which the Universal is referred, and therefore the element to which poetry has to look. I think the defenders of poetry would not mind saying that they are not prepared to abandon nature, because that would be the abandonment of metaphor, which in turn would be the abandonment of poetry' (John Crowe Ransom, *Poems and Essays* (New York, 1955), p. 181).

In view of the existence of these three similarities of structure between poetry and pantheism, it is not surprising that we find abundant historical examples of a mutual tolerance, and even attraction, between the two realms. We may distinguish two kinds of interest here: first, the actual evocation of pantheist sentiment as subject for poetic utterance, and secondly, the discernment of pantheist rationales in the attitudes and backgrounds of poets—although, of course, the two interests can and do appear together. In the first connexion we may think of Shelley's *Mont Blanc*:

> The everlasting universe of things
> Flows through the mind, and rolls its rapid waves . . .

or of Byron's *Childe Harold*:

> I live not in myself, but I become
> Portion of that around me; and to me
> High mountains are a feeling, but the hum
> Of human cities torture: I can see
> Nothing to loathe in nature, save to be
> A link reluctant in a fleshly chain,
> Classed among creatures, when the soul can flee,
> And with the sky, the peak, the heaving plain
> Of ocean, or the stars, mingle, and not in vain.

or of Wordsworth's *Tintern Abbey*:

> And I have felt
> A presence that disturbs me with the joy
> Of elevated thoughts; a sense sublime
> Of something far more deeply interfused,
> Whose dwelling is the light of setting suns,
> And the round ocean and the living air,
> And the blue sky, and in the mind of man:
> A motion and a spirit, that impels
> All thinking things, all objects of all thought,
> And rolls through all things.

Such examples are perhaps too familiar to require additional citations.

If the specific poems in which pantheism is expressly hailed, or subtly implied, are numerous, so too are the occasions on which we find pantheist preoccupations in the biography of the poet. It was the pantheist sense of the Oneness of the Many that lay behind Baudelaire's conception of a kind of oceanic One that he called 'the universal analogy', which contained all discrete and particular images that might be used for poetry: '. . . ces comparaisons, ces métaphores, et ces épithètes sont puisées dans l'inépuisable fonds de *l'universelle analogie*, et qu'elles ne peuvent être puisées ailleurs' (Baudelaire, *L'Art romantique* (Paris, 1868), p. 317). This can be identified, through hermetic-neoplatonic-cabbalistic transmissions, as the νοῦς of Plotinus, with its hypostases of universal first forms (e.g. *Enneads*, v. 1. 4). Of the various platonic transmitters available to Baudelaire, Swedenborg was undoubtedly the most important, even though identification of a specific source is sometimes made difficult by the fact that the transmitters were nurtured in a common tradition of reading and, besides, tended to borrow from one another (so St. Martin's *Tableau naturel des rapports, qui existent entre dieu, l'homme et l'univers* (Édimbourg [Lyon], 1782), often provides virtually the same correspondence-theory that Swedenborg does). In general, though, it can be said that Baudelaire's metapoetic sonnet, *Correspondances*, is probably fertilized chiefly by Swedenborg: 'First, what correspondence is: the whole natural world corresponds to the spiritual world, and not only the natural world in general, but also in particulars. . . . Whatever, therefore, in the natural world exists and subsists from the spiritual world is called correspondent' (Swedenborg, *Heaven and Hell*, Par. 89). Swedenborg in his turn could relate back, by many routes, to pantheisms of antiquity: 'First of all things is God . . . and second is the Kosmos, which has been made by God in his image'; 'The sensible Kosmos has been made in the image of that other Kosmos, and reproduces eternity in a copy' (*Hermetica*, i. 175, 351). But Swedenborg is especially relevant for poetry. Emerson, after citing one of his statements on the nature of correspondences, comments as follows: 'The fact thus explicitly stated is implied in all poetry, in allegory, in fable, in the use of emblems and in the structure of language' (*Works*, iv. 116).

Baudelaire was steeped in Swedenborgianism; he speaks freely of 'Swedenborg . . . avec ses *correspondances*' (*Les Paradis artificiels* (Paris, 1928), p. 51), and he says that Swedenborg demonstrates 'que tout, forme, mouvement, nombre, couleur, parfum, dans le *spirituel* comme dans le *naturel* est significatif, réciproque, converse, *correspondant*' (*L'Art romantique*, p. 317). See further John McFarland, 'Baudelaire and Swedenborg: The Unity of the Symbolic Tradition' (Harvard Undergraduate Honours Thesis, Unpublished, 1950); Jean Pommier, *La Mystique de Baudelaire* (Paris, 1932); André Ferran, *L'Esthétique de Baudelaire* (Paris, 1933); Auguste Viatte, *Les Sources occultes du romantisme* (Paris, 1928). Yeats, incidentally, was also fortified in his poetical sensibility by the pantheisms of Swedenborg: he says, for instance, of his important and recurring 'gyre' symbol, that 'there are gyres in Swedenborg' (note to *The Winding Stair*, in *The Collected Poems of W. B. Yeats* (New York, 1946), p. 454). And he says elsewhere, 'I had read Swedenborg and Boehme, and my initiation into the "Hermetic Students" had filled my head with Cabalistic imagery' (*A Vision* (London, 1937), p. 12). 'Swedenborg's schematizing . . .', summarizes a commentator, 'probably influenced Yeats very much' (M. I. Seiden, *William Butler Yeats; The Poet as a Mythmaker* (East Lansing, Michigan, 1962), p. 33).

As the statements of Yeats indicate, and as we should emphasize, all these poetry-feeding pantheisms tend to be interchangeable. When we find a poet paying attention to one, he will usually be found to pay attention to others. Thus Saurat, in his classic elucidation of Milton as a student of the Cabala, notes the interchangeability of Cabalism and Swedenborgianism in mystical currents: 'Was it possible after all that the "Puritan" Milton and the "Swedenborgian" Blake belonged to the same school? I am now in a position to answer that they did, that they were both kabbalists, and that this fact explains their common stock of ideas' (Denis Saurat, *Milton; Man and Thinker* (New York, 1925), p. v). And much the same could be said in terms of their common Hermeticism, or their mutual Behmenism (for Milton's Behmenism see Margaret L. Bailey, *Milton and Jakob Boehme* (New York, 1914)). Again, Jacques Gengoux discusses the Cabala in Rimbaud's background (*La Symbolique de Rimbaud; le système; ses sources* (Paris, 1947), p. 64 ff.), but finds also that Spinoza is very important in that background (pp. 201–6).

Probably no poet, however, equalled Yeats in the assimilation of heterogeneous pantheisms. Thus, rather than attempt to ground his key pantheist-poetic doctrine, that of the *Anima Mundi*, in Plotinus as such, we might accept his own description and refer to it as 'the Anima Mundi described by Platonic philosophers, and more especially in modern times by Henry More, which has a memory independent of embodied individual memories' (*Autobiographies* (London, 1926), p. 324). At the same time, of course, Plotinus lies behind Henry More and the 'Platonic philosophers'. The 'Anima Mundi' is thus an analogue of Baudelaire's 'l'universelle analogie', and it too validates by its pantheism the central poetic requirement that images be 'réciproque' and '*correspondant*'. 'If all our mental images', says Yeats cryptically, 'are forms existing in the general vehicle of *Anima Mundi*, and mirrored in our particular vehicle, many crooked things are made straight' (*Per Amica Silentia Lunae*, in *Mythologies* (New York, 1959), p. 352). Certainly Yeats took the notion very seriously: 'And certain men-at-arms there were/Whose images, in the Great Memory stored' (*The Tower*); '. . . a vast image out of *Spiritus Mundi*' (*The Second Coming*).

Whether Henry More or Plotinus be immediately responsible for 'Anima Mundi', it is certain that Plotinus occupied the prime place in Yeats's pantheon. Though he cries out in *The Tower* that 'I mock Plotinus' thought/And I cry in Plato's teeth', and appears to say in the same poem that Plotinus and poetry do not agree ('It seems that I must bid the Muse go pack,/Choose Plato and Plotinus for a friend'), the fact is that these intense statements occur inside, not outside, one of his important poems. Some of Yeats's correspondence in 1926, furthermore, gives us an etiological view of the common interest of poetry and pantheism. 'I have brought but two books', he writes on 25 May, but these, significantly, are 'Baudelaire and MacKenna's *Plotinus*'. And then he says, 'Plotinus is a most ardent and wonderful person.' On 2 July, he writes, 'I am in better health than I was and I do really believe that I owe it to Plotinus as much as to the Tower.' On 6 September he writes that 'I wrote a poem about Byzantium to recover my spirits' (*The Letters of W. B. Yeats*, ed. Allan Wade

(London, 1954), pp. 715, 716, 718). The genesis of one of his finest poems, therefore—*Sailing to Byzantium*—is associated with the reading of Plotinus.

So it was for Goethe. Though he felt his poetic concern would not accord with the study of Kant, Goethe was deeply impressed by Plotinus, especially by Plotinus as the friend of beauty. 'Of all the writings of Plotinus', says H. F. Müller, 'Goethe knew best the tractate on beauty (*Enneads*, i. 6). We might well say, that a congenial spirit spoke to him here' ('Goethe und Plotinos', *Germanisch-romanische Monatsschrift*, vii (1915), 53). And then Müller emphasizes that this food for the sense of beauty was for Goethe prepared by an urge to a pantheistic oneness with nature: 'Goethe had the need to feel himself one with the totality of nature; the consciousness of this unity, the *unio mystica* with the eternal and all-one, was his joy, his religion' (p. 59). See further, K. P. Hasse, *Von Plotin zu Goethe* (Leipzig, 1909); F. Koch, *Goethe und Plotin* (Leipzig, 1925); A. Liebert, 'Goethes Platonismus', *Kantstudien*, xxxvii (1932), 1–48.

The common denominator in all these dependences is the view of reality in which All is One and One is All, with the consequent licencing of poetic realignments of linguistic reference. 'I deem it impossible', says one of the Hermetic tracts, 'that . . . the Father or Master of all things can be named by a single name, though it be made up of ever so many others; I hold that he is nameless, or rather, that all names are names of him. For he in his unity is all things; so that we must either call all things by his name, or call him by the names of all things' (*Hermetica*, i. 333). And in Plotinus we find that particularities in the phenomenological realm (the realm of *psyche*) are resolved into universal identity in the transcendental realm of *nous*: 'Admiring the world of sense as we look out upon its vastness and beauty . . . let us mount to its archetype . . there we are to contemplate all things as members of the *nous*. . . . Soul (*psyche*) deals with thing after thing—now Socrates, now a horse . . . but the divine mind (*nous*) is All, and therefore its entire content is simultaneously present in that identity' (*Enneads*, v. 1. 4). But this doctrine is derived directly from Plotinus's pantheistic monism: '. . . the beginning must be a really existent One, wholly and truly One, while its sequent, poured down in some way from the One, is All, a total which has participation in unity *and whose every member is similarly all and one*' (*Enneads*, v. 3. 15—italics mine). Again: '. . . all entwines into a unity; and there is something wonderful in the agreement holding among these various things of varied source, even of sources frankly opposite; the secret lies in a variety within a unity' (*Enneads*, iv. 4. 38).

This last pantheist statement by Plotinus, 'difficult indeed, but under a rough and austere rind concealing fruit worthy of Paradise' (*Biographia*, ii. 239) brings the wheel full circle. As Coleridge says, the 'most general definition of beauty' is 'Multëity in Unity', or 'THE REDUCTION OF MANY TO ONE' (*Biographia*, ii. 232, 238). And yet the final word of all belongs to T. E. Hulme: 'In the least element of beauty we have a total intuition of the whole world. Every artist is a kind of pantheist' (*Speculations; Essays on Humanism and the Philosophy of Art* (London, 1949), p. 131).

EXCURSUS NOTE VII

Swedenborg

SWEDENBORG in himself is neither the most profound nor the most consequent of pantheists, though he is certainly one of the most prolix; but he has a special importance as a kind of clearing house for Romantically inclined pantheism (incidentally, he acknowledges ancient authority in his doctrine of correspondences: 'To the Ancients the chief of knowledges was that of correspondences, but today this is lost' (*Heavenly Arcana*, par. 3021)), especially in its role as friend to poetry. He was more accessible than Boehme or Bruno or Plotinus, less difficult and austere than Spinoza, more important than Oetinger or St. Martin or Kleuker, more public than Freemasonry or Rosicrucianism. In addition—as we can see from Kant's interest in him, culminating in the *Träume eines Geistersehers*—he was, by his claims to second-sight and special experience, a pique to the curiosity of the culture of the late eighteenth century. See, for Swedenborg in particular and for eighteenth-century mystical currents in general, Jacques Roos, *Aspects littéraires du mysticisme philosophique et l'influence de Boehme et de Swedenborg au début du romantisme: William Blake, Novalis, Ballanche* (Strasbourg, 1951); Eugene Susini, *Franz von Baader et le romantisme mystique* (Paris, 1942); Pauline Bernheim, *Balzac und Swedenborg; Einfluß der Mystik Swedenborgs und Saint-Martins auf die Romandichtung Balzacs* (Berlin, 1914). Most interesting of all, for our emphasis on the skeletal Spinozism underlying Swedenborg's torrent of words, is a parochial but none the less perceptive tract by Ethan Allen Hitchcock, who was later to become a Union general in the Civil War: *Swedenborg, A Hermetic Philosopher; Being a Sequel to Remarks on Alchemy and the Alchemists Showing that Emanuel Swedenborg was a Hermetic Philosopher and that his Writings may be Interpreted from the Point of View of Hermetic Philosophy. With a Chapter Comparing Swedenborg and Spinoza* (New York, 1858). The essay reflected the vogue for Swedenborg among the American intellectuals of the mid-nineteenth century; we recall Emerson's chapter in *Representative Men*; Bronson Alcott and the elder James were also his devotees.

Coleridge himself seems to have been too sophisticated philosophically to have fallen under Swedenborg's spell. He knew the seer's writings well ('all Swedenborg's works published within his lifetime would have been available to Coleridge', notes Kurtz, 'and it would be interesting to know exactly how many of these Coleridge possessed or had read. It is certain that on January 6, 1821, he was perusing a translation of the *Universal Theology of the New Church*, that he made a marginal note in the *De Cultu et Amore Dei* on September 22, 1821, and that at various dates he annotated the *De Caelo et . . . Inferno*, the *De Equo Albo et de Verbo*, etc., an English translation, *The Nature of the Intercourse between the Soul and the Body*, the *Oeconomia Regni Animalis*, etc., the *Regnum Animale*, etc., and three translations, viz., *True Christian Religion, The Wisdom of the Angels concerning Divine Love and Divine Wisdom . . .* and *The Wisdom of Angels concerning Divine Providence*. To these ten works, the *Prodromus . . .* must be added' (Benjamin P. Kurtz, 'Coleridge on Swedenborg with Unpublished

Marginalia on the "Prodromus" ', *Essays and Studies, University of California Publications in English Volume 14* (Berkeley and Los Angeles, 1943), p. 201). Coleridge thus knew Swedenborg's writings well, and admired him as a man, but he was more critical of his doctrines than almost any other prominent Romantic intellectual (Moehler's theological attack in his *Symbolismus* occurred after Coleridge's death, and was mounted by a man notably out of sympathy with Romanticism). At one point, significantly, Coleridge aligns Swedenborg with the great pantheists: 'I have often thought of writing a work to be entitled . . . Vindication of Great Men unjustly branded; and at such times the names prominent to my mind's eye have been Giordano Bruno, Jacob Behmen, Benedict Spinoza, and Emanuel Swedenborg' (*Works*, v. 526). But in general Swedenborg did not loom large in his preoccupations, and particularly not in relation to his poetry. He felt that 'as a moralist Swedenborg is above all praise; and . . . as a naturalist, psychologist, and theologian, he has strong and varied claims on the gratitude and admiration of the professional and philosophical student' (*Works*, v. 527), but he never doubted that Swedenborg was deluded in his psychic claims: this 'great and excellent man was led into his [mistaken beliefs] by becoming the subject of a very rare, but not (it is said) altogether unique, conjunction of the somnaitive [*sic*] faculty (by which the products of the understanding, that is to say, words, conceptions and the like, are rendered instantaneously into forms of sense) with the voluntary and other powers of the waking state . . . by some hitherto unexplained affections of Swedenborg's brain and nervous system, he from the year 1743, thought and reasoned through the *medium* and instrumentality of a series of appropriate and symbolic visual and auditaul [*sic*] images, spontaneously rising before him, and these so clear and so distinct, as at length to overpower perhaps his first suspicions of their subjective nature, and to become objective for him' (*Works*, v. 526–7). And in fact he elegantly guillotined the entire structure of Swedenborg's claims: 'this is the grounding, and at the same time pervading error, of the Swedenborgians;— that they overlook the distinction between congruity with reason, truth of consistency, or internal possibility of this or that being objectively real, and the objective reality as fact' (*Works*, v. 525).

Though Coleridge was too much a follower of Kant to allow himself to become involved with Swedenborg's semi-mysticism, the poet's need for pantheism is omnipresent, and Coleridge's involvement with Schelling testifies to that need in the same way that the involvements of Blake and Baudelaire with Swedenborg testified to it in their efforts. Of special interest with regard to the possibility of such a reciprocity is Friedemann Horn, *Schelling und Swedenborg*, (Zürich, 1954).

As to the similarity of Schelling and Swedenborg, we may adopt Emerson's conclusion: 'In short, he [Swedenborg] was a believer in the Identity-philosophy, which he held not idly, as the dreamers of Berlin or Boston, but which he experienced with and established through years of labor . . .' (*Works*, iv. 106–7).

None the less, Swedenborg's pantheism seems rather a pale prototype of Schelling's. The dynamisms of Schelling's metaphorical conception are quite at variance with a static—a musty, even—quality in Swedenborg. 'His perception of nature', says Emerson, 'is not human and universal, but is mystical

and Hebraic. He fastens each natural object to a theologic notion;—a horse
signifies carnal understanding; a tree, perception; the moon, faith; a cat means
this, an ostrich that. . . . The slippery Proteus is not so easily caught' (*Works*,
iv. 121). Thus, for Emerson, 'The vice of Swedenborg's mind is its theological
determination' (*Works*, iv. 134). He criticizes 'the incongruous importation of
a foreign rhetoric. "What have I to do," asks the impatient reader, "with jasper
and sardonyx, beryl and chalcedony; what with arks and passovers, ephahs and
ephods; what with . . . heave-offerings and unleavened bread, chariots of fire,
dragons crowned and horned, behemoth and unicorn?" ' (*Works*, iv. 135). And
of Swedenborg's vision of heaven and hell, Emerson says that 'an ardent and
contemplative young man, at eighteen or twenty years, might read once these
books of Swedenborg, these mysteries of love and conscience, and then throw
them aside forever' (*Works*, iv. 132). Again, Blake, in *The Marriage of Heaven
and Hell*, says that 'Swedenborg has not written one new truth. . . . Any man of
mechanical talents may, from the writings of Paracelsus or Jacob Behmen,
produce ten thousand volumes of equal value with Swedenborg's. . . .' In such
an enterprise, Boehme's *Signatura Rerum* would be a central document.

In its structure, Swedenborg's pantheism conceives of love and wisdom
emanating from God through a spiritual world to form a world of things: 'The
universe in the greatest and least things, and in the first and last, is so full of the
Divine love and Divine wisdom that it may be said to be Divine love and Divine
wisdom in an image. That this is so, is clearly evident from the correspondence
of all things of the universe with all things of man . . . the created universe is an
image representative of God-Man, and . . . it is this love and wisdom which in
the universe are presented in an image' (*The Divine Love and Wisdom*, par. 52).
Again, 'The visible things in the created universe testify that nature has produced nothing, but that the Divine produces all things from itself, and through
the spiritual world' (par. 349). Such formulations clearly owe something to
Plotinus: Ernst Benz points out the general agreement of Swedenborg scholars
that 'the historical prototype of the doctrine of correspondences is the ancient
Neoplatonic image-metaphysics' (*Emanuel Swedenborg; Naturforscher und Seher*
(München, 1948), p. 388). Even more surely, as Hitchcock saw, they are a
restatement of essentials of Hermetic thought. The researches of Frances Yates
have demonstrated how very much more pervasive than previously realized
was the dissemination of Hermetic philosophemes in the Renaissance; and we
can have little doubt that Swedenborg, like Bruno before him, was deeply
involved in this persistent subterranean tradition. In restating the macrocosm-
microcosm theory of correspondences (for the currency of which in the Renaissance, see, e.g., E. M. W. Tillyard, *The Elizabethan World Picture* (London, 1945),
pp. 77–93), Swedenborg insists on the Hermetic essential that man is not the
image of a dead world, but that the world is a living image of man (or of God,
who is, in Swedenborg's Hermetic-Cabalist conception, 'A Great Man'). Likewise, he constantly restates the central Hermetic identification of God and the
sun (e.g. *The Divine Love and Wisdom*, par. 353). Despite his division of a natural
world with a natural sun, and a spiritual world with a spiritual sun, Swedenborg
is a pantheist: his two worlds are, as in the divided realms of Plotinus, the inner
elaboration of a monistic One: 'All things in the world', says Swedenborg,

'exist from the Divine and are clothed with such forms in nature as enable them to be there and to perform use, and thus to correspond' (par. 108).

For the Hermetic tradition, and for its interfusions with Platonist, Gnostic, and Cabalist beliefs, see the four-volume work of A.-J. Festugière, *La Révélation d'Hermès Trismégiste* (Paris, 1950–4), and the extensive notes and commentary to the four-volume edition of W. Scott, *Hermetica* (Oxford, 1924–36). For brief treatments see F. A. Yates, *Giordano Bruno and the Hermetic Tradition* (Chicago, 1964), pp. 1–61, and C. H. Dodd, *The Interpretation of the Fourth Gospel* (Cambridge, 1953), pp. 10–53. The texts in the Scott edition are, by common consent, so loosely edited as to be virtually unusable, and for exact work only the texts established by Festugière and A. D. Nock (*Corpus Hermeticum* (Paris, 1945–54)) are adequate.

EXCURSUS NOTE VIII
The New Cosmology

As Cassirer says, 'The new cosmology, the heliocentric system of Copernicus' called into question 'man's claim to being the centre of the universe. . . . Man is placed in an infinite space in which his being seems to be a single and vanishing point. He is surrounded by a mute universe, by a world that is silent to his religious feelings and to his deepest moral demands' (*Essay on Man*, p. 30). Compare the restless and gloomy phrases of Nietzsche: 'Is there not since Copernicus an unbroken progress in the self-belittling of man, his *will* to self-belittlement? Alas, his faith in his dignity, uniqueness, irreplaceability in the chain of being is gone—he has become animal, literal, unqualified and unmitigated animal, he, who in his earlier belief was almost God. . . . Since Copernicus man seems to have been on an inclined plane—he rolls faster and faster away from the centre—where to? into nothingness?' ('Zur Genealogie der Moral', in *Werke*, vii. 474). So too Freud, who conceives Copernicus as having dealt the self-esteem of mankind the first of three great traumatic and humbling shocks (the second and third being, respectively, the work of Darwin and that of psychoanalysis itself): 'The central position of the earth was to man a surety for its ruling role in the universe, and corresponded with his inclination to feel himself master of this world. The destruction of this narcissistic illusion is connected for us with the name and work of Nicholas Copernicus in the sixteenth century. . . . When this work found general recognition, human self-complacency experienced its first, cosmological, shock' ('Eine Schwierigkeit der Psychoanalyse', *Werke*, xii. 6–7). For more specialized considerations of the impact of the new science on culture, see, e.g., Marjorie Nicolson, *The Breaking of the Circle; Studies in the Effect of the 'New Science' upon Seventeenth Century Poetry* (Evanston, Ill., 1950); Charles M. Coffin, *John Donne and the New Philosophy* (New York, 1937); Friedrich Kuntze, 'Pascals letztes Problem', *Archiv für Geschichte der Philosophie*, xxi (1908), 397–415,

469–91; Robert Grénoble, 'La représentation du monde physique à l'époque classique', *XVIIe Siècle. Bulletin de la societé d'étude du xviie siècle*, xxx (1956), 5–24.

The destruction of the medieval cover of assurances about man's place in the cosmos was a major factor in the formation of the widespread sense of alienation and gloom that students of literature term 'Jacobean melancholy'. Although it is true that one current of early seventeenth-century thought, which we associate with the progressive optimism of Bacon, does not fall within the general description of Jacobean melancholy, and although we should keep in mind Douglas Bush's scepticism about the very existence of any special melancholic strain in the attitudes of the time (Bush, *English Literature in the Earlier Seventeenth Century 1600–1660*, second edition (Oxford, 1962), pp. 3–4), I fail to see how sensitive reading in the literature of that era can do other than affirm the pervasive presence of gloom and disillusionment, in both England and France. 'All our wit/And reading brings us to a truer sense/Of sorrow', says the Duchess of Malfi. Our bodies serve to preserve earthworms, says Bosola, and as for the soul in our bodies, 'this world is like her little turf of grass, and the heaven o'er our heads, like her looking-glass, only gives us a miserable knowledge of the small compass of our prison'. I therefore agree with the more traditional view that melancholy and anxiety, whatever their cause, do characterize in a special way the psychic aura of various and important cultural manifestations, both in the early and late parts of the century. See, e.g., George Williamson, 'Mutability, Decay, and Seventeenth-Century Melancholy', *ELH*, ii (1935), 121–50; Victor Harris, *All Coherence Gone* (Chicago, 1949); Lawrence Babb, *The Elizabethan Malady; A Study of Melancholia in English Literature from 1580 to 1642* (East Lansing, Michigan, 1951); Herschel Baker, *The Wars of Truth; Studies in the Decay of Christian Humanism in the Earlier Seventeenth Century* (Cambridge, Mass., 1952), pp. 43–78. For a contrary opinion, which concurs with that of Bush, see C. J. Sisson, 'The Mythical Sorrows of Shakespeare', *Studies in Shakespeare; British Academy Lectures*, ed. Peter Alexander (London, 1964), pp. 9–32.

In any event, the new cosmology had a profoundly unsettling effect even when that effect was not one of melancholy. Montaigne's conviction that 'La plus calamiteuse & *fraile* de toutes les creatures, c'est l'homme' (*Essais*, ii. 158), and indeed his whole scathing exposure of human vanity, inanity, folly, and insignificance reflected, if it did not strictly follow from, the revelations of the new astronomy. What has induced man, he asks, to believe that the heavens were established for him: 'Qui luy a persuadé que ce branle admirable de la voute celeste, la lumiere eternalle de ces flambeaux roulans si fierement sur sa teste, les mouuemens espouuantables de cette mer infinie, soyent establis . . . pour sa commodité & pour son seruice? Est-il possible de rien imaginer si ridicule que cette miserable & chetiue creature . . . ?' (*Essais*, ii. 156). He says scornfully that the heavens revolved about our heads for three thousand years, or so everyone believed until Copernicus, and who knows but that in another thousand years still another opinion will replace these two: 'Le ciel & les estoilles ont branlé trois mille ans; tout le monde l'auoit ainsi creu, jusques à ce que *Cleanthes le Samien* . . . s'auisa de maintenir que c'estoit la terre qui se mouuoit . . . &, de nostre temps, Copernicus a si bien fondé cette doctrine qu'il s'en sert tresregléement à toutes les consequences *Astronomiques*. Que prendrons nous de là, sinon qu'il *ne nous doit chaloir le quel ce soit des deus*? Et qui sçait qu'vne tierce opinion, d'icy à mille ans, ne renuerse les deux precedentes ?' (*Essais*, ii. 322). It is thus that Montaigne can say, with gloomy wit, 'L'ignorance qui estoit naturellement en nous, nous l'auons, par longue estude, confirmée & auerée' (*Essais*, ii. 223)—we have, by long study, confirmed our natural ignorance. Deprived of his central position in a cosmos made and regulated for his benefit, man becomes an object of contempt: 'Nous auons pour nostre part l'inconstance, l'irresolution, l'incertitude, le deuil, la superstition, la solicitude des choses à venir, voire, apres nostre vie, l'ambition, l'auarice . . . la guerre, le mensonge, la desloyauté, la detraction & la curiosité. Certes, nous auons estrangement surpaié ce beau discours dequoy nous nous glorifions, & cette capacité de iuger & connoistre' (*Essais*, ii. 204).

If Montaigne's sceptical rejection of the idea of man's dignity was one kind of response to the new knowledge supplied by Copernicus, so, in another way, was the systematic scepticism of Descartes. Descartes, seemingly so cavalier towards the learning of the past, was actually a radical conservative, who attempted to save man's dignity by removing that dignity from any connexion with the natural world—amputating, as it were, at the hip when to other doctors only the foot seemed infected. It was Descartes' sweeping rejection of the learning of the past, rather than, as the handbooks would have it, the *Clovis* of Desmarets de Saint-Sorlin, that was the real trigger for the issues of the *querelle*. For the *querelle* was not really the trivial plaything of the literary court, but testimony to a psychological abyss opened up when the medieval alliance of religion and science was breached by Copernicus and Luther (compare Montaigne: '. . . lors que les nouuelletez de Luther commençoient d'entrer en credit & esbranler en beaucoup de lieux nostre ancienne creance' (*Essais*, ii. 141)), and when the comfortable familiarity of a closed medieval image of the cosmos gave way before the assault of Copernicus and Bruno. Although Digges preceded Bruno in the dramatization of the new immensity of the 'infinite spaces', it was Bruno who exerted pressure on religion. 'Giordano Bruno', as Heim says, 'was the first with audacious hands to strike the roof off the world, disclosing space without end. And with that the thought of a world beyond, in its former significance, became unframable. . . . The discovery of the infinitude of the universe—produced a new situation. Bruno himself not only made the discovery; he also showed the consequences for religion. With the breakdown of the Ptolemaic idea of the world as a self-inclosed system, he felt that the possibility of ever distinguishing God and the world from each other went also. The divine line was gone; the world and the world beyond were no longer to be separated' (Karl Heim, *God Transcendent; Foundation for a Christian Metaphysic*, trans. E. P. Dickie (New York, 1936), pp. 31, 34). Though Bruno was not a scientist himself, his conceptualization of the meaning of New Science mediated between Copernicus and such later developers of Copernican postulates as Galileo and Kepler. Compare the report of Kepler's complaining that Galileo neglected to record his obligations: 'I had this morning occasion for friendly dispute with Kepler', writes a mutual friend to Galileo—'He said concerning your book [*Sidereus nuncius*] that truly it has revealed the divinity of your talent, but that . . . you make no mention of those writers who gave the signal and the occasion for your discovery, naming among them Giordano Bruno as an Italian, Copernicus and himself' (quoted in Dorothea Waley Singer, *Giordano Bruno; His Life and Thought* (New York, 1950), p. 189). For the traditional view of the *querelle*, consult the book by Rigault, which is probably still the most complete on the subject (Hippolyte Rigault, *Histoire de la querelle des anciens et des modernes* (Paris, 1856)).

EXCURSUS NOTE IX

The Personal Influence of Jacobi

JACOBI, throughout his career, possessed a kind of submerged centrality for the thought of his peers and contemporaries, and his attitudes were respected by almost everyone (at least until the advent of Schelling's *Denkmal*); yet only a few of his contemporaries could bring themselves to accept the radical existentialism of his position. We see this curious amalgam of respect and distrust in one of Crabb Robinson's entries. In Voss's house, says Robinson in 1803, 'I once met the famous philosopher Frederick Jacobi, with whose personal dignity and beauty I was much struck. He was, take him for all in all, one of the handsomest men I ever saw. He was greatly respected. . . . Jacobi is at the head of a school of thought which has attracted men of feeling and imagination, but which men of a dry and logical turn have considered a corruption of philosophy. Yet opposed as he was to the critical philosophy on account of its dryness, and to the poets for their supposed want of religion, he was to no one's taste precisely. . . . Goethe . . . seemed never to be quite reconciled to his way of showing religious zeal' (Crabb Robinson, *Diary*, i. 170). Compare Friedrich Schlegel: 'Jacobi's living philosophy is a mature result of his individual experience, and a critical opponent of that philosophy which does business only with the dead letter' (August Wilhelm Schlegel und Friedrich Schlegel, *Charakteristiken und Kritiken* (Königsberg, 1801), i. 6). For confirmation of Robinson's report on the striking personal appearance of Jacobi, compare Goethe: 'Von stattlicher Figur, edler Haltung, feinen Manieren und würdigem Ernst, wüßte ich nicht leicht mir eine liebenswürdigere Erscheinung zu denken als eben Jacobi' (Goethe, *Gespräche*, iii. no. 2309, p. 161). Because he was 'to no one's taste precisely', Jacobi's overt influence was limited to only a handful of disciples: Friedrich Roth, who edited his correspondence; Kajetan Weiller, who published a two-volume work (*Der Geist der allerneuesten Philosophie der HH. Schelling, Hegel, und Kompagnie. . . . Zum Gebrauche für das gebildetere Publikum überhaupt* (München, 1803–5)); and Friedrich Köppen, whose *Schellings Lehre oder das Ganze der Philosophie des absoluten Nichts* (Hamburg, 1803) is an elegantly reasoned attack on Schelling that exhibits not only adherence to Jacobi's thought, but a remarkable echo of the very tone of his philosophical voice. In addition to these disciples, Jacobi had, as *Halbanhänger*, Jacob Salat, and, as comrades-in-arms, Fries and

Bouterwek. ('I believe', said Jacobi to Bouterwek, 'that all the difference between us lies in the fact that the proposition: "Reason can exist only in Person" is an axiom to me but not to you' (*Jacobi's Briefe an Bouterwek*, p. 159).) More impressive, however, than such overt witnesses to Jacobi's influence is the submerged dependence on him shown by some of his most important opponents. We have already had occasion to note two instances: Goethe's education in Spinozism, and Schelling's derivation of his methexic concept of 'potence'—although Jacobi possibly was unaware of this dependence himself, for in some disgusted remarks about the ultra-Schellingian tract by Eschenmayer (*Die Philosophie in ihrem Uebergang zur Nichtphilosophie*) he shows no possessiveness about the term at all: 'Truly has Eschenmayer done to his spiritual father, Schelling, what the daughters of Pelias did to their corporeal father: instead of bathing him to health and immortality, he has hacked and cooked him to death. . . . Enough of this confused little book. . . . With it the Schellingian system has now truly culminated. This modish inconsequence with *Potenz* and *Potenziren*, this mish-mash of scholastic and ill-applied mathematical terms, this mere trickery with names, appears here in its highest glory, and conducts itself so impudently that it is not to be borne' (*Jacobi's Briefe an Bouterwek*, 8 Jan. 1804, pp. 60–62). To these examples we may add another, more ironically revealing, from the development of Fichte's thought. Ostensibly Fichte's philosophy originated as an attempt to protect Kantianism from the sceptical assaults of Maimon and Schulze. In a long and admiring review of Schulze's *Aenesidemus* in the *Jenaer allgemeine Literaturzeitung* in 1794, Fichte concedes that 'many a reader of *Aenesidemus* will have given the critical philosophy up for lost', but then presents himself as the conditional champion of Kantianism, stating that 'this philosophy in itself, according to its inner content, stands as strongly as ever', needing however, 'still more work . . . in order to arrange the materials in a properly put together and unshakeable whole'; and he calls the intellectual world 'to contribute to this sublime goal' (Fichte, *Werke*, i. 24–25). In his own contribution to this sublime goal, the *Ueber den Begriff der Wissenschaftslehre oder der sogenannten Philosophie* (Weimar, 1794), Fichte accordingly begins with an obeisance to Schulze and Maimon: 'The author of this treatise was completely convinced by reading the new sceptics, especially Aenesidemus and the superb writings of Maimon, of what to him had earlier seemed highly probable: that philosophy, even through the most recent efforts of discerning men, is not yet raised to the rank of an evident science. He believed himself to have found the cause of this, and to have discovered an easy way of completely satisfying all the well-grounded demands of the sceptics on the critical philosophy, and to unite the dogmatic and critical system in their conflicting claims, just as the conflicting claims of the different dogmatic systems are united by the critical philosophy' (*Werke*, i. 29). Despite such explicit acknowledgement, at the outset of his philosophizing, of dependence upon Schulze and Maimon, however, we find that Fichte later, in his hour of philosophical need—that is, when confronted with the disapproval of the mighty Kant himself—apparently found their sceptical positions no adequate bastion for his thought; instead he abandoned these untenable fortifications and retreated, as it were, into the keep of the castle: into the sceptical anti-Kantianism of Jacobi. We have had occasion to quote earlier Kant's *Erklärung in*

Beziehung auf Fichtes Wissenschaftslehre, where he delivered, in 1799, an emphatic public 'Lossagen'—a wanting-no-part-of—concerning the *Wissenschaftslehre*. Prior to this public declaration, however, Fichte had learned of Kant's displeasure by private report. ('Herr Forberg', says Fichte in a rather pitiable and straw-grasping note, 'can "from the *best source* [presumably from a letter from Kant to him] certify, that Kant is of the opinion that my system is wholly different from the Kantian". . . . It may be that Kant has uttered such an opinion. But the question is whether he has spoken of the *truly read and truly understood* Wissenschaftslehre' (*Werke*, i. 469 n.).) So where in the *Erste Einleitung in die Wissenschaftslehre* of 1797 he confidently asserted a claim of inheritance to the Kantian philosophical fortune: 'I have always said, and say it here again, that my system is nothing other than the Kantian' (*Werke*, i. 420), he now has to amend this statement to one in which the Wissenschaftslehre 'keine andere sey, als die wohlverstandene Kantische' (*Werke*, i. 469)—is nothing else but the 'properly understood' Kantian. In such an understanding, the central Kantian conception of the external *Ding an sich* was dropped, and the *Ding an sich* was relocated in the ego—to the outrage of Kant and his followers, and to the destruction of the final meaning of Kantianism. Fichte therefore focuses all his fire upon 'was das wunderbarste bei der Sache ist — die Entdeckung, daß Kant von einem vom Ich verschiedenen Etwas nichts wisse' (*Werke*, i. 481). And at this moment of philosophical truth, with the thing-in-itself in the balance, Fichte summons to his aid, not Maimon, not Schulze, but Jacobi: 'Everyone could read the most thorough and complete proof of this ten years ago. It is in Jacobi's *Idealismus und Realismus, ein Gespräch* (Breslau, 1787) in the appendix, *Ueber den transcendentalen Idealismus*, pp. 207 ff. There Jacobi cited and brought together the most decisive and striking utterances of Kant on this point, in Kant's own words. I am not going to do again what is already done and what cannot be more fittingly done, so I refer the reader to Jacobi's book itself, since the whole book, like all the philosophical writings of Jacobi, may well even yet be one of the century's useful readings' (*Werke*, i. 481–2). For Fichte, Jacobi was to modern philosophy what Plato was to ancient (*Werke*, v. 470); he was 'without doubt one of the best stylists of the century' (*Werke*, viii. 35); he was 'along with Kant one of the reformers in philosophy' (*Werke*, ii. 334); he was 'the clearest thinker of our time' (*Werke*, i. 483).

These public testimonials by an established philosopher can be compared to an entry in the private diary of the youthful Franz von Baader in the 1780s: 'Jacobi's writings and the philosophical lectures on the new Testament, which I am now beginning to read, are thriving very much with me and seem *lastingly* to affect my spirit' (Baader, *Werke*, xi. 186). Later the youthful Schleiermacher, the youthful Feuerbach, and the youthful Kierkegaard likewise experienced the formative influence of Jacobi. This influence was sometimes difficult to assess, for, as Friedrich Schlegel said, 'the elastic point from which Jacobi's philosophy proceeded was not an objective imperative, but an individual optative' (*Charakteristiken und Kritiken*, i. 30). But it was extensive. 'Around the year 1800', writes David Baumgardt, 'Jacobi became the banner-bearer and place-holder for all the strivings that could not find enough room in the world of the broad, humanistically motivated classical idealism of German metaphysics. Instead of reliance on the spirit of the Stoa or a harmonizing eudaemonism, he was able to catch sight of, in many cases more deeply than his era, the austere and dark values of Christianity; instead of ethical pantheism, he urged theism; instead of conciliatory ethical monism, abrupt dualism; instead of an ethic of world-testing, an ethic of world-overcoming; instead of an ethic of all-conceiving reason, the inscrutability of ethical not-knowledge. And accordingly he was able to point the way beyond Baader to Kierkegaard' (*Der Kampf um den Lebenssinn unter den Vorläufern der modernen Ethik* (Leipzig, 1933), pp. 364-5).

Indeed, Schelling himself, even after the ferocities of the *Denkmal*, delivered after Jacobi's death a generous summary of his position, with the judgement that 'ist vielleicht Jacobi die lehrreichste Persönlichkeit in der ganzen Geschichte der neueren Philosophie' (Schelling, *Werke*, x. 168). As Lévy-Bruhl says, 'Would Schelling ever have thought, when he pitilessly crushed his aged adversary, that a day would come when he would be inspired by him? That is, however, what happened, in 1833, in his lessons on the history of modern philosophy. In order to criticize Hegel, Schelling "armoured himself", as Kuno Fischer says, with some of the arguments so frequently invoked by Jacobi. Like Jacobi, he explains that logic never coincides with the real, and that it is vain to attempt to deduce that which is. Indeed, one of these lessons is devoted almost entirely to Jacobi. Schelling renders full justice to his merit. He points out very well the place that Jacobi occupies at the beginning of the reaction against the rationalism of the eighteenth century, and calls him, from this point of view, "perhaps the most instructive personality in the whole history of modern philosophy" ' (Lucien Lévy-Bruhl, *La Philosophie de Jacobi* (Paris, 1894), pp. 227-8).

During his lifetime, however, especially after the appearance of the *Denkmal*, Jacobi was invariably underestimated by the young transcendentalists, at the same time that they almost all acknowledged debts to his insight. In Steffens's recollection of a visit to Jacobi, for instance, the Norwegian *Naturphilosoph* can on the one hand patronizingly refer to his aged host as a 'once not insignificant man', and on the other gratefully recall that it was Jacobi who had launched him on his philosophical career by directing his attention to Spinoza, and had in addition pointed the age to Giordano Bruno: 'I therefore visited Jacobi', says Steffens, and then, after an almost unique description of the eccentric household—or court, rather—of Jacobi, he muses, apropos Jacobi's supposed annihilation by Schelling, that 'I could not forget that Jacobi was the first one to win me to speculation, by making me acquainted with Spinoza. I believed, in fact, that he, by pointing out the depths of Leibniz's philosophy, had exercised a positive influence on the later time of philosophy. To be sure, this time had fallen apart in its beginning—a mightier one, against which he sought in vain to arm himself, had come. But I could not regard this defeat of a once not insignificant man, in his old age, without a certain sadness' (Steffens, *Was ich erlebte*, viii. 380, 387-8).

The range of Jacobi's influence was inevitably restricted by the limitations he imposed upon himself. As we have seen (p. 128 above), Coleridge's attitude towards him was ambivalent: much as he admired Jacobi he could not reconcile himself to the exclusiveness of Jacobi's aims. Jacobi was essentially a moralist.

'The secret of the moral sense and moral feeling is the secret of lasting life. . . . In the moral feeling there exists a presentiment of eternity. . . . Faith and experience are therefore the only way by which we can attain to knowledge of the truth' (Jacobi, *Werke*, vi. 138). Jacobi was 'highly gifted' (*genialisch*) but not a 'genius' (*Genie*), said Friedrich Schlegel, 'for what else is genius except the lawfully free inner community of several talents? The constitution of Jacobi's inner life, however, was not truly republican. . . . The theological talent dominated with an unlimited despotism over the philosophical and poetic talents, which had to render it slavish service, and it set itself up, on its own authority, as the universal lawgiver . . .' (*Charakteristiken und Kritiken*, i. 38). So exclusively did Jacobi limit himself that Mme de Staël found it necessary to give him a chapter all his own in her *De l'Allemagne* (we find 'Jacobi' following such headings as 'Du principe de la morale dans la nouvelle philosophie allemande' and 'De la morale scientifique'), where she emphasizes that it is 'surtout comme grand moraliste que sa réputation est universelle': 'It is difficult to find, in any country, a man of letters of a more distinguished nature than that of Jacobi; with all advantages of figure and fortune, he has devoted himself since his youth forty years ago to meditation. Philosophy is ordinarily a consolation or an asylum; but the man who chooses it when all circumstances promise him great success in the world is especially worthy of respect. Drawn by his character to recognize the power of feeling, Jacobi has occupied himself with abstract ideas, mainly in order to demonstrate their insufficiency. His metaphysical writings are highly esteemed in Germany, but it is as a great moralist, above all, that his reputation is universal' (*De l'Allemagne* (Paris, 1866), p. 514). She continues: 'He has fought primarily the theory that morality is founded upon self-interest, and, assuming as his own principle the religious feeling philosophically considered, he has constructed a doctrine distinct from that of Kant, who relates everything to the inflexible law of duty, and from those of the new metaphysicians, who seek, as I have just said, the means of applying scientific rigour to the theory of virtue.' In regard to this last, compare Jacobi's statement to Fichte that a strictly demonstrated theory of morals 'can with its law never become the heart of man, and truly lift him above himself; only his heart truly lifts man above himself, and is the real faculty of ideas—of ideas that are not empty' (Jacobi, *Werke*, iii. 40–41). Fichte's own philosophy culminated in an affirmation of absolute systematic morality; hence, until the *Jacobi an Fichte*, he thought, and others did too, that he and Jacobi were allies. Consider the hilarious little 'Tragedy in Four Acts' that Bouterwek composed about the course of the Jacobi–Fichte philosophical relationship:

> 'Beginning, Middle, and End of the Jacobian Philosophy in the High Transcendental-Ideal-Scientific School. A Tragedy in Four Acts.'

Erster Act.

Der Wissenschaftslehrer [i.e. Fichte] spricht sich aus und sprichte:

> Ich und Jacobi sind einverstanden.
> Jacobi's Nam' ertön' in allen Landen!
> [Jacobi and I are in agreement
> Let Jacobi's name resound into all lands]

—to which the 'Wissenschaftsschüler' (Schelling and other Fichtian disciples) reply:

> Vivat Jacobi! Vivat er wie wir!
> Denn wer nicht mit uns ist, der ist ein Thier.
> [Long live Jacobi, just like us,
> For who is not with us is a beast]

—but by the 'Third Act' (two couplets later):
Der Wissenschaftslehrer spricht:

> O weh! o weh! Jacobi ist ein Duns,
> Jacobi glaubt an Gott, und nicht an uns!
> [O woe is me, Jacobi is a dunce,
> He believes in God, and not in us]'

(*Jacobi's Briefe an Bouterwek*, pp. 39–40.)

The price Jacobi paid for his retreat to the moral feelings of the heart was very great, and perhaps Lévy-Bruhl, whose own empirical, scientific orientation was so opposite, indicates best (and with barely controlled impatience) from how much of man's mental activity Jacobi—unlike Coleridge—withdrew: 'Jacobi n'ignorait point la singularité, et, si l'on peut dire, l'excentricité de sa philosophie. Il en acceptait allègrement certaines conséquences, renonçant de grand cœur, par exemple, à toute prétention scientifique. Il en subissait certaines autres avec peine, et ce lui fut un amer chagrin de voir le mouvement philosophique de l'Allemagne s'éloigner de lui toujours davantage. Mais à aucun moment il ne songea à se départir de sa méthode'; 'La philosophie de Jacobi n'aura pas la . . . fécondité. Elle n'y prétendait pas; elle s'en serait plutôt défendue. Jacobi aime peu, au fond, l'esprit de recherche et d'examen, qui est l'âme de la philosophie. Il n'en a que faire, puisqu'il possède la vérité absolue. Cette vérité relève du sentiment, non de la pensée. L'entendement n'ayant pas contribué à l'établir, n'est pas non plus compétent pour la critiquer'; 'Personne aujourd'hui ne reprocherait à Jacobi de s'être fait sa philosophie. On lui reprocherait plutôt la façon dont il se l'est faite, avec un singulier mélange de hardiesse et de timidité, de passion et d'indifférence. Il va jusqu'au bout de certaines questions, il s'arrête au seuil de certaines autres. Il revient sans cesse à deux ou trois problèmes qui l'obsèdent, il en néglige d'autres qui sont étroitement liés aux premiers, et cela, sans autre raison que ses besoins personnels d'esprit et de cœur. "On croyait rencontrer un philosophe, et l'on trouve un homme." Jacobi n'eût sans doute pas refusé pour son œuvre cette épigraphe, qui en exprime à la fois l'originalité et le plus grave défaut' (Lévy-Bruhl, *La philosophie de Jacobi* (Paris, 1894), pp. 240; 248; 262). Thus Friedrich Schlegel could say that Jacobi was 'a philosopher not by profession but by character' (*Charakteristiken und Kritiken*, i. 3), and in another passage was able to realize the exclusiveness of Jacobi's 'I am' preoccupations: 'Inclined by nature to sink into himself and to luxuriate in his own ideas, Jacobi could at first be induced only through mistrust in his love [of an extramundane Deity] and doubt of the reality of its object to tear himself out of himself and direct his activity outward . . .; and likewise it was afterwards almost always an attack (as in the case of the *Briefen über Spinoza* . . .) or an inspiration from outside by which he was forced, as it were, to outer activity' (i. 30–31).

Jacobi's correspondence and publications are in many ways epitomes of the special tone of the elegant rationalism of the eighteenth century. It has been suggested that he was a 'mystic' (see p. 129 above). But only in the way that men like Washington or Mozart were interested in Freemasonry could he be said to be interested in mysticism—that is, as a dilettantish counterbalance to a discursively orientated intellectual commitment. True, he numbered among his personal friends Kleuker and, before his alliance with Schelling, Baader, and he recalls that he visited St. Martin in Paris ('Ich habe dieses Buch vor vielen Jahren . . . mit Mühe einmal durchgelesen, und seitdem nicht wieder angesehen. . . . Ich habe nun den Verfasser, Saint-Martin, in Paris kennen gelernt. . . . Da er sehr eingezogen, von allen Pariser Gelehrten, Theologen, Schöngeistern und Weltleuten verachtet lebt, und ich ihn nicht geradezu in seiner, auch nicht einmal leicht zu erforschenden, Wohnung aufsuchen wollte, so gelang es mir nur wenige Wochen vor meiner Abreise, mich ihm zu nähern. Nachher habe ich ihm viermal und jedesmal einige Stunden hinter einander gesprochen. Er hält Stand in philosophischen Untersuchungen, wie wenige, ist immer heiter und voll Witz und Laune. Beim Abschied sagte er zu mir: *Tout le monde vous avait dit, que j'étais un fou; vous avez vu, que du moins je suis un fou heureux . . .*' (*Briefwechsel*, ii. 309–11). But everything about this anecdote supports the view that Jacobi's interest in mysticism was merely the wide-ranging interest and tolerance of the cultivated eighteenth-century gentleman, and not the commitment of a disciple or an adept. For instance, we note that the actual visits to St. Martin were not even mentioned except in the casual context of a letter far later than the time of the visits; that Jacobi says he read the book of St. Martin (*Des Erreurs et de la vérité*) carefully—but only once, and had not looked at it since; that the visits to St. Martin were not the most pressing items on his agenda, as they occurred just before the end of a long sojourn in Paris, and then took place in an atmosphere far closer to cultivated curiosity-seeking than to one of awed reverence (imagine what Baader would have given to have had those interviews!); and the words actually ascribed to St. Martin, while friendly and humanly approving, at the same time tend to lessen his importance: 'They have told you I am a madman; you have seen that at least I am a happy madman.'

Jacobi was interested in people and in ideas; Spener and Zinzendorf were part of his intellectual heritage, but he was an eighteenth-century gentleman to the core ('mehr . . . ein angenehmer Mann der höhern Gesellschaft', was Steffens' impression on first meeting him, 'als ein Gelehrter' (Steffens, *Was ich erlebte*, viii. 387)), an elegant dilettante of rationalism. Thus in a letter to Goethe in 1808 (*Briefwechsel*, ii. 407) he says that an acquaintance 'believed that the mystical would be alien and repugnant to me. I assured him that on the contrary what was elevated and true in mysticism was too congenial to me for pretentious talk and phoney displays in its name to be tolerable.' In other words, Jacobi applauds any affirmation of what to him is the unarguable final truth: that our being derives from transcendent grounds—that is, any affirmation of Plato's position. But he rejects Freemasonry, Swedenborgianism, Cabalism, Rosicrucianism, and such other portentous ciphers of the transcendent (to use Jaspers' conception) that were the stuff of true mysticism in his time.

Jacobi was a product of the eighteenth century in its most typical emphases.

He had no sympathy at all for the characteristic attitudes of Romanticism. Thus he rejected Romantic egotism: 'You ask about my opinion of Rousseau's *Confessions*. The book has depressed me exceedingly, and I would give a lot if I could just forget it. Surely Rousseau was half crazy when he wrote it. . . . A sad performance!' (*Briefwechsel*, i. 356).

Likewise he showed little of the Romantic nature-sense. Instead of the raptures in the bosom of untamed nature that we associate with the attitudes of Chateaubriand or Tieck or Wordsworth or Novalis, we see Jacobi tending his garden (with '25 to 30' gardeners) in the high tradition of eighteenth-century distrust of external nature unmethodized: 'If you want to see *Pains Hill* again, dear Julia— without going across the sea—take a trip to Pempelfort. I have made the actual *Pains Hill* out of my garden (except for the grotto, the tower, the Gothic building and the like). It has become about as large once again as you have seen it. The Düsselbach has taken another course; mountains and valleys have arisen' (*Briefwechsel*, ii. 19).

He distrusted too the characteristic 'quest' of the Romantics as much as he distrusted Romantic nature; indeed, he is as dubious about the moral implications of wanderlust as Dr. Johnson was about its appearance in Cowley's retreat from London: 'I share little in your pleasure in travel. Read Homer, Sophocles, Herodotus, Plato, and you truly profit more thereby than by wandering through Spain or Wales' (*Briefwechsel*, ii. 13). Such a statement is coordinate with the 'Be Homer's works your study and delight' of Pope, and is as antipathetic to the 'quit your books' of Wordsworth as it is to the questing voyages of Byron or Lenau, Childe Harold or the Wandering Jew.

Coleridge's Discovery of Jacobi

The date of Coleridge's first acquaintance with Jacobi's work can be narrowed down to late March or early April 1799—perhaps to 5 April 1799. And the work Coleridge encountered could have been either the *Ueber die Lehre des Spinoza* or the *David Hume über den Glauben, oder Idealismus und Realismus*. My reasoning is as follows. Coleridge wrote to his wife from Göttingen in March 1799 and cited a list of the eminences that the university had boasted: 'Mosheim, Gesner, Haller, Michaelis, Pütter, Kästner, Heyne, Letz or Less, Blumenbach, Lichtenburg, Plank, Eichhorn, Meiners, and Jacobi' (*Letters*, i. 477). Then, on 6 April 1799, Coleridge wrote to Poole, and in the letter he quoted some French: 'La nature (says Pascal) "La Nature confond les Pyrrhoniens, et la raison confond les Dogmatistes. Nous avons une impuissance à prouver, invincible à tout le Dogmatisme: nous avons une idée de la vérité, invincible à tout le Pyrrhonisme"' (*Letters*, i. 478–9). Now, if it were someone other than Coleridge, with his deep antipathy for things French, and if the situation were different—that is, if he were not actually in Germany and immersing himself in German language and culture—we might simply conclude that he had been reading Pascal's *Pensées* and had come across a passage that pleased him. But, as it is, we tend to be suspicious. The passage is a conflation of two statements from Article VIII of that work (Article XXI), and to find it Coleridge would probably have needed to read a considerable portion of the book—in which case he characteristically should have found much besides this passage to emphasize (certainly others have); and, secondly, it is difficult to imagine that he would be reading a French book during his enthusiastic sojourn in Germany. There is, furthermore, considerable doubt that Coleridge at that time either knew enough French to have read Pascal, or, conversely, was enough aware of Pascal for such an undertaking even had his French sufficed. Thus in a letter of more than four years later—22 September 1803—he writes to Sir George and Lady Beaumont that he is 'a wretched French Scholar' (*Letters*, ii. 994). If he could describe himself as a 'wretched French Scholar' in 1803, he is unlikely to have been skimming through the *Pensées* in 1799. And this admission was on the occasion of his attempting to read Pascal himself. Not the *Pensées*, true, but Pascal none the less, and not in tones that suggest any previous first-hand knowledge of him:' Yesterday Afternoon I found among Southey's Books a Tetraglott Edition of Paschal's Provincial Letters/I seized it, O how eagerly! It seemed to me as if I saw Lady Beaumont with my very eyes; and heard over again the very sounds of those words, in which she had expressed her enthusiastic Admiration of him. Tho' but a wretched French Scholar, I did not go to bed before I had read the Preface & the two first Letters. They are not only excellent; but the excellence is altogether of a new kind to me!' (*Letters*, ii. 994). If, therefore, 'the excellence' of Pascal's French was 'altogether of a new kind' to Coleridge, it suggests that the quotation of 1799 did not come to him from Pascal's *Pensées* but from some other book. Very probably it was a German book, and quite possibly a book bearing the name of one of the Göttingen eminences that he had proudly noted. The last on the list was 'Jacobi' and Jacobi's best known and most widely circulated book was the *Ueber die Lehre des Spinoza*. There, near the end, Jacobi says: 'Mein großes Thema werde ich behalten; jene Worte des Pascal: "La nature confond les Pyrrhoniens, et la raison confond les Dogmatistes. — Nous avons une impuissance à prouver, invincible à tout le Dogmatisme. Nous avons une idée de la vérité, invincible à tout le Pyrrhonisme" ' (*Ueber die Lehre des Spinoza* (*Werke*, iv–1), p. 230). Thus the first edition of 1785, and the second edition of 1789. But the quotation may equally well have come from Jacobi's *David Hume über den Glauben, oder Idealismus und Realismus. Ein Gespräch*, published in 1787. Indeed, this is more likely, for there the same words appear on the very first page, under the title.

EXCURSUS NOTE X

Leibniz and Descartes

Leibniz, with his accepting, conservative temperament, found the excluding, sceptical temperament of Descartes antipathetic. Apparently too he needed, especially in his youth, to emphasize his autonomy, for the figure of Descartes of course loomed titanically over the intellectual life of the the time. In a youthful and intellectually fiery letter to Thomasius, Leibniz asserts in 1669 that 'me fateor nihil minus quam Cartesianum esse'—that he is anything but a Cartesian

(*Sämtliche Schriften*, Zweite Reihe, i. 15). Ten years later he writes to Malebranche that Descartes had a keen and judicious mind, but had produced only beginnings, without going to bedrock; that his mechanics were replete with mistakes, his physics hasty, his geometry too restricted, and his metaphysics all those things at once: 'Des Cartes a dit de belles choses; c'éstoit un esprit penetrant et judicieux au possible. Mais comme il n'est pas possible de tout faire à la fois, il n'a fait que donner de belles ouvertures, sans estre arrivé au fonds des choses; et il me semble qu'il est encor bien eloigné de la veritable analyse et de l'art d'inventer en general. Car je suis persuadé que sa mecanique est pleine d'erreurs, que sa physique va trop viste, que sa Geometrie est trop bornée, et enfin que sa Metaphysique est tout cela ensemble' (*Philosophische Schriften*, i. 327–8). To Philipp, also in 1679, Leibniz says that if Descartes had paid less attention to his imaginary hypotheses and more to experience, his physics would have been worth following. Leibniz conceded that Descartes had great penetration, but his geometry and analysis were less perfect than is claimed, and there were several errors in his metaphysics. Nevertheless, Descartes was well worth reading, and Leibniz preferred to have to do with Cartesians than with members of any other school (*Philosophische Schriften*, iv. 282). The reproach that Descartes did not pay enough attention to experience is perhaps an echo of Leibniz's early predilection for Bacon and certainly sounds very much like an echo of the *locus classicus* in the *Advancement of Learning*: 'Another error hath proceeded from too great a reverence, and a kind of adoration of the mind and understanding of man; by means whereof men have withdrawn themselves too much from the contemplation of nature and the observations of experience, and have tumbled up and down in their own reason and conceits. Upon these intellectualists, which are notwithstanding commonly taken for the most sublime and divine philosophers, Heraclitus gave a just censure, saying *Men sought truth in their own little worlds, and not in the great and common world*; for they disdain to spell and so by degrees to read in the volume of God's works; and contrariwise by continual meditation and agitation of wit do urge and as it were invocate their own spirits to divine and give oracles unto them, whereby they are deservedly deluded' (*Works*, iii. 292). But however much Leibniz leaned towards Bacon in order to criticize Descartes, and however much he agreed with Bacon in his emphasis on the community of learning and on the cumulative progress of knowledge, in the ultimate implications of his thought Leibniz considered Descartes—with all his faults—his spiritual predecessor. 'Enfin', he says to Philipp, 'je considere cette philosophie [the Cartesian] comme l'antichambre de la veritable' (*Philosophische Schriften*, iv. 282).

More searching than the criticisms from Bacon are those in Spinozistic terms, which if Leibniz had felt they extended to the core of Descartes' work would have made the Frenchman unusable to him. We should note them as a further example of the absolute centrality of the 'I am' position, with all its implications, in Leibniz's philosophical opinions. 'J'estime Mons. des Cartes', says Leibniz by way of broaching this criticism, 'presqu'autant qu'on peut estimer un homme, et quoyqu'il y ait parmy ses sentimens quelques uns qui me paroissent faux et même dangereux, je ne laisse pas de dire que nous devons presqu'autant à Galilei et à luy en matiere de philosophie qu'à toute l'Antiquité.' Leibniz then says that he can call to mind on the spur of the moment only 'une seule des deux propositions dangereuses' that Philipp had wanted him to point out, that it is one in the *Principia philosophiae* where Descartes speaks of 'materia formas omnes quarum est capax successive assumat'—of matter successively taking on all the forms it can. Leibniz then comments that there is no more dangerous proposition than this one, that it leads to Spinoza's view that justice, beauty, order, are things relating only to us, while God's perfection consists in a largeness of activity by which everything conceivable is brought into being, that these are also the sentiments of Hobbes, that in Leibniz's opinion this is the foundation of atheistic philosophy, even though it speaks of God in fine-seeming terms, that, on the other hand, the true philosophy gives us a different idea of God's perfection, one that serves both physics and morality, that, far from excluding final causes from the concern of physics, as Descartes tries to do, it is rather by final causes that everything is determined, because efficient causes of things are intelligent (*Philosophische Schriften*, iv. 283–84). The passage not only emphasizes Leibniz's unequivocal opposition to pantheism, but also his pervasive Platonism. It points to the lack of this Platonism in Descartes—in its emotional dimension, that is—as Leibniz's most important crux of disagreement with Cartesianism. Gueroult emphasizes that Descartes suppressed the Platonic 'intelligible world' (Gueroult, *Descartes*, i. 383), and if the 'intelligible world' is, as Wolfson says, 'the totality of ideas' (*Philo*, i. 228) then its special dimension as multiplicity rather than as merely 'other' is the true source of the Platonic 'threshold' theme. Wheelwright finds that 'the intimation of a something more, a beyond the horizon, belongs to the very nature of consciousness', that 'man lives always on the verge, always on the borderland of a something more' and arrives thereby at the formula (apparently without prior knowledge of Jaspers' *Von der Wahrheit*): 'the threshold character of human existence' (Philip Wheelwright, *The Burning Fountain; A Study in the Language of Symbolism* (Bloomington, 1959), pp. 8, 17). This, though he does not himself argue from Platonic hypotheses, helps to gloss Coleridge's central definition of the Platonic tone as the 'thirst for something not attained' (*Philosophical Lectures*, p. 158); and in either statement is an attitude correspondent only to the feeling of 'realm' in alterity, as opposed to the purely logical altereity of Descartes. Schlesinger suggests that the broken disc called *symbolon* by the Greeks (used as identification in etiquette situations—that is, if the piece held by one man fitted with the piece held by another, the holders were mutually accredited in a given situation) by Plato's time might have been cut down the middle rather than broken at random, and that therefore the multiple equality of the realm of objects and the realm of ideas, and their 'symbolic' connexion, would be further emphasized (Max Schlesinger, 'Die Geschichte des Symbolbegriffs in der Philosophie', *Archiv für Geschichte der Philosophie*, xxii (1909), 72, 76). The rapturous moral expansiveness characteristic of Platonism (see, e.g. *Phaedo* 85 A–B; *Phaedrus* 251 A–B; *Symposium* 211 D–212 A; *Republic* 517 A) is thereby the effect of purposiveness toward a transcendent realm (ὀρέγεσθαι), whereas the merely heuristic dualism of Descartes lacks the focus of realm (substituting instead the goal of *mathesis universalis*, a universal science of relationships) and thereby lacks, notably, the Platonic moral tone (Gueroult remarks that 'En contraste avec la science qui ... requiert l'ascétisme intellectuel et nous renvoie à Platon . . . la morale . . . se place expressément, au nom de son eudémonisme, non point sous le patronage de Platon, mais sous celui d'Epicure . . .' (*Descartes*, ii. 228–9)). Such was not the case with Leibniz; his tone is Platonic, and his philosophical ancestry is also: the monads are really little more than accommodations of the Platonic *paradeigmata*, for, as Leibniz explains them to Des Bosses, they are incorporeal, and physical necessity follows moral necessity (*Philosophische Schriften*, ii. 450–1). For further study of the relationship of Leibniz and Descartes, see Yvon Belaval, *Leibniz critique de Descartes* (Paris, 1960). For Coleridge's acceptance-rejection attitudes towards Descartes see Excursus Note XVII, p. 320.

EXCURSUS NOTE XI

Berkeley's Idealism and Pantheism

BERKELEY was a deeply pious man, and he not only waged a lifelong war against 'atheism', but even confidently said that 'My doctrines rightly understood, all that Philosophy of Epicurus, Hobbs, Spinosa, &c. wch has been a declared enemy of religion, comes to the ground' (*Berkeley's Commonplace Book*, ed. G. A. Johnston (London 1930), p. 100, M. 836). But in his war against atheism, Berkeley was like the British at Singapore, whose gun emplacements, directed against attack by sea, proved useless against an enemy who stole up by land. Berkeley's whole purpose was to establish, not the dualism of mind and matter, but the monism of mind, for 'Matter once allow'd, I defy any man to prove that God is not Matter' (*Commonplace Book*, p. 75, M. 634). His philosophy consequently, though perhaps not strictly speaking pantheist, is not a defence against pantheism, and in its implications actually favours pantheism.

Berkeley sets out with what seems a ringing affirmation of the 'I am': 'That neither our Thoughts, nor Passions, nor Ideas formed by the Imagination, Exist without the Mind, is what every Body will allow. And to me it is no less evident that the various Sensations or Ideas imprinted on the Sense, however Blended or Combin'd together (that is whatever Objects they compose) cannot Exist otherwise than in a Mind perceiving them . . . as to what is said of the Absolute Existence of unthinking Things without any relation to their being perceiv'd, that is to me perfectly Unintelligible. Their *Esse* is *Percipi*, nor is it possible they shou'd have any Existence, out of the Minds or thinking Things which perceive them' (Berkeley, *A Treatise Concerning the Principles of Human Knowledge* (Dublin, 1710), Part I, par. 3, pp. 43–44). He skilfully protects this view from 'crude egoismus' or Aenesidemean scepticism by insisting that 'The trees are in the park, i.e. whether I will or no, whether I imagine anything about them or no' (*Commonplace Book*, p. 11, M. 100); that 'whatever Power I may have over my own Thoughts, I find the Ideas actually perceiv'd by Sense have not a like Dependence on my Will. When in broad Day-light I open my Eyes, 'tis not in my Power to chuse whether I See or no, or to determine what particular

Objects shall present themselves to my View' (*Principles*, par. 29, p. 70). But at this point in his reasoning, Berkeley—crucially for the problem of pantheism—refuses to grant independent existence to these subsisting objectivities: 'We have been led into very dangerous Errors, by supposing a two-fold Existence of the Objects of Sense, the one *Intelligible*, or in the Mind, the other *Real* and without the Mind: Whereby Unthinking Things are thought to have a natural Subsistence of their own, distinct from being perceived by Spirits' (*Principles*, par. 86, p. 131). He insists instead that 'There is therefore some other Will or Spirit that produces' objects (*Principles*, par. 29, p. 70). If we sense that we have somehow been whirled on to a Neoplatonic tangent leading to the Stoic *anima mundi* or Plotinian *psyche*, our suspicions prove correct. 'Those things which are call'd the works of Nature, *i.e.* the far greater part of the Ideas or Sensations perceived by us, are not produced by, or dependent on, the Wills of Men . . . they belong to the aforesaid Spirit, *who works all in all*, and *by whom all* things *consist*' (*Principles* par. 146, p. 199). And as pantheism itself looms on the horizon, Berkeley refuses to deflect his course: 'But you'll say has Nature no share in the Production of Natural Things, and must they be all ascrib'd to the immediate and sole Operation of God? I answer . . . if by *Nature* is meant some Being distinct from GOD . . . I must confess, that Word is to me an empty Sound, without any intelligible Meaning annexed to it. Nature, in this Acceptation, is a vain *Chimera*' (*Principles*, par. 150, p. 204).

Not only does Berkeley's later work not repudiate this identification of God and nature, but his treatise on tar water of 1744 is a veritable anthology of Neoplatonic and Stoic pantheistic lore, lovingly and approvingly set forth by the Bishop. There is the *anima mundi*: 'Nature seems to be no otherwise distinguished from the anima mundi, than as life is from soul, and upon the principle of the oldest philosophers, may not improperly or incongruously be styled the Life of the world' (*Siris: A Chain of Philosophical Reflexions and Inquiries Concerning Virtues of Tar Water, and divers other Subjects connected together and arising one from another* (Dublin, 1744), par. 278, p. 195). Berkeley, significantly, finds no atheism in the conception: 'If nature be the life of the world, animated by one soul, compacted into one frame, and directed or governed in all parts by one mind; This system cannot be accused of Atheism' (*Siris*, par. 279, p. 196). But as Bayle more penetratingly saw, 'Le dogme de l'âme du monde qui a été si commun parmi les anciens, & qui faisoit la partie principale du système des Stoïques' is 'dans le fond celui de Spinoza' (Bayle, *Dictionaire*, ii. 1084 n.). And not only does Berkeley approve the Stoico-Spinozistic world soul, he approves τὸ ἕν: '. . . it will not seem just to fix the imputation of Atheism upon those philosophers who held the doctrine of τὸ ἕν' (*Siris*, par. 353, p. 250). Likewise, he approves τὸ πᾶν: 'Comprehending God and the creatures in one general notion, we may say that all things together make one universe, or τὸ πᾶν' (*Siris*, par. 288, p. 202). Still further, he approves the linkage of τὸ πᾶν and τὸ ἕν: 'those who thought the Whole, or τὸ πᾶν, to be ἐν ἑστώς, a fixed or permanent One, seem to have understood the Whole of real beings' (*Siris*, par. 349, p. 246). And finally, he approves the express conception ἕν καὶ πᾶν: 'τὸ ἕν may be conceived either by composition or division. For as, on the one hand, we may say the world or universe is ONE whole or ONE animal; so we may, on the other hand, consider τὸ ἕν by division or abstraction, as somewhat in the order of things prior to mind. In either sense there is no atheism, so long as mind is admitted to preside and direct the animal; and so long as the unum or τὸ ἕν is supposed not to exist without mind. So that neither Heraclitus nor Parmenides, nor Pythagoras nor Plato, neither the Aegyptians nor Stoics, with their doctrine of a divine whole or animal, nor Xenophanes with his ἕν καὶ πᾶν, are justly to be accounted atheists' (*Siris*, par. 354, p. 251).

Berkeley's thought, in short, dramatizes the inadequacy of the mere 'I am' starting-point as a guarantee against pantheism; to protect against pantheism, that starting-point must be bulwarked by ontological and cosmological dualism. The history of philosophy demonstrates this truth again and again. Thus Schopenhauer begins his chief work with the confident statement that 'The world is my idea' (Schopenhauer, *Die Welt als Wille und Vorstellung: vier Bücher nebst einem Anhange, der die Kritik der Kantischen Philosophie enthält* (Leipzig, 1819), p. 3). And he continues: 'No truth is therefore more certain . . . than this, that everything, which is there for knowledge, therefore the whole world, is only an object in relation to the subject' (*Die Welt als Wille und Vorstellung*, p. 4). But then we spot a slight cloud in this flawless sky: 'This truth is by no means new. Berkeley was the first who expressed it; he has thereby rendered an immortal service to philosophy' (p. 4). And our forebodings are confirmed; Schopenhauer finds that the 'will' which we discover within us is the true Kantian *Ding an sich*; therefore 'will' alone is real, and we, the poor individuals, are mere 'appearances': 'Since the Will is the Thing-in-itself, the inner form and essence of the world, and life, the visible world, the appearance but only the mirror of the Will, so will the visible world inseparably accompany the Will, like a shadow its body, and if Will is there, there is life and world' (p. 393). The 'I am' becomes lost—the individual becomes a momentary wave on the great ocean of blind 'Will': 'Indeed we see the individual arise and disappear! but the individual is only appearance . . . goes forth from nothingness, suffers by death the loss of that gift and goes back into nothingness' (p. 393). And 'Will' itself is purposeless and dark: 'the Will, whose objectification, human life, like every appearance' is 'a striving without goal and without end' (p. 462).

With less metaphor, different terminology, and less sombre splendour, the philosophy of Fichte follows this same pattern: initial affirmation of the 'I am', followed by eventual affirmation of a monistic one that absorbs all personality. See Excursus Note XIX, pp. 328–9.

Augustine, conversely, a true 'I am' thinker, not only begins with the 'I am' (see pp. 59, 337 n. 7), but also, as Gilson says, believes that *true philosophy implies an act of adherence to the supernatural order* (*The Christian Philosophy of Saint Augustine*, trans. L. Lynch (New York, 1967), p. 235).

We may wonder why the true 'I am' position must be validated by a two-world ontology, even though 'it is' positions involve only a one-world ontology. The answer is as follows. Our common sense makes us reject any attempt to say that 'things' are not really there: things are intuitively there. But that same common sense tells us that it is highly speculative as to whether a 'self' is anything other than an affect of the 'thing' of our physical organization: self is there only after we reflect about it. The burden of proof, so to speak, is on the man who denies 'things' an independent existence, not on the one who denies it to 'self'. As a result, the 'it is' thinker either can content himself with non-systematic acceptance of the world as he finds it—in which case he will be able to account for everything within the framework of physical reality (we recall LaPlace's famous statement that he had no need of the hypothesis of God)—or, if he accepts a syntactic extension into the question of 'God', will conclude, as does Spinoza, that all 'God questions' can be answered in terms of 'it is': God's essence, accordingly, is that of 'res extensa', his relationship to reality that of 'causa immanens'. Likewise, any pure idealism that also assumes only one substance finds that such a substance must be indifferently the self and things (or their idea), and it follows that the God-extension is also that indifferently of self and things; and here too the living self is drowned in a monistic sea. But the 'I am' thinker starts with his *existential* sense of self, and likewise with things as separate from that self; he is a dualist at the outset. He cannot, like Berkeley, extend his 'God' syntax into the world of things without abandoning, or compromising, this self, which is postulated at the outset as a unity unlike that of 'thing'. Rather, he must extend his 'God' syntax into the hypothetical realm beyond 'thing', where it can retain the unsullied characteristics of the existentially felt 'separate' self. Kant's *Ding an sich* implies such an extramundane God by positing—activating—the extramundane realm which is his locus; and yet the *Ding an sich*, as a positing, is really an act of faith on the part of the existential self (see below, note 56, p. 368).

At the same time that it is apparent why the 'I am' position must be dualistic, and why the 'it is' position must be monistic, it is also apparent that the 'I am' position can never complete its system, and the 'it is' can. The 'I am' breaks the systematic network at two points: (*a*) at the outset, with the idea of the existential self (the 'man of flesh and bone'), who stands outside of and prior to any system—who, indeed, is actually thinking the system—and by that token breaks the chain; and (*b*) at the conclusion, by the concept of a second realm, which stands outside all discursive possibility, and therefore outside that of system itself. The 'I am' position, accordingly, can point towards system, but only the 'it is' position can achieve its completion. The historical result of this discrepancy is that 'it is' thinkers, whether systematic or not, are content to remain within the implications of their postulates, but 'I am' thinkers, if they aspire to system, are always under pressure, in the interests of completion, to partake of, or draw near to, 'it is' conceptions and their extensions.

EXCURSUS NOTE XII

Adverse Criticisms of Schelling

THOUGH Ferrier and Ingleby, to belittle Coleridge, speak of Schelling as though his eminence were beyond dispute, he in fact encountered, in his own lifetime, as much ridicule and denigration as Coleridge. We should be aware of Kierkegaard's opinion: 'I am so pleased', he writes in 1841 from Berlin, 'to have heard Schelling's second lecture—indescribably. . . . Now I have put all my hopes in Schelling.' Yet by 27 February 1842 he is writing to his brother that 'Schelling drivels on quite intolerably. . . . Imagine parson R.'s meandering philosophising, his entirely aimless, haphazard knowledge, and parson Horn-syld's untiring efforts to display his learning, imagine the two combined and in addition an impudence hitherto unequalled by any philosopher . . . and you will have some idea of Schelling's philosophy. . . . My time is too precious to allow me to take in drop by drop what I should hardly have to open my mouth to swallow all at once. I am too old to attend lectures and Schelling is too old to give them. His whole doctrine of potency betrays the greatest impotency' (*The Journals*, pp. 102, 104). For similar adverse opinions on the part of Burck-hardt and of Boeckh, see Jaspers, *Schelling*, pp. 245–6. Again, we might consider the fact that Henry Crabb Robinson, who knew both Schelling and Coleridge in their primes, leaves little doubt that Coleridge seemed to him the greater figure.

There was a general tendency for an initial admiration of Schelling to fade into boredom or inattention. Robinson, who attended Schelling's lectures in 1802, spoke of them as representing 'a philosophy which in its pretensions is more aspiring than any publicly maintained since the days of Plato', and noted that 'in the sphere of Metaphysics' Schelling was at that time 'the Lord of the Ascendant' (*Diary*, i. 129). In 1829, however, Robinson visits Schelling and refers to him as 'the not-yet-forgotten famous metaphysician' (*Diary*, ii. 446). Compare Staiger's description of the young, bustling, confident, slightly spoiled Schelling ('. . . Schelling strode into the history of thought, impudent, pre-cocious, ambitious, a twenty-three-year-old youth who, spoiled by admiring friends, trusted himself to understand everything and dismiss difficulties and frustration with ease') with his judgement on Schelling's later position in Ger-man thought: 'He was a word out of a closed chapter of the German mind' (Emil Staiger, 'Schellings Schwermut', *Die Kunst der Interpretation; Studien zur deutschen Literaturgeschichte* (Zürich, 1955), pp. 182, 204). Compare Baader's acid statement of 1841, that 'this Schelling, whose philosophy is already dead, has only forgotten to have himself buried' (*Werke*, xv. 688). Baader displayed an especially wicked tongue when commenting on Schelling's self-proclaimed and portentous new stages of development. Coining the derisive appellation, 'Neuschelling' (*Werke*, x. 29), he at various times speaks of his former friend's changes as 'new wine in old bottles'; and also of his attempt 'to patch together the old pantheist garment with new rags' (*Werke*, xv. 455). In another metaphor, Baader tells Hegel that Schelling's later thought is a stew made out of the nourish-ing and spicy venison roast of his youthful nature-philosophy, cooked with all kinds of ingredients, including Christian ones (*Werke,* xv. 464). (For Schel-ling's counter-estimate of Baader see Guido Schneeberger, *Friedrich Wilhelm Joseph von Schelling; eine Bibliographie* (Bern, 1954), p. 178).

Not only did initial satisfaction with Schelling usually give way to generalized dissatisfaction, but he was also, from early in his career, taxed with specific errors in logic. As Berg said in 1804, 'How can Schelling by means of and according to thinking infer the opposite of thinking or something unthinkable? How does the reverse of the premises get into the conclusion? . . . By thinking Schelling finds his absolute, by thinking he treats of it, by thinking he seeks to make it free of objections. At the same time it is supposed in no wise to stand under the laws of thought. . . . That means, therefore—the absolute is in itself thinkable and unthinkable. That would be Schelling's *Geist*? I wish you luck if you can comprehend it . . .' (Berg, *Sextus*, p. 39). In addition to this deeplying logical flaw of attaching predicates to stipulated absolutes, Schelling is also guilty of the flaw of not bridging the gap between logic and reality, and this charge was brought more forcibly by Jacobi's disciple Köppen than by anyone else: 'Subject and Object are according to Schelling conceived in an opposition whereby they reciprocally condition one another. . . . All products, both subjective and objective, are appearances of the absolute, self-identical construction'—but, argues Köppen, 'out of logical knowledge, out of logical equating and opposing, out of indifference and difference, a thing, an object, can never be constructed. No real, no actual, no particular and finite subject and object begets itself out of the logical subject and predicate. . . . The Schellingian philosopher cannot concede this without giving himself up for lost. He must therefore transform the logical subject into the real subject, the logical predicate into the real object, in order to be able to construct with them in the finite world. This transformation takes place through mere substitution of names, since Schelling puts object in place of predicate' (Friedrich Köppen, *Schellings Lehre oder das Ganze der Philosophie des absoluten Nichts* (Hamburg, 1803), pp. 10, 18). Köppen accordingly characterizes Schelling's philosophy—which manipulates logic rather than describes realities—as an organization of 'not-knowledge': 'The philosophical systems, which believe themselves to produce a construction and creation of the universe through their own inner power, and which find in this creation the highest science and knowledge, are mere organizations of our not-knowledge (*Nichtwissens*), not-power (*Nichtkönnens*), not-proof (*Nichtbeweisens*)' (Köppen, p. 125). For still another attack on Schelling's postulates see Schopenhauer, *Werke*, ii. 214.

In addition to contemporary realizations of Schelling's logical errors, there was, on the part both of his contemporaries and of his later commentators, a persistent realization of his dependence on a wide variety of previous thinkers. Although such a dependence has not usually been considered a flaw in his thought, its existence should be noted, especially in view of the ridicule heaped upon Coleridge for his own use of Schelling.

Fichte, for instance, said in 1795 of 'Schelling's essay' (*Ueber die Möglichkeit einer Form der Philosophie überhaupt*) that it was 'entirely commentary on my thought' (*Briefwechsel*, i. 481). Eswein says that 'Aristotelian concepts', together with 'Platonic, Plotinian, Scholastic, Spinozistic, Leibnizian, Kantian and other elements', form 'the framework and scaffolding' from which Schelling built up his thought (Karl Eswein, 'Schellings Verhältnis zu Aristoteles', *Philosophisches Jahrbuch der Görres-Gesellschaft*, xlvii (Fulda, 1934), 84). Erdmann speaks of the 'taking in of Fichtean elements, which make Schelling receptive to the mysticism of Boehme and Baader and allow him to set up his revised doctrine, where the famous proposition, All Being is Will, cannot disavow its Fichtian origin'

(J. E. Erdmann, *Ueber Schelling, namentlich seine negative Philosophie* (Halle, 1857), p. 7). (In this work, incidentally, Erdmann pays unexpected tribute to Coleridge as the only thinker who understood the meaning of Schelling's conception of 'hunger for existence', p. 15.) Feuerbach, again, says that Schelling and Hegel are counterparts: Hegel represents the masculine principle, while Schelling represents 'the feminine principle of receptivity, of impressionability—first he took in Fichte, then Plato and Spinoza, finally Boehme' (*Werke*, ii. 260–1). And again, Walzel says that it will probably never be known whether and to what extent Schelling was influenced by Friedrich Schlegel, 'for both depend on the aesthetic and nature-knowledge of Goethe and Herder. Friedrich Schlegel seems, however, to have perceived the relationship of Goethe's artistic and physical *Denkformen* earlier than Schelling . . .' (Oskar Walzel, *Deutsche Romantik. I. Welt- und Kunstanschauung*, fünfte Auflage (Leipzig und Berlin, 1923), p. 45). Still again, about Schelling's conception of mythology as 'Mittelglied der Rückkehr der Wissenschaft zur Poesie', Walzel notes that Schelling's exposition in the lectures on the philosophy of art (1802–3) rests 'völlig auf den Schultern der romantischen Genossen' (p. 53).

EXCURSUS NOTE XIII

Coleridge's Theory of the Imagination

COLERIDGE—together with other Romantics, and indeed with virtually all who have thought on the matter—saw that 'imagination' (*a*) bears witness to the indispensability of nature—that is to say, an image must have as its content the representation of an external object (an 'it is')—and (*b*) that it simultaneously bears witness to the mind's independence of nature—that is to say, one can 'imagine' an image of nature even though the object itself is not present in space or time: I can babble of non-existent green fields or think of non-existent perfect islands; I can even make play with Berkeley's trees in the park— I can imagine them as oaks, and then I can imagine them as beeches, I can imagine them in the autumn, or budding in the spring, as saplings or full-grown, and when I am tired of imagining them, I can simply dismiss them from my mind. And in this possibility I realize that the imagination is intimately connected with the will—for in 'imagination', as distinct from that which we call 'reality', I change or alter the existence of images simply by willing to do so.

Now the Scylla and Charybdis that guard the approach to a true understanding of Coleridge's theory of imagination consist, on the one hand, in the error of Richards that takes 'imagination' out of its historical context in Romanticism and Coleridgean thought, and, on the other hand—and this is both a more common and a less noble error than the first—in the attempt to make the conception *merely* historical, and even merely quirkily and idiosyncratically Coleridgean. What in fact does Coleridge mean by 'imagination'? To this the answer is clear: *he means exactly what we all mean in ordinary language by the word imagination.* By 'imagination' Coleridge means what Descartes means by 'imaginatio'; what Kant means by 'Einbildungskraft'; what Wordsworth means by 'imagination'; what Fichte, and Schelling, and Herder, and the Schlegels, and all others, mean wherever they refer to the imaging faculty. For 'imagination' is a given in experience, not the property, nor the terminological construct, of a special philosopher. 'Imagination', as Spinoza say, is precisely 'the idea wherewith the mind contemplates a thing as present' (*Ethica* v. 24. Demonstratio.) The differences in the formulations of the nature of imagination are dictated by differing conceptions of the faculty's *function* in a systematic view of reality.

The resurgence of interest in the nature of the imagination during the Romantic era was a corollary of the resurgence of interest in the external world. The decline of trust in externally given forms that, for whatever reason, characterized Baroque and Neoclassic activity in the seventeenth and eighteenth centuries, led to a diminution in the importance attached to imagination by poetic theory and philosophical schematism. Thus the great Descartes makes *imaginatio* a faculty inferior to *intellectio* (which needs no images). Hobbes thinks of 'IMAGINATION' as 'nothing but *decaying sense*. . . . *Imagination* and *Memory*, are but one thing. . . . *Reason* is the pace' (*Leviathan* (London, 1651), pp. 5, 22). Conversely, the great revival of interest in external nature that became one of the hallmarks of Romanticism was necessarily accompanied by renewed interest in the scope and function of the previously despised *imaginatio*. Imagination now became this 'wonderful faculty' (Schelling, *Werke*, i. 332 n.), or that 'awful Power' (Wordsworth, *The Prelude*, Book VI, line 594), and was hailed with reverence—as, for instance, in Baader's musing about 'imagination' as 'a wonder of wonders', which is 'no mere word, but a microcosmos of secret forces within us' (Baader, *Werke*, xi. 85).

In this new assertion of the importance of imagination, however, Schelling's emphasis does not coincide with that of Coleridge. For Schelling, imagination was involved in the creation of reality itself. Since 'the system of Nature is at the same time the system of our Spirit' (*Werke*, ii. 39), it would follow that the imagination recognizes no essential difference between object and image. 'One might explain imagination as the power of transposing itself through complete self-activity into complete passivity' (*Werke*, i. 332 n.). The function of imagination in a system of absolute idealism is always constitutive and regulative, therefore, never, as with Coleridge, truly mediating and reconciling—for indeed, there is no need to mediate between 'nature' and 'spirit' when they are really the same. Thus Friedrich Schlegel can say that 'in der Einbildungskraft ist es die Natur, die in uns denkt' (*Philosophische Vorlesungen*, ii. 461)—a pantheist emphasis quite different from Coleridge's conception. Again, Fichte says that 'Alle Realität . . . blos durch die Einbildungskraft hervorgebracht werde' (*Grundlage der gesammten Wissenschaftslehre* (Leipzig, 1794), p. 195). And Schelling says that 'Einbildungskraft' is the 'only faculty' that can 'comprehend negative and positive activity and represent them in one common product'. But his context is an assertion that 'the object is not something which is given to us from outside, but only a product of the original spiritual self-activation, which by opposed activities creates and produces a third in common' (*Werke*, i. 357).

For Schelling, therefore, as for Fichte, imagination was the coordinator of the reciprocal energies by which (in the words of Schelling's youthful poem) 'Eine Kraft, Ein Pulsschlag nur, Ein Leben/Ein Wechselspiel von Hemmen und von Streben' poured out all reality (Plitt, *Aus Schellings Leben*, i. 287). Indeed a recent commentator, noting that Schelling's imagination 'can be formulated as participation of man in the creation of the world', goes so far as to term 'Schellings Philosophie eine *Mystik der Einbildungskraft*' (Rudolf Hablützel, *Dialektik und Einbildungskraft; F. W. J. Schellings Lehre von der menschlichen Erkenntniss* (Basel, 1954), pp. 81, 82). In Coleridge's view, on the contrary, imagination mediates between a nature of *real* objects and a *real* 'I am', creates poetry, not the world, and maintains the priority of the 'I am' over the 'it is'. Coleridge was closer to Kant than he was to Schelling, and closer to Kant than Schelling was to Kant, who maintains that 'die Einbildungskraft nach dem Assoziationsgesetz macht unseren Zustand der Zufriedenheit physisch abhängig', on the one hand, but on the other 'ist Werkzeug der Vernunft und ihrer Ideen' and therefore 'asserts our independence of the influences of nature' (Kant, *Werke*, v. 341). Yet Coleridge differed from Kant also by his practical emphasis on poetry, and by his active faith in religion. The function of imagination accordingly takes on in his thought a religious coloration which it does not have in the Kantian scheme.

Though an emphasis on imagination always means an emphasis on external nature, imagination itself is the exclusive faculty for mental *poiesis* or *fiction*—is, as Baader says, 'die Mutter der Poesie'. In his own poetry Coleridge, both in theory and in practice, conceived the imagination as a bulwark for the primacy of the 'I am'. Thus *The Ancient Mariner*, a poem of 'pure imagination', depends as little as possible upon the memory or reproduction of actual scenes or objects experienced in the external world, but is rather a willed creation and coordination of images by the 'I am'. Wordsworth's poetic practice, on the other hand, tended towards actual recollection of the real presence of external nature, or even present description of that nature, and hence it was that Coleridge was 'disposed to conjecture' that Wordsworth 'has mistaken the co-presence of fancy with imagination for the operation of the latter singly' (*Biographia*, i. 194). Compare Hartman: 'An unresolved opposition between Imagination and Nature prevents [Wordsworth] from becoming a visionary poet. It is a paradox, though not an unfruitful one, that he should scrupulously record nature's workmanship, which prepares the soul for its independence from sense-experience, yet refrain to use that independence out of respect of nature. His greatest verse *still takes its origin* in the memory of given experiences to which he is often pedantically faithful' (Geoffrey Hartman, *Wordsworth's Poetry 1787–1814* (New Haven and London, 1964), p. 39). Certainly one of the reasons why Coleridge divided the imaginative function into 'imagination' and 'fancy', the latter taking upon itself the inferior functional status of Descartes' *imaginatio* or Hobbes's equation of Imagination and Memory, was that he wanted to emphasize as much as possible the freedom of the poetic imagination from slavish dependence on the 'it is'. 'Fancy is indeed no other than a mode of Memory' (*Biographia*, i. 202), while 'Imagination' is 'essentially *vital*, even as all objects (*as* objects) are essentially fixed and dead' (*Biographia*, i. 202). In short, for Coleridge the theory of imagination allowed the recognition and use of the 'it is' while strongly insisting on the primacy and control of the 'I am', and in this sense was a 'reconciling and mediatory power' (*Works*, i. 436).

Though Coleridge's later definitions of imagination are more carefully elaborated than his early statements, they seem to elucidate rather than contradict them. In his full statement in the *Biographia Literaria* the 'primary IMAGINATION' is the 'living Power and prime Agent of all human Perception', a 'repetition in the finite mind of the eternal act of creation in the infinite I AM' (i. 202). Though this definition might well owe something to Fichte or Boehme (see below, Excursus Note XIX, p. 330), it is also, and at least, an expansion of that definition of 1804 in which 'Imagination' in the 'highest sense of the word' is a 'dim Analogue of Creation, not all that we can *believe* but all that we can *conceive* of creation' (*Letters*, ii. 1034). And this in its turn is a restatement of a formulation of 1796, where (though at that time without the term 'imagination') Coleridge enunciates the Platonism that 'Man . . . is urged to develop the powers of the creator, and by new combinations of these powers to imitate his creativeness' (*The Watchman*, p. 101). Again, the secondary imagination in the *Biographia Literaria* 'dissolves, diffuses, dissipates, in order to recreate' and 'at all events it struggles to idealize and to unify' (i. 202). And this emphasis is heralded by the definition in 1804 of 'Imagination' as the '*modifying* Power' (*Letters*, ii. 1034); still earlier by the 'shaping spirit of imagination' of the *Dejection* ode; again still earlier by the '*Imagination*' which in 1802 is the '*modifying*, and *co-adunating* Faculty' (*Letters*, ii. 866). These early flowerings open from still earlier buds—though not as yet named 'imagination'. Thus in December 1796 Coleridge speaks of 'my own shaping and disquisitive mind' (*Letters*, i. 271); in March 1796 of 'the catenating Faculty . . . the silk thread that ought to run through the Pearl-chain of Ratiocination' (*Letters*, i. 193). Likewise for Fancy. 'FANCY', in 1817, 'has no other counters to play with, but fixities and definites. The Fancy is indeed no other than a mode of Memory emancipated from the order of time and space.' In 1804 'Fancy' is 'the *aggregating* power' (*Letters*, ii. 1034); in 1802 'Fancy' is 'the aggregating Faculty' (*Letters*, ii. 865).

In his earliest statements Coleridge does not differentiate between 'Imagination' and 'Fancy'—using them (as indeed *Phantasie* and *Einbildungskraft* are customarily used in German) as synonyms. Thus in June 1796 he says that Thelwall's poetry lacks 'the *light* of Fancy' (*Letters*, i. 221), while in May of that year he says that Godwin lacks 'strength of intellect' and 'the powers of imagination'. None the less, though not fully schematized, the 'imagination' is, from early in his career, clearly important to Coleridge as a central and vital power of his poetic being. In 1799, for instance, he speaks of 'my Imagination' as 'tired, down, flat and powerless' (*Letters*, i. 470). Again, in December 1796 he says that Southey 'does not possess opulence of Imagination, lofty-paced Harmony, or that *toil* of thinking, which is necessary in order to plan a *Whole*' (*Letters*, i. 293–4)—and it is evident here that we see the beginnings of the theory by which 'imagination' struggles 'to idealize and to unify' (*Biographia*, i. 202). The later differentiation between the two terms actually puts the 'I am' more firmly in control of 'imagination' than when that faculty had also to bear the burden of Hobbes's equation of '*Imagination* and *Memory*'. Imagination, as it were, remains in the sled while the baby of 'fancy' is sacrificed to the 'it is'.

By allowing 'fancy' to discharge one necessary function of the imaging faculty—
that is, to image external reality by aggregation and memory—Coleridge is able to
emphasize the free creativity of the imagination, to co-ordinate it with 'the
eternal act of creation in the infinite I AM' (*Biographia*, i. 202).

Furthermore, Coleridge's distinction of imagination and fancy (despite his
own explicit claims, e.g. *Biographia*, i. 60–61) does not really divide the imaging
faculty, but only distinguishes its modes. Thus in a marginal note on the flyleaf
of Maass's *Versuch über die Einbildungskraft*, verbesserte Ausgabe (Halle und
Leipzig, 1797), Coleridge speaks of 'the sensuous Einbildungskraft . . . which
we call Imagination, Fancy &c. all poor & inadequate Terms. . .'. Coleridge's
feeling that he improves these 'poor & inadequate Terms' by fixing special
significances for the synonymous 'Imagination, Fancy' is actually licensed
by an ambiguity in the meaning of imagination in ordinary language. If we
examine our common understanding of the word 'imagination' we see that the
single term is used in two ways, one somewhat denigrative and one honorific:
(1) a child cries out in the night that a monster is in its room; its parents assure
the child that 'it's only your imagination'; while (2) the highest praise that can
crown recognition of capability is to say that a man has 'imagination'. It is
the existence of the unbidden mental phantoms of the first order that sanctions
Coleridge's 'fancy', and it is the unified, consciously willed, creative control of
the potential ramifications of a situation, signalized by the second use, that
sanctions Coleridge's 'imagination'.

So too the distinction between primary and secondary imagination. To
perceive any object we must have an image—the chair we perceive remains in
the room, and another chair, made up of impulses in our brains, occurs in our
consciousnesses. We could perceive nothing without such images, and hence
their faculty, the 'primary' imagination is 'the living Power and prime Agent
of all human Perception'. But we can 'imagine' the chair in another way: we
can leave the room, and then, by willing to do so, bring to mind the 'image'
of that same chair. This 'secondary' imagination, accordingly, is 'an echo of
the former, co-existing with the conscious will . . .' and can 'dissolve' and
'recreate' images into a poetic whole.

Of the studies of Coleridge's theory of imagination, the most suggestive still
seems to me I. A. Richards, *Coleridge on Imagination*, third edition (London,
1962). For fiercely adverse criticism of Richards—although of the *Principles of
Literary Criticism* more than of *Coleridge on Imagination*—see D. G. James,
Scepticism and Poetry (London, 1937), pp. 60–74 *et passim*. Probably the fullest
presentation of the theory of imagination and its ambiance is James Volant
Baker, *The Sacred River; Coleridge's Theory of Imagination* (Baton Rouge, La.,
1957). Brief but interesting treatments are in Basil Willey, *Nineteenth Century
Studies; Coleridge to Matthew Arnold* (New York, 1949), pp. 10–26, and in Willey,
The English Moralists (New York, 1964), pp. 303–12. Useful works on the more
general topic of Coleridge's aesthetic theory or critical presuppositions include
C. D. Thorpe, 'Coleridge as Aesthetician and Critic', *JHI*, v (1944), 387–414;
R. H. Fogle, *The Idea of Coleridge's Criticism* (Berkeley and Los Angeles, 1962);
J. A. Appleyard, *Coleridge's Philosophy of Literature; The Development of a Concept
of Poetry 1791–1819* (Cambridge, Mass., 1965).

EXCURSUS NOTE XIV

The Religious Heterodoxy of Hartley, Priestley, and Godwin

THOUGH Hartley is obviously quite sincere about his strange fusion of necessitarianism and Christianity, it is interesting to note that Priestley felt called upon, in 1775, to publish an abridged version of the *Observations on Man*, under the title of *Hartley's Theory of the Human Mind*, because the original was 'clogged with a whole system of moral and religious knowledge; which however excellent, is, in a great measure, foreign to it' (p. iii).

In the British Museum there is a copy of the *Observations on Man*, in a reprint of 1791, that contains only two annotations by Coleridge (and also many uncut pages—although doubtless Coleridge did not confine his reading to this one copy). The lightness of the annotation may well be an effect of Hartley's curious lack of philosophical intensity—on the very first page of his work, for instance, he vows allegiance to Locke and Newton and announces that he intends to set forth their ideas, and from such a beginning one scarcely anticipates high excitements to follow. Like Godwin, Hartley is clear, coherent, and rather prolix; like Godwin, he displays little overt learning and almost no attempts at novelty, paradox, or subtlety—both philosophies are garments of sturdy homespun. Unlike Godwin, however, Hartley uses the language of Christianity.

In the 'First Part' of Hartley's work 'The doctrines of vibration and association' are proposed, and he proceeds to 'Ideas, their Generation and Associations, and . . . the Agreement of the Doctrine of Vibrations with the Phaenomena of Ideas', as well as 'muscular Motion', the senses of 'Feeling', 'Taste', 'Smell', 'Sight', 'Hearing', 'The Desires of the Sexes towards each other', 'the Affections in general', 'Memory', 'Imagination, Reveries and Dreams'. In the 'Second Part' Hartley goes on to discuss 'the Being and Attributes of God, and of Natural Religion', and in 'Chapter II', laboriously to discuss 'the Truth of the Christian Religion' under sub-titles such as 'The genuineness of the Scriptures proves the truth of the facts contained in them', and 'The reception which Christ, his forerunners and followers, with their doctrines, have met with in all ages, is an argument of their divine authority'. Hartley eventually concludes, at the end of his second volume, with 'the doctrine of ultimate, unlimited happiness to all. This doctrine, if it be true, ought at once to dispel all gloominess, anxiety, and sorrow, from our hearts; and raise them to the highest pitch of love, adoration, and gratitude towards God, our most bountiful creator, and merciful father, and the inexhaustible source of all happiness and perfection. Here self-interest, benevolence, and piety, all concur to move and exalt our affections' (Hartley, *Observations on Man* . . . (London, 1791), ii. 438). Despite his optimism, however, Hartley worries about matters that 'threaten ruin and dissolution to the present states of *Christendom*' (ii. 441)—e.g. 'The great growth of atheism and infidelity . . . open and abandoned lewdness . . . sordid and avowed self-interest . . . licentiousness and contempt of every kind of authority, divine and human, which is so notorious in inferiors of all ranks'—and insists that 'If we refuse to let Christ reign over us, as our redeemer and saviour, we must be slain before his face, as enemies, at his second coming' (ii. 455). But Hartley has, as it were, given the game away beforehand; at the 'Conclusion' of the 'First Part', under the title 'Remarks on the Mechanism of the Human Mind', he says that 'Besides the consequences flowing from the doctrine of association . . . there is another, which is thought by many to have a pernicious tendency in respect of morality and religion. . . . The consequence I mean is that of the mechanism or necessity of human actions, in opposition to what is generally termed free-will. Here then I will First, state my notion of this mechanism or necessity . . . '—and he then attempts to justify the view from a religious standpoint (Hartley, i. 500). See further Richard Haven, 'Coleridge, Hartley, and the Mystics', *JHI*, xx (1959), 477–94; and Robert Marsh, 'The Second Part of Hartley's System', *JHI*, xx (1959), 263–73, where the fittingness of the religious overlay is defended. Coleridge, however, believed that '. . . the whole of the second volume is, with the fewest possible exceptions, independent of his peculiar system' (*Biographia*, i. 84).

Priestley was more fiery in his religious unorthodoxy. A sample of his polemical persuasiveness, and at the same time a summary of his position, is his contrast of '*socinianism*' with orthodoxy (or what he calls the '*Supralapsarian system*') : 'There is something *striking* and *consistent* in the genuine *Supralapsarian system*, of the eternally destined fall of man, an infinite penalty incurred by one, and by the imputation of his sin, affecting all, and an infinite atonement adequate to it made by an infinite being; by which means a small remnant of the human race are necessarily saved, while all the rest of mankind, including new-born children, unbelieving jews, mahometans and heathens, arminians and baxterians, arians and socinians, without distinction (as destitute either of faith, or the right faith) are consigned to everlasting torments with the devil and *his* angels; from whence results *glory* to a God, who, in all this dreadful scheme, is supposed to have sought nothing else.

'These are the *tremendous doctrines* which have over-awed mankind for so many centuries; and, compared with this, all the modern *qualified, intermediate systems* are crude, incoherent, and contemptible things. My antagonists may cavil at *election* and *reprobation*, or any other single article in the well-compacted system, but every part is necessary to the whole; and if one stone be pushed out of its place, the whole building tumbles to the ground. And when, in consequence of their ill-judged attempts to alter, patch, and repair, they have brought things to this catastrophe, there will be nothing left but the simple belief, that the merciful parent of the universe, who never meant any thing but the happiness of his creatures, sent his well-beloved son, *the man, Christ Jesus*, to reclaim men from their wickedness, and to teach them the way of righteousness; assuring them, for their encouragement, of the free and unbought pardon of their sins, and promising a life of endless happiness to all that receive and obey the gospel, by repenting of their sins, and bringing forth fruits meet for repentance.

'This is the essence of what is called *socinianism*; and though this simple doctrine may, on account of its excellence and simplicity, be a stumbling block to some, and foolishness to others, I believe it to be the sum and substance of the gospel of Jesus Christ, and the wisdom and power of God' (Priestley, *Three Tracts* . . . (London, 1791), pp. 175–7).

Elsewhere Priestley makes more clear the central doctrine of Unitarianism

(somewhat glossed over in the passage quoted above), that Christ is 'mere man':
'If you ask *who*, then, is Jesus Christ, if he be not God; I answer, in the words of
St. Peter . . . that *Jesus of Nazoreth was* a man *approved of God* . . . Acts ii. 22.
If you ask what is meant by *man* in this place; I answer, that *man*, if the word be
used with any kind of propriety, must mean the same kind of being with yourselves . . . that is, *a mere man*, as other Jews, and as we ourselves also are'
(Priestley, *An Appeal to the Serious and Candid Professors of Christianity* . . .
([London?], 1771), p. 16). Again: 'So clear, my brethren, so full, and so express,
is the uniform testimony of the scriptures to the great doctrine of the proper
unity of God, and of the subordination of Christ, and all other being to him, that
the prevalence of so impious a doctrine as the contrary must be, can be ascribed
to nothing but the *mystery of iniquity* . . .' (ibid., p. 15).

The youngest of this trio of homespun pantheists was Godwin, who, less
religiously orientated than either Hartley or Priestley, was most insistent of all
on necessitarian hypotheses. 'Man', says Godwin, 'is in no case strictly speaking
the beginner of any event or series of events that takes place in the universe, but
only the vehicle through which certain causes operate, which causes, if he were
supposed not to exist, would cease to operate' (*Political Justice*, i. 306). Again, he
defines necessitarianism as follows: 'He who affirms that all actions are necessary,
means, that, if we form a just and complete view of all the circumstances in
which a living or intelligent being is placed, we shall find that he could not in any
moment of his existence have acted otherwise than he has acted' (i. 285).

Although it is possible that Godwin had barely heard of Spinoza, and probable
that he had never studied that philosopher, so compelling is the mould provided
by the human reason proceeding from given assumptions that Godwin exhibits
a strange congruence to Spinoza's tone as well as to his position. Thus his view
of reality as a whole: 'This view of things presents us with an idea of the
universe as connected and cemented in all its parts, nothing in the boundless
progress of things being capable of happening otherwise than it has actually
happened. In the life of every human being there is a chain of causes, generated
in that eternity which preceded his birth, and going on in regular procession
through the whole period of his existence, in consequence of which it was
impossible for him to act in an instance otherwise than he has acted' (i. 305).
(Compare Seneca, *De providentia*: '. . . scio omnia certa et in aeternum dicta lege
decurrere. Fata nos ducunt. . . . Causa pendet ex causa, privata ac publica longus
ordo rerum trahit.') And Godwin surveys the human situation with a rather
noble calmness reminiscent of the great Jew's austere splendour of vision—even,
curiously enough, of the disembodied geometric images to which Spinoza
habitually appeals: 'A further consequence of the doctrine of necessity is its
tendency to make us survey all events with a tranquil and placid temper. . . . He
therefore who regards all things past, present and to come as links of an indissoluble chain, will, as often as he recollects this comprehensive view, be superior
to the tumult of passion; and will reflect upon the moral concerns of mankind
with the same clearness of perception, the same unalterable firmness of judgment
and the same tranquillity as we are accustomed to do upon the truths of geometry'
(*Political Justice*, i. 316).

Several modern commentators have noted the similarity of Godwin's thought to that of Spinoza, among them Frank Lea (in *Shelley and the Romantic Revolution*) and D. H. Monro. The latter says that 'The reason to which [Godwin] pins his faith is, in the last analysis, something like Spinoza's *scientia intuitiva*', that 'in his final conclusions about the nature of generalization, Godwin is curiously close to Spinoza', and that Godwin 'may not . . . have been directly influenced by Spinoza, but he comes very close to him' (D. H. Monro, *Godwin's Moral Philosophy; An Interpretation of William Godwin* (London, 1953), pp. 12, 22, 181). Godwin's pantheism, however, seems to have been largely untutored; in youthful expressions considerably predating the *Political Justice*, he says that God 'is all in all, and all in every part', and that 'He exists through all time, fills all space' (printed in C. Kegan Paul, *William Godwin: His Friends and Contemporaries* (London, 1876), i. 27). Even more explicitly, he says that 'Religion is among the most beautiful and most natural of all things: that religion which "sees God in clouds and hears Him in the wind," which endows every object of sense with a living soul, which finds in the system of nature whatever is holy, mysterious, and venerable, and inspires the bosom with sentiments of awe and veneration' (i. 28). We may adopt Kegan Paul's terse comment on the passage: 'It is plain that this is not orthodox...' (i. 28).

EXCURSUS NOTE XV

Existential Shipwreck in Coleridge's Thought and Life

I⊤ was a sense of repeated defeat (his failure to take a degree at Cambridge, his unhappy marriage, his opium addiction as early as 1796, his disappointments in friendship, the attacks of the reviewers) and the omnipresent and mysterious inability to work steadily and justify his genius—in short, the shipwreck of his life—that seems to have led Coleridge to the mystery of sin and fallenness on the one hand, and paradoxically, to his conviction of the utter uniqueness of the individual self on the other. Though such experience of shipwreck was quite foreign to the Victorian mind, it has become for our own time the mark of the truly authentic in life. Thus Ortega y Gasset (in many ways the earliest and truest prophet of our modern situation) says: '. . . life is at the start a chaos in which one is lost. The individual suspects this, but he is frightened at finding himself face to face with this terrible reality, and tries to cover it over with a curtain of fantasy, where everything is clear. . . . The man with the clear head is the man who frees himself from those fantastic "ideas" and looks life in the face, realizes that everything in it is problematic, and feels himself lost. As this is the simple truth—that to live is to feel oneself lost—he who accepts it has already begun to find himself, to be on firm ground. Instinctively, as do the shipwrecked, he will look round for something to which to cling, and that tragic, ruthless glance, absolutely sincere, because it is a question of his salvation, will cause him to bring order into the chaos of his life. These are the only genuine ideas; the ideas of the shipwrecked. All the rest is rhetoric. . . . He who does not really feel himself lost, is lost without remission; that is to say, he never finds himself, never comes up against his own reality' (Jose Ortega y Gasset, *The Revolt of the Masses*, trans. anon. (London, 1963), p. 120). By this standard, no one, not even Kierkegaard, or Nietzsche, or Rimbaud, presents more authentic credentials than Coleridge. 'He was not a glamorous or systematic Romantic sinner who, like Byron or Baudelaire, seized on the idea of evil as a stimulus,' says House, 'he was a genuine sinner, who did what he believed to be wrong against his conscience and his better judgement; he was an important sinner, whose sins were meanness, hypocrisy, self-deceit . . . a tortured, tearful, weak, self-humiliating sinner' (*Coleridge*, pp. 18–19). And in listing the special facts of Coleridge's psychic life, House emphasizes the paradox of 'An inability to cope with what presented itself as the plain immediate duty . . . coupled with a very exact knowledge of what the immediate duty was' (p. 37). Thus, as early as 1794, Coleridge complains to Southey that 'My very Virtues are of the slothful order' (*Letters*, i. 132). From all sides there pressed in on him a constant and shattering proof of the need for grace. Thus drugs: 'What crime is there scarcely which has not been included in or followed from the one guilt of taking opium? Not to speak of ingratitude to my maker for the wasted Talents; of ingratitude to so many friends who have loved me I know not why; of barbarous neglect of my family. . . . I have in this one dirty business of Laudanum an hundred times deceived, tricked, nay, actually & consciously LIED.—And yet *all* these vices are so opposite to my nature, that but for this *free-agency-annihilating* Poison, I verily believe that I should have suffered myself to have been cut to pieces rather than have committed any one of them' (*Letters*, iii. 490). Thus too failure in human relationship: 'Scarce a day passed without such a scene of discord between me & Mrs Coleridge, as quite incapacitated me for any worthy exertion of my faculties by degrading me in my own estimation' (*Letters*, ii. 875). Thus a constant and poignant sense of inadequacy and unfulfilled time: 'There *is* a something, an essential something wanting in me' (*Letters*, ii. 1102). 'I am no Elm!—I am a crumbling wall, undermined at the foundation! Why should the Vine with all it's clusters be buried in my rubbish?' (*Letters*, ii. 929). 'I am loving & kindhearted & cannot do wrong with impunity, but o! I am very, very weak—from my infancy have been so—& I exist for the moment!—Have mercy on me, have mercy on me, Father & God!' (*Notebooks*, ii. 2091). 'This is Oct. 19. 1803. Wed. Morn. tomorrow my Birth Day, 31 years of age!—O me! my very heart dies!— This *year* has been one painful Dream / I have done nothing!' (*Notebooks*, i. 1577). Increasingly he began to be haunted by the 'Sense of past Youth, and Manhood come in vain, / And genius given, and Knowledge won in vain' ('To William Wordsworth', lines 69–70, *Poems*, i. 407). And the jaunty Pelagianism of a Sartre was not possible for a man whose experience was 'To know and loathe, yet wish and do!', who knew first-hand of 'the powerless will / Still baffled, and yet burning still!', of 'shame and terror over all!', of 'Life-stifling fear, soul-stifling shame' ('The Pains of Sleep', lines 48, 21–22, 26, 32, *Poems*, i. 390).

In this massive complex of experience, therefore, we find the groundwork of Coleridge's profound religiousness, and the evidence for his conviction that 'the doctrine of Original Sin gives to all the other mysteries of religion a common basis, a connection of dependency, an intelligibility of relation, and a total harmony, which supersedes proof' (*Works*, i. 293).

But it is not only in Coleridge's psychic life that we encounter the condition of shipwreck. His work too testifies. We think of *Christabel*. A still more fitting witness is *Kubla Khan*, whose incompleteness is somehow the only completeness possible. And this—the completeness of incompleteness—is that *Scheitern* (shipwreck) that Jaspers makes one of the ineradicable criteria of existence. Most of all, perhaps, is Coleridge marked as a truly existential thinker in the shipwreck of the *magnum opus*. For, as Spranger says, 'existence philosophy' is not merely 'knowledge *of* shipwreck' (das Wissen *vom* Scheitern), but 'shipwrecked knowledge' (die Wissenschaft *im* Scheitern) (*Der unbekannte Gott*, p. 20). Jaspers himself emphasizes that 'thinking is by nature systematic', yet that, paradoxically, true philosophy can never be absorbed into a completed system (*Philosophie* (Berlin, Göttingen, Heidelberg, 1956), i. 271–3).

Coleridge's failure cannot be separated from his success. He was, said Stephen, like 'a vine deprived of its props, which, though most of its fruit is crushed and wasted, can yet produce grapes with . . . full bloom . . .' (Stephen, iii. 356). His intellect, said Southey in 1815, was 'clear and powerful', yet he was 'the slave' of 'degrading sensuality'; 'he labours under a disease of the volition' (*New Letter of Robert Southey*, ed. K. Curry (New York, 1965), ii. 117, 118).

EXCURSUS NOTE XVI

Coleridge's Relation to Later Theological Thought

ANY discussion of the movement of theological thought since Coleridge's time must take into account Schleiermacher's enormous influence. As Barth says, 'at the peak of a history of theology of modern times belongs, and will for all time belong, the name of Schleiermacher—and no one beside him . . . the nineteenth century was, in the field of theology, his century' (*Die protestantische Theologie im 19. Jahrhundert* (Zürich, 1947), p. 379). In view of Schleiermacher's dominant role, therefore, it becomes an event of first importance that he specifically declared pantheism no threat to religion and no concern of theology; only piety (*Frömmigkeit*) was needed for religion, and a pantheist could be as pious as a monotheist. It cannot be admitted 'that pantheism belongs in our regard as something special'. Even when pantheism is thought of by 'the customary formula ἑν καὶ πᾶν', it must be conceded 'that the piety of a pantheist can be fully the same as that of a monotheist, and that the difference of pantheism' from Christianity 'lies wholly in the speculative realm'. Furthermore, says Schleiermacher, there has never been 'a church community' that has arisen 'on the basis of pantheism'—indeed, the name 'pantheism' is never used to designate a group of thinkers, but is employed only as an 'insult'. Therefore the disputes about 'these modifications of theism' do not belong to theology (Schleiermacher, *Der christliche Glaube*, pp. 67–69). Schleiermacher's 'piety', and his love of the universe, owed much to Spinoza (see especially P. Schmidt, *Spinoza und Schleiermacher; Die Geschicke ihrer Systeme und ihr gegenseitiges Verhältniss* (Berlin, 1868), which considers both similarities and differences); and in general, as one commentator says, 'as far as the fundamental features of his *Weltbild* are concerned, Schleiermacher is in fact a representative of the vitalistic pantheism of Herder, Goethe, and Schelling' (Hermann Süskind, *Der Einfluß Schellings auf die Entwicklung von Schleiermachers System* (Tübingen, 1909), p. 32). Friedrich Schlegel early celebrated the intrinsic pantheism of Schleiermacher by the exhortation to 'learn the true religious idea of "universe", if you have not already understood Spinoza, by reading the *Reden über die Religion*' (Schlegel, *Kritische Schriften*, p. 107). And in the *Reden über die Religion* Schleiermacher said that 'The whole religious life consists of two elements: that man surrender himself to the universe and let himself be stimulated by the aspect which the universe turns towards him, and then, that he transplant into himself this contact . . . and take it up into the inner unity of his life and being; and the religious life is nothing else than the continual renewing of this procedure'.

With this background we can easily understand Coleridge's divergence from Schleiermacher's position. Furthermore Schleiermacher, in declaring the problem of pantheism out of bounds, removed a major obstacle to the influx of Hegelian pantheism in theology. On the one hand there arose F. C. Baur and the learned historicism of the Tübingen school; and on the other, the audacious man-worship of Feuerbach: it is 'not I' but 'religion', says Feuerbach, that claims 'God is man, man God'; it is 'not I, but religion' that denies a God who 'is not man, but merely an *Ens rationis*'; 'I do not say that God is nothing, the trinity is nothing . . . etc., I only show that they are not what they seem in theological illusion'—they are rather 'the mysteries of human nature. . . . Religion is the dream of the human spirit' (*Das Wesen des Christenthums*, pp. xii, xiv, xv). Though Feuerbach represents an extreme from which other nineteenth-century theologians at least verbally recoiled (Bloch, in pointing out that Feuerbach is 'without Hegel not thinkable', says that in setting up 'a kind of religious humanism' Feuerbach proceeded 'totally to atheism'—*Subjekt-Objekt*, p. 401), his man-worship, together with the *laissez-faire*, community-orientated, generalized religiosity of Schleiermacher, defines the essential position of most of the later theologians of the century.

It was not until the advent of Barth that this 'desiccated humanism' (as Douglas Horton calls it) received a major challenge, especially in the *Römerbrief* and *Das Wort Gottes und die Theologie*: 'one can *not*', insisted Barth in the latter work, 'speak of God simply by speaking of man in a loud voice'. And against the background of the Schleiermacher–Hegel–Feuerbach domination of nineteenth-century theology, Coleridge seems remarkably at one with Barth's call to a renewed theocentricity. Coleridge probably exhibits as many points of difference with Barth as of similarity, because in general Barth stands in the tradition of Augustine and Calvin, neither of whom was especially congenial to Coleridge, who works rather in the counter-tradition of Origen. And to some extent Coleridge may seem like Schleiermacher; certainly he was no fundamentalist (e.g. 'Think only of the vast inferiority of the other Apostles to John and Paul—

and the distinct marks in the writings of the latter that he was becoming more and more doubtful of the Jewish Literarity in which he as well as the rest had understood the Second Coming of our Lord. What is Christianity at any one period? The Ideal of the Human Soul at that period' (*Unpublished Letters*, ii. 369)). Yet he speaks with distaste of 'the petty pietistic cant of the Schleiermacher School' (*Inquiring Spirit*, p. 134). Likewise, he proleptically rejects the Feuerbachian man-worship, and it is significant that he equates this position with pantheism: 'the proper Question therefore is this, whether Atheism in the form of Polytheism is better or worse than Atheism in the form of Sebanthropism, i.e., the reverence of *man* as the highest known impersonation of the One and all—which is Spinozism. I should reply: the Question is useless . . .' (*Critical Annotations*, p. 41). On the other hand, Coleridge comes very close to the whole position of Barth when he speaks of 'the sophistic results of every pretence to understand God by the World, instead of the World by God. It is an attempt to see the Sun by Moonlight' (*Inquiring Spirit*, p. 120). And one of Coleridge's most compelling statements is, in its fundamental emphasis, virtually a Barthian formulation: 'Observe: we must not worship God as if *his* Ways were as *our* ways. We must not apply to him, neither as tho' God were the same with sensible Nature, or the sum total of the Objects of our bodily senses. For Nature in this sense must of necessity appear to us but as a more subtle and exquisite sort of Machine—and so to think of God is a *deathly* Superstition. And to speak aloud to God and by the sound and meaning of our words to suppose ourselves influencing him as we in this way influence our fellow men—this is a *delirious* Superstition. . . . —In short, God is neither Man nor Nature; but of whatever excellence either partaketh, that with all other perfection God essentially *is*—and in this sense it may be said, that being neither, he comprehendeth both transcendentally' (*Critical Annotations*, p. 47). And if Coleridge enunciates the Barthian essential of the otherness and primacy of God, Barth enunciates the Coleridgean essential of the danger of pantheism: 'The doctrine of creation, or more accurately, of the Creator, speaks of God in His relation to our existence as such and to our world. . . . The knowledge of God as the Creator and of man as His creature and therefore the knowledge of the difference between God and man . . . would not be subserved if man was going . . . to look upon himself as . . . *the* creature, the partner of God. . . . With the proposition: God is the Creator! we acknowledge that the relationship of God and world is fundamentally and in all its implications *not* one of equilibrium or of parity, but that in this relationship God has absolute *primacy*. This is no mere matter of course, but rather a mystery, which all along the line determines the meaning and form of this relationship. . . . Heaven and earth are *not themselves God*, are not anything in the nature of a divine generation or emanation. . . . In opposition to what even Christian theologians have on occasion taught, the world must not be understood as eternal . . . the creation of the world is not a movement of God in Himself, but a free *opus ad extra*, finding its necessity only in His love . . .' (*Credo*, pp. 29–31). Indeed, Heim holds up Barth's theocentricity as the chief answer to pantheism: 'If God is reality, and not to be explained away in the sense of idolatry and pantheism, then we cannot attain what he is and wants by means of our observation and our power of reasoning. We are dependent on God's revelation' (*Glaube und Denken*, p. 226).

Of all modern theologians, however, Emil Brunner is the one to whom Coleridge stands closest. The similarity is one not only of specific emphases, but of subtler matters of tone and presupposition; and there are many passages in *Der Mittler* and in *Wahrheit als Begegnung* where we might almost think ourselves reading Coleridge himself. Agreeing with Barth in his rejection of the Schleiermacher tradition in theology, agreeing also with Barth in his conception of God, rather than man, as the central truth of religion, Brunner softens the Barthian theocentricity into a kind of Christocentricity (he thinks of himself as standing in the tradition of Irenaeus), and this Christocentricity is much like that of Coleridge. 'Faith in Jesus Christ constitutes the Christian religion. The centre and foundation of the whole Christian faith is "Christology", that is, faith in Jesus Christ, the Mediator.' Christ is 'the window through which "the eternal Light streams in"; this is His significance, and His alone.' 'In His very nature the gulf between God and man has been bridged. He himself is the bridge which God throws across to us . . .' (*The Mediator*, trans. Olive Wyon (Philadelphia, 1947), pp. 232, 401, 491). Like Coleridge, and unlike Barth, Brunner finds philosophy relevant for religion, and hence, like Coleridge, he is intrigued by Schelling, but like Coleridge, rejects him: '. . . in our further inquiry we must leave Schelling . . . out of account' (p. 131). Like Coleridge, he admires Kant and at the same time feels that Kant did not go far enough: 'Kant . . . is the only one among the Idealistic thinkers . . . who has recognized and admitted that evil is the positive resistance of the will to the law of good.' 'He, the enemy of all muddled thinking . . . the relentless logician, is forced by the very nature of the problem to come to the paradoxical conclusion of "inborn guilt" ' (pp. 127, 128). Like Coleridge, Brunner insists on the need for redemption: 'Religion of every kind is concerned with redemption' (p. 515). Like Coleridge, he emphasizes the sinfulness of man—'every ethical system proves itself inadequate which does not recognize that man has been created by God, and has fallen away from God'—and emphasizes the disease of the will—'. . . how can a sinner be made a just man? The answer "through the will" is false, for the will itself is sinful' (pp. 601, 611). Like Coleridge, he places great stress upon 'personality' in Christianity: '. . . a personality stands at the heart of the message of the Bible . . .' (p. 490). And, again like Coleridge, he finds 'personality' the true distinction of Christianity from other conceptions of religion: 'If the Christian religion speaks of the Eternal Word, and the Eternal Son, it does not speak of Him like the Platonist Philo, nor like Hegel, nor like Meister Eckhart, for it is speaking of Jesus Christ. We differ from Platonism in this, that we know the Eternal Son and the Eternal Word only in Jesus, in this real historical fact: the life of Jesus' (p. 405). And finally, like Coleridge, he opposes pantheism (p. 567) and affirms the supramundane as the essence of Christianity: 'He who brings to us the secret mystery of God, the mystery which apart from His coming would be for ever hidden from our sight, is indeed supra-mundane and supra-human; His place is "yonder", where God is; . . . in the mystery of His Person the secret of the personality of God is revealed . . .' (p. 248).

Though I suspect that Coleridge would have admired Brunner and Barth, and would have been deeply interested in Heim's phenomenological attempt to demonstrate the transcendence of God, I also suspect that he would have recoiled strongly from the still newer theologizing variously represented by Tillich, Bonhoeffer, Bultmann, Van Buren, and J. A. T. Robinson—which, despite ostensibly important differences in aims, methods, and vocabularies, has in common an almost finger-snapping, 'get with it' concern about 'updating' theology to 'modern' needs, and seems to me, underneath various pieties about kerygma, ground of being, hermeneutics, linguistic analysis (and notwithstanding specific denials of pantheism), to be little more than Spinozism ornamented with notions from Schelling, Heidegger, and other secularists. Though certainly Bultmann and Bonhoeffer, and also Tillich, were exposed to the full power of the Barthian revolution, their relationship to Barth is not unlike the relationship of the post-Kantians to Kant. As one commentator has said, 'the impoverished secularised versions of Christianity which are being urged upon us for our acceptance today rest not upon the rigid applications of the methods of scientific scholarship nor upon a serious intuitive appreciation of the Gospels as a whole in their natural context, but upon a radical distaste for the supernatural' (E. L. Mascall, *The Secularisation of Christianity*, p. 282). There is something ponderous and comical about Bultmann and Jaspers settling for us the fact that 'a corpse cannot regain life and climb out of the grave' (Jaspers, Bultmann, *Die Frage der Entmythologisierung* (München, 1954), pp. 20, 62). The canons of both fact and logic are satisfied by a simple answer: 'it can if it does.'

EXCURSUS NOTE XVII

Coleridge and Descartes

COLERIDGE refers to his 'reception and welcoming' of Descartes' *cogito* in the formula 'Cogito quia sum, et sum quia Cogito' (see above, p. 209, n. 6). In his *Logic* he elucidates the 'quia' fully: 'I affirm of myself, that I am. If a reason were required of me, . . . I could only answer—I am because I am—sum quia sum, For "*I* am", in the first person, *implies* self-consciousness. The only reason I can assign for my being conscious of myself, is that I am a self-conscious Being' (MS. Logic in the British Museum, vol. i, Egerton 2825, p. 37 facing). Coleridge elsewhere rejects the Cartesian formulation: 'The Cartesian Cogito, ergo sum is objectionable, because either the Cogito is used extra Gradum, and then it is involved in the sum and is tautological; or it is taken as a particular mode or dignity, and then it is subordinated to the sum as the species to the genus . . .' (*Biographia*, i. 184 n.). In both instances we see a curious ambivalence in Coleridge's attitude: a certain rejection of Descartes combined with a certain dependence on the Cartesian standpoint.

For this ambivalence there are probably several reasons. His need for Descartes is made clear by the continuing argument of this book. His coolness towards Descartes involves several factors. First of all, we must not underestimate the eccentric, but none the less real, power of Coleridge's prejudice against all things

French. As he tells Sir George Beaumont, he was from an early age 'a Despiser & Abhorrer of French Philosophy & French Morals' (*Letters*, ii. 1002), and even though Descartes himself was exempted from such fierce judgement, so strong a general prejudice almost undoubtedly held back Coleridge's sympathies from the kind of fellow-feeling necessary to a true understanding of a great thinker.

Secondly, we must realize that Descartes is a deceptively difficult philosopher. Though he is ostensibly the most straightforward of reasoners, he not only baffled most of his contemporaries (as the Objections to his *Meditations* show), but it is probably fair to say that very few before Gueroult, Alquié, and above all, Husserl, really saw the extent of his achievement. Coleridge, in short, probably did not fully understand Descartes. For a single example of the deficiencies of his study we may consider a notation of 1801 that the 'Cartesians indicated Body, when they said it was a being extended in length, breadth, and thickness—or depth/but they hereby imperfectly indicated, because these qualities belong to Space likewise' (*Notebooks*, i. 903). What Coleridge here takes to be an inadvertent fault in Cartesian thought is in fact a quite deliberate assertion : thus Koyré notes that Descartes 'denies that there is such a thing at all as "space", an entity distinct from "matter" that "fills" it. Matter and space are identical and can be distinguished only by abstraction. Bodies are not *in space* . . . the space that they "occupy" is not anything different from themselves' (*From the Closed World to the Infinite Universe*, p. 102). Compare Descartes, *Principia philosophiae*, pt. II, par. 10.

Thirdly, not only did Descartes scorn Coleridge's beloved 'imagination', but in general he conceived nature as totally divorced from God. Though Coleridge welcomed help against pantheism, we must not forget that he was threatened by pantheism precisely because of his love of nature. Hence Descartes was for Coleridge quite unacceptable in his view of nature: '. . . Descartes was the first man who made nature utterly lifeless and godless' (*Philosophical Lectures*, p. 376), and the corollary of this was that 'in consequence of' the 'dross & verbal Impurities' of 'Des Cartes's system', the 'System of Locke is found . . . completely bodied out in it' (*Letters*, ii. 699).

Fourthly, Coleridge, like Leibniz, found Descartes's radical rejection of the historical dimension of thought alien to his own deeply felt systematic conservatism. Accordingly, he speaks of 'that pernicious custom . . . in no small degree fostered by Des Cartes, of neglecting to make ourselves accurately acquainted with the opinions of those who have gone before us. . . . It is even better to err in admiration of our Forefathers, [than] to become all Ear, like Blind men, living upon the Alms and casual mercies of contemporary Intellect. Besides, Life is short, & Knowledge infinite; & it is well therefore that powerful & thinking minds should know exactly where to set out from, & so lose no time in superfluous Discoveries of Truths long before discovered' (*Letters*, ii. 700-1).

Despite these antipathies, Coleridge did study Descartes respectfully—as we can see especially from four long letters of February 1801 to Josiah Wedgwood (*Letters*, ii. 677–703); see also J. I. Lindsay, 'Coleridge Marginalia in a Volume of Descartes', *PMLA*, xlix (1934), 184–95. Like Leibniz, who considered the philosophy of Descartes, notwithstanding its deficiencies, the 'ante-chamber of true philosophy', Coleridge based his own philosophy upon the rock of the *cogito*—albeit in the 'Cogito quia sum, et sum quia Cogito' formula he extrapolated from Fichte. He was not an 'implicit disciple', but he thought that 'Descartes had been much misinterpreted' (*Table Talk*, 20 April 1811).

Coleridge needed a philosophy that protected the both-and of the moral self and of nature. If the problem had been simply how to conceive God so as to protect the moral self, Coleridge might well have adopted the Cartesian solution. As Koyré says, 'Descartes' God is perhaps not the Christian God, but a philosophical one. He is, nevertheless, God, not the soul of the world that penetrates, vivifies and moves it.' But such a solution takes away all dignity from nature: 'Descartes' God, in contradistinction to most previous Gods, is not symbolized by the things He created; He does not express Himself in them. There is no analogy between God and the world; no *imagines* and *vestigia Dei in mundo*' (Koyré, *From the Closed World to the Infinite Universe*, pp. 122, 100). But, just as 'Nature ne'er deserts the wise and pure/No plot so narrow, be but Nature there' ('This Lime-tree Bower my Prison', *Poems*, i. 181, lines 60–61), so Coleridge could not desert nature. 'The utter rejection of all present and living communion with the universal Spirit impoverishes Deism itself, and renders it as cheerless as Atheism, from which indeed it would differ only by an obscure impersonation of what the atheist receives unpersonified under the name of Fate or Nature' (*Works*, i. 159). The abandonment of nature, in other words, was no more palatable to Coleridge than was pantheism itself. The 'moderns [Deists and Cartesian rationalists] take the 'Ο θεός as an hypothetical Watch-maker, and degrade the τὸ θεῖον into a piece of Clock-Work—they live without God in the world. The ancients are (at least some of them) chargeable with the contrary extreme—they take the τὸ θεῖον to the omission of the 'Ο θεός, and make the world the total God. True Philosophy begins with the τὸ θεῖον in order to end in the 'Ο θεός. . . . All false Systems may be reduced into these two genera— instead of the κόσμος ἐν θεῷ [the world in God] the former assumes a θεὸς ἔξω τοῦ κόσμου [God outside the world], the latter a θεὸς ἐν κόσμῳ [God in the world]. In the one the World *limits* God, in the other it *comprehends* him. Now the *falsehood* of both may be *taught*, both directly by subversion of the premises, and indirectly by the absurdity, and immoral *un*human nature, of the inevitable consequences' (*Letters*, iv. 768. To Tulk, Sept. 1817). We may question whether Coleridge's κόσμος ἐν θεῷ actually differs from the θεὸς ἐν κόσμῳ (see the Excursus Note on panentheism, p. 268) but we accept its enunciation as a sign of his both-and concern: to avoid pantheism and at the same time not to retreat from nature. If it seems that he thereby flirts with pantheism, our reply is that his whole career flirts with pantheism. Thus it is that Appleyard takes notice of his difficulty in freeing himself from 'the vaguely pantheistic implications of the whole unitive and integrative tendency in his earlier thought' (J. A. Appleyard, *Coleridge's Philosophy of Literature* (Cambridge, Mass., 1965), p. 208). In this respect, we should note the persistence of the 'one life' theme in his work. 'Nature has her proper interest', he writes in 1802, '& he will know what it is, who believes & feels, that every Thing has a Life of it's own, & that we are all *one Life*' (*Letters*, ii. 864). In 1817, the 'one life' reappears, in the errata to the

Sibylline Leaves, as the 'one Life within us and abroad', and in 1828 it is incorporated into *The Eolian Harp*, a poem first written in 1795. In short, hylozoism and the pantheist-leaning 'one life' are never far from Coleridge's thoughts: 'I cherish, I must confess, a *pet* system, a bye blow of my own Philosophizing; but . . . I must content myself with caressing the heretical Brat in private— under the name of the Zoödynamic Method—or the Doctrine of *Life*' (*Letters*, iv. 956. October 1819). Thus Coleridge never really gave up his commitment to the 'it is', and we must insist that if he had, his utterance would have lost its characteristic pregnancy and vitality, just as it would have done had he given up his allegiance to the 'I am'.

EXCURSUS NOTE XVIII

Coleridge and Scientific Thought

IT is evident from Coleridge's extensive marginalia in works of scientific speculation, from his correspondence (e.g. *Letters*, iv. 768–76), and from the *Theory of Life*, that he took his scientific interests seriously. A recent article, indeed, suggests that the *Theory of Life* actually fulfils the requirements projected for the *magnum opus* (Sam G. Barnes, 'Was *Theory of Life* Coleridge's "Opus Maximum"?', *Studies in Philology*, lv (1958), 494–514).

But it seems to me that Coleridge's scientific speculation—illegitimate in method and specious in conclusion—should be granted only a symbolical, not a substantive, role in any assessment of his thought. As scientific knowledge any validity it may prove to possess must be largely accidental. Not only does Coleridge seem to think that drawing a circle quartered by axes, or making thesis-antithesis-synthesis play with the conceptions of galvanism, light, gravity, and so forth, constitutes permissible scientific method, but, led on by the fancies of Schelling and his school, he renders opinions on subjects where he has no right to speak at all: e.g. 'Schelling & all others have attempted to explain the multeity (ex. gr. the Planets of the Solar System) out of the Unity (ex. gr. the Sun) by successive or simultaneous explosion. Now I take the reverse, and explain all out of the Multeity involved in each, and presupposed as the condition of its existence. This goes thro' the whole—the Earth *rose* in it's present position' (Henri Nidecker, 'Notes marginales de S. T. Coleridge IV. En marge de Steffens', *Revue de littérature comparée*, xi (1931), 282). Now why does such a statement, which in form is the same kind of assertion of opinion that we find so admirable in Coleridge's literary judgements, sound so inflated? Because, I suspect, Coleridge's opinions in literary and moral matters were in fact based on experience, thought, and knowledge, while his opinions on scientific matters were based merely on interest, and, doubtless, a certain amount of egotism. To be truly co-ordinate with his opinions on literature, the scientific opinions would have to represent hours in a laboratory and discipline in a method, and such a grounding they did not have. Accordingly, we may sympathize with the position of Lamb's brilliant friend, Manning: on an occasion in which, by Robinson's report, 'Coleridge was philosophizing in his rambling way', Manning 'sometimes smiled, as if he thought Coleridge had no right to metaphysicize on chemistry without any knowledge of the subject' (*Diary*, ii. 81).

To be sure, Schelling and his school sinned as flagrantly. As Wundt later contemptuously summed up the matter, *Naturphilosophie* is a 'Phantasiegebäude' (quoted in Carl Ihmels, *Die Entstehung der organischen Natur nach Schelling, Darwin und Wundt* (Leipzig, 1916), p. 79). And it is a fact of philosophical history that the over-reaching speculations of the German idealists in the area of natural science did more than anything else to discredit their thought and prepare the way for positivism. But in such a context, it is dismaying to realize that Coleridge's most ambitious forays into science were a mixture of slavish dependence on, and rivalry with, the school of Schelling. For instance, Coleridge's statement, 'as the Ideal is realized in Nature, so is the Real idealized in man' (*Letters*, iv. 769), appears as the final and summarizing quotation in a recent sympathetic attempt to salvage relevance from his scientific assertions (Craig W. Miller, 'Coleridge's Concept of Nature', *JHI*, xxv (1964), p. 96). But this statement, adduced as an apogee of Coleridge's scientific thought, is virtually a translation of Schelling's programmatic equation in the *Ideen zu einer Philosophie der Natur*: 'Die Natur soll der sichtbare Geist, der Geist die unsichtbare Natur sein' (Schelling, *Werke*, ii. 56). In general, to realize how much Coleridge depended on the daring phantasms of the *Naturphilosophie*, the reader unacquainted with German should consult J. B. Stallo, *General Principles of the Philosophy of Nature*.

In short, though we may not wholly agree with Beach that the *Theory of Life* is 'a bizarre farrago of pretentious nonsense' ('Coleridge's Borrowings from the German', *ELH*, ix (1942), 50), we should keep such harsh judgements in mind when we are tempted to overestimate the validity or importance of Coleridge's scientific opinions.

In terms of the general schematism of 'I am' and 'it is' relationships, however, Coleridge's *Theory of Life* and other scientific ventures are interesting as an attempt to formulate a system of nature that is not pantheistic. In the *Kritik der Urteilskraft* Kant had suggested that there were two possible ways of conceiving 'purpose' in nature: one, called 'Hylozoism', postulates 'ein belebendes inneres Prinzip, eine Weltseele', while the other postulates a 'mit Absicht hervorbringenden . . . verständigen Wesen' and is called 'Theism' (Kant, *Werke*, v. 470). The efforts of the *Naturphilosophen* had all been on the side of Hylozoism (in its pantheistic form); Coleridge, I suspect, was competitively trying to maintain the same degree of interest in nature in terms of Kant's second possibility, Theism. (Thus at one point in Schubert's *Ansichten von der Nachtseite der Wissenschaft* he remarks that 'The cause of this, as of almost every other, mistake of the Natur-philosophen is to be found in their Pantheism' (Henri Nidecker, 'Notes marginales de S. T. Coleridge III. En marge de Schubert', *Revue de littérature comparée*, viii (1928), 715)). In any event Coleridge took over the *naturphilosophischen* emphases: e.g. 'The vegetable and animal world are the thesis and antithesis, or the opposite poles of organic life'; '. . . *polarity*, or the essential dualism of Nature, arising out of its productive unity, and still tending to reaffirm it, either as equilibrium, indifference, or identity' (*Works*, i. 403, 391). At the same time he insists that he is 'convinced—by revelation, by the consenting authority of all countries, and of all ages, by the imperative voice of my own conscience, and by that wide chasm between man and the noblest animals of the brute creation, which no perceivable or conceivable difference of organization is sufficient to overbridge—that I have a rational and responsible soul . . .' (pp. 381–2). The proviso implies both dualism and theism.

Aside from its relevance to the problem of pantheism, Coleridge's *Theory of Life* is a document in the recognition of the organicism of natural life; indeed, in view of the fact pointed out by Abrams—that Coleridge's metaphorical consciousness tended to be dominated by images of trees and plants—one finds this strange and borrowed work curiously Coleridgean. In this respect, R. H. Fogle, making the *as if* plea that we disregard the whole question of Coleridge's borrowings, treats the *Theory of Life* as central testimony to Coleridge's preoccupation with ideas of 'organic unity' (*The Idea of Coleridge's Criticism* (Berkeley and Los Angeles, 1962), pp. 18–33). Likewise, if we extend Max Schulz's interesting conception of a 'farrago voice' in Coleridge's poetic utterance to other aspects of his practice, we find Beach's characterization of the *Theory of Life* as a farrago not so indicative of inauthenticity as might have been supposed (see Schulz, *The Poetic Voices of Coleridge* (Detroit, 1963), pp. 11–24).

EXCURSUS NOTE XIX

Coleridge and Boehme

BOEHME's constant preoccupation with the Trinity and his belief in the emergence of all things from God by means of a doctrine of contraries coincided to some extent with Coleridge's own philosophico-religious approach to the Christian mystery. Thus Coleridge says, in one of his marginalia, 'Not only the theosophical Truth, but the formal logical and theological accuracy and discrimination of Jac. Behmen's Explication of the Mysterious Tri-unity is worthy of reverential Wonder!' (Note on page 57, vol. i of the Law edition). Though it is not clear precisely how many of Boehme's works Coleridge read, he evidently read enough to be familiar with every aspect of Boehme's thought. Coleridge's marginal notes indicate that the treatises he studied most carefully are the *Aurora* and the *Three Principles*, and it is these two works that F. C. Baur, in *Die christliche Gnosis*, identifies as fundamental for a study of Boehme and his most perfect productions as well.

In at least the early stages of his own trinitarian reasoning, Coleridge found Boehme as useful as orthodox writers on the Trinity: 'Böem's (or as we say, Behmen's) account of the Trinity is masterly and orthodox. Waterland and Sherlock might each have condescended to have been instructed by the humble

Shoe-maker of Gorlitz, with great advantage to themselves . . .' (Marginal note at pages 39–40 of vol. i of the Law edition). But Coleridge later became more critical; in fact, it seems to have been his repeated exposure to trinal schemes among the pantheists that finally led him to realize that only the Christian Trinity—with its idea of person—could truly break the bonds of pantheism. Thus the 'Rock, on which Behmen still wrecks or rather bulges' is 'of itself . . . a proof how essential to . . . Religion a true Idea of the Trinity is—i.e. that it is the co-eternal Logos, in and by which God is manifest to himself . . . *not* the coagulation of Chaos, much less the Chaos itself. In short, there are but three possible coherent systems—I. That of Self-construction, according to which the Absolute organizes itself into the World = Pantheism. II. That of Self-mechanism, or rather of selfless Formation, according to which aboriginal Chaos is everlastingly mechanized into Particulars . . . & finally Consciousness, result = Atheism . . . III. That of the Trinity: and this third is the only possible escape from one or other of the two former' (Marginal note, page 23 of vol. ii of the Law edition). So when, in the *Mysterium Magnum*, Boehme writes that 'We Christians say, that God is threefold, but only one in *Essence*; But that we generally say and hold that *God is threefold in Person*, the same is very wrongly apprehended. . . . For God is no Person but only in *Christ*; but he is the eternal begetting power . . .', Coleridge comments: 'This opinion, which is likewise that of *Swedenborg*, has, I confess, in times past appeared just to me . . . if not directly asserted in the Gospel of St. John. . . . But deeper meditation has opened to me the error or ambiguity of the tenet, in the want of a previous definition of *Person*. If the word be confined to a manifestation ad extra, ex gr. in the present case, to all finite Being, the tenet is still defensible—in this sense God is a *person* only in the only-begotten Son, and *this* sense of Personality St. John expresses by exegesis. But if it be extended to the Self-manifestation of God as God, then it *burns*—i.e. borders too perilously on pantheism, and gives an atheistic sense to St. John's *In the beginning*: whereas St. John clearly meant the words 'Εν ἀρχῇ as synonymous with *Eternally* or From all Eternity. S. T. C.' (Marginal note, page 29 of vol. iii). And we can see also the main line of Coleridge's own trinitarian position emerging out of his reaction to Boehme: 'The Depth begetteth not, but in & together with the Act of self-realization the Supreme begetteth his substantial Ideas, the primal Self (I AM) its Other Self, and becometh God the Father, self-originant and self-subsistent even as the Logos or Supreme Idea is the Co-eternal Son, self-subsistent but begotten by the Father—while in the . . . inspiration and respiration of Love the Son is Deus alter et idem, and these words express the Triunity—Deus, Alter, Idem. i.e.: Deus: Deus alter: Deus idem . . .' (Marginal note, pp. 162–3, vol. iv).

We may well ask how successfully Coleridge extricated himself from the merely logical trinity of pantheistic speculation. His own habits of mind sometimes took him rather far from orthodox theology—indeed, in one of his musings he strikingly anticipates Freud: '. . . there are three analogous Acts in the human Consciousness, or rather three dim imperfect Similitudes; and if ever we have a truly scientific Psychology, it will consist of their distinct Enunciation, and Developement of the three primary Energies of Consciousness . . .' (Marginal note on page 40 of vol. i). Elsewhere he seems rather comfortably settled-in with thesis-antithesis-synthesis logic ('You may express the formula thus:—God, the absolute Will or Identity, = Prothesis. The Father = Thesis. The Son = Antithesis. The Spirit = Synthesis' (*Table Talk*, 8 July 1827).) Thus an unfriendly, but by no means foolish, nineteenth-century commentator charges that 'Coleridge's philosophy was a Neo-Platonized edition of Schelling's; . . . his theology had affinities with Popish rather than Protestant doctrine, but is essentially rather a semi-pagan theosophy or mysticism, baptized with a Christian and biblical nomenclature'—'in the Alexandrian philosophical Tri-unity he thought he had found the *nexus* between the philosophy of Schelling and the theology of St. John', but 'His Unitarianism, in fact, in later days, merely passed into a Neo-Platonized Sabellianism'. 'In what sense . . . Coleridge can be fairly considered a Trinitarian Christian, we cannot understand . . . his was practically a Sabellian view of the Trinity, under Neo-Platonic forms . . .' (James H. Rigg, *Modern Anglican Theology* (London, 1857), pp. 24, 10, 7, 12 n.). There can indeed be no doubt that Sabellianism (the merely logical or modal division of one god into three functions) was a heresy less repugnant to Coleridge than the other extreme of Tritheism (three separate gods), which was tantamount to polytheism. The Sabellian error at least had the virtue of holding to the one god of the Hebrews, and to Coleridge the *one* God took precedence over even the triune God. The 'truth of the essential unity of God has been preserved, and gloriously preached, by Christianity alone', he says, '. . . It has been objected to me, that the vulgar notions of the Trinity are at variance with this doctrine; and it was added, whether as flattery or sarcasm matters not, that few believers in the Trinity thought of it as I did. To which again humbly, yet confidently, I reply, that my superior light, if superior, consists in nothing more than this—that I more clearly see that the doctrine of Trinal Unity is an absolute truth transcending my human means of understanding it, or demonstrating it. I may or may not be able to utter the formula of my faith in this mystery in more logical terms than some others; but this I say, Go and ask the most ordinary man, a professed believer in this doctrine, whether he believes in and worships a plurality of Gods, and he will start with horror at the bare suggestion. He may not be able to explain his creed in exact terms; but he will tell you that he *does* believe in one God, and in one God only—reason about it as you may' (*Table Talk*, 13 April 1830).

Coleridge solved, to his own satisfaction if not to that of his critics, the threat of Sabellianism by invoking the I-Thou structure of person; thus it was 'from want of a previous definition of *Person*' that Boehme could make the mistake of saying that 'God is no Person but only in *Christ*'. In terms of the I-Thou, the 'pet text of the Arians', that 'My Father is GREATER than I', not only posed no threat to Coleridge's belief, but was actually necessary to the Trinity (*Works*, v. 538, 430). The I-Thou conception, in its Trinitarian application, not only works against Sabellianism, but, as formulated by Feuerbach in 1843, specifically repudiates Schelling's identity-philosophy. 'The absolute identity-philosophy', says Feuerbach, 'has totally displaced the standpoint of truth. The natural standpoint of man, the standpoint of the differentiation into I and Thou, Subject and Object, is the true, the absolute standpoint, thus also the standpoint of philosophy. . . . The Trinity was the highest *mysterium*, the central point of the absolute philosophy and religion. But the secret of the Trinity is, as was in the *Essence of Christianity* historically and philosophically proven, the secret of the communal, social life—the secret of the necessity of the Thou for the I—' (*Werke*, ii. 343, 345). Thus Coleridge's insistence on the 'Filial subordination in the Godhead' authenticated for him, in opposition to the abstract distinctions of Sabellianism and the polytheism of Tritheism, the true I-Thou relationship of Father and Son: an eternal togetherness and an eternal separation.

Scarcely less important for Coleridge than Boehme's analysis of the Trinity was his emphasis on 'will'. Though this concept came into philosophical prominence through Kant's analysis of the moral will in the *Kritik der praktischen Vernunft*, the dark, mysterious ultra-Romantic will of Schopenhauer's *Die Welt als Wille und Vorstellung* and Nietzsche's *Der Wille zur Macht* actually owes more to Boehme than to Kant, for Romantic 'will' is the Kantian moral will overlaid by Boehme's conception of God as 'the Will of the Abyss' (*Mysterium Magnum*, i. 2). 'We recognize the will as the eternal Omnipotence', says Boehme (*The Earthly and the Heavenly Mystery*, iii. 1). All things for Boehme arise out of nothing through the agency of will: 'The unground is an eternal nothing, but makes an eternal beginning as a craving. For the nothing is a craving after something . . . though this craving is also a nothing, that is, merely a will' (*The Earthly and Heavenly Mystery*, i). 'The life of man is a form of the divine will, and came from the divine inbreathing into the created image of man' (*The Divine Intuition*, ii. 2).

For the dissemination of Boehme's 'eternal, unfathomable will of life' (*The Divine Intuition*, ii. 8) in nineteenth-century thought, two works are of primary importance: Fichte's *Bestimmung des Menschen* and Schelling's *Über das Wesen der menschlichen Freiheit*. The latter work, published in 1809, utilizes 'will' to convert Schelling's philosophy from Spinozistic pantheism to a dynamic Boehmean variant. 'The first beginning of creation', says Schelling, 'is the longing of the One to give birth to itself, or the will of the depths' (*Werke*, vii. 395)—and such a statement is wholly Boehmean. 'In the final and highest instance', asserts Schelling, 'there is no other being than will, will is primordial being, and all the predicates of being apply to it alone—groundlessness, eternity, independence of time, self-affirmation' (*Werke*, vii. 350).

Though such dramatic emphases are clearly Boehmean, they are also in competition with, and doubtless to a large extent suggested by Fichte's *Bestimmung des Menschen*, which was published in 1800. In this dithyrambic discussion of freedom and necessity, Fichte recognizes that 'there is a forming power in nature' that produces 'flowers and plants and animals' (*Fichte's sämmtliche Werke*, ii. 177). He recognizes that 'I am an expression, defined through the universe, of a self-defining natural force' (p. 189), and that therefore 'I myself with everything I call mine am a link in the chain of strict necessity' (p. 179). But 'the system of freedom satisfies me, the opposed system of necessity kills and annihilates my heart', so he asks: 'What can I invoke against the idea of necessity?' (pp. 196, 198). His answer is 'will'—the force that rolls through both nature and man is not a material but a spiritual force: 'will'. 'The will is the living principle of reason, is reason itself . . .' (p. 288); 'My will, which I myself, and no foreign agent, ordain in the order of that world, is the source of true life and eternity' (p. 289). Just as, in his earlier thought, the individual ego was merely an expression of the absolute ego, so now does the individual will become a single expression of an 'infinite will', which is the mediator between 'the spiritual world' and 'me'; for this will is 'the ultimate source of both the spiritual world and myself' (p. 299). 'This will is the only true and unchanging essence, toward which my soul, out of its innermost depths, moves; all else is merely appearance and disappears, and turns back into a new illusion' (p. 299). 'That eternal will is therefore certainly the creator of the world . . .' (p. 303), and 'thus I live and am, and am unchangeable, secure and complete for all eternity; for the ultimate being is not one received from without, it is my own, unique true Being and Nature' (p. 319).

Plitt reports that when Tieck, in the autumn of 1799, was spreading the gospel of Boehme to an enthusiastic Schelling, Fichte 'wanted to know nothing about this fanatic or "confused dreamer"' (*Aus Schellings Leben*, i. 247). But Fichte, in the privacy of his study, seems to have done a bit of surreptitious homework on the 'confused dreamer'. One of Baader's editors says that 'it is definitely not to be doubted that Fichte knew Boehme's writings . . .' (Baader, *Werke*, xiii. 163).

Coleridge, like Fichte, Schelling, and other Romantic thinkers, was fascinated by the mysteriousness of 'will', and in the *Aids to Reflection* 'will' comes to the fore. The 'will' is the 'condition' of 'personality' (*Works*, i. 286). 'If there be aught spiritual in man, the Will must be such. If there be a Will, there must be a spirituality in man' (*Works*, i. 192). 'Unless . . . we have some distinct notion of the Will . . . insight into the nature of spiritual religion is scarcely possible . . .' (*Works*, i. 193). Will, in short, is a prime symbol of the incommensurability and transcendence of the ego: '. . . by *spiritual* I do not pretend to determine *what* the Will *is*, but what it is *not*—namely, that it is not Nature. And as no man who admits a Will at all . . . will suppose it *below* Nature, we may safely add, that it is super-natural' (*Inquiring Spirit*, p. 132).

Thus the 'will', like the 'I am' itself, appears in some of Coleridge's formulas for the Trinity: 'The Trinity is, —1. the Will; 2. the Reason, or Word; 3. the Love, or Life. As we distinguish these three, so we must unite them in one God. The union must be as transcendent as the distinction' (*Table Talk*, 15 May 1830). The similarities of this to Boehme's Trinitarian formula are obvious: '1. An Eternal Will. 2. An Eternal Mind of the Will. 3. The Egress from the Will and Mind' (*Mysterium Magnum*, i. 3).

Though similar, the two conceptions do not seem to have been identical. Thus when Boehme says that 'those Powers, which all lie in one Power, are the *Original of the Word*: For the one only Will comprises itself in the one only Power, wherein lies all hidden Secrets, and breathes itself forth through the Power into *Visibility*' (*Of the Election of Grace*, ii. 26), Coleridge comments: 'I fear that I have myself (thank God! the work is as yet only in MSS.) written incautiously on the absolute Will as the same with the ground of the Divine Existence, but this cannot be done without something of a Prolepsis. For the Will does indeed contain in itself Power and Intelligence as the Identity of both; but yet Might and Intelligence do not constitute Will—they are essential to it . . . but not *its* essence which is to be causative of Reality. Now here is the Abyss & the abysmal Mystery, that there is in the causativeness or All-might of God

more than God—an x y that God did not realize in himself . . .' (Marginal note
at page 162 of vol. iv of the Law edition). Again, when Boehme says 'the Will
is the *Beginning* and is called God the Father', Coleridge comments: 'In this
period commences Behmen's Error, and the false Leaven of his whole Theosophy. The Will is the beginning, only when considered as more and higher
than the *Ground* of Deity or the Abyss. But when used as = the Might, it is not
to be called God, much less God the Father' (Marginal note at page 162 of
vol. iv of the Law edition). It seems evident that Coleridge is here recoiling
from the kind of conception of the will that marks Schopenhauer's philosophy.

Less clearly relevant than the two preceding matters is the possibility of a
connexion between Coleridge and Boehme on the subject of imagination.
The formulation in the thirteenth chapter of the *Biographia Literaria* ostensibly
divides the imagination into two functions ('The IMAGINATION then, I consider
either as primary, or secondary'); but just as the 'secondary Imagination' is an
'echo' of the 'primary IMAGINATION', the 'primary IMAGINATION' itself is 'a
repetition in the finite mind of the eternal act of creation in the infinite I AM'
(*Biographia*, i. 202), and it becomes apparent that a third kind of imagination is
implied: a divine imagination. Coleridge's 'infinite I AM'—God—thus creates
the world by imagining it, and this conception we find in Boehme. As Koyré
says, 'Le Dieu de Boehme ne se borne pas à penser le monde avant de le créer: il
l'imagine' and 'imagination' is 'la puissance magique (*imaginatio = magia*) par
excellence; toutefois, elle ne confère pas à ses produits un être véritable, mais
seulement un être magique' (*La Philosophie de Jacob Boehme*, p. 214).

Just as Coleridge's 'secondary Imagination' is conceived as 'co-existing with
the conscious will' (*Biographia*, i. 202), so Boehme's imagination as divine magic
is bound up with the dark mysterious will: 'Magic is the mother of eternity, of
the being of all being; for it creates itself, and is understood in desire. It is itself
nothing but a will, and this will is the great mystery of all wonders and secrets,
but brings itself by the imagination of the desireful hunger into being. It is the
original state of Nature. Its desire makes an imagination (*Einbildung*), and
imagination or figuration is only the will of desire. But desire makes in the will
such a being as the will in itself is' (*Six Mystical Points*, v. 1–3). It is, indeed,
possible that Boehme's imagination as divine magic licenses Coleridge's statement, in the fourteenth chapter of the *Biographia*, about the 'magical power, to
which we have exclusively appropriated the name of imagination', and which is
'first put in action by the will . . .' (*Biographia*, ii. 12).

In the thirteenth chapter of the *Biographia Literaria* Coleridge seems to think
of 'imagination' as not only a mediator between 'I am' and 'it is', but as a mediator
between God and world. Dedicated to having both a personal God and a living
nature, he is, about this time, much exercised by the need for a relationship that
will not degenerate into pantheistic identity. Thus in the *Lay Sermon*, he speaks
of 'another book, likewise a revelation of God—the great book of his servant
Nature' (*Works*, i. 461), and the word 'servant' both indicates relationship and
disclaims identity. Likewise, at the very end of the *Biographia Literaria*, the
'I AM' and its 'filial WORD' has the 'universe' as its 'choral Echo' (*Biographia*, ii.
218), and the word 'echo' serves the same purpose. In this context, the Boehmean
idea of the world as 'imagined' out of God simply replaces the auditory image

of echo with the visual image of mirrored reflection. As Koyré says, 'La conception boehmiste de l'imagination est, selon toute probabilité, favorisée par le sens du mot *bilden*, qui veut dire former, d'où l'on peut tirer *einbilden* = informer et *sich einbilden* = *se former en* et *s'incorporer à*' (Koyré, pp. 218–19, n. 4). An imaginary world, however, is not really distinct from an imagining God; and probably it was Coleridge's eventual understanding of the hidden pantheism of the conception that accounts for the fact that in a copy of the *Biographia* examined by his daughter, he had crossed out the words that say the primary imagination is 'a repetition in the finite mind of the eternal act of creation in the infinite I AM' (*Biographia*, i. 272 n.).

On one important point, however, Coleridge found Boehme most unsatisfactory: Boehme did not properly distinguish between reason and understanding. 'Scarcely a Day of my Life passes in which I do not meet with some fresh instance of the Evils or Inconveniences arising from the misuse of the word, Reason, instead of the Understanding' (Marginal note at page 153, vol. iv). Again, in a comment on Boehme's remark that 'as Reason, which understands nothing of God, fancies . . .', Coleridge says: 'Reason has no *fancy*; but Behmen means the *Sense*, or the Understanding. . . . The Reason is a Participation of *Ideas*; & strictly speaking, it is no *Faculty*, but a Presence, an Identification of Being & Having. This sentence alone (and there are a hundred such in these volumes) would suffice to establish the sense of the word, *Reason*, in Behmen's use of the term, whether it be Vernunft or Verstand in the original—B. uniformly means that faculty . . . in *oppos.* to the *Reason*; i.e. the *Understanding*, or that which *stands under*, supports, and gives the form to, the *materials* supplied by the senses . . .' (Marginal note at p. 33, of vol. iii). Compare Koyré, *La Philosophie de Jacob Boehme*, p. 42 n.

As we have seen (p. 251 above) Coleridge in 1818 believed that he had 'extricated' himself from Boehme's errors. He had discovered Boehme to be a pantheist. But in a note at the beginning of Boehme's *Mysterium Magnum* he is writing: 'November 9th, 1819. With great delight I find, that Behmen guided by the light of a sincere love of truth, worked himself out of the Pantheism (God = Chaos) of his earlier writings: and seems in this Tract to have emerged into the full Day.' The following note, however, does not sustain the mood: '10 November, 1819. As I read on, I have found that this first Chapter is a deceptive Promise: that Behmen soon deviates into his original error . . . and places the polarities *in* the Deity, makes them eternal, confounding, first, correspondents with opposites, and *then* opposites with Contraries. . . . In short, Behmen remained, I fear and as far as I have hitherto read, a Cabiric Physiotheist' (Marginal note at p. 11 of vol. iii).

Coleridge's ambivalence about Boehme's pantheism, however, reflects not only his own inner conflict, but also inconsistencies in Boehme's position. Boehme does not always speak as though he were a pantheist, and he does always speak as though he were a Christian. Baader, accordingly, fiercely denies that he is a pantheist (e.g. '. . . die gegen Böhme erhobene Beschuldigung des Naturalismus und Pantheismus nur die Unkenntniss der Ankläger mit seinen Schriften beweiset' (Baader, *Werke*, xiii. 173); 'Wenn sich die neuere Philosophie mehr oder minder zum Pantheismus und Spinozismus neigte, so hält dagegen J. Böhme den Begriff eines supramundanen Gottes fest . . .' (ii. 373)). But Baader also says that Boehme is 'free' of all 'dualism' (xiii. 173), and the main difference between Boehme and Spinoza is that 'Bei Spinoza findet man nur das Petrefakt von diesem Begriff der göttlichen Substanz, den der Philosophus Teutonicus lebendig uns gab' (*Schriften Franz von Baaders*, hrsg. Max Pulver (Leipzig, 1921), p. 131).

Despite his deep piety, furthermore, Boehme in certain of his most important assertions seems clearly to favour pantheism: 'Da nun Gott diese Welt samt allem hat erschaffen, hat Er keine andere *Materiam* gehabt, daraus Ers machte, als sein eigen Wesen aus sich selbst' (*De Tribus Principiis*, i. 3); 'Höre du blinder Mensch, du lebest in Gott und Gott ist in dir; und, so du heilig lebest, so bist du selber Gott; wo du nur hinsehest da ist Gott' (*Aurora*, xxii. 46); 'So man nennet Himmel und Erden, Sternen und *Elementa*, und alles, was darinnen ist, und alles was über allen Himmeln ist, so nennet man hiemit den ganzen Gott, der sich in diesem oberzehlten Wesen in seiner Kraft, die von Ihm ausgehet, also creatürlich gemacht hat' (*Aurora*, ii. 33); 'Er ist aber von Ewigkeit zu Ewigkeit also unveränderlich, Er hat sich in seinem Wesen noch nie verändert. . . . Er ist von nichts herkommen oder geboren, sondern ist selber Alles in Ewigkeit: und alles was da ist, das ist von seiner Kraft worden, die von Ihm ausgehet' (*Aurora*, iii. 12).

NOTES

1 (p. 6). Evidently Hamilton's memory failed him on this point, because the charge had been incorporated by Ferrier into his *Blackwood's* article some six years before Hamilton's suggestion for the addition. Ferrier says: 'Before taking leave of the *Biographia*, we must plead, in a very few words, the cause of another German philosopher, pointed out to us by a friend [i.e. Hamilton], as having been very scurvily treated by Coleridge. In vol. i, p. 107, we find the name "Maasse" (*Maasz*, it should be) once mentioned by Coleridge, without however any commentary upon it, or any hint that he lay under the smallest obligation to the philosopher of that name. On looking, however, into this author's work [Ferrier's footnote at this juncture cites "*Versuch über die Einbildungskraft*. Halle and Leipzig: 1797"] we find that all the real information and learning put forth in *Biog. Lit.*, Chap. V, is stolen bodily from him. In B.L., pp. 100, 101, *et seq.*, a considerable show of learning is exhibited on the subject of the association of ideas; and of course the reader's impression is, that Coleridge is indebted for the learning here displayed to nothing but his own researches. But no such thing— he is indebted for it entirely to Maasz. He found all the quotations and nearly all the observations connected with them, ready-made to his hand in the pages of that philosopher. "Long before", says Coleridge, p. 100, "either Hobbes or Des Cartes, the law of association had been defined, and its important functions set forth by Melanchthon, Amerbach, and Ludovicus Vives, more especially the last." Maasz says precisely the same thing, p. 343. Then follows (p. 101) Coleridge's account of the distinction which Vives makes between *Imaginatio* and *Phantasia*. This distinction is distinctly pointed out by Maasz, p. 344. Then follow four quotations from Vives—all of which are to be found in Maasz, pp. 344, 345. In a word, all Coleridge's learning bearing upon Melanchthon, Amerbach, and Vives, is to be found in Maasz. Passing on to Coleridge's remarks on what Aristotle says on the subject of association, we find that here, too, his co-incidences with Maasz are a good deal *more* than coincidences' (Ferrier, pp. 296–7).

2 (p. 7). Thus at the very beginning of Carlyle's famous attack on Coleridge in the *Life of John Sterling* we find mention of Coleridge's status as interpreter of German thought, and Carlyle's excessive spitefulness on this occasion reveals quite clearly, I think, his sensitivity and envy: 'His [Coleridge's] express contributions to poetry, philosophy, or any specific province of human literature or enlightenment, had been small and sadly intermittent; but he had, especially among young inquiring men, a higher than literary, a kind of prophetic or magician character. He was thought to hold, he alone in England, the key of German and other Transcendentalisms . . . to the rising spirits of the young generation he had this dusky sublime character; and sat there as a kind of *Magus*, girt in mystery and enigma' (Carlyle, *The Life of John Sterling*, p. 53). In this connexion of mingled rivalry and spite we may recall Arnold's notice, on the one hand of Carlyle's own status as a purveyor of German culture to England, and on the other, of Carlyle's unfairness: 'The living writer who has done most to make England acquainted with German authors, a man of genius, but to whom precisely this one quality of justness of spirit is perhaps wanting,—I mean Mr. Carlyle . . .' (Arnold, 'Heinrich Heine', *Essays in Criticism; First Series*, p. 157). Again, we may see both effects—Scottish possessiveness towards the Germans and viciousness towards English intellectuals, especially Coleridge—in some amusing statements by Stirling. 'Hegel', he fantasizes in a moment of heavy good feeling, is 'a dry Scotsman who speaks

at, rather than *to* us . . .' (*The Secret of Hegel*, 1. liv), and 'Hegel is as a son of the border, home-spun, rustic-real, blunt . . . there are always the sagacious ways about him of some plain, honest, deep-seen, old Scotsman' (*The Secret of Hegel*, 1. lv). Such approval, however, is not extended to the interloper, Coleridge. His 'ignorance', we are told waspishly, 'is utter, and, considering the pretensions which accompany it, disgraceful' (*The Secret of Hegel*, 1. xxx–xxxi).

Inasmuch as Orsini has recently implied that we should, because of Stirling's role as a professional in matters of German philosophy, accept his judgements as to the deficiencies of Coleridge's knowledge of Kant, it is advisable to look at the matter a bit more closely. Stirling, it is true, had a considerable vogue in the mid-nineteenth century, and his *Secret of Hegel* received flattering commendations from German scholars as formidable as Erdmann (see the section on Stirling in J. H. Muirhead, *The Platonic Tradition in Anglo-Saxon Philosophy; Studies in the History of Idealism in England and America* (New York, 1931), especially pp. 170–1). None the less, there is little reason to think that Stirling penetrated any more deeply into the Critical Philosophy than did Coleridge. Watson attacks his knowledge of Kant in the most acerbic tones, e.g.: 'Dr. Stirling's appreciation of the *Aesthetic* seems to me to be inadequate; his view of the relations of sense and understanding, as expounded in the *Analytic*, I regard as a complete inversion of the truth'; 'I am compelled to reject unreservedly Dr. Stirling's explanation and criticism of the proof of causality'; 'I should like preliminarily to remark here, that Dr. Stirling's reconstruction of Kant's psychological state in writing the Second Analogy and the Prolegomena, I regard rather as complimentary to Dr. Stirling's power of imagination, than as based upon any real evidence' (John Watson, *Kant and his English Critics* (Glasgow, 1881), pp. 152, 229, 230–1). Again, Kemp Smith speaks of Stirling's Kantian scholarship with neither enthusiasm nor respect (*A Commentary to Kant's 'Critique of Pure Reason'*, second edition (New York, 1950), p. 366 n.).

To examine a single instance of Stirling's wilfulness in the denigration of Coleridge, he sneeringly says that 'it is not difficulty that Coleridge finds' in Kant, 'but, on the contrary "clearness and evidence". Hegel, for his part, found the study of Kant "difficult" and "hard"; and humanity in general have called him "dark". . . . Now Kant *is* obscure . . .' ('De Quincey and Coleridge upon Kant', pp. 212–13). A modern commentator, however, speaks as follows: 'That Kant was sometimes obscure as well as difficult I certainly do not deny, but I hold that much of what is frequently regarded as his obscurity is in fact nothing of the kind but is simply the natural and indeed the only way in which he could put what he wanted to say. I also think it unlikely that anyone will agree with me who does not approach his work historically and consider it as essentially the outcome of a development which took place over the whole of western Europe for two hundred years before the composition of the *Critique* as well as of Kant's own earlier philosophical training and outlook. It is indeed in the nature and working out of the system of Descartes that the problems of the *Critique* have their origin . . .' (T. D. Weldon, *Kant's Critique of Pure Reason*, second edition (Oxford, 1958), p. 3). Not to deny Stirling his own achievement, it is nevertheless fair to say that he, as a man of intelligence but modest learning, did not command the history of European thought for the two hundred years preceding Kant. Coleridge did. In any event, Paton avers that the 'obscurity to be found in Kant has been greatly exaggerated. As a writer he is very much clearer than most of his critics; and many of the alleged contradictions exist only in their imagination, and are due to misunderstandings for which Kant is not to be held responsible' (H. J. Paton, *Kant's Metaphysic of Experience* (New York, 1936), i. 49). On the flyleaf of his monumental commentary, moreover, in lone splendour like a benediction to his entire enterprise, Paton prints that very passage about 'the *clearness* and *evidence*, of the "CRITIQUE OF THE PURE REASON"'

(*Biographia*, i. 99) that Stirling finds so laughable an indication of Coleridge's fraudulent ignorance.

3 (p. 17). The Victorian emphasis on morality was of a heaviness that is by now legendary, and is rightly judged to be an identifying idiosyncrasy of the cultural situation of the time. But morals as such have, in the long stream of the Christian tradition, been little stressed by the great theologians; we will be saved by faith, not morals—and indeed, an over-emphasis on morals veers dangerously close to the heterodoxy of salvation by works. Christ's commandment of love is the fulfilment of the moral law, and in its dynamic demand rebukes the wooden restraints and the prideful righteousness that jut from moral codes. Hence Luther bids us to 'sin bravely', and Reinhold Niebuhr pointed out the common agreement of the best modern theologians that 'all human encounters must take place within the general presupposition that the difference between "bad" men and "good" men, though immediately important, becomes ultimately irrelevant; for no human virtue can meet the ultimate test'. It was Coleridge's misfortune to die at the very beginning of the Victorian Age of Morality, and as a result his peculiar neuroses and torments were for many years puffed up into 'moral' delinquencies in a way that still tends to obscure his true problems and his true contributions. It is a disheartening testimony to the incantatory power of the Victorian conception of the moral life that so humane, intelligent, and fair a man as Matthew Arnold could allow its vulgar entrance into his judgement; he is less the critic and more the medicine man exorcistically rattling his gourds, when he says: 'But that which will stand of Coleridge is this: the stimulus of his continual effort—not a moral effort, for he had no morals . . .', and again: '. . . Coleridge's memory, in spite of the dis-esteem —nay, repugnance—which his character may and must inspire . . .' (*Essays in Criticism; First Series*, pp. 274–5). To such presumption perhaps the best answer is Coleridge's own question: 'Is it or is it not true, that whoever supermoralizes unmoralizes?' (*Notebooks*, ii. 2358). We can understand today why a man with Thomas Arnold for a father would inevitably boast a powerful superego: a father at once so just and so powerful would arouse in the son the strongest and at the same time the most guilt-ridden resentments, the residue of which would achieve hypostasis as an exceptionally strong sense of inner check. John Stuart Mill, Samuel Butler, and Edmund Gosse, from different perspectives, have also borne witness to the overwhelming presence of the Victorian *paterfamilias*; and in general we can hardly doubt that the Victorian stress on restrictive morality was in large part bound up with the prominence of the father in that society. Coleridge's own ego, and his superego, on the contrary, appear to have been undernourished by the presence of a weak father. But I cannot persuade myself that Christian virtue is identical with the observance of Victorian morality; Matthew Arnold was a good and admirable man, but he was neither a better nor a more admirable man, nor a soul more worth the saving, than S. T. Coleridge.

4 (p. 30). Compare with Ferrier's bombastic horror about 'the extraordinary number of nineteen full pages, copied almost *verbatim* . . . an event in the history of literature altogether unprecedented', the ambivalences of Langbaine's charges that Dryden himself was a 'learned plagiary'. Indeed, Langbaine's attitudes reveal the slipperiness and contradictoriness of 'plagiarism' as a relevant literary category at all. On the one hand, we see him, as he candidly admits, writing a 'Censure' of Dryden's works (though to us it might seem a simple exercise in literary envy) in which Dryden's multifarious 'plagiarisms' are faults, and at the same time defending Jonson's 'plagiarisms' as virtues —to which end Langbaine takes approving note of 'plagiarism's' omnipresence in the greatest writers of the ancient world:
'Mr. *Dryden* . . . is for the most part beholding to French Romances and Plays, not

only for his Plots, but even a great part of his Language; tho' at the same time he has the confidence to prevaricate, if not flatly deny the Accusation, and equivocally to vindicate himself. . . .

'. . . As to [Fletcher's] Plots being borrow'd, 'tis what is allowed by *Scaliger* and others, and what has been practic'd by Mr. *Dryden* more than by any Poet that I know; so that *He* of all Men living had no Reason to throw the first Stone. . . .

'To come lastly to *Ben Johnson*, who, as Mr. *Dryden* affirms, has borrow'd more from the Ancients than any, I crave leave to say in his behalf that [Dryden] has far out-done him in Thefts. . . . I must further alledge that Mr. *Johnson*, in borrowing from the Ancients, has only follow'd the Pattern of the great Men of former Ages, *Homer, Virgil, Ovid, Horace, Plautus, Terence, Seneca,* &c., all which have imitated the Example of the industrious Bee, which sucks Honey from all sorts of Flowers and lays it up in a general Repository . . . there was an Illiad written before that of *Homer,* which *Aristotle* mentions, and from which . . . *Homer* is supposed to have borrow'd his Design. *Virgil* copied from *Hesiod, Homer, Pisander, Euripides, Theocritus, Aratus, Ennius, Pacuvius, Lucretius,* and others, as may be seen in *Macrobius* and *Fulvio Ursini,* which last Author has writ a particular Treatise of his Thefts. Notwithstanding, he accounted it no Diminution to his Worth, but rather gloried in his Imitation. . . .

'There is this difference between the Proceedings of these Poets, that Mr. *Johnson* has by Mr. *Dryden's* Confession *Design'd his Plots himself,* whereas I know not any One Play whose Plot may be said to be the Product of Mr. *Dryden's* own Brain. . . .

'But, tho the Poet be allow'd to borrow his Foundation from other Writers, I presume the Language ought to be his own; and when at any time we find a Poet translating whole Scenes from others Writings, I hope we may without offence call him a Plagiary; which if granted, I may accuse Mr. *Dryden* of Theft . . .' (Gerard Langbaine, 'Essay on Dryden', in *Critical Essays of the Seventeenth Century,* ed. J. E. Spingarn (Bloomington, 1957), iii. 111, 121, 122, 124, 125).

The extent and variety of these statements preclude their clarifying real issues. If we feel capable of drawing any clear conclusion at all from such a welter of contradictory attitudes, surely the most acceptable would be that 'plagiarism' is more a polemic weapon than a substantive category of literary history.

5 (p. 36). That importance can hardly be overestimated. As Spranger says at one point: 'Here, as so often, all lines and threads lead back to Shaftesbury, who, without being a thinker in the strictest sense sowed seeds on all sides that sprout up in the metaphysics, ethics, and aesthetics of the eighteenth century. In universality of effect he is like the very great: Socrates, Kant, or Leibniz' (*Humboldt und die Humanitätsidee,* p. 156). Compare the testimony of Josef Kremer: 'In Shaftesbury there lie the seeds of all the ideas which strove for possible clarity in the eighteenth century' (Kremer, *Das Problem der Theodicee,* p. 89). For other authority on this important matter see C. F. Weiser, *Shaftesbury und das deutsche Geistesleben* (Leipzig und Berlin, 1916); I. C. Hatch, *Der Einfluß Shaftesburys auf Herder* (Breslau, 1901); H. Grudzinski, *Shaftesburys Einfluß auf Chr. M. Wieland. Mit einer Einleitung über den Einfluss Shaftesburys auf die deutsche Literatur bis 1760* (Stuttgart, 1912); O. Walzel, 'Das Prometheussymbol von Shaftesbury zu Goethe', *Neue Jahrbücher für das klassische Altertum,* xxv (1910), 40–71, 133–65.

As to why Shaftesbury's influence was greater in Germany than it ever was in his native England, thus delaying the German Romantics in their discovery, in the Neoplatonists and above all in Plotinus, of prototypal patterns for their Romantic orientation, we may, I believe, find the clue in the influence of one man: Leibniz. Not only was Leibniz the most brilliant of German intellectuals during his lifetime, but he became after his death, through the academic endeavours of Christian Wolf, almost totally dominant in eighteenth-century pre-Kantian German thought (and Kant himself served his apprentice years in the Leibniz–Wolf philosophy). So when Leibniz threw all his great prestige into an admiring acceptance of Shaftesbury—a truly rapturous acceptance of Shaftesburian Neoplatonism as congruent to the central tenets of his own *Theodicy*—such an endorsement could not fail to have great weight with every aspiring young German intellectual of the mid-eighteenth century. Leibniz does in fact pull out all the stops in his praise of the most Neoplatonic section of Shaftesbury's *Characteristicks*; in a letter to Coste, accordingly, he says: 'I thought I had penetrated deeply into the opinions of our illustrious author [Shaftesbury], until I came to the treatise which is unjustly called *Rhapsody*. Then I perceived that I had been in the forechamber only and was now entirely surprised to find myself in the . . . sanctuary of the most sublime philosophy. . . . The turn of the discourse, the style, the dialogue, the new-Platonism . . . but above all the grandeur and beauty of the ideas, their luminous enthusiasm, the apostrophe to divinity, ravished me and brought me into a state of ecstasy. At the end of the book I finally returned to myself and had leisure to think about it. . . . I found in it almost all of my *Theodicy* before it saw the light of day. The universe all of a piece, its beauty, its universal harmony, the disappearance of real evil . . . It lacked only my pre-established harmony, my banishment of death, and my reduction of matter or the multitude to unities or simple substances' (Leibniz, *Philosophische Schriften*, iii. 429–30).

6 (p. 37). The ideational basis for the whole complex of Romantic philosophical distinctions: imagination, fancy, reason, understanding, symbol—as special and general, as lower and higher, powers of mind—is indubitably supplied by the traditions dating from antiquity. Thus, to cite an example, Richard Walzer summarizes Al-Farabi's theory of imagination as follows: 'Most remarkable is the theory of imagination adopted by Al-Farabi; its Greek author had probably taken as his basis Aristotle's view of φαντασία as modified by the Stoics but, under Neoplatonic influence, given it a new direction. . . . As the divine mind rules the universe, so reason should govern and control the life of man. No human faculty higher than reason can be conceived. . . . φαντασία, "imagination" or "representation", is intermediate between perception and reason; it not only provides reason with material derived from sense-perception but is also at the service of the rational faculty in other ways . . . cf., e.g., what the Neoplatonist Plutarch, following Iamblichus, has to say about the double aspect of φαντασία, and in particular its higher form. . . . Now, imagination is, according to Al-Farabi, also capable of an activity of its own, which is no longer dependent on the material supplied by the senses and preserved in the memory, and does not consist in combining or separating this material. . . . Through this creative φαντασία a kind of access to metaphysical truth with the help of images is open, this being a still higher activity . . . which manifests itself in translating metaphysical truth into symbols' (R. Walzer, 'Al-Farabi's Theory of Prophecy and Divination', *The Journal of Hellenic Studies*, lxxvii, Part I (1957), 142–6).

7 (p. 57). The opposition of the two thinkers, Husserl and Mach, whose writings laid the groundwork for the major divisions of twentieth-century thought into the existential and the positivist, can be most clearly schematized as the opposition of 'I am' and 'it is' viewpoints. Husserl departs from the Cartesian *cogito*: 'A radical and universal continuation of Cartesian meditations, or (equivalently) a universal self-cognition, is philosophy itself and encompasses all self-accountable science. The Delphic motto, "Know thyself" has gained a new signification. Positive science is a science lost in the world. I must lose the world by *epoché*, in order to regain it by a universal self-examination. *Noli foras ire*, says Augustine, *in te redi, in interiore homine habitat veritas*' [Do not wish to go out; go back into yourself; truth dwells in the inner man] (Husserl, *Car-

tesianische Meditationen, pp. 182–3). Mach, on the other hand, finds the 'I am' merely an illusory modification of the 'it is'. He speaks of the necessity to 'get rid of the conception of the Ego as a reality which underlies everything' (Ernst Mach, *The Analysis of Sensations*, trans. C. M. Williams (New York, 1959), p. 360). Mach makes the demand that the observer 'should consider the Ego to be nothing at all . . . resolve it into a transitory connexion of changing elements. . . . We see such unities as we call "I" produced by generation and vanishing in death' (p. 356). Consequently, he does not have 'the least objection to make to a criticism which decides that my position is incompatible with Kant's' (p. 367). 'In his philosophical notes', recalls Mach, 'Lichtenberg says : . . . "We should say, *It thinks*, just as we say, *It lightnings*. It is going too far to say *cogito*, if we translate *cogito* by *I think*. The assumption, or postulation, of the ego is a mere practical necessity." Though the method by which Lichtenberg arrived at this result is somewhat different from ours, we must nevertheless give our full assent to his conclusion' (pp. 28–29). For Lichtenberg's statement see *Georg Christoph Lichtenberg's vermischte Schriften*, hrsg. L. C. Lichtenberg und Friedrich Kries (Wien, 1817), ii. 84; see also *Georg Christoph Lichtenbergs Aphorismen*, hrsg. Albert Leitzmann (Berlin, 1902–8), v. 128, No. L 713. In regard to the continuation of the traditions of Husserl and Mach, we can identify Ryle's celebrated *The Concept of Mind* as embodying the presuppositions of the latter, and Merleau-Ponty's *Phénoménologie de la perception* the former. Both traditions verify William James's dictum that 'The history of philosophy is to a great extent that of a certain clash of human temperaments' (*Pragmatism: A New Name for Some Old Ways of Thinking* (New York, London, Toronto, 1948), p. 6).

8 (p. 72). Clarke provides an admirably succinct summary of Spinoza's position: 'Spinoza taught that there is no Difference of Substances; but that the Whole and every Part of *the Material World* is a Necessarily existing Being; and that there is no other God, but the Universe . . .' (p. 28); again: 'the Opinion of *Spinoza*, when expressed plainly and consistently, comes evidently to this: That *the Material World*, and every Part of it, with the order and manner of Being of each Part, is the only Self-Existent, or Necessarily-Existing Being' (p. 30). Clarke's *Demonstration*, which constituted the first Boyle Lectures, was delivered as a series of eight sermons at St. Paul's in 1704, and, though little read today, won extremely high praise, for its subtlety and logical consequence, from no less a figure than the seminally important mathematical logician, George Boole. As Boole says, 'The "Demonstration of the Being and Attributes of God", consists of a series of propositions or theorems, each of them proved by means of premises resolvable . . . into two distinct classes, viz., facts of observation . . . and hypothetical principles. . . . It is, of course, upon the truth of the latter, . . . that the validity of the demonstration really depends. But whatever may be thought of its claims in this respect, it is unquestionable that, as an intellectual performance, its merits are very high. Though the trains of argument of which it consists are not in general very clearly arranged, they are almost always specimens of correct Logic, and they exhibit a subtlety of apprehension and a force of reasoning which have seldom been equalled, never perhaps surpassed' (*An Investigation of the Laws of Thought*, pp. 186–7). Boole, in fact, rated Clarke's logical acumen higher than that of Spinoza himself: 'The Ethics of Benedict Spinoza is a treatise, the object of which is to prove the identity of God and the universe, and to establish, upon this doctrine, a system of morals and of philosophy. The analysis of its main argument is extremely difficult. . . . While the reasoning of Dr. Samuel Clarke is in part verbal, that of Spinoza is so in a much greater degree; and perhaps this is the reason why, to some minds, it has appeared to possess a formal cogency, to which in reality it possesses no just claim' (Boole, p. 187).

9 (p. 72). Bayle conceded that Spinoza had led a pure and blameless life, but refused

to admit that Spinozistic doctrine was thereby validated. In attempting to avoid the difficulties of a theistic position, Spinoza had, said Bayle, involved himself in far greater difficulties; Spinoza opposed dogma but was himself the most thoroughgoing of dogmatists; he denied the Biblical God and substituted a God partitioned into a million pieces. 'Ainsi dans le système de Spinoza tous ceux qui disent *les Allemans ont tué dix mille Turcs*, parlent mal & faussement, à moins qu'ils n'entendent, *Dieu modifié en Allemans a tué Dieu modifié en dix mille Turcs*: & ainsi toutes les phrases par lesquelles on exprime ce que font les hommes les uns contre les autres, n'ont point d'autre sens veritable que celui-ci, *Dieu se hait lui-même, il se demande des graces à lui-même, & se les refuse; il se persecute, il se tue, il se mange, il se calomnie, il s'envoye sur l'échafaut &c.* Cela seroit moins inconcevable, si Spinoza s'etoit representé Dieu comme un assemblage de plusieurs parties distinctes; mais il l'a reduit à la plus parfaite simplicité, à l'unité de substance, à l'indivisibilité. Il debite donc les plus infames & les plus furieuses extravagances qui se puissent concevoir, & infiniment plus ridicules que celles des Poetes touchant les Dieux du Paganisme' (Bayle, p. 1093.) Bayle's attack became the pattern, oft-repeated and deeply respected, of eighteenth-century anti-Spinozism—Diderot (see above, p. 76) follows it very closely in his great encyclopedia; and the learned Mosheim, in the notes to his Latin translation of Cudworth's *Intellectual System*, which was published at Jena in 1733 as *Systema intellectuale hujus universi*, observes: 'The partisans of Spinoza complain that his adversaries, and especially Bayle . . . have either wilfully perverted or egregiously misunderstood his meaning. And his new expositor [Boulainvilliers] repeats this complaint in his preface: although his book will convince all those who possess any knowledge of such matters, that most of this Atheist's [i.e. Spinoza's] opponents had a tolerably accurate conception of his meaning. . . . If I am not mistaken, Spinoza's friends were annoyed at finding his foul and flagitious doctrines expounded and set forth so lucidly and perspicuously [by Bayle]; and therefore, to save the reputation of the man, deemed it prudent to accuse his interpreter of ignorance' (J. L. von Mosheim, in Ralph Cudworth, *The True Intellectual System of the Universe*, trans. John Harrison (London, 1845), iii. 426 n.). And Voltaire, like Mosheim, accepts Bayle's view of Spinozism and defends Bayle against the charge of ignorance and unfairness: 'On reprocha au savant Bayle d'avoir attaqué durement Spinosa sans l'entendre: durement, j'en conviens; injustement, je ne le crois pas. Il serait étrange que Bayle ne l'eût pas entendu. Il découvrit aisément l'endroit faible de ce château enchanté; il vit qu'en effet Spinosa compose son Dieu de parties, quoiqu'il soit réduit à s'en dédire, effrayé de son propre systeme. Bayle vit combien il est insensé de faire 'Dieu astre et citrouille, pensée et fumier, battant et battu. Il vit que cette fable est fort au-dessous de celle de Protée. Peut-être Bayle devait-il s'en tenir au mot de *modalités* et non pas de *parties*, puisque c'est ce mot de *modalités* que Spinosa emploie toujours. Mais il est également impertinent, si je ne me trompe, que l'excrément d'un animal soit une modalité ou une partie de l'Être suprême' (*Œuvres de Voltaire*, avec préfaces, avertissements, notes, etc., par M. [Adrien Jean Quentin] Beuchot (Paris, 1829–40), xlii. 565).

Voltaire's 'battant et battu' suggests the opening of Emerson's *Brahma*, and, indeed, there is fundamentally little difference between the Spinozistic and Brahmanistic systems. For recent testimony, see S. Melamed, *Spinoza and Buddha; Visions of a Dead God* (Chicago, 1933), a work whose learning and perception are unfortunately somewhat obscured by its author's uncertainty in the handling of the English language.

10 (p. 73). Upon this and other occasions Malebranche expressed himself with vigour against Spinoza, yet so compelling is the Spinozistic expression of one universal tendency of thought that Malebranche himself was more than once during his lifetime reproached with Spinozism. Fénelon, in his *Réfutation du système du P. Malebranche sur*

la nature et la grace, tactfully but none the less explicitly posed a question concerning Malebranche's thought: 'N'est-ce pas ainsi que Spinosa, sous prétexte de raisonner avec l'exactitude géométrique sur les principes évidens de la metaphysique, a écrit des rêveries qui sont le comble de l'extravagance et de l'impiété?' (*Œuvres*, iii. 141–2). A like charge, in a context of great philosophical and human interest, was brought against Malebranche by the young scholar, Dortous de Mairan, in the course of a correspondence with Malebranche concerning Spinozistic thought. On 17 September 1713 Mairan wrote to Malebranche of his helplessness before the power of Spinoza's *Ethics*: 'En un mot, je ne sais par où rompre la chaîne de ses démonstrations.' Thus troubled, Mairan, having rejected 'les prétendues réfutations' of Spinozism, appealed to Malebranche—to 'la grandeur de votre génie et la justesse de votre esprit'—for help against Spinoza. On 29 September 1713 Malebranche responded that 'I was soon disgusted by the book, not only by the consequences of its doctrine, which are horrible, but again by the error of the pretended demonstrations of the author. He gives, for example, a definition of God that one might allow in taking it in one sense; but he takes it in another, from which he concludes his fundamental error, or rather in a sense that contains this error. . . . Take the trouble, Monsieur, to re-read the definitions, etc., that he cites in his demonstrations, and you will discover, if I am not mistaken, the equivocation that invalidates his proof. . . . The principal cause of the errors of this author, it seems to me, comes from his taking the ideas of creatures for the creatures themselves, the ideas of bodies for the bodies, and supposing that these are seen in themselves: a great error, as you know. For, being convinced internally that the idea of extension is eternal, necessary, infinite, and supposing besides that the creation is impossible, he takes the world or extended creation to be the intelligible world which is the immediate object of the spirit. Thus he confounds God or the sovereign Reason, which contains the ideas which illuminate our spirits, with the work that these ideas perform.' From this initial exchange there followed a series of letters in which, on Mairan's side, the horrified fascination by the power of Spinozism gradually gave way to something like an exposition and defence of Spinozism, and at last, Mairan's impeccable courtesy notwithstanding, resulted in the virtual charge that Malebranche's philosophy was itself Spinozism, or at least in its implications led to Spinozism: '. . . everything that you say in the beginning', said Mairan, 'about being in itself (l'être par soi) . . . could perfectly agree with the system of the author [Spinoza] . . .', and 'Thus the names *essence*, *representative*, *participable by the creatures* and *archetype of the bodies*, which you give your principle, and which seem to save or soften the consequence, reduce themselves, being well understood, to those of substance or of the essence of bodies . . .' (*Correspondance de Malebranche et de Mairan*, pp. 269, 270, 272, 297, 300, in Victor Cousin, *Fragments de philosophie cartésienne* (Paris, 1845), pp. 262–348). Baron d'Holbach, writing in 1771, made the charge more specific. The 'principes du célèbre P. Mallebranche,' he said, 'considérés avec l'attention la plus légère, semblent conduire directement au spinosisme . . .' (*Système de la nature* (Paris, 1821), ii. 100–1).

11 (p. 74). 'Ist was lächerlicher, als im Ernste zu sagen: diese Welt sey Gott? Dieser Staub, den wir mit Füssen treten, gehöre zu Gottes Wesen? Hasen, Hunde, Mücken wären Glieder Gottes? Ist was lächerlicher?' Mosheim's catalogue of absurdities—dust, hares, dogs, gnats as part of God's essence—was a customary anti-Spinozistic *reductio ad absurdum*. Thus More, half a century earlier, used a quite similar catalogue of absurdities in the effort to render Spinoza ridiculous: 'Hinc enim manifesto sequitur Materiam esse Deum, cum illa substantia & detur & facile a nobis concipiatur, & nulla tamen secundum hanc propositionem dari aut concipi possit praeter Deum. Hinc Lapides, Coenum, Plumbum, Stercus Deus erunt, ut quae sunt Materia' (*Opera*, p. 619). But we would probably be safe in assuming that Spinoza would have flinched neither

from Mosheim's 'dust, hares, dogs, gnats', nor from More's 'stones, dirt, lead, dung', for, in the *Ethica*, he had provided a general form of rebuttal to precisely such attacks: 'Many argue in this way. If all things follow from a necessity of the absolutely perfect nature of God, why are there so many imperfections in nature? such, for instance, as things corrupt to the point of putridity, loathsome deformity, confusion, evil, sin, etc. But these reasoners are . . . easily confuted, for the perfection of things is to be reckoned only from their own nature and power; things are not more or less perfect, according as they delight or offend human senses, or according as they are serviceable or repugnant to mankind' (Spinoza, *Ethica* 1, Appendix).

12 (p. 76). Noting that '*Spinosa* avait étonné et scandalisé l'Europe' by his theology, Diderot accuses him of violating the law of contradiction ('Les spinosistes ruinent cette idée . . .'), finds that 'le premier point d'égarement, qui est la source de l'erreur, se trouve dans la définition que Spinosa donne de la substance. . . . Cette définition est captieuse', and insists that 'les axiomes de *Spinosa* ne sont pas moins faux et captieux que ses définitions' (*Œuvres complètes de Diderot*, ed. J. Assézat et M. Tourneux (Paris, 1875–9), xvii, 173, 177, 192–3, 196).

The vigour of Diderot's attack is the more remarkable in view of the fact that his own ideas—e.g. Saunderson's speech in the *Lettre sur les aveugles*—approximated to those of Spinoza. Sainte-Beuve, among others, explicitly classes him among 'Les Panthéistes et Spinosistes' (*Port-Royal*, Bibliothèque de la Pléiade (Paris, 1953), i. 822). As another nineteenth-century commentator said: 'Sans le savoir et sans préméditation, Diderot se fit l'orateur du système dont Spinosa est le rédacteur géomètre: Diderot, c'est Spinosa en dehors, non qu'il ait eu l'intention expresse de répandre les principes du Juif d'Amsterdam: tant s'en faut, même dans l'Encyclopédie il le combat; mais Diderot fut aussi naturellement panthéiste que Spinosa; comme lui il fit une confusion idéale du monde et de Dieu' (E. Lerminier, *De l'influence de la philosophie du XVIIIᵉ siècle sur la législation et la sociabilité du XIXᵉ* (Bruxelles, 1834), p. 63). For extended discussion see Paul Vernière, 'Spinoza et l' "Encyclopédie" ', 'Le néo-spinozisme de Diderot', *Spinoza et la pensée française avant la révolution* (Paris, 1954), ii. 576–95, 595–611.

13 (p. 78). The phrase ἓν καὶ πᾶν, which after Jacobi's publication of his conversation with Lessing (see p. 81) became almost universally current as a synonym for pantheism, seems to have entered the western tradition through the Ἐκλογαί of Stobaeus, where it appears among excerpts from a lost work of Aëtius on the opinions of the Greek philosophers. As formulated by Aëtius the phrase describes the Eleatic philosophy of Zeno and Melissus: Μέλισσος καὶ Ζήνων τὸ ἓν καὶ πᾶν [sc. θεὸν εἶναι], καὶ μόνον ἀΐδιον καὶ ἄπειρον (*Aetii de placitis reliquiae* (*Plutarchi epitome, Stobaei excerpta*) i. 7, 27, in Diels's *Doxographi Graeci*, p. 303). The phrase, or something very much like it, was apparently in general use in antiquity as a description of the Eleatic theory of reality, but I believe that there is no exact duplication of its wording prior to the statement of Aëtius. Aristotle, for instance, speaking of Melissus, uses the phrase εἶναι ἓν τὸ πᾶν (*Physics* 185ᵇ7), while Heraclitus, earlier, says that all things are one—ἓν πάντα εἶναι (Diels, *Die Fragmente der Vorsokratiker*, i. 87 (Herakleitos B 50 (69, 13))). Plato, speaking of Melissus and Parmenides, uses the phrase ἕν τε πάντα (*Theaetetus* 180 E). For further discussion of the use in antiquity of πᾶν and πάντα in the predication of divinity, see Norden, *Agnostos Theos*, pp. 246–50. Neither Zeno nor Melissus, nor yet Heraclitus, however, was the first enunciator of the ideas underlying the doctrine of ἓν καὶ πᾶν for we have Aristotle's express statement that it was Xenophanes who was the first of these monists: Ξενοφάνης δὲ πρῶτος τούτων ἑνίσας (*Metaphysics* 986ᵇ21).

In this context, see J. G. Buhle, *De ortu et progressu pantheismi inde ex Xenophane Colophonio primo ejus auctore usque ad Spinozam* (Gottingae, 1790). Among modern scholars,

Werner Jaeger insists that 'Xenophanes is not to be dismissed with the word pantheist' (*The Theology of the Early Greek Philosophers*, p. 43). But W. K. C. Guthrie,
arguing specifically against Cherniss and Reinhardt, speaks of 'the conclusion which
has now become inescapable, that Xenophanes identified God and the world and to
that extent may be called a pantheist' (*A History of Greek Philosophy*, i (Cambridge,
1962), 381).

It is, incidentally, interesting to point out, in view of our concern with the question
of Coleridge's philosophical 'originality', that not even so early a figure as Xenophanes
can claim to be 'original'. Hence Jaeger, after summarizing his doctrines, concludes as
follows: 'Not one of all these ideas was new. They were at bottom the doctrines of
Anaximander and Anaximenes. But the work of Xenophanes was to preach them with
passionate conviction' (*Paideia; The Ideals of Greek Culture*, trans. G. Highet (New
York, 1960), i. 171).

14 (p. 79). There was no real doubt about the authenticity of Jacobi's report, but
only about the correctness of his interpretation. As Scholz says, 'That Lessing really
expressed himself as Jacobi has him talk can be doubted even less when the reported
utterances suggest a considerably different conception than Jacobi's exposition. Not
only the younger Reimarus and Herder so judged, but even Mendelssohn did not contest the possibility that Lessing might have thus expressed himself in a given situation.
Jacobi might rightly maintain that all who have known Lessing . . . certify that they
believe they are seeing and hearing Lessing' (*Hauptschriften*, p. lxiii). Mendelssohn
himself seems clearly to have thought that Jacobi lacked a sufficient knowledge of
Spinoza, or of philosophy in general, to judge correctly what he might have heard:
'Mendelssohn wants to know', wrote Elise Reimarus to Jacobi, 'precisely how Lessing
uttered these convictions. Whether he said, in so many words: I hold the system of
Spinoza as true and fundamental? And which system? That set forth in the *Tractatus
Theologico-Politicus*, or that in the *Principles of Cartesian Philosophy*, or the one which
Ludovicus Mayer after the death of Spinoza made known in his name? And if Lessing
referred to the system of Spinoza generally known as atheistic, then Mendelssohn asks
further, whether Lessing accepted the system as Bayle misunderstood it, or as others
have better explained it? And he adds: If Lessing were by way of agreeing so simply,
without more precisely defining his position, to the system of any man whatever, then
he was not himself at the time, or was in a special humour of maintaining something
paradoxical that he would reject at a serious hour. Did, however, Lessing perhaps say:
Dear Brother! The so very much decried Spinoza may well in some parts of his thought
have seen further than all the decriers . . .; in his ethics especially there are contained
excellent things, perhaps better things than in some orthodox moralities. . . . His
system is not so absurd as is believed' (Jacobi, *Werke*, iv-1, 43–44). Mendelssohn's later
tone, however, exchanged its patronizing tolerance for tight-lipped defensiveness:
'All friends and acquaintances of Herr Jacobi praise his rectitude; even extol his heart
above his intellectual gifts. How would his behaviour towards Lessing, however, be
reconciled with this rectitude?' (*Moses Mendelssohn an die Freunde Lessings*, p. 17). We can,
in fact, see in Mendelssohn's own description both his initially patronizing attitude
towards Jacobi, and his dawning realization that he was actually up to his neck—if not,
indeed, over his head—in philosophical controversy with a learned and subtle foe:
'I had never really known Herr Jacobi. I knew of his merits as a novelist; but I had
never seen anything of his in the field of metaphysics. Also I did not know that he
enjoyed Lessing's friendship and personal association. I therefore took this report to
be a mere anecdote that a traveller might perhaps have supplied him. This class of
traveller is well known in Germany—they carry their albums around from place to
place, and whatever they see or ascertain about a man of merit they dispose of here and

there in the greatest haste, or even dispatch for publication. Such a person, thought I, has perhaps picked up a half-understood word from Lessing, or perhaps Lessing has inscribed for him the Greek motto 'One and All' in his album, and the anecdote-hoarder immediately makes out Lessing to be a Spinozist. . . . The utterances of Herr Jacobi were therefore highly unwelcome to me, and I pressed for more precise explanation: how, on what occasion, and with what expressions did Lessing make known his Spinozism? The questions that I put to Herr Jacobi are perhaps somewhat too brightly expressed. . . . A letter directed to me by Herr Jacobi gave me sufficiently to realize that I had not known my man, that Jacobi had more deeply penetrated into the subtleties of Spinozistic doctrine that I supposed, that he had really had personal association with Lessing . . . and that therefore the report of Lessing's attachment to Spinoza was no mere anecdote-hoarding, but the result of these confidential conversations' (pp. 9–11). For a letter of Markus Herz to Engel, describing Mendelssohn's distress, just before his death, over the Jacobi controversy, see *Moses Mendelssohn; der Mensch und das Werk*, hrsg. Bertha Badt-Strauss (Berlin, 1929), pp. 242–6.

15 (p. 83). In general, Hamann's position was one of extreme nominalism; thus: 'Metaphysics has its language of the schools and of the court. I suspect both, and I am not in a position either to understand them or to make use of them. Hence I am inclined to think that our whole philosophy consists more of language than of reason, and the misunderstandings of countless words, the posing as real of the most arbitrary abstractions, the antitheses of pseudo-gnosis, and even the commonest figures of speech of the *sensus communis*, have produced a whole world of questions which have as little reason to be raised as to be answered' (*Schriften*, v. 21–22). Such an attitude is interesting as a forerunner of linguistic and positivistic orientations in modern philosophy, but it shares with modern philosophy a tendency towards over-simplification of problems and towards dismissal of all abstraction whatever as arbitrary; so when Hamann actually speaks of Spinoza, he seems to lose the forest of issues in the trees of linguistic quibbling. For instance: 'In Spinoza's first formula, *causa sui*, lies the whole error of logomachy. A relative term can by its nature not be thought absolutely without its correlatives. Therefore (*effectus*) *causa sui* is at the same time (*causa*) *effectus sui*. A father who is his own son, and a son who is his own father. Is there such an example in the whole of nature? Spinozism is therefore a view which contradicts nature, assuming as it does only one single existing thing, which is at the same time cause and effect, and can be infinitely thought and felt. One can as little identify what is thought and what is felt as one can identify cause and effect in one subject. Being is the cause and existence the effect! So idea and thing are one and the same? The word, a sign of the idea, and appearance, a sign of the thing, are one and the same? And there is no distinction, either in nature or in reason?' (p. 49).

16 (p. 83). It had, in fact, been Goethe's instinctive Spinozism that precipitated the epoch-marking conversation between Jacobi and Lessing. At their first meeting in July 1780 Jacobi, happening to have with him the manuscript of Goethe's poem *Prometheus*, handed the poem to Lessing as something with which the latter could while away the time while Jacobi himself wrote some letters. Jacobi made the remark, as he gave the manuscript to Lessing, that 'you have shocked some people yourself, so you might as well be shocked in return'. Lessing, after reading the poem, said: 'I was not shocked; all that can shock in this poem I experienced long ago at first hand.' Jacobi then agreed that the poem was a beautiful one, but Lessing countered with the remark: 'I mean something else. . . . Der Gesichtspunct, aus welchem das Gedicht genommen ist, das ist mein eigener Gesichtspunct'—the viewpoint from which the poem is written, that is my own viewpoint (Jacobi, *Werke*, iv-1, 51–54). And then Lessing,

as we have noted, amplified his statement by launching into praise of the ἕν καὶ πᾶν, was answered by Jacobi that in this attitude he would seem to be in agreement with Spinoza, and in his turn emphatically avowed his unequivocal Spinozism.

Of his philosophical apprenticeship to Jacobi at about this time, Goethe has left a beautiful and eloquent remembrance in his *Dichtung und Wahrheit*. There he speaks of 'Fritz Jacobi', whose nature 'worked in the deeps', who 'was far advanced before me in philosophical thought, even with regard to Spinoza', and who 'sought to guide and enlighten my dark striving'. 'Such a pure intellectual comradeship', says Goethe, 'was new to me and awakened in me a passionate longing for further communication. At night, when we had parted and withdrawn to our sleeping chambers, I would seek him out again. The moonlight trembled over the broad Rhine, and we, standing at the window, exulted in the fullness of the intellectual giving and taking that swelled so richly in that wonderful time of unfolding' (Goethe, *Gedenkausgabe*, x. 684–5).

Although Goethe felt himself inspired by Spinoza, his pantheism was fully developed long before he knew the Jewish thinker. Thus, a decade before he encountered Spinoza, he says in *Werther* (in Victor Lange's translation) that 'The rich and ardent feelings which filled my heart with a love of Nature' overwhelmed him with 'a torrent of delight, and brought all paradise' before him. 'When I used to gaze from these rocks upon the mountains across the river and upon the green valley before me, and saw everything around budding and bursting . . . when I heard the groves about me melodious with the music of birds . . . all this conveyed to me the holy fire which animates all Nature, and filled and glowed within my heart. I felt myself exalted by this overflowing fullness to the perception of the Godhead, and the glorious forms of an infinite universe stirred within my soul!' (Goethe, *Gedenkausgabe*, iv. 314–15). And at this early time too the panic predicate of a philosophy of Pan—the cost, that is, of such rapture—was likewise clear to Goethe: 'My heart is wasted by the thought of that destructive power which lies latent in every part of universal Nature. Nature has formed nothing that does not destroy itself, and everything near it. And so, surrounded by earth and air and all the active forces, I stagger on with anguished heart; the universe to me is an ever devouring, ever ruminating monster' (p. 316).

No large work on Goethe is complete without some consideration of his Spinozistic enthusiasm, but among the countless treatments, perhaps the most satisfactory individual study is Gerhard Schneege, *Goethes Spinozismus* (Langensalza, 1911).

17 (p. 91). As Jacobi argues, 'the Kantian philosopher wholly abandons the spirit of his system, if he speaks of objects (*Gegenständen*) that make impressions on the senses, thereby excite sensations, and in this manner bring about ideas (*Vorstellungen*): for according to Kantian doctrine the empirical object (*der empirische Gegenstand*), which is always only an appearance, cannot exist outside us and still be anything other than an idea (*Vorstellung*). Of the transcendental object (*der transcendentale Gegenstand*), however, we know according to Kant not the slightest thing; and also it is never of such an object that we talk when we are considering objects—its concept is at most a problematic concept.' It is the understanding, says Jacobi, which 'adds the object (*Object*) to the appearance, by connecting its manifold into one consciousness. Thus we say we perceive the object (*Gegenstand*) if we have brought about synthetic unity in the manifold of intuition; and the concept of this unity is the idea of the object = X. This = X is however not the transcendental object, for of the transcendental object we know not even that much. It is only assumed as intelligible cause of appearance in general, merely in order that we have something which might fit with the sensibility as a receptivity.' Even if 'it can be conceded that to these merely subjective realities—which are purely determinations of our own natures—a transcendental something may correspond as cause, where this cause may be, and what its relation to the effect may

be, remain hidden in the deepest darkness.' We have no experience whatever of this 'transcendental something', and can in no way or to any extent become aware of it. 'In respect to the way and manner in which we are affected by objects, we find ourselves in the most total ignorance. And as far as the inner arrangement or digestion of this material is concerned, by which it gets its form and the sensations in us become objects for us, this rests on a spontaneity of our being, whose principle is however completely and wholly unknown to us, and of which we only know that its first expression is the expression of a blind forward and backward connecting faculty that we call imagination (*Einbildungskraft*).' Thus 'our whole knowledge is nothing except a consciousness of connected determinations of our own selves, from which nothing further can be concluded'. 'In short, our whole knowledge contains nothing, absolutely nothing, which might have any truly objective significance' (Jacobi, *Werke*, ii. 301–7). As Friedrich Schlegel said, 'The polemical part of Jacobi's writings have great philosophical value: he has discovered the gaps, the consequences, the disjointedness, not merely of this or that system, but also of the century's dominating manner of thinking. And he has done so with critical intelligence and with the transporting eloquence of fair-minded indignation' (*Charakteristiken und Kritiken* (Königsberg, 1801), i. 34).

18 (p. 97). *Aenesidemus*, published in 1792 ostensibly as an attack on the Elementar-Philosophie of Reinhold, denies that Kant has refuted Hume and Berkeley and marshals singularly powerful attacks against all vulnerable points in the Kantian system. In his attack on the *Ding an sich* Schulze utilizes the following argument: the *Ding an sich* exists in the Kantian scheme as the assumed essence of any object or occurrence perceived as existing in the external world, and as such it is the hypothesized 'cause' of the phenomena; but since causality itself, if the Kantian axioms are accepted, is wholly a category of mind, with no real inherence in the external order, then causality cannot be attributed logically to the *Ding an sich*, and consequently the concept of the *Ding an sich* becomes meaningless.

'Reality', says Schulze, 'belongs of course to our knowledge, as even the *Vernunft-kritik* itself concedes, only in so far as the ideas of which knowledge consists stand in a connection with something outside them. Now if the things in themselves are *completely* unknown to us, then the connection of our ideas with the things in themselves, and even the possibility of such a connection, are also necessarily quite unknown. Whoever concedes the former must, if he wants to be consequent in his thought, also concede the latter. For if a thing is completely unknown to me according to all its predicates and conditions, then I cannot even know that it is there, that it stands in a connection with me, and that it is by way of effecting or occasioning anything. In so far, therefore, as the *Vernunftkritik* denies the reality and possibility of *all* knowledge of the thing in itself, and moreover explains even the principle of causality (from whose applicability to things in themselves one can demonstrate only that our ideas have causes of their origination outside themselves) as a principle that merely concerns the subjective association of our empirical intuitions in the understanding, and constitutes no objective law of the things themselves, to that extent it contests also the possibility of a knowledge of connections of our ideas with something outside them, and to that extent the assumption of a reality alongside certain of our ideas is, by the terms of the *Vernunftkritik*, a mere imagining' (Schulze, *Aenesidemus*, pp. 201–2). In another statement Schulze maintains that 'all real dependence of our ideas on things in themselves and outside us is absurd and unthinkable, and that furthermore according to the principle set forth by the *Vernunftkritik* all capability of the human mind of attaining to such a knowledge—as in the critical philosophy is certainly attributed to it with regard to the sensible world—must be totally denied. If the very concepts of existence (*Existenz*) and causality (*Caussalität*) are valid only in their application to that which belongs to the variations of our mind and takes place *in* our mind, if these concepts are only forms of thinking of perceptions, then a *real* dependence on supersensible things can be attached to no single idea in us, and it makes no sense at all when one attributes to these things . . . an existence and a causality in respect to certain ideas in us' (*Aenesidemus*, pp. 288–9).

We recognize such attacks as expansions of Jacobi's earlier objections. We also realize how important an impeachment of the *Ding an sich* was for the Spinozistic world view. For if, as Schulze would have it, the *Ding an sich* cannot be maintained as an existent external, then it makes no difference whether we simply drop the conception completely, or do as Fichte, Schelling, and Hegel did, 'save' the conception by identifying it with internal consciousness itself. In either case, we are left with a monistic systematization of the ego that is no less complete, nor less materialistic in its implications, than the system of Spinoza. As Jacobi says, in explication of the whole matter, 'it is undeniably the spirit of speculative philosophy . . . to make unequal the natural man's equal certainty of these two propositions: I am, and there are things outside me. It seeks to subjugate one of these propositions to the other, to deduce the "I am" from the "there are things outside me" or the "there are things outside me" from the "I am", in order that just one essence and just one truth may be seen. . . .' In these terms, says Jacobi, 'the two chief ways of philosophizing, materialism and idealism, have the same goal: the attempt to explain everything solely from a self-defining material, or from a self-defining intelligence. . . . Speculative materialism, worked out to a metaphysic, must ultimately transform itself into idealism. . . . Little was lacking for such a total transformation of materialism to have already been achieved by Spinoza. His substance, binding inseparably together the extended and the thinking essences, is nothing other than the unintuitable absolute identity of object and subject, confirmed only through deductions, on which the system of modern philosophy, the independent philosophy of intelligence, is based' (Jacobi, *Werke*, iii. 10–11). And, adds Jacobi, not only Schelling's Absolute Identity philosophy, but Fichte's *Wissenschaftslehre* is an 'umgekehrten Spinozismus'—a reversed Spinozism—transformed from materialism into 'a flame burning out of itself alone, having no place, and needing no fuel: *Transcendental Idealism!*' (p. 12).

Jacobi wrote to Bouterwek, on the occasion of the latter's praising Schulze's arguments, that 'you haven't done right by me. You attribute a service to Schulze that was already rendered by me five years earlier. My *Gespräch über Idealismus und Realismus* appeared in the year 1787, and his *Aenesidemus* first appeared in 1792. So far as I know, the third entity, assumed philosophically since Locke, that resides between the knowing subject and things to be known, was first properly got rid of by me' (*Jacobi's Briefe an Bouterwek*, p. 64).

19 (p. 106). Schelling's defence concedes a great deal, despite its ferocity: ' "The absolute *Identitätssystem* is in truth and fact the same as Spinozism" (which Herr Jacobi has for the last twenty-five years been explaining as atheism) p. 193 [of Jacobi's book] —I have in the preface to the first presentation of my system explained, that Spinozism in a certain (by no means Jacobian) sense is the one, chief, real side—necessarily underlying the ideal side—of all true philosophy. I hold to that assertion still, and I have tried to show how it is true. To that extent the statement that the identity-philosophy is Spinozist has nothing against it, so long as one adds that Spinozism is a part, an element; just as there is nothing insidious in saying that man is a physical substance, so long as this is not to mean he is only a physical substance.—That, however, the identity philosophy is nothing other than Spinozism, the proof of this matter we await from Herr Jacobi' (Schelling, *Werke*, viii. 26–27).

It is difficult to understand how Schelling thought he had answered Jacobi's objections, because Jacobi's whole point about Spinoza had always been that Spinozism's central reality was its logical submersion of all other views in itself—that its very nature was that it would not abide as a 'part' in another system. Thus, in terms of Schelling's analogy of the human being, Jacobi's simple answer would be that Spinozism is exactly that philosophy that does indeed claim that a human being is explainable as a physical substance and nothing more—that all his mental affects are merely apparent, not real, being transformations of physical effects—nerve impulses and the like. In other words, Schelling, like Schopenhauer (see note 2, p. 102), seems to think he covers himself with an armour of logic, while to us he appears to be wearing a tattered blanket of sophisms. Indeed, he customarily relies on purely metaphorical distinctions to salvage his thought from congruence with Spinoza's. The error of Spinoza, he says in a typical statement, does not consist in his having maintained 'an All-Oneness' (*All-Einheit*), but in that this All-Oneness is 'a dead, unmoving, unliving' All-Oneness (*Werke*, ii. 72).

In justice to Schelling, however, it might be argued that the Romantic sensibility tended to ascribe vast importance to metaphors of organic and dynamic kinesis. Thus Renan in effect agrees with Schelling when he says that 'L'univers pour Spinoza, comme pour Descartes, n'était qu'étendue et pensée; la chimie et la physiologie manquaient à cette grande école, trop exclusivement géométrique et mécanique. Étranger à l'idée de la vie et aux notions sur la constitution des corps que la chimie devait révéler . . . Spinoza n'arriva point à cet infini vivant et fécond que la science de la nature et de l'histoire nous montre présidant dans l'espace sans bornes à un développement toujours de plus en plus intense. . . . Spinoza ne vit pas clairement le progrès universel; le monde comme il le conçoit semble cristallisé . . .' (*Nouvelles études d'histoire religieuse*, pp. 508–9).

20 (p. 108). In his essay, 'Goethe and the Kantian Philosophy', Cassirer develops a statement in Eckermann—'. . . a curious remark, of great importance for [Goethe's] biography and for the history of ideas. . . . "Kant", says Goethe, "never took any notice of me, although independently I was following a course similar to his. I wrote my *Metamorphosis of Plants* before I knew anything of Kant, and yet it is entirely in the spirit of his ideas.'" Cassirer finds that Kant, by his *Kritik der Urteilskraft*, helped Goethe to formulate the distinctions by which he moved from the generic to the genetic in his biological approach. None the less, it seems to me that the real import of Cassirer's article is that this special and limited accord of the two thinkers took place within a general context of powerful oppositions, both psychological and theoretical. Thus at one point Cassirer writes: 'Was the idea Goethe formed of the Kantian theory adequate? Can we grant it objective historical truth? This question can hardly be answered with a simple yes or no. I should certainly advise no one to adopt Goethe's conception and account of the Kantian philosophy in a textbook on the history of philosophy. Goethe himself has told us that when he occasionally became involved in conversation about the Kantian philosophy and advanced his own idea of it, the Kantians present would shake their heads.' Discussing the fact that Kant 'aimed to extend, complete, and generalize Newton's ideas', Cassirer describes it as 'in sharpest conceivable contrast to Goethe's notion of nature'. He thus concedes that 'it is clear that there was for Goethe no approach to Kant through physics'. But then he also has to concede that there was no approach through pure philosophy either: 'Nor could Kant the logician, the critic of pure reason, offer [Goethe] any fundamental ideas. We know that in contrast to Herder he felt great admiration for Kant's masterpiece. He did not fail to make a real effort to understand it. His copy of the *Kritik der reinen Vernunft*, preserved in Weimar, shows the intensive study he devoted to it. But as a whole the work could never come to have for him the significance it held for Schiller.

It grew out of another way of thinking—and it lay outside the course of his life and training. He felt this clearly himself. "It was the entrance", he said, "which I liked. I never dared to advance into the labyrinth itself; my poetic gifts or my common sense soon stopped me, and I never felt I was getting much out of it" ' (*Rousseau, Kant and Goethe*, trans. James Gutman, P. O. Kristeller, J. H. Randall (New York, 1963), pp. 61–63, 96).

The fundamental antipathy between Goethe and Kant, again, reveals itself on the issue of Christianity versus pantheism. Shortly after the publication of Kant's *Religion innerhalb der Grenzen der blossen Vernunft*, Goethe wrote to Herder, 7 June 1793, that 'even Kant, who, throughout a long life, has tried to cleanse his philosopher's cloak from various disfiguring prejudices, has now deliberately allowed it to be stained with the shameful idea of radical evil, in order that even Christians will be drawn to kiss the hem of his garment'.

21 (p. 109). This sense of the 'panic' at the base of the philosophy of Pan crops out in all kinds of contexts in nineteenth and early twentieth-century writing. The meaning of panic is really the whole burden of Nietzsche's *Die Geburt der Tragödie*. Heavily indebted to Schopenhauer, it is quite simply a pantheist theory of tragedy—that is, a theory that sees the tragic combination of exhilaration and terror as stemming from the nullification of the personality in the face of the pantheist One. The origin of tragedy, argues Nietzsche (while calling for a Dionysiac reaffirmation in his own time), is the orgy of Dionysus, in which all individuality—the *principium individuationis*—is symbolically destroyed and merged into the primal One ('. . . the gulfs between man and man give way to an overpowering feeling of unity, which leads back to the heart of nature' (Nietzsche, *Werke*, i. 54–55)); the counter-principle of Apollonian rationality is of the order of dream, and its affirmation of individuality (though, under the aegis of Euripides and Socrates, it historically overcomes the Dionysian origins of tragedy) is ultimately mere illusion: 'Apollo stands before me as the transfiguring genius of the *principium individuationis*, through whom alone the redemption in appearance may truly be expected; whereas under the mystical Dionysian shout of joy the spell of individuation is broken and the way is laid open to the mothers of being, to the innermost kernel of things' (p. 110). Thus all culture and individuation is illusory, and true reality is the primal and terrible oneness of Pan. Nietzsche scorns the Arcadian pastoralism emphasized by earlier views of Greek culture, and he sees the sunlit deities of Olympus as mere masks placed over the terror of this true reality: 'Now it is as though the Olympian magic mountain opens itself to us and shows us its roots. The Greeks knew and perceived the terrors and horrors of existence . . .' (p. 31). 'In the Dionysian dithyramb man is incited to the greatest exaltation of all his symbolic capabilities; something never before experienced struggles for utterance—the annihilation of the veil of Maya, Oneness as the soul of the race, and of nature' (p. 28). But this revelation brings us face to face with the terror of individual existence: 'In the consciousness of the once perceived truth man now sees everywhere only the horror or absurdity of being' (p. 56). Confronted with 'dionysische Kunst', we are forced to look into the terror of individual existence (p. 117).

The same sense of the panic predicate of a philosophy of Pan appears in Freud's curious tractate, *Jenseits des Lustprinzips*, where the so-called 'Todestrieb'—death wish —is formulated as a corollary of a theory of instinct as the conservative tendency of any organism to revert to a former state. The basic instinct of life itself, therefore, is the urge to return to the lifeless state of undifferentiated nature from which existence is basically a deviation or abnormality (Freud, *Werke*, xiii. 39–40). Jaspers—antipathetic to Freud, although certainly not to Nietzsche—has expounded an analogous existential principle of 'Leidenschaft zur Nacht'—passion for the night (Karl Jaspers,

Philosophie (Berlin, Göttingen, Heidelberg, 1956), iii. 102 ff.). Also see above, note 16, p. 344.

22 (p. 110). Thus, in a few examples quite at random: '. . . an austere system of morals' (*Letters*, ii. 768); '. . . the *metaphysical* System of Des Cartes' (p. 699); 'My answer to Godwin will be a six shilling Octavo; and is designed to shew . . . the absurdities and wickedness of *his* System . . .' (*Letters*, i. 267); '. . . the Greek system' (*Table Talk*, 6 January 1823); 'Paley's whole system is reducible to this one precept . . .' (*Works*, v. 469). Catholicism was 'a complex bad system—a system, however, notwithstanding' (*Works*, v. 333). He speaks of 'the superiority of the Gospel as a system of religion . . .' (*Notebooks*, ii. 2971). Even Jesus had a 'system' (*Works*, v. 469; *Letters*, i. 293). And of his own effort, he almost always uses the word 'system'. 'The pith of my system', he says, 'is to make the senses out of the mind' (*Table Talk*, 25 July 1832). He tells Byron that the purpose of the first volume of what was to become the *Biographia Literaria* was 'to reduce criticism to a system' (*Letters*, iv. 598). And he felt that 'a true System of Philosophy . . . is *best* taught in Poetry' (p. 687). The *magnum opus* was to form 'a compleat and perfectly original system of Logic, Natural [Philosophy] and Theology' (p. 736). The concept of system so permeated his attitude, in fact, that he even saw the poem itself as a form of system: 'the common end of . . . *all* Poems is to convert a *series* into a *Whole*: to make those events, which in real or imagined History move on in a *strait* Line, assume to our Understandings a *circular* motion' (*Letters*, iv. 545).

23 (p. 110). Though the notes are not system, they are also not mere jottings. They reveal an intensely energetic mental activity, and vibrate with a kind of longing for reconciliation. In them, for instance, Coleridge speaks of '*Ego/* its metaphysical Sublimity—& intimate Synthesis with the principle of Co-adunation—without *it* every where all things were a waste—nothing, &c—' (*Notebooks*, ii. 2057). And again: '. . . I feel too intensely the omnipresence of all in each, platonically speaking—or psychologically my brain-fibres . . . is of too general an affinity with all things/ and tho' it perceives the *difference* of things, yet is eternally pursuing the likenesses . . .' (*Notebooks*, ii. 2372). As Beer maintains, 'Side by side with his visionary world of speculation, there is in his mind a positivist world of rationalist investigation, which he no doubt hoped would eventually be harmonized with it, but which none the less seems at times to contradict it flatly' (J. B. Beer, *Coleridge the Visionary* (London, 1959), p. 287). Schelling was able to achieve a systematic reconciliation only at the expense of this kind of fidelity of observation that Coleridge's notebooks show—there is nothing in Schelling, nor in any other of the German systematists, like these amazing intensities. It is in them that we see a quality of timelessness, not in the specious reconciliations of *Theory of Life*. When Coleridge says there that 'the whole *actual* life of Nature originates in the existence, and consists in the perpetual reconciliation, and as perpetual resurgency of the primary contradiction, of which universal polarity is the result and the exponent' (*Works*, i. 403), he not only takes over bodily the emphases of Schelling, but perverts his own authenticity in the process. It is not *achieved* reconciliation that constitutes Coleridge's authenticity, but the tension generated by the *longing* for reconciliation coupled with fidelity to experience, both internal and external. The notebooks, as we later argue, are mines of phenomenological *cogitationes*. Their harsh, minute, and faithful observations give the lie to all neat abstractions in which 'the vegetable and animal world are the thesis and antithesis, or the opposite poles of organic life' (*Works*, i. 403). See further, note 72, p. 380.

24 (p. 114). As early as December 1799, Coleridge complained to Southey that 'I have scarce poetic Enthusiasm'—a word, incidentally, that Coleridge tended to use in its

technical derivation—'. . . to finish Christabel' (*Letters*, i. 549). By September 1800 he lamented that 'Every line' of *Christabel* 'has been produced by me with labor-pangs', and then said bleakly: 'I abandon Poetry altogether—I leave the higher & deeper Kinds to Wordsworth' (p. 623). By February 1801, he was expressing the 'hope' that 'Philosophy & Poetry will not neutralize each other, & leave me an inert mass' (*Letters*, ii. 668–9), and by the end of March 1801, he was writing that 'I have *forgotten* how to make a rhyme' (p. 714). During this period, however, he speaks of himself as being almost totally absorbed in Leibniz and Kant, 'such a purus putus Metaphysicus am I become' (p. 676). Writing to Wedgwood in October 1802 he regards this not as a healthy manifestation, but as a form of escape from his personal troubles: 'Scarce a day passed without such a scene of discord between me & Mrs Coleridge, as quite incapacitated me for any worthy exertion of my faculties by degrading me in my own estimation. . . . I found no comfort except in the driest speculations—' (*Letters*, ii. 875). All these statements—whether about the abandonment of poetry, or the unhealthiness of metaphysics —reinforce, rather than invalidate, the conception of Coleridge as being fundamentally committed both to poetry and to philosophy; he defines his malaise in terms of the imbalance of these concerns ('. . . that which suits a part infects the whole' (*Poems*, i. 367))—and, ironically, he most profoundly laments the passing away of his poetic capacity in the 'Dejection' ode, which is surely one of the peaks of his poetic achievement.

25 (p. 125). And indeed, the kind of man associated with that body characteristically devoted much thought to the problem of pantheism, even if the word itself was not yet in vogue. Thus Robert Boyle, in 1685, in distinguishing different meanings of the word 'nature', issued a sombre warning against the tendency of the age to encourage pantheism: '. . . even in these times', he says, in what I take to be a reference to the Cambridge Platonists, 'there is lately sprung up a sect of men, as well professing Christianity, as pretending to philosophy, who (if I be not mis-informed of their doctrine) do very much symbolize with the antient Heathens, and talk much indeed of God, but mean such a one, as is not really distinct from the animated and intelligent universe, but is, on that account, very differing from the true God, that we Christians believe and worship. And though I find the leaders of this sect to be looked upon, by some more witty than knowing men, as the discoverers of unheard of mysteries in physics and natural theology; yet their hypothesis does not at all appear to me to be new'; or again: 'Since many of the most learned amongst the Naturists are Christians . . . it may not be improper . . . to add . . . that the next thing, for which I dislike the vulgar notion . . . of nature, is, that I think it dangerous to religion in general, and consequently to the Christian' (Boyle, *A Free Inquiry*, pp. 183, 191). In general, it can hardly be overemphasized that if, as Wolfson argues, Spinoza is concluding a philosophical dialogue originating in antiquity, it is equally true that he is speaking to issues current in his own day. For instance, though the *Tractatus* first appeared in Holland in 1670, a 'new edition' of Gerard Voss's *De origine ac progressu idololatriae* appeared in Amsterdam in 1668, and its enormous, double-columned folio volume was designed, states the preface, to show that the pantheistic formula 'Nature is God' is false, that God is not Nature, nor part of Nature, but rather the author of Nature: 'Cumque gentiles virtutem illam divinam quae est ab Deo, minime distinxerint ab altera, quae est in Deo; eoque ex naturae & mirandis collegerint, Naturam esse Deum: nobis contra propositum fuit, ostendere Deum non esse Naturam, vel partem illius; sed Naturae auctorem' (*De Theologia* in 'Benevolo lectori', the unpaginated preface to the new edition). Nor must we forget the formidable Hobbes, who in 1651 was claiming that 'The World (I mean not the Earth onely . . . but the *Universe*, that is, the whole masse of all things that are) is Corporeall, that is to say, Body; and that the dimensions of

Magnitude, namely, Length, Bredth, and Depth: also every part of Body, is likewise Body, and hath the like dimensions; and consequently every part of the Universe, is Body; and that which is not Body, is no part of the Universe: and because the Universe is All, that which is no part of it, is *Nothing*; and consequently *no where*' (*Leviathan*, p. 524). For further discussion of Spinoza's place in a complex of pantheistic and semi-pantheistic oppositions to Christian orthodoxy dating from the execution of Vanini in 1619, see J. S. Spink, *French Free-Thought from Gassendi to Voltaire* (London, 1960).

26 (p. 130). Montaigne said that he read much, but had trouble with his memory: his readers should not worry about where he took his statements, but about whether they were pertinent to what he said, that sometimes he availed himself of borrowings ('ce que i'emprunte') because their wording was better than his own, sometimes because their sense was—in any event, that he did not number his borrowings but rather weighed them. And he lightheartedly informs us that he sometimes deliberately inserts unidentified statements from Plutarch or Seneca merely to confound his critics—when they reproach him for incompetent opinion, they will make fools of themselves by blaming as his a passage from these revered ancients! (*Essais*, ii. 101–2).

Certainly Coleridge did not help his state of mind by his moralistic attitude towards his own borrowings, and one of the least lovely aspects of the whole curious matter is his psycho-analytical displacement activity—his being 'very sharp on plagiarism in others', as Stirling says. Thus, to cite a few examples, he charges Condillac with plagiarizing from Hartley ('. . . the Logic, which he basely purloined from Hartley' (*Letters*, ii. 947)); he accuses Madame de Staël of plagiarizing from Wilhelm Schlegel (*Letters*, iv. 667); he says, upon the appearance of *Childe Harold*, that he 'not only conceived' the same poem 'six years ago, but have the whole Scheme drawn out in one of my old Memorandum Books' (*Letters*, iii. 387); he tells Robinson that he had independently discovered the same theory of colour as Goethe (*Diary*, ii. 12); he is disingenuous about his own use of Wilhelm Schlegel (*Letters*, iv. 831, 839, 899, 924; iii. 845–6); and he taxes Sir Walter Scott with having plagiarized from *Christabel* (*Letters*, iii. 355–61). Elsewhere he announces that LaPlace commits an 'unprincipled plagiarism' from Kant (*Letters*, iv. 808), that Locke 'picked the pocket' of Spinoza (*Notebooks*, ii. 3217). But we should not too hastily condemn Coleridge for these accusations; they are psycho-analytically predictable once we realize that he accepted the Romantic conception of originality in a moral context. If he had been morally uninvolved, like Montaigne, or like Webster, who, as a recent commentator emphasizes, plagiarized serenely under the guarantee of Patricius that 'It is the custome of all writers almost, to enterlace other mens doings into their own . . . this is one kinde of fruit gotten by readinge . . .' (quoted in R. W. Dent, *John Webster's Borrowing* (Berkeley and Los Angeles, 1960), pp. 6–7), he would probably still have indulged his mosaic bent, but without either the guilt or the ugly displacement phenomena.

27 (p. 130). Underhill skirts the issue by distinguishing 'two extreme forms' of mystical philosophy: 'emanation-theory' and 'immanence-theory'. The latter, she more or less concedes, implies pantheism: 'Unless safeguarded by limiting dogmas, the theory of Immanence, taken alone, is notoriously apt to degenerate into pantheism; and into those extravagant perversions of the doctrine of "deification" in which the mystic holds his transfigured self to be identical with the Indwelling God' (Underhill, p. 119). The former, it is true, she attempts—with the hopeful inconsequence that we have come to recognize as the legacy of post-Kantian apologetics—to see as opposed to pantheism: 'at the opposite pole from this way of sketching Reality [i.e. the "theory of Immanence"]' is the "*Theory of Emanations*" (pp. 118, 116). But surely we understand by now that an emanatory system does not differ in any of its implications from Spinozistic

pantheism: if God and the world are not radically set apart (as vowel to consonant, in Jacobi's happy comparison: 'Je crois un Dieu comme je crois un monde sensible; je suis entre deux, et ma raison fait que je me trouve pour ainsi dire comme un mot composé de cette voyelle (Dieu) et de cette consonne (univers)'—*Briefwechsel*, ii. 354), then the system of their relationship will be pantheism. Thus, against Underhill's conception of immanatory pantheism and emanation-system as 'two apparently contradictory modes' (p. 116), we may invoke the authority of Eduard Zeller's great scholarship and insist on their identity: 'Hence it will now be clear with what right Plotinus's system is called an *Emanationssystem*. . . . It would perhaps be still more correct to call it a dynamic pantheism. The system is pantheistic, because it asserts a relation of the finite to Godhead according to which no independent being belongs to the finite. Everything finite is in this system mere accident, mere appearance of the divine' (*Die Philosophie der Griechen*, III. ii. ii. 560–1). Compare Novalis's laconic equation: 'Spinozism—Emanationssystem' (*Schriften*, iii. 170). And the nondistinction of emanation-system and pantheism is explicitly maintained by Jäsche: 'Thus the doctrine of emanation certainly rests on one and the same foundation as strict pantheism. The basic text of the ἑν καὶ πᾶν—union of all being in the being of God as the totality of all realities—is in both systems the same . . .' (*Der Pantheismus*, i. 80). Jäsche argues very extensively that emanation theory and immanence theory both reduce themselves to pantheism. The second section of his first volume, for instance, is 'Versuch einer wissenschaftlichen Begriffsbestimmung der Lehre des ἑν καὶ πᾶν in den Systemen der Immanenz und der Emanation nach ihren verschiedenen, aus dem pantheistischen Grundgedanken entwickelten Grundformen und Ausbildungsweisen' (i. 52–107), while in the second volume, the second part of the first section is 'Der orientalische Pantheismus in den Emanationssystemen der Kabbalistischen, Gnostischen und der Alexandrinisch-neuplatonischen Philosophie' (ii. 72–135).

28 (p. 134). Coleridge at one point in his writing expresses himself as favouring Schelling's view of Spinoza over that of Jacobi. 'We ourselves', he says, 'adopt neither statement entirely: tho' of the two we greatly prefer [Schelling's]' (Lore Metzger, 'Coleridge's Vindication of Spinoza: An Unpublished Note', *Journal of the History of Ideas*, xxi (1960), 293). We must realize, however, that this utterance was in a manuscript that dates from so close to the time of the *Biographia* as almost certainly to represent the same attitudes and enthusiasms. 'There is little doubt', concludes Metzger, 'that the MS. dates from some time between August 1817 . . . and January 1818' (p. 279, n. 6). In this manuscript, moreover, Coleridge 'vindicates' Spinoza in terms so extravagant (he asserts, for instance, that we do not 'possess any satisfactory proof' that 'Spinoza himself thought otherwise' than that his doctrines were 'in all essentials co-incident with the doctrines of Christianity, as declared in the Gospel of John, and the epistles of St. Paul' (Metzger, p. 284)) as to make the exorcising of Jacobi mandatory. Hence what seems significant is not that he here claims to prefer Schelling to Jacobi, but that his exorcism of Jacobi is so equivocal. Jacobi, he says, 'contends, first, that the System of Spinoza is atheistic; secondly, that it is a strictly consequent and the only strictly consequent Production of *demonstrative* or *ratiocinative* Theology; that all other works, that profess to demonstrate the existence and attributes of God . . . may be driven by fair argument to the same conclusions. . . . There is something to be said for all this: and Jacobi wanted neither subtlety or eloquence to say it in the most impressive manner' (Metzger, p. 291). And when Coleridge then comes to praise the 'celebrated Schelling', he says—rather wistfully, perhaps—that Schelling is 'a less polished, a less attractive writer than Jacobi' (Metzger, p. 292). Compare Friedrich Schlegel: 'Jacobi's authentic prose expression is not merely beautiful, but geniuslike—vital, intellectual, keen, and yet certain as Lessing's. He achieves this through a skilful use of charac-

teristic words and phrases from cultivated daily speech, and through sparing allusions to the true realm of the poet—as sophisticated as, but more soulful and sensitive than Lessing' (*Charakteristiken und Kritiken* (Königsberg, 1801), i. 37).

29 (p. 134). The sole mention of Jacobi in the *Biographia* is the humorous anecdote about the conversation of Jacobi and Lessing in Gleim's garden house, and its humour, I suggest, serves to divert attention—both ours and Coleridge's—from more serious conclusions about the meaning of Spinozism: 'SPINOZA and BEHMEN were, on different systems, both Pantheists; and among the ancients there were philosophers, teachers of the EN KAI PAN, who not only taught that God was All, but that this All constituted God. Yet not even these would confound the *part, as* a part, with the Whole, *as* the whole. Nay, in no system is the distinction between the individual and God, between the Modification, and the one only Substance, more sharply drawn, than in that of SPINOZA.' In this statement he probably takes his cue from Schelling: '. . . a more complete differentiation of things and God can hardly be conceived than is made in the teaching of Spinoza' (*Werke*, vii. 340). The passage then proceeds to the Gleim anecdote, which both distracts us from Spinozism and associates Jacobi with non-seriousness: 'JACOBI indeed relates of LESSING, that, after a conversation with him at the house of the poet, GLEIM . . . in which conversation L. had avowed privately to Jacobi his reluctance to admit any *personal* existence of the Supreme Being, or the *possibility* of personality except in a finite Intellect, and while they were sitting at table, a shower of rain came on unexpectedly. Gleim expressed his regret at the circumstance, because they had meant to drink their wine in the garden: upon which Lessing in one of his half-earnest half-joking moods, nodded to Jacobi, and said, "It is *I*, perhaps, that am doing *that*," i.e. *raining*! and J. answered, 'or perhaps I'; Gleim contented himself with staring at them both, without asking for any explanation' (*Biographia*, ii. 112–13).

30 (p. 142). For example, Heidegger says, 'Why are there essents, why is there anything at all, rather than nothing?'—obviously this is the first of all questions, though not in a chronological sense' (*An Introduction to Metaphysics*, p. 1). (Compare Leibniz: '. . . la premiere question qu'on a droit de faire, sera, *Pourquoy il y a plustôt quelque chose que rien?*', *Principes de la Nature et de la Grace, fondés en raison*, in *Philosophische Schriften*, vi. 602.) For a more generalized congruence with Coleridge's attitudes compare Husserl: 'Empiricists', he says, 'holding characteristically to an adopted standpoint, and in open contradiction with their freedom from bias, start out from unclarified, ungrounded preconceptions; we start out from that which *antedates* all standpoints: from the totality of the intuitively self-given which is prior to any theorizing reflexion, from all that one *can* immediately see and lay hold of, provided one does not allow oneself to be blinded by prejudice, and so led to ignore whole classes of genuine data. If by "*Positivism*" we are to mean the absolute unbiased grounding of all science on what is "positive", i.e. on what can be primordially apprehended, then it is *we* who are the genuine positivists. In fact we permit *no* authority to deprive us of the right of recognizing all kinds of intuition as equally valuable sources for the justification of knowledge, not even that of "modern natural science". When it is really natural science that speaks, we listen willingly and as disciples. But the language of the natural scientists is not always that of natural science itself . . .' (*Ideas; General Introduction to Pure Phenomenology*, p. 86). For further opposition to positivist views and a general affinity with Coleridgean attitudes, compare Jaspers: 'Positivism . . . rejects metaphysics as fantastic, although it can in no way overcome or nullify the reality of this fantasy in man. . . . Positivism can really not ask about transcendence at all, since it *does not leave the standpoint of consciousness itself*' (Jaspers, *Philosophie* (Berlin, 1932), iii. 12).

31 (p. 144). Coleridge's correspondence is voluminous by any standards. His note-books are extensive. He not only read many hundreds of books, but he annotated scores of them. He learned Greek, Latin, German, and Italian, and he could at least read French and Spanish. He knew some Hebrew. He actually published, further-more, several volumes in his own lifetime. In short, as Gillman insists, 'Coleridge never was an idle man' (Gillman, p. 91). To be sure, Coleridge did procrastinate, and his insights did outstrip his energies for organizing them, but his sloth was intertwined with a most unusual intellectual drive. 'It has not been altogether Indolence or my habits of Procrastination', he writes to Thomas Wedgwood in 1802, 'which have kept me from writing, but an eager wish, I may truly say, a Thirst of Spirit to have some-thing honorable to tell you of myself . . .' (Letters, ii. 874–75). And on still other occasions he is willing to acknowledge effort—thus, in the very act of self-blame for languor and neglect of duty, he can refer to himself as 'Intensely studious by Habit' (Letters, iii. 216), and he writes to Byron in 1815 that 'No one of my bitterest Censors have ever charged my writings with triviality; but on the contrary, they have been described as over elaborate, obscure, paradoxical, over subtle &c—and I know myself, that I have written nothing without as much effort as I should or could have employed whatever had been the Subject—' (Letters, iv. 604). To Davy, again, he speaks of 'a Life of intense Study and unremitted Meditation' (Letters, iii. 144).

32 (p. 144). Thus Creuzer, the Romantic editor of Plotinus, wrote to his mistress on the occasion of his very first acquaintance with Plotinus's thought (which he teasingly speaks of as 'something . . . out of the Greek and not by Plato—and never yet translated at all, except by me here for the first time') that it is a doctrine 'that I could pass off for Spinoza's' (Die Liebe der Günderode, p. 25). Again, Friedrich Schlegel says that 'Plotinus has the same basic premise as Spinoza: mind and matter both stem from a higher substance' (Philosophische Vorlesungen, i. 269). The resemblances, indeed, between Plotinus and Spinoza are so marked that many have speculated as to whether Spinoza might actually have derived the outline of his thought from Plotinus. Geb-hardt, for instance, finds that 'vom Geiste Plotins durchleuchtet ist das fünfte Buch der Ethik' and says that 'Das Kenntnis Plotins konnte Spinoza von zwei Seiten vermittelt werden', from Abraham Herrera and from Leone Ebreo (Carl Gebhardt, 'Spinoza und der Platonismus', Chronicon Spinozanum I (Hagae Comitis, 1921), p. 217). Plotinus's monism, especially when he is engaged in polemic against Gnostic dualism, is quite unequivocal, e.g., 'the Good, the Principle is simple. . . . When we speak of the One and when we speak of the Good we must recognize an Identical Nature. . . . Even in calling it The First we mean no more than to express that it is the most absolutely simple. . . . Deriving then from nothing alien, entering into nothing alien, in no way a made-up thing, there can be nothing above it. . . . The Divine Mind in its mentation thinks itself' (Enneads, ii. 9).

33 (p. 155). The full context of the statement displays a more finely articulated argu-ment than Watson's: '. . . all Schellings "Contradictions" are reducible to the one difficulty of comprehending the co-existence of the Activities, Agere et Pati, in the same subject—and that the difficulty is diminished rather than increased by the facts of human Art, in which the Pati and the Agere take place in different relations and at different Moments.—Likewise, that Schelling's position of opposites, viz. Nature and Intelligence as the same with Object and Subject already supposes Plurality, and this being supposed, the whole Hypothesis becomes arbitrary/ for the conception of Plurality once admitted, Object and Subject become [mere relative?] terms, & no reason can be assigned why each existent should not be both Object and Subject. But if he begins at the beginning, then the objection applies—viz. that Schelling arbitrarily

substantiates attributes. For in the very act of opposing A to B, he supposes an X common to both viz. Being, οὐσία; but this given, there is no necessary reason why Objectivity and Subjectivity should not both be predicable of both. . . .'

34 (p. 157). In other words, imagination, in any consistent ontological accounting, must always be a witness to the mystery of human freedom. Thus it is no accident that Sartre's two phenomenological analyses of imagination not only precede his *L'Être et le néant*, but are in fact its groundwork. For Sartre 'Imagination is not an empirical and superadded power of consciousness, it is the whole of consciousness as it realizes its freedom' (Jean-Paul Sartre, *The Psychology of Imagination* (New York, 1963), p. 270). The characteristic function of imagination is to 'grasp *nothing*', to 'posit *nothingness*' (p. 263). Thus 'the imagination . . . is the necessary condition for the freedom of empirical man in the midst of the world' (p. 271), for to 'posit an image is to construct an object on the fringe of the whole of reality, which means therefore to hold the real at a distance, to free oneself from it, in a word, to deny it. . . . For a consciousness to be able to imagine it must be able to escape from the world by its very nature, it must be able by its own efforts to withdraw from the world. In a word it must be free' (pp. 266-7). Sartre earlier had maintained that 'there are not, and never could be, images *in* consciousness. Rather an image is *a certain type of consciousness*. An image is an act, not some thing. An image is a consciousness *of* some thing' (*Imagination; A Psychological Critique*, trans. Forrest Williams (Ann Arbor, 1962), p. 146). Accordingly, 'imagination, far from appearing as an *actual* characteristic of consciousness, turns out to be an essential and transcendental condition of consciousness. It is as absurd to conceive of a consciousness which would not imagine as it would be to conceive of a consciousness which could not realize the *cogito*' (*The Psychology of Imagination*, p. 273). With such an ultimate ontological grounding, imagination guarantees freedom as a fundamental fact of the human mind.

35 (p. 158). Fichte himself starts with a search for the 'schlechthin unbedingten Grund-saz alles menschlichen Wissens' (*Grundlage der gesammten Wissenschaftslehre* (Leipzig, 1794), p. 3), which he finds in the law of identity—that is, if A, then A, expressed as A is A ('Den Saz A *ist* A . . . giebt Ieder zu . . . man anerkennt ihn für völlig gewiss und ausgemacht. . . . jener Saz sey *schlechthin d.i. ohne allen weitern Grund*, gewiss' (p. 5)). In this fundamental postulate of reason Fichte finds, not the existence of any *thing* ('Man sezt, durch die Behauptung, dass obiger Saz an sich gewiss sey *nicht*, dass A *sey* . . . man *sezt*: wenn A sey, *so* sey A'), but rather the existence of the 'I' that is positing the identity ('das Ich ist es, welches im obigen Saze urtheilt' (p. 6)). From his examination of the one absolute and unconditional proposition of all knowledge, there-fore, he discovers nothing except a positing 'I', and so he concludes that '*Das Ich sezt ursprünglich sein eignes Seyn*'—the 'I' originally posits its own being (p. 13). He insists that the 'sich sezende Ich, und das seyende Ich sind völlig gleich, Ein und eben dasselbe' (p. 13), and he notes that we do not derive 'the proposition I-am' from 'the proposition A equals A', but rather that we know the latter because of the former (p. 13). In an effort to widen the circle of reality thus set up, Fichte later distinguishes 'das intelligente' from 'das absolute Ich' (p. 222). The 'absolute ego' is unlimited activity, pure will, and contains in itself all reality. The 'intelligent ego' is 'nicht ein Wesen ausser dem Ich, sondern das Ich selbst soll die Intelligenz seyn, welches jene Einschränkung sezt' (p. 252); for 'the ego is everything, and is nothing, because it is nothing *for itself*, can distinguish no positing and no posited in itself' (p. 251). Though by his conception of 'absolute Ego' Fichte thinks, as he writes to Jacobi, to protect himself from the charge of practical 'Egoismus', he simply falls over backward into practical pantheism: 'my *absolute ego*', he tells Jacobi earnestly, 'is not the *individual*'—

and this in a letter in which he is hailing the 'conspicuous similarity of our philosophical convictions' [!] (Fichte, *Briefwechsel*, i. 501).

36 (p. 159). Not all hylozoism is atheism necessarily; thus Plato enunciates hylozoism in the *Timaeus* ('the world came into being—a living creature truly endowed with soul and intelligence': 30B; 33B–34B) but is defended against 'Hylozoic Atheism' by Cudworth. Leibniz was a hylozoist; a reviewer, indeed, asserts in 1737 that his *'Monades moitié matière, moitié esprit, sont toutes Stratoniciennes et Spinosistes par conséquent'* (quoted in W. H. Barber, *Leibniz in France from Arnauld to Voltaire* (Oxford, 1955), p. 114). Leibniz's denial of the existence of death is specifically adumbrated in the hylozoic pantheism of the Hermetic tracts: 'Now this whole Kosmos,—which is a great god . . .,—is one mass of life; and there is not anything in the Kosmos . . . that is not alive. There is not, and has never been, and never will be in the Kosmos anything that is dead' (*Hermetica*, ed. W. Scott (Oxford, 1924–36), i. 233). Doubtless the doctrine of hylozoism had a considerable attraction for Coleridge himself. But his reverence before the 'vegetable creation', which inspired in him 'a feeling similar to that with which we gaze at a beautiful infant that has fed itself asleep at its mothers bosom' (*Works*, i. 461) was prevented from spilling over into hylozoism not only by his fear of the moral consequences of pantheism, but specifically by the counter-pull of Kant. In the *Metaphysische Anfangsgründe der Naturwissenschaft* (which Coleridge greatly admired—see, e.g., *Biographia*, i. 99), Kant argued that all physics depends on the validity of laws of inertia, and that inertia in its turn is precisely the *lifelessness* of natural objects: 'Auf dem Gesetze der Trägheit (neben dem der Beharrlichkeit der Substanz) beruht die Möglichkeit einer eigentlichen Naturwissenschaft ganz und gar. Das Gegenteil des ersten, und daher auch der Tod aller Naturphilosophie, wäre der Hylozoism' (Kant, *Werke*, iv. 456). This last glittering statement our 'library-cormorant' bore off and embedded in the mosaic walls of his nest: 'The hypothesis of Hylozoism . . . is the death of all rational physiology, and indeed of all physical science' (*Biographia*, i. 89). Schelling and the *Naturphilosophen* (Treviranus, Troxler, J. J. Wagner, Oken, Steffens, Schubert), on the other hand, were all hylozoists.

37 (p. 159). It is interesting to note that Creuzer's edition of Proclus's commentary on the first Alcibiades (*Procli Successoris in Platonis Alcibiadem Priorem Commentarii Ex Codd. Mscrr. nunc primum edidit . . . Fridericus Creuzer* (Francofurti, 1820)), is dedicated in part to 'Friderico Guilielmo Josepho Schelling'. Coleridge knew the work of Proclus at least as early as the 1790s (e.g. *Letters*, i. 262), and in a memorable statement to Lady Beaumont in 1810 he says that 'The most beautiful and orderly developement of this philosophy, which endeavors to explain all things by an analysis of Consciousness, and builds up a world in the mind out of materials furnished by the mind itself, is to be found in the Platonic Theology by Proclus' (*Letters*, iii. 279). As Dodds points out, the *Elements of Theology* is 'the one genuinely systematic exposition of Neoplatonic metaphysic which has come down to us . . . its systematic character lends it an importance second only to that of the *Enneads* of Plotinus' (Proclus, *The Elements of Theology*, A revised text with translation, introduction, and commentary by E. R. Dodds (Oxford, 1933), p. ix). Proclus is a complete pantheist: almost all his propositions begin with the word πᾶν. Central to his conception is the idea of the 'One', from which all reality streams down in descending elaborations: 'Every manifold is posterior to the One' (Prop. 5); 'Every series of wholes is referable to an unparticipated first principle and cause; and all unparticipated terms are dependent from the one First Principle of all things' (Prop. 100). Much of his viewpoint is compressed into a corollary to Proposition 21: 'it is apparent that in the nature of body, unity and plurality coexist in such a manner that the one Nature has the many natures dependent from it, and con-

versely, these are derived from one Nature, that of the whole; that the soul-order, originating from one primal Soul, descends to a manifold of souls and again carries back the manifold to the one . . .; that for the One which is prior to all things there is the manifold of the henads. . . . Thus there are henads consequent upon the primal One, intelligence consequent on the primal Intelligence, souls consequent on the primal Soul, and a plurality of natures consequent on the universal Nature' (*Elements of Theology*, p. 25). The One passes into the Many by means of a doctrine of δύναμις— 'There is a perfect and an imperfect potency' (Prop. 78); 'All that comes to be arises out of the twofold potency' (Prop. 79)—that is virtually indistinguishable from Schelling's *Potenz*. (Schelling, indeed, in his later years became eager to identify his *Potenz* both with *potentia*—'Potenz ist das lateinische *potentia*' (Schelling, *Werke*, xiii. 63)— and with Aristotle's δύναμις (Schelling, *Werke*, xi. 291).) Proclus's δύναμις is, of course, taken over from Aristotle. As Dodds emphasizes, 'Proclus was not an innovator but a systematizer of other men's ideas . . . a systematizer who carried to its utmost limits the ideal of the one comprehensive philosophy that should embrace all the garnered wisdom of the world' (*Elements of Theology*, p. xxv).

38 (p. 160). As to why Coleridge should have been taken in, I suggest that, in addition to his being off form, he was (1) involved in an intense will to believe that Schelling had indeed achieved the reconciliation, and (2) he was still in the process of reading and thinking through Schelling's treatises—had not then even seen some of the more openly Spinozist ones. There are additional reasons in Schelling himself. We may note the fact of his exultant self-confidence: Staiger speaks of 'Schelling's language with its sonorous certainty of victory' ('Schellings Schwermut', *Die Kunst der Interpretation* (Zürich, 1955), p. 186); Bloch terms him 'der dithyrambische Schelling' (Bloch, *Subjekt-Objeckt*, p. 143). Again, Schelling never seems to show his whole hand—he constantly speaks as though his system is already complete, but each treatise is only 'one aspect' of that system. For instance, the *Wesen der menschlichen Freiheit* is introduced by the statement that 'up to the present the author has never set up' a 'finished and completed system', but has 'only presented special aspects of one and has very often shown these in certain relationships only, as, for instance in polemical connexions. Thus he explained his writings to be fragments of a whole, the connexions between which it would require a more acute power of insight to recognize than self-constituted followers are apt to have, and more good will than one commonly finds among opponents. As the only scientific presentation of his system was not completed, its essential purport was understood by no one or by very few' (Schelling, *Werke*, vii. 334). And yet this treatise itself is published in a book marked 'first volume' (*F. W. J. Schellings philosophische Schriften. Erster Band* (Landshut, 1809)). Thus Coleridge's realization of the incompatibility of his own position and that of Schelling was a slow and rather painful process; but, as we can see from one of his marginalia to the volume just cited, it was a certain one: 'Spite of all the superior airs of the *Natur-Philosophen*, I confess that, in the perusal of Kant, I breathe the free air of Good Sense and Logical Understanding with the light of Reason shining in it and through it; while in the Physics of Schelling I am amused with happy conjectures, and in his Theology am bewildered by positions, which, in their first sense are transcendental (*über fliegend*), in their literal sense scandalous' (Marginal note as reproduced at page 709 of volume iii of *Works*).

We can see, in the *Biographia*, the incompatibility of Schelling's attempt to reconcile 'I am' and 'it is' with Coleridge's own requirements for that reconciliation. Coleridge needed an answer that would maintain the reality of both realms, but when involved in Schelling's formulations, he can refer to 'essential prejudices' that are 'all reducible to the one fundamental presumption, THAT THERE EXIST THINGS WITHOUT US

(*Biographia*, i. 177); and can say that 'the true system of natural philosophy places the sole reality of things in an ABSOLUTE' (i. 187). These Schellingian formulations are quite opposed to what Coleridge indicates elsewhere—and what I take to be his own primary understanding of the matter—for, before embarking on the Schelling translation, he speaks of earlier feelings of 'the sacred distinction between things and persons' (i. 137). When he began to ask himself, 'what proof I had of the outward *existence* of anything ?', he saw 'that in the nature of things such proof is impossible; and that . . . the existence is *assumed* by a logical necessity arising from the constitution of the mind itself, by the absence of all motive to doubt it . . .' (i. 133). And he speaks slightingly of 'that compendious philosophy, which talking of mind but thinking of brick and mortar, or other images equally abstracted from body, contrives a theory of spirit by nicknaming matter' (i. 163)— although he apparently has not yet realized that Schelling's thought itself might, in its implications, be thus pejoratively characterized.

In general, it should be emphasized that a study of Coleridge's letters and marginalia reveals that he is not at all times equally clear about the consequences of given philosophemes. Some of his statements represent learner's work; others reflect his conflicted interests; still others reflect the different times at which they were written—for he habitually made his marginal comments over a period of years in the same work. Yet we should not therefore overestimate the interpretative importance of chronology; the marginalia and letters are not all of equal authority (for instance, his marginal comments almost never occur beside passages which he finds important enough to 'plagiarize'). Instead of referring them to a chronological scale, we should refer them for their evaluation to the coherence of his systematic concerns.

39 (p. 160). Thus Coleridge's most enthusiastic description of Schelling occurs in his vindication of Spinoza, and is elicited by Schelling's virtuosity in the defence of Spinoza. After summarizing Jacobi's attack on Spinoza, Coleridge says: 'Opposed point-blank, as to Jacobi's own anti-philosophical Philosophy, so especially to his representation of the philosophy of Spinoza, stands the celebrated Schelling . . . a man of prodigious acquirements and of vast intellectual powers, which however he does not wear too meekly . . . his own judgment is, that Spinoza's System is chargeable with deficiency and imperfection rather than with positive error; that the passages, that are least defensible, are not essential to the system, but engrafted on it by the mechanical philosophy of the age. . . . Of Spinoza's own piety he deems it calumnious to doubt' (Lore Metzger, 'Coleridge's Vindication of Spinoza: An Unpublished Note', *JHI*, xxi (1960) 292). Though Metzger cites Schelling's *Denkmal* as the source of these opinions, it seems more likely that Coleridge is referring to the *Wesen der menschlichen Freiheit* (*Werke*, vii), p. 349 *et passim*. Coleridge found the argument of the *Denkmal* 'so steeped in Gall, as to repel one from it', and 'In addition to the harsh quarrelsome and vindictive Spirit that displays itself in the Denkmal, there is a Jesuitical dishonesty in various parts that makes me dread almost to think of Schelling. I remember no man of any thing like his Genius & intellectual vigor so serpentine & unamiable' (note on the flyleaf of *F. W. J. Schelling's Denkmal der Schrift von den göttlichen Dingen* . . . (Tübingen, 1812), now in the British Museum).

40 (p. 163). Not only the constancy but also the curious intertwinement of Coleridge's concerns is suggested by the fact that it was apparently this childhood image of stars as suns in other worlds that engaged his interest in Bruno, who then fed back into his concern the doctrine of polar oppositions and their reconciliations: '[Bruno] contended that the Fixed Stars were Suns, each the Center of a Planetary System, and endeavoured to deduce this a priori from the centro-peripheric Process, or primary Law of Matter: which he elsewhere calls the Law of Polarity, in this as in many other instances anticipat-

ing the Ideas & discoveries generally attributed to far later Philosophies' (A. D. Snyder, 'Coleridge on Giordano Bruno', *Modern Language Notes*, xlii (1927), 432–3). In this multilevel connexion of Coleridge's interests, the 'universal Law of Polarity or essential Dualism' which, as Coleridge says in *The Friend*, Bruno 'made the foundation both of Logic, of Physics, and of Metaphysics', ties in with one of the functions of the imagination. For as Eliade points out, 'Images by their very structure are *multivalent*. If the mind makes use of images to grasp the ultimate reality of things, it is just because reality manifests itself in contradictory ways and therefore cannot be expressed in concepts. (We know what desperate efforts have been made by various theologies and metaphysics, oriental as well as occidental, to give expression to the *coincidentia oppositorum*—a mode of being that is readily, and also abundantly, conveyed by images and symbols.)' (Mircea Eliade, *Images and Symbols; Studies in Religious Symbolism*, trans. Philip Mairet (London, 1961), p. 15).

41 (p. 169). When Priestley argued, in 1777, that 'all the powers of man' belong 'to the *same substance*' (*Disquisitions Relating to Matter and Spirit* (London, 1777), p. 33), he had apparently not at that time read Spinoza. By the second edition of the work, however, he had either read Spinoza or been informed of Spinoza's position, for he there says that 'Nor, indeed, is making the deity to *be*, as well as to *do* everything, *in this sense*, any thing like the opinion of Spinoza; because I suppose a source of infinite power, and superior intelligence, from which all inferior beings are derived; that every inferior intelligent being has a consciousness distinct from that of the supreme intelligence, that they will forever continue distinct, and that their happiness or misery to endless ages, will depend upon their conduct . . .' (Priestley, *Disquisitions Relating to Matter and Spirit* (Birmingham, 1782), i. 42). Again: 'the Divine Being, and his energy are absolutely necessary to that of every other being. His power is the very *life and soul* of every thing that exists; and, strictly speaking, *without him, we* ARE, as well as *can* DO nothing' (i. 42). Though Priestley says such statements do not constitute Spinozism, their logic, if he himself were consequent, would amount to Spinozism. As one commentator says, 'The essence of Priestley's metaphysical belief was that there was no such thing as matter. What did exist was active force, and the apparent solidity of matter was only the resistance of this force. Thus the whole universe was spiritual force, and all action the direct act of God. Though such a system can only be distinguished from pantheism by Priestley's assertions that God, as well as being everything, was also additional to the sum of things, yet Priestley was a devout believer. He looked to the divine force for the fulfilment of the apocalyptic prophecies and the coming of the Millennium, and he saw the French Revolution as the first stage in this process' (H. W. Piper, *The Active Universe; Pantheism and the concept of Imagination in the English Romantic Poets* (London, 1962), p. 27). Also see Piper for discussion of Erasmus Darwin and other figures in the provincial English (and French *philosophe*) tradition of pantheism. For the almost universal involvement of the *philosophes* in vague forms of pantheism, see Paul Vernière, *Spinoza et la pensée française avant la révolution* (Paris, 1954), ii. 528–693; for briefer description see, e.g., Aram Vartanian, *Diderot and Descartes; A study of Scientific Naturalism in the Enlightenment* (Princeton, 1953), pp. 295–8; for general background to this whole time of ferment see Paul Hazard, *European Thought in the Eighteenth Century; from Montesquieu to Lessing*, trans. J. Lewis May (New Haven, 1954).

Despite his provincialism, however, Priestley was no dunce, and his name is invoked with respect by Kant (e.g. *Werke*, iii. 504; iv. 6). Indeed, Kant may even have modified one of his central doctrines in accordance with a hint from Priestley, for in the first *Kritik*, published in 1781, Kant, in a four-part exposition of the concept of space, argues, in his second exposition, that space must be a necessary *a priori* representation because 'we can never represent to ourselves the absence of space, though we can quite well think of it as empty of objects' (*Werke*, iii. 58). Although the first of these expositions, as Kemp Smith notes, is 'an almost verbal repetition of the first argument on space' in Kant's inaugural *Dissertation* of 1770 (Norman Kemp Smith, *A Commentary to Kant's 'Critique of Pure Reason'*, second edition (New York, 1950), p. 99, n. 3), the 'second argument is not in the *Dissertation*' (p. 103, n. 1). Between 1770 and 1781, in other words, Kant modified his doctrine of space to include the argument that space can never be done away with by thought. This argument Priestley adumbrates in 1777, in his *Matter and Spirit*, where, arguing against a provincial exponent of Leibniz's view of space, he says that 'it appears to me, that it is impossible, even *in idea*, to suppose the annihilation of space' (p. 59).

42 (p. 174). Wolfson believes that, starting in antiquity and continuing to Spinoza, there was a 'common philosophy of three religions—Judaism, Christianity, and Islam —consisting of one philosophy written in five languages', which can be regarded as both 'a continuation of pagan Greek philosophy' and also a 'radical revision' of that philosophy. This common philosophy deferred to scripture, to the idea of immutable laws of nature, and most especially to the idea of 'human freedom' and the 'divine origin of morality'. 'Philo is the founder of this new school of philosophy, from him it directly passes on to the Gospel of St. John and the Church Fathers' and 'continues uninterruptedly in its main assertions for well-nigh seventeen centuries, when at last it is openly challenged by Spinoza', after which it 'no longer held a dominant position. Henceforth, in order to gain attention at all, it had to disguise its meaning and adopt a new vocabulary' (*Philo*, ii. 446, 457). In such a context it is interesting to note that Coleridge was very sympathetic toward Alexandrian thinkers—e.g., '. . . I should use Philo (who has not been used half enough)' (*Letters*, iv. 803); he praises Origen as 'that very best of the old Fathers' (*Works*, v. 275); he hails Athanasius: 'I am a Christian of the School of John, Paul, Athanasius . . .' (*Inquiring Spirit*, p. 123).

43 (p. 176). It is permissible to speculate that the thought of Unamuno and of Coleridge, in this key emphasis, might have found its common progenitor in Joseph Butler. For Unamuno renders Butler handsome tribute: 'Another man, the man Joseph Butler, the Anglican bishop who lived at the beginning of the eighteenth century and whom Cardinal Newman declared to be the greatest man of the Anglican church, wrote, at the conclusion of the first chapter of his great work, *The Analogy of Religion*, the chapter which treats of a future life, these pregnant words: "This credibility of a future life, which has been here insisted upon . . . seems to answer all the purposes of religion." . . . The man Butler, whose works were perhaps not unknown to the man Kant, wished to save the belief in the immortality of the soul, and with this object he made it independent of belief in God . . . fundamentally [he] deduces the existence of God from the immortality of the soul' (Unamuno, pp. 5–6). Coleridge, for his part, writes in 1801 that Butler was one of the 'only three *great* Metaphysicians which this Country *has* produced . . .' (*Letters*, ii. 703). Even more significantly, he thought about collaborating with Estlin on an edition of the *Analogy*, and to that end wrote, in 1798, 'that Butler's Analogy *aided* by well-placed notes would answer irresistably all the objections to Christianity founded on a priori reasonings' (*Letters*, i. 386). Compare C. D. Broad's judgement that Butler's *Analogy* 'is perhaps the ablest and fairest argument for theism that exists' (C. D. Broad, *Five Types of Ethical Theory* (London, 1930), p. 5). Also interesting, in terms of the philosophical alignments we have emphasized in this volume, is Broad's judgement that it 'would be hard to find two writers of such eminence who were so unlike each other as Butler and Spinoza. The writer with whom

[Butler] has most affinity among those who are treated in this book is Kant . . .'
(Broad, p. 53). Certainly Coleridge, whether or not he echoes Butler specifically, fore-
shadows Unamuno's own essential position when he says, 'I cannot conceive a supreme
moral Intelligence unless I believe in my own immortality . . .' (*Inquiring Spirit*, p. 142).

With reference to the similarity of Unamuno's 'man of flesh and bone' and Coleridge's
'unity of consciousness', we may find most revealing Butler's dissertation 'Of Personal
Identity', appended to the *Analogy*: 'by reflecting upon that, which is my self now, and
that which was myself twenty years ago, I discern they are not two, but one and the
same self'—which statement goes straight to the heart of Jaspers' conception of
Existenz (*The Works of Joseph Butler*, i. 388). And then Butler makes the point that
'though consciousness of what is past does thus ascertain our personal identity to ourselves, yet to say, that it makes personal identity, or is necessary to our being the same
persons, is to say, that a person has not existed a single moment . . . but what he can
remember. . . . And one should really think it self-evident, that consciousness of
personal identity presupposes, and therefore cannot constitute, personal identity'—an
anticipation not only of Jaspers' *das Umgreifende, das ich bin*, but of all Coleridge's later
insistence on the incomprehensibility of the moral self (Butler, p. 388).

44 (p. 181). Coleridge's praise for this work ('the ablest philological support of the
Trinity, in existence' (*Letters*, iii. 69)) is doubtless to some extent conditioned by the
fact that its author was that same Middleton who, as a young scholar at Pembroke,
had been the object of Coleridge's youthful hero-worship, and whose failure to make
scholarly headway at Cambridge had been a precipitating factor in Coleridge's own
defection from the university (see Gillman, *Life of Coleridge*, pp. 43–44, 56). It is possible that in the work itself, Coleridge found the distinction between τὸ θεῖον and
ὁ θεός which crops up repeatedly in his later statements on the Trinitarian schematiza-
tion (e.g. 'True Philosophy begins with the τὸ θεῖον in order to end in the 'Ο Θεός'
(*Letters*, iv. 768)). Middleton pointed out that 'τὸ θεῖον, a Pagan appellation of God,
is not found at all in the LXX, and only once in the N.T., Acts xvii. 29, where St. Paul
in addressing the philosophers of Athens adopted their own phraseology. Neither
does the term τὸ ἕν, whatever Noun be understood in it [Porson had suggested that
τὸ ἕν should be explained by supplying θεῖον] appear to have been very familiar to the
Writers of the N.T. nor to the LXX.: for though they speak of God some thousands
of times, and of his Unity in particular very frequently, they no where call him τὸ ἕν:
they say of Him, that he is εἷς θεός' (Thomas F. Middleton, *The Doctrine of the Greek
Article; Applied to the Criticism and Illustration of the New Testament* (London, 1808),
p. 639). With respect to θεός, on the other hand, 'θεός is God or *a* God, either true or
false, real or imaginary, but never *superior or inferior*' (p. 292)—which, of course, would
militate against Arian or Socinian interpretations of Christ as either subordinate God
or mere man.

Though Middleton's book is not polemical either in tone or intent, at one point he
speaks against Socinian methods of interpretation. Referring to John xvii. 3, he says:
'It has usually, I believe, been regarded as one of the strong holds of Socinianism; and
much use is made of it by *Crellius* in his tract *de Uno Deo Patre*, in the Collection of the
Polish Brethren. But, as *Schleusner* and others have observed, τὸν μόνον ἀληθινὸν θεόν is
here opposed to the false gods of the Pagan worship: compare 1 Thess. i. 9; 1 John ii. 8,
v. 20; Apoc. iii. 7. It ought, then, to be considered, that the Socinian, in quoting this
text in support of what he calls *Unitarianism*, commits the common mistake of interpreting phrases rather from opinions subsequently adopted, than from those which
prevailed at the time, when the words in question were employed, and to which all the
words were intended to refer'—and after further argument Middleton concludes that
'It is, therefore, perfectly frivolous to introduce this passage into the Trinitarian

dispute' (Middleton, pp. 372–3). For the importance of the distinction between τὸ θεῖον and ὁ θεός in Coleridge's thought, see further, p. 377, n. 69.

45 (p. 188). For instance, in a marginal note to De Boyer's *Kabbalistische Briefe* Coleridge, commenting on De Boyer's statement that Spinoza was dominated by the desire to hand down his name to posterity, writes (*Critical Annotations*, p. 28): 'Detestable Calumny! If ever man of Genius was free from the lust of a wide reputation, Spinoza was he.' (Compare A. Wolf, 'Spinoza the Conciliator', *Chronicon Spinozanum II* (Hagae Comitis, 1922), p. 3: 'Spinoza never sought fame or popularity.' Again, Lucas, his first biographer, reported that 'He had such a great propensity not to do anything for the sake of being regarded and admired by the people, that when dying he requested that his name should not be put on his *Ethica*, saying that such affectations were unworthy of a philosopher' (*The Oldest Biography of Spinoza*, ed. A. Wolf (London, 1927), p. 62).) In another notation Coleridge roars that 'This coxcomb Frenchman probably never looked into the Ethic of Sp. . . ., but certainly did not, could not, understand a sentence of it' (*Critical Annotations*, p. 28). Again, Coleridge accuses Spinoza's 'inveterate Antagonist, Bayle, the Founder and Father of modern Scepticism and religious Indifference' of 'sensual grossnesses', of 'all-unhinging Sophistry', of 'bitterness and intolerance to Spinoza'. Bayle's attacks 'were provoked not by Spinoza's being in *error*, but by his being in *earnest*: not by what is heterodox but by what is most christian-like in his writings, by the austerity of his moral system, by his steadfast faith in the possibility of arriving at Truth and a satisfying conviction, and in the obligation to seek after it with seriousness and singleness of Heart' (Lore Metzger, 'Coleridge's Vindication of Spinoza: An Unpublished Note', *JHI*, xxi (1960), 286).

46 (p. 189). Inasmuch as Coleridge was a trinitarian in philosophy before he became one in religion (*Biographia*, i. 114), we note the fact that most of the pantheists who interested him employed some sort of trinitarian schematism. Boehme's logic and belief were expressly trinitarian (cf. Koyré: 'Boehme, ne l'oublions jamais, est un Chrétien. . . . Son Dieu est un Dieu-Trinité'—*La Philosophie de Boehme*, p. 72); Coleridge supposed that Bruno's 'polar logic' actually involved trichotomic distinctions (*Works*, v. 355); Schelling's Subject, Object, and Absolute accorded with the thesis-antithesis-synthesis logic also used by Fichte and later by Hegel; the Cabala in its first three Sephiroth ramified into a trinitarian scheme (see above, p. 228, n. 6); and Plotinus, in the distinction of *to hen*, *nous*, and *psyche* likewise afforded a trinitarian pantheism: Muirhead says that the Coleridge manuscript in the possession of the Huntington Library has a chapter which 'begins with a carefully drawn out criticism of the Plotinian idea of the Trinity as contrasted with the Christian' (*Coleridge as Philosopher*, p. 269). It seems likely, therefore, that Coleridge's repeated encounters with trinitarian logic and trinitarian schematism within the framework of these monistic systems finally led him to realize that only a trinity involving *person* could truly be anything other than modal (Sabellian). Thus, for instance, he says that 'the true doctrine of the Trinity', in its 'theological necessity', rescues 'our faith from both extremes, Cabalo-Pantheism; and Anthropomorphism. It is, I say, to prevent the necessity of the Cabalistic inferences that the full and distinct development of the doctrine of the Trinity becomes necessary in every scheme of dogmatic theology' (*Works*, v. 463). Beer points out that there 'is some evidence that Trinitarian speculations had occupied him while he was still at Christ's Hospital', that in any event 'it appears that beneath the innocent Platonic Trinitarianism of Coleridge's early days there lay a wealth of speculation', and that most of this speculation was Sabellian (J. B. Beer, *Coleridge the Visionary* (London, 1959), pp. 78–83).

47 (p. 206). Coleridge equated 'the *una et unica substantia* of Spinosa' with 'the World-

God of the Stoics' (*Works*, v. 267). The similarity of Spinozism and Stoicism was frequently noted in the abusive tractates of the late seventeenth and early eighteenth centuries, and Dilthey has pointed out that the Stoic revival in the Netherlands in the late sixteenth century (effected largely through the proselyting endeavours of Justus Lipsius, especially in his *De constantia* and his *Manuductio ad Stoicam philosophiam*) made available to Spinoza, on his own home ground as it were, a full presentation of Stoic doctrine (see Wilhelm Dilthey, 'Spinoza und die stoische Tradition', *Gesammelte Schriften*, ii (Leipzig und Berlin, 1914), pp. 283–9). See also Fortunat Strowski, 'Le courant stoïcien', *Pascal et son temps*, troisième édition (Paris 1909), i. 18–125. For an examination of Lipsius's thought see J. L. Saunders, *Justus Lipsius; The Philosophy of Renaissance Stoicism* (New York, 1955). Another source of Stoic doctrine available to Spinoza was Thomas Gataker's commentary on Marcus Aurelius, published in 1652. Norden, writing in 1913, speaks wonderingly of Gataker's 'ungeheure Gelehrsamkeit'— enormous learning—and says that any scholar who reads the commentary 'will be thankful all his life to this old man' (*Agnostos Theos*, p. 240, n. 1). In general, and leaving aside the question of how the knowledge might have been mediated to him, Spinoza, as Pohlenz summarizes the matter, 'took up fundamental ideas of the Stoa when he considered spirit and extension as the two sides of the divine substance, and regarded individual things, just as did Chrysippus, as the modes of this primal substance' (*Die Stoa*, i. 470).

48 (p. 208). Compare, for instance, Jaeger: 'In the *Phaedrus* Plato tells us that the written word is useless in the transmission of real scientific knowledge. We have believed only too long that we could disregard this view, fundamental though it be to the comprehension of the dialogues; and only now do we begin to see that it has its basis in the actual relation obtaining between literary production and oral teaching in Plato's Academy, and that every general view of the dialogues that does not see them on the background of this comprehensive pedagogical activity represents a displacement of the centre of gravity' (*Aristotle*, p. 317). Again, compare Stenzel: 'However little we know of the content of this philosophy which was not included in the Dialogues, the fact *that* such a philosophy existed, side by side with them, must be observed, if we would judge from the correct standpoint the meaning of the doctrines contained in the surviving sources' (*Plato's Method of Dialectic*, p. 2). Still again, compare Burnet: '. . . the doctrines of Plato, if we mean by that, as we should mean, the doctrine taught by Plato in the Academy, is not to be found in his best known dialogues' (*Platonism*, p. 113). (It should be said, however, that Burnet thinks Plato's own doctrines, as opposed to those of Socrates, are to be found in *The Laws*.) See further Jaeger, *Studien zur Entstehungsgeschichte der Metaphysik des Aristoteles* (Berlin, 1912), p. 140, where he stresses that it is only 'for lack of other sources' that we base our understanding of Plato's ideas and mathematical doctrine on the dialogues.

The statements in the *Phaedrus* are at 275C–278B. Even more explicit are passages in the *Seventh Epistle*, 341A, 341C, and 344C.

49 (p. 209). In a passage that Sartre has described as containing the whole of Baudelaire, we find also the whole of the Platonic tone: 'C'est cet admirable, cet immortel instinct du Beau qui nous fait considérer la Terre et ses spectacles comme un aperçu, comme une *correspondance* du Ciel. La soif insatiable de tout ce qui est au delà, et que révèle la vie, est la preuve la plus vivante de notre immortalité. C'est à la fois par la poésie et *à travers* la poésie, par et *à travers* la musique, que l'âme entrevoit les splendeurs situées derrière le tombeau; et quand un poème exquis amène les larmes au bord des yeux, ces larmes ne sont pas la preuve d'un excès de jouissance, elles sont bien plutôt le témoignage d'une mélancolie irritée, d'une postulation des nerfs, d'une nature exilée dans

l'imparfait et qui voudrait s'emparer immédiatement, sur cette terre même, d'un paradis revélé.

'Ainsi le principe de la poésie est, strictement et simplement, l'aspiration humaine vers une Beauté supérieure . . .' (Baudelaire, *L'Art romantique*, ed. Raynaud (Paris, 1931), p. 131). Not only do Baudelaire's 'soif insatiable' and Coleridge's 'thirst for something not attained' (*Philosophical Lectures*, p. 158) exemplify Platonic 'longing' but they accord with the Christian longing of Dante's 'La sete natural che mai non sazia/ se non con l'acqua onde la femminetta/ sammaritana dimando la grazia'—the natural thirst which is never quenched except with the water which the woman of Samaria begged as a favour (*Purgatorio*, xxi. 1–3).

As analogue to the passage from Baudelaire, compare the *Phaedrus*: 'Of the place beyond the heavens none of our earthly poets has yet sung, and none shall sing worthily. . . . It is there that true being dwells . . .' (247C); 'Few indeed are left that can still remember much, but when these discern some likeness of the things yonder, they are much amazed, and no longer masters of themselves' (250A). As Guy Michaud says, '. . . chez la plupart des Symbolistes, l'idéalisme comporte un mysticisme plus ou moins avoué et teinté de platonisme . . .' (*La Doctrine symboliste (documents)* (Paris, 1947), p. 23).

50 (p. 212). The Aristotle-Plato psychological division of attitudes does not wholly coincide with the Spinoza-Kant schematic division, because Kant's dry, eighteenth-century rationalism is alien to the Platonic tone. Kant is, as it were, suspended between the two psychological poles. Hence in 1820 Coleridge writes that 'there neither are, have been, or ever will be but two essentially different Schools of Philosophy: the Platonic, and the Aristotelean. To the latter, but with a somewhat nearer approach to the Platonic, Emanuel Kant belonged; to the former Bacon and Leibnitz and in his riper and better years Berkeley—And to this I profess myself an adherent . . .' (*Unpublished Letters*, ii. 264–5). This alignment, interestingly enough, coincides with that of Cassirer. Invoking the well-known distinction in the *Farbenlehre* in which Goethe, like Coleridge, divides attitudes into those of Plato and those of Aristotle, Cassirer says that Kant does not fit into this either-or, but rather partakes of both tendencies: 'For in fact the fundamental tendencies, which Goethe opposed to one another in the characterization of Aristotle and Plato, join and interpenetrate in Kant, and both stand here in perfect balance' (*Kants Leben und Lehre*, p. 446). But whereas for Cassirer the fact, that Kant 'in the fundamental direction of his intellect stands outside the universal intellectual opposition formulated by Goethe', bears witness to the 'comprehensiveness and depth of Kant's philosophical genius' (Cassirer, p. 446), for Coleridge it represents a limitation in Kant. As Deschamps puts it: 'La critique kantienne s'était rigoureusement limitée à l'étude des facultés de l'esprit et de leur fonctionnement; elle s'était interdit d'explorer le monde inaccessible de la chose en soi; et le pont avec une réalité objective, complètement supprimé dans la *Critique de la Raison Pure*, avait été difficilement rétabli dans la *Critique de la Raison Pratique*. C'est une limitation que Coleridge n'accepte pas; comme les platoniciens, et les néo-platoniciens plus encore, il croit à la réalité des idées; il veut connaître à tout prix ce monde que Kant juge illégitime d'explorer . . .' (*La Formation de la pensée de Coleridge (1772–1804)*, pp. 477–8). It is the issue of 'la réalité des idées' that Coleridge identifies as composing the technical ground of Kant's deviation from Plato: 'that which is neither individual (that is, a sensible intuition) nor general (that is, a conception), which neither refers to outward facts, nor yet is abstracted from the forms of perception contained in the understanding; but which is an educt of the imagination actuated by the pure reason, to which there neither is nor can be an adequate correspondent in the world of the senses;—this and this alone is = an Idea. Whether ideas are regulative only, according to Aristotle and

Kant; or likewise constitutive, and one with the power and life of nature, according to Plato, and Plotinus . . . is the highest problem of philosophy, and not part of its nomenclature' (*Works*, i. 484). For Coleridge's knowledge of Goethe's Aristotle-Plato distinction see *Letters*, iv. 911.

51 (p. 212). As Cassirer emphasizes about the Cambridge school, the '*a priori* of pure morality is the starting-point of their doctrine' (*The Platonic Renaissance in England*, p. 41), and to that extent they were congenial both to Leibniz and to Coleridge. But Cassirer then notes that 'in content and systematic significance the philosophy of the Cambridge School is by no means commensurate with the philosophy of Leibniz', though it 'fulfilled . . . a common mission in the history of thought' (pp. 84–85). Feilchenfeld summarizes the relation of Leibniz to More's thought in this way: 'More acquainted Leibniz with certain elements of the mystic-Neoplatonic world-view, and also spurred him to study Boehme, with whom Leibniz busied himself in the next few years, though without really gaining anything. More also led Leibniz into the world of the Cabala, and for this the philosopher retained his interest. For the rest, Leibniz learned less from More than because of More. He could take over almost nothing without reservation, and most needed energetic reinterpretation—if indeed progress did not actually grow out of a direct opposition. If these relationships none the less deserve the greatest attention, it is because the works of More fell into Leibniz's hands precisely in the most decisive time of his life. Under the impress of this reading, masses of materials which were stored up as dead, unrelated knowledge were set in motion and crystallized into a significant structure. . . . This structure, however, was no new creation; it rather adapted its inner organization from the pyramidal edifice of the Neoplatonic system' (Walter Feilchenfeld, 'Leibniz und Henry More', *Kantstudien*, xxviii (1923), 331–2).

52 (p. 212). Tulloch praises Coleridge for understanding the differences between the Platonism of the English Platonists and the Platonism of Plato; interestingly enough, in this respect also Leibniz and Coleridge are similar. Compare Panofsky: 'The Neo-platonists . . . attempted . . . to abolish the borderline not only between philosophy, religion and magic but between all kinds of philosophies, all kinds of religions and all kinds of magic, including Hermeticism, Orphism, Pythagoreanism, Cabala, and the ancient mysteries of Egypt and India. This wild mixture could not resist the criticism, both scientific and philological, which was to set in during the seventeenth century. But we should not forget that in this case, too, chaos was the prerequisite of order. It was only the indiscriminate acceptance of too many kinds of Platonism which made it necessary to isolate the real Plato from all the later accretions (the first to perceive this problem was, characteristically, the great Leibniz)' (Erwin Panofsky, 'Artist, Scientist, Genius: Notes on the "Renaissance-Dämmerung" ', *The Renaissance; Six Essays* (New York and Evanston, 1962), pp. 129–30). Compare Leibniz: 'Platonici posteriores ad loquendi portenta sunt lapsi' (*Philosophische Schriften*, iv. 468). Compare further Cassirer: 'Leibniz . . . sees the Platonic doctrine of ideas in a new light. He was the first European thinker to emancipate himself inwardly from the conception of Platonism devised by the Florentine Academy, and to see Plato again with his own eyes. He protested especially against that syncretism which confused Plato's original thought with later admixtures and made a medley of Platonic and neo-Platonic elements. "We cannot judge [says Leibniz] Plato's teachings by Plotinus or Marsilio Ficino, for they have perverted his fundamental doctrine in their scurryings after the miraculous and the mystical. . . ." Such judgment and critical analysis were possible only to a thinker who, like Leibniz, had rediscovered for himself the fundamental problems of Plato's logic and dialectic' (*The Platonic Renaissance*, pp. 154–5).

53 (p. 212). It is mainly on this rock that Lovejoy's curious thesis founders. I use the word 'curious' advisedly. Lovejoy feels free to make the large claim that 'in his "Copernican revolution", his "transcendental" idealism, his apriorism' Kant was 'merely the elaborator and systematizer of the general doctrine of the English Platonists'. At the same time he admits that he has not seen the work of Burthogge—who is one of the leading exponents of this point of view—and must therefore patch together translated passages from the French of Lyon's book on English idealism ('Kant and the English Platonists', in *Essays in Honor of William James*, pp. 302, 279). The gulf between Kant and the English Platonists Lovejoy dismisses by saying that 'it is, of course, true that these English Platonists made no such definite and methodical attempt to discriminate and precisely enumerate the several *a priori* elements in knowledge, as did the peculiarly systematic and taxonomic mind of Kant' (Lovejoy, p. 277). But it is precisely 'the peculiarly systematic and taxonomic' characteristics of Kant's thought that make him usable, and precisely the absence of these characteristics in Henry More's work that elicits Coleridge's description of it as 'a sad jumble'. Indeed, Coleridge himself was aware of the kind of antecedence Lovejoy argues for, but he did not accept its validity. Hence, speaking of Kant ('the most profound of modern Logicians & the proper Inventor & Founder of transcendental Analysis'), he comments on 'proper': 'i.e. unless the honors of Discovery can be justly or honestly withheld from the man who *first* saw & communicated the truths in their full extent, & with systematic comprehension under the pretence of a few scattered hints in some ancient or modern books the . . . bearings of which were not even suspected by the writer himself' (MS. Logic in the British Museum, vol. ii, Egerton 2826, p. 210). Thus when Lovejoy claims that the English anticipated Kant's 'apriorism', we might concede the point and at the same time insist that their anticipation is useless. 'In their defence of the *a priori*', says Cassirer, 'most of the thinkers of the Cambridge School do not distinguish between the "logical" and the "temporal" sense of the *a priori* concept. Hence they argue not only for the *a priori* validity of theoretical and ethical principles, but also for the "innateness" of these principles. . . . The union of the *a priori* with the "innate" is especially noticeable in Henry More'; and, emphasizes Cassirer, 'a confusion of this sort is not conditioned or demanded by the principle which the Cambridge School was defending' (*Platonic Renaissance*, p. 59, n. 1). How uncongenial to Coleridge was More's logical and systematic fuzziness can be gauged to some extent from his own precision on this very issue: the 'phrase, *a priori*,' says Coleridge, 'is in common, most grossly misunderstood. . . . By knowledge, *a priori*, we do not mean, that we can know anything previously to experience, which would be a contradiction in terms; but that having once known it by occasion of experience (that is, something acting upon us from without) we then know, that it must have pre-existed, or the experience itself would have been impossible. By experience only I know, that I have eyes; but then my reason convinces me, that I must have had eyes in order to the experience' (*Biographia*, i. 193 n).

54 (p. 214). In November 1798 Coleridge writes to his wife that he has seen 'a very, very fine picture of Lessing. His eyes were uncommonly like mine' (*Letters*, i. 437). By January 4, 1799 he is writing to Poole about a 'work I have planned', which turns out to be 'a Life of Lessing—& interweaved with it a true state of German Literature, in it's rise & present state.—I have already written a little life, from three different biographies' (*Letters*, i. 454–5). But, significantly, Coleridge had not yet read Lessing himself: 'at Gottingen I will read his works regularly . . . & the controversies, religious & literary, which they occasioned' (*Letters*, i. 455). To Josiah Wedgwood in May 1799 he announces that 'I have read & made . . . very large collections for a Life of Lessing', and he explains that 'I chose the Life of Lessing . . . because it would give me an opportunity of conveying under a better name, than my own ever will be, opinions, which

I deem of the highes[t] importance' (*Letters*, i. 518–19). Accordingly his 'main Business at Göttingen has been to read all the numerous Controversies in which L. was engaged' (*Letters*, i. 519)—including, doubtless, the *Pantheismusstreit*. Again, in December 1799 Coleridge writes to Southey that 'Immediately on my leaving London, I fall to the Life of Lessing' (*Letters*, i. 552–3), while to Tobin in September 1800 he writes that 'From the commencement of November next I give myself exclusively to the Life of Lessing' (*Letters*, i. 623). Apart from its testimony to Coleridge's long-standing pre-occupation with the man who occasioned the *Pantheismusstreit*, the project for a life of Lessing illustrates Coleridge's characteristic procedure of developing his interest in a thinker before—in response to his own needs—rather than after a study of that thinker's works. (For preliminary notes to the Lessing biography, see *Notebooks*, i. 377.)

55 (p. 216). In general the members of the Marburg School might be described as seeking the subordination of history to philosophically formal considerations, in investigations that are conventionally viewed as historical. Cassirer's vast *Erkenntnisproblem* is the most impressive and most typical illustration of their aims: the transposition and unification of past thought in terms of an abstract theory of knowledge. As epistemologists, the Marburg philosophers were followers of Kant, and their thought —including Cassirer's *Philosophie der symbolischen Formen*—is a kind of neo-Kantianism. Their critics, indeed, claim that they distort history in order to refer all problems to the Kantian analysis: Gueroult, for instance, complains that 'L'erreur de Natorp, et d'une facon générale de l'école de Marburg, réside dans un préjugé contraire à toute saine méthode historique, et qui consiste à faire rentrer coûte que coûte tous les philosophes, antérieurs ou postérieurs à Kant, dans les perspectives de la philosophie kantienne, en métamorphosant les premiers en précurseurs plus ou moins inconscients et les seconds en disciples plus ou moins infidèles' (*Descartes selon l'ordre des raisons*, i. 33). In their own estimation, however, the Marburg philosophers were guided not by any slavish adherence to Kant, but by the fact that Kant and epistemology, like Homer and nature, are the same. Thus Natorp defends their position: 'Therefore all argument is to be rejected . . . that would have one seeking to interpret Plato as a Kantian before Kant, and even as a Marburg Kantian before Marburg. He who can overlook in Plato the characteristics that prefigure Kant, and in Kant those that refer back to Plato, must have understood both philosophers equally ill. But he who considers a Marburg philosopher capable of wanting to prove Plato a Kantian in the Marburg sense falsifies the whole meaning of the philosophical endeavour that is honoured with the title "Marburg School". No century, no school, no individual will ever be able to do anything else than give expression to the timeless eternal, which operates beyond all limits of schools and individualities. The era, the community of scholarship in which each of us stands, and the special nature of the individual all make such expression possible' (Paul Natorp, *Platos Ideenlehre*, pp. 462–3). In such an orientation, it is not to Kant as a historical figure, but to Cohen's interpretational principle of 'erkenntnistheoretische Legitimirung' that the Marburg philosophers look (Hermann Cohen, *Platons Ideenlehre und die Mathematik* (Marburg, 1879), p. 30). As Natorp says, 'It was not until the rebirth of Kantian idealism that the time was also ripe for a full understanding of the idealism of Plato. I do not hesitate to name Hermann Cohen as the one who has opened our eyes both to Kant and to Plato' (*Platos Ideenlehre*, p. x). Though the method of Natorp is opposed by a scholar like Jaeger, who is committed to historicism—to chronologism, even—Coleridge's emphasis on the common service to philosophy of Plato and Kant, which receives its scholarly exposition in Natorp, finds therein a most formidable confirmation. Compare Stenzel's tribute: '. . . my work . . . will diverge from the "philosophical" exposition practised by the Marburg school; my only purpose is to restore Plato's views, if possible, in his own sense and in that of his time. Even where I have

argued philosophically, it is with the purpose of interpretation. Hence my frequent disagreement with Natorp's study of the Theory of Ideas, a work which is indispensable for any inquiry which pretends to go deeply into Plato's thought. For just this reason, however, the author feels that he must strongly endorse a remark often made by his teacher Wendland, that "at no time are Platonic problems so clear as when one engages in careful study of Natorp"' (*Plato's Method of Dialectic*, pp. 24–25).

56 (p. 217). As to whether Kant meant, by his conception of *Ding an sich*, to imply the existence of a God supramundane, neither commentary nor his own words supplies a wholly unambivalent answer. Clearly he did not mean to do so in the rather cryptically Platonic way that Coleridge suggests; equally certain, however, is the fact that the conception has an extra-logical dimension. Jacobi claimed that the whole Kantian philosophy was grounded upon the idea of a 'higher power', and that this was true not only at its end (in practical reason), where this 'höheres Vermögen' was necessary as a keystone to the philosophical structure, without which it would 'fall together and plunge away into an abyss of scepticism opened up by the master-builder himself', but was true also at its beginning, where the idea of a 'higher power' lays 'the foundation and the cornerstone of the structure with the absolute positing of a *Ding an sich*, which reveals itself to the faculty of knowledge neither in the appearances, nor through them, but merely with them, in a completely positive or mystical way, inconceivable to the senses and the understanding' (*Werke*, ii. 22–23). Commenting on this passage, Erich Adickes says that with Kant we 'surely cannot talk of mysticism and a higher power', but he then concedes a germ of truth to Jacobi's assertion. His own explanation is that Kant's positing of the *Ding an sich* reflects a primordial personal experience, which consisted 'in feeling a breath of the transcendent in the empirical material of objects of appearance' (*Kant und das Ding an sich* (Berlin, 1924), pp. 15, 14).

Kant himself gives various reasons for his adoption of the *Ding an sich*. Logically, it appears as a problem unavoidably bound up with the limitation of our sensibility—as a limiting concept or *Grenzbegriff* (*Werke*, iii. 241)—and only in this aspect does Hermann Cohen, in his *Kant's Theorie der Erfahrung*, grant it validity. Historically, however, it arises from Kant's preoccupation with the platonizing distinction of reality into *mundus sensibilis* and *mundus intelligibilis* (e.g. *Werke*, iii. 222). As a commentator points out, 'The two concepts of *mundus sensibilis* and *mundus intelligibilis*, translated into the German terms "Sinnenwelt" and "Verstandeswelt", which are rendered in English by "world of the senses" and "world of the understanding", run through all Kant's works, not only the later works but also the *Critique of Pure Reason*' (Gottfried Martin, *Kant's Metaphysics and Theory of Science*, trans. P. G. Lucas (Manchester, 1961), p. 190). A third reason is that common sense demands the *Ding an sich* to avoid 'the absurd conclusion that there can be an appearance without anything that appears' (*Werke*, iii. 23). Kant so clearly begs the question here, that we find ourselves once more in the realm of the extra-logical—in that realm of 'personal knowledge' (to adopt Polanyi's phrase) where the most important decisions are sometimes made.

In the second edition of the first *Kritik*, Kant sets up a distinction between noumenon in a positive sense, and noumenon in a negative sense (*Werke*, iii. 219–20). He says that 'what we entitle "noumenon" must be understood as being such only in a negative sense', and he thereby concedes the absolute unknowability of positive noumena and also their possible identity with objects of religious hope. In the second *Kritik*, this 'empty space' (*Werke*, iii. 224) protected by the first *Kritik* is filled with freedom immortality, and God.

Moreover, in his *Reflexionen zur Metaphysik*, No. 4135, Kant says that 'The phenomenon of a thing is a product of our sensibility. God is the originator of things in themselves' (*Kant's gesammelte Schriften*, hrsg. von der preussischen Akademie der

Wissenschaften (Berlin und Leipzig, 1910 ff.), xvii. 429). Again, in No. 5981 he says that 'One should really not say that God has created appearances, but that he has created things, which we do not know, and ordained a sensibility in us corresponding to them' (*Schriften*, xviii. 414).

Therefore, despite the many attacks on the *Ding an sich*, from Jacobi to Natorp, the conception seems necessary to Kant's emotional position, and favourable to religious predications. We perhaps need not go so far as Max Wundt, who says that 'the idea of God and its working out in knowledge of the world is the final goal of the Kantian philosophy' (*Kant der Metaphysiker* (Stuttgart, 1924), p. 389). But we might conclude with Paton that 'The distinction between a phenomenal world which we know and a world of things-in-themselves which we do not know is fundamental to Kant's metaphysics. It enables him both to explain our *a priori* knowledge of the phenomenal world, and also to justify our belief in God and in human freedom' (H. J. Paton, *Kant's Metaphysic of Experience* (New York, 1936), i. 64–65). 'In Kant's whole discussion of phenomena and noumena I can see no suggestion that he gave up for a moment his belief in things-in-themselves. . . . Nor can there be any reasonable doubt that without the presupposition of things-in-themselves—whether we regard it as justified or not —the whole of the Critical Philosophy falls to pieces' (ii. 461–2).

57 (p. 217). Also above Kant's own early *Beobachtungen über das Gefühl des Schönen und Erhabenen* (Koenigsberg, 1764), which is rather an ordinary instance of the eighteenth-century preoccupation with the sublime (for which see S. H. Monk, *The Sublime; A Study of Critical Theories in XVIII-Century England* (New York, 1935); W. J. Hipple, *The Beautiful, The Sublime, & The Picturesque in Eighteenth-Century British Aesthetic Theory* (Carbondale, Ill., 1957)). No doubt it was the wondrous Platonism in the 'sublime' of the *Kritik der Urteilskraft* that so entranced Coleridge. As negative evidence we may note the fact that though he usually speaks of Burke, the statesman, with respect (e.g. *Biographia*, i. 125), he says that 'Burke's Essay on the Sublime and Beautiful seems to me a poor thing' (*Table Talk*, 12 July 1827). Again, in a marginal note to a statement that an ode of Sappho's was 'produced by Longinus as one of the noblest and completest examples of the *sublime*', he snorts: 'No such thing. Longinus was no very profound critic; but he was no Blunderer. Of the energetic, of the language of high excitement, elevated from passion, in short ὑψότητος παθητικῆς, of this indeed it was, & probably ever will be, the most perfect specimen. But as to Sublime you might as well call it Blue, or Small-poxed' (*Critical Annotations*, p. 45). Probably Coleridge rejected Longinus and Burke on the sublime because Kant's 'das Erhabene' of the third critique beggared them by its Platonism. For the influence of Longinus on Kant, see R. W. Bretall, 'Kant's Theory of the Sublime', *The Heritage of Kant*, ed. G. T. Whitney and D. F. Bowers (Princeton, 1939), pp. 379–402.

58 (p. 219). It is precisely this that Natorp regards as the irreducible common emphasis of Plato and Kant: the Platonic *epekeina* and the Kantian 'Begriff des "Transzendental"' are epistemologically identical conceptions (*Platos Ideenlehre*, p. 463), and also historically related conceptions (Natorp cites the dissertation of Knittermeyer, *Der Terminus transzendental in seiner historischen Entwickelung bis auf Kant* (Marburg, 1920)). For an emphasis on the similar function of '*Ding an sich*' and Platonic 'idea' compare Schelling: ' "The principle of the sensible cannot be found in the sensible; it must lie in the supersensible." So said Kant, as have all true philosophers before him, and among those of his own time, none more clearly and excellently than Jacobi.—For the character of all things sensible is precisely that they are conditioned, that they do not have their ground in themselves. Now Kant symbolized this supersensible ground of everything sensible by means of the expression *things in themselves*—an expression which, like all

symbolic expressions, encloses in itself a contradiction, because Kant seeks to represent the unconditioned through a conditioned, to make the infinite finite. Such contradictory (absurd) expressions, however, are the only ones by which we are able to represent ideas at all. We have known for a long time what unaesthetic heads can make out of such an expression. Plato exhausted himself in words in order to express the fact that ideas contain a being (*Seyn*) that reaches far beyond all empirical existence (*Daseyn*). None the less one can still hear even today the argument that Plato's ideas are real substances, just as are Kant's *things in themselves*' (*Philosophische Schriften*, pp. 276–7).

59 (p. 219). *Works*, ii. 420. In the same way, but now echoing Leibniz, Coleridge says that the great philosophical question is why does the world correspond to our reason, and that the 'only answer which Plato deemed the question capable of receiving, compels the reason to pass out of itself and seek the ground of this agreement in a supersensual essence, which being at once the ideal of the reason and the cause of the material world, is the pre-establisher of the harmony in and between both. Religion therefore is the ultimate aim of philosophy . . .' (*Works*, ii. 422). And in the *Opus Maximum* Coleridge speaks at greater length of 'the dialectic so highly and mysteriously extolled by Plato as the very wings of philosophy by which we ascend from the conditional to the absolute. . . . If we examine in what this dialectic consisted, as in the Parmenides of Plato . . . we shall find that it consisted in taking two positions each undeniable as the premises, undeniable I mean according to the principles of the understanding. . . . From each premise the reasoner arrives and forces his antagonist to follow him by the most legitimate deductions to an inevitable conclusion. In both trains the premises are granted, the deductions are faultless . . . the conclusion inevitable, and yet they are in direct and exclusive contradiction to each other. The inference is evident, though Plato commonly leaves it to his reader's own reflection, namely, either that all reasoning is a mere illusion . . . or there must exist a class of truths to which the measures of time and space and the forms of quantity, quality and contingent relation are not applicable . . .' (Snyder, *Coleridge on Logic and Learning*, pp. 131–2).

60 (p. 223). Leighton was less a trinitarian expositor than a spiritual commentator. In the set of his works annotated by Coleridge, only one article explicitly deals with the Trinity ('An Exposition of the Creed', *The Whole Works of Robert Leighton, D.D.*, (London, 1820), iv. 1–37), although Coleridge—even before the appearance of this edition—had found Leighton peculiarly congenial to his way of thinking, and later, of course, virtually elevated him to the status of co-author of the *Aids to Reflection*. Of the other Anglican theologians, Coleridge apparently found most light in Daniel Waterland, *The Importance of the Doctrine of the Holy Trinity Asserted* . . . second edition (London, 1734), and in the Nicene defence of George Bull (*Defensio Fidei Nicænae* . . . (Oxonii, 1685)). Bull's work was often reprinted and translated, had a great reputation throughout Europe (Leibniz cites it with respect), and was generally accounted one of the ablest of all defences of the Trinity. As Henry Nelson Coleridge said, 'Mr. Coleridge's admiration of Bull and Waterland as high theologians, was very great. Bull he used to read in the Latin Defensio Fidei Nicaenae, using the Jesuit Zola's edition of 1784, which, I think, he bought at Rome. He told me once, that when he was reading a Protestant English Bishop's work on the Trinity, in a copy edited by an Italian Jesuit in Italy, he felt proud of the church of England, and in good humour with the church of Rome' (*Table Talk and Omniana*, p. 51 n.).

Though 'Bull and Waterland are the classical writers on the Trinity' (*Table Talk*, 8 July 1827), we should not overestimate Coleridge's debt to these theologians. They reassured him about the historicity of the Trinity, and orientated him towards the standard theological arguments, but his actual thinking was more philosophical than

theological. Indeed, he could be strongly critical of 'the classical writers on the Trinity':
'O, if Bull and Waterland had been first philosophers, and then divines, instead of
being first, manacled, or say articled clerks of a guild' (*Works*, v. 408). He has no
hesitation about declaring his disagreements, especially with Waterland: 'Here I differ
toto orbe from Waterland, and say with Luther and Zinzendorf, that before the Baptism
of John the *Logos* alone had been distinctly revealed, and that first in Christ he declared
himself a Son, namely, the co-eternal only-begotten Son, and thus revealed the Father'
(*Works*, v. 411). And he indicates a very serious ground of disagreement when he says
of Waterland that 'everywhere in this invaluable writer I have to regret the absence of
all distinct idea of the I Am as the proper attribute of the Father; and hence, the
ignorance of the proper Jehovaism of the Son; and hence, that while we worship the
Son together with the Father, we nevertheless pray to the Father only through the
Son' (v. 410). Again, he felt that 'that great truth, in which are contained all treasures
of all possible knowledge, was still opaque even to Bull and Waterland. . . . They most
ably vindicated the doctrine of the Trinity, negatively, against the charge of positive
irrationality. With equal ability they showed the contradictions, nay, the absurdities,
involved in the rejection of the same by a professed Christian. They demonstrated the
utterly un-Scriptural and contra-Scriptural nature of Arianism, and Sabellianism, and
Socinianism. But the self-evidence of the great Truth, as a universal of the reason,—as
the reason itself—as a light which revealed itself by its own essence as light—this they
had not had vouchsafed to them' (v. 407). It was, we know, the study of Kant and
Plato that vouchsafed it to Coleridge.

61 (p. 224). Thus Priestley: 'Be not backward or afraid, my brethren, to make use of
your reason in matters of religion, or where the scriptures are concerned. . . . Distrust,
therefore, all those who decry human reason, and who require you to abandon it,
wherever religion is concerned. When once they have gained this point with you, they
can lead you whither they please, and impose upon you every absurdity which their
sinister views may make it expedient for them that you should embrace' (*An Appeal*,
p. 4). The reason to which Priestley appeals was the fundamental bedrock of Socinianism, as is witnessed by Hazard's summary of Socinian activity in the late seventeenth-
century: in 1695, in Holland, 'Wiszowaty, a grandson of Socinus, published his *Religio
rationalis*, a book which the Socinians regarded as a sort of second bible. . . . According
to Bossuet, the main plank in the Socinian platform is the assertion that we cannot be
compelled to accept what is not clear to our understanding. *Socinianismus*, wrote Poiret,
fidem et scripturam subjicit rationi. According to Pufendorf, the Socinians regard Christianity as nothing more than a system of moral philosophy. Jurieu got it into his head
. . . that he saw Socinianism everywhere; and perhaps after all he was not far wrong,
so widespread and so unmistakable was the general lapse into rationalism. The
Socinians, he cried, declare that it is a matter of indifference what religion a man holds.
They reject the element of mystery' (*The European Mind (1680–1715)*, pp. 94–95). It was
against Wiszowaty that Leibniz composed his defence of the logical basis of the
Trinity (*Defensio trinitatis per nova Reperta Logica contra adjunctam hic Epistolam Ariani non
incelebris*).

62 (p. 224). Coleridge was quick to defend Leibniz's *Théodicée* against Voltaire's ridicule
('the Philosophy of Leibnitz,' says Coleridge, 'whose mortal sin in the Mind of Voltaire
& his Journeymen was, not his monads, but that intolerable Doctrine of the Theodicee,
that the system of the Universe demanded not only the full acquiescence of the Judgement in its perfection, but likewise the deepest devotion of Love & Gratitude' (*Letters*,
ii. 702–3). But when he was not on the defensive he tended to be rather noncommittal
about this particular work. Thus in 1818, in outlining a course of reading to Pryce, he

recommended the *Nouveaux Essais* and the logical defence of the Trinity, but says that
the 'Theodicee I would pass over at present' (*Letters*, iv. 851). Earlier he may vainly
have sought help from that very source, for one of his jottings of 1804 is a reminder to
'read the Theodicee & take notes for my Consolations' (*Notebooks*, ii. 1993). None the
less, though Coleridge, because of his own experience of original sin, was in a final
sense at variance with Leibniz's optimism, he unfailingly spoke of the mighty German
thinker with deep reverence: Leibniz was 'this great man' (*Letters*, ii. 702); 'the Bust
of Leibnitz' impressed on his 'whole soul a sensation which has ennobled and enriched
it!—It is the face of a God!—& Leibnitz *was* almost more than a man in the wonderful
capaciousness of his Judgment & Imagination!' (*Letters*, i. 472); 'Even Germany,—
though curst with a base and hateful brood of nobles and princelings . . . is still
remembered with filial love and a patriot's pride, when the thoughtful German hears
the names of Luther and Leibnitz' (*Works*, ii. 267).

In his curiously optimistic Christianity Leibniz diverged not only from Coleridge,
but from his own contemporaries as well. Although he knew the Fall of Man to be a
central dogma of Christian commitment, he was notably tranquil in his faith—as
though man, even though fallen, were somehow unscathed. And this stance he maintained in an era noteworthy for the deepness of its malaise and sense of human insignificance (as well as for a troubled scepticism that failed to ruffle his serene belief). We
are perhaps justified, therefore, in seeking a psycho-analytical explanation for his
attitude. In any event, almost the only childhood recollection this titanic intellect
chose to emphasize for posterity was a double memory of his father, whom he lost in
his sixth year. Leibniz remembered, first, that 'the Father' had taught him to read from
a 'little book' that syncretized secular and Biblical history, and had been pleased by his
progress toward knowledge; and secondly, that one day, his mother being at church,
the child Leibniz, not yet clothed, had climbed upon a table and fallen off, but was not
hurt—and that 'the Father', who had been ill, was suddenly well, and instead of being
angry, rejoiced and was well pleased that his son was unharmed (Guhrauer, *Leibnitz*,
i. 7). Can we fail to see, in this dual recollection, not only the structure of Leibniz's
optimism, the calmness of his belief that progress in learning would not lead to a fall
of Icarus, and that the Fall of Man (not yet clothed) mysteriously gave joy to 'the
Father', but also the origin of his motivation towards learning? The character of that
learning, even, is adumbrated by the 'Büchlein' that mixed the secular and the Biblical
—to the approval of 'the Father'. And if 'the Father' approved of learning in the
instance of this one book, he also left behind him a library in which his son later
immersed himself ('a stock', says Lamprecht, 'of the best philosophical, legal, and
theological books, in which perhaps the most considerable part of his fortune was
bound up' (*Leben des Leibnitz*, p. 6).

63 (p. 225). Though 'God' was an almost intuitive truth to Coleridge, the 'Trinity' was a
secondary and contingent truth, deriving from meditation. Thus in the 'four main
classes of Truth' for '*Christian* Philosophers', the first is 'God', and only the second is
'The living tri-une God' (*Letters*, iv. 809). Again: 'the mystery of the Trinity I believed
to be a truth, *pointed* toward, and even negatively proveable, by *Reason*; existing in all
ages, under more or less disfigurement, by *Tradition* from the patriarch Noah; but first
rendered an article of necessary *Faith* by the Incarnation and Redemption' (*Letters*,
iv. 894–5). 'The Trinity is not the doctrine (of the Logos); but one of the explanations
of it—that which after 300 years' experience the Church found to be the only tenable
explanation' (*Letters*, iv. 850).

64 (p. 226). In a letter to Pryce in 1818 Coleridge elaborates this contention, taking in
the distinction between τὸ θεῖον and ὁ θεός to which he so frequently has recourse

(see above, note 44, p. 361; see below, note 69, p. 377): 'The only possible mode of conceiving God as at once infinite and yet personal, is that of assuming that in the former sense it is God, as τὸ θεῖον, in the latter sense only Ὁ Θεός: that these are bonâ fide distinct—and the contra-distinction of God from all finite Beings consists in God's having the *ground* of his existence in himself, whereas all other Beings have their *ground* in another. Therefore God alone is a self-comprehending Spirit; and in this incommunicable *Adequate* Idea of himself (Λόγος) his Personality is contained—πρὸς τὸν Θεόν (very ill translated by the preposition, with) καί Θεός.—Philo has asserted the same, and anxiously guards against the misconception that the Logos is an Attribute or Personification or generic or abstract term.—*Est* enim, et est Deus alter et idem.—St John effects the same by interposing the account of *John*, a concrete, a man, and then adds— *He* was not the Logos. Can any thing be conceived more absurd than to affirm that John was not one of God's *Properties*?—In the beginning of this Mahogany Table was redness; and this Redness was in indivisible approximity to this Table, and was the Table—There was likewise a Looking-glass in the same Parlour—But this Looking-glass was not the Redness, of which I am speaking—&c.—Now Philo & John were Contemporaries—either therefore Philo learnt the doctrine from the Christians, of which there is no proof or probability—or (of which there are many proofs) he wrote long before John wrote the Gospel. In the latter case John could not have used words so familiar to all the Hellenistic Jews for whom his Gospel was written, in a sense utterly different, and without giving them the least hint of this change, without intentional delusion. Rationally or irrationally, the Logos in his time meant a personal Being—' (*Letters*, iv. 850). Although it is very difficult to fill in the ellipses of Coleridge's thought with respect to Philo, we should at least note that the Philonic *logos* (which is not identified with person) serves explicitly to prevent pantheism by separating deity and world. The ὁ θεοῦ λόγος is the 'world descried by the mind', the intelligible world (*De opificio mundi* VI) and is the Platonic pattern of the bodily world. Philo writes especially against those 'who, having the world in admiration rather than the Maker of the world, pronounce it to be without beginning and everlasting . . . whereas we ought on the contrary to be astonished at His powers as Maker and Father, and not to assign to the world a disproportionate majesty' (*De opificio mundi* II). In *John* a trinitarian division of Godhead in terms of a *logos* theory is simply given ('In the beginning' was (1) the Word, (2) the Word . . . with God, and (3) God), while in Philo there appears a philosophical-Platonic argumentation for a *logos* theory.

Although both Philo and John are opposed to pantheism, John is for Coleridge more decisive than Philo. 'Would it not follow', he asks Green in 1820, 'that a redemptive power must be necessary if immortality be true, and man a disordered being? And that no power can be redemptive which does not at the same time act in the ground of the life as one with the ground, that is, must act in my will and not merely *on* my will. . . . Under these views, I cannot read the Sixth Chapter of St. John without great emotion. The Redeemer cannot be *merely* God, unless we adopt Pantheism, that is, deny the existence of a God; and yet God he must be . . . Christ must become man' (*Letters of Samuel Taylor Coleridge*, ed. E. H. Coleridge (London, 1895), ii. 710). The emphasis here, in its relation to Coleridge's endorsement of Philo, may be made more clear by a series of interpretative statements by C. H. Dodd. 'Now Philo was a theist', says Dodd, 'whose Jewish training led him to believe in a transcendent God not to be identified with the world or any part of it; a God who is the Creator of the world.' But, although 'there is a formal similarity', 'reflection will suggest the immense difference, all the more striking for the similarity, between Philo's cosmological speculations and the personal realism of the (fourth) gospel.' Noting 'that whatever other elements of thought may enter into the background of the Fourth Gospel, it certainly presupposes a range of ideas having a remarkable resemblance to those of Hellenistic

Judaism as represented by Philo', Dodd stresses that 'The treatment of those ideas is indeed strikingly different. In particular there is one decisive difference: the evangelist conceives of the Logos as incarnate, and of the ἀληθινὸς ἄνθρωπος as not merely dwelling as νοῦς in all men, but as actually living and dying on earth as a man. This means that the Logos, which in Philo is never personal, except in a fluctuating series of metaphors, is in the gospel fully personal, standing in personal relations both with God and with men, and having a place in history. As a result, those elements of personal piety, faith, and love, which are present in Philo's religion but not fully integrated into his philosophy, come to their own in the gospel. The Logos of Philo is not the object of faith and love.' But the Fourth Gospel 'is a record of a life which expresses the eternal thought of God, the meaning of the universe. It is through a knowledge of this life that the eternal Logos is apprehended, and not otherwise. Though the evangelist recognizes a "reception" of the Logos apart from the incarnation, yet this is a given possibility for mankind only because the Logos is He who became flesh, and, Christ having come, it is in "believing in His name" that the Logos is received. We do not start with cosmology, ascending to knowledge of God through His works in creation and the eternal forms behind them. We start with faith in Jesus, which involves the recognition that the meaning which we find in Him is the meaning of the whole universe—that, in fact, that which is incarnate in Him is the Logos. That is the direction of thought, and that is where John differs decisively from Philo and other thinkers of a similar tendency. Cosmology is not for him a path to knowledge of God and eternal life. Only he who knows God in Jesus Christ, knows that the Logos is, by which the world was made. In the light of its conclusion, the beginning of the Prologue may be read in this fashion: "The ground of all real existence is that divine meaning or principle which is manifested in Jesus Christ. It was this principle, separable in thought from God, but not in reality separate from Him, that existed before the world was, and is the pattern by which, and the power through which, it was created. The life that is in the world, the light that is in the mind of man, are what we have found in Christ." The evangelist does not, like some "Gnostics", set out to communicate an account of the origin of the universe, as a way to that knowledge of God which is eternal life, and then fit Christ into the scheme. He says, in effect, "let us assume that the cosmos exhibits a divine meaning which constitutes its reality. I will tell you what that meaning is: it was embodied in the life of Jesus, which I will now describe" ' (*The Interpretation of the Fourth Gospel* (Cambridge, 1953), pp. 66, 327 n., 73, 284–5).

65 (p. 228). Though Spinoza did know, and use, the Cabala (*Opera*, iii. 135–6), the extreme emphasis of Coleridge's statement derives historically from the judgement of Wachter in 1699 that 'Spinoza hat seine Künsten aus der *Cabala* gelernet' (Johann Georg Wachter, *Der Spinozismus im Jüdenthumb oder die von dem heutigen Jüdenthumb und dessen Geheimen Kabbala Vergötterte Welt* . . . (Amsterdam, 1699), p. 34). See also *Elucidarius Cabbalisticus sive reconditae Hebraeorum philosophiae recensio, epitomatore J. G. Wachtero* (Romae [Halle], 1706). Of the relation of the two works Leibniz says, 'Wachter, who had met Moses Germanus at Amsterdam, wrote a book against him called "The World Deified" in which he attacks Spinoza, Moses Germanus, and the Cabala, because it confounds God with the world, but later he thought that he understood the matter better, and now defends the Cabala and Spinoza and claims that they distinguished between God and the world; but on this point he is not very satisfactory' (Foucher de Careil, *Réfutation de Spinoza par Leibniz*, p. 4). Leibniz seems, for his own part, to have accepted the large role of the Cabala in Spinoza's thought, for he writes to Bourguet that 'Spinosa vero ex combinatione Cabale et Cartesianismi, in extremitates corruptorum, monstrosum suum dogma formavit' (*Philosophische Schriften*, iii. 545). The judgement was revived for the Romantic consciousness by Jacobi's dictum that

'Cabalistic philosophy is, as philosophy, nothing else than undeveloped, or newly confused, Spinozism' (*Werke*, iv–1. 217–20). Herder, in response, denied the legitimacy of the equation: the sublime Spinoza should not be compared to that visionary mishmash called the Cabala (*Werke*, xvi. 524). Maimon, however, who speaks with authority on matters of rabbinical lore, said that 'the Cabala is in fact nothing other than an expanded Spinozism. Not only does it explain the origin of the world as a limitation of the divine being, but it also deduces the origin of each kind of being and its relation to all others from a special property of God' (*Lebensgeschichte* (Berlin, 1792), i. 141).

In general, along with the revival of Neoplatonic and Hermetic thought in the late seventeenth century, there was a revival of interest in the Cabala (which is, indeed, little more than a Jewish version of that thought), effected mainly through the proselyting zeal of Knorr von Rosenroth (*Kabbala Denudata*) and Henry More (*Conjectura Cabbalistica*). For a modern survey of the history and content of cabalistic thought, see G. G. Scholem, *Major Trends in Jewish Mysticism* (New York, 1946). To realize the interchangeability of Hermetic and Cabalistic doctrine, and their confluence in a major pantheist, see F. A. Yates, *Giordano Bruno and the Hermetic Tradition* (Chicago, 1964), where the conclusion is reached that 'Bruno's philosophy and religion are one and the same, and both are Hermetic', and that Bruno 'can be described as belonging into [*sic*] the Hermetic-Cabalist tradition', even though the 'persistence of Cabalistic ideas in Bruno's mind' was 'secondary' to his Hermetic preoccupation (pp. 249, 257, 267).

66 (p. 231). Thus Coleridge says that 'it is most dangerous, and, in its distant consequences, subversive of all Christianity to admit, as Taylor does, that the doctrine of the Trinity is at all against, or even above, human reason in any other sense, than as eternity and Deity itself are above it' (*Works*, v. 229). In this view he was in agreement with Leibniz: 'The more reason harmonizes with Religion, the more all things are improved', and 'Since truth accords with truth, the Theology which wars with reason will be suspect' (*Réfutation de Spinoza par Leibniz*, pp. 72, 74). The *credo quia absurdum*, which is the general medieval formula of Tertullian's 'certum est, quia impossibile est' (see Gilson, *La Philosophie au moyen âge*, p. 98) is one of the great patterns of Christian thought, that which eschews the spoiling effects of 'philosophy and vain deceit' (Colossians ii. 8) and which finds countless adherents down to and including Barth. Its great opponent is the tradition of Origen. As Wolfson says, 'To [Tertullian] faith unadorned by reason or philosophy . . . is sufficient for salvation. . . . Quite the opposite of the view of Tertullian is that of Origen. "There is a great difference", he says, "between knowledge conjoined with faith (πιστεύειν ἐγνωκέναι) and faith only (πιστεύειν μόνον)." The former is to him superior' (*Philosophy of the Church Fathers*, pp. 102, 106). To this tradition both Coleridge and Leibniz subscribed. For Coleridge, Origen was 'almost the only very great scholar and genius combined amongst the early Fathers' (*Table Talk*, 12 Jan. 1834). It is difficult, therefore, to agree with Wellek that 'Coleridge sometimes teaches the old adage: credo quia absurdum est' (*Kant in England* (Princeton, 1931), p. 129). Not only does Coleridge speak against the '*Certum est quia impossibile est*' (*Works*, i. 237), but he expressly says that the 'sum total of my convictions' would comprise such a system 'that of all Systems that have ever been presented, this has the least of *Mysticism*, the very Object throughout from the first page to the last being to reconcile the dictates of common Sense with the conclusions of scientific Reasoning' (*Letters*, iv. 706).

67 (p. 235). Thus 'It is to me evident that if the Holy Ghost does not proceed through and from the Son as well as from the Father, then the Son is not the adequate substantial idea of the Father' (*Works*, v. 243). The real difficulty for Coleridge was to realize that 'No Christ, no God.—and conversely, if the Father, then the Son' (v. 441). Not only

for Coleridge but for theology itself, once Christ and God are conceived in parity—'I and my Father are one' (John x. 30); 'the Father is in me, and I in him' (John x. 38)— then both the demands of logic by which a dichotomy is simultaneously a trichotomy, and the clearly stated existence of the Paraclete, invite the Trinitarian formulation. The existence of the Holy Ghost—outside expressly Trinitarian groupings—is very strongly affirmed in the New Testament, e.g., the unforgivable 'blasphemy against the Holy Ghost' (Matthew xii. 32), and the 'Comforter, which is the Holy Ghost, whom the Father will send in my name' (John xiv. 26), also John xv. 26, xvi. 7, 13–15. 'If the Divinity of our Saviour be satisfactorily proved', says a theologian contemporary with Coleridge, 'and we are assured of the second Person, the Son of God, the third follows of course, and cannot but be admitted. When our Saviour gave his last command to his disciples, and ordered them to *teach all nations, baptizing them in the name of the Father, and of the Son, and of the Holy Ghost* . . . we cannot suppose, that on so solemn an occasion, after mentioning two Persons, he would thirdly mention along with them, and exactly in the same manner, a mere mode, or attribute, and that too an attribute of one of those persons. . . . It is not to be supposed, that the Apostles would have spoken so repeatedly of the Holy Spirit and it's operations, if no such operator had existed. They could as easily have referred these blessings, and this influence, immediately to the Father, and to the Father alone; had there not been a third Person . . .' (Bryant, *Sentiments of Philo,* pp. 54–55).

68 (p. 235). Though Bishop Pike has recently brought forward once more the Socinian claim that the Trinity is not founded upon Biblical testimony, the weight of the evidence, to my mind, is clearly against him. Not only is the Trinitarian formulation most explicitly stated at Matthew xxviii. 19 ('Go ye therefore, and teach all nations, baptizing them in the Name of the Father, and of the Son, and of the Holy Ghost') and at 2 Corinthians xiii. 14 ('The grace of the Lord Jesus Christ, and the love of God, and the communion of the Holy Ghost, be with you all'), but it appears in more or less explicit forms in numerous other places (e.g. Ephesians iii. 14–17; Romans viii. 9–11; v. 1–5; Galatians iv. 4–6; 2 Thessalonians ii. 13–14; 1 Thessalonians i. 3–5; v. 18, 19; 1 Corinthians xii. 4–6). For a brief and sharp defence of the formulation, and a discussion of the relative chronology of its appearances, see J. Tixeront, *Apologetical Studies; The Trinity, Jesus Christ, The Church, Penance* (London and St. Louis, 1917). Again, the 'Scope and Design' of Bull's *Defensio Fidei Nicænae* was 'clearly to show that all the approved Fathers of the Church, before the *Nicene* Council, nay, even from the Apostolic age, taught the same thing . . . concerning the Divinity of the Son, which the *Nicene* Fathers determined, against Arius, and the other Heretics' (*The Defence of the Nicene Creed,* in *The Works of the Right Reverend George Bull,* trans. Fr. Holland (London, 1725), i. 11). Compare Coleridge: '*All* Scripture from Genesis to the Apocalypse declares, there is but one God. In the New Testament three distinct Agents are spoken of, the Father, the Son, and the Paraclete or Holy Ghost. (My *Father* and *I* will come and *we* will dwell with you.—Sins against the Father and against the Son may be expiated; but not against the Holy Ghost, &c. &c.). . . . Ergo, there are three, and these Three are One—This is the Scripture Trinity; and what other is contained in the Nicene Creed?' (*Works,* v. 536).

69 (p. 235). But Coleridge almost never wholly abandoned a position; he could usually salvage something from an intellectual experience, and it seems probable that this early realization of the non-personal aspects of deity were useful in preventing him from falling into a kind of proto-Feuerbachian man-worship, just as the later emphasis on person kept him from pantheism (in Trinitarian terms, Sabellianism). If God is *merely* person (or three persons), then Feuerbach is right and man is God; if God is not

person (but rather the logical interdependence of a thesis-antithesis-synthesis logic) then the Schelling–Spinoza position is correct and nature is God. The only solution can be to conceive God as both infinite and beyond all limit (τὸ θεῖον) *and* person (ὁ θεός); hence Coleridge came to see the 'Trinitarian' solution as 'the only consequent Medium between the Atheist and the Anthropomorph' (Marginal note at page 40 of the first volume of the Law edition of Boehme's works in the British Museum).

In the Biblical τὸ θεῖον and ὁ θεός therefore, Coleridge found, not a random interchange of terms, but a special indication of the conflict resolved in the Trinity. According to Karl Rahner, the New Testament asserts 'with complete assurance that everything is, moves and lives in . . . God as τὸ θεῖον; it sees the πατὴρ πάντων (Eph. iv. 6) at work everywhere, in Nature too. . . . But close observation shows that the New Testament completely lacks any expression of numinous feeling for the cosmos, excited by the world, its greatness and its glory. . . . Thus on the one hand the New Testament is capable of seeing God powerfully at work in the whole of reality and history, and on the other God never becomes for it the mysterious glimmer of an Absolute immanent in the world, the world is never deified but remains always the creature of the Lord beyond all world who shapes it freely by his Word' (*Theological Investigations*, pp. 105-6). 'Ο Θεός, on the other hand, refers to God as Father: 'We may outline our results as follows', says Rahner at the conclusion of an exhaustive discussion—'Nowhere in the New Testament is there to be found a text with ὁ θεός which has unquestionably to be referred to the Trinitarian God as a whole existing in three Persons. In by far the greater number of texts ὁ θεός refers to the Father as a Person of the Trinity. . . . Besides this there are six complete texts in which ὁ θεός is used to speak of the Second Person of the Trinity, but still in a hesitant and obviously restricted way. . . . In addition, ὁ θεός is never used in the New Testament to speak of the πνεῦμα ἅγιον. These findings are sufficient in themselves to justify the assertion that when the New Testament speaks of ὁ θεός, it is (with the exception of the six texts mentioned) the Father as First Person of the Trinity who is signified' (Rahner, pp. 143-4). Compare Coleridge: 'ὁ θεός becomes Πατήρ [the Father] by the act of realizing in the Son' (*Unpublished Letters of Samuel Taylor Coleridge*, ed. E. L. Griggs (London, 1932), ii. 372).

For Coleridge, 'True Philosophy begins with the τὸ θεῖον in order to end in the 'Ο Θεός' (*Letters*, iv. 768); and 'The only possible mode of conceiving God as at once infinite and yet personal, is that of assuming that in the former sense it is God, as τὸ θεῖον, in the latter sense only 'Ο Θεός' (*Letters*, iv. 850). The τὸ θεῖον, therefore, is the God demanded by our universal consciousness of our situation—the 'perfect being' implied by our own imperfection, as in the ontological proofs of Anselm and Descartes, or that on which, in Schleiermacher's terminology, our universal feeling of dependence leads us to depend, or in the Spinozistic conception of Bishop Robinson, the God who 'is, by definition, ultimate reality. And one cannot argue whether ultimate reality *exists*. One can only ask what ultimate reality is like . . .' (J. A. T. Robinson, *Honest to God* (London, 1963), p. 29). The 'Ο Θεός, on the other hand, is not the God of philosophical need; 'Remember', says Coleridge, 'that the Personality of God, the living I AM, was the distinctive privilege of the Hebrew Faith' (*Unpublished Letters*, ii. 401). Thus, in a sense, we can see Coleridge's whole programme for the reclamation of Spinozistic thought as a progression from τὸ θεῖον to 'Ο Θεός.

70 (p. 236). 'By man, whom he considers as the highest subject of philosophy', says Buber, 'Feuerbach does not mean man as an individual, but man with man—the connexion of *I* and *Thou*. "The individual man for himself", runs his manifesto . . . "does not have man's being in himself, either as a moral being or a thinking being. Man's being is contained only in community, in the unity of man with man—a unity which rests, however, only on the reality of the difference between I and Thou." Feuerbach

did not elaborate these words in his later writings. Marx did not take up into his concept of society the element of the real relation between the really different *I* and *Thou*,
and for that very reason opposed an unreal individualism with a collectivism which
was just as unreal. But in those words Feuerbach, passing beyond Marx, introduced
that discovery of the *Thou*, which has been called "the Copernican revolution" of
modern thought [by Karl Heim], and "an elemental happening which is just as rich in
consequences as the idealist discovery of the I" and "is bound to lead to a new beginning of European thought, pointing beyond the Cartesian contribution to modern
philosophy." (Heim, *Glaube und Denken* [1931], p. 405 ff.) I myself in my youth was
given a decisive impetus by Feuerbach' (*Between Man and Man*, pp. 147–8). It was not
until his 'Nachwort' in *Die Schriften über das dialogische Prinzip* (Heidelberg, 1954)—*Ich
und Du* was published in 1923—that Buber finally assigned Jacobi priority in the history
of the I–Thou distinction (though Bollnow pointed out the priority some two decades
before). Compare Maurice S. Friedman, *Martin Buber; The Life of Dialogue* (London,
1955), pp. 164, 162 n. For the Ich–Du distinction in Feuerbach see *Grundsätze der
Philosophie der Zukunft*, par. 58, 59, 60, 62, 63, in Feuerbach, *Werke*, ii. 344–5. Compare
Coleridge in 1818: 'Does not personality necessarily suppose a *ground* distinct from the
Person . . .? Conscire, = scio et me et alterum simul vel scio me dum scio alterum—
Ergo, Sui Conscientia = scio me quasi alterum. The *Me* in the objective case is clearly
distinct from the *Ego*' (*Letters*, iv. 849).

71 (p. 238). Thus 'The first lesson, that innocent Childhood affords me, is—that it is
an instinct of my Nature to pass out of myself, and to exist in the form of others'
(*Inquiring Spirit*, p. 68). Again: 'My nature requires another Nature for its support, &
reposes only in another from the necessary Indigence of its Being' (*Notebooks*, i. 1679).
Curious though the suggestion may at first seem, it is quite possible, even probable,
that Coleridge's plagiarisms are a kind of bizarre obeisance to the I–Thou principle.
In this respect, it is interesting to note that he not only takes, but gives—hence the
statement that he plans to write his Life of Lessing 'because it would give me an
opportunity of conveying under a better name, than my own ever will be, opinions,
which I deem of the highes[t] importance' (*Letters*, i. 519). In the same connexion,
we realize that Wordsworth's great philosophical poem would have been in fact
Coleridge's *magnum opus*! 'I must recall to your mind what my *expectations* were', writes
Coleridge to Wordsworth in 1815. '. . . I looked forward to the Recluse, as the *first*
and *only* true Phil. Poem in existence. . . . I expected the Colors, Music, imaginative
Life, and Passion of *Poetry*; but the matter and arrangement of *Philosophy*. . . . I supposed you first to have meditated the faculties of Man in the abstract, and their correspondence with his Sphere of action . . . to have laid a solid and immoveable foundation
for the Edifice by removing the sandy Sophisms of Locke, and the Mechanic Dogmatists,
and demonstrating that the Senses were living growths and developements of the Mind
& Spirit. . . . Next . . . to have affirmed a Fall in some sense, as a fact, the possibility of
which cannot be understood from the nature of the Will, but the reality of which is
attested by Experience & Conscience . . . to point out however a manifest Scheme of
Redemption from this Slavery, of Reconciliation from this Enmity with Nature . . .—
and to conclude by a grand didactic swell on the necessary identity of a true Philosophy
with true Religion . . .' (*Letters*, iv. 573–5). And in 1832 Coleridge says that he 'cannot
help regretting that Wordsworth did not first publish his thirteen books on the growth
of an individual mind—superior . . ., upon the whole, to the "Excursion". Then the
plan laid out, and, I believe, partly suggested by me, was, that Wordsworth should
assume the station of a man in mental repose . . . prepared to deliver upon authority
a system of philosophy. He was to treat man as man,—a subject . . . in contact with
external nature, and informing the senses from the mind, and not compounding a mind

out of the senses . . .; thence he was to infer and reveal the proof of, and necessity for, . . . a redemptive process in operation, showing how this idea reconciled all the anomalies. . . . Something of this sort was, I think, agreed on. It is, in substance, what I have been all my life doing in my system of philosophy' (*Table Talk*, 21 July 1832).

72 (p. 244). The Spinozistic argument could, in formal terms, be blocked by the phenomenological approach of Husserl. This was not quite Coleridge's answer, for his 'abnormal speed of cerebration, but of rather a peculiar kind' (House, p. 37) never exhibits itself properly in terms of formal process. But when Coleridge says that Spinoza's '*unica substantia*' is, in fact, a mere notion,—a *subject* of the mind, and no *object*' (*Table Talk*, 30 Apr. 1830), and that Spinoza's 'God as an *Object*' forgets 'that an Object . . . presupposes a Subject' (*Letters*, iv. 548 n.), he enunciates an insight that translates easily into Husserlian terms. The 'idea rei alicujus singularis actu existentis'—the idea of some particular thing actually existing—that Spinoza stipulates (*Ethica*, ii. 11) as awakening the mind to consciousness, cannot, in the Husserlian view, be transformed to substance. For the moment the first reductive question is asked (e.g. 'what is it?'), the 'res aliquis', as such, would be 'ausgeschaltet' (disconnected) or 'eingeklammert' (bracketed); the question would then still be valid, but would not be a question about the *fact* (Tatsache) of the 'res aliquis', but about the 'idea' itself. It would be the first step in a 'phänomenologische Reduktion', which, in this case, would be 'transzendent gerichtet' (transcendently directed), and the eventual 'syntactic objectivity' of 'substantia' would be an 'eidetische Wahrnehmung' (eidetic perception), not an impeachment of the fact of the 'something', nor of the existence of the self, because it is precisely eidetic *cogitationes* that consitute the 'intentional Being' of the Ego. 'Jedes "cogito" ', says Husserl, 'jeder Akt in einem ausgezeichneten Sinne ist charakterisiert als Akt des Ich, er "geht aus dem Ich hervor" ' (*Ideen*, p. 194). For Husserl the *cogito* is the irreducible ground of thought: 'what to me, the meditator, thereby becomes my own is my pure life with the universe of *phenomena* in the sense of phenomenology. The ἐποχή is the radical and universal method through which I purely grasp myself as ego and with my own pure life of consciousness, in which and through which the whole objective world is for me. . . . Everything worldly, all being in space and time is for me—that is, is valid for me, in that I experience it, perceive it, remember it, somehow ponder it, judge it, desire it, etc. All this Descartes signified under the title *cogito*. The world is for me in general nothing else at all than a being conscious and valuing to me in such a *cogito*' (*Cartesianische Meditationen*, p. 60). Yet, though Husserl accepts the *ego cogito* as given and unquestionable, he also accepts the existence of *Tatsachen* as given and unquestionable; the 'Einklammerung' that begins the reduction does not in any way contest the reality of the 'external world': '. . . this whole natural world, which is constantly "there for us", which is "present", will always remain there as conscious "reality", even if we choose to bracket it (*einzuklammern*). If I do so, as I am fully free to do, then I do not negate this "world", as though I were a sophist, nor doubt its existence, as though I were a sceptic' (*Ideen*, p. 67). Again, Husserl states 'quite explicitly that in regard to transcendental-phenomenological Idealism, I . . . hold every form of current philosophical realism to be in principle absurd, as no less every idealism to which in its own arguments that realism stands contrasted. . . . Our phenomenological idealism does not deny the positive existence of the real (*realen*) world and of Nature. . . . Its sole task and service is to clarify the meaning of this world . . . as really existing' (Husserl, Author's Preface to the English Edition, *Ideas*, pp. 19, 21). Though Coleridge and Husserl were different in temperament (Husserl was a mathematician by training) and ultimate aim (Coleridge looked towards system, whereas Husserl looked toward a universal scientific method), none the less Husserl's acceptance of the strict evidential validity of eidetic as well as factive phenomena is consistent

with Coleridge's own orientation. Both Husserl and Coleridge are characterized by a kind of philosophical egalitarianism in conceding equal theoretical importance to all phenomena—not the Wittgensteinian attitude that 'All propositions are of equal value' (*Tractatus* 6. 4), but the attitude that all experiences whatsoever are equally real. In this sense Coleridge's notebooks, where he muses on first forms and on waste paper, on anxiety and on Skiddaw, are a kind of mine of Husserlian phenomenological *cogitationes* (Coleridge's 'note-books abound', says Gillman, 'with "his hints and first thoughts;" as he says, his "Cogitabilia rather than actual cogitata à me" ' (Gillman, *Life of Coleridge*, p. 176). Likewise, in the key conception of 'idea', Coleridge and Husserl are close. An 'idea is a power δύναμις νοερά, which constitutes its own reality', says Coleridge, 'and is in order of thought necessarily antecedent to the things in which it is more or less adequately realized' (*Works*, v. 47). The conception here is at least as near Husserl's *eidos* as it is to the 'idea' of either Kant or Plato. The largest common factor in the thought of Husserl and Coleridge is, however, their insistence upon the primacy and incommensurability of the 'I am'. For Husserl the 'wonder of all wonders' was the pure ego and pure consciousness, and, says a commentator, the 'wonder about this phenomenon seems to have been the focal and fundamental experience of Husserl's philosophical existence. . . . The central mystery to Husserl was not Being as such, but the fact that there is a such a thing in this world as a being that is aware of its own being and of other beings' (Spiegelberg, *The Phenomenological Movement*, i. 87).

73 (p. 245). Thus Boehme 'approaches . . . perilously near to Pantheism—while yet, his Heart trembling truthward, there was still an unseen presence, a desiderium, a presensation by a sense of *missing* . . . of the more glorious Antecedent' (Marginal note, p. 125 of the first volume of the Law edition). In general, it seems likely that Boehme and Bruno represented the Platonic *oregesthai* to Coleridge in their feeling for the *dynamic*. Now Coleridge, like other Romantics, was fascinated by the conception of organism and dynamic process. The dynamic was for him an attribute of nature (hence a symbol of its dignity and vitality), and also an attribute of consciousness. As a common denominator in will, imagination, conscience, and other functions, it was a symbol of the incommensurability, the non-thingness, of the personality. He accordingly espoused 'Dynamic Philosophy in opposition to the merely mechanic' (*Letters*, iv. 579, 687), and 'St. Paul' and 'Plato' were 'dynamic philosophers' (*Works*, v. 221). To some extent, however, the dynamic/mechanic opposition, because it applied to nature as well as to mind, lay athwart rather than precisely coincided with the theism/pantheism alignment. Thus part of Schelling's attraction for Coleridge was that, against the 'Mechanic, Locke, Hartley, and Condilliac System' (*Letters*, iv. 670), Schelling—'beyond doubt a Man of Genius'—asserted a 'System' that was of 'permanent value' as an 'attack on the mechanic and corpuscular Philosphy' (*Letters*, iv. 883). In such an orientation both Boehme and Bruno assume great importance. Noting Boehme's vast 'influence on romanticism and occultist currents', Berdyaev says that 'Boehme is the fountainhead of the dynamism of German philosophy, one might even say of the dynamism of the entire thought of the nineteenth century. He was the first to conceive cosmic life as an impassioned battle, as a movement, as a process, as an eternal genesis' (*Unground and Freedom*, p. xxxiii). So also for Bruno. His tone, says Cassirer, was a 'new tone of feeling the world',—Bruno 'embraces the infinite universe with all the ardour of a passionate emotion . . . the scales are turned by a dynamic feeling for the world, not, as with Kepler and Galileo, by the form of a new science of dynamics' (*Individuum und Kosmos*, pp. 197–8).

74 (p. 246). Coleridge scrupulously continues, however, that it is also true that the first principles of Behmen are found '(but mixed with gross impieties) in Paracelsus;

but it is not true that they are easily known, and still less so that they are communicable in common familiar terms. But least of all is it true that there is nothing original in Behmen.' Again, in a marginal note to Boehme's *Three Principles*, he says that 'many passages in this work would suggest the conjecture that J. B. had read Plotinus and Proclus' (Marginal note at the second page 73 of the first volume of the Law edition) —though Coleridge then says that he doubts whether Boehme knew the learned languages. Henry More had early noted the congruence of Boehme with Neoplatonism, even at times with Plotinus himself: 'This is extremely Platonic', he says of one of Boehme's emphases, 'even to the sublime degree of Plotinus himself' (*Philosophiae Teutonicae censura . . . quae responsum complectitur ad Quaestiones Quinque de Philosopho Teutonico Jacobo Behmen illiusque philosophia, Opera*, p. 558); and he pointed out the similarity of many of Boehme's doctrines to the Cabala: 'There are indeed remarkable tendencies towards the ancient Cabala in many passages of his [Boehme's] writings' (*Censura*, p. 558).

75 (p. 249). Coleridge's 'obligation' to the 'polar logic and dynamic philosophy of Giordano Bruno' (*Biographia*, i. 103) is more symbolical than functional. Coleridge did not *use* a polar logic, even though he loved to collect examples of how extremes meet. The favourite Coleridgean doctrine of 'the reconciliation of opposites' shows (*a*) his systematic, inclusive habit of mind, and (*b*) his recognition of the multiplicity of his interests. But it does not form a logical basis for philosophical conclusions. As Miss Snyder says, 'A theoretical insistence upon inclusiveness, in all spheres, and a temperament that found in abstract metaphysical entities, in mere words, real emotional values of almost enervating ultimateness, made it natural that Coleridge should pin his faith to the principle of the Reconciliation of Opposites. And it is natural that he should employ the logical form of this principle, in which the opposites to be reconciled are words and philosophical concepts rather than the forces and elements of a mechanically constructed universe. The principle in this form serves primarily to define that which is positively inclusive, and absolute; at the same time it gives room for all the negations, oppositions and double meanings that must arise in any fundamental dealing with words and metaphysical concepts' (*The Critical Principle of the Reconciliation of Opposites*, p. 17). We can see the special inertness of Coleridge's reconciliation of opposites principle in an 'EXTREMES MEET' notation of 1803: 'Nothing & intensest absolutest Being' (*Notebooks*, i. 1725)—for we realize that this very insight forms the basis of the first triad of Hegel's logic, and indeed of his entire panlogism, while for Coleridge it is merely noted as an observation.

One point, however, should be noted with respect to the consistency of Coleridge's attitudes: namely, that his 'reconciliation of opposites' principle works towards the same symbolical end as his espousal of the 'dynamic'. For Coleridge, as for Schelling and the other German thinkers, the emphasis on the dynamic, though later fertilized by Bruno and Boehme, took its departure from Kant's analysis of the 'Metaphysische Anfangsgründe der Dynamik' in the *Metaphysische Anfangsgründe der Naturwissenschaft* (1786). And Kant there insists that the dynamic can only be conceived as the tension of two opposing forces (e.g. Kant, *Werke*, iv. 417).

A final point. The historical groundwork of Cusanus's *coincidentia oppositorum*, as Cassirer has made clear in a virtuoso demonstration, is the dualism of Plato, in which the counterparts of the sensible and intelligible realms were reversed (*Individuum und Kosmos*, pp. 7–48). We can therefore realize that the 'reconciliation of opposites' principle, though used by the German thinkers in the service of pantheism, does not necessarily imply pantheism, and derives indeed originally from the idea of theism and the supramundane.

For Bruno's espousal of polar logic, see his conclusion, following a number of mathematical examples, that 'he who wants to know the greatest secrets of nature should regard and contemplate the minima and maxima of contraries and opposites. It is a profound magic (*profonda magia*) to know how to draw out the contrary after having found the point of union' (*Dialoghi italiani* . . . con note da Giovanni Gentile, terza edizione a cura di Giovanni Aquilecchia (Firenze, 1958), p. 340). For Cusanus's doctrine of opposites, see, e.g., *The Vision of God*, trans. Emma Gurney Salter (London, Toronto, New York, 1928), p. 43: '. . . I observe how needful it is for me to enter into the darkness, and to admit the coincidence of opposites, beyond all the grasp of reason, and there to seek the truth where impossibility meeteth me.' Again, p. 53: '. . . I behold Thee, my God, in Paradise, girt by that wall of the coincidence of opposites . . .'

INDEX

PRINTED IN GREAT BRITAIN
AT THE UNIVERSITY PRESS, OXFORD
BY VIVIAN RIDLER
PRINTER TO THE UNIVERSITY